# HISTOR.

## STUDIES IN POPULAR PROTEST
## AND POPULAR IDEOLOGY
## IN HONOUR OF

## GEORGE RUDÉ

# HISTORY FROM BELOW

## STUDIES IN POPULAR PROTEST
## AND POPULAR IDEOLOGY
## IN HONOUR OF

## GEORGE RUDÉ

*Edited by*

FREDERICK KRANTZ

CONCORDIA UNIVERSITY
MONTRÉAL, QUÉBEC
1985

Legal Deposit Third Quarter
Bibliothèque nationale du Québec

**Canadian Cataloguing in Publication Data**

History from below: studies in popular
protest and popular ideology in honour of George Rudé

Includes some text in French.
Includes index.
Bibliography: p.
ISBN 0-88947-009-X

1. Revolutions — History — Addresses, essays,
lectures. 2. Social movements — History —
Addresses, essays, lectures. 3. Ideology —
Addresses, essays, lectures. 4. Rudé,
George, 1910- — Addresses, essays, lectures.
I. Krantz, Frederick II. Rudé, George, 1910-

HM283.H48 1985     303.6'4'09     C85-090182-0

Concordia University
1455 de Maisonneuve Boulevard West
Montréal, Québec H3G 1M8

*for George and Doreen*
*(and for Lenore)*

# CONTENTS

# THE CONTRIBUTORS

**Alan H. Adamson** is Professor of History, and Fellow of Liberal Arts College, at Concordia University in Montreal. He is the author of *Sugar Without Slaves. The Political Economy of British Guiana, 1838-1904* (1972) and of studies of Western hemisphere slavery and Victorian literature and society.

**Pierre H. Boulle**, Associate Professor of History at McGill University in Montreal, works on early modern French social and cultural history. The author of studies of the eighteenth-century *chambres de commerce* and of the port of Nantes, he is currently writing a book on racism in early modern France, and chairing the Canadian Historical Association's Commission de Recherche pour la Célébration du Bicentenaire de la Révolution Française.

**J.S. Bromley,** Emeritus Professor of Modern History, University of Southampton, England, and Fellow of the Royal Historical Society, is the editor of *The Rise of Great Britain and Russia, 1688-1725* (1970, Vol. VI of *The New Cambridge Modern History)* and of *The Manning of the Royal Navy: Selected Public Pamphlets* (1974). He brought out, with E.H. Kossmann, *Britain and the Netherlands,* 5 vols. (1959-75), and is currently completing work on *The French Cruising War, 1688-1713.*

**C.M.H. Clark**, Professor of History at the Australian National University in Canberra, is editor of *Sources of Australian History* (1957) and author of *A History of Australia,* 4 vols. (1962-78), as well as of numerous studies of Australian society and culture.

**George C. Comninel** took his doctorate in 1984 from the Graduate Programme in Social and Political Thought, York University, Toronto, where he also worked with George Rudé, there as a Visiting Professor. His *Revolutionary Bourgeois and "Bourgeois Revolution": Class Relations and the French Revolution,* is to be published by Verso Books (London).

**Carolyn Fick** recently took her doctorate, under George Rudé, in the Department of History, Concordia University, Montreal, with a dissertation on *The Black Masses in the San Domingo Revolution.* She is currently in Haiti completing research for a book on Saint Domingue and the French Revolution.

**William J. Fishman,** Professor of Political Studies at Queen Mary College, University of London, works in late nineteenth-century London radical history. He is the author of *Jewish Radicals: from Czarist Stetl to London Ghetto* (1974), *East End Jewish Radicals, 1875-1914* (1975), and *The Streets of East London* (1979), and has acted as an adviser to the BBC in areas related to his field of research.

**Christopher Hill,** Fellow of All Soul's College and former Master of Balliol College, Oxford, is the author of *Puritanism and Revolution* (1958), *Intellectual Origins of the English Revolution* (1965; 1980), *God's Englishman: Oliver Cromwell and the English Revolution* (1970), *The World Turned Upside Down: Radical Ideas during the English Revolution* (1972) and many other studies of seventeenth-century English politics and thought. He is a Fellow of the Royal Society and Member of the British Academy.

**Eric J. Hobsbawm**, Reader in History at Birkbeck College, University of London, is the author of *Primitive Rebels* (1959), *Age of Revolution: Europe 1789-1848* (1962), *Labouring Men* (1964), *Industry and Empire* (1968), *Captain Swing* (with George Rudé) (1968), *Bandits* (1969) and *Revolutionaries* (1973). He teaches as well at the New School for Social Research in New York, and his *Worlds of Labour* appeared in 1984.

**V. G. Kiernan**, Professor Emeritus of Modern History at Edinburgh University, Scotland, is a student of modern European social and political history. He has written on *The Lords of Human Kind: European Attitudes to the Outside World in the Imperial Age* (1969), *State and Society in Europe, 1550-1650* (1980), and *European Empires from Conquest to Collapse* (1982), and is at work on a book on religion in history.

**John F. Laffey** is Professor of History, and Fellow of Liberal Arts College, Concordia University, Montreal. He has published studies of French colonialism in Indo-China and of modern European intellectual history. Recent articles have been devoted to Pierre Janet, John Stuart Mill, and Karl Mannheim, and he is completing a monograph on *Shattered Intellect, Broken Will: The Genesis and Development of Contemporary Consciousness.*

**Walter Markov** is Professor of Modern and Contemporary History at the Karl-Marx-Universität, Leipzig, and Member, Comité Directeur, *Annales historiques de la Révolution française.* He is the author, among many works, of *Jacques Roux: Scripta et Acta* (1969), *Volksbewegungen der Französischen Revolution* (1976), and editor (with Albert Soboul) of *Die Sansculotten von Paris, 1793/94* (1957), and of *Maximilien Robespierre 1758-1794*, rev. ed. (1961).

**William J. Murray** is a student of the press during the French Revolution. A professor of history at La Trobe University, Bundoora, Australia, he did his B. A. honours degree under George Rudé at Adelaide. He has published (with J.T. Gilchrist) *The Press in the French Revolution: A Selection of Documents,* and his *The Right-Wing Press in the French Revolution, 1789-1792* is forthcoming.

**Caroline Ralston**, after doing history honours with George Rudé at Adelaide, took her doctorate in Pacific history from the Australian National University in Canberra. Senior Lecturer in history at Macquarie University in Sydney, her publications reflect her major interest in the early "contact history" of Western penetration and indigenous popular reaction in Hawaii.

**R.B. Rose** is Professor of History at the University of Tasmania and a Fellow of the Australian Academy of the Humanities. He works on popular protest and popular ideology, and in addition to studies of price- and tax-riots in England and France, is the author of *The Enragés: Socialists of the French Revolution* (1965), *Gracchus Babeuf 1760-1797, The First Revolutionary Communist* (1978), and the forthcoming *The Making of the Sans-Culottes: Democratic Ideas and Institutions in Paris 1789-1792* (Manchester University Press).

**Albert Soboul**. The late Albert Soboul, dean of French Revolutionary historians, directed the Institut d'Histoire de la Révolution Française of the University de Paris. Among his many notable works are *Les Sans-culottes parisiens en l'an II. Mouvement populaire et gouvernement révolutionnaire,* 2nd ed. (1962--Engl. transl. *The Parisian Sans-Culottes and the French Revolution 1793-4* [ *1964* ]), *Précis d'histoire de la Révolution française,* 2nd ed. (1967--Engl. transl. *The French Revolution 1787-1799,*

2 vols. [1974]), and *La France à la veille de la Révolution, I. Économie et société* (1969).

**Hugh Stretton**, Reader in History at the University of Adelaide and a Fellow of both the Australian Academy of the Humanities and of the Social Sciences, is author of *The Political Sciences* (1969), *Ideas for Australian Cities* (1970, rev. ed. 1975), *Housing and Government* (1974), and *Capitalism, Socialism and the Environment* (1976).

**Kåre Tønnesson** is Professor of History at the University of Oslo and Member of the Norwegian Academy of Sciences. He is the author of *La défaite des sans-culottes. Mouvement populaire et réaction bourgeoise en l'an III* (1959; 2nd ed. 1978) and *Sentraladministrasjonens historie 1914-1940* (1979). He is currently completing the 1750-1815 volume of a joint Norwegian-Swedish fifteen-volume "History of the World".

**Pierre Vilar** has taught at the Sorbonne, the École des Hautes Études en Sciences Sociales, and been Director of the Institut d'Histoire Économique et Sociale. He is the author of Vol. VI [Catalonia] of *Estudios de Historia Moderna* (1956-9), of *La Catalogne dans l'Espagne moderne; recherches sur les fondements économiques des structures nationales,* 3 vols. (1962), of major articles on the formation of capitalism (in *Past and Present,* 1965, and *Sur le féodalisme* [1971]), of *A History of Gold and Money, 1450-1920,* transl. Judith White (1976), and of *Iniciacion al vocabulario del analisis historico* (1980).

**Ellen Meiksins Wood** is Associate Professor of Political Science at Glendon College, York University, Toronto. She is the author of articles on Lev Kopelev, C.B. Macpherson, and E.P. Thompson, and of *Mind and Politics: An Approach to the Meaning of Liberal and Socialist Individualism* (1972) and (with Neal Wood) *Class Ideology and Ancient Political Theory: Socrates, Plato and Aristotle in Social Context* (1978). She is currently working on a study of *Ancient Greece and the Sources of Western Development.*

**Neal Wood**, Professor of Political Science at York University, Toronto, has written on *Communism and the British Intellectuals* (1959) and (with Ellen Meiksins Wood) on *Class Ideology and Ancient Political Theory: Socrates, Plato and Aristotle in Social Context* (1978). His *The Politics of Locke's Philosophy: A Social Study of "An Essay Concerning Human Understanding"* appeared in 1983, *John Locke and Agrarian Capitalism* in 1984, and a book on Cicero's social and political thought is forthcoming.

# PREFACE

*Habent sua fata libelli.* This book, almost five years in the making, has been a labour of love for all concerned with it, editor, contributors, and many others. Through his manifold works George Rudé, one of our truly great European historians, has played a major role in creating and shaping what is today an established field of historical endeavour, "popular" history, "crowd studies", or, more generically, "history from below". Not only is George a fine historian: he is also a remarkable teacher, whose students warmly reciprocate his genuine concern for them, and a decent, caring human being, whose life is a rare example of the integration of scholarly creativity and human commitment. As scholar, teacher, and *Mensch,* warm, concerned person, he touches all who know him and changes them for the better. It is, then, my privilege, as friend, colleague, and editor, to present to him this book, *"History from Below": Studies in Popular Protest and Popular Ideology in Honour of George Rudé.* I do so in the name of the authors of the studies contained herein, and of all his former and current students and colleagues, in Australia, where he spent many fruitful years, and here in Canada, in Montreal, where he continues to teach and to write in the Department of History of Concordia University.

That this is an international book is reflected not only in the authors of its articles, but also in the different national traditions of expression and style they represent. I have made an effort to ensure general expressive and bibliographical coherence without, however, doing complete violence to the different traditions. It was decided, for the Soboul and Vilar articles, to let these masters speak in their own tongue, one central, moreover, to George Rudé's own life and work. That this book is also in a sense a collective work, is reflected in the fact that its final publication was made possible by a kind of academic "popular movement" in George's use of the term. There are too many "faces" in this crowd to list individually here; the following must, however, be noted: first, and above all, Doreen de la Hoyde Rudé, whose gentle (and sometimes *not* so gentle) Irish prodding pushed the project ahead at critical junctures; Hugh Stretton at Adelaide, V. G. Kiernan at Edinburgh, Barrie Rose at Tasmania, and Bill Fishman at London, all of whom in different ways provided support and aid beyond the call of ordinary contributorial duty. The late Albert Soboul, George's great friend and colleague, finished and submitted his piece despite serious illness. Carolyn Fick, a former doctoral student of George's, is largely responsible for "George Rudé: A Bibliography", itself a contribution, and in addition to her own article for the book; Peter Altenburg, a graduate student in History at Concordia, translated Walter Markov's German article; Reford Mac-Dougall, one of George's "mature" students, and his wife Natalie, made the "Index" and pre-publication publicity possible; Jill Capri, Executive Assistant of Liberal Arts College, and Kathleen O'Connell, of the Provost's office, gave much of their own time to the editorial work; and Don Wilson, of the *Institute for Research on Public Policy* (Montreal), gave invaluable advice on the composition and printing of the manuscript.

Special thanks must go to Martin Singer, Provost of Concordia University, a friend and colleague of George's in History, without whose help and good offices this book might not have been published. Pierre H. Boulle (History, McGill University) brought to the project at a critical moment the support of the Canadian Historical Association's Commission on the Bicentenary Celebration of the French Revolution. My good friend and colleague Harvey Shulman, Acting Principal of Liberal Arts College, Concordia University (of which George was a founding Fellow in 1977), provided his usual sound critical advice and unfailing personal support. Above all, my wife, Lenore Hammel Krantz, enabled me to complete final work on the manuscript through a difficult time.

*Habent sua fata libelli:* perhaps this book was, finally, fated to find its home where George and Doreen have made theirs, just as its publication, reflecting George's own work and life, was a collective, international effort. The reader will, I think, find that this is a book which pays its well-deserved homage in the most appropriate way: by re-creating in its wide-ranging contributions the lived experience and struggles of those "ordinary men and women" to whose historical memory George Rudé, the tireless master-craftsman of "history from below", has dedicated his scholarly life. *"History from Below": Studies in Popular Protest and Popular Ideology in Honour of George Rudé* has, indeed, been a labour of love, and of deep respect and comradeship. Whatever is of value in these pages is owed to the fine work of our contributors; and if the good critiques of the manuscript's external readers rescued the editor from many *gaffes,* responsibility for the inevitable remaining errors is of course his.

Frederick Krantz
Principal, *Liberal Arts College*
Associate Professor, Department of History
Concordia University
Montréal, Québec.

March, 1985.

# INTRODUCTION

.

Frederick Krantz

# "SANS ÉRUDITION, PAS D'HISTOIRE": THE WORK OF GEORGE RUDÉ

*I*

This book is both a *Festschrift,* a celebratory volume in honour of George Rudé, one of the finest contemporary students of European "popular protest", and a contribution in its own right to the field he has done so much to create. Rudé's wide-ranging *œuvre* includes pioneering studies of pre-industrial popular movements in France and England, of the Revolutionary crowd and of crowds in general, works on the nature of popular ideology, of criminality and transportation to Australia, general histories of the eighteenth century and of the historiographical traditions pertaining to it, monographs on Hanoverian London and on Robespierre, and much more. The complete bibliography of his work compiled for this volume lists twelve monographs (with a thirteenth about to appear and a fourteenth already on the way)[1], and over three-score articles and editions: astonishingly, this production issues from an academic career begun when Rudé was already forty years old. He is, in many respects, an historian's historian, combining scrupulous archival research with detailed, almost *pointilliste,* quantitative analysis, and unfailingly clear exposition and writing with comparative perspectives and historiographical mastery. He is a Marxist open, somewhat uncharacteristically, to the modern "social sciences", and writing from a supple and rather deceptively "common-sensical" analytical stance, one ever-sensitive to the complexities of social, political, and cultural interaction and to the role of personality and events in historical unfolding. Equally at home with *histoire des structures* and *histoire événementielle,* he has consistently sought to understand and to value the role of "ordinary people" in those two great Revolutions, French and British, political and industrial, which have shaped the modern Western, and contemporary, world.

The contributors represented in these pages--his colleagues, students, and friends--are all practitioners of the special branch of historical research George Rudé has so assiduously cultivated. The work collected in this book represents a rich contemporary counterpoint on themes either opened up or elaborated by him in his own groundbreaking studies. In Part One, Hugh Stretton, Manning Clark, and Alan Adamson shed light on Rudé's life and work in England, France, Australia and Canada. Part Two contains predominantly conceptual and pre-modern articles whose discussions illuminate subsequent interpretive issues. Eric J. Hobsbawm's "History from Below — Some Reflections" is a general discussion by a leading practitioner in the field. It is followed by Christopher Hill's analysis of the

3

ideological nature, and social limits, of the term "the people" in seventeenth-century England, opening perspectives reflected in V. G. Kiernan's study of the Scottish Covenanters' religiously-expressed resistance, into the eighteenth century, to changing social and political circumstances. Ellen Meiksins Wood's study of the socially democratic meaning of Rousseau's "General Will", by rooting the discussion in a comparative analysis of Ancien Régime and English socio-political structure and political theory, acts as a conclusion to Part Two and a conceptual bridge to Part Three.

Part Three, focusing on Revolutionary France, the starting-point of Rudé's researches into popular movements, opens with George C. Comninel's discussion of current approaches to the popular context of the Revolution, and of *sans-culotte* politics within it. Barrie Rose's evaluation of a peasant riot (and of Babeuf's role in it) in 1791 evokes forms of rural protest pre-dating, and a vision of mass action post-dating, 1789, while William J. Murray's study of D.-J. Garat as "philosophe" moves through, and beyond, the Revolution. The subtly different approaches of the late Albert Soboul and of Walter Markov to the complex problem of the Revolutionary *"curés rouges"* touch on ideological issues already marking V. G. Kiernan's piece on religion and protest. Pierre H. Boulle's essay on the colonialist origins of racial ideology in Ancien Régime and early Revolutionary France also provides context for Carolyn Fick's "Black Peasants and Soldiers in the Saint Domingue Revolution", which probes the popular impact of Revolutionary ideas and policies. John F. Laffey's analysis of French social ideology after 1815 takes us through the 1830 and 1848 revolutions and their consequences, to close Part Three.

Part Four groups a series of studies pre- and post-dating the Revolution, and crossing Rudé's 1848 dividing-line for popular movements. Neal Wood discusses the impact on St. Augustine's social theology of North African peasant terrorism, while J.S. Bromley's analysis of the social origins, organizational forms, and ideological values of seventeenth- and eighteenth-century Caribbean "boucaniers" and freebooters also touches on issues in the Boulle and Fick articles of Part Three. Pierre Vilar follows Catalan popular rebellion across the pre-industrial/industrial protest divide signalled by Rudé's work, reinforcing observations arrived at by Kåre Tønnesson in his evaluation of the Thrane movement and Norwegian protest to 1855. Caroline Ralston applies a number of Rudé's categories to a non-European movement in her study of "the ordinary Hawaiians", and William J. Fishman concludes this book by bringing us into the twentieth century, and back to England, with an account of a London "people's journée" in 1936 (and a reference to the young George Rudé doing on-the-spot "crowd research").

*"History from Below": Studies in Popular Protest and Popular Ideology in Honour of George Rudé* is a rich collection of contemporary studies of popular protest and popular ideology. Its authors, whether already masters in their own right or still younger journeymen scholars, and no matter how diverse their individual concerns, owe a debt to George Rudé's work and example, one they gladly consented to discharge by participating in this *Festschrift*. The ensemble of their collected articles, with its rich documentary and bibliographic resources, compliments, broadens, and extends Rudé's own extensive corpus. This "Introduction" will turn now to an examination of the major themes informing Rudé's writing and thought,

both to indicate its range and quality and to situate the articles which follow. I will stress exposition, rather than critique, and--knowing well, in this case, the "face" belonging to the "name"--will, to the extent possible, let the master (unlike his "pre-industrial" subjects) speak with his own voice. Some repetition of points made in the second part of Hugh Stretton's perceptive "George Rudé", which opens Part One, is inevitable, although our emphases being somewhat different, a number of disparate issues and materials will be addressed.

## *II*

George Rudé's concern with the study of "popular movements" issues, as Hugh Stretton notes below, from the human commitments which have marked his life. He came to scholarship relatively late, his career beginning--he was already forty--with his University of London doctoral dissertation of 1950 (done under Alfred Cobban), "The Parisian Wage-Earning Population and the Insurrectionary Movements of 1789-1791". Over the succeeding thirty-five years he has deepened and extended his understanding of popular movements, all the while pursuing a busy university teaching career beginning at Adelaide, in Australia, and continuing now at Concordia University in Montreal. His concerns were comparative almost from the beginning: the Gordon Riots of 1780 soon joined Parisian insurrection as a focus of study, and the first article limning out what would later be *Wilkes and Liberty* (1962) was published two years before the appearance of the great *The Crowd in the French Revolution* (1959).[2] Comparative historiography, demanding as it does multiple competences, is rather rare among historians; beginning, for Rudé, with the studies of Britain and France collected in *Paris and London in the Eighteenth Century* (1970) and extending in a work like *Ideology and Popular Protest* (1980) from the medieval period through colonial America and twentieth-century Latin America, it has led to a rich harvest of empirical and conceptual insights. His comparative range, one of his great strengths as an historian, is even more evident in the series of large-scale societal and historiographical studies, perhaps better known to the public than to the profession, which have flowed from his pen: *Revolutionary Europe,* 1783-1815 (1964), *Hanoverian London* (1971), *Debate on Europe 1815-1850* (1972), *Europe in the Eighteenth Century* (1972).

Indeed, over the years two *genres,* at first sight somewhat antithetical, have marked his writing: the deservedly famous detailed analyses and re-creations of specific popular movements, rooted in painstaking archival research and quantitative method, and the broader, reflective works of synthesis. How these two strands of his achievement in fact reinforce one another generally and come together to inform one of his finest studies, *Robespierre: Portrait of a Revolutionary Democrat* (1976)--a work unique in Rudé's *œuvre* in its sustained confrontation of an *individual* making, and being made by, history--will be the subject of the final part of this "Introduction".

\*

"Popular" in Rudé's lexicon means, almost literally, "of or pertaining to the people"; the "lives and actions of the common people... the very stuff of history", as he put it in 1970,[3] not of those of the dominant classes or "elites" (or their agents), is the focus of his work. "Pre-industrial" locates popular history temporally; its *terminus ad quem* politically is the February, 1848 Revolution in France and Chartism, again to 1848, in England; in economic terms, the break comes with the impact of the industrial revolution, first in England and later in France, reflected for Rudé's purposes above all in new forms of organization (both imposed "from above" and developed "from below") for rural and urban labor. This decisive turning-point witnesses the shift from generally spontaneous and "backward-looking" crowd action--the food riot, machine-breaking, urban window smashing and "pulling-down" of selected houses--to more organized and "forward-looking" expressions — mass demonstrations and petitions, formation of labor unions, emergence of "permanent" leaders, autonomous working-class action. Ideologically, the "backward"-"forward" dialectic is also central: from traditional concepts of "just" prices and wages, of "natural justice" ("the way it has always been") and the "freeborn Englishman's 'ancient liberties'", expressed in *taxation populaire,* peasant rebellion and urban riot, to clearer economic and political perceptions of longer-term popular needs (the *sans-culotte* movement in Paris by 1793, Owenite and French "utopian" socialism, the "New Model" English trade unions of the 1850s and 1860s). Methodologically, since by and large pre-industrial people spoke through their actions, and, in turn, written transcriptions of this concrete language ("a short argument, fire", as Carlyle put it) issued from those hostile or, at best, indifferent to them, Rudé sought to re-create the "crowd", to identify its members (and, later, their victims) individually and to vindicate them as historical actors in their own right. Here he followed in the footsteps of his revered George Lefebvre, the "master of the study of the Revolution 'from below'", whose own working motto--*Sans érudition, pas d'histoire*--Rudé appropriated and exemplifies in all his work.[4]

In his first book, *The Crowd in the French Revolution* (1957), Rudé refused to view the popular elements composing the *sans-culottes*--craftsmen, small shop-keepers, journeymen, laborers--"from above", as a "disembodied abstraction and personification of good or evil", as either Michelet's virtuous and homogeneous "*le peuple*" and Aulard's "*tout Paris*", or (more easily dispensed with for Rudé) Burke's "mob" or "swinish multitude" and Taine's "*gens sans aveu*". Instead, he sought, using new sources such as police and judicial records, to re-create the revolutionary crowd "from below", as a "thing of flesh and blood", with its own "distinct identity, interests, and aspirations". At Rudé's hands the Parisian *menu peuple* on the eve of the Revolution, rooted in traditional forms of protest, become, through exposure to democratic ideas and participation in the great revolutionary *journées,* the *sans-culottes,* increasingly aware politically and playing a major role in defending the Revolution and driving it forward. *The Crowd in the French Revolution* asks, and answers, what would become characteristic "Rudéan" questions about the crowd and popular movements in general:

> ... how it behaved, how it was composed, how it was drawn into its activities, what it set out to achieve and how far its aims were realized.[5]

Analysis of the lists of the 662 "*vainqueurs de la Bastille*" and of those arrested or killed on other Revolutionary *journées* indicates that they were not *canaille*, thieves and bandits, Taine's "*la dernière plèbe*", but characteristic Parisian working-people, generally "of fixed abode and occupation", no more criminals than "the ordinary run of Parisian citizens from whom they were recruited". Nor, though impelled by the traditional need of the poor for cheap and assured bread, were their actions simply a series of *émeutes de la faim:* "The new ideas of 'liberty' and the 'rights of man' were... gaining ground among the *menu peuple*...".[6] A gunsmith arrested at Versailles in 1789 demands a fair hearing on the basis of "le droit de l'homme"; a cook arrested after signing the Champs de Mars petition, following the King's "flight to Varennes" in July, 1791, describes its purposes in her interrogation as "*à faire organiser autrement le pouvoir exécutif*".[7]

What of leadership? Obviously, from the Orléanists through the Jacobins, bourgeois parties gave "cues" to the popular crowds; but was there a peculiarly *sans-culotte* leadership stratum, able to guide the people's own, more authentic, action? Before 1791, Rudé answers, no; after--through participation in the Commune and the Paris sections--, yes. This concern with the problem of the relationship between leadership and spontaneity will mark all his subsequent work; here, after noting the shift from "external" direction in the early years of the Revolution to a later phase of more "internal" guidance, he concludes that there nevertheless "remains an element of spontaneity that defies a more exact analysis".[8]

The narrative (always stage-front in Rudé's work) ends with Thermidor and its aftermath. Jacobin backtracking on the *Maximum* legislation of September, 1793, forced on them by popular demands for price-controls, "snapped the link" binding them to the *sans-culottes*. Robespierre was greeted by workers' cries of "*foutu Maximum*" as his tumbril passed to the guillotine on 10 Thermidor (28 July, 1794). Subsequent popular risings against the Directory's "free-trade" policies, which had produced spiralling bread-prices and a drop in real wages, were put down by General Dubois' 40,000 troops in Germinal and Prairial of the Year III (April-May, 1795). When the royalists rose against the Directory in Vendémiaire (October, 1795), the Faubourg Saint-Antoine watched passively as Napoleon dispersed the dissident bourgeois with his "whiff of grapeshot". "The days of 'revolutionary crowds'... were over for many a year".[9]

The final part of the book, "The Anatomy of the Crowd" (playfully echoing Crane Brinton's *Anatomy of Revolutions,* with its rather different vision of crowds), seeks to reap the conceptual harvest of the preceding empirical chapters. The more politically conscious *sans-culotte* elements, when they emerged, were rarely wage-earners; but laborers, wage-earners, journeymen and women predominated in the *journées* and in *taxation populaire,* forced reduction of prices in markets and shops. If the "active elements" adopted political ideas and goals derived "from above", they did so because these "coincided with their own interest in the fight against the old régime and to safeguard the Republic". Yet such goals "cannot be regarded as the particular demands of wage-earners, small shopkeepers, and workshop masters as such" — "Where, then, draw the line?" Rudé's answer is that it is a *question mal posée:* the "line" of social and political consciousness is a continuum, based on the fundamental need of the *menu peuple* for cheap and sufficient food, with ascending awareness a function of the interaction between continuing need and the unfolding of the Revolution itself as an "educational" process: from initial support for *le tiers état* to support for the execution of the king and for a republic, to more radical, *Hébertiste-* and *Enragé*-assisted, social demands. Specifically, and across time, "It is, in fact, this element of mutation and transformation that marks the revolutionary crowd in its most typical form". Immediate "panic-fear", involving threat to "three matters of vital moment--property, life, and the means of subsistence"--often sparks initial actions. The peasants' "Grand Peur" of 1789, *sans-culotte* fear of a *complot aristocratique* (behind the "September Massacres" of 1792), bourgeois and small rural and urban property holders' fear of the *loi agraire,* the radicals' demand for the re-distribution of property — all entered into the unfolding of the popular movement. Popular action occurred in contexts within which "economic crisis, political upheaval, and the urge to satisfy immediate and particular grievances all played their part".[10]

The last chapter, "The 'Revolutionary Crowd' in History", already points to the more general concerns of Rudé's third book, *The Crowd in History* (1964). If some features of *sans-culotte* protest reach back into the eighteenth century, others reach forward, to June, 1830 and February, 1848, when masters and journeymen again marched together to the barricades. Yet the June days of 1848, reflecting changing economic and social structures, expess something new, a marked increase in the proportion of wage-earners among the insurgents, who, "organized in their own clubs, marched under their own banners and leaders, and far from responding to the ideas and slogans of the *bourgeoisie,* were deeply imbued with the new ideas of Socialism". And in England, as we shall soon see, a similar process was under way, and even earlier on. "A new kind of 'revolutionary crowd'--to use the term in its broadest possible sense--with new social objectives and new modes of expression was evolving in western Europe...".[11]

In 1962, after "warming up" through a series of shorter studies of English riots, Rudé published *Wilkes and Liberty. A Social Study of 1763 to 1774.* He tells us, in the "Introduction", that his concern is not so much biographical as to relate Wilkes' life, career and opinions "to their social background and to trace the nature, course and outcome of the movements that sprung up in their wake".[12] Writing eight years later, he noted that what was original about his second book "was not so much the subject or the conclusions as the method used to arrive at the results".[13] Wilkes' supporters went beyond the social equivalents of the *sans-culottes,* and extended out into the counties and northern towns as well as London and Middlesex. This meant painting on a much wider canvas, and using a far greater range of documentary materials — records of the London livery companies, rate-books and land-and tax-registers, city directories, lists of justices of the peace, petitions, and so on.

Wilkes, educated son of a well-to-do distiller, entered the Commons in 1757 and in 1762 became editor of an opposition weekly, *The North Briton.* "No. 45" of the paper, in April 1763, led to a complicated train of events in the course of which he was arrested for publishing "a seditious and treasonable paper" and, finally, expelled from his Commons seat when he re-issued "No. 45" and used the paper to print *An Essay on Woman,* an obscene parody of Pope's *Essay on Man.* Charming, politically adroit, and not without courage, Wilkes, who had averred his support for "the middling and inferior sort of people, who stand most in need of protection", became a popular hero. Crowds shouted "Liberty! Liberty! Wilkes for ever!" at his first trial and "Wilkes and Liberty!" at the great processional escorting him home upon his release. As his dismissal from Parliament became a constitutional issue, he was elected, in March, 1768, MP for Middlesex, London's major "outparish". His re-imprisonment, without bail, in April touched off two weeks of rioting in London; on 10 May, the day Parliament opened, a crowd of over 20,000 from all parts of London, gathered in his support in St. George's Field, was fired on by government troops, killing four or five and wounding fifteen. Waves of street riots ensued, with selective window-smashing and the "pulling-down" of magistrates' houses; at a massive riot outside the House of Lords cries of "Wilkes and Liberty!" mingled with others that "bread and beer were too dear & that it was as well to be hanged as starved".[14]

A farcical duel between King and Administration and Wilkes and his City supporters was fought out in the Commons, with Wilkes repeatedly elected and, in turn, repeatedly disqualified by the House majority. Finally, Wilkes having defeated a hand-picked Court candidate, the Commons, in exasperation, simply declared him ineligible and seated his defeated opponent. This time, however, in addition to support in the street, Wilkes became the focus of a Middlesex electors' petition campaign, which would soon spread across England.

Much of the Wilkite movement is comparable with the Parisian phenomena Rudé had already studied. Utilisation of criminal records showed that, at the "lower" level, Wilke's supporters were "servants, journeymen, small craftsmen, or petty traders... nearly all lived in lodgings". Again, as for Paris, there is a correlation between Wilkite protest and rising bread prices (though food-rioting in well-provisioned London was the exception, rather than the rule). And, again, Rudé concludes that, nevertheless, such correspondence "can only serve as a partial explanation" of the movement--popular support for the "Revolution principles" of City magistrates and the Opposition, which predated "Wilkes and Liberty", must be factored in. Here, as in Paris, the ideas accompanying the street actions of "the inferior sort" were often those "more lucidly and decorously expressed by the 'middling sort'", issuing especially, in the case of London, from the City's Common Council, long proud of its independence and often (over economic policy and war) in opposition to Court and Administration. William Beckford, twice Lord Mayor and "Pitt's principal henchman in the City", standing for Parliament in 1761, had attacked the importance of "'little, pitiful boroughs' and thus fired the opening shot in the City's campaign for parliamentary reform". Wilkes' own political vocabulary drew on "the traditional stock-in-trade of Whigs and other upholders of the Good Old Cause", the constantly-repeated refrain that "the Englishman's liberties were... being violated by a tyrannical executive... and required to be defended". It was a viewpoint drawing on old causes and myths, nourished by the "country party", Chathamites and City radicals, and echoed in the streets by Wilkite demonstrators.[15]

What Rudé identifies as the centrally important aspect of "Wilkes and Liberty", and really fascinates him about it, is that the movement, for the first time, is "metropolitan in scope rather than limited... to the confines of the City". And, further, that, from the beginning, it acted as a rallying point for previously disparate social elements, both within and without London. If, aside from the popular strata, Wilkes' support came in London and Middlesex from the "middling" and lesser sorts of merchants, represented by the Common Council, Rudé's close analysis of the country-wide petition campaigns of 1769 shows Wilkite support there "more solidly and directly founded on the deeper sentiments of the mass of the county freeholders and the freemen and householders of the bigger trading cities". Remarkably, the 60,000 signatories represented one-quarter of the voting population. When the King rejected the petitions by ignoring them, Edmund Burke reminded his supporters in the Commons that when the gentry deserted the freeholders under Charles I, "The body of freeholders got up; the gentlemen were trampled down: they were made slaves to draymen & brewers"; and William Beckford insisted that "The 40s. freeholder has as good a right as any large property-owner to send a man to Parliament. I never measure the patriotism of a man by the number of his acres. I have known the greatest rascals in the Kingdom in laced coats".[16] To criticisms that "people of family and fortune" were insufficiently represented among the signatories, John Robinson replied that the mere weight of numbers was a factor that "would never be quieted".[17]

The Wilkite movement, Rudé concludes, contributed to a coalition which brought into political action "freeholders and freemen unstirred by earlier agitation" and thousands more beyond London and its counties "previously considered outside the 'political nation' and... untouched by parliamentary or municipal elections". In time, and despite setbacks, this incipient "mass radical movement" would acquire a more stable base and migrate north, to the new industrial towns. If 1780 witnessed the "No Popery" Gordon Riots in London, a throwback to an earlier tradition of protest, the same year saw the beginnings of the campaign by the Yorkshire Association -- founded by a kinsman of a Wilkite petition signer -- for Parliamentary reform.[18]

*

With two major monographs, and a series of smaller "five-finger exercises" on popular movements now behind him, Rudé was anxious "to write a synthesis of my studies on England and France".[19] The result, *The Crowd in History. A Study of Popular Disturbances in England and France* (1964) is a rich, deservedly famous work, combining the by now evident control of detail with a more consciously comparative, and reflective, framework. The book opens with a careful methodological discussion, and closes with general reflections on "Motives and Beliefs" and "The Pattern of Disturbances and the Behaviour of Crowds"; intervening chapters give detailed examinations of French and English rural and urban riots, Luddism, political riots, labour disputes in the French Revolution, "Church and King", "Captain Swing", and "Rebecca" riots, Chartism, and 1848 in France. Two summary paragraphs constitute a kind of "phenomenology of the crowd" and are worth citing in full. First, what are the general characteristics of "pre-industrial" crowds?

... the typical form of social protest is the food riot, not the strike of the future or the millenarial movement or the peasant *jacquerie* of the past. Those engaging in popular disturbances are sometimes peasants (as in the past), but more often a mixed population of what in England are termed "lower orders" and in France *menu peuple* (or, for a short time in the 1790's *sans-culottes):* they appear frequently in itinerant bands, 'captained' or 'generaled' by men whose personality, style of dress or speech, and momentary assumption of authority mark them out as leaders; they are fired as much by memories of customary rights or a nostalgia for past utopias as by present grievances or hopes of material improvement; and they dispense a rough-and-ready kind of 'natural justice' by breaking windows, wrecking machinery, storming markets, burning their enemies of the moment in effigy, firing hayricks, and 'pulling down' their houses, farms, fences, mills, or pubs, but rarely taking lives. The riot, then, is the characteristic and ever-recurring form of popular protest which, on occasion, turns into rebellion or revolution.[20]

"Stereotypical" approaches, from Burke and Michelet through Taine to Gustave Le Bon's "psychological" racial and animal metaphors (and his view of revolutionary crowds as composed of criminals and degenerates) reduce the men and women involved to disembodied abstractions, what Carlyle called a "dead logic formula". How, then, escape the stereotypes?

...we should attempt from the start to place the event in which the crowd participates in its proper historical context.... Next: how large was the crowd concerned, how did it act, who (if any) were its promoters, who composed it, and who led it? [ We must examine ] what Asa Briggs has called 'the faces' in the crowd in terms of the individuals and groups that compose it, their social origins, ages (sometimes) and occupations. Next: who were the target or the victims of the crowd's activities? ... what were the aims, motives, and ideas underlying these activities? ... without such enquiry we shall have to fall back on the purely 'psychological' and 'behaviorist' explanations of the crowd... how effective were the forces of repression, or of law and order?.... Finally, what were the consequences of the event, and what has been its historical significance? And so, having dissected the crowd and its components, its leaders and victims, we return to the question from which we started -- *the nature and importance of an event* in history.[21]

In the course of *The Crowd in History* Rudé addresses several key conceptual problems. How, for instance, apply modern conceptions of "class" to pre-industrial societies which were organized, thought, and acted in terms of "orders", "ranks", "degrees" and so on? Reading the past in terms too close to the present distorts it (he takes D. Guérin's *La lutte des classes sous la 1re République* [ Paris, 1946 ] to task for mistakenly presenting the *sans-culottes* as "a modern proletariat in embryo", a topic to which he will later return in *Robespierre).* But historical understanding has its advantages, even as one must beware of the opposite error, "which is to be bound too closely and too literally by the social labels used by contemporary writers and observers":

Whatever contemporaries may have thought about it, society is continuously evolving and developing and there is bound to be a time-lag separating the emergence of new forms and their recognition in the 'language of class' used by dictionaries and encyclopedias.... Here, of course, the historian, though so often at a disadvantage, has the advantage of being able to look back at the whole course of development, and can thus gauge more precisely the exact point of transition and devise social labels appropriate to the occasion....[22]

The question of leadership is also clearly addressed: "how far is the crowd representative of the social groups from which its component parts are drawn?" The "militant"-"passives" distinction should not be carried too far — there are indeed *meneurs* or activists who play a role even in spontaneous movements, but crowds composed of "dedicated militants" emerged in Paris only after the Revolution had produced a "political élite from among the *sans-culottes* themselves", and in England, "where riot never reached the stage of revolution", this kind of crowd emerged only later. On occasion, the crowd imposes assent by terror or force, yet often the majority extends its approval and exhibits "an evident bond of sympathy and common interest linking the active few and the inactive many".[23] Insofar as motivation is concerned, what crowds do is what we must suppose they intended — "we must, therefore, not be so subtle or devious as to ignore the overt or primary intention". Yet the issue is complex, there may be deeper causes, and, where mixed social groups participate, motives may vary, "and not only between one action and the next, but between different groups participating in the same disturbance".[24]

The connection between action and motive now leads Rudé into a "cultural" distinction to be elaborated in *Ideology and Popular Protest* sixteen years later. He distinguishes between *dominant* and *underlying* motives, with the former, "for the sake of clarity", divided into "economic" and "political" aspects. Food-riots, strikes and peasant movements issue from "dominant" economic concerns, and constitute the majority of pre-industrial protests. City riots (Wilkite and Gordon riots), and large-scale movements like the French revolutions of 1830 and 1848, issue from "dominant" political concerns, yet are often impinged upon by contextual "economic" factors (rising prices or food shortages). And dominant motivation can be multiple—*sans-culottes* rising against the Directory in May, 1795 "wore on their blouses the twin slogans, 'The Constitution of 1793' and 'Bread'". Alongside such generally "forward-looking" dominant motives often lie other, more directionally ambiguous, *underlying* motives, what "crowd psychologists and social scientists have termed 'fundamental' or 'generalized' beliefs". The "levelling instinct", impelling crowds to seek justice at the expense of *les grands,* the rich, those in authority, is most common. Here, beyond political slogans, is where "the militant sans-culotte meets the 'Church and King' rioter or the peasant in search of his millenium". And underlying motives like the levelling instinct can be Janus-faced, "as readily harnessed to an anti-radical as to a radical cause". Jacobins (in carriages) were attacked in the streets of Naples in 1799, Vendée peasants hated bourgeois more than local landlords, Priestly and friends were abused in Birmingham as men of wealth and status even though dissenters and radicals.[25]

In the 150 years at hand, the transformation of countryside, town, and city transformed too the people's conditions of life. Traditional notions of "just" price and wage faced, opposed, and gave way to the new notions of "natural" prices and wages set within competitive markets. Starting earlier in England, but with a "sharp thrust forward" in France in the 1760s and 1770s, in both countries "the process was largely completed by 1800". And if older forms still survived into the new century, in the collective traditions of French villages and the Speenhamland System's poor-rate subsidized agricultural wages, the future forms of modern protest lay elsewhere. Noting Reinhard Bendix's distinction between "pre-democratic" and "democratic" protest, Rudé once again emphasizes the decisive impact of "the new and essentially forward-looking ideas of 'the rights of man' and 'popular sovereignty' which, once they had gripped the popular imagination'', informed popular riot with a new dimension and a previously lacking "stable ideological content". Still, traditional beliefs might yet, despite changed conditions, be not so much abandoned as transformed — "in this sense, there is no radical departure from the old yearning for 'protection' in the socialist ideal of a more fully collectivist society".[26]

With the powerful *Captain Swing. A Social History of the Great English Agricultural Rising of 1830,* written in 1968 with Eric Hobsbawm, Rudé moved from the urban orientation of his earlier work into the countryside, and to an evidentiary base wider and richer even than the *Wilkes and Liberty* materials. He sought, too, to address what he now felt were several lacunae in his approach:

> ... it has been easier [in *Swing*] to present a living picture of both the riots and the rioters and of the agricultural population out of which they grew. It has been possible, too, to trace the laborers' history over a longer period, from 'trough' to 'peak' and back to 'trough' in two directions: into the aftermath of rural incendiarism and union organisation, and, for those transported, into their enforced exile in the Australian colonies ... I think this work marks a considerable advance on what I have been able to do, largely unaided and with other records, in the past.[27]

In Hobsbawm, Rudé had an able, experienced, and eloquent collaborator, whose own work in *Primitive Rebels. Studies in Archaic Forms of Social Movement in the 19th and 20th Centuries* (1959) had been extended by the essays in *Labouring Men. Studies in the History of Labour* (1964). The turbulent Sixties were a period in which popular history became genuinely "popular"; E.P. Thompson's influential *The Making of the English Working Class,* in which Rudé is acknowledged as "the foremost pioneer" in urban crowd studies, had appeared in 1963. Rudé, writing in 1972 of the new life breathed into "history from below" in these years, noted two broadly different emphases within the field, the "impressionistic" and the "statistical" or "analytical". Thompson exemplified the former: his concern was to "evoke the mood, the mentality and degree of class consciousness of a developing working class"; he and Hobsbawm represented the latter:

> ... our enquiry was both descriptive and analytical, but mainly it was analytical; we wanted to know, as precisely as possible, who the rioters were, why they rioted, how they behaved, and why their behavior was different in one place from what it had been in another. We were admittedly, like Thompson, concerned with motives and mentality, but even more with economic factors (such as prices, wages, Poor Law allowances, tithes, rents and profits), topography and patterns of behavior. In consequence, the records we consulted were often analytical and statistical, less often literary and impressionistic.[28]

The "Swing" riots of 1830 (named after the protesters' threatening letters -- "Revenge for thee is on the wing from thy determined Capt. Swing") -- broke out in Kent, an area close to London and the sea, and hence to news of the 1830 Revolution in Paris, and one also marked by rural and smalltown political discontents. Hobsbawm and Rudé relate the movement to its larger context, the period 1750-1850, across which a "traditional, hierarchical and paternalist" rural society was transformed into one dominated by the "cash-nexus" between farmer and laborer. The proletarianised rural worker was "deprived of those customary rights as a man (though a subordinate one) to which he felt himself to have a claim". "Hodge", the inarticulate country worker, left behind, aside from gravestones and children, only the "marvelous surface of the British landscape" which, unlike the masons' cathedrals, bore no signature;

> The task of this book is the difficult one ... of reconstructing the mental world of an anonymous and undocumented body of people in order to understand their movements, themselves only sketchily documented.[29]

*Captain Swing* is a remarkably integrated collaborative work, but not quite a seamless web; Rudé's hand is clearly present in the sections noted as primarily worked up by him (Chapters Five through Eight, the bulk of "The Rising" section; Ten through Fourteen, "The Anatomy of Swing"; "Repression" and "Australia" in Part IV; and the detailed quantitative-analytic Appendices — "Distribution of Disturbances by Counties", "Summary of Repression", "Table of Incidents", and "The Problem of the Threshing Machine"). His method and techniques inform one of the central sections of the book, which addresses the major problem of why some villages were riotous and others not.[30] On the basis of a close quantitative-statistical analysis, over time, Rudé sketches a "provisional 'profile' of the village disposed to riot". Such a village tended to be above average in size, to have a higher laborer-to-employing farmer ratio than others, a distinctly higher number of local artisans, and (possibly) a higher percentage of people independent of squire, parson, and large farmers — small family cultivators, shopkeepers, and so on. Interestingly, such a village also held groups "with a greater than average disposition to religious independence": nonconformity meant a nucleus of independence vis-a-vis squire and parson, "for few more overt gestures of independence can be conceived than the public refusal to attend the official church". Landownership in "high profile" villages tended to be "open" (held by many small owners) rather than "close" (owned by one or a few large landlords), and the former pattern characterized the rural slum areas, sources of surplus labor for neighboring parishes. The proximity of local communications centers, markets and fairs, and more pauperism and unemployment than tranquil villages, also come into play, but above all the presence of tillage and grain (rather than pastoral) farming or production of specialized crops dependent on a fluctuating labor demand, were clearly contributing factors.

Taken together, and factoring in the role of a prior history of local disputes over enclosures and perhaps local administration and politics, these simultaneously socio-political, geographical-economic, and cultural-ideological considerations constitute a fully three-dimensional, empirically-grounded analytic "model". This discussion -- in which, importantly, past history and development within the time period of "Swing" and after, play an important role -- is a remarkable expression of Rudé's now enlarged range and concerns, and clearly defines the village disposed to riot or, even, "to become one of those local centres of militancy whence riot radiated out over the surrounding region".[31] Similar quantitative inventiveness, and thoroughness, may be found in Appendix III's forty-six page "Table of Incidents", where seventeen categories, from arson through food riots to destruction of threshing machines and "sedition", are analyzed on a daily basis across 1830 in terms of "place", "county", "type of disturbance", "target" and "value" (cost of destroyed property).[32]

*Captain Swing* is a brilliant example of the new social history "from below", a complete re-creation of the nature, purposes, causes, rhythms, consequences, and importantly, the human agents of this agrarian protest movement. National in thrust, but concentrated in the low-wage South and East, and directed above all against the introduction of mechanical threshing machines (387 of which would be destroyed before "Swing" was over), its basic unit was "a small village group, composed of neighbours or bound by family ties". Town and village craftsmen, and sometimes even the farmers themselves, sympathetic to the laborers' cause, took part. The rioters themselves tended to be young or in early middle age and the proportion of married men was high; by and large, few had any previous criminal record. Across the entire period of protest the rioters -- but not the agents of their repression -- caused "not a single life" to be lost. In general, they "fully deserved the good reputations their employers and neighbours gave them":

> ...they believed in 'natural right' -- the right to work and earn a living wage -- and refused to accept that machines, which robbed them of this right, should receive the protection of the law...like most 'primitive rebels', and like Sir John Hampden 200 years before, they were firmly convinced that justice -- even the law -- was on their side.[33]

They were wrong. The new Poor Law of 1834 destroyed their last illusion, that society "would not let poor men starve like dogs. As the song put it:

> 'If life was a thing we could buy,
> The rich man would live -- what thousands he'd give!
> While a poor man he might die'". [34]

The answer to the final question Hobsbawm and Rudé pose -- "What, if anything, did the Swing movement achieve?" -- is complex. It may have played a role in the passing of the 1832 Reform Act, and in the Poor Law Amendment Act of 1834 and the Tithe Commutation Act of 1836 — but there is little direct evidence for this. If wages and conditions improved in some areas, this was short-lived. About one of the rising's results, however (with the exception of the eastern counties) there is "considerable confidence": "The threshing machines did not return on the old scale. Of all the machine-breaking movements of the 19th century that of the helpless and unorganised farm-labourers proved to be by far the most effective. The real name of King Ludd was Swing".[35]

*

Out of *Captain Swing* issued two subsequent studies, one (to which a chapter of the 1968 book had already been devoted) on *Protest and Punishment. The Story of the Social and Political Protesters transported to Australia 1788-1868* (1978) and the other, reflecting the growing concern across Rudé's writing with cultural dynamics, on *Ideology and Popular Protest* (1980). (Two intervening large-scale studies, which we will examine subsequently -- *Hanoverian London* [1971] and *Debate on Europe 1815-1850* [1972] -- had already begun to address, more clearly than before, the issues of crime and ideological process.) *Protest and Punishment,* too, touches for the first time on Canadian protest (Rudé had come to Québec in 1970), and one senses in *Ideology and Popular Protest* the Montréal refraction of the then-current Marxist-structuralist ideological debates raging in Paris.

One of the striking features of *Protest and Punishment,* aside from its moving elegiac conclusion, is the presence and utilisation of a large number of individual case-histories. Another is the way in which close study of the ca. 3,600 transportees (one in forty-five of the total across 1788-1868) acts as a kind of mirror in which we see reflected the basic transformation of British society and changes within Australia itself. Rudé points out that, precisely in these years, British (if not Irish) society was transformed: major urban populations, especially in London and the new northern industrial towns, doubled or tripled; population rose from 10½ to 16 million, and indictable crimes increased by over 600%. Transportation was, next to the death penalty, the most dreaded punishment the courts could mete out, yet despite -- or, perhaps, because of -- the steady softening of the British penal code in this period (by 1849 only high treason and arson endangering life were capital crimes), it was frequently imposed. But if Chartism and the Welsh "Rebecca" riots made 1842 a peak year for both protest and general crime, it was the severely-punished rural "Swing" riots of 1830 which yielded "the bumper year for protest activity and transportation", with 483 convicted rioters out of 1,350 indictments sent to Australia. Yet 1842 also produced a new kind of "industrial" convict, the seventy-five urban workers sentenced to transportation for the northern "Plug-Plot" riots. Conversely, changes in Australian society affected transportation, as well; increasing resistance to the acceptance of convicts saw Tasmania "close its doors" in 1852 (Sydney had already done so in 1841), with Western Australia, where the need for labor was greater, following suit later, in 1868. Within the colonies, and while conditions overall were harsh, authorities and employers often distinguished between the "politicals" and others, sentences were eased, and aid extended in individual re-settlement and family patriation. With the help of friends in their home countries, some transportees eventually returned home; most, however, remained, and died, in their land of exile.[36]

Rudé focuses on the 3,600 transportees--2,250 Irish, 1,200 Britons (England, Scotland, Wales), 154 French and English Canadians, 120 women -- "whose aim was to have rebelled or protested against the social conditions or institutions of the country from which they came." Rejecting both strictly "juridical" definitions, for which protest as such does not exist as a criminal category, and "radical" approaches, for which all crime, as a product of poverty and deprivation, is "social", he stresses transgressive acts with a clear social or political content and a collective or communitarian dimension.[37] He relates the incidence of transportation to the rhythms of home-country protest, and uses the case-histories -- as he did in *Swing* -- to sketch in the "troughs" between protest and transportation "peaks". The book ends with a "Selective List of Prisoners" giving the names and occupations of almost 500 individuals.

What emerges across the usual tightly-argued and statistically-supported discussion (supplemented now by a good deal of eloquent "literary" documen-tation) is a detailed and sympathetic treatment of the convicts. The faces in this immense, long-term "crowd" come alive in what is, clearly, one of Rudé's finest achievements. In part, too, he is addressing the much-vexed national-historio-graphical problem of the impact of transportation on Australian society and culture. If the Hammonds painted too "rosy" a picture of the convicts as idealistic "village Hampdens" and modern Australian historians like A.G.L. Shaw and Manning

Clark have, more critically, pointed to the high percentage of "young urban thieves" among them, Rudé stresses the need to ask "not only *who* were the convicts but how did they change from one generation to the next?"[38] Insofar as his social and political protesters are concerned, it is precisely "the ubiquitous urban thief" of the general run of transportees "which is virtually missing from our protest chart". And when the "necessary" statistical as well as literary evidence is consulted, it also emerges that the crime-rate of his "politicals" *within* the colony falls "well below" that recorded for all transportees. And so it is among these 3-4,000 men that "we must look for the village Hampdens", men whose sentences, in the face of their otherwise exemplary records, should not be allowed "to deny them the respect that their descendants owe them". *The Australian Dictionary of National Biography,* however, lists only two dozen of them, and so Rudé urges, in an uncharacteristically elegiac vein, that they

> ...no longer deserve to be hidden in the shadows with all the others -- unsung heroes, let them be allowed to emerge and bask a little in the appreciation that posterity has too long refused them.[39]

It is tempting to leave *Protest and Punishment* with this celebration of the connection between quantification and the re-creation of lived, and too-often ignored, lives. It would, however, be remiss, in a book published in Canada, not to note *Protest and Punishment's* Canadian dimension. Rudé devotes two chapters to Canadian protest and transportation, issuing from the simultaneous "dual rebellion" of 1837 and 1838 in Upper (present-day Ontario) and Lower (Quebec) Canada, "which led to the Australian exile of fifty-eight French-Canadians and ninety-six Anglo-Canadians and citizens of the United States". Common factors behind the rebellion (the only Canadian protest movement resulting in transportation to Australia) were growing middle-class and farmer resentment over British domination (heightened after the Reform Bill of 1832), the impact on Canada of the great economic crises of 1836-37, and "the close proximity of the hoped-for 'liberator', the United States". In Lower Canada, survival of the *système féodal,* including payment of tithe to the Church, complicated *bourgeois* and *habitant* resentments and fed the "Patriot" cause. Both movements sought reforms and an extension of political democracy, and both had radical wings in favor of national independence.[40]

Both rebellions were, in the event, easily suppressed. Some 2,200 rebels and suspects were imprisoned, and about thirty eventually hanged; their respective leaders, like Louis-Joseph Papineau and the more-committed William Lyon Mackenzie, fled into exile across the border. On 22 September, 1839, the convict ship *Buffalo* sailed for Hobart from Quebec with seventy-eight Upper and fifty-eight Lower, Canadian transportees (twelve others had already sailed for Van Diemen's Land). Over time the Canadians, well-regarded by the authorities and aided by friends and families, returned home, to take up former occupations as lawyers, merchants and farmers. Rudé, an inveterate walker, had come across the commemorative "Monument des Patriotes" in the large Côte des Neiges cemetery on the Mountain soon after coming to Montreal. When researching *Protest and Punishment* he had discovered that the Monument oddly omitted the names of a number of the fifty-four Quebecers who had in fact returned from exile. Lest they, any more than their British and Irish comrades in Australia, be forgotten, he pursued the issue and, in a note, proudly proceeds to list their names.[41]

\*

If *Protest and Punishment* succeeds better than any of Rudé's previous work in putting faces on the individuals within the crowd, *Ideology and Popular Protest* (1980) takes the next step, and tries (as he put it in one of the *Paris and London* essays of 1969) "to get into the skulls of the participants".[42] After the completion of *Swing* Rudé had set himself the task the new book addresses:

> ... to fill in another gap in my studies of the 'crowd': to trace the origins and course of the ideas that 'grip the masses' (Marx's phrase) ... If the labour or social historian really wants to see 'mind put back in history' this is one of the jobs he will have to undertake.[43]

Rudé develops this observation in the opening pages of *Ideology and Popular Protest*, the most explicitly "theoretical" work in his *œuvre,* noting the shift in his concerns from "who" to "why". Now, in order to do justice to "the full range of ideas and beliefs that underlie social and political action", terms like "motives" or "generalized beliefs", used in *The Crowd in History's* earlier discussion of "dominant" and "underlying" popular culture, will no longer do. Instead, Rudé prefers to use the more analytic term, "ideology of protest": he recognizes that Marx and Engels initially restricted "ideology" to the "ideas of the ruling class", one of its means of exerting domination or hegemony over subordinate classes, but notes that their usage subsequently broadened to include "other intermediate forms of ideology".[44] And if, within the Marxist tradition, Georg Lukàcs' dualistic Hegelian distinction between "true" ("proletarian") and "false" ("bourgeois") consciousness is not of much use for heterogeneous pre-industrial strata, Antonio Gramsci's distinction between "fundamental" or "organic" (the modern bourgeoisie, or capitalists) and "traditional" (the non-industrially engaged common people) class ideology is. If, even in a twentieth-century industrial society (however important Italy's peasants were), Gramsci had to develop a flexible theory of ideology more pertinent to wider social groups, "how much more must it be so when an author is writing not of an industrial, but of a 'pre-industrial' society in which the two major classes dividing society today were still, *if they existed at all,* in the process of formation!".[45]

Gramsci, however, does not demonstrate how the "non-organic" or "non-fundamental" popular ideology is related to, or becomes merged with, "the more structured or sophisticated ideas of the 'fundamental' classes of which he writes". Yet this is, precisely, the conceptual issue which must be addressed in the socially transitional period within which Rudé's studies fall; and, he notes, it is one not addressed by other, contemporary students of ideology, from Marxists like Althusser and Coletti through non-Marxists like Geertz, Lichtheim, Plamenatz and C. Wright Mills. Definitions of ideology as a highly-structured set of ideas are not useful in relation to popular expressions, nor are notions like *"mentalité"* (Leroy Ladurie, Mandrou) or the "culture of poverty" (Oscar Lewis) which are either too broad and general, or too "passive".[46] Open to other approaches, but staying within a Marxist *optique,* Rudé is really trying to develop a theoretical approach to the ideological expressions of pre-modern social formations, in a period when *"popular* ideology" is not directly equivalent to "ideology as 'class consciousness'". What Rudé means by "popular ideology" is that

It is most often a mixture, a fusion of two elements, of which only one is the peculiar property of the 'popular' classes and the other is superimposed by a process of transmission and adoption from outside. Of these, the first is what I call the 'inherent' traditional element -- a sort of 'mother's milk' ideology, based on direct experience, oral tradition or folk-memory and not learned by listening to sermons or speeches or reading books. In this fusion the second element is the stock of ideas and beliefs that are 'derived' or borrowed from others, often taking the form of a more structured system of ideas, political or religious, such as the Rights of Man, Popular Sovereignty, *Laissez-Faire* and the Sacred Rights of Property, Nationalism, Socialism, or the various versions of justification by faith. So two things are important to note: one is that there is no such thing as a *tabula rasa,* or an empty tablet in place of a mind on which new ideas may be grafted where there were no ideas before (a notion dear to the proponents of the 'mindless rabble'); and the second is that there is also no such thing as an automatic progression from 'simple' to more sophisticated ideas... But it is equally important to realize -- and this is closely related to what has just been said -- that there is no Wall of Babylon dividing the two types of ideology, so that one cannot simply describe the second as being 'superior' or at a higher level than the first. There is, in fact, a considerable overlap between them. For instance, among the 'inherent' beliefs of one generation, and forming part of its basic culture, are many beliefs originally derived from outside by an earlier one.[47]

Examples of Rudé's "popular ideology" include the "Norman Yoke" notion of the original "liberties" taken by William the Conqueror from freedom-loving Englishmen "which, enriched by later experience, became an important popular legend" doing service into the Chartist era, and Lutheran and Calvinist ideas, thundered from the pulpits, which, by the seventeenth century, became, "in one form or another...part of the 'inherent' ideology or culture of the people at large".[48]

"Derived" ideology, however, "can only be effectively absorbed if the ground has already been well prepared" — poor Spanish peasants in 1794 rejected the Rights of Man, and recently-tribal or feudal African peoples and Pacific Islanders "find it hard to accommodate themselves to the blessings of *laissez-faire"*. And not only receptivity, but also reciprocity, is involved — "it is perhaps even more significant that the derived or more 'structured' ideas are often a more sophisticated distillation of popular experience and the people's 'inherent' beliefs". Marx himself, whose theory was rooted in reflection on historical reality, was "possibly the greatest purveyor of 'derived' ideas in history": and Rudé cites Althusser's observation, that "Marx has given back to the workers' movement in a theoretical form what he took from it in a political and ideological form".[49]

Given these dialectically subtle overlaps and interpenetrations, "where, then, more exactly, should one draw the line between the two ideologies?" "By 'inherent' beliefs I mean, for one thing the [universal] peasant's belief in his right to land", individually or collectively, and the small consumer's belief in his right "to buy bread at a 'just' price, as determined by experience or custom, or the worker's claim to a 'just' wage".[50] Yet the issue is complex; popular ideology contains not only inherent and derived elements, but other, more general components from what E. P. Thompson calls "the plebeian culture" and Michel Vovelle *sensibilité collective.* Together, these constitute a mixture or "amalgam" within which distinguishing what is truly inherent from what is more recently derived is often extremely difficult. Rudé cites, as an example, Hobsbawm's wonderful Italian brigand's proclamation, from the 1860s: "Out with the traitors, out with the beggars, long live the fair kingdom of

Naples with its most religious sovereign, long live the vicar of Christ, Pius IX, and long live our ardent republican brothers".[51]

On the other hand, "inherent" ideology alone, which may carry protesters into food riots, strikes and peasant rebellions, cannot lead them to transform their historical circumstances: "it cannot bring them all the way to revolution, even as junior partners of the bourgeoisie". What Thompson calls "the self-activating culture of the people derived from their own experiences and resources", despite its real achievements, nevertheless only "almost led them into believing they were 'free'". Pre-industrial popular movements relying wholly on their own "inherent" resources reach inevitable blockage, unless "supplemented by ... 'derived'" elements, political, social or religious. Yet even here, if such amalgams tend to be "forward-looking"--"No taxation without representation", *Vive le tiers État* or *Parlement,* "Wilkes and Liberty!"--they can also, depending on the nature of what is "derived", become "backward-looking", conservative or even counter-revolutionary — "Church and King", the Vendée peasants. Rudé points out that if the Tsarist fleet can become the Bolshevik navy, the latter can also become the Kronstadt sailors.[52] The *precise* form such mixtures take depends less on "the nature of the recipients or of the 'inherent' beliefs ... than on the nature of the 'derived' beliefs compounded by the circumstances then prevailing and what E.P. Thompson has called 'the sharp jostle of experience'".[53]

The "empirical" chapters of *Ideology and Popular Protest* develop a broad typology of ideological forms rooted in specific social formations, from the medieval period (where a tenth-century Norman peasant is reported to have cried *"nus sumes homes come il le sunt"*) through Absolutism and eighteenth- and nineteenth-century French, American and English movements, to contemporary Latin America.[54] The book ends with a final chapter, "Postscript: Industrial Britain", carrying the story into the present. This last chapter, concerned "with failure rather than success", is uncharacteristically personal in tone. Socialist hopes, raised by the decision in 1890 of the British trade unions to join the first International May Day celebrations, were soon dashed. Unequal distribution of the "fruits of Empire", the emergence of an "aristocracy of labour", bourgeois "liberalisation" aimed at re-stabilizing society and industry, propagandists within labour's ranks for "class mutualism" and "social peace", all combined to divide and to set back an emerging working-class movement. *Ideology and Popular Protest* closes its characteristically clear handling of a complex subject crucial in Rudé's work by repeating that "inherent" values are insufficient "to win decisive battles"; for this, "an injection of 'derived' ideas ... which Marx and Engels, writing on separate occasions, quite simply gave the name of 'theory'" was (and, as his last chapter indicates, still is) necessary.[55]

## III

If the crowd and popular movement studies from 1957 to 1980 constitute the clear *basso continuo* of Rudé's work, another, more discursive, kind of writing, starting with *Revolutionary Europe 1783-1815* (1964), provides important thematic and historiographical counterpoint. Four major works (and two ample and carefully-introduced source collections -- *The Eighteenth Century* [1965] and *Robespierre* [1967])--parallel, complement, and reinforce the unfolding "histories from below". This second body of work, employing a larger canvas than the first, is more explicitly concerned with narrative and personality, the role of "the event" and of individuals (as well as of cities, societies and nations) in the historical transition from early-eighteenth to mid-nineteenth centuries. A parallel reading of these two aspects of his writing reveals, as in the interactions between his "inherent" and "derived" ideologies, mutually enriching and reinforcing overlaps. The fruits of his crowd studies are quickly integrated into the general books, lending them a freshness and social dimension lacking in other works of similar range, and, reciprocally, the comparative-historiographical dimensions of the larger-scale syntheses are often brought into play to "locate" the crowd studies. This latter aspect is important, for it enables Rudé to ask questions about the larger implications and subsequent development of the specific movements under review.

*Revolutionary Europe* is emblematic of much of this production. After an initial "situating" chapter stressing basic, and changing, social structures, the different impacts and socio-political appropriations of the French Revolution are traced chronologically and geographically across Europe. Along the way there are masterful chapters on "Why was there a Revolution in France" and "1789", an incisive portrait of Robespierre, and three chapters discussing Napoleon and "The Napoleonic Era". The result is a fresh, sophisticated, high-level work of synthesis, and a model of clear, analytic narrative writing. Rudé's studies from 1955 on of London protest, including the essays collected in *Paris and London in the Eighteenth Century* (1970), come together now in extended form in his major urban history of 1971, *Hanoverian London 1714-1808*. Here not the crowd, but the great metropolis itself, is his subject. The reader watches London overtake Paris across 1714-1750 as perhaps the largest city in the world, and is taken inside the City's Common Council and its "rate-payer's democracy", unique in the world and closely connected to popular protest. London's geographical growth, the gradual social differentiation of neighborhoods, the plight of the poor and the growth of crime, improvements in sanitation and public health, the emergence of a new non-aristocratic "city" culture with the novel as bourgeois form, and a new kind of urban architecture — all are amply discussed and related. Using Daniel Defoe's 1709 social classifications. Rudé calculates that "The *middle sort,* who live well", constituted about one in seven of the population, or 125,000 persons, just after 1800, while "The *miserable,* that really pinch and suffer want", were one in eight, or 115,000 people, just before. Across the century City-based "popular egalitarianism", rooted in the great Revolution and the Good Old Cause and the tradition of the Englishman's "liberties", countered a continuing aristocratic social and political dominance. By 1801, much had changed — iron water-pipes, gas lamps, and water-closets had made their appearance. But Rudé, ever-sensitive to complexity and nuance, ends *Hanoverian London* by noting that "the new still rubbed shoulders uneasily with the old": in that year of the first census and the first steamboat on the Forth-Clyde Canal, "a woman was ducked in the Thames at Kingston, on the periphery of the new 'greater' London, in the traditional scold's chair'".[56]

*Debate on Europe 1815-1850* (1972) followed a year later. It is one of Rudé's finest texts, a reflective and self-reflexive historiographical masterpiece (Stretton, below, terms it "the most widely and wrongly neglected of his works"). Behind its careful and fair presentation of the major interpretive currents of European social, political and cultural history between 1815 and 1850 lies a genial, rather common-sensically disarming, and altogether Rudéan, "philosophy of history".

*Debate* opens with the observation that historians "often differ so widely" because of four factors: nationality; class and generation; nature of evidence used; and differing social, political, and religious views, with the mutual interactions of the variables complicating things further. Rudé concludes, given this, that "there can be no single received or universal truth"; if he himself, as a Marxist, chose to emphasize "material" factors and conflict in *Debate on Europe,* "In so doing I make no more claim to strict objectivity or 'value-freedom' on my part than I do for any of the historians whose work I am discussing":

> Man is a political animal and, once more, the historian is no exception. As he responds to the call of nationality or generation or religion, so he responds equally or with even greater vigour to the promptings of his political assumptions. The response may be a muted or a subtle one, or it may be crude or blatant, and even grotesque; but, in one guise or another, his work cannot escape it entirely.[57]

Yet there *is* a kind of relative objectivity — labels like "Tory", "Whig", "liberal" "conservative", "socialist", "Marxist" "are supposed to be reasonably objective definitions and not to separate goats from sheep or to be approbatory or condemnatory". If a "Marxist" is supposed to be someone stressing class struggle, putting "matter" before ideas yet weighting both, and praising revolutions and peoples' movements, such generalizations "never exactly fit". There are shadings, and "some [Marxists] are more subtle and perceptive and less given to dogmatic pronouncements than others; and this makes them better historians and, no doubt, better Marxists, too".[58] Still, there is something inescapably subjective about historical analysis, even of the less polemically-ridden "new economic history":

> If it were a matter of method alone, there could be no dispute about it -- the computer is neutral enough.... But method is only a part... the new economic history is as much indebted to new economic theory as it is to new means of quantification.... And theory implies evaluation and selection, including the questions historians ask; and these in turn will, irrespective of the neutrality of mechanical aids, reflect his 'values' and help determine the nature of his findings.

What to do about such continuing controversies? Rudé smiles, and disarmingly points out that we need not be alarmed, for "Controversy lies at the heart of all historical enquiry, and scholarship would be meaningless without it".[59]

*Debate on Europe* closes with a discussion of recent historiography on the February and June risings of 1848 in Paris. Is there evidence to support Marx's view of 1848 as "the first great battle...between the two classes that split modern society"? Rudé cites Peter Amann's view, that to see 1848 as a struggle between modern proletariat and bourgeoisie is "historical folklore": Paris was still, as in 1789, a city of small workshops and crafts, and Rémi Gossez is brought in with the reinforcing observation that, while social conflict was real enough, it was still traditional, between "rich" and "poor". Yet Rémi Gossez goes on to point out the "vanguard" role of a new kind of industrial worker in 1848, and Rudé concludes that "this was something new and showed that a modern 'proletariat', if not yet fully developed, was already in the making".[60] And this vision of 1848 as the *terminus ad quem* after which traditional, spontaneous popular protest begins to be replaced by newer forms of organized, "forward-looking" industrial protest, closes *Debate on Europe* and marks all of Rudé's subsequent crowd studies.

Rudé's productivity in the period 1962-1972, across which he changed continents and universities and directed Montreal's *Centre Interuniversitaire d'Études Européennes,* is striking. In 1972 *Europe in the Eighteenth Century. Aristocracy and the Bourgeois Challenge,* the fourth in this series of major large-scale works, appeared. Here not crowds or the city or historical interpretation, but the two "fundamental" classes confronting one another across the eighteenth century, is Rudé's subject. The subtle and richly-illustrated discussion ranges over the varying national forms of these internally-differentiated classes, touches on aspects of their pre-modern specificity, and compares their French and English variants on the eve of 1789. Differing with Godechot and R.R. Palmer on the reality of a cross-national "Atlantic Revolution", Rudé at the same time concludes that, with a number of important qualifications, the stress on British social and political "uniqueness", issuing from Toqueville, has "closed more doors than it has opened".[61] *Europe in the Eighteenth Century*'s conceptual range and sophistication (the latter, as in much of Rudé's work, somewhat obscured by the deceptively simple clarity of his writing) draws on the hard-earned insights of his specific crowd studies, and in turn, situates them over the equally important historical *longue durée*.

These two, intertwining, series of focused and large-scale monographs constitute together a remarkable corpus of eighteenth-century studies, singular in depth, range, and historiographical sensitivity. These qualities come together in yet another work of this period, the great *Robespierre. Portrait of a Revolutionary Democrat* of 1975, which deserves a special place in the growing list of Rudé's masterpieces.

\*

Rudé's *Portrait* of Robespierre, a sustained confrontation of the problem of individual action in history, is a work unique in his production. Despite its opening *Wilkes and Liberty*-like observation, that this is a "political rather than a personal biography", it is clear before "Part One"'s detailed narrative is over that Robespierre, and not the Parisian popular movement or the Revolution itself, is the subject of the book. And Robespierre is clearly a subject with whom Rudé identifies: we follow his career, from abandoned orphan in Arras through provincial "poor man's" lawyer and representative of Artois to the Estates-General of 1789, to "The Incorruptible" of 1791 ("The man will go far", Mirabeau observed, "he believes all he says"), dominant force in the Jacobin Club and leader of the left-democratic group in the Assembly.[62] "Part Two"'s broad-ranging historiographical survey of Robespierre's reputation (including east, as well as west, European historians) is followed by the heart of the book, the discussions in "Three" and "Four" of the interaction, from 1791 through Thermidor, between his thought, his political action, and the unfolding internal and external context of the Revolution.[63] From these pages, as individual greatness and historical inevitability come together in Robespierre's revolutionary practice, emerges what deserves recognition as one of the most dramatic examinations in recent historical writing of the fundamental individual-society-history dialectic.

Rudé's Robespierre, though possessed of the usual bundle of Enlightenment ideas and unswervingly committed to popular sovereignty, is not the rigidly abstract, messianic figure of hostile interpreters (Richard Cobb's "Saint-Maximilien"). Rudé stresses that "it was through the logic and pressure of events far more than through obedience to 'philosophical' precepts" that Robespierre arrived, by the autumn of 1793, at his vision of the "single will" necessary to protect the fragile Republic from internal and external threats. He cites Robespierre's great speech" of 25 December 1793:

> The theory of revolutionary government is as new as the Revolution that created it. It is as pointless to seek its origins in the books of the political theorists, who failed to foresee this Revolution, as in the laws of the tyrants... The object of revolutionary government is to preserve the Republic; the object of constitutional government is to establish it.[64]

Earlier, in his reply to the Girondins outraged by the Jacobin-backed popular storming of the Tuileries and capturing of the King, Robespierre had noted that

> ... all these things were illegal, as illegal as the Revolution, as the overthrow of the throne and the Bastille, as illegal as liberty itself! Citizens, *did you want a revolution without a revolution...* Who can determine, after the event, the precise point at which the flood of popular insurrection should have stopped?[65]

From December, 1793, in response to pressing need, Robespierre fashioned a new Jacobin "strong government", tightening controls in Paris and beyond, crushing an emerging Dantonist-Hébertiste opposition, and breaking with his former *sans-culotte* supporters: Saint-Just observed that "La Révolution est glacée". The *Maximum Général* of September, 1793, never seen by Robespierre as more than a temporary expedient, is eased to ensure "middle class" support for the revolutionary war. This, with the closing down of popular assemblies in Paris, alienates the *sans-culottes,* a factor of crucial importance when, in June, Jourdan's victory over the Prussians at Fleurus, by easing the external threat, leads to an anti-Robespierre coalition of moderate Jacobins, the Plain, and "terrorist" opponents. Robespierre, inexplicably withdrawing from public activity in precisely this period -- "a fatal gesture, or miscalculation" -- is arrested, fails to call on the residual nucleus of *sans-culotte* support that rallied to him, and is guillotined on 10 Thermidor (28 July) 1794. With him, Rudé observes, "perished not only a man or a group but a system. The democratic Republic of the Year II, created with the aid of the *sans-culottes,* gave way to the property-owners' Republic of Thermidor and the Directory...".[66]

Rudé's handling of Robespierre's policy in this period turns on a careful analysis of his social and political thought in relation to the pressing need to defend the revolutionary Republic. He notes, first, Robespierre's remarkable ideological consistency; he was, from his Arras days forward, "a champion of the *menu peuple...* easily moved to sympathy for the condition of the poor...". Beginning, like most bourgeois coming to Paris in 1789, with vague *laissez-faire* notions, Robespierre nevertheless moved leftwards as the Revolution, and his contact with the people, unfolded, arriving finally at a view of the necessity to put certain limits on the free disposition of property. In 1793, during the debates on the new Constitution and Declaration of Rights, he observed that

... to none of the people has it ever occurred that property carries moral responsibilities... We have justly said that this right [liberty] was limited by the rights of others. Why have we not applied the same principle to property, which is a social institution, as if the eternal laws of nature were less inviolable than the conventions evolved by man? You have drafted the numerous articles in order to ensure the greatest freedom for the exercise of property, but you have not said a single word to define its nature and legitimacy, so that your declaration appears to have been made not for ordinary men, but for capitalists, profiteers, speculators and tyrants.[67]

He went on to suggest a clause limiting the exercise of property rights when this impinged on "the security, or the liberty, or the existence" of others' property, as well as others stipulating an extension of the right to work to all *"citoyens malheureux"* and referring to "the international brotherhood of man". Rudé notes that "even the new Jacobin Convention of June 1793" refused to follow his suggestions. In February, 1794, in a speech on "the principles of public morality", he reminded the Convention that "It is only in a democracy that the State is really the fatherland of all the individuals that compose it and can count as many defenders devoted to its cause as it has citizens within its borders". Rudé comments that "The meaning is clear enough: it is only by satisfying their basic social and political wants that the common people can become firmly attached to the republican cause...".[68]

So Robespierre developed a social vision for a time congruent with the emerging popular movement which rallied to the Jacobin cause. The Revolution would help bring about a society of independent petty producers, owning their land and workshops and exchanging directly with one another: "It was a social ideal that many craftsmen and shopkeepers and small peasant proprietors could readily share with him...". Yet Robespierre was more sympathetic to the small producer than to the small consumer, and if he was repelled by the grasping *capitaliste* or *agioteur* emerging after 1789 he was also uneasy with "a third social phenomenon" issuing from this "transitional, pre-industrial society" — the *ouvrier,* the wage-earner or "proletarian" with "no recognizable status of his own". For him, as for Marat, Saint-Just and others, wage-labor was a transitory phenomenon, and one making for instability. The *ouvriers,* property-less, tied to their masters, without the natural "virtues" of free and independent craftsmen, were easily misled and provided a potentially dangerous pool of support for counter-revolutionary aristocratic activities. Robespierre never forgot the uncontrolled popular destruction of the "September Massacre" of 1792, and had denounced "patriots" rioting over food prices in February, 1793, for their concern with *de chétives marchandises.* He had Jacques Roux, the *"curé rouge",* arrested after he demanded radical measures against hoarders, and, no friend of the extreme-left *Enragés,* ridiculed Hébert's view of trade as a form of "despotism", noting that without it Paris and the other large cities could not be provisioned.[69]

Rudé observes that Robespierre deserves his reputation as a founder of French social democracy, but not, as some historians would have it, as an early socialist. "We must recognize the limits of his thinking, circumscribed as it was bound to be by the society in which he lived and the possibilities for change it appeared to offer". If to be a socialist means to believe in state ownership of the basic means of production and the redistribution of wealth, Robespierre was never a socialist, "either in theory or performance". And as for contemporary radical demands for the re-distribution of property -- the so-called *loi agraire* -- "he strongly disapproved of them and, at best, dismissed them as a chimera or visionary's dream". It was one thing to recognize, as Robespierre put it, that "extreme disparities of wealth lie at the root of many ills and crimes", and quite another to advocate equality of property, which he saw as an impossibility in civil society since "it must necessarily be based on community, which is still more obviously a fantasy in a country like ours...".[70]

When, by the winter of 1793-94, the popular movement gained "a degree of independence incompatible with the needs of a revolutionary gouvernement charged with the conduct of a revolutionary war", the limits of the Jacobin-*sans-culottes* alliance were reached. "Democracy", Robespierre noted in a speech of 17 Pluviose (5 February) negatively mirroring popular demands, "is not a state in which the people, continually assembled, directly controls all public affairs".[71] Familiar with Rousseau's "the people always wish the good, but does not always see it", Robespierre acted on his own maxim, that the people's mandatory must lead, and not merely follow, and, in order to save the Republic, he backed away from the Convention's progressive social legislation. Rudé presents Robespierre in this last, critical period as caught in an inescapable contradiction, between the limits of his own social vision and sense of practical necessity, and his inability and unwillingness to compromise with the other, emerging "wing" of the Revolution, those groups involved in the new capitalist relations of production which represented its concrete future. In this latter respect, some of his more "corrupt" fellow-citizens, Rudé notes, were "more perceptive than he was". The Revolution as a petty-producers' alternative to capitalist development was, at the end of the day, as much a Robespierrean "chimera" as that of the *loi agraire*. And so the real tragedy -- and irony -- of Thermidor was that Robespierre and the *sans culottes* "fell together, and that those who reaped the rewards were the monied men...the enemies of both".[72]

*Robespierre. Portrait of a Revolutionary Democrat* closes with an appreciation of Robespierre as "the Revolution's outstanding leader... the first great champion of democracy and people's rights". Unlike subsequent revolutionary leaders, he had no real models to guide his action: his policy reflected the strengths, and the limits, of his own values and perceptions, his own political development as events unfolded, and the necessary, and increasingly rigid, constraints of what Saint-Just called "*la force des choses*". Responsible for the Terror, but no *buveur de sang* (Collot and Fouché, behind the "Great Terror" of June and July, which he condemned in his last speech of 26 July to the Committee of Public Safety, warrant the term far more than he does), Robespierre's justified claim to greatness lies in his successful defense of the Revolution. Like Winstanley before, and Lenin after, Robespierre, in spite of his own limitations and those of compelling historical circumstance, made history.[73] And like Rudé's other, more collective "heroes" -- the urban crowds and rural laborers and transported convicts -- Robespierre, in personal defeat, nonetheless bequeathed an enduring human legacy to our own times.

*

*Robespierre* is a great book, in some respects perhaps Rudé's finest work. In it the hallmarks of his historical production -- the specificity of the crowd studies, his comparatist-historiographical range, the sure feel for underlying social structure, and his commitment to the centrality of narrative unfolding and "event" -- come together in sustained drama and beautifully-expressed creative synthesis. His remarkable scholarly productivity, of course, continues: we await the forthcoming *Criminal and Victim. Crime and Society in Early Nineteenth Century England,* and he is already at work on its successor, a study of crime, protest and ideology across three continents and two centuries. The rich materials that follow in this book written for him, *"History from Below"*: Studies in Popular Protest and Popular Ideology in Honour of George Rudé, reflect and extend his achievement. We offer them in homage to a master craftsman of the people's history, and an exemplar of Lefebvre's great motto, "Sans érudition, pas d'histoire".

# NOTES

1. *Criminal and Victim. Crime and Society in Early Nineteenth Century England* (Oxford, Oxford University Press, forthcoming); the next book analyses crime, protest and popular ideology before and after 1800.

2. "Wilkes and Liberty, 1768-69", *The Guildhall Miscellany,* 8 (July 1957), 3-24. As Stretton notes below, Rudé's "The Gordon Riots: A Study of the Rioters and their Victims" (*Transactions of the Royal Historical Society* [ser. 5] 6 [1956] 93-114) won the Historical Society's Alexander Prize; it is also an early example of Rudé's use of the social origins of the victims of popular movements to illuminate the social and political purposes of the rioters.

3. "The Changing Face of the Crowd", in L.P. Curtis, Jr., ed., *The Historian's Workshop. Original Essays by Sixteen Historians* (New York, 1970), pp. 187-204, at p. 189. In the same unusually reflective essay, Rudé notes that "I did not approach my subject[s] without commitment... I have always felt a bond of sympathy with them, whether their activities have been peaceful or rebellious"; believing that conflict, not equipoise, is "a normal and a salutary means of achieving social progress", Rudé adds that "I have not hesitated in looking back on the past to identify myself more closely with some parties in the conflict than with others" (190-91).

4. Rudé acknowledges his historical-methodological debt to Georges Lefebvre (from his studies of peasant movements in *Les Paysans du Nord* [1924] to his work on revolutionary crowds and rural rumor and panic -- "La Grande Peur" --) across his own production. Lefebvre aided Rudé in his initial researches in Paris; in "The Changing Face of the Crowd" Rudé observes that "all who came under his spell took away with them valuable lessons on what he considered indispensable to 'la bonne méthode' in all historical enquiry: *Sans érudition, pas d'histoire"* (192).

5. *The Crowd in the French Revolution* (Oxford, 1959), p. 9; pp. 1-4 for Michelet, Aulard, Taine and Burke (and Carlyle's crowd as "Victorious Anarchy"). (All citations to Rudé's monographs will be to first editions unless otherwise noted; see "George Rudé: A Bibliography" following this essay for complete bibliographical information, including translations into languages other than English.)

6. *Ibid.,* p. 196; p. 106 for those killed and wounded at the 10 August 1792 capture of the Tuileries and p. 187 for the *vainqueuers de la Bastille.*

7. Pp. 196-97 for the gunsmith (who had disparaged Lafayette) and the cook, Constance Évrard; of the some 130 persons arrested in connection with the Champs de Mars

demonstration, "the great majority" had expressed "political opposition to the National Assembly, the city administration, or the armed militia" (198). Rudé notes that political ideas, as such, were "mainly *derived* from the bourgeois leaders" [ my italics, to note a term which will loom larger in his later discussions of popular ideology], but that without the *sans-culottes'* ability to "adopt and adapt" them, the Revolution would have had a course and outcome "far less substantial than it in fact was" (p. 209).

8. The problem of leadership, from bourgeois "intermediaries" through indigenous *sans-culottes,* is discussed across pp. 219-231, in the context of the generally "defensive" actions of the *menu peuple* against the "innovations" of ministers, capitalists, speculators, "improvers", and so on.

9. "Thermidor", "Germinal-Prairial", and "Vendémiaire" are detailed in three chapters, pp. 128-77. The "new" repressive element here, the army, "stayed in occupation under the Directory and paved the way for the military dictatorship of Bonaparte" (177).

10. Pp. 178-190 for the social composition of the revolutionary crowds; p. 190 for the question "Where, then... draw the line?", with the answering discussion on pp. 191-209.

11. Pp. 210-39 for the general presentation of "the revolutionary crowd" after 1795, including a brief reference to "Wilkes and Liberty" and Gordon riots in London in 1768-69 and 1780; at p. 239 for the "new type of 'revolutionary crowd'".

12. *Wilkes and Liberty. A Social Study of 1763 to 1774* (Oxford, 1962), xiv: "It is, in fact, 'Wilkes and Liberty' rather than John Wilkes himself that is the central theme of this volume".

13. "The Changing Face of the Crowd" in L.P. Curtis, ed., *The Historian's Workshop* (1970), p. 195, where Rudé is also quick to disclaim a *Punch* reviewer's barb, that he had "Namierized the Mob".

14. *Wilkes and Liberty,* pp. 17-56 for biographical-political details and St. George's Field "Massacre".

15. *Ibid.,* pp. 54-73 for Wilkes' defeat of Henry Lawes Luttrell, the Court candidate, and pp. 74-89 for Rudé's analysis of his support by the Middlesex electors. The discussion of "City" political thought, and William Beckford on "little, pitiful boroughs", is drawn from the "London Background" chapter, at pp. 15-16.

16. Broadly speaking, the social evolution of London (to be more fully presented in Rudé's *Hanoverian London, 1714-1808* [ 1971 ]), and not Wilkes, lay behind "Wilkes and Liberty!" (Wilkes himself, seated in Parliament in 1774, ended his days defending the Bank of England, gun in hand, against the Gordon rioters of 1780). Chapter VII, pp. 105-48, analyses "The Petitions of 1769", with Burke and Beckford cited on pp. 136-7; Beckford, a particular favorite of Rudé, is quoted in a number of his works — he appears in the essay on "The London Mob of the Eighteenth Century" in Rudé's 1969 collection of articles, *Paris and London in the Eighteenth Century,* where he defines "the people" in terms strikingly close to those of Christopher Hill's conclusions in his "The Poor and the People in Seventeenth-Century England" in this book: "I don't mean the mob... I mean the middling people of England, the manufacturer, the yeoman, the merchant, the country gentleman, they who bear all the heat of the day" (p. 293 — Beckford is speaking in Parliament, in 1761).

17. P. 148. The Commons majority stressed the need for the presence among the petition signatories of "the soberest & most weighty part of the nation", not merely the weight of numbers, if they were to be taken seriously (p. 136) — this eighteenth-century aristocratic convention reaches back to medieval distinctions, in monastic and guild elections, between the *maior* (majority) and *sanior* (numerically smaller but socially weightier) *partes.*

18. Pp. 196-8. The Wilkite crowds, and the Wilkite movement as a whole, demonstrated not "to promote a purely outside interest, but in a cause which they believed, however vaguely and incoherently, to be their own.... This was something new in the nation's political live...."; and Wilkes, whatever his vagaries, "and eventual apostasy", is entitled to the simple device he had inscribed on his casket — "A Friend of Liberty" (196-7).

19. "The Changing Face of the Crowd", p. 196. The new book would go beyond the eighteenth century, and, building on some lessons learned from E. P. Thompson's *The Making of the English Working Class* (1963) and "more" from E. J. Hobsbawm's *Primitive Rebels* (1959), would "lend more weight than I had done before to the irrational in human motivation, to the phenomenon of violence in crowd behavior, to the forces of law and order, to the relations between leaders and followers in riots and revolutions, to the survival of archaic forms of thought and action carried over from an earlier age, to the role of religion and millenarian fantasies as adjuncts of disturbances, to the coexistence in popular movements of 'backward-looking' and 'forward-looking' concepts, to the special characteristics of counter-revolutionary (or 'church and king') movements, and to the transformation of ideas in the process of assimilation and adaptation" (197).

20. *The Crowd in History. A Survey of Popular Disturbances in France and England 1730-1848* (New York, 1964), p. 6. Rudé goes on to note that pre-industrial formations suffer from a "reading back" into their structure and dynamics of "liberal-democratic" notions associated with the "working class" and issuing from studies of the historiographically "better served" modern or industrial crowd (he cites J. M. Thompson in England, Tarlé in the Soviet Union, and Levasseur in France) (p. 7).

21. *Ibid.,* pp. 10-11, my italics, to indicate how Rudé, however "sociological" his approach, always returns to a popular disturbance as a lived, human "event". All of his writing has a narrative frame, an "event"-ful unfolding of *actions* in and across time; his generalisations emerge from his study of these events, and not, in the first instance, from the working-up of a then retrospectively-applied "model".

22. P. 197. The often-complex problem of applying "post"-industrial analytic terminology to pre-industrial social and cultural formations is one Rudé will return to often, most notably in the historiographical discussions of *Debate on Europe, 1815-1850* (1972) and his most "theoretical" book, *Ideology and Popular Protest* (1980). In a 1971 "conversation" about "The French Revolution" he describes the difficulties posed by using terms like "aristocracy" and "bourgeoisie", which have developed an "economic" emphasis in Marxist discussions, in pre-Revolutionary contexts, and cites the view of his great friend and colleague, Albert Soboul, that not only were the Jacobins not "socialists" but that, on the whole, "the Revolution did not immediately foster capitalism" (in Norman F. Cantor, ed., *Perspectives on the Past. Conversations with Historians* [New York, 1971], 40-61 at p. 47 and pp. 58-60).

23. *The Crowd in History,* pp. 210-12.

24. *Ibid.,* pp. 217-18.

25. Pp. 214-34, "Motives and Beliefs", where it is noted (p. 217) that "The crowd may riot because it is hungry or fears to be so, because it has some deep social grievance, because it seeks an immediate reform or the millenium, or because it wants to destroy an enemy or acclaim a 'hero'; but it is seldom for any single one of these reasons alone". At p. 227 Rudé notes that the persistence of traditional forms of behavior, tied to the "levelling instinct", tended to "drive a deeper wedge between the riotous crowd that clung to these old customs and the forward-looking, reforming, radical or revolutionary middle class or liberal aristocracy".

26. *Ibid.,* and at p. 234 for the concluding quotation.

27. "The Changing Face of the Crowd", p. 202.

28. *Debate on Europe 1815-1850* (New York, 1972), pp. 195-6. The statement is in a way a response to criticisms of Rudé's earlier work by E. P. Thompson and, probably, Richard Cobb (see *Times Literary Supplement* for 30 December 1965 and 7 April 1966 — Rudé discusses these reviews in "The Changing Face of the Crowd", pp. 198-9). Cobb had referred to Rudé's mode of enquiry as "Rudéification" (p. 200).

29. *Captain Swing* (New York, 1968), pp. 11-16; p. 12 for the "difficult", but "rightly" tempting, task of reconstructing the laborers' "mental world".

30. The discussion unfolds in the context of Chapter 9, "The Distribution of Riots", pp. 173-192. The typically Rudéan procedure here exemplifies another of his master Lefebvre's aperçus: "D'abord, il faut constater les faits; ensuite, il faut chercher à les expliquer" (cited in *Paris and London in the Eighteenth Century,* p. 10).

31. *Captain Swing,* pp. 188-9.

32. *Ibid.,* pp. 311-58. The more descriptive, "number-less" Appendix IV, "The Problem of the Threshing Machine", with its detailed economic history, carries a clear "Hobsbawmian" signature.

33. P. 249.

34. P. 286, from a Southrop (Glos.) song, "The Prop of the Land" — a particularly striking example of the use, throughout *Captain Swing,* of "literary and impressionistic", as well as "analytical and statistical", sources.

35. P. 298, closing the long analysis of "what lay at the core of the whole 'Swing' movement: the breaking of threshing machines" (169).

36. *Protest and Punishment. The Story of the Social and Political Prisoners transported to Australia 1788-1868* (Oxford, 1978), pp. 13-23 for the changing social context of protest crime and punishment, and pp. 61-70 for the softening criminal law's impact on transportation, and for changing Australian policy.

37. *Ibid.,* pp. 2-4, where the necessity insofar as *protest* crime is concerned "to distinguish between the common-law offender who, however acute the provocation, simply helps himself or settles a purely private score and the one who either acts with others or appears to do so in pursuit of common political and social goals" is emphasized. Rudé had stressed "the importance of *community* as a backdrop to protest" earlier, noting that, "strange as it may sound, it is not instability but stability--of social ties and shared experience--that is the seed-bed of riot and rebellion..." ("Urbanization and Popular Protest in Eighteenth-Century Western Europe", *Eighteenth-Century Life* 2 No. 3 (March, 1976), 46-8, at p. 48).

38. *Protest and Punishment,* Part Five, Chapter 2, "Who were the Protesters?", pp. 242-7 at 242.

39. P. 247.

40. The Canadian discussion at pp. 42-51 and 82-8. At the Twelfth (Vienna) International Congress of Historical Sciences, in 1965, Rudé had met the Canadian historians Fernand Ouellet and S. B. Ryerson; all three were then at work on 1837. The Vienna exchanges helped create a link between the historians and historiography of Australia (Rudé was then at Adelaide) and Canada. Rudé's work on the Canadian transportees was aided by Ouellet's *Histoire économique et sociale du Québec,* Ryerson acknowledges the list of transported *Patriotes* sent him by Rudé in his *Unequal Union* (1968), and Rudé noted the "virtue" of the latter book's having placed the two rebellions "in a common context" (*Protest...,* p. 44, n. 3, with references to other Canadian historians). Rudé's contacts with Canadian historians increased, of course, after his arrival in Montreal in 1970; in 1976 he delivered the Distinguished Historian's Address at the Quebec City meeting of the Canadian Historical Association, on the theme "The Study of Revolutions", noting, characteristically, that "Frankly, I want to have it both ways: to look at the general as well as the particular; to look at the general pattern of revolutions as well as the individual case-histories of those taking part. In short, I want to indulge in the luxury of looking through the telescope at both ends" (C. H. A., *Historical Papers/Communications Historiques* [1976], pp. 13-19 at 18-19).

41. Description of the Canadians' transportation on pp. 202-04; the five -- reduced to two by later research -- missing names are given on p. 204, n. 47.

42. Rudé, pleading "guilty" to the charge that his concern with the question "who" amounts almost to an "obsession", offers no apology — how know what popular movements or revolutions are about "if one does not take the trouble to find out who played the most active part in them?"; and when, once having determined "Whose, in fact, were 'the faces

in the crowd'", the next step was "to get into the skulls of the participants... to unravel the motives and impulsions..." (*Paris and London in the Eighteenth Century,* pp. 10-12).

43. "The Changing Face of the Crowd", p. 203.

44. *Ideology and Popular Protest* (London, 1980), pp. 7-9. Rudé defends his term "ideology of protest" (not heretofore used in any preceding work) against potential charges that it is too loose, a "catch-as-catch-can" phrase. Like Gramsci, he too needs a category able to contain the "simpler and less structured ideas" of the "traditional" classes of peasants and craftsmen, which cannot be explained in terms of Marxist ideology-theory developed in relation to the late nineteenth-century bourgeoisie and working-class.

45. *Ibid.,* p. 9, editor's italics. The problems of precisely when, and whether, prior to 1789 or 1815, recognizably "modern" classes emerged are confronted by Rudé throughout his work (see the discussion of his handling of the French "1848" in *Debate on Europe* [1972] and of supposed English "exceptionalism" in *Europe in the Eighteenth Century. Aristocracy and the Bourgeois Challenge* [1972] below). The related problem of whether the popular strata, rural or urban, constituted a "class" in the modern sense at all, is a constant issue in his work (see notes 20 and 22 above, and the discussion of *Robespierre. Portrait of a Revolutionary Democrat* [1975] below).

46. Pp. 27-31.

47. Pp. 16-37, at p. 28. Rudé had spoken of popular political ideas as "derived" in his first book, *The Crowd in the French Revolution.* As his concerns about the question "Who?" sharpened, so did his categories, from the political and economic "dominant", and more basic "underlying", beliefs and motives of the 1964 *The Crowd in History,* to the "indigenous (that is, directly experienced)" and "derived, or borrowed or adapted from another quarter", motives of the 1969 *Paris and London* essays, and to the 1970 "Changing Face" essay's stress on the way "ideas themselves become a 'material force' when they pass into the active consciousness of men". One of the practical consequences of this conceptual focus is the rich harvest of individual case-histories which breathe such vivid life into the pages of *Protest and Punishment* (1980) — here, as in a good deal else, *Captain Swing* in 1968 seems to have been a crucial transitional work.

48. Pp. 28-29. He adds the example drawn from "the Australian", Felix Raab, of the Elizabethan "reception" of Machiavelli's ideas: "what was anathema to one generation was acceptable to the next and just a yawn to the third".

49. Pp. 29-30.

50. P. 30.

51. For the really quite rich notion of pre-industrial popular ideology as "amalgam", pp. 30-31; for Hobsbawm's brigand (from *Primitive Rebels* [Manchester, 1959], p. 29), p. 31.

52. Pp. 32-37 (the Kronstadt sailors example is a bit of a *risposte* to E.P. Thompson — see p. 38, n. 20).

53. P. 35. Rudé goes on to point out that "the process of [ideological] grafting was never a simple A + B affair" — "in the case of all classes, and not of the 'popular' classes alone, all 'derived' ideas in the course of transmission and adoption suffer a transformation or 'sea-change': its nature will depend on the social needs or the political aims of the classes that are ready to absorb them" (p. 36).

54. "Part Two", p. 41-77, discusses the ideological dimensions of peasant movements in Europe and Latin America; Part Three, "Revolutions", deals with England, America, and France to 1848 (pp. 81-130). The tenth-century "We are as much men as they" is at p. 43 (where a late-thirteenth century peasant cry of *"nulli servire volumus"* is also noted).

55. "Postscript: Industrial Britain", pp. 158-165, is the concluding chapter of "Part Four", "Transition to Industrial Society", which opens with a discussion of England in the eighteenth century. The juxtaposition of "derived" ideology with "theory" in the last-cited quotation (p. 164) occurs at a number of points in *Ideology and Popular Protest* and is not a confusion. Rudé generally intends by the former term clear socio-political

perceptions, rooted in relatively objective analysis of the basic contours of a given or developing social structure. Although the issue is not explicitly joined, it is clear that for him there is no obvious sense in which all thought is "simply" class-bound and "ideological". What emerges from *Ideology and Popular Protest* is a pragmatic, nuanced "theory" of pre-industrial cultural formations, resting on a loose Marxian *optique* but, characteristically, "open" and sensitive to historical specificity.

56. *"Hanoverian London 1714-1808* (London, Berkeley and Los Angeles, 1971), pp. 1-19 for The Growth of the Metropolis", 20-36 for "Economic Life" (Defoe's seven-part classification -- including the *great,* the *rich,* the *working trades,* the *country people* and the *poor,* as well as the *middling sort* and the *miserable* -- appears on p. 38, where "Men of Property" are discussed) and 64-81 for "Social Life, the Arts and Entertainment". Change and continuity are examined in Chapter 12, "London and the French Wars", with the traditional "scold's chair" ducking on p. 255.

57. *Debate on Europe 1815-1850* (New York, 1972), vii-xvi, with "Man is a political animal" at xii. Time, too, sheer *durée,* is an important factor: whatever the historian's *prise de position,* Europe by 1850 was simply no longer the same, socially, politically, culturally, as she had been in 1815, a *fact* which affects interpretation (x, citing E.H. Carr's "dictum about history being a dialogue between the present and the past...").

58. A characteristically Rudéan position, reflecting a private communication of 1972 to this writer, in which Rudé noted that "in spite of my devotion to Marx, I am essentially a pragmatist...". Here, he notes his friend Hugh Stretton's observation, that while conservatives can sometimes be romantic or even radical about the past, "Marxists are more consistent...'to be Marxist about the present is usually to be Marxist about the past'" (xiv, citing Stretton's *Political Sciences*).

59. xvi. See note 3 above for an earlier observation on conflict in history and in historiography. Here, as elsewhere, Rudé cites the work of Charles Tilly with warm respect.

60. Pp. 213-66, with the work of Amann and Rémi Gossez at 224-26. This discussion is paralleled earlier in a section dealing with why there was so little response to socialism in England, where Rudé cites G.D.H. Cole's observation that in Great Britain, unlike France, "Socialism declined *before* 1848, not because it shared in a *bourgeois* defeat, but because it was robbed of its appeal by a *bourgeois* advance" (p. 120). The June Days of '48 as the beginning of something new is, of course, an old *topos* in Rudé's work, but it is stated here in lapidary form.

61. *Europe in the Eighteenth Century. Aristocracy and the Bourgeois Challenge* (London, 1972), pp. 1-4 and, specifically on British "exceptionalism", pp. 80-82, where James Watt complains that "our landed gentlemen reckon us poor mechanics no better than slaves who cultivate their vineyards". Rudé, noting that in both countries (England and France) it took "three generations for a merchant's family to be assimilated" into the aristocracy, cites David Landes' "The real test is not the union; it is what follows..." and observes "In short, it is one thing to marry the girl; it is quite another to ask Dad and Mum to tea". Rudé concludes that, nevertheless, "The English appear to have been more willing to do so than the French and to have shown a greater capacity for social mixing in general" (p. 82).

62. *Robespierre. Portrait of a Revolutionary Democrat* (London, 1975), p. 10 for this is a "political rather than a personal biography", pp. 15-52 for the (characteristically entitled) detailed presentation of "The Man and the Events".

63. The very rich bibliographical discussion here takes up an issue already raised in *The Crowd in the French Revolution* (1957), Daniel Guérin's mistaken -- in Rudé's view -- presentation of the *sans-culottes* as a "pre-proletariat" (in Guérin's 2-vol. *La lutte de classes sous la Ire République: bourgeois et «bras-nus»* [1793-97]), which in turn leads Guérin to present Robespierre as a reactionary betraying the popular movement. It is a view not sustained by Rudé's close social analysis of the pre-industrial *sans-culottes* as a heterogeneous amalgam — yet it does reflect what Rudé terms the post-1945 tendency of a new history to "play down personal vice and virtues and to pay greater attention to the historical role and the social forces that leaders like Robespierre represented or unleashed", with "the

present volume" as a "case in point" that not even biography, "that last redoubt of the cult of personality", has escaped this influence (pp. 87-8). (Rudé returns to Guérin, and to the fact that the *sans-culottes* were neither a "working-class" in the modern sense nor "a single social class at all", at p. 187.)

64. *Robespierre. Portrait...*, p. 40 (and the discussion of the passage at p. 113); p. 39, and again at p. 129 for "it was only through his own direct experience of war and revolution, and through the logic of events...a process of self-education" that he became, "as Georges Lefebvre described him, not only the 'historic leader of political democracy, but of social democracy as well'".

65. *Ibid.,* pp. 169-70 (I have retained Rudé's italics).

66. Pp. 41-52, at p. 52 for with him "perished... a system".

67. P. 135; the context is the discussion in Chapter 2 of "The Social Democrat" (in Part III, The Ideologue"), pp. 129-152.

68. Pp. 139-40. Robespierre had observed earlier, in the autumn, 1792 debates concerning food riots and rural demands for price controls on grain, that "Food that is necessary for man's existence is as sacred as life itself. Everything that is indispensable for its preservation is the common property of society as a whole. It is only the surplus that is private property and can safely be left to individual commercial enterprise" (p. 133).

69. The discussion of Robespierre's social views occurs largely in Part Three, "The Ideologue", cited above, no. 67. This careful, lucid chapter, sensitive to complex and changing social structure and thought, is one of the finest examples of Rudé's "practical theory" at work.

70. The "socialism" discussion on pp. 150-52, with Robespierre's striking observation about "community" in civil society on 151; see too pp. 82-92.

71. P. 190, where Rudé observes that "the *sans-culotte* idea of [directly participatory] democracy was almost exactly what Robespierre...said it was not". And, by this period, the *sans-culotte* idea of *social* democracy had already gone beyond Robespierre's limits as well — Rudé cites a resolution of 2 September 1793 at the Jardin des Plantes Section in Paris, which opens with "Let the maximum of wealth be fixed; Let no individual possess more than this maximum..." (p. 189).

72. P. 195.

73. Part IV, chapter III, "The Revolutionary Leader", pp. 196-213. Robespierre, like his contemporaries, knew little of the Levellers and Diggers, and saw in Oliver Cromwell a tyrant abusing the people (pp. 158, 198); Marx and Engels (no friends of the "Republic of Virtue"), and Lenin, differently, were better placed, having Robespierre to work with, as it were.

# GEORGE RUDÉ: A BIBLIOGRAPHY

"The Parisian Wage-earning Population and the Insurrectionary Movements of 1789-1791." Ph.D. dissertation, University of London, 1950, 2 vols.; 457 pp.

"La composition sociale des insurrections parisiennes de 1789 à 1791." *Annales historiques de la Révolution française* 127 (juillet-août 1952): 256-88.

"Les émeutes des 25, 26 février 1793 à Paris." *Annales historiques de la Révolution française* 130 (janv.-mars 1953): 46-61.

"The Motives of Popular Insurrection in Paris during the French Revolution." *Bulletin of the Institute of Historical Research* 26 (1953): 53-74.

"14 July 1789: The Fall of the Bastille." *History Today* 4 (July 1954): 448-47.

[with A. Soboul] "Le maximum des salaires parisiens et le neuf thermidor." *Annales historiques de la Révolution française* 134 (janv.-mars 1954): 1-22.

"Prices, Wages and Popular Movements in Paris during the French Revolution." *Economic History Review* 6 (1954): 246-67.

[with R. Cobb] "Le dernier mouvement populaire de la révolution à Paris, les journées de germinal et de prairial an III." *Revue historique* 214 (1955): 250-81.

"The Gordon Riots, 1780." *History Today* 7 (July 1955): 429-37.

"The Outbreak of the French Revolution." *Past and Present* 8 (November 1955): 28-42.

"I 'Tumulti di Gordon' (1790)." *Movimento Operaio* (Milano) (1955): 833-53.

"The Gordon Riots: A Study of the Rioters and their Victims." *Transactions of the Royal Historical Society* (ser. 5) 6 ( 1956): 93-114.

"Note sur les manuscrits de Bertrand de Moleville conservés au British Museum." *Annales historiques de la Révolution française* 142 (janv.-mars 1956): 48-56.

"Some Financial and Military Aspects of the Gordon Riots." *The Guildhall Miscellany* 6 (February 1956): 31-42.

"La taxation populaire de mai 1775 à Paris et dans la région parisienne." *Annales historiques de la Révolution française* 143 (avril-juin 1956): 139-79.

"Wilkes and Liberty, 1768-69." *The Guildhall Miscellany* 8 (July 1957): 3-24.

"The Common History Syllabus in the Comprehensive School." In *New Trends in English Education: a Symposium,* pp. 151-8. Edited by Brian Simon. London, 1957.

"Die Arbeiter und die Revolutionsregierung." In *Maximilien Robespierre, 1758-94,* pp. 301-22. Edited by W. Markov. Berlin, 1958.

*The Crowd in the French Revolution.* Oxford: Clarendon Press, 1959, 267 pp.; Oxford University Press, 1967; reprint ed., London: Oxford University Press, 1972. [Also published in German (Munich and Vienna: Oldenbourg, 1961); Japanese (Tokyo: Mineruba shobô, 1963); and French (Paris: Maspéro, 1972).]

"The London 'Mob' of the Eighteenth Century." *Historical Journal* 2 (1959): 1-18.

"'Mother Gin' and the London Riots of 1736." *The Guildhall Miscellany* 10 (September 1959): 53-63.

"Les sans-culottes parisiens et les journées de vendémiaire an IV." *Annales historiques de la Révolution française* 158 (oct.-déc. 1959): 332-46.

"The Study of Eighteenth-Century Popular Movements." *The Amateur Historian* 4 (Winter 1959-60): 235-41.

"Georges Lefebvre et l'étude des journées populaires de la révolution française." *Annales historiques de la Révolution française* 160 (avril-juin 1960): 154-62.

"The Middlesex Electors of 1768-1769." *English Historical Review* 75 (October 1960): 601-17.

Review of *Les sans-culottes parisiens en l'an II,* by A. Soboul. *English Historical Review* 75 (April 1960): 315-18.

*Interpretations of the French Revolution.* London: Routledge and Kegan Paul for the Historical Association (General Series, no. 47), 1961, 32 pp.; reprint ed., Cox and Wyman, 1967.

"La taxation populaire de mai 1775 en Picardie, en Normandie et dans le Beauvaisis." *Annales historiques de la Révolution française* 165 (juillet-sept. 1961): 305-26.

Review of *An Age of Crisis,* by Lester G. Crocker. *Science and Society* 26 (Summer 1962): 359-62.

"John Wilkes and the Re-birth of British Radicalism." *Political Science* 14 (September 1962): 11-29.

[with S. Lotté, A. Soboul and J. Zacker] "Quelques réflexions sur la composition, le rôle, les idées et les formes d'action des sans-culottes dans la révolution française." In "I Sanculotti: una discussione tra storici marxisti." *Critica storica* (Rome) 1, no. 4 (1962): 369-98.

*Wilkes and Liberty: A Social Study of 1763 to 1774.* Oxford: Clarendon Press, 1962, 240 pp.; reprint ed., London: Lawrence and Wishart, 1982.

Review of *Les armées révolutionnaires.* 2 vols., by Richard Cobb. *Times Literary Supplement,* 27 September 1963, p. 735.

Review of *The Debate on the French Revolution,* by A. Cobban. *Science and Society* 27 (Fall 1963): 478-81.

Review of *French Ecclesiastical Society under the Ancien Régime,* by J. McManners. *Australian Journal of Politics and History* (May 1963): 123-25.

Review of *A Social History of the French Revolution,* by N. Hampson. *New Statesman,* 6 September 1963, pp. 291-2.

"The Study of Popular Disturbances in the 'Pre-Industrial' Age." *Historical Studies, Australia and New Zealand* (Melbourne) 9 (May 1963): 457-69.

Review of *The Age of Revolution, 1789-1848,* by E.J. Hobsbawm. *Science and Society* 28 (Spring 1964): 242-45.

"'Captain Swing' and Van Diemen's Land." *Tasmanian Historical Research Association: Papers and Proceedings* (Australia) 12 (1964): 14-21.

*The Crowd in History: A Study of Popular Disturbances in France and England, 1730-1848.* New York: Wiley, 1964, 281 pp.; reprint ed., London: Lawrence and Wishart, 1981. [Also published in Spanish (Buenos Aires: Siglo XXI, Argentina Editores, 1971; Madrid: Siglo XXI de España, 1978), German (Frankfurt: Campus Verlag, 1977), Japanese (Tokyo: Tuttle-Mori, 1982), Italian (Rome: Riuniti, 1984) and Russian (Moscow: Progress, 1984).]

Review of *The French Revolution from its Origins to 1793,* by Georges Lefebvre; trans. by E.M. Evanson. *Science and Society* 28 (Winter 1964): 115-17.

*Revolutionary Europe, 1783-1815.* London: Collins, 1964, 350 pp.; Meridian Books, 1964; reprint ed., New York: Harper and Row, 1966; Collins (Fontana), 1967; Colophon Books, 1975. [Also published in Swedish (Stockholm: Aldus Bonnier, 1967) and Spanish (Madrid: Siglo XXI de España, 1974).]

Review of *The Social Interpretation of the French Revolution,* by A. Cobban. *New Statesman,* 2 October 1964, pp. 504-06.

"The Anti-Wilkite Merchants of 1769." *The Guildhall Miscellany* 2 (September 1965): 283-304.

"The Bread Riots of May 1775 in Paris and the Paris Region." In *New Perspectives on the French Revolution: Readings in Historical Sociology,* pp. 191-210. Edited by J. Kaplow. New York: Wiley, 1965.

"'Captain Swing' in New South Wales." *Historical Studies. Australia and New Zealand* (Melbourne) 11 (April 1965): 467-80.

[ed.] *The Eighteenth Century, 1715-1815.* New York: Free Press, 1965, 248 pp.; London: Collins-Macmillan, 1965.

Review of *Elbeuf during the Revolutionary Period: History and Social Structure,* by J. Kaplow. *Science and Society* 29 (Winter 1965): 109-11.

"'Feudalism' and the French Revolution." *The Monash Historical Review* (Australia) 1 (1965-66): 15-21.

"The Outbreak of the French Revolution." In *New Cambridge Modern History* 8, pp. 653-79. Edited by A. Goodwin. Cambridge: The University Press, 1965.

Review of *Terreur et subsistances,* by R. Cobb. *Times Literary Supplement,* 4 November 1965, p. 978.

"Collusion and Convergence in Eighteenth-Century British Political Action." *Government and Opposition* 1 (1966): 511-28.

Introduction to *1848: The Making of a Revolution,* by Georges Duveau; trans. by Anne Carter. New York: Pantheon Books, 1966; xxxi pp.

Review of *The Enragés: Socialists of the French Revolution,* by R.B. Rose. *Labour History* (Canberra) (November 1966): 69-71.

Review of *France and the Atlantic Revolution of the Eighteenth Century,* by J. Godechot; trans. by H. Rowen. *William and Mary Quarterly* 23 (July 1966): 495-97.

"Robespierre vu par les historiens anglais." In *Actes du Colloque Robespierre,* pp. 215-24. Paris: Société des Études Robespierristes, 1966.

Review of *The Single Duty Project: A Study of the Movement for a French Customs Union in the Eighteenth Century,* by J. F. Bosher. *Annales historiques de la Révolution française* 1983 (janv.-mars 1966): 107-09.

"English Rural and Urban Disturbances on the Eve of the First Reform Bill, 1830-31." *Past and Present* 37 (July 1967): 87-102.

Review of *Lectures on European History, 1789-1914,* by J. McManners, *Teaching History* (Sydney) (February 1967): 23-24.

"The Mass Portrait Gallery." *The Listener* 16 (March 1967): 349-51.

"La population ouvrière parisienne de 1789 à 1791." *Annales historiques de la Révolution française* 187 (janv.-mars 1967): 15-33.

[ed.] *Robespierre.* New Jersey: Prentice Hall, 1967; 182 pp.

[with E.J. Hobsbawm] *Captain Swing.* New York: Pantheon Books, 1968, 384 pp.; London: Lawrence and Wishart, 1969; Penguin Books, 1973; Norton, 1975. [Also published in Spanish (Madrid: Siglo XXI de España, 1978); and Portuguese (Rio de Janeiro: Alves, 1982).]

"The Study of Revolutions." *Arena* (Melbourne) 15 (1968): 12-29.

" The 'Pre-Industrial' Crowd." *Flinders Journal of History and Politics* (Australia) 1 (1969): 4-18.

"Why Was There No Revolution in England in 1830 or 1848?" *Studien über die Revolution* (Berlin) (1969): 231-44.

"The Archivist and the Historian." *Tasmanian Historical Research Association: Papers and Proceedings* (Australia) 17 (October 1970): 111-27.

"The French Revolution and 'Participation'." In *A World in Revolution,* pp. 15-24. Canberra: Australian National University, 1970.

"The Changing Face of the Crowd." In *The Historian's Workshop. Original Essays by Sixteen Historians,* pp. 187-204. Edited by L.P. Curtis, Jr. New York: Alfred A. Knopf, 1970.

*Paris and London in the Eighteenth Century: Studies in Popular Protest.* London: Collins, 1970, 350 pp.; Viking, 1971. [Also published in Spanish (Barcelona: Ariel, 1978).]

"The French Revolution." In *Perspectives on the European Past: Conversations with Historians,* pp. 40-61. Edited by Norman F. Cantor. New York: Macmillan, 1971.

*Hanoverian London, 1714-1808.* London: Secker and Warburg, 1971; Berkeley: University of California Press, 1971; 271 pp.

*Debate on Europe, 1815-1850.* New York: Harper and Row, 1972, 277 pp.

*Europe in the Eighteenth Century: Aristocracy and the Bourgeois Challenge.* London: Weidenfeld and Nicolson, 1972, 291 pp.; New York: Praeger Books, 1973. [Also published in Italian (Bari: Laterza, 1974); German (Munich: Kindler, 1978); and Spanish (Madrid: Alianza Editorial, 1978)].

Introduction to *The Great Fear of 1789: Rural Panic in Revolutionary France,* by Georges Lefebvre; trans. by J. White. London: NLB, 1973; Pantheon, 1973; xvi pp.

"The Growth of Cities and Popular Revolt, 1750-1850." In *French Government and Society, 1500-1800.* Edited by J. F. Bosher. London: Athlone, 1973; pp. 166-90.

"Early Irish Rebels in Australia." *Historical Studies, Australia and New Zealand* (Melbourne) 16 (April 1974): 17-35.

"Revolution and Popular Ideology." In *France and North America: The Revolutionary Experience,* pp. 142-58. Edited by M. Allan and G. R. Conrad. Lafayette, La., 1974.

*Robespierre: Portrait of a Revolutionary Democrat.* London: Collins, 1975; Viking, 1976; 254 pp. [Also published in Italian (Rome: Riuniti, 1979).]

"The Two Nations: Industrialization and its Discontents." In *The Long March of Everyman.* Edited by Theodore Barker. André Deutsch, 1975: 82-100.

"Ideology and Popular Protest." *Historical Reflections / Réflexions historiques* (Waterloo, Ont.) 3 (Winter 1976): 69-77.

"The Study of Revolutions." *Historical Papers / Communications historiques: A Selection of the Papers Presented at the Annual Meeting.* Canadian Historical Association. (1976): 13-19.

"Urbanization and Popular Protest in Eighteenth-Century Western Europe." *Eighteenth Century Life* 2 (March 1976): 46-48.

"La participation populaire à la révolution française." *Histoire sociale* 20 (1977): 277-84.

"Popular Protest and Ideology on the Eve of the French Revolution." *Vom Ancien Régime zur Französischen Revolution / De l'ancien régime à la Révolution française,* Göttingen, 1978): 420-35.

*Protest and Punishment: The Story of Social and Political Protesters Transported to Australia, 1788-1868.* Oxford: Clarendon Press, 1978; 270 pp.; Melbourne: Oxford University Press, 1981.

"L'idéologie de la contestation populaire à l'époque pré-industrielle." *Europa: A Journal of Interdisciplinary Studies/ Revue d'Études Interdisciplinaires* (Montréal) 3 (1979-80): 7-17.

*Ideology and Popular Protest.* London: Lawrence and Wishart, 1980, 176 pp.; Pantheon Books, 1980. [Also published in Spanish (Barcelona: Editorial Critica, 1981); Portuguese (Rio de Janeiro: Zahar, 1982); Japanese (Tokyo: Tuttle-Mori, 1984); and Russian (Moscow: Progress, 1984).]

"The 'Poverty of Theory' Debate" (review-article). In *Saothair* [Ireland] 7 (1981): 62-8.

"Les Débuts d'une idéologie révolutionnaire dans le petit peuple urbain en 1789." In *Die Französische Revolution — Zufälliges oder notwendiges Ereignis?* (Akten des Internationalen Symposiums an der Universität Bamberg vom 4-7 juni 1979), pp. 29-39. Edited by E. Schmitt and R. Reichardt. Munich-Vienna, 1983.

*Criminal and Victim: Crime and Society in Early Nineteenth-Century England.* Oxford: Oxford University Press, forthcoming.

# PART ONE

Hugh Stretton

# *GEORGE RUDÉ*

Early in this century Colonel Elliot, a banker, lived with his wife rather grandly on Richmond Hill, despising people who engaged in trade. In 1906 their daughter Amy as part of her "finishing" spent some months in Dresden studying the violin. It happened that Jens Rude, a Norwegian engineer from rougher social origins than hers, came to stay at the same *pension*. They met across the dining table without formal introduction and he presently offered her a cigarette. She thought that was an ill-bred way for a man to behave to a young lady. She told him so, left the room, would not speak to him for some days, and married him the next year. They went to live in Oslo where their second son was born in 1910 and christened George Frederick Elliot. He spent his first nine years there speaking Norwegian as his native language, except for a few months of 1915 when he and his mother ran the submarine blockade to visit England and George began to learn English.

In 1919 they all moved to England. Jens Rude had no regular job there. He was an inventor, a pioneer of smokeless fuels, but he rarely made any money. They lived chiefly on Amy's small private income. Jens was a conservative man in most ways but in one way he was not: he admired much of the contemporary art of the time and taught his children to like and understand it; George remembers being taken to see London's first Epstein sculpture. But in most respects George grow up as a product of his mother's culture and social outlook rather than his father's. The culture included a standard public school education. He boarded for five years at a proper prep school (Seabrook Lodge at Hythe in Kent) where to survive among English schoolboys he was advised to change the pronunciation of his name by giving it a French accent. He then financed his own education with scholarships first at Shrewsbury, then at Trinity College, Cambridge. At Cambridge he was some way into a modern languages course when his father persuaded him to switch to economics. He read economics for a year, disliked it and failed his first exam in it (at the hands of Denis Robertson, whom he also disliked). He returned to modern languages having lost a year of working time, and graduated in 1931 with upper second class honours. More than one public school offered him work and he went as a modern languages master to Stow.

So far, aged twenty-two, he had no political interests or convictions. At Cambridge he had once paid five shillings to join a Conservative club, but only because he fancied its pink-striped silver tie. He spent his vacations in European galleries looking at paintings and sculpture and became quite knowledgeable in the history of art (the work of Piero della Francesca, especially). Then at a party in London in the summer of 1932 he chanced to meet an amiable young athlete from Oxford who was about to visit Russia and who persuaded him to join the same conducted tour. What he saw in Soviet Russia and learned from his touring companions in those six weeks changed his life: he set out uninterested in politics and mildly impressed by Mussolini and came back a committed communist and anti-fascist.

He set about re-educating himself. He read the Marxist classics and also became a thorough daily reader of *The Times* and a popular contributor to the "present day" discussion classes of the senior forms at Stow. In June 1935 he joined the British Communist Party. There was not much party work for him in the conservative countryside around Stow but as an intellectual he was well received by Emile Burns and other in London and before long he was surprised and pleased to be sent as a *Labour Monthly* observer to the first popular front conference of communist and non-communist labour unions in Paris, where among other notables he saw and was deeply impressed by the young Thorez. He had resigned from Stow to take a job in industry which however failed to materialize. He moved to London and worked with a London party branch, making a sparse living by tutoring and part-time teaching until another public school (St. Paul's) took him on as a full-time modern languages master. He shared lodgings with a number of other people behind an antique shop in Berkeley Square. He did various kinds of party work, some more intellectual than others. Taking part in a protest against a fascist demonstration in the East End, he was arrested, convicted and fined for "obstruction". One wet November night he hired a barrel organ and played it around Kings Cross to collect pennies for an unemployed relief fund; some street kids robbed him and besides losing the collection he had to pay from his own pocket for the hire of the organ. But in one at least of his party activities he showed signs of the kind of historian he later became. He worked on various party committees with trade unionists, especially engineers and transport workers. In one particular conflict it occurred to him that it would be useful to know precisely *which* workers were represented by the National Union of Municipal and General Workers: what numbers of which trades were in the union and what numbers of which eligible trades were not in it; in short, the actual class and occupational composition of the union. He did the necessary research and used the results in a speech to the London district congress of the party in 1938. That speech was noticed and he was put on the panel for the London district committee of the party, on which he served on and off over the next ten years.

Meanwhile at a dance one night, while sober but nevertheless singing "Eskimo Nell", he had met Doreen de la Hoyde, an Irish girl recently returned from an Australian convent upbringing. She was not actually much interested in politics but because of her nationality and the company she kept in Dublin and London she had some spurious reputation as a Trotskyist and an Irish revolutionary. She asked him if he was a Stalinist and was depressed to hear that he supposed he was. Before long they were married. They appear to have lived happily ever after: if so, it has been a triumph of complementarity rather than similarity. The scholar-puritan labours long hours at desk or archive or microreader, to a strict working schedule, industrious and thoughtful and relentlessly productive, apparently oblivious of the eventful interior decoration and diverse sensual attractions with which she surrounds him, of which professional French cooking, amateur Irish hoydenry and plentiful Australian claret are only a few of the more mentionable. Punctually at six p.m. each day for more than twenty years now he has looked up in a surprised way and noticed these vulgar temptations for the very first time, and shut his books for the day.

Their first twenty years together were not as easy as these last twenty, or as free after six p.m. During the war George worked (full-time) in the London fire service. Then, bored with teaching languages, he took a history degree at London University by part-time evening work while continuing to teach full-time by day, and working for the party at night and weekends. For most of the next twelve years that treble life continued: he did his party work, earned his living as a teacher, and began his historical research and writing, first for a London Ph. D. and then as an independent scholar. In 1949 St. Paul's School dismissed him because of his out-of-school political activities. He took the opportunity to spend a year in Paris working in the archives of the Revolution. He had to go alone, leaving Doreen in London with their foster daughter. He had only a £70 grant; he lived austerely and lost weight; but Albert Soboul fed him once a week and the great Georges Lefebvre noticed and helped his work. Back in London he first taught French at a grammar school then moved to teach history at a comprehensive school in Holloway, in north London. Those were years of long daily hours of very hard work.

Towards the end of the 1950s, with a Ph. D., the Alexander Prize for historical research, some articles in print and *The Crowd in the French Revolution* written, George began to apply for academic jobs. In Britain he got none. British universities were not sacking communists through that cold war decade but they were not hiring many, nor were they hiring middle-aged school teachers, least of all one who had made a rake's progress from the heights of Stow to the depths of Holloway. Polytechnics as well as universities turned him down. He applied further afield. At the University of Tasmania the relevant appointment committee nominated him for a lectureship. The Vice-Chancellor, an economist fresh from Belfast, held up the appointment because the nominee was a communist. The University of Tasmania had already been torn apart by its famous Orr case and might have been torn further by a Rudé case, but at that moment George was offered a senior lectureship at the University of Adelaide and went there instead. Even that more enlightened place still had some cold warriors on its governing Council, but an unusual trio -- the Vice Chancellor (an English public servant who had been head of the Singapore Harbours Board), the Chancellor (an octogenarian Chief Justice) and the Chairman of the Finance Committee (a rich merchant who had been head of Australian Military Intelligence)--to their great credit conspired privately to keep their Council ignorant of Dr. Rudé's politics until his appointment was secure.

His politics were anyway under stress by then, though the people appointing him did not know it. He did not leave and was not expelled from the British Communist Party after the Hungarian revolution. I guess (without knowing) that his view of the events of 1956 may not have been very different from those of colleagues like Eric Hobsbawm or Christopher Hill, but he felt very strong fraternal loyalties to the comrades and the good causes of the depression and wartime years. Neither then nor since has he denounced the party or his ex-comrades in it, even under strong inducement — for example to qualify himself for U.S. residence when excellent jobs which he would have liked to take in excellent American universities were open to him. But when he emigrated in 1960 he left the Communist Party by the negative method of not joining the Australian party. In an interview (17 August 1981) which he knew was for the record he was asked whether he saw that change in 1960 as a retreat from active politics to pure scholarship or as a shift from one way of trying to reform the world to another way of trying to reform it. "A bit of both", he said, "but mostly the second."

*

Thus he arrived in Adelaide at the age of fifty to begin an academic career. Contrary to some academic expectations his school-mastering experience has positively helped him to be a good undergraduate teacher. As lecturer and tutor he is easy, informal, lucid, and takes care to adapt the work to the students' capacities. He also knows how to keep them interested. He has other useful dominie skills. For example he is as helpful a critic of students' written work, and as reliable an examiner, as any I know, but he is also the *fastest* I ever saw at both those activities. He is an excellent and fertile supervisor of research. In Adelaide his undergraduate teaching was richly welcome, a few good graduate students worked with him, he was soon made a Professor and took his turn as an able administrative head of department. He was an outstandingly friendly, generous and popular colleague. But it was as a researcher and writer that he inspired most awe and envy in what was already quite an able and productive company. In his first year, while lecturing for the first time to large first-year classes and taking plenty of tutorials, he wrote all but the first chapter of *Wilkes and Liberty,* and also discovered the potential value to English "history from below" of the convict records in the Sydney and Hobart archives. (He had trouble getting access to both those archives, until suspicion of the communist was overcome by working experience of what one surprised reactionary was moved to call the "scholar and gentleman".) Then an American publisher asked him to write a world history of political crowds. George proposed instead something more manageable: a comparative survey of English and French popular movements through the century from about 1750 to 1850 that he knew something about. Even so, there was a serious shortage of materials for such work in Australia. He spent some months planning what might be done with what materials there were, and arrived at the structure and outline of what became *The Crowd in History.* The plan called for twelve historical chapters of fifteen pages each and four general or theoretical chapters of twenty pages each. The publishers approved it and George began to write it. His teaching and other activities continued as usual but punctually every second Friday the office typist received a manuscript chapter of a length to make exactly fifteen pages of print. The four twenty-page chapters then came at three-week intervals, just as punctually. The rest of us ground our teeth, beat our wives and children, muttered darkly of sausage machines and instant history, and secretly hoped the work would be as dull as its production appeared to be routine. Alas, the writing routine seemed to do no more harm than Trollope's famous writing habits did to the quality of the product. Worst of all, the man never worked after six p.m. From seven onwards he and Doreen were exchanging excellent dinners with a diverse and rapidly expanding sample of Adelaide society.

Soon after that he was asked to write a volume for William Collins' general history of Europe, and did so: *Revolutionary Europe* (1964). He selected and edited a couple of volumes of texts: *The Eighteenth Century* (1965) and *Robespierre* (1967). He began a study of criminal offenders in some English counties in the nineteenth century and in processing that material became as far as I know the first historian in Australia to make practical use of a computer. His reputation grew steadily. The "history from below" in his first three books had linked exemplary archival research to a very practical and flexible variety of Marxism: the mixture was specially popular in Japan and the product was widely appreciate in North America. He went as visiting professor to Columbia in 1965 and to the University of Tokyo in 1967. Those appointments helped him to move around, and he also used Adelaide research grants and his own savings to revisit sources in England and Sydney and Hobart; so he was able to collaborate with Eric Hobsbawm to produce *Captain Swing* (1969). There were still no invitations to English universities but in 1967 he was appointed to the foundation chair of history at the new University of Stirling in Scotland. He and his wife did not much like the gritty Scottish society. He distressed his new employers by asking them to convert his appointment to a visiting one for one year only. He returned to Adelaide, this time to Flinders University. Two years later he moved to Sir George Williams University which has since merged into Concordia University, in Montreal, where he has been employed since 1970. Since 1968 his exile from the United Kingdom should perhaps count as voluntary. It ended in 1975 when he "retired" to live and work for some months of each year in a converted oast house in the Sussex countryside.

In Montreal he was soon involved in another enterprise. There was thought to be too little cooperation between the French and English branches of Canadian historical scholarship. To improve their relations the bilingual, multi-university *Inter-University Centre for European Studies / Centre Interuniversitaire d'Études Européennes* was founded. George Rudé was its first Director, 1972-74, and is the current honorary President of the now-interdisciplinary Centre in 1985. Since he reached the statutory retiring age in 1975 Concordia has maintained his position as a half-time Professor, and in that capacity he has spent each Fall Semester there, except for a year of leave which he spent as a visiting professor at William and Mary College in the U.S. in 1980-1. Australians also keep in touch with him. Historians of modern Europe working in Australia conduct a biennial "George Rudé Seminar" and Rudé revisits Australia every second year to attend it. He made the 1980 seminar specially memorable by taking Albert Soboul with him. And there are other Australian engagements — the book *Ideology and Popular Protest* (1980) had an early trial as a visiting course of undergraduate lectures at the University of Adelaide.

Through all those energetic years his location in Adelaide and Montreal, remote from most of his sources, seems to have done remarkably little harm to his scholarly work. It may even be that others suffered more than he did from two specially regrettable features of his career. No English university would employ him when he wanted to work in England; and as an ex-communist who would not denounce his ex-comrades Rudé was denied by the United States the permanent residential status which he needed in order to take permanent employment in an American university. Those barriers kept him out of big graduate schools in reach of his main sources, and must have deprived many young scholars of the chance of working with him.

But there are other ways of learning from his work. He travels widely and his books are widely read — *The Crowd in the French Revolution* has appeared in five languages. And the work brings him into splendid company. Among historians "from below" he is the common member of two famous trios. In the French archives he worked with Albert Soboul and Richard Cobb — Lefebvre called them the three musketeers. In the equivalent English field he encounters Edward Thompson and Eric Hobsbawm. The four Englishmen make a formidable and sometimes stormy quartet. Unavoidably they review one another's books, but they could not be accused of doing it too cosily. Rudé and Hobsbawm are unfailingly courteous, balanced, clear, cool. Cobb and Thompson are passionate, showy, capable, when high principles or low spirits prompt them, of severe criticism of their old comrades' works. The hot pair are also prolix, writing their histories and their polemics at great length. Asa Briggs may have been gently reproving those two when he wrote of Rudé's *Protest and Punishment* (in the *New Statesman,* 24 Novembre 1978):

> As always, it is the human reckoning which concerns him. He starts with numbers and ends with individual cases. The research behind his book, meticulously detailed, has required a rare combination of patience, diligence, imagination and sympathy. An additional quality is also apparent in the final result - economy. Many historians would have needed a thousand pages: he is content with 270. Everything is superbly condensed and yet still direct.

Those few sentences are themselves well condensed, and make an appropriate introduction to a short review of Rudé's work as a whole.

\*

The best account of George Rudé's work was written by himself and appeared in L. P. Curtis (ed.), *The Historian's Workshop: Original Essays by Sixteen Historians* (N.Y.: Knopf, 1970). Richard Cobb once wrote (in *The Spectator,* 27 January 1979) that Rudé likes his history "to be tidy, to speak out clearly, and to be 'developing'". That also characterises the essay in *The Historian's Workshop.* It is informative, economical, clear. It is severely self-critical by the hard method of acknowledging the force of other people's criticism. With too much credit to the critics and too little to himself it describes the development of his ideas from each work to the next. In the beginning, about 1949,

> Who actually took the Bastille, stormed the Tuileries, expelled the Girondin leaders from the National Convention, or stood silently by as Robespierre was hustled to the scaffold? Not only who were they, but how did they get there? What were their motives and social aspirations, and by what means did they acquire them?... I began to think that a more precise analysis of *who,* if it could be made, would throw a useful light not only on the activities, but on the outlook and motives of the common people who, as everyone conceded, had played an important part in the course and the outcome of the Revolution. I soon discovered, with Cobban's help, that it was not for lack of appropriate records that historians had dodged the issue: there was even a list in the Archives Nationales in Paris, fully described in Tuetey's sixty-year-old *Répertoire* of Parisian revolutionary manuscripts, that gave the names, addresses, ages, occupations, and militia units of every one of the 600-odd civilians who had been proved to have taken an active part in the siege of the Bastille. For the rest, I had mainly to make do with the police records of the Paris Châtelet and Prefecture of Police, which I supplemented in later work with the official lists of those receiving

awards, pensions and compensation, or jail sentences (according to the event) for the part they played in the great revolutionary *journées* of August 1792, June 1793, and May 1795. These proved to be a mine of information about those who had been arrested, killed or wounded, or against whom information had been laid; but, of course, they provided only a sample - and sometimes a rather fortuitous one at that - and had, in consequence, to be used with discretion and with ample reservations. Still, while conscious of its limitations, I have made this type of record a basic part of my research equipment ever since. *(The Historian's Workshop,* p. 190)

He has indeed used those methods ever since, but there has been a continuous development of the philosophy which guides their use — no historian ever started work so late in life but continued to develop his ideas with such fertility. The Ph. D. thesis merely asked what role the Paris wage-earners played in the revolutionary events of 1789-91, a question which could be understood as asking how far a particular class, with particular motives, fulfilled a particular Marxist expectation. Nine years later *The Crowd in the French Revolution* not only extends the study to the years 1787-1795, it also asks and answers different questions: *who* did whatever was done through those years by popular force, *what* motivated them, *what* social forces did they represent? The questions are still prompted by the author's Marxism and his general class sympathies but they are now open questions, and the fine archival research yields some unideological, partly unexpected answers. The criteria of class are not quite the same after the research as they were before. Rudé quotes Engels: history can never be deduced from theory, "all history must be studied afresh".

Meanwhile he had begun to apply similar methods to the study of English popular movements. With the Gordon Riots of 1780 he had the bright idea of studying the identity and class of the victims as well as the rioters, as a further aid to identifying the rioters' perceptions and purposes. The sources and methods were as ingenious as the idea: "The Gordon Riots: A Study of the Rioters and their Victims" won the Alexander Prize of the Royal Historical Society in 1955. In *Wilkes and Liberty* (1962) he applied similar ingenuity to more diverse sources to find out who actually supported Wilkes, and why. With the social sciences booming as they did though the 1960s it was unusual that a researcher so interested in the sociology and statistics of the Wilkite movement should also be so interested in its individual members and the ideas in their heads. This was the book which prompted A.J.P. Taylor, no great friend of Marxist work, to declare that Rudé had "put mind back into history and restored the dignity of man".

Rudé himself was less happy with the way he had related the mind to the history. It was one thing to find out what the members of popular movements thought about the world and what they were trying to do about it, that is, to discover as far as the evidence allowed *what* their ideas were. But how did they come by those ideas? Which of their ideas did they inherit, which did they borrow and from where, which if any did they invent? The traditional Marxist and non-Marxist debates about ideas and action did not really throw much light on the origins and role of the ideas that animated ordinary people in town and country, some literate and some not, in the conflicts of the eighteenth and early nineteenth century. "In particular", Rudé wrote in *The Historian's Workshop,* p. 197,

I wanted to lend more weight than I had done before to the irrational in human motivation, to the phenomenon of violence in crowd behavior, to the forces of law and order, to the relations between leaders and followers in riots and revolutions, to the survival of archaic forms of thought and action carried over from an earlier age, to the role of religion and millenarian fantasies as adjuncts of disturbances, to the coexistence in popular movements of 'backward-looking' and 'forward-looking' concepts, to the special characteristics of counterrevolutionary (or 'church and king') movements, and to the transformation of ideas in the process of assimilation and adaptation.

He did his best with some of those questions in *The Crowd in History* (1964). Then with the help of Hobsbawm, first as critic then as collaborator, he added one more to the battery of questions. Given the ideas in the suffering people's heads, what determined who would disturb the peace and who would not? In the English agricultural labourers' risings of 1830, for example, why did some villages rebel while others did not? Of the attempts to answer that question in *Captain Swing* (1969) he wrote in *The Historian's Workshop* (p. 203):

> Even if the evidence suggested (as, in fact, it did) that a riot-prone village tended to be larger than the average; to contain a higher ratio of laborers to farmers; to have a larger proportion of craftsmen, small landholders, and shopkeepers; to have an 'open' or 'mixed' rather than a 'close' landownership; to have a larger measure of religious independence; to lie closer to markets and fairs: to have a longer history of local disputes: to have (on balance) a larger proportion of unemployed; and (more decidedly) to be engaged in tillage rather than pasture - all this could, on occasion, be made almost irrelevant by the simple fact of the powerful contagion that a concerted movement among its neighbors might exert on the most peaceful and least riot-prone village lying in its path. So the question might elicit no firm and conclusive answer. Yet the question was well worth asking; and to ask it was, at least, the beginning of a wisdom that I, for my part, had previously neglected.

That passage is the best text for an argument, below, about the limits of sociology. But first there is a continuing history of Rudé's dealings with ideas. He was still interested in those earlier questions about the provenance of the popular ideas themselves. It may have been specially troublesome or challenging to a Marxist to find such mixtures of progressive and reactionary ideas in popular class movements. Some theory for use with such phenomena can be seen developing through all Rudé's "histories from below", to be stated explicitly, at length, in *Ideology and Popular Protest* (1980). It is very simple and open theory: a loose model which suggests questions to ask in each historical case. People grow up with an inherited understanding of the world, ideas received from parents and the surrounding culture. In the course of growing up and experiencing life (individually) and in the course of historical change (socially) people are offered a variety of other ideas from other sources — often, especially in Rudé's period, from other classes. Those available ideas are variously rejected, picked over, accepted. They are often changed in the course of adapting them to new purposes and grafting them onto the inherited picture of the world. Thus one generation's acquired ideas, with or without modification, become part of the next generation's inherited ideas.

These are suggestions about the processes by which, over time, people's ideas and conscious purposes are related to their class and social situations. In Rudé's model and in his historical uses of it ideas are never independent forces, nor are they ever mechanical expressions of material interest, merely. Interests are linked through consciousness to action by historical processes which need to be researched in each case, which take time, and which allow plenty of scope for invention, persuasion, error and irrationality, nostalgia and other sentiments. It is through those processes, consistently with the more flexible of Marx's and Engels' observations on the subject, that "ideas themselves become a material force when they pass into the active consciousness of men".

Generalizing about ideas in action is only one instance of the wider problem of generalizing about *anything* in social history and experience. Most of Rudé's research includes two elements: There is a conscientious attempt to see how far counting, classifying and formal analysis can go — what quantitative generalizations they can establish, what regular associations or relationships they seem to indicate. Then there is research of a doubly detailed kind: it typically looks more directly for any relationships suggested by the statistical work by searching for those relationships where they would actually have to operate, in the motivation and behaviour of the people concerned; and it also puts "open" questions to the faces in the crowd, using whatever evidence is available to identify them and allow them to speak (and if appropriate, generalize) for themselves. Rudé does both kinds of research with ingenuity, but also with great care not to run his conclusions beyond what the evidence will really support. Very few of his generalizations have been attacked as insufficiently supported, none of his individual portraits have been attacked as romantic or fictionalized. Some critics -- most consistently perhaps Asa Briggs -- have appreciated the virtues of both elements of the work and the critical relations between them. But more critics have not: if they liked one element they disliked the other. Doctrinaire Marxists criticize the lack of "structure"; scientistic sociologists want more generalizing; Cobb and Thompson sometimes seem to want none at all. I offer my own opinion that in pushing the statistical and sociological work to its workable limits, in recognizing what those limits are in each case, and in relating those elements of the work to its individual and qualitative elements, Rudé sets an example of honesty and excellence to both disciplines — or to all three, if you are irreverent enough to count history, sociology and Marxism as one each. He works with unsurpassed skill precisely where C. Wright Mills argued (in *The Sociological Imagination,* 1960) that most social scientists should work, at the critical points "where history and biography intersect" — where historical forces determine individual experience, and at the same time take their character from common characteristics of individual experience and behaviour.

Similar virtues appear in his dealings with questions of historical interpretation. They appear throughout his work indirectly in the structure, selections, themes, explanations and emphases of his history books, and they also appear directly in his writings *about* history books. He is well aware that his values shape his books. Partly because he knows they do, no writer subjects the effects of his guiding values more scrupulously to the appropriate disciplines of factual research and fair selection. As one effect, the two general histories of Europe -- *Revolutionary Europe* (1964) and *Europe in the Eighteenth Century* (1972) -- are models of their kind. As another effect, so are the two direct studies of interpretation, the Historical Association pamphlet *Interpretations of the French Revolution* (1960) and *Debate on Europe 1815-1850* (1972). The latter is the most widely and wrongly neglected of his works. A publisher planned a many-volumed history of Europe of a new and interesting kind. It was to be a history of European self-knowledge, with each volume narrating the history of changing and conflicting interpretations of its period, from when it happened to now. Punctual, productive George Rudé finished his volume in good time and nobody else finished one at all, because the project collapsed for commercial reasons. That solitary volume is an interesting and important one: both a novel history of ideas, and a model of the self-knowledge and understanding of the sources of historical disagreement which every working historian ought to have, and all too few do have.

\*

I think it worth while to press this theme a little further. That may be partly because I am a doubly inappropriate person to review Rudé's work — I do not work in his field of history and I have never been any sort of Marxist. What I do study is chiefly the role of the social sciences in modern societies. I think some of those sciences, especially economics and for a time sociology, have been corrupted, and the societies which nourish them have been ill-served, by two widespread misuses of social and economic theory. First, too many academics have come to regard theories as consumption goods, things to be valued for themselves for their qualities of novelty or intricacy or elegance or mathematical interest. They should of course be valued for their social uses alone. To put the same point in another way, theories have begun to serve the social purposes of the disciplines and people who generate them rather than the social purposes of the surrounding society. Second, privileged theories are used as tests of loyalty: class loyalty, party loyalty, cliquish academic loyalties. Thus there is little relation between the economic problems of contemporary society and the algebra that fills the pages of the leading Economics journals, least of all any traditional relation between "pure and applied" science. There was no relation between the social problems of contemporary society and the structural-functional jargon that filled many sociological journals through the nineteen fifties and sixties. I do not believe the workers of the world can expect much benefit from the feuds which entangle some contemporary Marxists in the concerns of Althusser, Habermas and other obscure but rigid elaborators of Marx. And so on.

In short, much harm comes of valuing theory for its own sake, or as a test of loyalty. Good theory is a vital ingredient of most useful social research and action, including good historical writing, but it should be judged by its values in use, by its actual product of understanding or action. Most good social and economic theory does one or both of two related things: (1) it offers selective simplifications of social relations and processes, simplifications which help people to investigate the relations and processes in particular cases and to understand and, where appropriate, to act on them; and (2) it debates social values and the rights and wrongs of social interests and purposes and directions of action. The two qualities are related because the selective simplifications have to express both technical and valuational judgments: they have to be useful *technical* guides to what are judged to be politically or socially or morally *important* aspects of social life.

The point of this disgression is that social theories and their intellectual and political uses should not be judged by the narcissistic and scientistic tests which have too often prevailed in academia. They should be judged by the value of understanding and action to which they lead, and by unavoidably controversial judgments of the values which they necessarily incorporate. This is an unfashionable or at best a minority opinion — except in the discipline of history. There, the prevailing scientistics of the neighbouring social sciences have often appeared so offensive to common sense and intellectual honesty that many historians have erred in the opposite direction: they have scorned theory altogether and refused to believe it could be of any use to them. One ill effect has been to deter too many of them from serious study or conscious ordering of their own working values and assumptions.

It has followed (it seems to me) that however well George Rudé's factual "history from below" has been received, his dealings with social theory have been trebly unfashionable. Scientistic sociologists, finding neither jargon nor algebra, have patronised the theoretical parts of the work as weak and old-fashioned. Traditional historians have overlooked the theory and hurried on to the factual faces in the crowd. Theoretically-minded Marxists have found the work merely pragmatic —and prone to some error and backsliding because of its lack of proper "theoretical rigour". Rudé actually knows and actively rejects Althusserian structuralism and some other of the more tortuous variants of contemporary Marxist theory. He rarely says so because he hates feuds and all the sectarian accompaniments of those theoretical wrangles. So for professional and personal reasons -- and probably also from unreasonable modesty -- he himself has generally represented his work as detailed, pragmatic history of little theoretical interest.

I take this opportunity to disagree. No doubt the straightforward history from below in "The Gordon Riots", *The Crowd in the French Revolution, Wilkes and Liberty, Captain Swing, Protest and Punishment* and the current study of criminals and their victims in early nineteenth-century England will continue to be regarded by most historians as his main achievement: "history from below" characterized by patient, ingenious and extremely careful use of novel sources to uncover the membership, and some at least of the mind and motivation, of historically important crowds and popular movements in France and England at the onset of their industrial revolutions. I share the universal respect for the fact-finder who gives identity and life and voices to all those faces in the crowd, and does it with the good-mannered, respectful sympathy which George Rudé seems to feel for eighteenth-century peasants and artisans and for twentieth-century students and colleagues without distinction of age, sex, class or literacy. But however just, I think that is still an unperceptive judgment. In addition to that achievement, and also as a necessary part of it, Rudé has considerable theoretical capacity.

His choice and use of received theories is sure-footed. When he needs new theory he develops it — but unobtrusively, for productive use, not for sale or display for its own sake. The theoretical skill appears, as I have suggested, in the developing concerns of the histories from below. It appears in the coherent values and the order and clarity of the general histories of Europe and the study of Robespierre. It appears directly in his work on historical interpretation, of the uses of sociological theory "where history and biography intersect", and on relations between ideas and action and the ways in which historians may best understand those relations. Throughout, the theoretical work is thoughtful and unobtrusive; it is economical, developing new theory only when actually needed; and the theory is everywhere subordinate to the substantive work of discovering and understanding and valuing what the author's values judge to be the more important facts and relations and directions of historical life. Those are the qualities that make his theoretical work unfashionable, and excellent. It would be a better world if similar principles had disciplined all the social sciences in recent times.

The same virtues may be rare in some Marxist circles, but happily they are not at all rare among English Marxist historians. Rudé shares with Christopher Hill, Eric Hobsbawm, Edward Thompson, Raphael Samuel and others an exceptionally flexible, humane and unobstructive variety of Marxism. A last quotation from *The Historian's Workshop* (p. 189) gives his own account of it:

> Marx's historical ideas have been so long and so insistently misrepresented in certain countries that it may be a surprise to some that a professor of history should actually claim that a reading of Marx was of any solid advantage to him in his craft. What I learned from Marx was not only that history tends to progress through a conflict of social classes (a view, incidentally that was held to be perfectly 'respectable' a hundred years ago), but that it has a discoverable pattern and moves forward (not backward, in circles, or in inexplicable jerks) broadly from a lower to a higher phase of development. I learned also that the lives and actions of the common people are the very stuff of history, and though 'material' rather than institutional and ideological factors are primary, that ideas themselves become a 'material force' when they pass into the active consciousness of men. Moreover I have also learned from Engels that, whatever the excellence of historical 'systems' (like his own and Marx's, for example), 'all history must be studied afresh'. What I never at any time learned from either of them was that history should be interpreted in terms of a narrow economic determinism

*

Perhaps his Australian exile was not so regrettable after all. By removing him in a "non-political" way from the British Communist Party it may have freed his Marxism from some sectarian constraints. By removing him from the French and English archives it turned him for some years to more reflective and theoretical work. Certainly no one who was his colleague there can regret his time in Australia. It was one of two specially happy events in my own academic life. In Oxford in 1953 I was one of those who offered his first post-war job to Edward Hallett Carr, then starting the fourth volume of the *History of Soviet Russia,* when the British universities had disgraced themselves by outlawing him for many years. In 1959 in Adelaide I read that untidy proof copy of *The Crowd in the French Revolution* and joined in offering work to George Rudé. If there is ever an academic Judgment Day, those two items should easily outweigh any others.

C.M.H. Clark

# *ON MEETING GEORGE RUDÉ IN CANBERRA*

Sometimes when meeting a man or a woman well known in the academic world there is a moment of surprise, even of astonishment of heart. They do not correspond with the picture formed in the mind from reading their work and listening to the mockers of the tea room or the knockers of the bar. But George Rudé had no surprises for us. From the moment my wife, who has an eye and an ear for such things, said to him that with the name of Rudé (from Rude) he must be Norwegian by origin, they began to sing Norwegian folk songs together; they began to imitate Norwegians talking to each other, and George told the story of an ancestor of his who always tossed the gold coin to the maid in the same lordly way as Lord Byron greeted a French chamber maid in a channel boat after a lively morning on the sea.

I could see then why so many were drawn to George—so many, that is, in Australia, because at that time the English had kept the light of George Rudé severely under the bushel, seemingly determined to allow it to burn out in some obscure school. But Australia gave him his chance. Of course, they had made their rather silly attempt to keep him out of an academic position in Australia.

But happily Adelaide, which was supposed to be, in the eyes of the academic heavy-weights of Sydney and Melbourne, that citadel inside which the giant of British philistine culture would make his last-ditch stand against the forces of progress in Australia, welcomed him. That was not only their good fortune: that was their sound judgement.

Adelaide was then on the eve of astounding Australia by playing a leading role in the liberation of our academic and intellectual life from the almost dead hand of conventional bourgeois, evangelical and Jansenist morality. Adelaide had become to the other cities in Australia a city with a morality, but without a faith. It was ripe for the loosening of what remained of the morality.

Adelaide, rather like the other provincial cities of Australia, seemed to be searching for a new mythology. The mythology of the bushman was as dead as a dodo. Catholicism and Mammon were the main contenders to fill the vacuum created by the withdrawal of the bourgeoisie. George had something to say to those who were looking for answers to such questions as what held the world together in its innermost heart.

That night in Canberra held many delights. The man knew all about those things to which those with the walnut hearts remain eternal strangers. George was clearly to be one of the enlargers of life, not one of the straiteners. That was why later on as I got to know him better, reading his work, listening to some of his lectures in

Canberra, and talking to him in Adelaide and Canberra, and at other centres where academic behaviour provides evidence for the world's belief that when two or three are gathered in the same place there is a third invisible to the persons present, the qualities of the man took shape.

He knew his philosophy of history. He had his own position, a Marxist position which illuminated everything he wrote and everything he said. But he was singularly free of the shouting and bullying tendencies of those who believe there is only one way of writing about either the past or the present, and they happen to know it. George was a Europeanist, but unlike some of the members of that team in Australia, especially those Europeans and British who sniff at Australians as a society of second-rate Europeans, George quickly won the respect and the affection of those who were or who were rapidly becoming Australian-centred.

George had about him an aura which allowed him to transcend loyalties of background, class and creed and political or religious conviction. The Thomists knew where he stood on all the great questions: they treated him with respect. The faces of the most extreme wing of the women's liberation movement, the ones who painted on the walls of University buildings the slogan "Castrate all heterosexual males" (who said we Australians were a quiet people?) were wreathed in smiles when George's name was mentioned in their company.

This gift to gather all manner of men and women around him came out in his published work in Australia. George who had been the centre of controversy in England, a victim possibly of some of the worst features of British philistinism, significantly worked here on a subject which used to cause a rush of blood to the head. He not only worked on convicts: he worked on political convicts: he worked in the archives in Hobart — often in flames of human passions. He was not a Tasmanian.

But as so often with what he did he charmed those who might otherwise have accused him of despitefully using them. The ones who had hissed and mocked at other less worthy performers in the same field applauded and called for more. Once again George had shown it was possible to employ a sweet reasonableness, in subjects which previously had seemed to illustrate the point that the writing of history is an example of human madness and folly.

I do not propose to discuss why George had, and has, such a gift. That will be for a biographer, indeed for someone much wiser and more discerning. For me he is one of those rare human beings who has the gift to inspire others to give of their best. The spite and malice were singularly absent when George was around. The other historian who had that gift in abundance was Keith Hancock. It is perhaps hopeful for the future of all of us here that both of them are men of faith, men who did not lose their faith even after quite a long residence in what now threatens to become the "kingdom of nothingness".

Alan H. Adamson

# *GEORGE RUDÉ IN CANADA*

When George Rudé arrived in Montreal in November 1970, the melodrama of our October crisis was still playing itself out. Pierre Trudeau had invoked the War Measures Act, the streets were lined with soldiers and the jails were filled with innocents suspected of subversion. George might well have believed himself to have dropped into one of his beloved revolutionary situations. As events turned out, however, this was not the beginning of a popular movement so much as the termination of a decade of infantile leftism.

For Rudé, however, this modest Canadian contribution to the repertoire of *opéra bouffe* was to mark the beginning of perhaps the most fruitful period of an uncommonly fruitful career. In 1970 George was sixty, an age when most scholars begin to think of resting on their oars. Not George Rudé. His capacity for work is the envy and the scourge of us all. I can remember many a country week-end when we sought in mindless outdoor action some short reprieve from thought. But not George. He always had a paper to read, a book to review, or a chapter to finish. And he would emerge just before lunch with a genial smile, his work done, ready for a short walk and a modest glass. We were physically exhausted but, miserable offenders, had left undone those things which we ought to have done. He was a man with a clear conscience.

The results are reflected in his publishing record over the last fourteen years. *Hanoverian London, Debate on Europe,* and *Europe in the Eighteenth Century* appeared one after the other in 1971 and 1972. The publication of *Robespierre* in 1975 brought with it a quaint and unexpected honour. One day George received a letter from a direct descendant of Samuel Clemens, informing him that he had been dubbed a Knight of the Order of Mark Twain. He had been admitted to this exclusive fraternity, which joined him in unlikely brotherhood with Winston Churchill, Lester Pearson, and Jimmy Carter, because he had "unmonstered" Robespierre and restored him to his rightful dignity. *Protest and Punishment: the Story of the Social and Political Protesters Transported to Australia. 1788-1868* (1978) is surely George's most imposing "Canadian" work. Its preparation involved research across three continents and included, to the occasional perplexity of some of his colleagues, a certain amount of footwork among Canadian graveyards, including the last resting place of George Loveless, the Tolpuddle martyr, in London, Ontario, and the Côte des Neiges cemetery in Montreal, where George noted that the names of some of the 1837 rebels returned from Australian transportation had not been inscribed on the *Monument aux Patriotes. Ideology and Popular Protest* appeared in 1980, while *Criminal and Victim: Crime and Society in Early Nineteenth-Century England* is to be published in 1985.

One book every other year would be enough to absorb the energies of any normal organism, but it has formed only one part of George's Canadian career, at the centre of which has been his teaching in the History Department of Sir George Williams University (Concordia University after it absorbed Loyola College in 1974). His graduate seminar, *Aspects of the Study of Revolution,* and his undergraduate seminar, *The Comparative Study of Popular Protest,* have acted as magnets attracting many of the department's brightest students, one of whom, Caroline Fick, has contributed to this volume. Nor did the labours of this compulsive pedagogue cease when the week's work in Montreal was done. We all remember George packing his Gladstone of a Friday and heading off to speak at a conference somewhere in Canada or the U.S.A. Indeed there must hardly be a major campus on the continent -- including Toronto, Columbia, Yale, Harvard, Wisconsin and Michigan -- where he has not cast his shadow. In addition to these academic one-night stands he managed to run a seminar on revolutionary movements at York University in Toronto as part of their interdisciplinary graduate programme in social and political thought (one of his students there, George Comninel, has a piece in this book); in 1980-81 he occupied the Pinckney Harrison chair of history at William and Mary College, a somewhat incongruous but nonetheless successful experience for a specialist in popular protest.

Beyond the writing, the teaching, the lecture tours and the visiting professorships, George has made some important contributions to what may be termed innovative academic organisation. He was a founding member and, in 1972 and 1973, the first regular (and now honorary) president of the post-graduate, interdisciplinary *Inter-university Centre for European Studies / Centre Interuniversitaire d'Études Européennes.* Later he lent his influence and support to the founding of Concordia's multidisciplinary Liberal Arts College. When that now-flourishing institution opened its doors in 1979 he delivered its first public lecture, which has subsequently become an annual fall event of the College, given by a major academic figure, and now known as the *George Rudé Inaugural Lecture.* This last, incidentally, is only one of the many honours which have fallen on George's shoulders. In 1976, the year of the American Bicentenary, he gave the Distinguished Historian's Address at the May meetings of the Canadian Historical Association in Quebec City, on "The Study of Revolutions". In 1978 a group of Australian historians established the *George Rudé Seminar,* a gathering held every two years at a different Australian University and generally organised around some theme in modern French history. And in October, 1982 the History Department of Concordia University presented a three-day *George Rudé Colloquium,* focussed on the theme of *Popular Protest and Popular Ideology.* 100 scholars and graduate students from across Canada and the U.S. heard a paper on the influence of the seminal *The Crowd in History* and others on French, English and American subjects, as well as a talk by George on his own work at the Colloqium's concluding banquet.

Even a condensed account of George's Canadian years would be incomplete without some mention of his impact on students. After all, he has always been first and foremost a teacher; and if teachers tend to fall into two categories -- those who genuinely love their students, and those who like Gulliver with his wife find their odour so offensive that they must always keep their noses well stuffed with rue and lavender -- George clearly belongs among the former. He does not tolerate the young, he actually enjoys them. The reason is not hard to find. Despite inevitable twinges he has retained his youthful juices, continues to look upon the world with fresh eyes, and communicates his enthusiasms to the young — who respond in kind. When George was seriously ill in the winter of 1983-84, a virtual round-the-clock service of students visited him in hospital, brought him soup from Doreen, papers and correspondence from the office and even helped organise his infamous card files so that he could continue work on the current manuscript. Now that he is restored to his usual vigour, they and all his other friends and colleagues can only rejoice and pray him many more productive years.

PART TWO

Eric J. Hobsbawm

# HISTORY FROM BELOW—SOME REFLECTIONS

Grassroots history, history seen from below or the history of the common people, of which George Rudé is a distinguished pioneer, no longer needs commercials. However, it may still benefit from some reflections on its technical problems, which are both difficult and interesting, probably more so than those of traditional academic history. To reflect on some of them is the purpose of this paper.

But before turning to my main subject let me ask why grassroots history is so recent a fashion — i.e. why most of the history written by contemporary chroniclers and subsequent scholars from the beginning of literacy until, say, the end of the nineteenth century, tells us so little about the great majority of the inhabitants of the countries or states it was recording, i.e. why Brecht's question "Who built Thebes of the Seven Gates" is a typically twentieth-century question. The answer takes us both into the nature of politics--which was until recently the characteristic subject of history--and the motivations of historians.

Most history in the past was written for the glorification of, and perhaps for the practical use of, rulers. Indeed certain kinds of it still have this function. Those fat neo-Victorian biographies of politicians which have recently become the fashion again are certainly not read by the masses. Who reads them, apart from a handful of professional historians and a sprinkling of students who have to look into them for essays, is not clear. I have always been gravely puzzled by those alleged best-seller lists which always seem to contain the latest block-buster of this type. But certainly politicians gobble them up like popcorn, at least if they are literate. This is natural enough. Not only are they about people like themselves, and activities like the ones they are engaged in, but they are about eminent practitioners of their own trade, from which -- if the books are good -- they can learn something. Roy Jenkins still sees himself living in the same universe as Asquith, just as Harold Macmillan certainly saw people like Salisbury or Melbourne as in some sense contemporaries.

Now the practical business of ruling class politics could, for most of history until the latter part of the nineteenth century and in most places, be normally carried on without more than an occasional reference to the mass of the subject population. They could be taken for granted, except in very exceptional circumstances — such as great social revolutions or insurrections. This does not mean either that they were contented or that they didn't have to be taken into account. It merely means that the terms of the relationship were arranged in such a way as to keep discontent within acceptable bounds, i.e. in such a way that the activities of the poor did not normally threaten the social order. Furthermore, mostly they were fixed at a level below that on which the top people's politics operated — for instance locally and not nationally.

Conversely, the ordinary people accepted their subalternity most of the time, and mostly confined their struggles, such as they were, to fighting those oppressors with whom they had immediate contact. If there is one safe generalisation about the normal relation between peasants and kings or emperors in the period before the nineteenth century, it is that they regarded the king or emperor as by definition just. If he only knew what the landowning gentry were up to -- or more likely a particular named nobleman--, he would stop them or him oppressing the peasants. So in a sense he was outside their world of politics and they were outside his.

There are naturally exceptions to this generalisation. I am inclined to believe that China is the main one, for that is a country in which, even in the days of the Celestial Empire, peasant risings were not occasional freak phenomena like earth-quakes or pestilences, but phenomena which could, did, and were expected to be capable of, overthrowing dynasties. But by and large they were not. Grassroots history therefore becomes relevant to, or part of, the sort of history that was written traditionally--the history of major political decisions and events--only from the moment when the ordinary people become a constant factor in the making of such decisions and events. Not only at times of exceptional popular mobilisation, such as revolutions, but at all or most times. By and large this did not begin to happen until the era of the great revolutions at the end of the eighteenth century. But in practice of course it did not become significant until much later. Outside the USA even the typical institutions of bourgeois democracy — i.e. elections by general male suffrage (the women's vote is an even later development) were exceptional until the early nineteenth century. The economy of mass consumption is, in Europe at least, a phenomenon of this century. And the two characteristic techniques for discovering people's opinions--market research by sampling, and its offspring, the public opinion poll--are quite implausibly young by historical standards. In effect they were products of the 1930s.

The history of the common people as a special field of study therefore begins with the history of mass movements in the eighteenth century. I suppose Michelet is the first great practitioner of grassroots history: the Great French Revolution is at the core of his writing. And ever since, the history of the French Revolution, especially since Jacobinism was revitalised by socialism and the Enlightenment by Marxism, has been the proving-ground of this kind of history. If there is a single historian who anticipates most of the themes of contemporary work, it is Georges Lefebvre, whose "Great Fear", translated into English after forty years, is still remarkably uptodate. To put it more generally: it was the French tradition of historiography as a whole, steeped in the history not of the French ruling class but the French *people,* which established most of the themes and even the methods of grassroots history, Marc Bloch as well as Georges Lefebvre. But the field really began to flourish in other countries only after World War II. In fact its real advance only began in the middle 'fifties, when it became possible for Marxism to make its full contribution to it.

For the marxist, or more generally the socialist, interest in grassroots history developed with the growth of the labour movement. And though this provided a very powerful incentive to study the history of the common man -- especially the working class -- it also imposed some quite effective blinkers on the socialist historians. They were naturally tempted to study not just any common people, but the common people who could be regarded as ancestors of the movement: not workers as such so much as Chartists, trade unionists, Labour militants. And they were also tempted -- equally naturally -- to suppose that the history of the movements and organizations which led the workers' struggle, and therefore in a real sense "represented" the workers, could replace the history of the common people themselves. But this is not so. The history of the Irish revolution of 1916-21 is not identical with the history of the IRA, the Citizen Army, the Irish Transport Workers Union or the Sinn Fein. You have only to read Sean O'Casey's great plays about Dublin slum life during this period to see how much else there was at the grass-roots. Not until the 1950s did the left begin to emancipate itself from the narrow approach.

Whatever its origins and initial difficulties, grassroots history has now taken off. And in looking back upon the history of ordinary people, we are not merely trying to give it a retrospective political significance which it did not always have, but we are trying more generally to explore an unknown dimension of the past. And this brings me to the technical problems of doing so.

Every kind of history has its technical problems, but most of these assume that there is a body of ready-made source-material whose interpretation raises these problems. The classical discipline of historical scholarship, as developed in the nineteenth century by German and other professors, made this assumption which, as it happens, fitted in very conveniently with the prevailing fashion of scientific positivism. This sort of scholarly problem is still dominant in a few very old-fashioned branches of learning such as literary history. To study Dante, one has to become very sophisticated in interpreting manuscripts and in working out what can go wrong when manuscripts are copied from each other, because the text of Dante depends on the collation of medieval manuscripts. To study Shakespeare, who left no manuscripts but a lot of corrupt printed editions, means becoming a sort of Sherlock Holmes of the early seventeenth-century printing trade. But in neither case is there much doubt about the main body of the subject we are studying, namely the works of Dante or Shakespeare.

Now grassroots history differs from such subjects, and indeed from most of traditional history, inasmuch as there simply is not a ready-made body of material about it. It is true that sometimes we are lucky. One of the reasons why so much modern grassroots history has emerged from the study of the French Revolution is that this great event in history combines two characteristics which rarely occur together before that date. In the first place, being a major revolution, it suddenly brought into activity and public notice vast numbers of the sort of people who previously attracted very little attention outside their family and neighbours. And in the second place it documented them by means of a vast and laborious bureaucracy, classifying and filing them for the benefit of the historian in the national and departmental archives of France. The historians of the French Revolution, from Georges Lefebvre to Richard Cobb, have vividly described the pleasures and troubles of travelling through the French countryside in search of the Frenchmen of the 1790s — but chiefly the pleasures, for once the scholar arrived at Angoulême or Montpellier or wherever, and got the right archival series, practically every dusty packet of ancient paper -- beautifully legible, unlike the crabbed hands of the sixteenth or seventeenth centuries -- contained nuggets of gold. Historians of the French Revolution happen to be lucky — luckier than British ones, for instance. In most cases the grassroots historian finds only what he is looking for, not what is already waiting for him. Most sources for grassroots history have only been recognized as sources because someone has asked a question and then prospected desperately around for some way--any way--of answering it. We cannot be positivists, believing that the questions and the answers arise naturally out of the study of the material. There is generally no material until our questions have revealed it. Take the now flourishing discipline of historical demography, which rests on the fact that the births, marriages and deaths of people were recorded in parish registers from, more or less, the sixteenth century. This was long known, and many of these registers were actually reprinted for the convenience of the genealogists who were the only people to take much of an interest in them. But once the social historians got going on them, and techniques for analysing them were developed, it turned out that tremendous discoveries could be made. We can now discover how far people in the seventeenth century practised birth control, how far they suffered famine or other catastrophes, what their life expectancy was at various periods, how likely men and women were to remarry, how early or late they married etc. — all questions about which, until the 1950s, we could only speculate for the pre-census periods.

It is true that once our questions have revealed new sources of material, these themselves raise considerable technical problems: sometimes too much so, sometimes not enough. Much of the time of historical demographers has been taken up simply with the increasingly complex technicalities of their analysis, which is why much of what they publish is at present interesting only for other historical demographers. The time-lag between research and result is unusually long. We must learn that a lot of grassroots history doesn't produce quick results, but requires elaborate, time-consuming and expensive processing. It is not like picking up diamonds in a river-bed, more like modern diamond or gold-mining which requires heavy capital investment and high technology.

On the other hand some kinds of grassroots material have not yet stimulated enough methodological thinking. Oral history is a good example. Thanks to the tape-recorder a lot of this is now practised. And most taped memories seem sufficiently interesting, or have sufficient sentimental appeal, to be their own reward. But in my opinion we shall never make adequate use of oral history until we work out what can go wrong in memory with as much care as we now know what can go wrong in transmitting manuscripts by manual copying. The anthropologists and African historians have begun to do so for the inter-generational transmission of facts by word of mouth. For instance we know over what number of generations certain kinds of information can be transmitted more or less accurately (e. g. genealogies) and that the transmission of historical events is always likely to lead to chronological telescoping. To quote a personal example, the memory of the Labourer's Rising of 1830, as preserved in and around Tisbury, Wilts., today, remembers as contemporary things which happened in 1817 and in 1830. But most oral history today is personal memory, which is a remarkably slippery medium for preserving facts. The point is that memory is not so much a recording as a selective mechanism, and the selection is, within limits, constantly changing. What I remember of my life as a Cambridge undergraduate is different today from what it was when I was thirty or forty-five. And unless I have worked it up into conventional form for the purpose of boring people (we are all familiar with those who do this with their wartime experiences), it is likely to be different tomorrow or next year. At the moment our criteria for judging oral sources are almost entirely instinctive or non-existent. It either sounds right or it doesn't. Of course we can also check it against some verifiable independent source and approve it because it can be confirmed by such a source. But this doesn't get us nearer the crucial problem, which is to know what we can believe when there is nothing to check it against.

The methodology of oral history is not simply important for checking the reliability of the tapes of old ladies and gentlemen's reminiscences. One significant aspect of grassroots history is what ordinary people remember of big events as distinct from what their betters think they should remember, or what historians can establish as having happened; and insofar as they turn memory into myth, how such myths are formed. What did the British people actually feel in the summer of 1940? The records of the Ministry of Information present a somewhat different picture from what most of us now believe. How can we reconstruct either the original feelings or the formation of the myth? Can we separate them? These are not insignificant questions. My own view is that they require not merely the collection and interpretation of tapes or retrospective questionnaires, but experiments — if necessary in conjunction with psychologists. There is plenty of the methodological, hypothetical, and what is more arbitrary involved here. The curve of support for the Liberal - Social Democratic Alliance, indicated by monthly questions about how people would vote if a general election were held tomorrow, indicates nothing about their political behaviour except how they answer this particular question and the assumption that voting intention is the crucial variable in politics. It is not based on any model of how people actually make up their minds about politics, and it does not investigate their political behaviour, but their present view about one particular political act in hypothetical circumstances. But if we discover the equivalent of retrospective opinion polls, we are investigating what people actually thought or actually did.

Now sometimes this can be done by actually discovering their opinions. For instance Hanák analysed opinions about World War I in the different nationalities of the Habsburg empire by working through the censored letters from and to soldiers at the front, and Kula in Poland has published a collection of letters from emigrant relatives to Polish peasants in the late nineteenth century intercepted by the Tsarist police. But this is rare, because for most of the past people were generally illiterate anyway. Much more commonly we infer their thoughts from their actions. In other words we base our historical work on Lenin's realistic discovery that voting with one's feet can be as effective a way of expressing one's opinion as voting in the ballot box. Sometimes, of course, we are halfway between opinion and action. Thus Marc Ferro investigated the attitude of different groups to war and revolution in Russia by analysing the telegrams and resolutions sent to Petrograd in the first weeks of the February Revolution — i.e. before public meetings, workers', peasants' or soldiers' councils or whatever had acquired party labels or character. To send a resolution to the capital is political action — though at the beginning of a great revolution it is likely to occur more frequently than at other times. But the content of the telegram is opinion, and the differences between e.g. worker's, peasants and soldiers' opinions is significant. Thus peasants "demanded" much more often than they petitioned. They were more opposed to the war than workers, who were also less self-confident. Soldiers were not at this point opposing the war at all, but complaining about officers. And so on.

But the prettiest sources are the ones which simply record actions which *must imply* certain opinions. They are almost always the result of searching for some way -- any way -- of asking a question already in the historian's mind. Also, they are generally quite conclusive. Suppose, for instance, you want to discover what difference the French Revolution made to monarchist sentiment in France. Marc Bloch, investigating the belief that the kings of France and England could work miracles, which was widespread for many centuries, points out that at the coronation of Louis XVI in 1774 2,400 sufferers from scrofula came forward to be cured of the "king's evil" by the royal touch. But when Charles X revived the ancient ceremonial of coronation at Rheims in 1825, and was reluctantly persuaded to revive the ceremony of royal healing also, a mere 120 people turned up. Between the last pre-revolutionary king and 1825 the Shakespearean belief that "there's some divinity doth hedge a king" had virtually disappeared in France. There is no arguing with such a finding.

The decline of traditional religious beliefs and the rise of secular ones has similarly been investigated by analysing wills and funeral inscriptions. For though Dr. Johnson said that in writing lapidary inscriptions a man is not on oath, it is even more true that he or she is more likely to express their real religious views in such a context than at other times. And not only these. Vovelle has illustrated very prettily the decline in eighteenth-century Provence of the belief in a stratified hierarchical society by counting the frequency of the testamentary formula "to be buried according to his or her rank and condition". It declines steadily and quite markedly throughout the century. But -- interestingly enough -- not more steeply than, say, the invocation of the Virgin Mary in Provençal wills.

Suppose we look for other ways of discovering changes in attitude towards traditional religion, and decide to turn from burial to baptism. In Catholic countries the saints provide the main body of given names. Actually, they only do so overwhelmingly from the time of the Counterreformation on, so that this index can also tell us something about the evangelisation or re-evangelisation of the common people in the period of Reform and Counterreform. But purely secular names become common in some parts in the nineteenth century, and sometimes deliberately non-Christian, or even anti-Christian, names.

A Florentine colleague got his children to do a small bit of research on Tuscan telephone directories, to check up on the frequency of first names taken either from deliberately secular sources — e.g. Italian opera and literature (for instance, Tasso, Dante or Rigoletto), or even from politics (for instance, Spartaco). It turns out that this correlates particularly well with the areas of former anarchist influence — more so than with those of socialist influence. So we can infer -- what is also probable on other grounds -- that anarchism was more than a mere political movement, and tended to have some of the characteristics of an active conversion, a change in the entire way of life of its militants. It is possible that the social and ideological history of personal names has been investigated in England (other than by that gentleman who annually keeps track of the names in the *Times* announcements), but if so I have not come across these studies. I suspect there aren't any, at least by historians.

So, with more or less ingenuity, what the poet called the simple annals of the poor — the bare records of, or connected with, birth, marriage and death, can yield surprising quantities of information. And everyone can try his or her own hand at the historian's game of discovering ways of not merely speculating about what songs the sirens sang (Sir Thomas Browne), but actually finding some indirect records of those songs. A lot of grassroots history is like the trace of the ancient plough. It might seem gone for good with the men who ploughed the field many centuries ago. But every aerial-photographer knows that, in a certain light, and seen at a certain angle, the shadows of long-forgotten ridge and furrow can still be seen.

Nevertheless, mere ingenuity doesn't take us far enough. What we need, both to make sense of what the inarticulate thought, and to verify or falsify our hypotheses about it, is a coherent picture, or if you prefer the term, a model. For our problem is not so much to discover one good source. Even the best of such sources -- let's say the demographic ones about births, marriages and deaths -- only illuminate certain areas of what people did, felt and thought. What we must normally do is to put together a wide variety of often fragmentary information: and to do that we must, if you'll excuse the phrase, construct the jig-saw puzzle ourselves, i.e. work out how such information *ought* to fit together. This is another way of repeating what I've already stressed, namely that the grassroots historian cannot be an oldfashioned positivist. He must in a way know what he is looking for, and only if he does, can he recognize whether what he finds fits in with his hypothesis or not; and if it doesn't, try and think of another model. How do we construct our models? Of course, there is an element -- a rather strong element -- of knowledge, of experience, of simply having a sufficiently wide and concrete acquaintance with the actual subject. This enables us to eliminate obviously useless hypotheses. To quote an absurd illustration. An African candidate in the London external BA once answered a question about the industrial revolution in Lancashire by saying the cotton industry developed there because Lancashire is so suitable for growing cotton. We happen to know that it isn't, and therefore think the answer absurd, though it might not seem so in Calabar. But there are plenty of our answers which are equally absurd, and could be avoided by equally elementary information. For instance, if we do not happen to know that in the nineteenth century the term "artisan" in Britain was used almost exclusively to describe a skilled wage-worker, and the term "peasant" generally meant a farm-labourer, we might make some substantial howlers about nineteenth-century British social structure. Such howlers have been made -- continental translators persistently translate the term "journey-man" as "day-labourer" -- and who knows how many discussions about seventeenth-century society are hamstrung by our ignorance of what exactly the common meaning or meanings of the term "servant" or "yeoman" was. There simply are things one has to know about the past, which is why most sociologists make bad historians: they don't want to take the time to find out. We also need imagination — preferably in conjunction with information, in order to avoid the greatest danger of the historian, anachronism. Practically all popular treatments of Victorian sexuality suffer from a failure to understand that our own sexual attitudes are simply not the same as those of other periods. It is plain wrong to assume that the Victorians -- all except a small and rather atypical minority -- had the same attitude to sex as we have, only they suppressed it or concealed it. But it is fairly hard to make the imaginative effort to understand this, all the more so since sex seems to be something fairly unchanging and we all think we are expert on it.

But knowledge and imagination alone are not enough. What we need to construct, or to reconstruct, is, ideally speaking, a coherent, preferably a consistent, *system* of behaviour or thought. And one which can be, in some senses, inferred once we know the basic social assumptions, parameters and tasks of the situation, but before we know very much about that situation. Let me give you an example. When communities of Indian peasants in Peru occupied the land to which they felt they were entitled, notably in the early 1960s, they almost invariably proceeded in a highly standardised manner: the whole community would assemble, with wives, children, cattle and implements, to the accompaniment of drums, horns and other musical instruments. At a certain time -- generally at dawn -- they would all cross the line, tear down the fences, advance to the limit of the territory they claimed, immediately start building little huts as near the new line as possible, and begin to pasture the cattle and dig the land. Curiously enough, other land-occupations by peasants in different times and places -- for instance in Southern Italy -- took exactly the same form. Why? In other words, on what assumptions does this highly standardised, and obviously not culturally determined, behaviour make sense?

Suppose we say: *First* the occupation has to be collective, a) because the land belongs to the community and b) because all members of the community must be involved to minimise victimisation and to prevent the community being disrupted by arguments between those who stuck out their necks and those who didn't. For after all, they are breaking the law and unless there is a successful revolution, they will certainly be punished — even if their demands are actually conceded. Can we verify this? Well, there is considerable supporting evidence about the importance of minimising victimisation. Thus in Japanese peasant risings before the Meiji restoration, a lot of villages were conventionally "coerced" into joining the rising, meaning that their village authorities were provided with an official cover for participation. Lefebvre made similar points about French villages in 1789. If everybody can say "I'm sorry, but I had no option but to join", it is likely that the authorities in turn will have an official excuse for limiting the punishment which they feel obliged to mete out for rebellion. For of course they have to live with the peasants just as the peasants have to live with them. The fact that one lot rules and the other is subaltern doesn't mean that the rulers need take no account of the ruled.

Very well. Now what is the most familiar way of mobilising the entire community? It is the village *fiesta* or its equivalent — the combination of collective ritual and collective entertainment. And of course a land occupation is both: it is bound to be a very serious and ceremonial affair, reclaiming land which belongs to the village, but it is also probably the most exciting thing that has happened to the village in a long time. So it is natural that there should be an element of the village fair about the rising. Hence the music — which also serves to mobilise and rally the people. Can we verify this? Well, time and again we have evidence in such peasant mobilisations of the people -- especially the young people -- putting on their Sunday best; and we certainly have evidence in regions of heavy drinking, that a certain number of pints are being sunk.

Why do they invade at dawn? Presumably for sound military reasons — to catch the other side napping and to give themselves at least some daylight by which to settle in. But why do they settle in with huts, animals and implements, instead of just waiting to repel the landlords or the police? Actually, they hardly ever try seriously to repel the police or the army, for the good reason that they know very well they can't, being too weak. Peasants are more realistic than many of the ultra-left insurrectionaries. They know perfectly well who is going to kill whom if it comes to a confrontation. And what is more important, they know who can't run away. They know that revolutions can happen, but they also know that their success doesn't depend on them in their specific village. So mass land occupations are normally by way of being a try-on. Generally there is something in the political situation which has percolated to the villages and convinced them that times are a-changing: the normal strategy of passivity can perhaps be replaced by activity. If they are right, nobody will come to throw them off the land. If they are wrong, the sensible thing is to retreat and wait for the next suitable moment. But they must nevertheless not only lay claim to the land but actually live on it and *labour* it, because their right to it is not like bourgeois property right, but more like Lockean property right in the state of nature: it depends on mixing one's own labour with the resources of nature. Can we verify this? Well yes, we know quite a lot from nineteenth-century Russia about peasants' belief in the so-called "labour principle". And we can actually see the argument in action: in the Cilento, south of Naples, before the 1848 revolution "every Christmas Day the peasants went out onto the lands to which they laid claim in order to carry out agricultural labours, thus seeking to maintain the ideal principle of possession of their rights." If you don't work the land, you cannot justly own it.

I could give you other examples. Indeed I've tried this sort of construction --which, I confess, I think I learned from the social anthropologists--on other problems—for instance, on the problem of social banditry, another phenomenon which lends itself to this type of analysis, because it is highly standardised.

It implies three analytical steps: *First,* to identify what the doctors would call the syndrome—namely all the "symptoms" or bits of the jig-saw puzzle which have to be fitted together, or at least enough of them to go on with. *Second,* to construct a model which makes sense of all these forms of behaviour; i.e. to discover a set of assumptions which would make the combination of these different kinds of behaviour consistent with one another according to some scheme of rationality. *Third,* we must then discover whether there is independent evidence to confirm these guesses.

Now the trickiest part of this is the first, since it rests on a mixture of the historian's prior knowledge, his theories about society, sometimes his hunch, instinct or introspection, and he is generally not really clear in his own mind about how he makes his initial selection. At least I've not been, even though I try hard to be conscious of what I'm doing. For instance, on what grounds does one pick out a variety of disparate social phenomena, generally treated as curious footnotes to history, and classify them together as members of a family of "primitive rebellion" — of what you might call pre-political politics: banditry, urban riots, certain kinds of secret societies, certain kinds of millennial and other sects and so on? When I first did so I did not really know. Why do I notice, among the numerous other things I could notice (some of which I obviously don't), the significance of clothes in peasant movements: clothes as a symbol of the class struggle, as in the Sicilian hostility between the "caps" and the "hats", or in the Bolivian peasant risings in which the Indians occupying the cities force the city people to take off their trousers and wear peasant (i.e. Indian) costume? Clothes as symbols of rebellion itself, as when the farm-labourers of 1830 put on Sunday best to march to the gentry with their demands, thus indicating that they are not in the normal state of oppression which equals labour but in the state of freedom which equals holiday and play? (Remember that even in the early labour movement the concept of the strike and the holiday are not clearly separated: miners "play" when they are on strike, and the Chartist plans for a general strike in 1839 were plans for a "National Holiday"). I don't know, and this ignorance is dangerous, for it may make me unaware of introducing my own contemporary assumptions into the model, or of omitting something important.

The second phase of the analysis is also tricky, since we may simply be placing an arbitrary construction on the facts. Still, insofar as the model is capable of testing -- unlike many beautiful models, such as, say, a lot of structuralist ones -- this is not too troublesome. More troublesome is a certain vagueness about what one is trying to prove. For to assume that a certain kind of behaviour makes sense on certain assumptions is not to claim that it is sensible, i.e. rationally justifiable. The great danger of this procedure -- and the one to which a lot of field anthropologists have succumbed -- is to equate all behaviour as equally "rational". Now some of it is. For instance, the behaviour of the good Soldier Schweik, who, of course, had been certified as a bona fide half-wit by the military authorities, was anything but half-witted. It was undoubtedly the most effective form of self-defence for someone in his position. Time and again, in studying the political behaviour of peasants in a state of oppression, we discover the practical value of stupidity and a refusal to accept any innovation: the great asset of peasants is that there are many things you simply can't make them do, and by and large no change is what suits a traditional peasantry best. (But of course, let us not forget that many of these peasants don't just play at being dense, they really *are* dense). Sometimes the behaviour was rational under some circumstances, but is no longer rational under changed circumstances. But there are also plenty of kinds of behaviour which are not rational at all, in the sense that they are effective means of achieving definable practical ends, but are merely comprehensible. This is obviously the case with the revival of beliefs in astrology, witchcraft, various fringe religions and irrational beliefs in the West today, or with certain forms of violent behaviour -- e.g., to take the most common example -- the madness which seizes so many people once they get into a car. The grassroots historian does not -- or at least he ought not to -- abdicate his judgment.

What is the object of all these exercises? It is not simply to discover the past but *to explain it,* and in doing so to provide a link with the present. There is an enormous temptation in history simply to uncover what has hitherto been unknown, and to enjoy what we find. And since so much of the lives, and even more of the thoughts, of the common people have been quite unknown, this temptation is all the greater in grassroots history, all the more so since many of us identify ourselves with the unknown common men and women -- the even more unknown women -- of the past. I don't wish to discourage this. But curiosity, sentiment and the pleasures of antiquarianism are not enough. The best of such grassroots history makes wonderful reading, but that is all. What we want to know is *why,* as well as *what.* To discover that in seventeenth-century Puritan villages in Somerset, or in Victorian Poor Law Unions in Wiltshire, girls with illegitimate children were not treated as sinners or as "unrespectable" if they genuinely had reason to believe that the father of the child had intended to marry them, is interesting, and provides food for reflection. But what we really want to know is why such beliefs were held, how they fitted in with the rest of the value-system of those communities (or of the larger society of which these formed a part), and why they changed or didn't change.

The link with the present is also obvious, for the process of understanding it has much in common with the process of understanding the past, quite apart from the fact that understanding how the past has turned into the present helps us understand the present, and presumably something of the future. Much about the behaviour of people *of all classes* today is, in fact, as unknown and undocumented as were much of the lives of the common people in the past. Sociologists and others who monitor developments in everyday life are constantly trailing behind their quarry. And even when we are aware of what we are doing as members of our society and age, we may not be conscious of the role which our acts and beliefs play in creating the image of what we would all wish to regard as an orderly social cosmos -- even those who regard themselves as being outside of it --, or in expressing our attempt to come to terms with its changes. Much of what is written, said and acted out today about family relationships, clearly belongs to the realm of symptoms rather than diagnosis.

And as in the past one of our tasks is to uncover the lives and thoughts of common people and to rescue them from Edward Thompson's "enormous condescension of posterity", so our problem at present is also to strip away the equally presumptuous assumptions of those who think they know both what the facts and what the solutions are, and who seek to impose them on the people. We must discover what people really want of a good or even a tolerable society, and, what is by no means the same--because they may not actually know--, what they *need* from such a society. That is not easy, partly because it is difficult to get rid of prevailing assumptions about how society should work, some of which (such as most liberal ones) are very unhelpful guides, and partly because we do not know actually what makes a society work in real life: even a bad and unjust society. So far in the twentieth century all countries I know have failed to solve by deliberate planning a problem which, for many centuries, appeared to pose no great difficulties for humanity, namely how to construct a working city which should also be a human community. That should give us pause.

Grassroots historians spend much of their time finding out how societies work and when they do not work, as well as how they change. They cannot help doing this, since their subject, ordinary people, make up the bulk of any society. They start out with the enormous advantage of knowing that they are largely ignorant of either the facts or the answers to their problems. They also have the substantial advantage of historians over social scientists who turn to history, of knowing how little we know of the past, how important it is to find out, and what hard work in a specialised discipline is needed for the purpose. They also have a third advantage. They know that what people wanted and needed was not always what their betters, or those who were cleverer and more influential, thought they ought to have. These are modest enough claims for our trade. But modesty is not a negligible virtue. It is important to remind ourselves from time to time that we don't know all the answers about society and that the process of discovering them is not simple. Those who plan and manage society now are perhaps unlikely to listen. Those who want to change society and eventually to plan its development ought also to listen. If some of them will, it will be due partly to the work of historians like George Rudé.

Christopher Hill

# THE POOR AND THE PEOPLE IN SEVENTEENTH-CENTURY ENGLAND

*I*

I must make one obvious point to start with. The word "people" is often abused today, as when politicians say "the people want this" or "the people won't stand for that", when they haven't a clue statistically about what the people want. But the fact that we can see that they are abusing the word shows that there is an agreed meaning. "The people of England" means the inhabitants of England, all of them, male and female, rich and poor. As we shall see, things were not quite so simple in the seventeenth century. Very few indeed who used the word "people" included all inhabitants.

Linguistic usage relates of course to political practice. It comes as quite a shock to recall that it is only in the present century that all adults have been regarded as people in the sense of having a vote for Parliament. Nineteenth-century historians took quite seriously seventeenth-century claims that Parliament represented the people of England, because it seemed to them that *their* Parliaments represented the people, though only a minority of the population had the vote. Only in the present century did historians become aware of the significance of this blind spot. As so often, history has to be rewritten not because new evidence has been discovered but because of changes in the society in which the historians live. In this instance, introduction of universal suffrage has made historians more aware of its absence in the seventeenth-century.

When civil war broke out between King and Parliament in 1642, Parliament had to find arguments to justify its stand against the King. He was accepted as the Lord's Anointed, ruling by divine right, and also by tradition, by historical and legal right. What moral claim had Parliament to oppose him? The answer found was that Parliament represented the people of England, and that the whole people was superior even to the King. Some even claimed, to the horror of conservatives, that the Biblical text "Touche not mine anointed" "refers to inferior subjects.... This dangerous tenet", wrote a pamphleteer as early as 1642, "hath been buzzed into the ears of the people, as if they only were anointed, none but they".[1] But even if the people were superior to the King, awkward questions were raised in the free discussion of the sixteen-forties about the extent to which Parliament was really representative. The royalist Sir Robert Filmer had great fun pointing out that so far

75

from representing the people of England, the Parliamentary electorate in fact included perhaps one out of every ten Englishmen — the upper ten. Levellers made the same point from the other side; but they -- unlike Filmer -- thought that the franchise should be extended so as to make Parliament representative of the whole male population.

Parliamentarian political thinkers got themselves into deep waters here. The rhetoric of the prosecution at Charles I's trial, when he was condemned to death as a traitor to the people of England, and of the legislation abolishing monarchy in 1649, made great play with the superiority of "the people" to the King. But even if the Long Parliament did represent the people, it was notorious that before the King could be brought to trial a majority of M. Ps. had to be purged by Colonel Pride. The Rump that was left of the Parliament, sitting on the bayonets of the New Model Army, hardly looked like the people of England — less so even than the Army itself, many contemporaries thought.

But then who were the people? The question remained. It had been asked a century earlier. When one of Henry VIII's propagandists, William Marshall, translated Marsiglio of Padua's *Defensor Pacis* in 1535, he had to interrupt irritably from time to time with marginal notes explaining to his readers that, despite appearances, when Marsiglio spoke of the people he did not mean the whole people. "In all this long tale he speaketh not of the rascal multitude but of the Parliament"; "wheresoever he speaketh of such multitude he meaneth when it is assembled in the Parliament".[2] In Elizabeth's reign Sir Thomas Smith declared that the "commonwealth consisteth only of freemen". "Day labourers, poor husbandmen" and others who have no free land "have no voice nor authority in our commonwealth, and no account is made of them but only to be ruled".[3] The point was insisted on by a frightened baronet in 1641: - "the primates, the nobiles, with the minores nobiles, the gentry, consult and dispose the rules of government; the plebeians submit to and obey them".[4] By 1641 the plebeians were not submitting and obeying entirely as was expected of them. But after 1660 the Duke of Albermarle was able with more confidence to reassert that "the poorer and meaner people have no interest in the commonwealth but the use of breath".[5] The men of property in the seventeenth century inherited a horror of the Many-Headed Monster, an ignorant, irrational populace.[6]

So upper-class writers tended to exclude the poor from the "free people", though in no very precise or self-conscious way. They just did not think of the lowest classes (any more than they thought of women) when speaking of "the people" whom Parliament represented. The anonymous *The Lawes of England*, probably written by a Puritan in the sixteen-twenties or -thirties, gave as one of the rights of "the people" - "those *jura familiae*, consisting in wives, children, servants, goods and lands", over which all fathers of families are "lords and kings in their own houses".[7] The best known example is Captain Adam Baynes, Yorkshire M.P., speaking in the Parliament of 1659. Discussing the causes of the civil war, he said "the people were too hard for the King in property; and then in arms too hard for him.... Property generally is now with the people.... All government is built upon property, else the poor must rule it". The poor appear not to be people, because they have no property.[8]

The question had come up earlier, in October-November 1647, in the General Council of the Army, meeting at Putney. The Army had just won the war against the

King, and this General Council, consisting of the generals, some officers, representatives of the rank and file and some London Levellers, were discussing what should be the future constitution of England — a unique occasion. Colonel Rainborough and the Levellers called -- or appeared to call -- for manhood suffrage, on the ground that every man had a natural right to the vote. The Levellers and their supporters at Putney were very confused when Commissary-General Ireton suggested that the same arguments could be used to defend a natural right of all men to property — i.e. to justify communism. Most of the Levellers were in favour of private property, and perhaps had not fully thought out the implications of resonant phrases like Lilburne's "the poorest that lives hath as true a right to give a vote... as the richest and greatest".[9] Rainborough uttered the famous words: - "the poorest he that is in England hath a life to live as the greatest he; and therefore... I do think that the poorest man in England" ("every man born in England") "is not at all bound in a strict sense to that government that he hath not had a voice to put himself under". Ireton, echoing Sir Thomas Smith, retorted that "a man's being born here" gives him no right to a vote: the franchise is attached to property. By the people, Ireton maintained, is meant those "that are possessed of the permanent interest in the land". Colonel Rich added that if master and servant should be equal electors, then "the majority may by a law ... destroy property". If any property qualification at all was retained, he said, five-sixths of the people would be excluded from the franchise. What guarantee have you, Rich and Ireton asked, that if you give the vote to the poor they will not vote for communism and share out the property of the rich?[10]

The Levellers had no thought-out answer. They were probably divided among themselves. Some of them distinguished between the free people and the poor. "All inhabitants that have not lost their birthright", said Maximilian Petty, "should have an equal voice in elections". He suggested that the poor had lost their birthright freedom by becoming -- at least temporarily -- dependent on others. This also applied to apprentices and living-in servants. A few days later the General Council of the Army voted to extend the franchise to all except servants and beggars.[11]

But Petty's was rather a sophisticated distinction. Most Parliamentarian political theorists continued to speak of "the people", making it clear only when pressed that they did not include the poor. Thus Marchamont Nedham, propagandist for the republican government in the fifties, declared "when we mention people, we do not mean the confused promiscuous body of the people"; "by the people we mean such as shall be duly chosen to represent the people successively in their supreme assemblies".[12] He might almost have been reading Marshall's marginal notes to his translation of Marsiglio, and it is the nearest he gets to a definition. Robert Norwood in 1653 asserted that Parliaments are "the people meeting together", who "choose from all the parts of the land men from amongst themselves". Answering the question, who are to judge the justice of Parliament's laws, he replied "Why all Englishmen, the whole people of England, in and by their several courts and officers,...hundred courts, county courts, courts of inquest, sheriffs, juries and the like".[13] Here "the whole people" means at most all householders.

Thomas Hobbes came near to a break-through when he argued that the state was founded on the consent of the people, and that all men were in this respect equal. But Hobbes had included competitive individualism within his basic psychology of man, and the object of his analysis was far from being the establishment of a democracy. Rather he argued that the form of government is irrelevant so long as subjects are protected from the anarchy to which their inherent competitiveness would otherwise inevitably lead. So the effect was to defend the *status quo* -- any old *status quo* -- against change of any sort: though once change had taken place it must be accepted.

James Harrington (Baynes was a Harringtonian) elaborated a republican political theory in which he always speaks of government as based on the people, but in his ideal commonwealth servants were not citizens. The distinction between freemen and servants seemed to him "as it were natural", not deriving from the constitution but existing before the state was set up.[14] Servants neither had the vote nor were allowed to bear arms. In England, he argued, economic power in the century before 1640 had passed to "the people" who had upset the traditional balance by purchasing land from crown, church and aristocracy. The revolution of the sixteen-forties had simply been a matter of adjusting the political superstructure so as to restore the balance. By people Harrington clearly meant men of some property. "The peasantry, partaking not of the balance, can (in relation to government) be of no account", and therefore "is not called the commons but only the third estate; whereas the yeomanry in England" are the commons, the true people.[15] So there are distinctions to be drawn between people and people. In one of Harrington's dialogues Publicola asks: "The Parliament declares all power to be in the people; is that in the better sort only?" Valerius (who appears to represent Harrington) replies: "The Parliament consisted wholly of the better sort.... It was, you will say, no democracy.... Yet this derived from the free election of the people". Publicola was still dissatisfied. "How free? Seeing the people then under lords dared not to elect otherwise than as pleased those lords". "Something of that is true", Valerius admitted; "but I am persuaded that the people, not under lords, will yet be most addicted to the better sort". "That is certain", Publicola agreed.[16]

In October 1659 Henry Stubbe, who had read his Harrington, distinguished between on the one hand "the nation" (all men except servants, who ideally should have the right to vote in a free commonwealth) and on the other "the people" (in effect the supporters of the Good Old Cause). Stubbe recognized that his was not the normal use of "people": "to be a part of the people it is not necessary that one actually have land". Landless soldiers should enjoy the rights of citizens. "The people" would control the Senate; Parliament would be "chosen by the whole nation, and not the people only".[17]

For Algernon Sidney too (later the hero of the Whigs) not all the people were full citizens. "No man whilst he is a servant can be a member of a commonwealth; for he that is not in his own power cannot have a part in the government of others".[18] Locke echoed Harrington. His state originated in a social contract between the people. But "the people" who founded Locke's state had servants in the state of nature before the state existed: "the turfs my servant has cut" belong to me. James Tyrell, friend and follower of Locke, did "by no means allow the rabble or mob of any nation to take arms against a civil government, but only the whole community of the people of all degrees and orders, commanded by the nobility and gentry thereof". Servants without property in goods or land had no more reason than children "to have voices in the institution of the government". (And no more reason than women: this attitude helps to explain why even the Levellers never advocated votes for women). Eighteenth-century Whigs tended to think "the people" meant "the gentry".[19]

Seventeenth-century practice was clearer than seventeenth-century theory, but equally unfavourable to the poor. In 1640 it was "the sense of the House" (of Commons) that "no beggar or man that received relief or is not subject to scot and lot is capable of giving his voice in election of burgesses".[20] This was normal practice in elections in Parliamentary boroughs. Similarly in parish elections those who did not pay poor and church rates had no vote.[21] This seemed to seventeenth-century men of property only just: those who were elected spent the money of tax- and rate-payers; therefore they should be elected by and responsible to them. In the countryside, moreover, Richard Baxter pointed out, "in most parishes the major vote of the vulgar... is ruled by money and therefore by their landlords". Those whose poverty is "so great as to make them servants of others and deprive them of ingenious freedom" should lose their right to vote.[22] Sir Simonds D'Ewes who in 1640 rather surprisingly argued that the poor ought to have the vote qualified this a year later so as to exclude vagrants. Even so he was more liberal than most of his contemporaries.[23] The Presbyterian minister Thomas Edwards for instance regarded it as a *reductio ad absurdum* of any idea of universal suffrage that it would give the vote to paupers and women.[24] "Had women and children and servants and madmen and fools", asked Archbishop Ussher, "freedom of suffrage as well as men of age and fortune and understanding?"[25] The Earl of Shaftesbury, in about 1680, declared that "every paterfamilias... has... the votes of all his family, man, woman, and child, included in his". Locke took it for granted that the poor, servants and women were all disenfranchised.[26] For similar reasons "the meaner sort of people and servants" were normally excluded from service in the militia.[27] They were however the main source of conscripts for military service overseas.

## II

There is a theological background to such attitudes which is perhaps worth dwelling on for a moment. When in the reign of Elizabeth Presbyterian Puritans argued that lay elders should be elected by parish congregations to share with the minister in administering the discipline of the state church, there were loud outcries that this would mean that "the dregs of the people" would select those who would supervise the moral behaviour of their social betters. Archbishop Parker deplored any system which allowed "the people to be orderers of things".[28] Defenders of Presbyterianism were at great pains to explain that they did not intend that sort of democracy. William Stoughton, for instance, in 1604 spoke of the "birthright" of the people whilst specifically excluding "the multitude" from the right to elect elders. "The multitude" were the poor as distinct from "the people". "Men of occupations",

Stoughton insisted, would be elected elders. There should be no fear of the word democracy, provided the thing which the word represented was not dangerous.[29] Only Anabaptists advocated equality of servants and masters, William Gouge asserted.[30] "The Anabaptists are men that will not be shuffled out of the birthright of the free-born people of England", one of them later asserted.[31]

Richard Hooker in 1593 drew attention to the ambiguity in Presbyterian arguments: "When they hold that ministers should be made with the consent of many, they understand by *many* the multiple or common people; but in requiring that many should evermore join with the bishop in the administration of church censures, they mean by *many* a few lay elders, chosen out of the rest of the people to that purpose".[32] Half a century later the Levellers were equally "going round in a circle by failing to define what they meant by 'the people'".[33]

Later Puritans were more cautious than Stoughton. When the Pilgrim Fathers sailed to America, "some of the strangers amongst them" let fall "discontented and mutinous speeches" suggesting that "none had power to command them" and that "when they came ashore, they would use their own liberty". "The people therefore", as Thomas Prince put it a century later, "before they landed, wisely formed themselves into a body politic... by solemn contract" — which effectively excluded servants as well as the "strangers".[34] In New England exclusion from church membership meant exclusion from the franchise. This made explicit what was implicit in England, where the parish had become both an ecclesiastical and a political unit. The same persons had the vote in each. "Rogues, beggars, vagabonds", William Perkins and other Puritans argued, "commonly are of no civil society or corporation"; "they join not themselves to any settled congregation for the obtaining of God's kingdom". They were outside church and commonwealth unless and until they could be restored by labour discipline and hard work.[35]

There is a curious analogy between the theory we have been considering, that some of the people are full citizens whilst servants and the poor are not, and the dual meaning which Calvinists gave to the word church. In one sense the church is the whole community; in another sense it is the godly within that community. In an ideal world both church and state would be run by the godly minority. This was rarely achieved in practice because of the difficulty of identifying the elect on earth: there were backsliders and hypocrites. But the theoretical distinction remained clear. It derived from theology. The elect were predestined to salvation from all eternity. Therefore in one sense Christ died for all men, in another he died for the elect only. Persons brought up in this theological tradition, who thought of the church as both the whole community and as the elect minority within that community, easily slid from thinking of the people as all inhabitants to "the people" as the respectable minority. Milton thought of "the people" as heads of households. "By people we mean all citizens of every degree", but apparently more especially "the middle class, which produces the greatest number of men of good sense and knowledge of affairs".[36] He was virtually echoing the arguments of the Dutch rebels sixty-five years earlier. The States not only represented but were selected ("made") by the people. But excluded from the people were "what we call the rabble... as against the good, the decent citizens".[37]

The two concepts were linked in Stoughton's assumption that elected elders would be "men of occupations". In the Parliamentary ordinance of 1646 which set up a Presbyterian state church in England, elders were to be elected by members of congregations who were not "servants that have no families".[38] Nor indeed was the slide from people to elect peculiar to Presbyterians. Bishop Lancelot Andrewes likewise had distinguished between "the common sort" and "true Christians".[39]

## III

Religious thinking thus contributed by analogy to explain why men forgot "the poor" when speaking about "the people". But there were also social developments which help to explain why it was so easy. In the first place we must recall the patriarchal nature of seventeenth-century society. A very large part of the population -- probably the majority -- lived in households which were units of production, whether industrial workshops or family farms. The head of the household was manager of the firm, supervising not only his wife and children but also his apprentices and living-in servants. He was held responsible for their moral and religious welfare, and for their education and vocational training, no less than for that of his own children. The exclusion of women, children, servants and prentices from the vote was justified on the assumption that they were "virtually represented" by the head of their household.[40] When an apprentice or living-in servant married and set up his own household, then he too became "free" and possibly eligible for the vote. In 1647 it was argued that "very many in the Army" were "servants and prentices not yet free", and so by definition were *incapable* of representing any-body.[41] Paupers and vagrants did not count at all.

Secondly of course, all political ideas were formulated by intellectuals, by men of some education. This was true even of interregnum radicals like the Levellers, Diggers and Ranters. Of the three leading Levellers, Richard Overton had had a university education, William Walwyn -- grandson of a bishop -- was a very sophisticated reader of Montaigne; Lilburne -- a gentleman's son -- had had some legal training; Winstanley the Digger was educated at a grammar school and quoted Latin. In the century before 1640 the lines of educational division in society had hardened. It is the century of what Professor Stone has called the "educational revolution". There are far more schools in England, thanks largely to generous endowments by merchants and gentlemen. As English society was increasingly commercialized, far more people were needed who could read, write and keep accounts.

But the century of the educational revolution was also the century of the great economic divide. Some merchants, yeomen and artisans were prospering — the skillful, the lucky, those who lived near an expanding urban market (London especially), those in the countryside who had long leases at fixed rents to protect them against rising prices. These were a minority; but they were an up-and-coming self-confident minority, from whom much of the support for the radical revolutionaries was soon to be drawn. The mass of the population had to face an inflation in which the price of food rose faster than that of other commodities, and the price of the food of the poor rose more sharply than that of the food of the rich. One consequence was that landlords were encouraged to meet rising prices by racking rents, enclosing and over-stocking commons, and by a myriad other devices which saved them at the expense of the poor. Enclosure by agreement between the richer occupants of a village fortified their power over the community.

The net result was that a class of permanent poor established itself, at a time when economic opportunities were opening up for the fortunate few. Mass poverty was of course nothing new: what was new was the possibility that some members of social groups below the gentry might break through the barrier between indigence and prosperity. Education was vital to crossing this barrier. The poor could not spare the labour of their children, could not afford to maintain them at school once they had reached the age at which they were able to contribute to the income of the household — seven or eight years.[42] Only a tiny minority of the children of the poor were lucky enough to find a patron who would pay for them to receive a grammar school education; still fewer went on to a university. The universally observed phenomenon, that children of the gentry were usurping free places in schools that were originally designed for poor children, is not so much evidence of the greed and self-interest of the gentry as of the economic helplessness of the poor. So the lines of social division hardened: the vast mass of the children of the poor were excluded from access to the educational ladder up which some of the children of their more fortunate betters were climbing rapidly. It was almost impossible for a pauper to escape from the inheritance to which he was born.

The Elizabethan poor law had been codified after the famine years of the 1590s. Accepting the existence of a permanent class of paupers, it recognized and legitimized payment of relief to the deserving poor, as distinct from idlers, rogues and vagabonds; and it put the administration of the poor law, under the J. Ps., into the hands of village constables and churchwardens.[43] These were normally drawn from the middling sort, below the gentry, from the upper ten per cent of the villagers who were relatively prosperous. As a class of permanent poor differentiated itself from the parish élites in the desperately hard days of the 1590s, 1620s and 1640s -- economic crisis and wartime taxation -- so the problem of maintaining law and order became one which increasingly pre-occupied parish élites as well as the gentry.[44] The poor were rightless, helpless, illiterate: their only resource in near starvation was blind revolt. Not only did they exist only to be ruled: maintaining them in subjection and making them work was a major object of government and the possessing classes, joined now by the middling sort.

An Act of 1610 declared that any able-bodied man or woman who should *threaten* to run away from his or her parish was liable to be sent to the house of correction and treated as a vagabond.[45] The poor could be conscripted to labour as they were conscripted into the armed forces when necessary; but "the meaner sort of people and servants" were normally excluded from the militia, the army of property, because "the government feared to arm and train the lower orders".[46] This increasingly sharp division between "the poor" and the rest of the population helps to account for the trend in English Puritanism, from William Perkins in the 1590s onwards, which stressed the wickedness, the apparently irredeemable wickedness, of the poor. Calvinist doctrines of the predestination of the majority of mankind to eternal damnation reflected the social realities of English life in the early and mid-seventeenth century.[47]

Oliver Cromwell in a speech to his Parliament of 1654 said that the Levellers wanted to reduce "all to an equality", an aim he thought likely to appeal to "all poor men and...all bad men". Harrington similarly spoke of "robbers or Levellers".[48] (Most of the Leveller leaders in fact were defenders of private property. Cromwell and Harrington were probably thinking of Winstanley and the True Levellers, whom I shall be discussing shortly.)

The wickedness of the poor also helps to explain Puritan and Parliamentary emphasis on labour discipline, on the sinfulness of idleness. The "debauched" and "profane" lower classes notoriously preferred idleness to work, observed every saint's day as a holiday in a regrettably papist way: the poor law distinguished sharply between the deserving poor and idle rogues. Men assumed that the poor would work only to avoid starvation.[49] A statute of 1550 had protected small cottagers building on wastes and commons. They formed a convenient pool of the cheapest labour for new rural industries. Commons and wastes gave them something to live on when there was no employment. "There are fewest poor where there are fewest commons", observed Samued Hartlib. But improvement of England's agricultural production, and the profits of farmers, depended on bringing waste land under cultivation. The well-to-do came to dislike these "housed beggars", as Bacon called cottagers.[50] Enclosure, said Adam Moore in 1653, "will give the poor an interest in toiling whom terror never yet could inure to travail". Workhouses were deliberately made unpleasant in order to discourage applicants for relief.[51]

The ability to squat on uncultivated land was the last refuge of the vagrant poor. In the course of the seventeenth century forests were brought under cultivation, and other steps were taken to curb lower-class mobility. The 1662 Act of Settlement was accompanied by a drive against cottages. This was possible because the population explosion had ended: indeed, soon it was necessary to allow limited mobility for economic reasons.[52] At the beginning, fear of over-population; at the end, fear of shortage of hands: from import to export of corn. Sir Dalby Thomas expressed the new view when he said in 1690 that people are the wealth of the nation. But he hastened to add that by "people" he meant the laborious and industrious people, not the unemployed such as serving-men and beggars — and, he naughtily added, "gentry, clergy, lawyers".[53] Swift similarly distinguished between poor artisans, meaner tradesmen and labouring men on the one hand, and the idle rabble on the other.[54]

Looked at from the other side, we must recall the hatred which many of the poor felt for a life of permanent wage-labour as unfreedom. Permanent wage-labour and the poor law arose together.[55] Bernard Mandeville in the early eighteenth century expressed the distinction between the poor and the rest of society by saying "We have hardly poor enough to do what is necessary to make us subsist". (Note the distinction between "them", the poor, and "us", for whom they work.) "Men who are to remain and end their days in a laborious, tiresome and painful station of life, the sooner they are put upon it at first, the more patiently they'll submit to it *for ever after*" (my italics).[56]

If we look at seventeenth-century developments in this perspective, several points relevant to our theme emerge. John Morill recently argued persuasively that the seventeenth century had no word to cover those yeomen, artisans and merchants who were prospering at the time of the great economic divide; and he argued, less convincingly, that therefore historians should not try to distinguish them as a special social group linked by their economic position.[57] But I think we can see by now that the seventeenth century did have a word for them, though the usage of the word is so different from our own that we have failed to notice it. The word is "people" — those between the gentry above them and the permanent poor below them from whom they are in process of distinguishing themselves.

Secondly, the work of Derek Hirst has shown how in the early seventeenth century the Parliamentary electorate -- the middling and lower sort above the very poor in the towns, yeomen and freeholders in the counties -- was taking a quite novel and increasingly active interest in national politics, in Parliamentary elections.[58] In the severe economic depression of the twenty years before 1640 -- which Professor Bowden sees as perhaps the worst in all English history for the poor[59] -- there was continuing fear of popular revolt. In the early sixteen-forties leaders of the Long Parliament used appeals to the people and the threat of mob violence to pressure the King, though ultimately they got more than they bargained for.

Thirdly, the most radical amongst the Parliamentarian revolutionaries were drawn mainly from the middling sort in town and country, from those self-confident prospering men who were excluded from social and political privileges but who were distinguished by education and knowledge of affairs from the permanent poor. Such men were prepared to break with tradition and convention. There were many of them in the New Model Army: Oliver Cromwell deliberately recruited his Ironsides from "freeholders and freeholders' sons", "plain russet-coated captains". Such men from the middling sort were ready to emphasize the rights of the people as against the privileges of peers, gentry and big merchants: they wanted the franchise to be extended to them, and had no inhibitions about using lower-class support. But -- except in moments of emotion -- they did not really want the poor to be enfranchised. The well-to-do in urban and rural parishes wanted their growing say in affairs to be officially confirmed; but in the last resort such men of small property had more in common with the gentry than with the unpropertied. That is why the Levellers collapsed once they had failed to capture the Army.

Fourthly, the role of Archbishop Laud and his followers perhaps looks rather different in this perspective. Laud was criticized by Puritans because his theological and ceremonial innovations were thought to be leading England back to popery. But the Laudians, who dominated in church and state in the 1630s, were objected to on social no less than on theological grounds. Under Laud church courts positively encouraged idleness by punishing men for working on saints' days. The Book of Sports issued in 1633 encouraged men and women to engage in the traditional village pastimes on Sundays. Puritans thought they ought to have been improving their minds, or at least resting after their six-days' labour; parish élites agreed with Puritans that the pagan fertility rites which underlay the traditional sports were disruptive of the labour discipline they were struggling to impose. Laud opposed enclosure, because eviction from small holdings meant loss of taxpayers, of trained men for the militia and of tithe-payers for the church, as well as creating the danger of riots and unrest. In the 1630s the Privy Council interfered with local control of poor relief and of wage regulation. The Laudians were not so much *for* the poor as *against* parish élites, against the growing control of local affairs by the middling sort in alliance with town oligarchies and the gentry. We take so much for granted that there was to be a steady growth in power of local oligarchies in the course of the seventeenth century that we forget the Laudian attempt to reverse the process. So we miss the vital *social* significance of their overthrow in 1640, and of the abolition of the church courts which enforced Laudianism. When church courts were restored in 1660 they did not resume the attempt to control social and economic life.

*IV*

All this may perhaps help us to understand the restoration of monarchy in 1660. After the civil war things looked like getting out of hand — Agitators in the Army were demanding manhood suffrage, mechanic preachers were collecting congregations of the lower classes and preaching sedition with no control at all. Regicide and the abolition of the House of Lords seemed to call all social subordination in question. Levellers, Diggers, Ranters, early Quakers were organizing the lower classes. The more moderate revolutionaries felt genuine outrage and fear. They had been let down by those whom they had liberated. An Independent in 1650 said that the rule of the Great Turk would be better than that of the rabble rout.[60] Such social anxieties were to lead the men of property to restore Charles II — not quite the Great Turk, but certainly better than the rabble rout.

For a time in 1647-9 it had been claimed that the New Model Army *was* the people and indeed it was arguably a fairer cross-section than the electorate, since it included conscripts from the poor. "The people in gross", declared William Sedgwick in 1649, are "but a monster, a rude unwieldy bulk of no use; but here they are gathered together into one excellent life.... For an army has in it all government and parts of government, order, justice, &c, in highest virtue". So in the Army the defects of the poor, their ignorance and helplessness, were overcome; "they are truly the people, not in a gross heap, or a dull, heavy body, but in a selected, choice way".[61] They were controlled by "the people".

That may have been plausible in 1647-9, when the New Model Army, claiming to be "no mere mercenary army", took over power. But in the fifties the Army was repeatedly purged of radicals, was professionalized and used increasingly to repress the people it claimed to represent. So though a pamphleteer of 1653 still argued that the Army was "the people's power, chosen by the people, entrusted with the people's welfare and defence", he had to admit that "by people is meant the sound, well-affected part, the rest are the conquered or subdued part, who can challenge no right in that free election which is the fruit of conquest".[62] The Army became increasingly unpopular as the fifties wore on, and left a lasting heritage of dislike for standing armies, which was shared by radicals no less than conservatives. It was merely pathetic when in 1659 a pamphleteer claimed that "the Army is the principal body of the people", representing "the ordinary and common bulk of the people" better than Parliament. Power should rest with "the good people embodied in an army together with those that adhered to them".[63]

I am suggesting that the distinction between "the poor" and "the people" was deeply embedded in the social reality of seventeenth-century England. The dilemma of the radicals in the English Revolution -- and the dilemma reappeared in later revolutions -- was that the poor had for centuries been kept away from politics and education. In 1642 Milton denounced the bishops who first "with a most inhuman cruelty... put out the people's eyes" and then "reproach them of their blindness". Milton was happy with the way in which "that iron flail, the people" rather roughly overthrew the bishops' government in 1640-1. But such actions offered no long-term solution to England's problems; Milton rapidly lost confidence in the people once he had seen them in action. ("Licence they mean when they cry liberty"). In the sixteen-fifties he among others realized that the likely consequence of introducing the wide franchise the Levellers advocated would not be a democratic republic but a return of the royalists to power: he contrasted "the people" with "the mob". The governors of the Commonwealth "are themselves now the people".[64] "Everywhere the greater party are for the King", wrote an Independent in October 1648. "If the common voice of the giddy multitude rule,... how quickly would their own interest, peace and safety be dashed and broken?"[65] In the sixteen-forties Richard Overton had listed "Rude Multitude" among the supporters of Mr. Persecution.[66] The Presbyterians had shown that they could use City "mobs" for conservative purposes, no less than did the Independents for their purposes. In 1688 Roger Morrice had ominously noted that "there was another power (though it was unwarrantable) that the mobile had" beside that of the "natural rulers" of the country.[67] But by the end of the century "the mob" was notoriously fickle: Tories could stir up church and king mobs to rabble dissenters.

So what could the answer have been? Cromwell advocated "what's for their good, not what pleases them". Thomas Scot spoke of "our new people, scarce yet proseletized". "We... would have enfranchised the people", declared the regicide John Cook, "if the nation had not been more delighted in servitude". Hugh Peter spoke of using the Army to teach peasants to understand liberty.[68] It is Rousseau's paradox of forcing men to be free, the dilemma which the Soviet Communist Party tried to resolve by the dictatorship of the proletariat. But the CP became divorced from the people just as Cromwell's army did: what Trotsky called "substitutism", the rule of a minority in the name of a people whom in theory they represent, inevitably degenerates into something less admirable. The problem did not cease with the seventeenth century's failure to solve it: Shelley in 1817 admitted that "the consequences of the immediate extension of the elective franchise to every male adult would be to place power in the hands of men who have been rendered brutal and torpid and ferocious by ages of slavery".[69]

Laurence Clarkson the Ranter in October 1647 was one of the very few who tried to stir up the poor to act upon a class analysis of politics. It is, he declared, "naturally inbred in the major part of the nobility and gentry to oppress the persons of such that are not as rich and honourable as themselves". They "judge the poor but fools and themselves wise, and therefore when you the commonalty calleth a Parliament they are confident such must be chosen that are the noblest and richest .... Your slavery is their liberty, your poverty is their prosperity.... Who are the oppressors but the nobility and gentry? And who are the oppressed, is it not the yeoman, the farmer, the tradesmen and the labourer? .... Have you not chosen oppressors to redeem you from oppression?"[70] Starting from similar assumptions to those of Harrington (see p. 78 above), Clarkson advocated startlingly different conclusions.

Many reformers spoke with alarm, especially in the starvation years 1648-9, of the dangerous consequences that might result if something was not done to relieve the lot of the poor, hard hit by bad harvests on top of heavy war-time taxation, free quarter and plunder. In January 1648, "the poor" were seizing corn going to market and dividing it "among themselves, before the owners' faces, telling them they could not starve".[71] On 3 April 1649, Peter Chamberlen declared his fear lest the many who were starving for want of bread would proceed to direct action unless something was done for them. He advocated the nationalization of lands confiscated from church, crown and royalists for the poor to cultivate, together with commons and fens.[72] But only one thinker, I believe, followed Clarkson in looking at the problem from the point of view of the poor, and advanced beyond him in proposing specific, thought-out measures which would not have been merely palliatives but which aimed at the total abolition of poverty — a possibility which Bacon had conceived, but which no one had done anything to realize. This was Gerrard Winstanley, leader of the True Levellers or Diggers.

## V

The Diggers started digging up the common land near Cobham, Surrey, in April 1649. In defending their action, Winstanley quite deliberately spoke on behalf of "all the poor oppressed people of England" and indeed of "the whole world". "England is a prison", he said, "and poor men are the prisoners". "All laws", he declared in 1652, after the suppression of the colony, "were made in the days of the kings to ease the rich landlord". "The poor labourers were left under bondage still". These laws enslaving the poor to the rich were backed up by the clergy, who promised the poor recompense in heaven, in the after life. Winstanley and the Diggers wanted a more tangible heaven, on earth, now. Victory over the King in the civil war had been won by the people, including the poor, who indeed had done most of the fighting as well as bearing the heaviest burden of taxation and free quarter: it was only right that they should now benefit by victory over kingly power.[73]

Winstanley believed that "that Scripture which saith, the poor shall inherit the earth" was "really and materially to be fulfilled"; but he noted the reluctance of the gentry to share the fruits of victory with the common people. "The gentry's hardness of heart against the poor" might lead to disaster in case of foreign invasion. For "the poor see, if they fight and should conquer the enemy, yet... they... are like to be slaves still". They say "We can as well live under a foreign enemy working for day wages as under our own brethren". It was therefore on all grounds essential to recognize that "the common people" (among whom Winstanley specifically included "poor labourers") are "part of the nation".[74] It was a direct challenge to traditionalists who held that the poor "existed only to be ruled".

"This is the bondage the poor complain of, that they are kept poor by their brethren in a land where there is so much plenty for everyone". A rational economic organization, based on collective ownership, would end the oppression and exploitation of the poor; this was the only way in which real equality could be established. Winstanley's solution was similar to Chamberlen's, but instead of urging the rich to make charitable concessions he called on the poor themselves to occupy and cultivate waste and common lands, which by right belonged to them and were withheld only by "murdering governing laws". For "the poorest man hath as true a title and just right to the land as the richest man". So he extended "natural rights" arguments from the franchise to property, just as Ireton had predicted in the Putney Debates. The Diggers thought it their duty to demonstrate that "everyone" should as his just inheritance "have the benefit and freedom of their creation, without respect of persons". "Will you be slaves and beggars still when you may be freemen?" they asked.[75]

"The declaration of righteous law shall spring up from the poor", Winstanley believed. "Magistracy signifies the greatest bond...that ties people together in love", preserves all and despises none. And he asked: "Is the magistracy of the nations like this?" The answer could only be No: it favours the rich, despises and slights the poor. "In many parishes", Winstanley noted, "two or three of the great ones bear all the sway in making assessments, over-awing constables and other officers" — the parish élites to whom we have referred. Yet true magistracy is to be sought "among the poor despised ones of the earth, for there Christ dwells". Winstanley hoped that the Revolution in England would mark the beginning of a better state of affairs, in which true freedom would be made possible by the abolition of private property and wage labour and the establishment of an egalitarian communist society.[76] In the ideal commonwealth which he sketched in outline manhood suffrage would be established, though supporters of Charles I during the war and speculators in confiscated lands would be disfranchised. Apprentices were also disfranchised during their prenticeship (for the traditional reasons), as were those who should be deprived of their "freedom in the commonwealth" for particularly heinous offences such as buying and selling or preaching for money. All magistrates were to be elected annually, (including judges, peace makers and ministers) by "the whole body of the parish"; they and M. Ps. were to be responsible to "their masters, the people who chose them". The sanction which Winstanley invoked was the might of the whole armed people, who would defend the liberty of the commonwealth against a foreign enemy, "degenerated officers" or against any others who "through treachery do endeavour to destroy the laws of common freedom". There was to be no standing army.[77]

Winstanley, then, took seriously the equality of servants and masters proclaimed earlier by Anabaptists, (p. 80 above). He envisaged a reorganization of society which would enable the poor to assert themselves as part of the nation. He was the only man, to my knowledge, who really tried to grapple with the problem of fitting the whole people to run a democracy. He recognized that this would call for a long period of education and political re-education to liberate people from dependence on the gentry and clergy from whom they had always taken their political ideas. He proposed laws and institutions which would incorporate the true interests of the people, but the people itself would always retain control over the representative government which administered the laws, backed by the ultimate authority of the armed people. And by people Winstanley really did mean all the people. We may think his proposals inadequate (though they are worked out in far more detail than I have been able to indicate). He himself finally despaired of their being accepted. But at least they acknowledge and try to face some of the problems in setting up a communist society — in this well ahead of his time.

As the failure of Levellers and Diggers demonstrates, the poor in the seventeenth century were not only ill-educated but also divided by their economic situation. The Levellers appealed to men of small property, and Lilburne attacked the Diggers' communist experiment, though some of his followers were more sympathetic.The Levellers drew their initial support mainly from London and the Army. In 1649 they initiated a propaganda campaign in towns outside London, and began to turn to the countryside, laying a new stress on opposition to enclosure and defence of the property rights of small occupiers. They were immediately suppressed. The Diggers came at the socially dangerous point where rural and urban poor joined hands. They too were suppressed, perhaps co-incidentally, after they had sent emissaries from Surrey to ten or more groups of sympathizers scattered through the Midlands. What later alarmed the respectable classes most about the very unrespectable and unpacifist early Quakers was that they repeated many Leveller and Digger ideas and that they had a national organization. Such anxieties played a big part in creating the social panic which led to the restoration of Charles II. The question now, Richard Baxter told the House of Commons in April 1660, is not whether bishops or no but whether discipline or none.[78] He was an old enemy of bishops, but now theological considerations had to yield place to social fright.

## VI

We started then with a problem in political theory: how was it that serious political thinkers in the seventeenth century could not see that the poor were people? I suggested a possible analogy in Puritan theology: Christ died for all men, but especially for the elect. But we have been led ultimately into social history: differentiation between people and poor can be understood (which does not mean justified) only if we grasp something of the depressed and ignorant state of the poor in English pre-industrial society, just as we can only understand the similar blind spot in relation to women if we recognize how totally patriarchal that society was.

The point I want to end by stressing is not the inability of the men of the seventeenth century to include the poor within the people: that might lead us to conclude smugly that we are much cleverer and nicer than they were. What I want to emphasize is that the thinking of some of them got far enough for the question of whether the poor were people to arise at all. It was raised nowhere else in Europe in the seventeenth century, and not again in England till the nineteenth century, after the Industrial Revolution had transformed "the poor" into the working class. It was not solved in practice, formally at least, until the present century. The seventeenth-century radicals made a fantastic intellectual leap in the revolutionary circumstances of the sixteen-forties, culminating in Winstanley's proposals for a reorganisation of society which would enable the poor to assert themselves as "part of the nation". The intellectual leap, I suggest, was made possible by the rapid evolution of the household economy as capitalism developed in agriculture and industry. It was the unique preponderance of the household in the English economy and of householders among supporters of Parliament that made the conception of the sovereignty of the people theoretically possible; it was the stratification which took place among the householders that made it impossible for the poor to be accepted as people.

# NOTES

1. [Anon.], *The Soveraignty of Kings: Or An absolute Answer and Confutation* (of schismatics) (1642), Sig. A 1v.

2. G.R. Elton, "The Political Creed of Thomas Cromwell", *Transactions of the Royal Historical Soc.*, 1956, p. 86. In *The Tudor Constitution* (Cambridge University Press, 1960), Elton appears to share this assumption that Tudor Parliaments represented the people, "everyone" (pp. 230, 300, 303).

3. Ed. L. Alston, *De Republica Anglorum, A Discourse of the Commonwealth of England* (Cambridge University Press, 1960), pp. 20-2.

4. Sir T. Aston, *A Remonstrance against Presbytery* (1641), Sig. I 4v.

5. G. Monck, Duke of Albermarle, *Observations Upon Military and Political Affairs* (1671), p. 146.

6. I have discussed this at greater length in *Change and Continuity in Seventeenth-Century England* (1974), chapter 8.

7. Quoted by M.A. Judson, *The Crisis of the Constitution* (Rutgers University Press, 1949), p. 337.

8. Ed. J.T. Rutt, *Diary of Thomas Burton* (1828), III, pp. 147-8.

9. J. Lilburne, *The Charters of London* (1646), p. 4.

10. Ed. A.S.P. Woodhouse, *Puritanism and Liberty* (1938), pp. 53-6, 63.

11. *Ibid.*, p. 53; D.E. Underdown, "The Parliamentary Diary of John Boys, 1647-8", *Bulletin of the Institute of Historical Research*, XXXIX (1966), pp. 152-3.

12. *Mercurius Politicus*, No. 78, 27 November-4 December, 1651, p. 1237; cf. No. 77, p. 1222, and Marchamont Nedham, *The Excellencie of a Free State* (1656), p. 244, quoted in J. Frank, *Cromwell's Press Agent: A Critical Biography of Marchamont Nedham, 1620-1678* (Lanham, Maryland, 1980), pp. 99-100.

13. Robert Norwood, *An Additional Discourse* (1653), pp. 44-8.

14. Ed. J.G.A. Pocock, *The Political Works of James Harrington* (Cambridge University Press, 1977), pp. 786-8.

15. *Ibid.,* pp. 436-7.

16. *Ibid.,* pp. 786-8; cf. p. 764.

17. H. Stubbe, *A Letter to an Officer of the Army* (1659), pp. 52-4, 59-62, quoted by J.R. Jacob in his *Henry Stubbe, Radical Protestantism and the Early Enlightenment* (Cambridge and New York 1983), chapter 2. I am grateful to Professor Jacob for having allowed me to read and quote from this book in advance of publication.

18. A. Sidney, *Discourses Concerning Government* (1698), p. 79.

19. James Tyrrell, *Patriarcha non Monarcha* (1681), pp. 83-4, quoted by J. Richards, L. Mulligan and J.K. Graham, "'Property' and 'People': Political Usages of Locke and Some Contemporaries", *Journal of the History of Ideas,* XLII (1980), p. 34; cf. p. 42, and H.T. Dickinson, *Liberty and Property* (1977), p. 78. I owe this last reference to Antony Arblaster.

20. M.R. Frear, "The Election at Great Marlow", *Journal of Modern History,* XIV, p. 435; M.F. Keeler, *The Long Parliament, 1640-1641: A Biographical Study of its Members* (Philadelphia, 1954), pp. 33, 35; Derek Hirst, *The Representative of the People? Voters and Voting in England under the Early Stuarts* (Cambridge University Press, 1975), chapter 5.

21. H. Prideaux, *Directions to Churchwardens* (Norwich, 1701), p. 51.

22. R. Baxter, *The Holy Commonwealth* (1659), pp. 243, 218-19.

23. G.P. Gooch and H.J. Laski, *The History of English Democratic Ideas in the Seventeenth Century* (1927), p. 154.

24. T. Edwards, *Gangraena,* Part II (1646), p. 16c.

25. J. Ussher, *The Power communicated by God to the Prince* (3rd. ed., 1710), Sig. D 6v-7. First published, posthumously, in 1661. Ussher died in 1656.

26. Shaftesbury, "Some Observations", in *Somers Tracts* (1809-15), VIII, p. 401; J. Dunn, *The Political Thought of John Locke* (Cambridge University Press, 1969), pp. 122-3, 131.

27. See p. 82 below.

28. Quoted in P. Collinson, *Archbishop Grindal: The Struggle for a Reformed Church* (1979), p. 289; cf. pp. 205, 247-8.

29. W. Stoughton, *An Assertion for true and Christian Church-Policie* (1604), pp. 193-5, 362-72.

30. W. Gouge, *Of Domesticall Duties* (1626), pp. 331-2.

31. [J. Sturgion], *Queries for His Highness to Answer* (1655), quoted by D.B. Heriot, "Anabaptism in England during the 17th century", *Transactions of the Congregational Hist. Soc.,* XIII (1937-9), p. 29.

32. R. Hooker, *Works* (Oxford University Press, 1890), II, p. 405.

33. J. Frank, *The Beginnings of the English Newspaper, 1620-1688* (Harvard University Press, 1961), p. 343, referring to *A Modest Narrative,* No. 7, 12-19 May, 1649.

34. W. Bradford, *History of Plymouth Plantation* (Collections of the Massachusetts Hist. Soc., III, 1856), pp. 89-90; T. Prince, *A Chronological History of New England in the Form of Annals,* Part II, Section I (1736), in *An English Garner* (ed. E. Arber, 1895-7), II, pp. 410-11.

35. See my *Puritanism and Revolution* (1958), pp. 225-7; *Society and Puritanism in pre-Revolutionary England* (1964), pp. 274-5.

36. Ed. D.M. Wolfe, *Complete Prose Works of John Milton* (Yale ed., 1953- ), III, pp. 236-7; cf. IV, pp. 389, 471, and my *Milton and the English Revolution* (1977), p. 186.

37. P. Geyl, "The Interpretation of Vrancken's *Deductio* of 1587 on the Nature of the Power of the State of Holland", in *From Renaissance to the Counter-Reformation: Essays in Honor of Garrett Mattingly* (ed. C.H. Carter, New York, 1965), p. 239.

38. Ed. C.H. Firth and R.S. Rait, *Acts and Ordinances of the Interregnum* (1911), I, p. 749.

39. L. Andrewes, *XVI Sermons* (2nd. ed., 1631), p. 459.

40. See for instance John Eliot, *The Christian Commonwealth* (1659), pp. 5-6.

41. [Anon.], *The Case of the Army Soberly Discussed* (1647), p. 6.

42. Joan Simon, *Education and Society in Tudor England* (Cambridge University Press, 1966), pp. 195, 217, 370.

43. R.H. Tawney, *The American Labour Movement and other Essays* (ed. J.M. Winter, Brighton, 1979), pp. 179-80; cf. my *Puritanism and Revolution*, p. 233; *Change and Continuity in Seventeenth-Century England* (1974), p. 202.

44. See K. Wrightson and D. Levine, *Poverty and Piety in an Essex Village: Terling, 1525-1700* (1979), *passim;* also William Hunt, *The Puritan Moment* (Cambridge, Mass., 1983), which he kindly allowed me to read in advance of publication.

45. My *Reformation to Industrial Revolution* (Penguin ed.), p. 58.

46. L. Boynton, *The Elizabethan Militia, 1558-1638* (1967), pp. 62, 108-11, 220-1.

47. *Society and Puritanism*, pp. 274-5.

48. Harrington, *Works*, p. 292; cf. pp. 129-30, 657-60, 840.

49. See my *Century of Revolution* (revised ed., 1980), pp. 18-21, 131, 177-8.

50. *Reformation to Industrial Revolution*, pp. 56, 98-9.

51. Adam Moore, *Bread for the Poore* (1653), p. 39.

52. P. Styles, *Studies in Seventeenth-Century West Midlands History* (Kineton, 1978), pp. 186-93.

53. Dalby Thomas, "An Historical Account of the Rise and Growth of the West India Colonies" (1690), in *Harleian Miscellany* (1744-5), II, p. 343.

54. J. Swift, *Works* (1814), VIII, pp. 111-12.

55. I argued this in *Change and Continuity*, chapter 10.

56. [Bernard de Mandeville], *The Fable of the Bees* (3rd. ed., 1724), I, pp. 328-30; cf. pp. 210-13.

57. J.S. Morrill, *Seventeenth-Century Britain, 1603-1714* (Folkestone, 1980), pp. 108-9.

58. D. Hirst, *op. cit., passim.*

59. P.J. Bowden, "Agricultural Prices, Farm Profits, and Rents", in *The Agrarian History of England and Wales*, IV, *1500-1640* (ed. J. Thirsk, Cambridge University Press, 1967, p. 621.

60. John Price, *The Cloudie Clergy* (1650), p. 14.

61. W. Sedgwick, *A Second View of the Army Remonstrance* (1649), p. 13; cf. M. Kishlansky, *The Rise of the New Model Army* (Cambridge University Press, 1979).

62. T. Lock, *The Extent of the Sword* (1653-4), p. 2.

63. [Anon.], *The Armies Vindication of This Last Change* (1659), pp. 3-6, quoted by Austin Woolrych in his Introduction to Vol. VII of *The Complete Prose Works of John Milton* (Yale University Press), 1980, VII, pp. 124-5.

64. Milton, *Complete Prose Works*, I, pp. 932-3, IV, p. 635.

65. [Anon.], *Salus Populi Solus Rex* (1648), quoted by H.N. Brailsford, *The Levellers and the English Revolution* (1961), pp. 345-6.

66. R. Overton, *The Araignement of Mr. Persecution*, in *Tracts on Liberty in the Puritan Revolution*, ed. W. Haller (Columbia University Press, 1933), III, p. 213.

67. Quoted by Howard Nenner, "Constitutional Uncertainty and the Declaration of Rights", in *After the Reformation: Essays in Honor of J.R. Hexter,* ed. Barbara C. Malament (Manchester University Press, 1980), p. 294.

68. *Mr. Peters Last Report of the English Warres* (1646), p. 6.

69. P.B. Shelley, *A Proposal for Putting Reform to the Vote* (1817), in *Prose Works* (1912), I, p. 365.

70. L. Clarkson, *A Generall Charge or Impeachment of High Treason in the name of Justice Equity, against the Communality of England* (1647), pp. 10-18.

71. J. Wildman, *Truths triumph* (1648), p. 4.

72. P. Chamberlen, *The Poore Mans Advocate* (1649), *passim.*

73. Gerrard Winstanley, *The Law of Freedom and other Writings* (Penguin ed.), pp. 97, 108-9, 136, 170, 201-2, 373-4.

74. *Ibid.,* pp. 182, 372-4.

75. *Ibid.,* pp. 49, 104-6, 340; ed. G.H. Sabine, *The Works of Gerrard Winstanley* (Cornell University Press, 1941), p. 408.

76. *The Law of Freedom,* pp. 244-5, 281; Sabine, *op. cit.,* p. 205; my *The Religion of Gerrard Winstanley (Past and Present* Supplement, No. 5, 1978), pp. 26-7.

77. *The Law of Freedom,* pp. 314-21, 324, 345, 356-7, 361-2, 383-9.

78. R. Baxter, *A Sermon of Repentance* (1660), p. 43.

V.G. Kiernan

# THE COVENANTERS:
# A PROBLEM OF CREED AND CLASS

Part of the function of both religion and nationalism has been to provide substitutes for class consciousness among the poorer, with a resultant benefit to the richer. In this process of displacement, complex workings of both social psychology and political manipulation have been involved, for whose study Scotland offers special attractions. As a nation it was a peculiar hybrid. On a Celtic people, Gaelic-speaking in much of the Lowlands as well as Highlands until well on in the middle ages, were superimposed urban settlements and a feudal ruling class, originally brought in from Norman England by the first Celtic kings to strengthen their hold. An amalgam of feudal with tribal characterized all the Celtic fringes of the British Isles, and lent them a character of their own in feudal Europe, and Scotland particularly as their only independent monarchy.

As heads of clans, as well as lords, the dominant landowning class had a patriarchal status, which could make the peasant think himself bound in duty to submit to them, and pride himself on being distantly related to them. "This gave a deceptively friendly air to a relationship which was dictatorial and could be tyrannical."[1] Government being weak, taxation minimal, it was the landlord, not the tax-collector as in early modern France, who was the real oppressor, and ought to have been the target of popular discontent. Tenurial conditions in the sixteenth and seventeenth centuries were worsening for the cultivator, usually a tenant at will with no security, or no more than a one-year lease could give him. On top of this, and going on as in France into the eighteenth century, were feudal obligations which meant that the farmer was "at the beck and call of his master continually and always at times when work on his own holding was imperative".[2] English visitors over many years were astonished and repelled by the misery of Scottish life and housing. Most Scots, one of themselves wrote in the 1640s, were "by continual custom, born slaves and bondmen, their ordinary food pease and beans".[3]

With the Reformation some stirrings of protest broke in on this feudal limbo. An early nineteenth-century critic of Calvinism, writing when the alarums of 1789 were still fresh in mind, accused it of spreading everywhere a "restless and revolutionary spirit", and Scottish Calvinists of being "infected with as vile a spirit of insubordination as any of their brethren on the Continent".[4] Opponents at the time did not find it hard to accuse the Kirk of aiming at a theocracy. "The Ministers sought to establish a democracy in this land, and to become *tribuni plebis* themselves," James VI declared.[5] Popular support could be gained by talk of devoting old ecclesiastical revenues to poor relief, all over Christendom one of the purposes for which Church endowments had been intended. A right was claimed by the Kirk of punishing, not merely reproving, offenses against morals, and these included cheating with false measures and "oppression of the poor by exactions".[6]

On the other hand, in this economic sphere the Kirk was restrained by the fact that, the urban middle classes being as yet weak, Reformation was dependent on support by the nobles with axes of their own to grind, and in possession of most of the old Church lands and income. There could be no thought of summoning the poor to rise up against noble exactions, and by offering its own ineffectual protection the Kirk helped to divert them away from self-help. Calvinism might be politically revolutionary, but it was very rarely associated with social revolt by the poor. Whatever dream of social renovation the Kirk, or rather its more idealistic minority, set out with, was soon being rarified into a dual programme of doctrinal purity and moral purgation. After four decades of this treatment it could not help recognizing the state of the country as one of thorough-going alienation of rich and poor, instead of the interweaving of a feudal society in equilibrium: "little care and reverence of inferiours to their superiours; as suchlyke of superiours in discharging their dewtie to the inferiours...."[7]

In the past anything like a jacquerie had been "virtually unknown in Scotland"[8], and Reformation had no such effect as in Germany where its first breath brought the upheaval of the Peasants' War. Enough of old inertia survived to keep Scotland almost the only country in Europe free of peasant revolt, and this in spite of its being a country inured to war and civil broils, full of men with military experience. Opportunities of service abroad as mercenaries drew away many who might have made trouble at home. Others turned their backs on insoluble problems by giving themselves up to drunkenness and whatever other consolations they could afford. Calvinism seems to have polarized the village between the lax immorality the Kirk was perpetually denouncing, and the humourless gravity of the pious, as though Reprobate and Elect were each coming out in their natural colours. Such cleavage was one more obstacle to any united action by the poor, and would make the serious-minded, who should have been their vanguard, all the more inclined to turn away from worldly grievances to higher, spiritual things.

For these men and women there was much nourishment in the doctrine they heard from the pulpit. It could lift hungry scratchers of soil owned by others above the penury of their lot. Calvinism with its strong doctrinal fabric, built on infinities and eternities, could be a shelter from the perplexities of daily life. It had the appeal to a backward country, somewhat as Marxism has had for the Third World, of offering an all-embracing scheme, whose main propositions could be understood by anyone and give him a confident sense of understanding the universe, while its subtleties conferred on those able to grasp them the pride of intellectual achievement. By the puritan élite of the Scottish masses their faith came to be hugged with a dogged tenacity only comprehensible if it is recognized as a replacement for the frustrated social reform which the Reformation had seemed at first to promise. Like all such historical substitutions it came to be invested with an unreasoning emotional intensity.

With it there was growing attachment to the Kirk, a good deal as an institution round which inchoate national sentiment could gather. National consciousness was an ingredient in the Reformation from the outset, as in all other countries. It showed from the later sixteenth century in scholarly interest in Scottish history, while printings of the old tales of Wallace and Bruce met the popular taste, as they still did in the early nineteenth century.[9] This Scottish identity was all the more keenly felt because after 1603 and the union of crowns with England its survival seemed more and more in jeopardy. Scotland's kings became absentees; its parliament or Estates had no such weight or standing as England's; the Kirk might well appear the most authentic national institution, and its annual General Assembly the country's most representative gathering.

The "National Covenant" signed in 1638 by thousands of all classes, as a pledge to protect Kirk and creed against Charles I's interference, was a compendium modelled on an earlier one of 1580. "Covenants" or "bands" were a feature of the Reformation; they had antecedents in the "bands" (bonds) entered into by feudal factions, but now one of the high contracting parties was God. "Full of formal legalism",[10] and ambiguously worded so as to be "all things to all men", the document had a vigorously nationalist flavour, supplying "national conceit with a theological foundation" by playing on the idea, already time-honoured, of Scots being a chosen people, the equivalent in this age of the Hebrews in antiquity.[11] A poor country sinking into dependence needed a myth so magnificent to bolster its self-respect. (Welshmen too liked to fancy that they were part of the original chosen people, speaking a language akin to the first human speech, Hebrew.) A much less welcome sequel in 1643 was the Solemn League and Covenant with the Parliamentary party in England, which to Englishmen was only a grand title for a military alliance against the royalists, but which left many Scots obsessed with a quixotic belief in their mission to presbyterianize England. From this "enormous mistake"[12] they failed to move forward to any more common-sense programme; in the civil wars they floundered from side to side, becoming more and more deeply divided in the process. In the end defence of country and creed, first championed by the higher classes, largely though not exclusively from self-interest, would descend to the lower, to a plebeian mass which had failed and continued to fail to comprehend its own interests.

Elimination of bishops gave a fuller share of control of the Kirk to laymen of the propertied classes, serving as elders; this was regulated by the "Form of Presbyterial Church-Government" adopted in 1645. It sought for the Kirk a balancing or moderating role; care of the poor had its place in the schedule of duties of pastors and parish officers. The 1647 "Catechism" in its elaborate commentary on the ten commandments equated society and family, in true feudal-clan style, by extending the fifth commandment to cover relations between all "superiors" -- who clearly seem to include employers -- and "inferiors", and dilating on their mutual responsibilities. The eighth is made a peg for numerous social maxims; hard work is inculcated, but injury to others, for instance by "unjust enclosures" of common lands, is condemned. Theologically the catechism derived from the *Westminster Confession* painfully hammered out in 1647 by a joint Scottish and English commission. It represents the most elaborate edifice of Calvinist -- perhaps of Christian -- thinking ever reared, at the moment when this extraordinary system of ideas was about to begin crumbling under its own weight, and fading away everywhere except in backwaters like Scotland or New England.

Among some nobles who signed the 1638 "Covenant", like Montrose, fears had been expressed almost from the start that if the crown were too seriously weakened the masses might take the bit between their teeth, and go on to sweep aristocracy away into the bargain.[13] There was similar anxiety in the Kirk over the spread of conventicles, or irregular prayer-meetings, since even before 1638.[14] By the strait-laced they were suspected of being tainted with sectarian ideas akin to those of the Brownists, or the Family of Love, which had disturbed conservative repose in England and elsewhere, and might be said to hover -- as did so much religion in England during those years -- on the borderline between doctrinal and social heterodoxy. In Scotland there is very little sign of any of the consequences so much feared, even when the country came under the rule of an English government committed to Independency and wide toleration. In the spring of 1652 Edinburgh witnessed a mushrooming of sects hitherto unknown there -- Brownist, Antinomian, Familist --, and baptizing of Anabaptists in the Water of Leith;[15] a stream with hardly enough water to baptize a child, as shallow as this current of religious novelty proved to be, even in the urban areas to which it was limited.

A Cromwellian soldier in Berwickshire spoke pityingly of a peasantry huddled in its hovels, evicted at the landlord's whim.[16] During the occupation the authorities showed much "concern for social justice".[17] It was their cue, as an observer noted, to detach "the poor Commoners" from thraldom both to the aristocracy and to the clergy: it would be a good idea, he thought, to station good English preachers in the chief towns, to draw people away from "their Pharisaical and rigid Presbyterian Teachers".[18] At Edinburgh orders were issued for street-cleaning, and throwing of dirt out of windows was banned.[19] Such interference with cherished custom might have been enough to antagonize the capital, but Colonel Robert Lilburne, in command in Scotland in 1653, had cause everywhere to lament "the spirit of the generality of people here, who have a deadly antipathy against us".[20] In May 1654 union with England was imposed, and helped to ensure "firm and good government", with more impartial justice than Scotland had ever known. Yet it made no dent on old clannish prejudice. "Cromwell was in Scottish eyes almost another Edward I."[21] Nationalism has been at least as often an obstructive as a progressive force. In a not dissimilar fashion women through the ages have submitted to ill-usage from their lords and masters, and often taken part with them against outsiders. Molière has a scene of a wife indignant at a stranger who interposes against the husband who is beating her.

Scotland was capable neither of reforming itself nor of accepting reform from outside. It was cutting off its nose to spite its face when it hailed the Restoration in 1660 with loud satisfaction. The hated union was dissolved, and good rule from London was exchanged for bad rule from London. "The enemies of God", in the language of a stern Covenanter, were regaining power "with the favour and the fawnings of the foolish Nation".[22] It must be said in mitigation that there had been too little time before 1660 to permit economic recovery from the damage done by the wars. English occupation and the contacts it brought had done something, all the same, to widen horizons and stimulate the improving bourgeois outlook. In the towns some impatience of perpetual clerical squabbling had begun to be shown, and a turning away towards more mundane concerns. There was little public protest at the suppression of the ministers' assembly in 1653; and the despotic attitude of the bigots, when they were in the saddle, led to "a strong reaction against the Covenants and even against presbyterianism."[23] On the whole the decades following 1660 were a time of economic and cultural growth.

By the Kirk too the Restoration was welcomed uncritically, among both the "Resolutioners" who had taken the Stewart side against Cromwell in 1650 and their "Remonstrant" or "Protestor" opponents. When it speedily proved that return to monarchy meant return to episcopacy, regarded once more by royalists as an indispensable prop to the throne, moderates made the best of it; the more readily because presbyterianism was not being subverted, but only placed under supervision of bishops, and church services were scarcely affected. But the need to obtain "collation", or confirmation of their ministerial posts by the patron (now restored to his right of presentation) and the bishop, was more than the intransigent could bear; and in 1662 nearly three hundred, a considerable proportion of the total, were ejected from their pulpits.

They were giving a fresh display of the curious semi-republicanism Scotland had nurtured since the Reformation, or even earlier. It was riddled with contradictions, reflecting all the unclarity of an era of change and confusion. These unyielding men "were not prepared to admit that lay rulers had the right to control the religion of their subjects."[24] But the Kirk, meddling in politics, had often ignored its own precept of the Two Kingdoms, the spiritual and temporal each supreme in its own sphere. Moreover the zealots demanded action by government against everyone's religion but their own; in their eyes an essential part of the duty imposed on all good Scots by the Covenants was "the extirpation of Popery, Prelacy, Superstition, Heresie, Schisme, Profanenesse".[25] They were as far as could be from advocating freedom and toleration: theirs was the tribal insistence on all brethren facing the same way. A "free people", they might eloquently declare, should be ruled by civil law, "not by military force and cruelty";[26] but clearly only the strictest presbyterians, a dwindling minority, were entitled to this right.

Fidelity to the Covenants was their watchword. Veneration of these compacts with Heaven as immutable requirements of the faith, never to be relegated to the past as they were by the conformists, served as a bond of unity, in default of any more rational one, but unity in essence negative. A "Covenanting" movement quickly took the form of illicit services, or conventicles, often held privately, but more defiantly as field-preachings, combined with non-attendance at churches occupied by conforming or intruded ministers. Such behaviour necessarily had an anti-English hue, which lost nothing by the fact that some of the new "curates" were English, and hence doubly detested. Patriotic feeling must have helped to win sympathy, if not support, for the Covenanters. Their goal was salvation for the whole Scottish community, not for individuals merely; in this, theology can be seen as a chrysalis of nationalism. It was a counterweight to the isolation of the predestined soul, and of the tenant farmer, as much at the mercy of the landlord's caprice as his soul of God's.

Dislike of the new ecclesiastical order was widespread, but regional variations were strongly marked. It is easier from some points of view to see the Scotland of that time as a congeries of regions rather than of classes; the region formed an intermediate stage between the clan, with its denial of class, and the nation, within which classes are free to take shape. Conventicles were scarcely known north of the Tay; they were most numerous in the south-west. This had a rehearsal in earlier events. During the 1630s several of the group of pastors most resentful of episcopal encroachments came from there. It was there too that unofficial prayer-meetings spread most readily after 1638, with the encouragement of some outstanding ministers. It was there again that "Protestors" were most numerous, and from there that the "Whiggamore raid" of Kirk stalwarts marched to Edinburgh in 1648, starting the party nickname of "Whig" on its long career. All this betokened no disposition to approve of the Cromwellian presence. A list of prisoners captured by an English force at Dumfries in 1651 is a long one.[27]

Among the ejected pastors nearly all those of Galloway could be counted, besides more than two thirds of those attached to the synods of Ayr and Glasgow. It was in districts off the highroad of history that zealotry was likeliest to persist, provided that they were not too torpid for Reformation teaching to have sunk into men's minds. Geography was one simple reason for the obduracy of the south-west. Fife and the Lothians were too close under the eye of a government whose military strength was fortified by civil war experience, with a standing army now come to stay. Gatherings there were usually domestic, and tended towards a pietistic withdrawal from the iniquity of the times. Ayrshire, Dumfriesshire, and the neighbouring Borders were rich in trackless moors, bogs, hills, where unlawful meetings could avoid detection or baffle pursuit, as smugglers and cattle-reivers had done in times still not quite gone by. Paden's Hill in the midst of the Cheviot Hills, even today not easily explored, is only one of several secluded haunts on which the name of the celebrated preacher Alexander Peden came to be bestowed. Galloway in the far south-west -- the county of Wigtownshire and the county or "Stewartry" of Kirkcudbrightshire -- was not easy of access by land; John Knox had once taken refuge there. But unlike the landlocked Borders it was washed by sea and Solway Firth, and its bays and inlets and little ports assisted small-scale local trade. The nearness of Ulster, where Peden could find sanctuary at need in a Scottish settlement planted by the sword, with a Presbyterian fervour kept in constant heat by confrontation with popery, must have reinforced the intransigence of the south-west.

Regional feeling requires some measure of social solidarity, always largely illusory but sometimes favoured by circumstances. In most of Scotland landownership was concentrated in not many hands; in the south-west with its scattered patches of cultivation there were many survivors of the class of "bonnet lairds", or "small working landowners",[28] who formed a link between those above and below them. Trade helped to make for a gradation of ranks, up to a nobility itself not very wealthy. Cattle-rearing was a staple in Ayrshire and Lanarkshire, with export of herds to England, but still more in Galloway. Drovers and shepherds with their knowledge of hill and moorland could be useful guides or scouts, and might be of more independent temper than the ploughman. Bible-readers in country like this may have been more responsive than most others to the pastoral imagery of Scripture.

After 1660 the growing ascendancy of the government was likely in all areas to bring about a widening rift within Scotland's too numerous and penurious nobility between families content with a provincial status, and others which chose to associate themselves with the court: individuals ambitious of treading a wider stage, and able to catch the royal or ministerial eye, who might also be men who had overspent themselves and needed a financial blood-transfusion which the government alone could supply. A convenient means by which it could do so was furnished by the fines imposed on suspects or opponents. Of the plunder represented by forfeited lands, half went (or was supposed to go) to the crown, half to the commissioners empowered to act for it. A vulture aristocracy was continuing its predatory mode of subsistence in new guise.

One magnate of the south-west, the Earl of Annandale, was among those -- "bankrupt in estate as well as in morals"[29] -- who escaped ruin by getting large subsidies from this source; in the last years of persecution he was one of its strenuous agents. But in that oldfashioned corner of Scotland most of the prominent families were still rooted in the local soil, and it was they, accustomed until not many years since to rule the roost without much reference to Edinburgh, who had the most tangible interest in preservation of regional autonomy. Over a Kirk free from official control they would have the greatest share of influence. Some were, besides, unquestionably sincere in their presbyterian principles. There was an "ultra-protestant" tradition among them;[30] this as well as dislike of the monarchy's centralizing policies enlisted their support for the Covenant. In the reforming Assembly of the Kirk at Glasgow in 1638 the earls of Galloway, Dumfries, Wigtown, and Cassilis all took part, and for several years there prevailed an unwonted "unanimity of the Galloway baronage".[31]

In the previous century the French wars of religion had turned into a defence by the Huguenots of provincial and municipal self-rule in their southern strongholds, far away from Paris. In Scotland now the old type of feudal insubordination, chronic to the end of the sixteenth century, was no longer practical politics. Noblemen could not summon their vassals to take up arms; and when the common folk rose they "acted for the first time on their own initiative".[32] But in less dramatic ways local notables were ready enough to display their disapproval of government proceedings.

Foremost among them was the head of the Kennedy clan, John, sixth Earl of Cassilis. Such a man might well be shocked into better ways by memories of ancestral crime, like the Borgia who became Saint Alexander, for his two predecessors, one of them known as the "king of Carrick", had been among the worst feudal ruffians of their times. The present holder of the title was one of three Scots laymen deputed to attend the Westminster assembly. He was one of only two in the parliament of 1661 who spoke against the royal supremacy in church affairs, and paid the penalty by being declared incapable of any public office. After his death in 1666 his son followed the same course, and his was the solitary protest in parliament against the "Black Act" of 1670 which made field-preaching a capital crime.[33]

Another who fell foul of authority was John Maclellan, third Baron Kirkcudbright, like the second lord a staunch presbyterian who had stood against both king and Cromwell. His fortune was crippled by costs of raising troops during the wars, and wiped out after the Restoration by fines for resisting the intrusion of a curate into the church at Kirkcudbright. In 1663 he was arrested for alleged sympathy with a riot there, in which women took a prominent part, and next year he died. The fourth Viscount Kenmure was an ardent royalist in the civil wars, and the sixth was to lose his life in 1715 as a Jacobite rebel; in between, a distant relative who succeeded to the title in 1663 went very much the other way. Like Cassilis, and the Earl of Galloway, not hitherto in the same camp, he was among those stripped of offices and jurisdictions for refusing the oath under the Test Act of 1681, when the accession of the Catholic heir, James, was approaching; he was deprived of his hereditary bailliary of Tongland.

Such men could use their positions as magistrates, and their local influence, to extend some covert protection to their humbler neighbours. To act in such a manner as the people's guardians was in line with the kind of "populism" which had a place in feudal societies. They would be the more desirous of putting a check on the arbitrary conduct of officials and soldiery because their own estates suffered, if only indirectly, from the depredations. In 1667 a complaint by two noblemen and Sheriff Agnew about army extortion obliged the government to set up an enquiry. A few years later, when attitudes had hardened further, a petition to the king was ignored, and a deputation of western "noblemen and gentlemen" wanting to protest to the privy council at Edinburgh about grievances like the quartering of troops on their districts was unceremoniously turned away.

From the first the government tried to get all landowners to cooperate with it. Some did, for fear of trouble or in hope of enhancing their own power by acting as its myrmidons. Many must have had mixed or wavering feelings. They might not be sorry to see tenants banging their heads against a brick wall, instead of combining against *them*. On the other hand it may sometimes have struck them, as it did the more apprehensive of the Covenanting nobility after 1638, that defiance of government might one day turn into defiance of rent-collectors. Yet, again, neighbourhood feeling was pervasive, the same common dislike of pressure from outside which sometimes drew or dragged French seigneurs into anti-tax riots. In 1678 even those well-disposed towards presbyterianism made haste to assure the Council that they had no complicity in the scuffles with soldiers which were breaking out;[34] but they were clearly unwilling to accept the duty it wanted to thrust on them of keeping their plebeians in order.

Landlord authority being so extensive, the official assumption that they could do this if they chose was not unnatural; and without a good deal of malingering on their part it is hard to see how Covenanting could have held out so long. Trying to break down the obstacle, the government was no respecter of persons. Refractory nobles, not peasants, had always been its stumbling-block in the past. In 1682 Kenmure was ordered out of his mansion by Claverhouse to make room for a garrison.[35] There were financial motives too for striking at men of property. Tenants paid their rents mostly in kind; they could be laid under contribution chiefly by having soldiers billeted on them, but cash had to be looked for higher up. It was complained in 1666 that ninety-one persons in the Stewartry had been mulcted in a total of £47,860, and many gentry and other families ruined.[36] There is some ground for the statement that after the 1679 rising "The Galloway gentlemen were the first sacrifices."[37] Thirty-five estates in Galloway and Drumfriesshire were forfeited, either because their owners were suspected of disloyalty or as a warning to the rest of their class that they would not be allowed to stay neutral.

Among the zealots there were no doubt carpings at the reluctance of the bulk of the upper classes to come forward more boldly. All the same, their temporizing attitude may be supposed to have softened the bitterness which tenants as individuals must often have felt, and might come to feel collectively. Still more of a blurring of class relations may be ascribed to the part in the movement played by women of all classes, from highest to lowest. All women had grievances of their own against the social order, which could not yet find articulate expression, but could only merge themselves in a response to a more general summons. A Duchess of Hamilton did her best in the 1660s to shield Covenanters from prosecution. The Duke of Rothes, for some time the government's chief manager in Scotland, and among many other things chief collector of fines, had a conventicling wife. In 1672, while the Earl of Wigtoun was a member of the privy council, his lady was heavily fined for attending conventicles. When Claverhouse was man-hunting in Wigtownshire ten years later he reported that lairds were outwardly conforming, but allowing disaffected persons to haunt their houses, and having their children baptized by "outed" ministers; when challenged, they laid the blame on their wives. He meant to put a stop to this comedy, he added grimly.[38] Kenmure married the widow of a laird, John Bell, shot by the military in 1685. At the bottom of the scale there was often a fierce devotion to Kirk and Covenants among servant-women, and wives of peasants, like Cuddie Headrigg's mother in *Old Mortality,* who could find in the exaltation of the cause and its perils a release from the harsh, narrow existence to which they were condemned.

Ousted ministers who took to field-preaching were another link between the classes. Ejected preachers and tenants always liable to eviction were fellow-sufferers, and the latter could appreciate the sacrifice of security their pastors had made. Some of these were of humble birth, and knew the hardships of the poor, and were now sharing them again; but as scholars, whose high standing came from their learning, they would prefer to rise above vulgar bread-and-butter questions and soar into the empyrean of divinity. A fair number of others had gentry connections; since the earlier days of the Kirk the ministry had become, in terms of financial rewards, a respectable profession. Manses were always likely to be occupied by members of nearby families, and in Galloway their abandonment by nearly all their occupants must have owed much to local ties. Birth entitled men who accompanied their flocks into the hills to added respect; while many of those foisted into their places were taxed with both low origins and -- unjustly, it would seem[39] -- with scanty attainments.

Covenanters were always divided between more moderate and more extreme, and it may be further supposed that ministers with landed connections were likelier to belong to the first, as well as to be even more immune than the rest to any social incendiarism. John Welsh, the leading moderate, was the son of a Nithsdale laird, though reported to have led a very wild life on the Borders before his conversion; a change that might be said to epitomize the evolution of the Border valleys from clan forays to a more spiritual sort of independence. Peden is described as an Ayrshire peasant proprietor's son, of bonnet-laird descent. James Renwick, in religion an extremist, was a weaver's son. Besides differences over ecclesiastical principle, however, there was another -- as among Chartists later -- about whether physical force could rightly be resorted to. Richard Cameron, who gave his name to the movement in its last years and was killed fighting, came from a town tradesman's family. But within the rural orbit individuals from higher ranks, traditionally involved in the faction-fighting that had been Scotland's politics, might be readier than others to draw the sword. Donald Cargill's father was a small laird and lawyer. Laymen would be more thorough-going than preachers. Two of the men, in another part of the country, who brought fiercer persecution of the Covenanters by murdering Archbishop Sharp in 1679, were lairds.

Age was another differential. Welsh came from an earlier, more unsettled Scotland. Peden was thirty-four at the Restoration, Renwick only twenty-six when he was executed in 1688 just before the Revolution: his whole brief life belonged to the time of persecution. But youth did not correspond with an advance towards appreciation of social issues. It may sometimes indeed have been the other way about. We are told that Samuel Rutherford, inducted at Anwoth in 1627, showed sympathy with the common people's plight, for instance by remonstrating with a laird who in true feudal style raised his rents to defray the cost of his son's wedding.[40] Such an attitude preserved something of the Reformation clergy's concern with the state of the poor, which had some partial revival in the early 1640s. Doubtless conscientious ministers expected or hoped that study of the catechism would make landlords more benevolent, as well as tenants and labourers more docile. But their desire, all the more natural under stress of persecution, was to unite well-fed and hungry on the rock of Scripture, not to divide them over the affairs of this transient world.

It is going too far to say that their following came "almost entirely from the peasantry and small tenant farmers".[41] Any peasant movement regularly requires some admixture of other elements, for leaven or stiffening, as has been observed of agrarian revolts in China. Lists of names of those who fell under official displeasure do not usually specify their occupations, but there is a sprinkling of others than cultivators, a few described as "merchants", or relatives of lairds, but mostly of modest callings, such as smiths, tailors, weavers, down to servants.[42] Many of these must have had family links with the ploughmen, and it was very common for small farmers to have other employments besides. They were all close enough in each district for mutual trust. There were occasional informers, but if there had been many the government would have found its work far easier. Their faith and its hazards were a relief from the isolation of their separate lives, as tenants competing for farms, or simply as shepherds alone in the hills, as well as from the dreary monotony which must have been painfully felt by the mentally more alert.

In a slippery world, as treacherous as one of their upland bogs, their treaty with God, a perpetual bond never to be broken, was a comforting certainty to which they could hold fast. Neighbourhood sentiment might be strong, but Scots villagers had no such organization of their own as the commune of old Russia, or Vietnam, with fixed rights of cultivation and a traditional leadership. Only an unearthly vision, a pole star invisible to others, could lend them the sense of fraternity they needed. Devotion to their image of the Kirk may be seen as the false consciousness of a class, a coming together in defence of ideals instead of interests. Covenanters had a deep sensation of being wronged and oppressed, but they turned their indignation against an imaginary oppressor, a giant or monster called Erastianism, casting a still more horrid shadow of Popery and Idolatry. Rejection of bishops was an unconscious rejection of the social order.

Their cause had some able controversialists, in exile, like the author of *Jus Populi Vindicatum,* whose treatise followed those of the old Huguenot writers in denying royal absolutism and asserting the right of resistance to abuse of the authority created by "a voluntary compact, and consent of the Subjects".[43] But learnedly lengthy treatises like this, or *A Hind let loose,*[44] were far removed from the realities and miseries of rural life. Their philosophy could not go beyond a tacit assumption that godly rule and fulfilment of the Covenants would make all well for all good Scots, besides putting a stop to "the present overflowing and abounding of Idolatry, Superstition, Sodomy, Adultery, Uncleannesse, Drunkennesse, Atheisme...."[45]

To help to imprison Covenanters in their infatuation there was the grip of Calvinist dogma. In Scotland this creed could perform the negative task of sweeping away an older cult, and much that went with it, but it was far less capable of anything positive, because the social and economic foundations necessary for progress were not present, as they were in England or Holland. A theology can lend impetus to social drives, but cannot initiate them. In Scotland it remained a thing in itself, historically purposeless, except as unconscious symbol of rejection — rejection of life itself, it might often seem to the profane, or at any rate a hindrance instead of help to any useful new thinking. Religious excitement dammed up by the want of rational purpose turned into irrational obsession.

For men who could only turn their back on their world and dream of rising above it, instead of striving to alter it, such a doctrine might be appropriate enough. It is a salient difference between them and the irregular sects of the previous decades, in Scotland and far more in England, that instead of unorthodox beliefs mingled with social aspirations they took their stand on unswerving orthodoxy. In the England of the Commonwealth the sects were a retreat into religious emotionalism after the defeat of the Levellers, the failure of revolutionary hopes, by groups of disoriented individuals who had no external links to sustain them. Covenanters were men on whom hope of revolution had not even dawned, the rearguard of an idealized past instead of the forlorn hope of an ideal future. For them all truth was already written. They combined with their afflatus a hard Calvinist intellectuality. As faithful adherents of a cause not long since subscribed to by the entire nation, they could feel that they were no mere sect; while their regional base gave them a cohesion which the sectaries had to win from outbursts of collective excitement. Repression and censorship made it harder for any novel thinking to filter into the beleaguered south-west. Here was another reason for the movement -- or rather *stand-still* -- being countenanced by sections of the propertied classes; its creed offered no threat to them, as the notions of breakaway sectaries might.

Most of the resisters came from a downtrodden mass exploited since time out of mind by superiors against whom they had never attempted to rise. For them to rise up now and challenge authority was an immense feat in itself. They could only achieve it by having another, higher authority to look to; by virtue of firm conviction that God, through accredited representatives and the words of Scripture, commanded them so to act. They were exchanging one obedience for another. As for the meaning of what they were bidden to do, God's intentions were inscrutable. For men and women haunted by fear of damnation, to defy earthly penalties by joining in prayer on a wild moor might be the most potent reassurance. Scottish Calvinism has been reproached with seeing God only as "King and Judge", instead of Father. "The Scottish theologian had not emerged from the sphere of feudalism."[46] If so, it would seem that feudalism in Scotland in its later phases had very little of a paternal character.

Just as defence of the Covenants was the first independent act of these hard-handed toilers, their first entry into public affairs, this theology was their introduction to the world of intellect. Through the two things together the old servile abasement of the Scottish peasantry before birth and rank, its pathetic eagerness to claim kinship however remote with them, was being replaced by respect for moral and mental qualities; here at least they were taking a stride forward, with more meaning for some of their descendants in a far-off future than for their own prospects. Well-versed in the niceties of the catechism, and in Scripture, they could be keen dissecters of abstruse sermons, each listener with his favourite predilections. Very often the thinking faculty has been exercised and developed on more arid matter. Even the meanest, Bishop Burnet lamented, were ready with Biblical texts to justify a veto on royal interference in religion: they were "vain of their knowledge, much conceited of themselves, and were full of a most entangled scrupulosity."[47] They were sons of a legalistic, if often lawless, nation, and of an era in which codification of law was going ahead; theirs was a religion of controversy and dialectic.

Protestantism and the English Bible had helped to banish Gaelic speech,[48] and were held on to all the more firmly as the induction into a new era. But Galloway had been the last Lowland area to lose its old tongue, and something of a Celtic temperament was still left. All theology, however academic, is a refinement of very primitive belief, and the south-western hills made a natural setting for what was semi-magical or fetishistic in the obsessive loyalty to the Covenants. Prayer-meetings in such surroundings, with nerves highly strung by danger, must have fostered stirrings of feeling more elemental than the ordered pattern of Calvinist doctrine. It was still the age of witchcraft and witch-hunting, and there was an appetite for the marvellous. Supernatural gifts, of prophecy especially, were attributed to Peden. Some who fought at Rullion Green in 1666 were convinced that their enemies, the ogre Dalziell of the Binns most of all, were protected by a pact with Satan against any but silver bullets.[49]

Covenanting was an early trial of passive resistance, or civil disobedience. At Urr near Dalbeattie when a new man, John Lyon, appeared in the pulpit "The parishioners immediately began to manifest their antipathy to the 'curate', by general abstention from his services, and indirect obstruction of his work." Like most others of his species he was believed to aid the dragoons with information, and sometimes even accompany them on their raids.[50] Retaliation in kind was rare, even in hours of tumult; "mob violence was never more leniently exercised against defenceless men."[51] But one of the most interesting features of the agitation was its devising something very like the boycott method hit on by the Irish peasantry two centuries later.

Within a few years intruded ministers were driven to represent to the government that after their expenses of removal to this unruly quarter they were meeting with ill will, and finding their stipends grudgingly and irregularly paid.[52] Refusal to listen to their sermons was followed by refusal to work for them. It was a trenchant weapon out here, as Captain Boycott was to learn in the wilds of county Mayo. In 1680 the authorities were still having to promise protection to incumbents from "the fury of some blind zealots", thanks to which "even the necessaries of life, and the help of servants and mechanics are denied unto them for their money".[53] Similar tactics might have been resorted to, there and in Scotland at large, against exorbitant rents and other burdens; a peasantry can do much to baffle landlord greed without going to the length of revolt. But for this a degree of unity is required which in seventeenth-century Scotland only the celestial trumpet could arouse.

From armed revolt the Covenanters were withheld at most times by their preachers, but also by the contradictoriness of their whole outlook, that of a movement disoriented from the real needs of its class, with no tangible aims to fight for, however much it might alarm the government into brutal repression. It was clearly believed that there was a threat of revolution in the west country: men would not imperil themselves so deeply for any lesser stake, and it could not be forgotten in London that the "Great Rebellion" had been inaugurated in Scotland. In official eyes Covenanters were dangerous "fanatics":[54] this word, coined in the previous century with the meaning "mad", "possessed", was now acquiring its modern sense. It was to be used incessantly by nineteenth-century imperialists of opponents like the jehadists and dervishes of the North-West Frontier or the Sudan, with whom Covenanters had indeed some affinity.

Stevenson travelling with his donkey was haunted by thoughts of the Camisard rebels who, just after the time of the Covenanters, fought for years "a war of wild beasts" in the Cevennes, built up "an organization, arsenals, a military and religious hierarchy", and made their deeds the talk of Europe.[55] They were Protestants resisting Catholics, instead of erring fellow-Protestants; and they were poor country-folk left in the lurch by Huguenot citizens and gentry, to find leadership of their own. They were resentful of royal taxes as well as bigotry. By contrast the Covenanters' position was more complex and confusing, since apart from the fines imposed on them they were victims materially less of government than of their own gentry, to some of whom they owed a measure of protection. It was only in passive resistance that they could stand together.

They were not pacifists, and more and more as time went on their meetings were guarded by armed men; but except in immediate self-defence they only twice took up arms, and then only in an unplanned, unprepared reaction to molestation. They might then have made use of their hills to wage a guerrilla resistance, emulating Wallace's men who once ambushed the English by Loch Trool in the heart of Galloway, rolling rocks down on to their heads. Instead, on each occasion they marched out to confront their enemy in the open, in 1666 making for Edinburgh, in 1679 briefly occupying Glasgow. A rebellion must advance, it is true, but it must first consolidate its base, and be sure of support awaiting it outside. No such support was forthcoming. In these risings there was a gleam of the same unquestioning faith in God's readiness to stand by His true servants, a sense of the impiety of any distrust of this, of any hanging back, which had some part at least in hurrying the Scots army to destruction at Dunbar in 1650. No men of action comparable in talent with the leading preachers came forward to take command.

After their first defeat the government felt safe in reducing its forces and issuing the Indulgences of 1669 and 1672, which allowed vagrant ministers to come to terms, and preach in church instead of under the sky. Its aim was to split the ranks and isolate the irreconcilable, and it had some success. But the hard core remained strong enough to provoke in 1678 an extreme measure of coercion. A "Highland Host" of freebooters (not all in fact were Highlanders) was let loose. It was an equivalent of the *dragonnades* by means of which Charles II's cousin and exemplar, Louis XIV, was trying to break the spirit of his Huguenot subjects. Fifteen hundred men were quartered on the Cassilis estates, so impoverishing the owner that a good part of them had to be sold. Memories of this occupation by ruffians licensed, as Defoe wrote in 1717, to commit "rapine, violence, robbery and wickedness", were still vivid enough in 1745 to keep Ayrshire and Galloway even more anti-Jacobite than the rest of the Lowlands.[56]

Goaded into revolt again in 1679, the Covenanters won a first engagement at Drumclog, but then wasted their time listening to wrangles between the more and less inflexible of their ministers, until a few weeks later they were crushed at Bothwell Bridge near Hamilton. Led by Welsh, the moderates would have been content with freedom of conscience; those whose spokesman was Donald Cargill rejected any compromise with episcopacy, or reconciliation with the "indulged" ministers who had made their peace. Next year the "Sanquhar declaration" by the militants amounted to a withdrawal of allegiance, and in September Cargill followed it up by formally excommunicating the king and all his accomplices. This was going much too far to be countenanced by any men of respectable position. Moreover the obstinate stand of the remnant "cut against feudal and clannish dependence"; and Cameron was reported to have predicted before his death in 1680 that when these troubles were over the hour would be at hand for nobility and gentry to disappear.[57] Towards the end landowners, in Wigtownshire particularly, were showing willingness to collaborate with the government.

Persecution intensified into what were remembered as "the killing times". With scarcely any ordained ministers left the survivors could no longer function as a regular church, but they maintained a loose organization, as "Societies United in Correspondence" -- the first "corresponding societies" in modern political history --, holding their meetings in more remote, inaccessible spots, ready to defend themselves if interrupted. Fantasy could swell their slender numbers with reinforcements from on high, where they believed Providence to be giving its closest attention to their barren hills. Their dreams, kindled by Old Testament reading, were of "divine thunderclaps, irresistible legions, lethal swords of the Spirit...."[58] Short of miracles, little more was left, as for Wordsworth in his years of embitterment against an evil government, than to feed on the day of vengeance yet to come; and that day was receding beyond the boundaries of time. A rude epitaph in Glasgow cathedral, denouncing the executioners of nine martyrs there, ends

> They'll know at resurrection day
> To murder saints was no sweet play.

Yet in the end they were still capable of an astonishing burst of energy. When William landed in England in 1688, and in November James II had to withdraw his troops from Scotland, they flocked together in arms, and "for some months the Cameronians were masters of the south of the kingdom."[59] That winter they marched across the Lowlands unopposed, ejecting episcopalian clergymen. In 1689, with Claverhouse raising the Highlands against William, they were invited to form a regiment; there were debates and scruples, but a sufficient number agreed to enlist. Their spirited defence of Dunkeld nullified the Jacobite victory at Killiecrankie, and saved the situation. They were proving that they could fight as well as Cromwell's Ironsides, given proper leadership and the concrete task of defeating counter-revolution.

Thus in a sense the cause had triumphed, but only illusorily; these Covenanters were emerging from their lair into a Scotland where they were strangers, and where there could be little place for them. Shut up in their hills they could have no notion of how the world was changing round them. Theirs was the "enthusiasm" of a class which had received a powerful injection of ideas without a practical outlet, a class not yet reduced to the condition of wage labourers, as their descendants would soon be, but with only a spurious independence, idealized into dedication to independence for Kirk and country. They were at the same time stragglers of a fading social order, feudal and oppressive but with a rough and ready spirit of brotherhood.

Early in 1690 the Cameronian regiment was removed to Flanders, one of several from Scotland to take part in the wars of William and Marlborough against the French. In 1706 there were still three hundred armed men, described as Covenanters, ready to march into Dumfries and burn a copy of the unpopular treaty under which next year Scotland was drawn into another and longer-lasting union with England. Once more they were a rearguard destined to defeat. But their instinct was true; for many years to come the poor had good reason to detest the Union. Incorporation into capitalist England accelerated tendencies towards unrestricted profit-making, achieved -- as in England from an earlier date -- by a combination of feudal power with capitalist appetite.

Already in 1695 the Scottish Parliament had passed Acts to abolish the old practice of joint cultivation known as run-rig, doubtless primitive and inefficient, and to speed up consolidation of holdings and division of common lands, guided of course by the golden rule that to him that hath, more shall be given. In the south-west one stimulus was the growth of Glasgow, by 1715 as Scott noted in *Rob Roy* the commercial metropolis of Ayrshire and Dumfriesshire as well as its own environs. In Galloway large-scale enclosures began about 1720, with increased export of cattle to England since the Union making it profitable to substitute cattle-rearing for cultivation.[60] This made it necessary to get rid of many small farmers there and in neighbouring areas. Their removal was defended with the argument that the Galloway people were "very lazy", and mismanaged the land.[61] This may have been in a way true. Shiftlessness in workaday life, indifference to comfort or neatness, might well go, as it did in the Highlands, with a martial spirit, a readiness for adventure, all the more so because in the conditions of the Scottish countryside labour was likely to be so unrewarding. Such men as the Covenanters could not walk, like ordinary beings, but could only soar; they were better capable of exalted and sacrificial moods than of grappling with humdrum daily tasks.

The class from which most of them had come was now being brought down from the clouds to face economic reality; and the exhausting fight for the now-defunct Covenants may have made it less easy, or more impossible, for this class to rally together now. There was much bitterness, and in 1724 some hundreds of families turned adrift were pulling down stone walls built by the enclosers in parts of Dumfriesshire and Kirkcudbrightshire; but these "Levellers", as they were nick-named, were soon quelled by dragoons sent from Edinburgh. An account of Galloway dating from about 1730 speaks of bare-footed peasants leading a "coarse and dirty" existence in "most miserable hovels", many for want of bed or mattress sleeping on the ground.[62] They had always been poverty-stricken, but a statement that few could read suggests a falling back since the days of the Bible-conning rebels.

Compensations for lost independence were in store for Scotland, or for some Scots, opportunities to be grasped by enterprising individuals from all ranks.

Protestantism could not be the midwife to a social revolution the country was unready for, but it could in some ways deputise for an absent or feeble national development by forging a national character or mentality in many respects "bourgeois", even while the framework of society was still feudal. Thanks to this historical detour there was being moulded in advance of economics a nation many of whose members were ready, as soon as circumstances detached them from their past, for a new, modern life. Opportunity beckoned most enticingly of all from an expanding empire; though for the poor, removal to the colonies might be an eviction from Scotland resembling eviction from their farms. A symbolic anticipation may be found in the story of the Covenanter transported to Jamaica and sold into plantation slavery, who was half-killed by his master for refusing to work on Sunday, but then by faithful service won his confidence and the hatred of the blacks over whom he was made overseer, and who tried to poison him.[63] To strain at the Sabbatarian gnat while swallowing the camel of nigger-driving was quite in harmony with the Covenanting bent for abstractions, as well as with Scottish peasant attachment to any master, however bad.

As for the Cameronian regiment, in more pedestrian phrase the 64th Foot, its part in the suppression of a Highland regiment's mutiny at Edinburgh in 1778 might be called a long-delayed tit for tat for the Highland Host of exactly a century before. But like so many other Scottish troops it was quickly found work in the empire; it was in at the crushing of the Indian Mutiny, and went on to assist in the conquest of Zululand. A vestigial link with the heroic past was always preserved, in an annual church service before which pickets were placed round the building and an officer with a lantern made a search for lurking enemies, as if a conventicle were meeting once more to sing its psalms in the hills.

The Kirk as remodelled after 1688 was not one that would hinder the rich from becoming richer and the poor poorer. Elimination of bishops left the presbyterian organization again, as it had been earlier, "admirably adapted to be an instrument of the aristocracy and gentry."[64] Patronage, abolished in 1690, was restored in 1712, though enveloped in much complexity and uncertainty. More important, the elders, who were coming to hold office for life, were drawn from the propertied classes, oftener by cooption than by election. Covenanters and their heirs could scarcely think of trying to democratize the system; in their fieriest days they had not pretended to believe in majority rule, for the majority would always be recalcitrant to the rule of the Saints.

Social control became the Kirk's primary function, and it enjoyed great though informal power of coercion through its control of poor relief and its ability to get any individual it disapproved of refused a tenancy or a job. Lay elders were often also magistrates; to a remarkable extent "the instruments of economic, social and political power were delegated to the Kirk."[65] This facilitated the further squeezing of the masses on which the Scottish Enlightenment, the eighteenth-century flowering of upper-class culture, depended. Capitalist farming led to agricultural improvements, but it was only after about 1780 that they made a significant contribution to national wealth.[66] Until then landowning income was being improved, as usual in a feudal society trying to catch up quickly -- Peter the Great's Russia, for instance --, by the privileged taking more from the unprivileged.

As always since the Reformation, the rural masses seem to have been oddly divided into puritanical and libertine, many soberly pious, many others having to be incessantly disciplined and dragooned. It would not be surprising to find that the demoralized now were those who had sunk into wage-servitude or pauperism, and the virtuous those still struggling, by austere abstention from cakes and ale, to keep their footing. Their struggle went with fidelity to everything traditional in religious practice and belief, like the old clinging to the life-line of the Covenants. From this conservatism the better-off were moving away; religious divergence reflected a widening social gap. Arminianism, a Calvinist writer complained, was creeping into Scotland by 1750, chiefly among the higher classes, and many of the clergy shunned themes like predestination in their sermons, though the masses were still tenaciously attached to them.[67] Horrific doctrines like Calvin's, an Anglican divine wrote with strong distaste, are only suited to the vulgar, who relish coarse, pungent stimulants.[68] A poor man might not always feel certain of his own salvation, but he would suffer from few doubts about his landlord's or the government exciseman's damnation. Arminian sentimentality, redemption for all, would rob him of his revenge, the social revolution to begin on the Day of Judgment.

Among Scots still stuck in the old ruts, theology as fantasy-solution for material grievances, or means of rising above them, is well brought out by a report from a parish in Elgin in the 1790s--while France was having its terrestrial revolution--that almost the sole pleasure of the inhabitants was "conversing about some of the abstrusest doctrines of Calvinism...varied by occasional reflections on the degeneracy and oppressions of the age."[69] Twenty years later still an agricultural description of Ayrshire regretted that the distinction chiefly coveted by the peasantry was not skill with the plough but "an extensive acquaintance with the mysterious, abstruse and disputed points of systematic divinity".[70] Only removal to a fresh environment would enable them to apply the mental dexterity thus acquired to more useful avocations.

All classes in their various ways felt a lingering dislike of the Union, and either smouldering Scottishness or political opportunism might bring them together now and then, as, most explosively, in the affair of the Porteous riots at Edinburgh in 1736. Patriotism of this sort was the successor to older regional loyalties, and likewise helped to keep social friction within bounds. It was felt most strongly, though inarticulately, by the poor, who got least from the Union. But national consciousness can regress, as well as evolve, and turn back to more elementary symbols. On the Half-Moon Battery of Edinburgh castle the guns had come to be known as the Seven Sisters, a name originally bestowed on some cannon made in the castle foundry which saw action against the English at Flodden. When they were carried off to London in 1716 to be melted down for scrap, it "was like to break all the old women's hearts in town".[71]

Among more important monuments, or badges of Scottish identity, the Kirk stood easily first, with all its rights intact after the Union except religious monopoly, and it was not always subservient to London. It was the people's church, but not under the people's control. Its managers, a pamphleteer of the next century wrote, the elders who flocked to Edinburgh for the annual Assembly, were not "Cameronian, plaided, blue bonneted men from the muirs and upland pastures", but lairds, provosts, lawyers.[72] All the more was the common man anxious that it should be held fast to creed and catechism, as the true Scottish inheritance, now being abandoned by the anglicizing gentry with their taste for heathenish philosophy. Lurking bitterness against the higher classes, xenophobia against England, could thus go together.

Among the more modern-minded, old-fashioned Calvinism might be harder and harder to salvage, but as time went by the Covenanters could be looked back on as religion's most selfless paladins, and as part of what the Kirk stood for in cherished national tradition. A poet of the early nineteenth century extolled them as men who

Perish'd that Scotland might be free.[73]

A painter depicted the drama of a Covenanter hiding in a hole in the rocks, about to be seized by unpitying soldiers.[74] Memorials, grand or humble, littered the country. Like so much else in later-day Scottish patriotism, many tributes were no more than conventional tinsel. Christopher North brought into one of his dialogues a piece of fustian rhetoric about a maiden martyr drowned on the sands;[75] one might prefer Aytoun's honester Tory jibe about a tuneless hymn sounding as if "composed by the Reverend Saunders Peden in an hour of paroxysms on the moors".[76] But Scott, repelled by the Covenanters as bigots and mutineers, despite his Toryism was fascinated by them as well.

A law-abiding admirer was careful to except from his praise the two armed risings, putting them on the same bad level as the Radical disturbance in Scotland in 1820, fresh evidence that attempts to cure public ills by force only make them worse.[77] But Scottish Chartists were fond of seeing themselves as heirs of the Covenanters. So was Keir Hardie, the Scottish socialist. One more turn of the wheel brought 1914, when their legend as patriots was invoked in recruiting propaganda because "Nothing stirs the enthusiasm of Scotsmen more than the story of the trials and triumphs of the Covenanters".[78] Since then, if the man in the street has been forgetting them, Scottish historians have not, and lately these have been joined by Marxists, compelled to think more about such corners of the past now that the present has come to look so intractable.

What's Hecuba to him, or Covenants to a Galloway peasant? All men in action are actors, playing parts often genuine enough but always with some admixture of the histrionic, through which inner impulses of diverse character find expression. They have habitually turned earthly ailments and aspirations into a sort of anagram, or pictorial language supplied by ideas floating in the air of their time and place. In retrospect, or from an outsider's viewpoint, incongruities between the two planes will always be evident. As collective and perpetual obligations binding on all, the Covenants are reminiscent of the feudal oath of fealty that bound lord and vassal together. Speaking of the oddly familiar, even peremptory Presbyterian style of addressing the Almighty (foreigners were often struck by the rude familiarity of Scotsmen talking to their superiors, even to their sovereign while he still dwelt among them) Notestein cites an account of a pastor's prayer for God's aid when the movement was nearing final defeat:

'And if', said he, 'Thou wilt not be our secondary, we will not fight for Thee at all, for it is not our cause but Thy cause; and if Thou wilt not fight for our cause and Thy own cause, we are not obliged to fight for it.'[79]

This is very much what clansmen or feudal tenants, called out to serve their lord in war, must have felt when He was not seen fighting in their ranks; and it sounds curiously as if, close to despair, some Covenanters were catching a glimpse of reality through the Maya-veil of theology.

They were men of a decaying social order who got into a blind alley and spent their energies there. History teems with examples of high gifts futilely expended, and the cumulative wastage, like that of stifled individual talents, must have been very great, and one of the causes of mankind's faltering progress. Within a generation of 1688 a British government would understand that a challenge like that of the Covenanters could be ignored; whether they listened to sermons in their pews or on their hillsides mattered very little. Both sides had been fighting an atavistic war of the past. It may still be said that without that long-drawn wrestling match, that "last weird battle in the west", rulers would have been slower to learn the lesson. If so, there is substance in Froude's tribute to the Covenanters as the men who forced open the door for David Hume, Adam Smith, and the steam engine.[80] It was not a compliment that any of their ghosts can have relished; but if valid it is a notable illustration of how history makes use of mortals' toils to bring about results quite other than what they tried to achieve.

In a more general view, it may be permissible to think of a conservation of moral energy, thanks to which its loss is never total. Whatever their narrowness of outlook, one chronicler of the Covenanters wrote, they embodied certain vital qualities in the national life.[81] By showing that nameless poor men could stand up against tyrannical authority they were giving proof of something that would be the keystone of Burns's poetry. In the Scottish consciousness they may have come to symbolize an uneasy sensation of a riddle left unsolved, a primitive virtue lost in the scramble, a promised land foregone for the fleshpots of England and India. They were the uncompromising opposite of everything that modern Scotland drifted into being, gaining a good share of the world and perhaps losing its soul.

Some part of their moral make-up must be discoverable in all mankind's idealists. There must be, running through human nature, something aloof from the common satisfactions which content most people at most times, and justify Marxism in its materialist theory of history, its equivalent of the Newtonian law of gravity. It is something that comes to life in individuals and minorities, and turns them into dissenters. But if history can in some measure be made by men and women like the Covenanters, it may also be marred by them. The chosen few are liable to plunge in odd directions, and to tilt at windmills. The Covenanters may be charged with misleading their class, debarring it from a practical grapple with its ills, by engaging its emotions for generations on behalf of martyrs suffering for a chimera. Yet if their gospel was too other-worldly to cope with hardships like hunger, the simply bread-and-butter movements of our day have proved equally incapable of lifting men's minds to anything so ideal, so distant, so necessary, as socialism. How to reconcile the two visions, pushed so far apart by our society and its maladies, is what Marxists hitherto have been as far as anyone else from discovering.

# *NOTES*

1. C.V. Wedgwood, *The King's Peace 1637-1641* (1955; London edn., 1966), p. 53.

2. J.E. Handley, *Scottish Farming in the Eighteenth Century* (London, 1953), pp. 88-90.

3. Patrick Gordon, cited by Andrew Lang, *A History of Scotland* (3rd edn., Edinburgh, (1924), Vol. 3, p. 151.

4. James Nichols, *Calvinism and Arminianism* (London, 1824), pp. xli, 205.

5. *Basilikon Doron* (1603), cited by Lang, *op. cit.* Vol. 2, pp. 438-9.

6. T.I. Rae, *Scotland in the Time of Shakespeare* (Cornell Univ. Press, 1965), p. 21.

7. A. Peterkin, ed., *"The Booke of the Universall Kirk of Scotland"* (Edinburgh, 1838), pp. 434-5.

8. William Ferguson, *Scotland's Relations with England: a Survey to 1707* (Edinburgh, 1977), p. 120.

9. Rae, *op. cit.*, p. 30; Anon. (?James Myles), *Chapters in the Life of a Dundee Factory Boy* (Dundee, 1887), p. 27.

10. J.M. Reid, *Kirk and Nation. The Story of the Reformed Church of Scotland* (London, 1960), pp. 68-9.

11. Gordon Donaldson, *Scotland, the Making of the Kingdom, James V - James VII* (1965; Edinburgh edn., 1978), pp. 315-6.

12. Reid, *op. cit.*, p. 75.

13. David Stevenson, *The Scottish Revolution 1637-1644. The Triumph of the Covenanters* (Newton Abbot, 1973), pp. 224-6.

14. *Ibid.*, p. 200.

15. James Grant, *Old and New Edinburgh* (London, n.d.), Vol. 3, p. 90.

16. Lang, *op. cit.*, Vol. 3, p. 204.

17. Ferguson, *op. cit.*, p. 138. Cf. Sir R. Coupland, *Welsh and Scottish Nationalism* (London, 1954), pp. 88-90.

18. C.H. Firth, ed., *Scotland and the Commonwealth (1651-53)* (Edinburgh, 1895), pp. 339-40. (a report from Dundee, 14 Nov. 1651).

19. *Ibid.*, pp. 347-8.

20. Ibid., p. lii.

21. W. Notestein, *The Scot in History* (London, 1946), p. 145.

22. Anon. (Alexander Shields), *A Hind let loose, or An Historical Representation of the Testimonies of the Church of Scotland* (s.l., 1687), p. 97.

23. Donaldson, *op. cit.*, p. 365. Cf. W.L. Mathieson, *Scotland the Union. A History of Scotland from 1695 to 1747* (Glasgow, 1905), pp. 16-18.

24. Reid, *op. cit.*, p. 76.

25. Anon. (Sir James Stewart), *Jus Populi Vindicatum, or The People's Right, to defend themselves and their Covenanted Religion, vindicated* (s.l., 1669), pp. 3-4.

26. *Ibid.*, p. 5.

27. Firth, *op. cit.*, pp. 321-2.

28. W. Thompson, "From Reformation to Union", in T. Dickson, ed., *Scottish Capitalism* (London, 1980), p. 75. See also the same writer's "The Kirk and the Cameronians", in M. Cornforth, ed., *Rebels and their Causes* (London, 1978).

29. J.K. Hewison, *The Covenanters. A History of the Church in Scotland from the Reformation to the Revolution* (Glasgow, 1908), Vol. 2, p. 119.

30. Donaldson, *op. cit.,* p. 338.

31. A.S. Morton, *Galloway and the Covenanters* (Paisley, 1914), p. 79.

32. Donaldson, *op. cit.,* p. 317.

33. For details of these and other magnates, see Sir R. Douglas, *The Scottish Peerage,* ed. Sir J.B. Paul. Much scattered information will be found in P.H. M'Kerlie, *History of the Lands and their Owners in Galloway,* 5 vols. (Edinburgh, 1870-79). On some lurid episodes of the Cassilis past, see C.H. Dick, *Highways and Byways in Galloway and Carricwk* (London, 1916), chap. 27.

34. I.B. Cowan, *The Scottish Covenanters 1660-1688* (London, 1976), p. 93.

35. Morton, *op. cit.,* pp. 199-200.

36. *Ibid.,* p. 118-9.

37. *Ibid.,* p. 173.

38. *Ibid.,* p. 197.

39. Donaldson, *op. cit.,* pp. 367-8.

40. James Barr, *The Scottish Covenanters* (Glasgow, 1946), p. 173.

41. Cowan, *op. cit.,* p. 157.

42. Some lists are given by Morton, *op. cit.,* pp. 223 ff.; cf. Barr, *op. cit.,* p. 228.

43. P. 144; cf. pp. 471-2, etc.

44. *Jus Populi* runs to 472 pages, *A Hind* to 742.

45. *Jus Populi,* p. 438.

46. Alexander Webster, *Theology in Scotland* (London, 1915), p. 95.

47. Notestein, *op. cit.,* pp. 158-9.

48. *Ibid.,* pp. 159-60.

49. Morton, *op. cit.,* p. 272. Nine witches were strangled and burned at Dumfries in 1659; Dick, *op. cit.,* p. 3. On witches in Covenanting areas and in Scottish Calvinist thinking, see Christiana Larner, *Enemies of God. The Witch-hunt in Scotland* (London, 1981), pp. 32, 163 ff., 172, 199, etc.

50. D. Frew, *The Parish of Urr... A History* (Dalbeattie, 1909), pp. 30-1.

51. Lang, *op. cit.,* Vol. 3, pp. 418-9.

52. Morton, *op. cit.,* p. 108.

53. *Ibid.,* pp. 176-7, 185.

54. *Ibid.,* p. 148.

55. "The Country of the Camisards", in *Travels with a Donkey* (1879). See also Charles Tylor, *The Camisards* (London, 1893).

56. James Fergusson, *John Fergusson 1727-1750* (London, 1948), p. 99.

57. Angus Calder, *Revolutionary Empire* (London, 1981), p. 278.

58. Hewison, *op. cit.,* Vol. 2, p. 327.

59. Sir Herbert Maxwell, ed., *The Lowland Scots Regiments* (Glasgow, 1918), pp. 243-4.

60. Handley, *op. cit.,* p. 199.

61. *Ibid.,* p. 200n.

62. James Murray, *Life in Scotland a Hundred Years Ago* (Paisley, 1900), pp. 64-7.

63. Morton, *op. cit.,* pp. 444-5. He relates the story without seeing any incongruity in it.

64. Donaldson, *op. cit.,* p. 321.

65. K. Burgess, "Scotland and the First British Empire, 1707-1770s", in Dickson, *op. cit.,* p. 119.

66. T. Dickson and T. Clarke, "The Making of a Class Society", *ibid.,* p. 147; Cowan, pp. 156-7. On the Scottish agrarian background see also T.M. Devine and D. Dickson, eds., *Ireland and Scotland 1600-1850* (Edinburgh, 1983), chs. 3, 8, 13, 19; on religion and the economy, ch. 17.

67. Nichol, *op. cit.,* p. xxix.

68. Rev. A. O'Callaghan, *The Bible Society against the Church and State* (London, 1817), pp. 8-9.

69. Murray, *op. cit.,* pp. 91-2. Dumfriesshire, however, was regarded in 1797 as a hearth of radicalism, and there was a tumult at Wigtown: S. Mullay, *Scotland's Forgotten Massacre* (Edinburgh, 1979), pp. 11, 48.

70. David Daiches, *The Paradox of Scottish Culture. The Eighteenth-Century Experience* (London, 1964), p. 7.

71. D.H. Caldwell, *The Scottish Armoury* (Edinburgh, 1979), p. 32.

72. *Our Zion; or, Presbyterian Popery, By Ane of That Ilk* (Edinburgh, 1840), p. 9.

73. Morton, *op. cit.,* pp. 308-9. Fred Kaplan, discussing Carlyle's early religious environment, notes that "The tradition of the Covenanters was strong in Annandale" *(Thomas Carlyle. A Biography* [ Cambridge, 1983 ], p. 21). In 1844 Lord Cockburn commented on the respect still felt for their memory *(Circuit Journeys,* ed. Kelso, 1983, p. 157).

74. W.F. Douglas, "The Recusant's Concealment Discovered".

75. *Noctes Ambrosianae,* Dec. 1829.

76. W.E. Aytoun, *Stories and Verse,* ed. W.L. Renwick (Edinburgh, 1964), p. 29 (1845).

77. Barr, *op. cit.,* p. 207.

78. Morton *op. cit.,* pp. 6, 21.

79. Notestein, *op. cit.,* p. 166.

80. Cited by Hewison, *op. cit.,* Vol. 2, p. 542.

81. Hewison, *op. cit.,* vol. 2, p. 484.

Ellen Meiksins Wood

# THE STATE AND POPULAR SOVEREIGNTY IN FRENCH POLITICAL THOUGHT: A GENEALOGY OF ROUSSEAU'S "GENERAL WILL"

Rousseau's political thought--like that of most political thinkers--has suffered from a tendency to treat his ideas without concern for the real historical issues to which they were addressed and without consideration of the specific forms in which these issues were conventionally contested. When Rousseau's work is not considered in complete abstraction from actual political conflicts (as it is, for example, when his writings are treated as simply the neurotic outpourings of an "authoritarian personality"), or as a contribution to timeless debates about the "perennial questions" of politics, it is likely to be judged, at least implicitly, by the standards of political controversies belonging to a different historical "problematic", in particular an English one.

To understand Rousseau's *answers* we must first know the questions he was addressing; and to know the questions is to understand them not simply as if Rousseau posed them idiosyncratically to himself but as an historically constituted set of problems. It will be argued in what follows that French political discourse was long dominated by two essential historical problems, which never figured centrally in English history: a divided polity which could not overcome the political "parcellization" and corporate fragmentation of its feudal past; and a state conceived as a kind of private property, a resource for princes and office-holders, an instrument for extracting what might be called a form of rent from direct producers, specifically peasants, by means of taxation. The set of problems associated with this political configuration shaped the political thought of both supporters and critics of royal absolutism and produced a "tradition of discourse" the contours of which are clearly visible in the work of Rousseau.

*I*

The historical configuration of political questions that confronted Rousseau in eighteenth-century France and the conceptual instruments, the particular "traditions of discourse," that had evolved to deal with them, can be traced back at least as far as the centralization of the feudal monarchy and its gradual consolidation into an "absolutist state." The divergences between French and English patterns of feudal centralization, the different structures of class forces that underlay these divergent paths of state-formation, can be discerned not only in the future development of class and state in the two countries but also correspondingly in their "traditions of discourse" about class and state.[2] In France, the monarchy grew out of competing feudal powers and the ascendancy of one such power "over and against others," while in England, the crown was "at all times closely connected with the self-centralization of the feudal class as a whole."[3]

The French mode of feudal centralization produced a monarchy that never quite overcame the particularisms and "parcellized" power of its feudal origins, always contending with -- and yet, in many ways dependent upon -- the survival of seigneurial powers, privileges, and exemptions, as well as a variety of corporate institutions, local liberties, and competing jurisdictions. This mode of centralization was reflected in the character of French representative institutions — for example, in the corporate and regional fragmentation of the Estates, in sharp contrast to the unitary and national organization of the Engish Parliament. At the same time, the monarchy established a strong apparatus of centralized state power. The power of this state derived not only from the need of the feudal ruling class for improved instruments of political administration and military coercion to support its private powers of surplus-extraction and maintain order, but also from the new system of *centralized* surplus-extraction which it made available in the form of state *office*, as well as the opportunities it offered for plunder, internal and external, through war.

This development of the French state as a centralized instrument of private appropriation, an extension of feudal "extra-economic" surplus-extraction, defines many of its essential characteristics: the monarchy's reliance on the proliferation and distribution of offices, not only to maintain fiscal solvency by the sale of offices but to constitute its power-base; the dependence of the propertied classes on the state, not only as a means of enforcing its private powers of appropriation but as a private resource in its own right; the particular salience this gave to the problem of taxation -- and exemptions from it -- both for those who benefitted from them and for those who bore the burden.

This tax-office structure implied complex and ambiguous relations between the state and various classes. The state served as a source -- direct or indirect -- of private income for members of the landed classes, while at the same time competing with them for the same peasant-produced surplus; the bourgeoisie stood to gain from the proliferation and venalization of offices, which might give them access to power and a lucrative resource, and yet also suffered from the resulting increases in the burden of taxation; and the peasantry, the major source of tax revenue and the social base on which the whole tax-office structure rested, had to be preserved by the monarchy from destruction by rent-hungry landlords in order to be squeezed by a tax-hungry state. The role of the state as a private resource and the consequent structure of social relations based on the tax-office nexus remained a central theme of French political life in theory and practice, up to and beyond the Revolution, and long continued to determine the issues and shape the contours of political discourse.

The English state generated a different set of problems. While feudal central-ization here too had the function of enhancing the powers of "extra-economic" surplus extraction, English landed proprietors were able more successfully to develop private and increasingly "economic" means of extraction -- with the coercive support of the state -- and never came to rely so much on the state as a direct resource. The state also remained largely free of fragmentation inherited from feudal corporate institutions, regional privileges, and politically autonomous urban com-munes. A strong centralized state thus coexisted with -- indeed rested upon -- a strong propertied class much less fragmented than the French. Royal taxation never played the same role for the English propertied classes that it did for the French; the state never had the same reasons for either squeezing or protecting the peasantry as did the French absolutist state; and the English peasantry duly succumbed to larger landed proprietors. Thus, the relations among classes, and between class and state, differed considerably from the French, as did -- necessarily -- the issues contested among them.

Each form of state and class-rule naturally generated its own characteristic grievances, provoked its own resistances, and erected its own defenses. The relative importance of different modes of surplus extraction and accumulation, and the varying functions of the state in furthering or hindering them, played a central role in establishing the terms of struggle. English property owners, when seeking to protect and augment their increasingly "economic" means of appropriation, might struggle to defend their private rights of property against incursions by the crown, to establish the supremacy of Parliament as an association of property-holders, to thwart the consolidation of an absolutist monarchy by establishing "limited government," while at the same time staving off threats from below. The propertied classes of France, who confronted the state both as a competitor for surplus-product and as a means of access to it, contended over taxation, the proliferation of offices and the means of distributing them, often struggling less to limit the state than to acquire property in it or prevent others from doing so. The English commoner, in defense against the landlord's efforts to augment his economic powers of extraction, struggled against the enclosure of common and waste land. The French peasant, more oppressed by "political" forms of extraction, rebelled against royal taxation and seigneurial privilege. Englishmen asserted their individual rights; Frenchmen defended their corporate and regional privileges.

Many of the essential qualities of the French political "problematic" can be summed up by contrasting the English concern with the relation between the state and private property and the French concern with the state *as* private property. French anti-absolutism was not simply a matter of resistance to political tyranny but also an attack on the state as, so to speak, a private racket, a "semi-institutionalized system of extortion and embezzlement."[4] Popular resistance, too, often focused on exploitation by the state. Thus, for example, exploitation by means of direct seigneurial exactions might take second place to taxation (or the tax-exemptions of others) as an object of grievance, just as the landlord might be less concerned about losing economic powers such as the right of enclosure than about relinquishing tax-exemptions and political privileges.[5]

French political thought, then, was preoccupied with a complex of problems at the centre of which stood a fragmented polity consisting of many particularisms whose unifying principle was yet another particularistic power, yet another proprietary interest: the monarchical state and its growing administrative and fiscal apparatus conceived, if not as a means of production, certainly as a means of appropriation.

In absolutist political thought itself, the justification of monarchy -- especially its right to distribute offices and impose taxes -- often took the form of claims for its generality against the partiality and particularity of other elements in society. The king embodied the *public* aspect of the state as against the private character of his subjects. Such arguments suggested that a single, superior *will* was required to bind together the particular interests in the polity and produce a common good.[6] Arguments against absolutism voiced concern not only with the particularisms that divided the polity but also with the particularity of the state apparatus itself and the consequences of its use as private property — the proliferation of unnecessary offices, the corruption of administration, the tax burden. Even here, however, the public interest or common good might be presented as an emanation of a unifying will or mind; though now, the unifying, generalizing will of the monarch, who was "particular and single," was replaced by the collective will of the public council, "one mind compounded out of many."[7]

The contrast with England is striking. It is, of course, often argued that England never experienced absolutism at all, or at least that English absolutism was short-circuited. If the tax-office structure so characteristic of French absolutism and associated with the evolution of the state as a mode of appropriation is regarded as an essential characteristic, then English absolutism hardly existed — and in this respect, the problem of the state as private property hardly arose. It is no doubt significant that only two thinkers have entered the canon of English political thought as spokesmen for royal absolutism, Hobbes and Filmer; and of these only Hobbes is acknowledged as one of the "greats". Hobbes stands out, however, not simply because absolutist thinkers are relatively rare in England and great ones even more so, but because he alone among major English theorists regards an indivisible sovereign power as the essential condition of the polity's very existence, without which civil society itself would dissolve. This is an idea that is much less at home in England that in "parcellized" France. Indeed, the concept of sovereignty itself is a matter of little concern to early modern English thinkers. Given the long years spent by Hobbes in France and his close association with French thinkers, it is tempting to say that he is precisely the exception that proves the rule.

## *II*

A look at some landmarks in the development of French political thought, from a particularly seminal period in the late sixteenth and early seventeenth centuries, will serve to illustrate how the terms of confrontation, of resistance and defense, were established. The latter half of the sixteenth century was a period of virtual civil war in France. The Reformation, the spread of Protestantism, the Wars of Religion, followed by the decline of the Huguenots and the rise of the Catholic League, brought to a head underlying social conflicts and provided ideological vehicles for conducting battles over taxation and tithes, privileges and exemptions, the powers of local patrician oligarchies, and royal absolutism itself. While the objects and intensity of struggle, as well as the nature and scope of social alliances, varied according to regional differences and variations in local privileges, parts of the country saw the outbreak of violent peasant protests and sometimes regional revolts in which peasants were allied with urban classes. Such outbreaks might begin as revolts against taxation and tithes and end as attacks on the whole system of power and privilege.[8]

Not surprisingly, the period was rich in ideological expressions at every level of sophistication — the *cahiers,* the Huguenot resistance tracts, the political philosophy of Bodin. The degree to which even classics of political philosophy were generated by an engagement with immediate struggles and a dialogue not only with great thinkers of the past but with political actors and the common people of the present -- the complex interplay between what George Rudé has called "inherent" and "derived" ideology[9] -- is nowhere more strikingly manifested than in the continuities among these various levels of discourse.

An example drawn from the *cahiers* of the period, belonging to a province that experienced one of the country's bloodiest regional revolts in 1579-80, will indicate the points of contact between the "discourse" of popular protest and the more exalted idiom of political philosophy.[10] Jean de Bourg, archepiscopal judge of Vienne, representative of the third estate to the provincial Estates and Estates General, wrote the petition of grievances for the Dauphiné third estate to be presented at the Estates General at Blois in 1576. He drew on philosophical principles and the classics of antiquity to support complaints and proposals for reform typical of his estate. The list of grievances he rehearsed focused on the privileges of the other two estates, especially their exemptions from taxation; the proliferation of useless offices with high salaries, secular and ecclesiastical; the tax burden imposed on the common people; and the inequitable political structure which gave the advantage of power to the privileged estates, so that they could manipulate the fiscal system for their own gain at the expense of the third estate. To these complaints -- shared by the bourgeois, craftsmen, and peasants -- he added several of special concern to his own class, the urban bourgeoisie, and a few grievances of particular interest to the peasantry.

De Bourg's proposals for resolving these grievances included measures to strengthen the third estate, relieving its tax burden, augmenting its political powers in office and in the assemblies of Estates, and increasing the role of regional representative institutions. There were also suggestions in which the bourgeoisie's grievances against local oligarchies and seigneurial privilege converged with peasant complaints about rural administration. It is significant that these were met in part by proposals for restoring certain powers of local administration to the king in order to diminish the provincial powers of seigneurs, even though de Bourg pressed at the same time for reductions in the royal bureaucracy in order to reduce the burden of taxation.

De Bourg adduced philosophical arguments to support these proposals for reform. In particular, he developed a doctrine of *corporate equality*. He drew, for example, on Plato's concept of justice and especially Cicero's conception of a natural order based on a harmonious balance among the various social orders, to define a principle of social equality, not among individuals but among the three estates as corporate entities, and also (in particular, for purposes of tax assessment) among regions and cities.

The defense of a corporate balance among estates, especially with regard to taxation, based on the organic unity and harmony of the social order, remained the central focus of protest as voiced by de Bourg's successors, the provincial lawyers who continued to do battle for the third estate in this region after the period of bloody revolt. Attacking the tax exemptions of the nobility, they invoked various organic metaphors, the mystical body of the state, or the musical metaphor of harmonious proportion so popular among the ancients from Pythagoras to Plato and Aristotle, in order to establish the fundamental unity of the state and the interdependence of its parts. By these means they sought to demonstrate the nobility's duty to the social whole and the essential function of the third estate in sustaining the body politic.

These protestors were not, however, democrats. Men of substance, they represented essentially the interests of the urban bourgeoisie. The equality for which they strove was a corporate equality in which they would predominate over lesser members of their corporation, and a *proportionate* equality, an equality in difference, which acknowledged the hierarchic structure of the social whole. "We ... are not for government by the people nor for equality, as the Nobles falsely claim," maintained Claude Delagrange in 1599. "But our privileges are equal to [theirs].[11] In other words, this was not so much an attack on the system of privilege, such as peasants or artisans might have wished, as it was a demand for access to it. "The Third Estate needs the rules of harmonics, not arithmetic," writes Antoine Rambaud, echoing Jean Bodin. "It does not want to make law of equality.... It wants equal justice. But it does not want equal justice that follows arithmetic, with all things equal in weight and form. It wants the harmonic balance made up of different parts. Order and justice founded on proportional and harmonic equality, blending into one, are necessary to the survival of the State."[12]

What makes these arguments especially significant from our point of view is that these conceptions of the state as a "body," an organic unity, tended to be accompanied by a notion of a public or common good which was more than simply the sum of its parts, a principle of *unity* over and against the particularities comprising the body politic. Needless to say, the object of invoking this common good was to demonstrate that the nobility must subordinate its particular interests and privileges to the interests of the whole: "The Nobles use the privileges of the provinces as if they were theirs alone," complained Jean Vincent in 1598. "The Nobles think they are born only for themselves. But according to Pericles as quoted by Thucydides, one should love the public good above all [and] ... consider oneself born not for the self but for the world."[13]

For these bourgeois and far from radical protestors, the unity of the state, the "One" to which the "Multiple" must be subordinated, was embodied in the person of the king, the "Father of the Common Welfare," as Vincent called him.[14] "Aspiring to unity," explained Rambaud, "does not mean making everything equal. Unity in music is nothing other than Monarchy in a State."[15] It is not surprising that the lawyers should adopt this view, since the third estate might actually stand to gain from the appropriation of some (though not their own) corporate powers by the monarch. The corporate egalitarianism of these provincial lawyers, therefore, was based on a view of society in which the unity of the state and the "harmonious" balance of its constituent parts were expressed in and maintained by the sovereign power of the king. In this, they seem to have been true disciples of Bodin.

In contrast, outright resistance to royal absolutism was expressed by the Huguenot constitutionalists. They not only attacked the system of privilege and patronage, fiscal and administrative corruption, but placed the blame squarely on the monarchy itself, with its bureaucratic apparatus in which royal office, including the office of king, was conceived as private property. The solution, then, was to augment the powers of other public institutions, notably the Estates; and the case for these "public councils" was formulated as a defense of the "people's" inalienable right to resist.

The Huguenot constitutionalists were, however, no more (and, perhaps, in certain senses less) democrats than were the more moderate constitutionalists who still looked to the monarchy for relief. In some respects, in fact, the doctrine of resistance had more to recommend it to elements of the nobility who sought to entrench their corporate powers against an encroaching sovereign monarchy. It is not surprising that a substantial number of Huguenots and some of their leading spokesmen came from the ranks of the lesser, provincial nobility, precisely that section of the landed classes that had least to gain and most to lose from the growth of a strongly centralized appropriating monarchy. These interests are strikingly visible in the resistance tracts.

Again, the argument is based on a corporate and hierarchical conception of society; and the constitutionalists are at great pains to stress that the right of resistance belongs to the "people" not as private individuals but as properly constituted authorities, magistrates, and corporate bodies: the assemblies of estates, or towns and districts in the persons of their officials.[16] Thus, *rights* are not individual but corporate, and they reside not in ordinary citizens but in the notables who preside over them — the magistrates of towns, *and* (in keeping with the feudal interests of the nobility) the dukes, marquises, counts, and barons who "constitute a part of the kingdom" and are established as "guardians...for the several regions."[17] Indeed, in this argument -- where the issue is not simply an appeal to the monarch to correct the imbalances among estates but a call to revolt against the monarch himself -- the egalitarian aspect of the corporatist argument recedes and its function as a *limitation* on popular rights comes to the fore at the very moment that the "people's" rights are being so eloquently asserted.

The right of resistance is based on the principle that it is the "people" who constitute the king and not the reverse. In order to make this point, the Huguenot resistance movement transforms the familiar idea of a unity in multiplicity, a common good emanating from a single unitary will, which others had used to justify the power of the king. Significantly, they do not abandon the idea, or even suggest -- as the English were to do -- a definition of the common good as a public interest whose substance consists merely of private interests and rights. Instead, they simply transfer the source of the unifying will from the monarch to the "public councils" of the people. Much of their argument rests on contrasting the private, particular character of the king to the public, universal character of the "people" embodied in their officers and councils, "one mind compounded out of many." The king as a person is "particular and single";[18] the majesty of his office, its public character, derives from the people.

The Huguenot constitutionalists thus in effect responded in kind to the advocates of royal power, adopting important aspects of their "discourse"; and they did so because this idiom was well-suited to deal with their grievances in a state conceived as private property. In particular, it provided useful language with which to assert the authority of the Estates to control the two major "public" functions which lay at the heart of many grievances, the apportionment of taxes and the distribution of offices. While the "particular and single" king, they argued, can dispose of his own private treasure at will and appoint his own personal counsellors, a careful distinction must be made between his private patrimony and that of the *kingdom,* the public treasury and public offices which are rightfully the province of the "elders and experienced statesmen" who constitute the collective "mind" of the kingdom.[19]

The whole issue is summed up in the question: "Is the King the Owner of the Kingdom?" More specifically, "Does the king, then, have private property in the royal, or public, patrimony?"[20] The answer, of course, is no. And: "Let me ask, furthermore, whether royal status is a possession or an office *(functio).* If it is a possession, then is it not at least a form of possession whereby the people, who conferred it, retain the proprietary right?"[21] As for the power of taxation, since taxes are intended for "public purposes" -- specifically the conduct of war -- it cannot be the province of the king any more than the public domain is his private property. "To guarantee that taxes will be used for public purposes," they must be authorized by the Estates, on the principle that the people "taken collectively... are properly the owners of the kingdom"[22] and their officers, as it were taken collectively, the only truly public being.

Nothing symbolizes more clearly the difference between French and English "problematics" than this defense of representative institutions such as the assembled Estates on the grounds that they embody the public "mind" as against the private will of the king, in contrast to the typically English justification of Parliament on the grounds that it represents private interests against an encroaching public power. In a sense, the relation between the crown and the "people" in Parliament reverses this view of the relation between the king and the Estates. In one case, the people assert their private rights and interests against encroachment by the public sphere embodied in the state; in the other, the people assert their corporate rights and the public interest against the private, particular character of the state; in one case, the struggle is to rescue from the public sphere that which is rightfully private, in the other it is to render truly public that which has been wrongfully treated as private.

At a different level of discourse, Jean Bodin addressed himself to the same constellation of problems. His theory of sovereignty drew together several issues that were being contested in the struggles of the sixteenth century. The standpoint from which he sought to resolve these issues has much in common with that of our legal spokesmen for the third estate — and, indeed, Bodin was himself a lawyer and representative of the third estate for Vermandois at the Estates General of Blois in 1576. It is undoubtedly true that, when he wrote the *Six Books of the Commonwealth* in which his famous theory of sovereignty appeared, he was motivated in part by the desire to assert the sovereignty of the king against the dangers of rebellion and civil strife most dramatically embodied in the Huguenot resistance movement;[23] but he also wanted to reform the structure of the state, the system of office, the inequitable distribution of burdens created by the system of privilege and exemptions. Despite his advocacy of an absolute sovereign power vested in the king, he clearly believed in enhancing the role of the Estates General, insisting, for example, that no tax could be levied without consent of the Estates. Indeed, his theory of sovereignty is not so distant from the views of those provincial lawyers who relied on the monarchy to maintain unity in a fragmented polity and to correct the social imbalance among its corporate constituents, in part by appropriating to itself the feudal prerogatives of the privileged estates.

Bodin insists that *sovereignty* implies not only supreme but absolute and *indivisible* power, and rejects any arguments (like those of the Huguenot constitutionalists) that might suggest divided "sovereignty" and limited government. The idea of indivisible sovereignty has been described in an important study of Bodin as an error, an aberration, a failure of ingenuity, an idea "less adaptable" to the conditions of France; and it has been suggested that this alleged departure from the mainstream, and even from his own earlier work, was Bodin's reaction to the threat of rebellion.[24] It can, however, be argued that whatever logical inconsistencies there may be in Bodin's notion of indivisible sovereignty, it is addressed precisely to the conditions of France, and, for all its innovations, in terms not at all foreign to his contemporaries. Bodin's concern in constructing his theory of sovereignty was not simply to stave off rebellion of the Huguenot type but to deal with the underlying structural problems inherent in the French state and its political "parcellization." Whether he wanted to curtail the powers of the traditional nobility on behalf of the third estate or to strengthen the ruling class in spite of itself by bringing order to the anarchy of competing jurisdictions, he intended to transfer their particularistic, quasi-feudal powers to the monarchy, denying that noble prerogatives and offices belonged to their possessors by proprietary right (hereditary or otherwise) and rendering them dependent upon sovereign authority. The issue at stake, moreover, was not simply the location of supreme and ultimate power, but also the location of *unity,* the source of integration in a system of regional and corporate fragmentation: "...a commonwealth without a sovereign power to unite all its several members, whether families, colleges, or corporate bodies, is not a true commonwealth. It is neither the town nor its inhabitants that makes a city-state, but their union under a sovereign ruler...".[25]

Bodin's conception of absolute sovereignty, then, represents in some respects an attack on feudal remnants, but it also presupposes a polity still organized on feudal, corporatist principles. It is in this light that his commitment to *indivisible* power must be understood. For representative institutions to share "sovereignty" with the king would aggravate precisely that corporate fragmentation and political parcellization which Bodin's sovereign power was designed to overcome. He did not, however, envisage a society organized in a fundamentally different way, a society, like England, less divided into corporate fragments and integrated into a unitary state with a unitary representative body, like the English Parliament. Indeed, in some respects his argument was designed to strengthen certain corporate principles, and he regarded corporations as fundamental to the maintenance of social ties. It was the function of sovereign power to integrate and harmonize these necessary particularities.

The notion of divided "sovereignty" and limited government, it can be argued, could be fully developed only in a polity that was not itself essentially divided and parcellized. It required a state which, like England, had achieved "feudal centralization" with a relatively unified nobility, without territorial potentates like those of the Continent, with towns that lacked the political autonomy of Continental urban Communes, and with unitary representative institutions for the ruling class, assemblies that were national in extent and represented a community of property-holders not internally divided by region and estate.[26] Perhaps the unity of the English state, reflected in Parliament, made "divided sovereignty" less threatening and more practicable; or perhaps the relative unity and strength of the ruling class made it inevitable. At any rate, the English Parliament quite early acquired legislative powers -- at least the negative power to check the legislative activity of the king -- thereby, in effect, dividing between king and Parliament the very power which for Bodin constitutes *sovereignty*. In contrast, the French monarchy, whose power rested in part on the regional fragmentation of the state and the "parcellized" power of the nobility, remained largely free of limitation by representative bodies in this respect — if not in other respects, such as fiscal powers. In short, Bodin's concept of sovereignty reflects precisely the historical conditions of France.

At the heart of Bodin's political theory, then, is a tension between a still feudal, corporatist, and fragmented social order and a centralized sovereign state, a tension characteristic of his time and place. The ruling class was still "feudal" to the extent that its mode of exploitation represented a fusion of economic and political power, still rooted in the "parcellization" of the state. The centralizing state itself was feudal in conception in the sense that the tax-office structure simply centralized or "displaced upwards" this fusion of political and economic power in a system that Boris Porshnev summed up in his characterization of absolutist taxation as "centralized feudal rent";[27] and yet the state was at the same time *anti*-feudal in its attack on the parcellization of political power. This tension is captured perfectly in the economic doctrines of the period, often called "mercantilist," to which Bodin himself contributed. Like the political theory of Bodin, these economic doctrines depend upon both the maintenance of certain corporate powers, privileges, and liberties, and on their transcendence by a powerful monarchy.

It is in this context that Bodin draws an analogy between the state and the household, an analogy which, as we shall see, has important implications for Rousseau. The family, he suggests, is the origin of the state and its basic constituent unit; and household management is the model of good government.[28] In both cases the purpose of management is the "acquisition of goods," the provision and prosperity of the household or state (as a condition, of course, for the good life in a higher sense); and this object is best achieved under the supreme authority of a single head — the father in one case, the king in the other.

The household/state analogy as formulated by Bodin, then, represents a state dominated by an absolute ruler who, in promoting the "acquisition of goods" and increasing the prosperity of the state, guides and encourages the public "economy", just as the father manages the household. Furthermore, since like the family the unity of the state should be grounded in concord and "love," it is the task of the state management to reconcile and bind together the constituent parts of the polity by creating a balance based on "harmonic" justice. In short, the presupposition of the analogy is an absolutist monarchy which presides over a "mercantilist" economy while it respects and protects the private property and (selectively?) the corporate liberties of its subjects.[29]

This brief survey of a particularly fruitful episode in the development of French political thought, during an especially turbulent period in French history, gives some indication of the major issues at stake and the terms in which these issues were joined. The "parcellization" of political power in France, the survival of feudal prerogatives and privileges, their extension into new forms of patronage and proprietary offices, the persistence of regional and corporate particularisms, whether viewed from the perspective of the monarchy or the "people," were often confronted theoretically by the notion of a single unifying mind or will which would bind them together. Even in radical attacks on royal absolutism, the public will of the state was not generally opposed, as in England, by asserting private interests or individual rights against it, or by redefining the common good as a public interest essentially constituted by private interests, in order to counter the public claims of a crown encroaching upon private rights.[30] Instead, the public character of the absolutist state itself was questioned and the location of the public will was shifted to representative institutions, the officers of the "people," "intermediate bodies." And even where the common good was conceived as emerging from a harmony of private interests, the state -- indeed, the monarchy -- tended to appear as the necessary agent of harmony, the unifying will that would integrate corporate particularities and partial interests. The specific threats posed by the state itself were thus met not so much by attempts to defend the "private" sphere from encroachment by the "public," as by proposals for transforming the "private" state into a truly public thing.

*III*

If these themes survived to appear in the political thought of Rousseau, it is not simply because of the inertial pull exerted by an abstract "tradition of discourse" but because of a fundamental continuity in the issues of social conflict. The reformers of the eighteenth century were still addressing themselves to the evils of the proprietary state, patronage, excessive taxation, venal offices — though, as the state long continued to be a major resource, even beyond the Revolution and the Napoleonic state, complaints may often have been directed less at the inherent evils of the state as an instrument of appropriation than at the inequalities of opportunity blocking access to its fruits. The lack of legal, administrative, and economic unity continued to be a nuisance, not least to those engaged in trade. Social critics decried the oppression of the peasantry imposed by a corrupt court, an inflated royal bureau-cracy, and an exploitative system of taxation which served not only public purposes but private gain. In these grievances and proposals for reform, the state generally took centre stage, both as the object of complaint and as the proposed agent of reform, often in the same breath; and reformers often presented their cases in the form of claims for the *public* sphere against the essentially *private* character of the feudal principles still embodied in the state and the system of privilege.[31]

It is against this background that Rousseau's political theory must be understood. The core of his political thought and many of its key concepts -- the "general will," the distinction between "government" and "sovereignty" -- received their first elaboration in the essay on "Political Economy"; and in this work written for the *Encyclopédie* probably with the intent, like many other contributions, of commenting critically on contemporary institutions, we may find a means of tracing the central ideas of his political theory as a whole to their foundations in history and in live social struggles.

A wealth of historical meaning is contained in the idea of "political economy" itself. In its original French usage--referring to the management of national resources to increase the nation's prosperity--it implies an analogy between the house-hold or family and the state (the Greek *oikos* and *polis*). While the state economy is designated *political* to distinguish its generality and its public character from the particularity and the private nature of the domestic economy, the distinction *presupposes* a significant similarity between the art of state management and "oikonomia", the art of household management. In other words, the concept of "political economy" is based on precisely the kind of analogy between household and state which figures so prominently in the works of Bodin and Montchrétien, with all the historical presuppositions of that analogy. It is this analogy -- and the historical conditions for which it stands--that Rousseau questions in the article on Political Economy; and it is in this context that the "general will" appears.

The "general will" is usually treated by commentators -- whether hostile or sympathetic to Rousseau -- as simply a principle governing the conduct of *citizens*. In the "Political Economy", however, Rousseau's general will has a different object. Here, Rousseau's argument is, in the first instance, directed not at the individual citizen but at the "magistrate" or rulers. His purpose in attacking the household/ state analogy is to demonstrate that the magistrate cannot legitimately act in accordance with principles appropriate to the head of a household. "The principal object of the efforts of the whole house," argues Rousseau, "is to conserve and increase the patrimony of the father...."[32] This principle of private, domestic "economy", if applied to the state -- treating the state as a means of increasing the "patrimony" of the magistrate -- is fatal to the public interest. The magistrate must follow "no other rule but public reason, which is the law."[33] The general will is the uniquely public principle which should regulate the governance of the "political economy."

At this stage in Rousseau's argument, then, the concept of the general will represents an attempt to define the state as a truly *public* thing, not a form of private property, and to locate the legitimacy of government in its adherence to the public will and interests of the people and not the private will and interests of the magistrate. The household/state analogy--in which the state is treated, in effect, as a private estate -- for Rousseau simply confirms the reality of the French state and the use of public office, including the office of king, as private property. His insistence on a completely different principle to regulate the state -- opposed to the private motivations of household management, with its goal of increasing the patrimony of the master -- is thus directed against the theory and practice of French absolutism.[34]

Having criticized the analogy on which the notion of "political economy" is based, he must then go on to redefine "political economy" itself accordingly, in keeping with the uniquely public purpose of the state. It is here that he introduces the distinction between sovereignty, the supreme legislative power, and government or "public economy," which merely executes the will of the sovereign, though the theory of sovereignty is left to be developed in the *Social Contract.*[35] Rousseau was not the first to draw a distinction between sovereignty and government. Significantly, the credit for this distinction must go to Bodin. The differences between Bodin and Rousseau on this score, however, are even more striking than the similarities. Bodin distinguishes between the form of state, based on the location of sovereignty, and the form of government, based on the principle by which lands, offices, and honours are distributed — so that a monarchy, for example, can be governed aristocratically or democratically, according to how the sovereign monarch chooses to grant honours and preferments. His purpose is clearly to demonstrate that, however powers and offices may be distributed, these powers are ultimately vested in the sovereign and that it is in effect by the will of the sovereign that they are so distributed. The powers of officeholders or nobles are not held by proprietary right but by virtue of delegation from the sovereign — ideally, the sovereign in the person of a monarch. In this respect, the distinction between state and government, and the implied distinction between the sovereign legislative power and the subordinate power of execution, serve to reinforce Bodin's attack on feudal prerogatives and baronial anarchy, as well as on any other proprietary claims to political power apart from those of the sovereign. This feudal "parcellization" of power, rather than "divided sovereignty" in the English parliamentary sense, is, again, the main object of his insistence on the indivisibility of sovereignty. His practical object in distinguishing the form of government from the form of state, therefore, is to sustain and to enhance the authority of the monarchy against other particularistic claims to political power.

Rousseau's purpose in adopting a similar conceptual device is precisely the opposite of Bodin's. Although like Bodin he identifies sovereignty with the power of legislation and maintains the indivisibility of sovereign power, his object in doing so is quite different. Rousseau's distinction -- again in a sense like Bodin's -- is intended to relegate the functions of the magistrate or government to a subordinate position, subject to and dependent upon a higher principle or "general will". His intention, however, is not to consolidate but to undermine the power of rulers. The "Magistrate" stands not only for lesser officials but for all rulers including kings; and the general will becomes not the will of the ruler, not an expression of his supremacy, but a token of his subordination to the community. In a sense, where Bodin subordinates the particularity of the people to the universality of the ruler, Rousseau subordinates the particularity of the ruler to the universality of the people. For Rousseau, the sovereign will is not something which constitutes a community out of particular and partial interests by imposing itself from without through royal legislation and the art of public management or "political economy." Instead, it is something which emanates from the community itself, expressing its actual common interests, and is imposed on those--the magistrate, the government, the agents of "public economy" -- whose function is merely to execute that will. The logic of this argument demands that it culminate in a radical theory of popular sovereignty, giving full effect to the principle that the sovereign will emanates from the community by actually vesting the sovereign legislative power in a popular assembly. Whether or not in the "Political Economy" Rousseau was already prepared to pursue that logic to its conclusion, he certainly did so in the *Social Contract.*

If Rousseau's argument owes a great deal in its form to the idiom of absolutism (as commentators have suggested)[37] and to the language of a single, supreme and indivisible public will, he turns that idiom against itself. As many theorists have done, he adopts the form of his adversary's argument to attack its substance. There may be an element of truth in the proposition that the only French "tradition of discourse" to which Rousseau was "not much indebted" was constitutionalism and that, while "...he was one of the great proponents of the rule of law...his dedication to that principle was distinct from that of French constitutionalists such as Domat or Montesquieu." In particular:

> In Rousseau's theory, law is identified with the sovereign will, as it was in the absolutist tradition, rather than an external bridle on that will, as it was in the constitutive laws of the French polity. His hostility to intermediate bodies in the state and scorn for representative assemblies, set him off clearly from the constitutionalist tradition.[38]

If Rousseau departed from the constitutionalist tradition, however, it is, in part, because the mainstream of French constitutionalism (and arguably even its radical Huguenot form) did not imply -- as did English constitutionalism -- a transfer of sovereign legislative power to the "people" even as embodied in representative institutions.[39] To "bridle" the sovereign will meant to guide or direct it, not to limit or check the power of the sovereign by appropriating a piece of his sovereignty. Rousseau's concern is not merely to "bridle" the absolutist monarchy but to overturn it, not simply to guide sovereign power but to transfer it. In this respect, one might argue that, despite his dismissal of English representative institutions no less than French, Rousseau has something in common with the mainstream of English constitutionalism, if not French, to the extent that the English conception of limited, constitutional government has identified -- in theory and practice -- the limitations of royal power not simply with juristic "bridles" but with the actual transfer of legislative authority. There is, however, another sense in which Rousseau's argument is, after all, best understood in relation to French constitutionalism, at least in its more radical forms as exemplified by the Huguenot resistance movement.[40]

The ideological strategy adopted by the Huguenot constitutionalists in their assault on absolutism was, as we have seen, to confront absolutism on its own ground by stressing the particularity of the monarch, attacking his treatment of the state as private property. They insisted instead on the "people's" proprietary right in the state, asserting that the "people" constitute the "majesty" of the king, and transferring the public "mind" from the king to the "people" embodied in their officers and representative institutions — "one mind compounded out of many." Rousseau's strategy is strikingly similar — except in one decisive respect. He also proceeds by attacking the proprietary character of the absolutist state and the particularity of the ruler, and counterposes to them a common public will residing in the community; and he also maintains that the ruler is constituted by the people. However, he perceives a threat not only in the particularity of the monarch but in that of the "Magistrate" in general. He, therefore, locates the public will not in the "public council," in officials and "intermediate bodies," or in assemblies of Estates, but in the people themselves.

Rousseau's attitude toward "intermediate bodies" is often regarded as one of the more alarming aspects of his thought, an attack on the most cherished principles of liberalism, the freedom of association and opinion, of individual dissent and minority rights, and so on; but this is, again, to misread Rousseau's meaning by extracting his argument from its historical setting. Rousseau's refusal to lodge the public will in intermediate institutions does indeed cut him off from the French constitutionalist tradition even in its most radical forms. His rejection of these institutions, however, should not be understood as a ("totalitarian") violation of constitutionalist principles but rather as an attempt to extend and democratize them. Rousseau shares with the radical constitutionalists their concern for transforming the state into a truly "public" thing which derives its public or general character from the people. That is precisely the message of the "Political Economy." In the *Social Contract,* if not so unequivocally in the earlier article, he advances from the creation of a truly public magistrate -- a magistrate answerable in some unspecified way to the demands of the common good, the "general will" -- to the actual embodiment of that common good and the general will in a functioning popular sovereign. If in the process he resumes the language of absolutism, in order to vest in the people the powers hitherto lodged in the absolute monarchy, he travels that route not past but through the concerns of constitutionalism and the tradition of popular resistance.

It is again a question of historical perspective. The "intermediate bodies" that concern the French constitutionalists are not the "voluntary associations" so dear to the heart of English liberals, organizations in the private sphere as distinct from -- and, at least potentially, against -- organs of the state.[41] The French "intermediate bodies" are the corporate and representative institutions -- estates, parlements, municipalities, and colleges -- which constituted part of "la police", organs of the polity, whose role in the state constitutionalists proposed to increase — in varying degrees and with varying preferences for some such institutions over others. Neither, however, are these "bodies" legislative assemblies on the model of the English Parliament. These institutions were, in effect, feudal remnants, fragments of the feudal "parcellized" state, and were recognized -- and defended -- as such by constitutionalists even as late as Montesquieu, who regarded these elements of "Gothic" government as essential to the "moderation" and legitimacy of the French monarchy. This implied, too, that the notion of intermediate bodies was -- in the eighteenth century as before -- often closely associated with the defense of *aristocratic* power and might be not only undemocratic but anti-democratic in spirit. In the eighteenth century, even more explicitly than before, the principle of "particular" or intermediate powers interposed between king and people was invoked to support the enlargement of power for the nobility, as in the so-called "thèse nobiliaire." In these formulations, moreover, the claims of the nobility against the absolutist monarchy were likely to be equally claims against the third estate.

The notion of constitutional checks and balances thus assumed a clearly aristocratic cast, and the theory of intermediate powers was opposed to popular power more unequivocally than were English theories of representation, however undemocratic the intentions of the latter might be. Those who, like Montesquieu, preferred the *parlements* as the model of intermediate powers only partly modified the aristocratic character of the principle by extending it to include the *noblesse de robe*. Even in more radical and anti-absolutist or constitutionalist formulations, as we have seen in the case of the Huguenots, the insistence on intermediate bodies had the deliberate effect of limiting not only monarchical but also popular power — for example, by stressing that the right of resistance belonged to the "people" only as embodied in their officers and corporate representatives. Given the historical meaning and ideological function of these institutions in French political experience, the defense of intermediate bodies did not lend itself so easily to democratic extrapolation and extension — not even to the extent permitted by English theories of Parliamentary representation.[42] A democratic argument such as Rousseau's would, in that context, almost inevitably be formulated as an attack on intermediate institutions.

In the end, the question comes down to the particular social interests at stake. For those who felt aggrieved at their inadequate access to the means of extra-economic appropriation provided by the state, for those who -- even when they were subject to the state's appropriation through taxation -- themselves appropriated the labour of others, constitutional reforms designed to give them a piece of the state might serve very well. But these were not the interests represented by Rousseau. His concern -- clearly expressed in the article on "Political Economy" -- was for those on whose labour the whole structure of privilege, office, and taxation rested; the small producers and notably the peasantry. Much of the "Political Economy" is devoted to the problem of taxation, and Rousseau's proposals for reforming the fiscal system are explicitly designed to relieve the peasants who bear its brunt. It is here that he provides the clearest insight into his view of the existing state as a system of private appropriation and exploitation — and this is the specific target of his proposals for reform:

> Are not all advantages of society for the powerful and rich? Do they not fill all lucrative posts? Are not all privileges and exemptions reserved for them?
>
> ...whatever the poor pay is lost to them forever, and remains in or returns to the hands of the rich; and, as it is precisely to those men who take part in government, or to their connections, that the proceeds of taxation sooner or later pass, even when they pay their share they have a keen interest in increasing taxes.[43]

Thus, suggests Rousseau, the terms of the social contract between the two conditions of men can be summed up as follows:

> You need me, because I am rich and you are poor; let us therefore make an agreement: I will permit you the honour of serving me, on the condition that you give me the little that remains to you for the pains I shall take to command you.[44]

This, then, is the principle on which taxation is now based. Rousseau proposes a system of taxation based on opposing principles, by reforming the state to eliminate the use of taxation as a means of private appropriation and by transferring the tax burden for clearly public purposes to those more able to bear it, in a system of progressive taxation. He dismisses with contempt the idea that the peasant will lapse into idleness if not compelled to work by the demands of taxation: "Because for him who loses the fruits of his labour, to do nothing is to gain something; and to impose a fine on labour is a very odd way of banishing idleness."[45]

To the extent that Rousseau's political ideas, unlike the proposals for reform suggested by other Enlightenment thinkers, intended to attack the state not simply as an inefficient, unequal, or illiberal system of administration and representation but as a system of exploitation, he had eventually to conclude that only absolute popular sovereignty, as the sole means of displacing altogether the proprietary state, would suffice. Once he had decided on the necessity of true popular sovereignty if the state and its officers were indeed to be subject to "public reason," Rousseau was obliged to consider how the "general will" could actually operate — not merely as a notional standard for the behaviour of rulers and citizens, but as a real and active principle of political organization, a "will" actually emanating from the people and expressed in practice as law.

The typical French solution to the problem of the "common good," as we have seen, conjured up a single public will, usually embodied in the monarch, or a collection of partial and selfish interests woven together by the king and the officers of the state. None of these solutions -- not even those which replaced the monarchical will with "one mind compounded out of many" -- simply redefined the common good as a public interest constituted by private interests which would magically coalesce by the workings of an invisible hand, or aggregate themselves in the process of deliberation and legislation by a Parliament representing private interests. When Montesquieu argued that republican government required special virtue, and that monarchy had the advantage of allowing the implementation of the common good with minimal virtue or self-sacrifice on the part of its subjects, he was expressing an assumption common to all these formulations: that while self-interest could serve as the basis of society, the common good would not naturally emerge out of the interplay of private interests but required either the virtuous suppression of natural self-love or the active intervention of a "harmonizing" state.

If, in contrast, the English (and their Scottish spokesmen) thought -- or purported to think -- otherwise, especially in the eighteenth century, their optimism did not reflect a greater faith in human nature or an absence of deep divisions in English society. It had more to do with the particular conditions of their economy during that brief period in the development of English capitalism when England's commercial empire reigned supreme, and perhaps also with the traditionally unitary character of English representative institutions and the relatively secure and united propertied classes whose triumph over both king and people was expressed in the supremacy of Parliament.

French pessimism on this score, however, did not prevent political thinkers from proposing self-love and interest as the proper motivating forces of the body politic. Indeed, it became a common theme to suggest that selfish passions translated into interest could be the basis of public well-being, and even that society could fruitfully be conceived as a commercial transaction. The essential point, however, was that this view of society, far from disputing the need for strong monarchical power -- as similar views might do in England -- in fact generally served to emphasize its necessity. The disruptive and divisive character of commercial transactions, in which all parties pursue their own selfish gain, was perhaps as essential to this imagery as were the benefits of commerce. Thus, arguments that in England might serve to support the doctrines of laissez-faire and limited government, in France might appear in defense of royal absolutism. In any case, whether such arguments were marshalled in support of absolutism or "moderate" constitutional monarchy, the notion of a polity based on the harmony of selfish interests tended to postulate as its necessary condition an alien integrating will.

This is the context in which Rousseau formulated his conception of the general will as an expression of the common good emanating from the sovereign people. Much of his work, even before the *Social Contract,* had been devoted -- directly or indirectly -- to attacking the conception of society as a commercial transaction in which everyone sought his own gain in the other's loss or enlisted the aid of others only by persuading (or, more likely, deceiving) them to see their own profit in granting it. It is the consequence of property and inequality, he wrote, that each man

> ... must seek constantly to interest others in his fate, and to make them find, in reality or in appearance, their own profit in working for his. This makes him deceitful and artificial with some and imperious and harsh with others, and obliges him to abuse all those whom he needs, when he cannot make them fear him, and if he does not see his own interest in being useful to them.[46]

For Rousseau, such mutual deception was not a cure but a symptom. It was madness to suppose that the social bond and the common good could be based on the antagonisms of interest that divided people. Rousseau was bound to be especially hostile to this self-contradictory notion in view of its association with the idea of an external mediating will in the person of a powerful ruler. It clearly seemed to him especially absurd to imagine that a single, monarchical will -- or even the will of a plural magistrate -- which itself represented a very particular interest, could weld together a common good of these antagonistic particularisms. At the same time, it was entirely in keeping with his conception of personal autonomy to adopt the view that self-love ought to act as the source of the public good. He therefore set himself the task of discovering how self-love and self-interest could produce a common good without the mediation of "commercial" transactions or mutual deception and without the intervention of an alien will. His object, then, was to find a form of social organization in which the social bond was based not on what divided people but on what actually united them, a common interest composed of interests that people really had in common.

It is, therefore, a mistake to think that in his concept of the general will Rousseau is proposing the suppression of natural instincts and the submergence of self-interest in an abstract "general will," the individual in the collectivity. Individual interests are not in principle opposed to the general will, any more than *amour de soi* is synonymous with *amour propre*. Interests are "partial" as *opposed* to "general" only when circumstances put them necessarily and essentially in opposition to the interests of others, in the sense that one person's gain is another's loss. Society as it is now constituted forces interests into such mutual antagonism. Rousseau simply acknowledges that no amount of reason or enlightenment will induce these divisive impulses to serve as the basis of social cohesion — at least not without mass delusion or autocratic imposition, both of which are not only undesirable but unreliable. The point is precisely that people cannot be made to will what is against their self-interest. Summarizing the argument of his "Discourse on the Origin of Inequality," Rousseau writes elsewhere:

When finally all particular interests conflict with one another, when self-love *(amour de soi)* in ferment becomes egotism *(amour propre),* so that opinion, making the whole universe necessary to each man, makes men born enemies to one another and compels each man to find his advantage only in the other's loss, then conscience, weaker than inflamed passions, is extinguished by them, and remains in the mouths of men only as a word designed for mutual deception. Each one then pretends to wish to sacrifice his own interests to those of the public, and all of them are lying. No one wants the public good unless it accords with his own; thus this accord is the object of true politics which seeks to make people happy and good.[47]

This is far from saying that self-interest is in principle opposed to the common good; indeed, it is to assert that it *must* be the source of the common good. If the "general will" has any meaning, it is only on the understanding that people actually do have individual self-interests in common — interests that are common not only when mediated by commerce or an external will, but intrinsically; and politics must be built on this common foundation.

The *Social Contract* outlines the political principles appropriate to a society so organized; and though Rousseau is never unequivocally clear about the social pre-conditions for such a political order, his social criticism -- especially in the first and second Discourses -- suggests very strongly that a complete transformation of society would be required. Elsewhere, he gives indications of how his ideal society might be constituted: a small community of independent petty producers, more or less self-sufficient peasants and artisans.[48] However utopian this picture may be, it expresses clearly the principle which for Rousseau is the basis of a free society, that no one should be able to appropriate the labour of others or be forced to alienate his own. In the *Social Contract,* he suggests that the fundamental principles of the common good are liberty -- the absence of individual dependence -- and equality, which is the condition of liberty; and these require a distribution of power and wealth in which no citizen can do violence to another and "no citizen is rich enough to buy another, and none poor enough to be forced to sell himself."[49]

These, then, appear to be the conditions which make possible the general will. In order to will the general will as an expression -- not an unnaturally (and impossibly) virtuous or forcible violation -- of their own self-interest, people must actually, objectively, have interests in common. The common ground shared by interests in society as it is actually constituted is simply too narrow; and to widen the scope of commonality requires the removal of those social relations and institutions -- most especially, inequality -- that render people in reality and necessarily enemies by interest. Democracy, it appears, is the necessary condition for a state based on "public reason," rather than on the private interest of the magistrate; and social equality, the breakdown of the division between appropriators and producers, is the condition of democracy.

Rousseau's controversial concept of the "general will", therefore, must be treated not as an idiosyncracy but as an innovation on an old French theme, not as a disturbingly illiberal answer to English questions about the relation between private rights and public interests but as a radically democratic answer to French questions about the source of universality and the public will. This is not to say that his genius is circumscribed by the immediate historical conditions of France and that he has nothing to say about "durable dilemmas." Just as the particular conditions of

English history gave the world a lasting legacy of liberal values -- "durable" no matter how much they are traceable to and delimited by the particular interests of the propertied classes -- Rousseau translated the particular "dilemmas" of the French state into a "durable" and universal statement of democratic values. One might say that an engagement with immediate and urgent struggles, aimed at visible and living targets, concentrated his mind more effectively than reflection on "perennial questions" alone might ever have done.

## NOTES

[This article has appeared in a slightly modified and somewhat longer version in *History of Political Thought*, vol. IV no. 2, Summer 1983, with an acknowledgement that it was written specifically for this volume in honour of George Rudé.]

1. See, for example, Lester G. Crocker, *Rousseau's Social Contract: An Interpretive Essay* (Cleveland: Case Western Reserve University Press, 1968), p. 36. This book disregards the many ways in which Rousseau's idiom belongs to his time and place and attributes it simply to his own disordered psyche. See also J. L. Talmon, *The Origins of Totalitarian Democracy* (London: Sphere Books, 1970), pp. 38-40. Such approaches make it unnecessary to confront Rousseau's political thought as serious social criticism; and they have much in common with those treatments of social protest that reduce protesting crowds to irrational "mobs," driven not by genuine grievances directed at real targets but by their own moral or psychic failings, or by the external and natural laws of "collective behaviour." As George Rudé has shown us, the answer to such attempts to neutralize or trivialize social protest is to place it in its proper historical context, avoiding stereotypes by probing into the actual and specific historical objects, targets, aims, and ideas underlying the act of protest. See, for example, *The Crowd in History: 1730-1848* (New York, London, Sydney: John Wiley and Sons, 1964), pp. 10-11. What applies to the collective protest of the crowd in the street applies equally well to the solitary protest of the social critic in his study.

2. A ground-breaking discussion of the differences between English traditions in medieval political thought and their relation to the differences in historical experiences appears in an unpublished doctoral dissertation by Cary Nederman, entitled *State and Political Theory in France and England, 1250-1350: Marsiglio of Padua, William of Ockham and the Emergence of "National" Traditions of Discourse in the Late Middle Ages* (York University, Toronto, 1983). Some of these themes are also explored for a later period in England and France in another important dissertation by David McNally, entitled *The Political Economists and Agrarian Capitalism: A Reinterpretation of Classical Political Economy in Britain and France* (York University, Toronto, 1983).

3. Robert Brenner, "Agrarian Class Structure and Economic Development: A Reply to Critics," to be published in *Past and Present* as a reply to the debate which followed his "Agrarian Class Structure and Economic Development in Pre-Industrial Europe," *Past and Present*, no. 70, February, 1976. The following discussion of English and French "feudal centralization" is indebted to these essays.

4. Julian Franklin, ed. and transl., Introduction, *Constitutionalism and Resistance in the Sixteenth Century: Three Treatises by Hotman, Beza, and Mornay* (New York: Pegasus, 1969), p. 16.

5. For an example of such a case, see Emmanuel Le Roy Ladurie, *Carnival in Romans* (New York: Braziller, 1980), p. 72.

6. See Nannerl O. Keohane, *Philosophy and the State in France: the Renaissance to the Enlightenment* (Princeton, Princeton University Press, 1980), *passim,* for indications of how the concept of "will" and the "general will" were used in French traditions of discourse and their association with the idea of monarchical power acting as a unifying force among particularistic powers and interests. Other writers have also traced the lineage of the "general will," but from a somewhat less historical and more abstractly philosophical point of view: for example, Charles W. Hendel, *Jean-Jacques Rousseau: Moralist* (Indianapolis and New York: Bobbs-Merrill, LLA, 1934); Robert Derathé, *Jean-Jacques Rousseau et la science politique de son temps* (Paris: J. Vrin, 1970); Patrick Riley, "The General Will before Rousseau," *Political Theory,* vol. 6, no. 4, 1978, pp. 485-516.

7. François Hotman, *Francogallia,* in *Constitutionalism and Resistance...,* p. 68.

8. See, for example, Emmanuel Le Roy Ladurie, *The Peasants of Languedoc* (Urbana, Chicago, London: University of Illinois Press, 1976).

9. George Rudé, *Ideology and Popular Protest* (London: Lawrence and Wishart, 1980), pp. 27-37.

10. I am relying for this account of de Bourg and the other lawyers on Le Roy Ladurie, *Carnival in Romans.*

11. *Ibid.,* p. 357.

12. *Ibid.,* p. 358.

13. *Ibid.,* p. 353.

14. *Ibid.*

15. *Ibid.,* p. 359.

16. The Calvinist doctrine of the "lesser magistrate" is both radical in its justification of resistance and conservative in its restrictions on the right to resist. There were attempts to defend a more inclusive right of resistance by extending the meaning of the "lesser magistrate" to include private individuals, each acting as his own "magistrate"; but this extension clearly -- in effect, by definition -- violates the meaning and intent of the original doctrine.

17. Philippe du Plessis-Mornay (?) *Vindiciae contra Tyrannos* in *Constitutionalism and Resistance...,* p. 195. (The authorship of this tract remains in doubt.)

18. Hotman, *op. cit.,* p. 78.

19. *Ibid.,* p. 79.

20. Mornay, *op. cit.,* p. 173.

21. *Ibid.,* p. 174.

22. *Ibid.,* pp. 175-7.

23. *Cf.* Julian Franklin, *Jean Bodin and the Rise of Absolutist Theory* (Cambridge: Cambridge University Press, 1973), esp. pp. 41-53.

24. *Ibid.,* p. 52. In contrast to Franklin, Nannerl Keohane writes: "Bodin's assertion that sovereignty is indivisible was taken as axiomatic by his countrymen." *Op. cit.,* p. ix.

25. Jean Bodin, *Six Books of the Commonwealth,* ed. M.J. Tooley (Oxford: Blackwell, 1967), p. 7.

26. For a discussion of the contrast between England's "unitary government" and the fragmented polity of France and other Continental states, see Perry Anderson, *Lineages of the Absolutist State* (London: New Left Books, 1974). especially pp. 113-116.

27. Perry Anderson refers to the "displacement upwards" of extra-economic coercion in *ibid.,* p. 19, and on p. 55 cites Porshnev, *Les Soulèvements Populaires en France de 1623 à 1648* (Paris, 1965).

28. Bodin, *op. cit.*

29. An argument strikingly reminiscent of Bodin's, in substance and language, appears in Antoine de Montchrétien's *Traité de l'œconomie politique* (1615), apparently the first book with a title referring to "political economy", a concept based on the household/state analogy. Montchrétien is discussed in the longer version of this article, *op. cit.,* pp. 298-300. Something like this household/state analogy has, of course, also appeared in English political thought, notably in Sir Robert Filmer, who defends royal absolutism by invoking patriarchal authority as the origin and model of political authority. The English argument is, however, significantly different from the French, even when it is used to defend absolute monarchy. As Gordon Schochet has pointed out in *Patriarchalism in Political Thought* (New York: Basic Books, 1975), Bodin, for example, does not adopt a patriarchal defense of political obligation. Schochet goes on to suggest that "the combination of doctrines and interests that made possible a patriarchal theory of political obligation seems to have been peculiar to the England of the seventeenth century." (pp. 35-6). One might add that, while Bodin's concern is not primarily to construct a theory of obligation at all, if anything he reverses the patriarchal doctrine of obligation, suggesting that the father's right to obedience is analogous to that of the king. His household/state analogy works both ways: for example, the state like the household has the purpose of "getting goods" and increasing the material well-being of its members, while the household like the state is marked by obedience to its head. The king's right to obedience is here treated as given, and the analogy with the household serves other purposes — arguably in keeping with French, as distinct from English, realities.

    For another discussion of the relation between political power and paternal power in Rousseau and his predecessors, see Derathé, *op. cit.,* pp. 183-192.

30. See J.A.W. Gunn, *Politics and the Public Interest* (London: Routledge and Kegan Paul, 1969), for a discussion of the uniquely English character of this "individualistic rendering of the public interest" (p. xi) and its association with particular historical circumstances.

31. See Harry C. Payne, *The Philosophes and the People* (New Haven and London: Yale University Press, 1976), p. 65.

32. Rousseau, "Discours sur l'économie politique", *Œuvres Complètes.* Vol. III (Paris: Gallimard, 1964), p. 242.

33. *Ibid.,* p. 243.

34. In the *Social Contract,* Rousseau, in apparent opposition to his earlier argument, suggests briefly that "The family is then, one might say, the first model to political society...." *(Œuvres Complètes,* vol. III, p. 352). He draws the analogy, however, in a paradoxical way which undermines the absolutist argument by stressing the temporary and even contractual character of paternal authority; and the lesson he derives from the family is that all are born free and equal, with a right to judge for themselves the best means of self-preservation. This he concludes from the fact that, once children reach the age of reason, they remain in the family only voluntarily and by agreement. While apparently accepting the model of paternal power, Rousseau thus adopts an argument very similar to one used by Locke against Filmer's patriarchalism in the *First Treatise of Government.* The distinctions Rousseau drew earlier between household and state still apply, while the similarities he now cites merely confirm the attack on royal absolutism.

35. *Ibid.,* p. 244.

36. Bodin, *op. cit.*

37. See, for example, Keohane, *op. cit.,* pp. 442-449.

38. *Ibid.,* p. 442.

39. Even the Huguenot tracts speak of the fiscal powers of the Estates and their right to be regularly *consulted,* but it is not clear that representative institutions are conceived as *legislative* bodies.

40. Rousseau's own association with Geneva and Calvinism should, of course, not be forgotten.

41. As for Rousseau's view on voluntary associations, it is worth considering his remarks on the *cercles* of Geneva in the *Lettre à d'Alembert* and his answers to criticisms of these remarks voiced by his friends among the burghers of Geneva who felt that the *cercles* corrupted the republic's artisans and gave them an excessive taste for independence. Rousseau suggests in reply that these *cercles* provide the appropriate education for free citizens, midway between the public education of Greece and the domestic education of monarchies "... where all subjects must remain isolated and must have nothing in common but obedience." Letter to Theodore Tronchin, November 26, 1758, *Correspondance Complète,* ed. R.A. Leigh (Geneva: Institut et Musée Voltaire, 1965--), vol. V, p. 743.

42. John Locke, for example, vests a right of resistance not in intermediate bodies or "magistrates" but in the "people" themselves *against* "magistrates." While his conception of the "people" is certainly exclusive and restrictive, the category "people" is, as it were, more fluid, less easily controlled, and more readily expanded by democrats than the category "magistrates" which figures in Huguenot resistance doctrine.

43. "Discours sur l'œconomie politique," pp. 271-2.

44. *Ibid.,* p. 273.

45. *Ibid.*

46. "Discours sur l'origine et les fondements de l'inégalité parmi les hommes," *Œuvres complètes,* vol. III, p. 175. The idea that society is based on a kind of mutual deception, inducing people to serve each other's interests as in a commercial exchange, was stated most effectively in the *Maxims* of La Rochefoucauld.

47. "Lettre à Christophe de Beaumont," *Œuvres Complètes,* vol. IV, p. 937.

48. For example, in the *Lettre à d'Alembert* or the *Projet de constitution pour la Corse* (though this should be taken rather as a general indication of his values than as a literal blueprint for a Utopia).

49. *Contrat social, Oeuvres complètes,* vol. III, pp. 391-2.

# PART THREE

George C. Comninel

# THE POLITICAL CONTEXT OF THE POPULAR MOVEMENT IN THE FRENCH REVOLUTION

The recognition of several different "revolutions" -- those of the aristocracy, bourgeoisie, peasantry, and urban *menu peuple* -- within the complex whole of the French Revolution was one of the great legacies of the historian Georges Lefebvre.[1] Yet Lefebvre also strongly upheld that "social interpretation" which saw in the Revolution a purposeful attainment of social ascendancy by the bourgeoisie. This combined conception was in turn much enriched by historians of the popular movement, who rescued the autonomous political history of the *menu peuple* from the grand sweep of the Revolution. The popular movement was the critical driving force of the Revolution, responsible both for its initial accession to power and for the victory of successive radical challenges within it, and study of the people's interaction with the bourgeoisie during the Revolution has added a dynamic complexity that the social interpretation had previously lacked.[2]

Over the last twenty years, however, interpretation of the Revolution as a purposeful social conflict has been vigorously challenged by "revisionist" historians.[3] They reject any interpretation which would identify the political conflict of the Revolution with the social interests of any one group — and particularly the Marxist class analysis of *bourgeois revolution.*

The social interpretation has proved vulnerable because it has done little more than *assert* the conjunction of political and social conflict in the Revolution, regrettably reflecting the mechanical conception of economic base and social superstructure once prevalent in Marxist thought.[4] Marx himself never really analyzed the Revolution *as* a bourgeois revolution. He did not even develop the concept, but adopted it whole from earlier liberal historians to account for the emergence of the "bourgeois" capitalist class society that was his real concern.[5] What the revisionists have challenged is precisely the idea that bourgeois capitalist class interests were behind the Revolution.

The revisionists argue that the Revolution's antagonists did not have the social characteristics long presumed by Marxists, and that the Ancien Régime's social structure was not essentially transformed by the Revolution, only further developed; on these grounds, they deny that there was any basis for fundamental social conflict. They follow Alfred Cobban in separating the "political" from the "social", and agree that "The supposed social categories of our histories -- bourgeois, aristocrats, *sans-culottes* -- are all in fact political ones."[6] As a result, they conceive of the Revolution as a political conflict without fundamental social purpose — in this sense at least, a purely political, not social, revolution.

Colin Lucas has observed that the revisionists have not been convincing in explaining the revolutionary conflict as a political "clarification" of social changes already in place.[7] Nevertheless, the idea that a continuous social movement linked the National Assembly and the Revolutionary Government is now widely rejected. The Revolution is said to have "skidded" off course, its leaders accused of pure political opportunism. At the same time, the primary blame for *unnecessary* revolutionary violence falls to the people. In revisionist histories, popular political consciousness and commitment is played down; traditional responses, the motivations of misery, degradation and alcohol, and the influence of jealous petty leaders are highlighted.[8] The revisionist analysis offers a Revolution without political or social coherence, and tends to account for the popular movement in terms that recall "the mob".

The purpose of this essay is to reconsider the political role of the popular movement in light of the issues raised by the revisionist challenge. Clearly, any analysis of the popular movement must be rooted in a particular conception of the Revolution. It will be argued that, while the Revolution cannot indeed be explained as a conflict between "feudalism" and "capitalism", it did nonetheless express a fundamental *social* conflict between bourgeois *"Nationaux"* and noble *"Aristocrates"*. The significant point is that this social conflict took the specific form of a *political* revolution, and the various social interests at issue in the Revolution defined themselves in specifically political terms. It is not, therefore, a question of searching for "social" forces in the revolution apart from its political conflict, nor of complementing the political categories of *"bourgeois"*, *"aristocrate"* or *"sans-culotte"* with other, underlying, "social" categories. Instead, what is needed is a social interpretation of the political conflict itself.

*   *   *

The importance of the actions of the Parisian people during the French Revolution has always been clear to historians. Yet only in recent years, through the work of such historians as George Rudé and Albert Soboul, has the political role of the popular movement been fully appreciated as *both* autonomous *and* integral to the Revolution's history. The popular movement thrust the Revolution forward at each critical juncture prior to Thermidor. For the most part it did so in its own manner and for its own reasons, yet with ideological links to the anti-aristocratic crusade launched by the Third Estate.

The *menu peuple* did not initiate the Revolution. A major point of their historians is that they could not have. The *menu peuple* were an amalgam of social groups of restricted means, sharing a limited common interest and tradition in their dependence on an affordable bread supply.[9] As the *sans-culottes*, however, they became an integral element in the day-to-day political life of the Revolution, breaking ground in the exercise of direct democracy as they stamped the anti-aristocratic struggle with distinctive popular characteristics. In the development of their own ideology, the *menu peuple* prepared the terrain for later popular concern over "the social question".

*Menu peuple,* in fact, became *sans-culottes* precisely as they assumed an ongoing political role beyond their episodic identity as the revolutionary crowd. Under the tutelage of patriotic and revolutionary politicians -- but equally propelled by the experience of their own, crucial, revolutionary role -- their occasional struggle against "aristocratic intrigue" among those in power became a continuing and direct struggle against all expressions of "aristocracy". Through the logic of their ideology, they arrived at an intrinsic opposition to parties in power, per se. The *sans-culottes* had no social program beyond the provision of necessities and essential social benefits, concern with which roughly demarcated their social frontier. They were defined by a political program that amounted simply to the destruction of "aristocracy" and the exercise of direct popular sovereignty. The *sans-culottes* were not a class, comprising as they did petty shop proprietors, artisans, and hired workers — which is not to say that they had no *class interests* in common. Their anti-aristocratic ideology sought a Utopian classlessness among politically responsible, petty-producer citizens.

In this ideology, the *sans-culottes* did not radically differ from the Montagnards, among whom could be found those -- including Robespierre -- who ranked social justice (slightly) above property rights.[10] The Mountain was no less anti-aristocratic, upheld the principle of popular sovereignty, and had long championed egalitarian democracy. But the Jacobins had a positive, *national* political purpose — to establish in peace the Republic of the sovereign "general interest", not (for most Conventionnels *especially* not) merely to liberate the people. This fundamental difference between a fully social (if not "disinterested") national revolutionary purpose, and the "particular" interest of a specific group, suffused all the concrete policy differences and general disenchantment by which the *sans-culottes* were alienated from the Revolutionary Government during the Year II.[11]

The *sans-culottes* both engaged in the vital political life of their Sections, and pressed the Revolutionary Government with their demands. The true popular *role* in the Revolution, however, was to aid in the defeat of "aristocratic" or irresolute parties at the level of government, making way for challengers from the Left. In this they acted as partners, not pawns. This role ended with the victory of the Mountain and creation of the Revolutionary Government. The leading position of the Robespierrists was secured by their determination to provide that government of "a single will" -- the government of *virtue* -- that was necessary to save the Republic. There was no Left opposition to the Revolutionary Government at the level of the Convention, and it needed only to be politically adroit to eliminate its extra-legislative opponents. When, in fear, the Convention's majority finally struck out at the Robespierrists -- as the "single will" threatened to turn from the receding threat of counter-revolution to the "corrupt" among the Revolution's leaders -- no structural basis remained for a popular championing of the Left. A stable Nation with effective government had been achieved, and no future confluence of interest and ideology between Jacobins and the *sans-culottes* could again win the acquiescence of a governing majority. With their ideology and practice of direct sovereignty, but their reliance upon state intervention, the *sans-culottes* lacked both the objective and the conceptual capacity for seizing power themselves. Though the acme of the autonomous *sans-culotte* political career lay ahead in the *journées* of Germinal and Prairal, its actual role in the national Revolution had ended.

The popular movement, then, was a political phenomenon *within* the Revolution. As a whole, the Revolution took the form of a political struggle lead by the "bourgeois" revolutionaries of Paris and other cities against "aristocracy" (being both the counter-revolutionary leadership, and social inequality itself). The special merit of the histories of the popular movement produced by Rudé and Soboul is their focus on the interaction of the people with the bourgeois revolutionary leadership, clarifying the operation of their alliance and the ways in which the leadership of the one never negated the independence of the other.[12] George Rudé particularly has focused on questions of ideological linkages, of leadership and political motivation, to probe that relationship by which the people served the Revolution while forging their own political identity. Precisely because the popular movement was the key to the success of the Revolution as a whole -- of the revolutionary leadership -- its political role must not be taken for granted.

The context in which this political role has been recognized has been the social interpretation of the Revolution. The interpretation of the Revolution as, in a sense, a "single thing" (in Clemenceau's expression), having the continuous concrete purpose of achieving bourgeois class interests, was long the established one. From the days of the Restoration, dating to before Marx's birth, a political tradition sympathetic to the Revolution upheld this interpretation in substantially the same terms found in the *Communist Manifesto*.[13] The social interpretation became the "official" interpretation of the Third Republic, embraced by both Establishment liberals and Marxists, despite their differing conceptions of class and bourgeois democracy.

In liberal versions, the progressive bourgeoisie fought a moribund aristocracy to realize "economic liberty" and representative democracy. Marx and Engels took the bourgeois-led Revolution as the political foundation of "bourgeois" capitalist society, and saw in economic liberalism a central contradiction between the "feudal" class relations of privilege and bourgeois capitalist relations.[14] They argued that bourgeois opposition to the "particularistic" interests of aristocratic privilege provided unique grounds for a claim to represent the "general interest", and a basis for mobilizing not only the whole bourgeoisie, but also the popular social classes. The bourgeoisie had ruling class power to gain from this alliance, while for the popular classes there were only limited democratic gains, and material rewards for a very few. Most of the people, they argued, would succumb to the new tyranny of property and become proletarians.

This analysis accords well with the history of the popular movement, the classes of the one corresponding to the observable "political" groups of the other. Even in its liberal versions, therefore, there lay the chief implication of the Marxist analysis: it is the opposition of fundamental class interests which underlies historical development and political conflicts. While this social interpretation of the conflict troubled many scholars, it enjoyed the status of historiographical orthodoxy because of its political coherence.

The central thrust of the revisionist concept of the Revolution, however, is that it formed no "whole" and served no group's interests. The revisionists offer instead a proliferation of social groups -- and particularly of "elites" -- with complex and often overlapping identities and interests, that cannot be reduced to the opposed sides of a "fundamental" social conflict. The revisionists believe in "social history", but they tend to mean a history of social institutions, attitudes, and demography; a history of social *tendencies.* It is by cataloging social life, charting socio-professional categories, and compiling the evidence of social consciousness that they seek "social" revolution.[15]

Understanding Marxists to mean by "class" a political-economic concept, the revisionists argue that it is anachronistic to apply it to pre-capitalist society — that it forces groups into a "class" mould where possible, and robs groups of their real social identity where not. It has even been suggested that Marxism would deny the *sans-culottes* a fully social identity, because their group character lies in their ties as *consumers,* not producers.[16] It is argued that a full demographic investigation is needed to know the *sans-culottes,* to reveal their ties to the countryside — and to understand their "elite" of militants, who supposedly vied with the Jacobin "elite" of talents.[17]

The credibility of the revisionist "demographic" alternative is largely based on its initial challenge to the Marxist class analysis: that no significant differences existed between the forms of property of the "feudal" aristocrats and the supposedly capitalist bourgeois. By calling into question the fundamental classes of the Marxist analysis, they have undermined the whole idea of a social interpretation of the Revolution in any but general terms. Given the reluctance of many scholars to embrace "class struggle" in the first place, it is not surprising that, as William Doyle has reported, a new international consensus is emerging.[18] If the Revolution was not after all a "bourgeois revolution", few if any non-Marxists would go in search of a new interpretation in class terms.

With the social interpretation dispatched as "myth", a variety of options are open for the revisionists. A few see the Revolution as devoid of any social meaning, a *purely* political event (a concept which even most revisionists cannot support).[19] The more sophisticated François Furet sees the Revolution as the product of a structural crisis of power, based on growth, that "opened" French society — legitimizing the revolutionary ideology of equality, and setting in train an "autonomous political and ideological dynamic" of struggle among contending "elites" that diverted the Revolution's course.[20] In Doyle's synthesis of the "new consensus", the Revolution "merely clarified" the fact that French society would be dominated by a unified elite of "notables" defined by property instead of birth; merely clarified, that is, because no revolution was required to bring about this already-existing situation.[21]

The popular movement was an important focus of the social interpretation, accounting for the victory of the bourgeoisie, yet also providing the Revolution with that complex -- even dialectical -- dynamism that made sense of its crisis-ridden course. The revisionists, however, conceive of the Revolution as a contingent political crisis that expressed a long-term structural change. Their task is to explain the existence of revolutionary struggle among a culturally and economically *homogeneous* elite; an elite which, despite social "diversity", presented not even an ideological cleavage to coincide with a bourgeois/aristocratic conflict. This is the context for the revisionist conception of the popular movement: in a Revolution propelled and deflected by *social crisis* -- without social purpose, or goals to achieve beyond initial political reform -- it is the people who are cast in the role of "social crisis".

While seeming to accept the history of the popular movement, the revisionists profoundly distort it. In the first place, the revisionist analysis rips from the history of the popular movement that context of a Revolutionary whole, the continuous process of revolutionary development, which gave it political coherence. In denying there was real need for revolutionary struggle between the National Assembly and Thermidor, the revisionists deny the people a role as *ally*. Instead, the popular movement is reduced to a "social phenomenon" of the Revolution: the *sans-culotte* militants become one "elite" -- albeit an inferior one -- among the many in contention; the *menu peuple* as a whole are left as a seething, directionless force — bursting at times, and at times cajoled, onto the political stage.[22]

Though the revisionists pay lip service to Lefebvre's idea of several revolutionary movements in a single Revolution, they rob these movements of distinctive characteristics. The popular movement is no longer taken to be a specific political expression of popular social interests, effected through alliance with a class having more broadly social political motivations. The *sans-culottes* are instead divided between a political elite, parallel to but demographically distinct from the bourgeois elites, and an "inchoate" social mass lacking real political identity.

Not only are the people denied the identity of a political movement, but the revisionists incline towards total de-politicization of the mass of the *menu peuple*. It was the people's *hunger* -- not their socially motivated *politics* -- which Cobban identified as the "hidden factor" behind the course of the Revolution, providing "a continual supply of inflammable material to feed the fire of revolution."[23] The revisionists have also emphasized *humiliation* as a source of popular violence, and emphasized the persistence of *tradition* in popular protests and ideologies, while failing to give credence to the development of popular political consciousness through the Revolution.[24] It is, however, especially the differentiation of an "elite" of the *sans-culotte* militants -- drunken, jealous, venal, deluded, "completely contemptible", and resentful of Jacobin power and talents, as the revisionist histories have it -- that marks the de-politicization of the *menu peuple*, who are portrayed as essentially passive except when stirred by hunger and agitators or bullied by the militants of their Sections.

A final distortion of the revisionists is their contention that a recognition of the *political* character of the *sans-culottes*, and of the revolutionary crowd more generally, in some sense contradicts Marxist social analysis.[25] The revisionists have noted with barely restrained irony the emphasis given by Rudé and Soboul to the specifically *political* character of the *sans-culottes*, because they construe Marxism to be a form of economic determinism, based exclusively on the economic delineation of classes. This completely misrepresents Marxist social analysis, both in reducing class to a merely "economic" category, and in imposing upon Marxism that separation of the "political" from the "social" which is in fact a hallmark of the revisionists. Moreover, the revisionists' own de-politicization of the popular movement makes their irony incongruous, for it is their conception of the *sans-culottes* as a political "elite" which would deny that the popular movement was an expression of the common social interests of the *menu peuple*. The analysis of Rudé and Soboul, on the contrary, provides precisely what is required of a social interpretation — an understanding of how social interests are concretely expressed in political conflict.

The revisionist conception of the popular movement is, above all, implicit in the context the revisionists provide for popular political action in the Revolution. In the absence of a continuing social conflict to carry the Revolution forward, the revisionists must attribute the tumultuous and violent course of the Revolution to either the interplay of the people with contending ambitious elites, or to the people alone. In either case, the people are conceived of in a manner that recalls the "mob": a seething mass of popular resentments and hunger--the social crisis incarnate-- unleashed through a tragic failure of the system, then manipulated by ideologues.

Even if the revisionists are willing to accept the implications of this view in order to explain the "irrational" dynamism and persistence of the Revolution -- and they so far seem to be -- they are left with a fundamental problem. For what the revisionists all have in common, besides their rejection of Marxism, is an inability to explain the political conflict that was *central* to the Revolution, once they deny that it had any underlying social basis. They assert that the Ancien Régime had already acquired an economically undifferentiated elite of both nobles and *roturiers*. Socially, this elite is said to have comprised diverse socio-professional "elites" — riven with differing ideologies, but straddling the boundary of noble status (a status which was, in any case, open to acquisition and marked no real social frontier). This conception, they believe, precludes seeing the elite either as a single class, or as comprising two opposed classes. Yet it is undeniable that the issue over which the Revolution broke out and continued to be fought was "aristocracy". In denying that there was any social basis for conflict between a "bourgeoisie" and an "aristocracy", the revisionists are at a loss to explain the intense revolutionary struggle that followed precisely these lines.

Colin Lucas makes this point in reviewing Doyle's conception of the Revolution as the institutionalization of the society of notables, in the course of which "a political crisis unlocked social tensions into a social crisis" of peasant and urban popular mobilization, which set in train the rest of the Revolution. Lucas objects that this is not adequate even to explain the initial, but far-ranging reforms of the Constituent Assembly: "It is difficult to understand the sustained intensity of the revolutionary will to impose a new social organization without a pre-history of social conflict."[26] Yet even Lucas is inclined to look for the "prehistory" of conflict at the level of *mentalités,* locating it in the "tensions" engendered by a society of property which has not surrendered the privileges of status.[27] Such contradictions of "traditional and new forms," "within minds, between individuals and between groups," make pretty thin gruel for a profound revolutionary conflict. And, as with all the revisionist analyses, there is no satisfactory basis for explaining the peculiar relationship between the popular movement and the bourgeois revolutionary leadership — joined apparently in the same cause at one level, but with growing divergence at another.

\*       \*       \*

The intellectual well-springs of the revisionist challenge lie in the denial of the role of class in history. While a rigorous analysis of the Marxist concept of class is not possible here, it is important to clarify the means of identifying class relations, and to dispense with the notion that class is an "economic" category. Class is a social *relation*, both suffusing social relationships generally, and specifically located in the complex of social relations of production / distribution / domination by which surplus is extracted and shared among members of the exploitive / ruling class. Exploitation presupposes the overcoming of resistance — both in limited "normal" forms and in episodic outbreaks of violent opposition. Class is therefore necessarily *both* "economic" (surplus-extractive) and "political" (dominating) in all of its manifestations within social relations, whether in production, law, or the state. More to the point -- and here is where the revisionist separation of "political" and "social" is particularly glaring -- in some societies exploitation takes a *directly* "political" form, as in the classic case of manorial feudalism.

The organization of class relations is fundamentally different between societies whose basic "modes of production" -- which is to say, modes of *exploitation* -- are different.[28] As Marx observed in the third volume of *Capital*, the key to under-standing class relations, and "the hidden basis of the entire social structure," is to be found in "the direct relationship of the owners of the conditions of production to the direct producers" — the specific form of unpaid surplus-labor and the means of its extraction.[29] The classes of capitalism, for example, are defined by the extraction of surplus in the specific form of *surplus-value* through the wage relationship — to the existence and furtherance of which all other social relations must be bent to one degree or another. Wage employment in itself, however, does not automatically define capitalist and proletarian. The extraction of *surplus-value* cannot occur in isolation, but must be systematic and socially fundamental. Capitalism is necessarily a *system*, predicated on a body of property law, universal commodity circulation, free and general commodification of human labor–power, and the structural compulsion to continue the "self-expansion" of capital through constant re-investment of profits in production. Some capitalists, in such a system, may function merely as merchants; but though they buy cheap and sell dear like merchants in all societies, they fill a role within the specifically *capitalist* organization of social production, and their character as "capitalists" is derived from this role.[30] It follows that no merchant -- and for that matter no mere "industrialist" employing wage labor -- is genuinely *capitalist* in the absence of such a generalized system. Where surplus extraction does not take the specific form of surplus-value, some mode of class exploitation *other* than capitalism must be identified.

While no revisionist has yet demonstrated any understanding of the Marxist concept of class or of the nature of capitalism, they have produced a wealth of evidence to establish that there was no opposition of capitalist bourgeoisie and feudal aristocracy in the Revolution. Taking their lead from Alfred Cobban's seminal argument in *The Social Interpretation of the French Revolution*, the revisionists have shown that the Revolution's leadership corresponds to *no one's* idea of capitalists, and that "capitalism" in its loosest sense was almost as important to the nobility as land-ownership was to the bourgeoisie.[31] It remains, however, for this historical evidence to be subjected to a Marxist social analysis in order to reveal the real class relations, and to provide the social context necessary for interpretation of the Revolution. The social detail of the demographic histories can be extremely useful in looking for the relations of surplus extraction — even if as a consequence of their method the really relevant questions are rarely considered. In any case, the historical research on which the revisionists' contention rests remains far superior to that available to Marx.

This is a significant point, since Marx relied on "bourgeois" historians not only for the facts, but for the very concept of bourgeois revolution. Raphael Samuel has recently emphasized that the French historians of the Restoration not only described the French Revolution in class terms, but the English Revolution as well.[32] Marx and Engels clearly saw their contribution as the "materialist conception of history": not the discovery of classes in history, but a *methodological overview* of historical class analysis. Marx's comments on the Revolution cannot be compared to the class analysis of capitalism he developed through his critique of political economy; concerned with understanding and changing *capitalist* class society, Marx never similarly criticized liberal history.

Marx's point about bourgeois revolution, in any case, was that it resulted from the social relations of *class,* and that bourgeois class relations were the basis of modern bourgeois society. Most of his political observations on the bourgeoisie are not affected by rejecting the simple equation of "bourgeois" with "capitalist", and recognizing instead that in the Ancien Régime the bourgeoisie were *non-capitalist* exploitive proprietors. For, without touching on more than the most essential features of surplus extraction in the Ancien Régime, its class relations can be seen to provide a basis for fundamental social conflict between such a bourgeoisie and a privileged aristocracy.

*     *     *

It is necessary to sweep aside anachronistic usages and return to the *bourgeoisie,* a social group of the Ancien Régime.[33] A contemporary social definition would have included all those who clearly lacked noble status, and either possessed adequate property (primarily in land or interest-bearing *rentes*) to live properly as *bourgeois rentiers,* or who were in any case not reduced to "dishonorable" employment in a manual or petty trade.[34] This neatly approximates the level at which surplus extraction can meaningfully be said to exist, and conveniently excludes the petty shopkeepers and master artisans who actually labored — leaving comparatively few ambiguous cases.

The great majority of this *bourgeoisie,* as Cobban noted, had nothing to do with commerce, industry or banking. Most owned venal offices in the state, or had careers as legal professionals (closely tied to the state through the courts) — and most of the rest simply lived as *rentiers.* It is clear from the evidence that neither in the Ancien Régime as a whole, nor in any of its economic sectors (perhaps only excluding agriculture in recently annexed Flanders)[35] was surplus-value extracted through the productive circulation of capital. Profit-making of various sorts was quite common -- if not so common as revenue from land, *rentes* and venal offices -- and commerce and industry boomed. But the nobility were as keenly interested in profit-making (on their lands, or in trade of sufficient scale) as the *bourgeoisie,* nobles were important in the expansion of industry, and *bourgeois* who were really successful in business purchased noble titles and retired from trade.[36] Neither commerce nor industry possessed the structural characteristics of capitalism, nor a clear dynamic of its formation (though the growth of putting-out by petty rural *fabricants* in the textile industry of the North might perhaps be construed to have been "proto-capitalist").[37]

It is agriculture, however, which must be the primary focus of this analysis. As Robert Brenner and others have forcefully argued, English capitalism developed in *farming,* and it remained overwhelmingly agrarian in character right through the eighteenth century.[38] The capitalist farm, as leased from a landlord, had been transformed from traditional peasant fields and wastes into a heavily capitalized and specialized unit of production for hired labor — far greater in its size and its livestock and other capital requirements than a family could handle. It was completely severed from the rhythms and practices of interdependent peasant agriculture, and followed instead the dictates of "improved" farming to maximize yields while dispensing with the fallow land and other impediments of the peasant "commons". Competition among farmers led to innovations in techniques and implements, and peasant production became increasingly uneconomic as the countryside was turned into a powerful food "factory", with a surplus of available laborers.

This was in stark contrast to France, where the vast majority of land was either owned by peasants, or leased to peasant producers in units of family-size or less. Over most of France the peasant community, or the more isolated peasant household, clearly dominated agrarian production.[39] Even in the extremely fertile and profitable grain region about Toulouse, the estates of noble grain magnates were worked by peasant householders — and the *fermiers* who leased estates elsewhere often did so to sub-let to peasant families.[40] Indeed, the only area in which anything resembling the English farms could be found was the Paris basin — where the *fermiers* leased large estates and worked them with hired laborers. Yet this was precisely the region in which the ancient "open field" peasant community persisted. The *fermiers* entirely conformed to the traditional peasant community practices of fallow, gleanage, etc., without any of the basic methods of improvement, or investment in land or equipment, which were fundamental to capitalist farming.[41]

The English methods were not unknown, but they were alien to the fabric of French social production: the land could not be separated from the social relations of the peasant community, with all its demands and restrictions. Unlike the English farm, the French *ferme* could not be reduced to an element of the circuit of capital, its production organized to maximize a capitalist farmer's profits. Wage employment on the *ferme* was an important *traditional* element in the peasant economy of the highly commercial Paris region, and had been for centuries.

It was the *peasants* of France -- overburdened with rent and taxes, and constituting four-fifths of the population -- who were the fundamental producers of social surplus. The overwhelming bulk of surplus production was in agriculture, and the central means of surplus extraction were *rent* and *taxes.* Non-capitalist agrarian revenue was the basis of surplus extraction for holders of land, state offices and *rentes,* and supported in turn both commerce and the professions.

As the revisionists argue, there was no social frontier in the pattern of property holdings corresponding to the *status* difference between *bourgeois* and noble.

*Seigneuries* with privileged feudal property rights were owned by noble and *roturier* alike. Land, offices and *rentes* were the universal forms of wealth in the Ancien Régime; the revisionist picture of a unified propertied elite has this much basis in fact. In searching for the *class* relations of surplus extraction, noble status is simply a red herring. What the revisionists have ignored, however, is that *within* the nobility there existed a genuine and well-established *aristocracy,* defined by truly extensive wealth and an especially privileged relationship with the state.

Among the aristocracy we must first include the royal household, the Princes of the Blood, the Peers of France, the highest church officers, and the Court nobility. Then, perhaps a few hundred great houses of "ancient" nobility which had maintained their "names" and the prospect of royal favor by preserving and renewing inherited wealth and cultivating connections. The magistrates of the *parlement* of Paris also ranked high among this aristocracy, far from being *"bourgeois"* as is sometimes claimed.[42] That virtually all the *parlementaires* had nobility of recent vintage was irrelevant: their present status was very great, nearly all were already noble at their accession -- if perhaps as *anobli* or sons of *anobli* -- and they all had enormous wealth in land and *rentes.*

Of lesser standing, yet recognized to be entering the aristocracy, were the financiers — the nobility of the tax farm and other royal fiscal offices.[43] Nomination to the company of the *Fermiers-Généraux,* in fact, was a form of cooptation: a royal favor that bestowed very great fortune, noble status and aristocratic rank. Sons of the *fermiers* rarely remained in royal finance, but purchased magistracies or other positions more suitable for aristocrats.[44] The financial nobility were in the process of "arriving". The whole financial administration, in fact, was a means by which the state pumped surplus directly from the peasantry into the aristocracy -- whose established members lent money to the financiers at interest -- as also were the huge royal subventions to the Court, and many other royal favors. The state thus both sustained and renewed the aristocracy.

Once possessed of the wealth and privileges of aristocracy -- and above all, access to high office and royal favor, for which "rank" was a major determinant -- the state continued to be the focus of the aristocratic "career". A brief sojourn as a *parlementaire* (itself a worthy career) could lead a young aristocrat to purchase of a position as *maître des requêtes* and the possibility of rising in rank to intendant, councilor of state, or other high royal office.[45] The senior positions of royal administration were recruited from among the aristocracy -- with the exception of Necker, a foreign banker -- and, together with those of the church and the magistracies of the *parlement,* they offered power, significant income, the prospect of great favors, and the potential for glory of those aristocrats who were not content with careers of influence, investment, and indulgent living.[46]

Besides this most powerful and privileged aristocracy, there were the houses of the provincial aristocracies. These also were truly rich, if on a lesser scale, and their aristocratic rank was even more concentrated.[47] Provincial *parlementaires,* for example, belonged to a small circle of the province's richest houses, and were usually of far older lineage than the "upstarts" in Paris. The provincialism of these aristocrats did not extend to economic affairs: the *parlementaires* of Toulouse dominated the commercial grain trade of that favored region with advanced business practices adapted to peasant production; the *parlementaires* of Bordeaux dominated wine production there.[48] Provincial aristocrats rarely advanced to national status, and enjoyed far less privileged relations with the monarchy, but they had significant income from their magisterial offices, and strongly defended their privileges and traditions. Finally, the great majority of the nobility -- whether urban *anoblis* or petty rural *gentils-hommes* -- were closer in scale to the *bourgeoisie* in both their property and the offices they held.

The social relations of production of the Ancien Régime were above all based upon peasant agriculture. The most important form of surplus extraction was *rent,* primarily contractual and "economic" -- but not capitalist -- with surviving "feudal" rents of varying significance. Also of great importance, however, was extraction of surplus through the state and the church — "rent" in the form of taxes, tithes, fees for service, and so on. The distribution of surplus through the state was complex, based on both decentralized private offices and central royal power. Still, it is clear that while there were distinct spheres of surplus extraction in land and in the state / church complex, both spheres were vitally important to both the nobility and the *bourgeoisie* (particularly when the quasi-official status of the men-at-law is considered). Within the sphere of the state, however, a special relationship of access to privileged surplus extraction existed for the exclusive (if cooptive) circles of the aristocracy. This aristocracy excluded the great majority of nobles, and monopolized the administration and politics of the Ancien Régime.

Political life, in fact, revolved about the ambitions, special interests, and ideological differences of politically active aristocrats: loyal ministers, enlightened thinkers, courtly intriguers, archbishops, intendants, financiers, and jurists. The dominant ideological positions of the Ancien Régime pitted "aristocratic constitutionalists" against "royal absolutists".[49] Aristocratic ideology had been taken beyond traditional conceptions of the ancient constitution of a privileged aristocratic "race", primarily by the equally aristocratic but not very ancient *parlementaires,* led by Montesquieu. The legitimate role of aristocratic magistrates in balancing the power of the monarchy was much emphasized, a role which the *parlementaires* took seriously in a series of vigorous disputes with the Crown.

The royalist position had been widely subscribed to by the *bourgeoisie* and those rising through royal service, as well as the leaders of the royal and ecclesiastical administrations. It, too, was acquiring a new slant, for some now rejected royal "despotism" in favor of a *national* conception of sovereignty. This national ideology was loosely associated with the ideas of Rousseau, and to some extent also with emulation of England and America — especially in terms of trade and agrarian productivity. These perspectives commingled in the goal of a constitutional monarchy, based on "progressive" national economic policies, "merit", and the "national interest" — not privilege. Many nobles had adopted at least some of the Enlightenment's often contradictory ideas; but more significantly, a few politically active aristocrats of property and stature were coming to embrace the new, genuinely liberal ideas of the "patriots".[50]

Aristocratic politics therefore had many bases: specific social interests, personal ambitions, rivalry between aristocratic and royal institutions, and developing ideologies. Passing over the problems of royal administration, it is still not surprising that the crisis which led to the Revolution emerged from a struggle between the state and an array of aristocratic forces. The "aristocratic revolt" or "pre-revolution", in fact, was a conflict over aristocratic constitutional prerogatives. Opposition to Calonne's proposals by the Assembly of Notables, which won near-consensus among aristocrats, did not center on his sweeping tax reforms, the creation of provincial assemblies (as such), or free trade.[51] The contentious issues were directly constitutional: the prerogatives of the church, the omission of distinctions of Order in the new assemblies, and the subordination of provincial estates to the royal intendants. The Notables demanded convocation of the Estates General to consider constitutional reforms, which opened a conflict over the balance of state power that had a structural basis, but no pre-determined outcome.

The *parlements* fought bitterly in their turn over a series of constitutional issues: approval of new taxes by the Estates, revival of provincial estates in place of the establishment of royal assemblies, royal acknowledgement of "fundamental law", and their own legislative role. Patriots, conservative aristocrats, and nobles in general supported the *parlements* — but the *bourgeoisie* as a whole did not. In Provence, the revival of the provincial estates by the aristocracy early in the pre-revolution led to opposition by the *bourgeoisie* as a whole to what they perceived to be an unwarranted and dangerous seizure of provincial power. Yet when the royal "coup" against the *parlements* brought a reconciliation of lawyers and the city of Aix (seat of the *parlement)* with the aristocrats and nobles, against royal "despotism", most of the *bourgeoisie* did not join in.[52] In Brittany, the pre-revolution even saw conflicts in the towns between royalists and supporters of the *parlements.*[53] Apart from the few ideological "patriots", and those closely associated with the *parlements,* the *bourgeoisie* were not engaged in or especially supportive of the struggle against the regime — it was not their interests that were at issue.

The calling of the Estates General was a clear victory for constitutionalism over absolutism; it remained to be determined which sort of constitutionalism had prevailed. Aristocratic champions such as d'Eprémesnil and Duport parted ways over the extent of constitutional reform needed, and constitutional traditionalists balked at any at all. Even for progressive aristocratic constitutionalists such as d'Eprémesnil (who was amenable to the doubling of the Third Estate) the convening of the Estates signaled victory of the *aristocracy,* as constitutional guardians of the regime. The Paris *parlement*'s decree dictating observance of the "form observed in 1614" was a warning to the ministers that the aristocracy would brook no tampering with their constitutional victory, that they were determined to shape the new order of things that would emerge from the Estates.[54] This decree came as a sharp blow to patriots and liberal aristocrats like Duport, for they looked to the Estates for a *national* constitutional renewal, for the "assembled nation" to ensure "the happiness of the people" through liberal reforms.[55] The loose associations of liberal aristocrats and patriotic pamphleteers that had come together during struggle against the Crown -- such as the "Committee of Thirty" which met at Duport's -- now turned their energies against the "aristocracy", focusing precisely on the issue of constitutional privilege.

Struggle over constitution of the state in the Ancien Régime, whether within the aristocracy or between aristocracy and *bourgeoisie,* cannot be seen as "merely" political. No political conflict is ever "disinterestedly" political, in that the politics of class society are rooted in exploitation; whatever the individual's motivations, political action touches profoundly on social interests related to surplus extraction.

But given the specific relations of surplus extraction of the Ancien Régime, there was a far more immediate connection between the political and the social. The profound, specifically political conflict that was at the heart of the French Revolution was directly derived from the fundamental nature of constitutional issues in a state which was itself a central focus of surplus extraction. The conflict of the French Revolution was not between feudal property and bourgeois enterprise: if these interests were even in conflict (unlikely, in that the property relations of the *bourgeoisie* and aristocracy were identical) they could have been mediated by the state. The Revolution was not required to force freedom of trade, sanctity of property, rational administration, and the prohibition of workers' associations on a recalcitrant nobility. The conflict was over the state because the state played a *direct* role in surplus extraction and the accumulation of property, and systematically benefited a specific, especially privileged group. Regardless of exactly how the classes of the Ancien Régime are defined -- for the demarcation of class boundaries is less important than identification of essential class relations and interests -- it can clearly be discerned that the aristocracy was attempting to secure a constitutional guarantee for its uniquely privileged position, and to end the ambiguities and mediations of the absolutist state by assuming predominant ruling power directly, as a group.

Yet the surplus extracting role of the state was not important to the aristocracy alone. If anything, the state played a proportionally larger and more regular role in surplus extraction for the less-propertied *bourgeoisie.* An exclusively aristocratic constitutional coup represented a direct and obvious loss of effective *class power* to the *bourgeoisie* (whether or not they should be seen as part of the same class). Not only would aristocrats retain their monopoly of ruling and enriching positions, but *bourgeois* influence over state policy would be minimized in any future conflict with aristocratic interests. With the ambiguities of ruling class power resolved to the disadvantage of the *bourgeoisie,* they might find themselves shut out of state offices entirely. The state's power of taxation might even pose a threat to *bourgeois* property interests. An exclusively aristocratic victory therefore posed an immediate and potentially fundamental threat to the class interests of the *bourgeoisie,* and did so specifically in their political capacity as the Third Estate. The revelation of the aristocratic constitutional intentions of the Paris *parlement* abruptly led to bitter opposition by the whole *bourgeoisie,* across France -- through hundreds of resolutions, petitions, and illegal assemblies -- as had occurred at no previous stage of conflict.[56]

The position of the nobility as a whole, however, was ambiguous and fraught with contradictions. The poorer "ancient" nobility perhaps saw an opportunity to end the domination of lesser noble offices by the rising *anoblis.* Yet even the rural *gentilshommes* -- for all their ideological inclinations -- did not have interests as irreconcilably opposed to *bourgeois* interests as the aristocracy itself. Though the lines of conflict were drawn on the constitutional issue of *noble* privilege, per se, the nobility as a social group sinks from sight during the course of the Revolution — privilege is represented by the aristocracy, and the equality of a nation of property owners by the *bourgeoisie.*

The opposition of the *bourgeoisie* was general, but not, at first, the fundamental constitutional challenge that patriots such as the Abbé Sieyès proposed. Most of the *bourgeois* petitions and resolutions confined themselves to the issues of double representation and voting by head, which Sieyès rushed to point out was not sufficient to prevent effective aristocratic domination.[57] Yet despite the pamphleteers' urgings, *bourgeois* opinion remained generally moderate and was simply opposed to the immediate and outright constitutional domination of the aristocracy posed by the forms of 1614. It is often supposed that if the state had now mediated to impose the settlement later attempted in the royal session of 23 June, the result would have been widely accepted: a "natural" aristocratic dominance of the Estates would likely have existed, unless directed against *bourgeois* interests, while an aristocratic veto on the affairs of nobility and clergy would assure their continued domination.[58]

In the event, the conflict remained unmediated and each side perceived a loss of fundamental class interests in backing down. When the Third Estate followed Sieyès in proclaiming itself the National Assembly, and asserted its sovereignty against the aristocracy, the royal position lost its ambiguity and the state stood for the aristocracy. *Bourgeois* victory against this unified aristocratic state is impossible to imagine without the popular movement.

\*    \*    \*

As George Rudé's work has clearly established, the *menu peuple* -- the whole of the urban population which, aside from minor relations of surplus extraction which may have existed among themselves, had in common their *exclusion* from the primary class relations of agrarian surplus appropriation -- were faced with a social crisis of subsistence in 1789. With regard to the political conflict, they had no direct social interest in either side. Their primary interests lay as ever in the good order and steady price of bread. This popular social interest in a stable bread supply, however, had long required the intervention of the state. The monarchy had abrogated this responsibility at the start of the constitutional conflicts by freeing the grain trade — arguably more in the interests of the aristocratic grain dealers and large estate owners than the *bourgeoisie;* certainly the Physiocrats were aristocrats. In any case, the social crisis required action, change — and between the contending parties only the Third Estate stood for change.

The focus of patriotic agitation at this stage was the moderate majority of the *bourgeoisie,* but in the politicized circumstances, and given their own crisis, the *menu peuple* quickly came to understand that the choice was between change and the Nation, on one hand, or obstruction and privilege, on the other. Whatever meaning the "unity" of the Third may previously have had for the people -- and it likely was not great -- the Third Estate now represented progressive changes in state policy to resolve the social crisis. How else are "Vive le Roi," "Vive M. Necker," and "Vive le Tiers État" to be linked as the slogans of a riot over subsistence?[59] The people now identified themselves as the Third Estate and looked to their champions in the Estates to fight for change against the aristocracy — who stood for the status quo and popular misery.

"Inherent" popular ideology included both invective against aristocrats and acceptance of their ideological perspective. It was above all popular understanding of the need for change, and aristocratic opposition to it, that determined the role of the popular movement.[60] From this followed both the popular conception of "aristocratic plot" -- a refraction of social reality that suggests the *pacte de famine* of their inherent ideology -- and the adoption of anti-aristocratic and national slogans drawn from the patriots. Much as they later defined themselves as *sans-culottes* through their opposition to "aristocracy" in its broadest sense, so at this point the *menu peuple* identified with the "Third Estate" as the total body of political opposition to the obstructionism and famine of the aristocrats.

As both the social crisis and the political crisis deepened, the patriots intensified efforts to popularize the fundamental conflict between the aristocracy and the Nation, and the Orléanists were certainly ready to help foment unrest. The message filtered into popular ideology: the *"noblesse"* were equated with the "enemies" of Parisians, and the "Nation" with opposition to the enemies; the popular insurrection of July, 1789 became "bringing help to the Nation."[61] Popular actions began as *protest,* in a traditional manner that expected relief from the state, once properly informed and unhindered. In the rush of mounting political crisis, faced with the certain defeat of their champions and urged on by the patriots, the people transformed protest into direct popular political action.

This was the initial and fundamental bargain between the people and the *bourgeois* revolutionaries they came to see as mandatories. The people would provide support to the *bourgeois* renewal of power, and join in founding the Nation, in return for suppression of popular enemies and maintenance of the necessities of subsistence. The "bargain" was not exclusively with the *bourgeoisie,* but also with the king, with whom they particularly were to "review" the terms over the next several years. In the course of these subsequent *journées,* the people not only broke constitutional deadlocks in favor of the more resolute opponents of aristocracy, but they developed their own ideology of revolutionary egalitarianism as the true general interest. Experience taught the people the need for revolutionary zeal and suspicion of "natural" aristocrats. They learned of popular sovereignty from the Cordeliers and the Jacobins, but they learned its form and real meaning in the *journées* of the Revolution — events which were at once political action and subsistence protest; spontaneous, and politically intentional.[62]

Ultimately, the lesson was learned that opposing aristocracy was a *permanent* struggle, and popular sovereignty a permanent responsibility; that only egalitarian democrats would represent popular interests, and that political violence was a necessary tool for the achievement of social justice. So long as the fundamental issue remained opposition to constitutional aristocracy, there was a natural confluence of interest between the popular movement and the revolutionary leadership. The course of revolutionary struggle selected out the most fiercely anti-aristocratic and "national" of the leadership, and when faced with the need for a viable national state, the choice narrowed to the radical Jacobins and those who acquiesced in their lead. In any constitutional conflict -- to which political crisis was continually reduced by the Revolution -- the people found their voice in the sternness and national imagery of the Left, and the Left found their base in the people. But with the victory of the Mountain over the Girondins, the chain of this logic was broken: the Jacobins would carry the struggle against aristocracy as far as civil society would allow, and no farther.

This history of the popular movement is the history of the evolving political purpose of the *sans-culottes* — a unique and specific purpose, based on concrete social needs, which defined them as a political group. At first it led only to defense of the moderate reformers who appeared to represent their interests: the insurrection of 1789 was not a long step beyond popular protest. Yet it sealed a bargain which, by linking the interests of the people to the success of the Revolution, provided the *bourgeoisie* with the means of creating an effective revolutionary government. Over the following five years this political purpose was redefined through practical revolutionary experience and exposure to *bourgeois* ideology. It never acquired the same "social" quality as that of the *bourgeoisie* -- whose "general" and "national" interests defined a class society -- but the "political" character of the *sans-culottes'* struggle for egalitarian democracy was a real expression of popular social interests. It drew concepts from the national democratic ideology of the *bourgeois* revolution, but had its own base in popular experience and ideas.

The conjunction of popular subsistence crisis with *bourgeois* struggle against the aristocracy was the basis for an alliance that was thrust upon the *bourgeoisie* -- its apprehension made manifest in the National Guard -- by a popular movement which made the *bourgeois* issue of opposition to aristocracy into its own. Not only was the popular movement essential to the success of the *bourgeois* revolution, but a coherent *bourgeois* struggle against the aristocracy was necessary for the emergence of the popular movement. The internal contradiction of this movement lay in the logic by which its political purpose became a tool of the *bourgeoisie* in creating a strong national state, while the *menu peuple* lacked the capacity to keep this from taking the form of a class state based on property interests.

The dictatorship of the Revolutionary Government revealed itself to be a form of the purely "political" state peculiar to civil society — indeed, it was ruthless in its opposition to other than "political" uses of political power: the *virtuous* state. Yet, as Marx observed in *The Holy Family* (in a point Furet tries to turn against the idea of a consistent *bourgeois* revolution), by the very *virtue* with which the Jacobin dictatorship embraced national and democratic ideology, it alienated itself from that "bourgeois liberalism" for which the democratic state was a *means* and not an end.[63] Indeed, a substantial *bourgeois* interest in a large and corrupt state bureaucracy existed well into the nineteenth century; not until the Third Republic was there much demand for the virtuous state. Once the Jacobins' tireless efforts to preserve the nation, create the instruments of national revolutionary war, and tame the "excesses" of the people were successful, those "ideologues" who madly attempted to practice what they preached could be dispensed with. The Revolution had secured its supreme objective — blocking the establishment of an unmediated aristocratic state.

## *NOTES*

[I would like to thank Ellen Meiksins Wood for her very helpful comments and criticism.]

1. The classic statement is found in Georges Lefebvre, *The Coming of the French Revolution* (Princeton, 1947).

2. See particularly: George Rudé, *The Crowd in the French Revolution* (Oxford, 1959); *Ideology and Popular Protest* (New York, 1980); Albert Soboul, *The Parisian Sans-culottes and the French Revolution, 1793-4* (Oxford, 1964); *Les sans-culottes parisiens en l'an II: mouvement populaire et gouvernment révolutionnaire, 2 juin-9 thermidor an II* (Paris, 1958).

3. William Doyle, *Origins of the French Revolution* (Oxford, 1980), presents both an excellent summary and a synthesis of the revisionist arguments.

4. For an excellent brief discussion of the major concepts of Marxism, see Raymond Williams, *Marxism and Literature* (Oxford, 1977).

5. See discussion below. I pursued this question of the non-Marxist origins and doubtful *validity of the concept of "bourgeois revolution" at some length in my dissertation, *Historical Materialism and Bourgeois Revolution: Ideology and Interpretation of the French Revolution,* which is to be published in revised form by Verso Books.

6. Alfred Cobban, *The Social Interpretation of the French Revolution* (London, 1964), pp. 8-14, 162-163.

7. Colin Lucas, "Notable against notable," *Times Literary Supplement* (London, 8 May, 1981, p. 525.

8. Cobban, *Social Interpretation,* pp. 126-128, *A History of Modern France,* vol. I (Penguin, 1963), pp. 137-138, 226-228; François Furet and Denis Richet, *La Révolution française,* 2nd. ed. (Paris, 1973), pp. 204-207, 211-213.

9. Rudé, *Ideology,* pp. 104-115; Soboul, *Parisian Sans-culottes,* p. 69.

10. For a discussion of Robespierre's commitment to social justice, see George Rudé, *Robespierre, Portrait of a Revolutionary Democrat* (London, 1975).

11. Soboul, *Parisian Sans-culottes,* pp. 249-261; Rudé; *Robespierre,* pp. 109-121, 188-192.

12. François Furet appears to hold the opposite opinion; see F. Furet, C. Mazauric, and L. Bergeron, "The Sans-culottes and the French Revolution," in Jeffrey Kaplow, ed., *New Perspectives on the French Revolution* (New York, 1965), pp. 226-53.

13. Classic statements of the concept of bourgeois revolution, as applied to the French and the English Revolutions respectively, are found in François Mignet, *History of the French Revolution. From 1789 to 1814* (London, 1913) (first published in 1824), and Augustin Thierry, "Vue des révolutions d'Angleterre," in *Dix Ans d'Études Historiques,* vol. 6 of *Œuvres Complètes* (Paris, 1851) (first published in 1817). See also: Albert Soboul, "L'Historiographie classique de la Révolution française," *La Pensée,* 177 (1974), 40-58, and Raphael Samuel, "British Marxist Historians, 1880-1980: Part One," *New Left Review,* 120 (1980), 21-96, pp. 32-35.

14. Karl Marx and Frederick Engels, *The German Ideology* (New York, 1963), pp. 11-41.

15. On "Demographic history", see Robert Brenner, "Agrarian Class Structure in Pre-Industrial Europe," *Past and Present,* 70 (1976), 30-75.

16. See Furet, in Furet *et al.,* p. 228.

17. See Bergeron, in Furet *et al.,* pp. 242-253.

18. The arguments against the feudal / capitalist model are summarized by Doyle, pp. 11-24, and also by François Furet, "Le catéchisme révolutionnaire," in *Penser la Révolution française* (Paris, 1978), pp. 113-172.

19. George V. Taylor, "Noncapitalist Wealth and the Origins of the French Revolution," *American Historical Review,* LXXII (1967), 469-96.

20. Furet, "Le catéchisme", pp. 142-153, 170-171.

21. Doyle, p. 24.

22. Cobban, Furet and Richet, and Bergeron all offer this differentiation, and the "mob"-like characterization of the *menu peuple.*

23. Cobban, *History,* pp. 137-138.

24. Doyle, p. 179; Furet and Richet, p. 211.

25. Cobban, *Social Interpretation,* p. 126; Furet, in Furet *et al.,* p. 228.

26. Lucas, "Notables".

27. Lucas, "Notables", and "Nobles, Bourgeois and the Origins of the French Revolution," *Past and Present,* 60 (1973), 84-126.

28. On the complex question of class relations in pre-industrial society, see the three important articles by Robert Brenner: "Agrarian Class Structure," *op. cit.,* "On the Origins of Capitalist Development: a Critique of Neo-Smithian Marxism," *New Left Review,* 104 (1977), and "The Agrarian Roots of European Capitalism," *Past and Present,* 97 (1982), 16-113. Also, see the seminal "transition" debate, collected as Rodney Hilton, Paul Sweezy, Maurice Dobb, *et al., The Transition from Feudalism to Capitalism* (London, 1976).

29. Karl Marx, *Capital,* vol. III (Moscow, 1959), p. 791.

30. These points follow the central line of argument in *Capital.*

31. The evidence is drawn from many monographic studies of the towns, regions and institutions of the Ancien Régime, such as: Paul Bois, *Paysans de l'Ouest* (Paris, 1971); Paul Butel, *Les négociants Bordelais, l'Europe et les Iles au xviiie siècle* (Paris, 1974); Robert Forster, *The House of Saulx-Tavanes* (Baltimore, 1971), *The Nobility of Toulouse in the 18th Century* (Baltimore, 1960); Maurice Garden, *Lyon et les Lyonnais au xviiie siècle* (Paris, 1970); Pierre Goubert, *Beauvais et le beauvaisis de 1600 à 1730* (Paris, 1960); Georges Lefebvre, *Études orléanaises,* 2 vols. (Paris, 1963); T. J. A. Le Goff, *Vannes and its Region* (London, 1981); Herbert Luthy, *La Banque protestante en France, de la révocation de l'édit de Nantes à la Révolution,* 2 vols. (Paris, 1959). The evidence is just as clear in a Marxist work such as Régine Robin, *La société française en 1789: Semur-en-Auxois* (Paris, 1970).

32. Samuel, p. 35.

33. Henceforth, the term *bourgeoisie* will only be used to refer to that social group specific to the Ancien Régime, and will be italicized to denote a contemporary term of that society.

34. Elinor Barber, *The Bourgeoisie in 18th Century France* (Princeton, 1955).

35. Georges Lefebvre, *Les Paysans du Nord pendant la Révolution française,* 2nd. ed. (Paris, 1972). A discussion of the small area of French Flanders would require a comparative analysis of agriculture in the Low Countries that is beyond the scope of this article.

36. See Guy Chaussinand-Nogaret, *La Noblesse au xviie siècle. De la féodalité au lumières* (Paris, 1976), plus the works by Forster, Butel, Taylor, and Doyle; but nearly all the major regional studies make these points to one extent or another.

37. See Goubert, *op. cit.*

38. Besides the Brenner articles cited above, on the contrast between English and French agriculture see Eric Kerridge, *The Farmers of Old England* (London, 1973), or the Introduction by G. E. Fussell to Lord Ernle's *English Farming, Past and Present,* 6th ed. (London, 1961), and Robert Forster, "Obstacles to Agricultural Growth in 18th Century France," *American Historical Review,* 75 (1970), 1600-1612.

39. For overviews of French agriculture in each of its major geo-social zones, see E. Labrousse, P. Léon, P. Goubert *et al., Histoire économique et sociale de la France moderne,* Vol. 2 (Paris, 1970), and G. Duby and A. Wallon, eds., *Histoire de la France rurale,* Vol. 2 (Paris, 1975).

40. See Robert Forster, *Nobility of Toulouse,* "Obstacles to Growth," plus "Seigneurs and their agents," in E. Hinrichs, *et al., Vom Ancien Régime zur Französischen Revolution,* (Göttingen, 1978), and "The 'World' between Seigneur and Peasant," in R.C. Rosbottom, ed., *Studies in Eighteenth-Century Culture, Vol. 5* (Wisconsin, 1976).

41. Labrousse, Léon, Goubert, *et al.,* and Duby and Wallon have good discussions of the Paris region; also Jean Jacquart, *La Crise rurale en Ile-de-France 1550-1670* (Paris, 1974), plus Gilles Postel-Vinay, *La Rente foncière dans le capitalisme agricole* (Paris, 1974), for an effort to read the transition to capitalism into these agrarian relations.

42. François Bluche, *Les Magistrates du Parlement de Paris au xviiie siècle (1715-1771)* (Paris, 1960).

43. J. F. Bosher, *French Finances 1770-1795: From Business to Bureaucracy* (Cambridge, 1970); Yves Durand, *Les Fermiers-Généraux au xviiie siècle* (Paris, 1971).

44. Durand, pp. 60-87, 98, 219.

45. Bluche, pp. 65-68.

46. For the careers and fortune of a great house, see Forster, *Saulx-Tavanes.*

47. See Chaussinand-Nogaret.

48. Forster, *Nobility of Toulouse,* and "The Noble Wine Producers of the Bordelais in the Eighteenth Century," *Economic History Review,* xiv (1961).

49. Nanerl Keohane offers a full discussion of these ideological perspectives in *Philosophy and the State in France* (Princeton, 1980).

50. Chaussinand-Nogaret, *op. cit.,* makes a great deal of the "enlightened" ideology of the nobility.

51. Jean Egret, *The French Pre-Revolution, 1787-1788* (Chicago, 1977), pp. 1-24.

52. Jean Egret, *The Pre-Revolution,* and "The Pre-Revolution in Provence (1787-1789)," in Kaplow, pp. 153-170.

53. Jean Egret, "The Origins of the Revolution in Brittany (1788-1789)," in Kaplow, pp. 136-152.

54. Egret, *The Pre-Revolution,* pp. 197-203.

55. Egret, *The Pre-Revolution,* p. 88.

56. Egret, *The Pre-Revolution,* pp. 205-210.

57. E. M. Sieyès, *What is the Third Estate?* (London, 1963), pp. 67-69.

58. Doyle, p. 175.

59. As George Rudé so cogently asks, *Ideology,* p. 111.

60. For "inherent" ideology, and the influence of experience, see Rudé, *Ideology,* pp. 28-37.

61. Rudé, *Ideology,* p. 111.

62. Rudé, *The Crowd,* pp. 210-231.

63. Karl Marx and Frederick Engels, *The Holy Family,* Marx-Engels *Collected Works,* vol. 4, pp. 122-124; Furet, "Le catéchisme", p. 169.

R.B. Rose

# JACQUERIE AT DAVENESCOURT IN 1791: A PEASANT RIOT IN THE FRENCH REVOLUTION

On the morning of 25 February 1791 the bell began to ring in the Parish church of the little Picard village of Davenescourt, and as the peasants flocked in from the fields, rumours began to spread about alarming events at the local château, the château of the Countess de la Myre. The mayor and municipal officers, it was said, had gone up to the château early that morning, formally and peacefully, to discuss certain matters in dispute between the Countess and her tenants, only to find themselves trapped in the fortified tower of the château and held there while the Maréchaussée were sent for from the neighbouring District capital, Montdidier. At all costs they must be rescued. And so a crowd gathered outside the château until, about ten o'clock, it burst through the doors of the tower, forcing the portcullis with iron bars, and poured inside. There was a struggle with one of the family retainers over a gun, the gun went off, and the old man fell bleeding at the feet of the Countess.

So began a reign of terror for the occupants of the château which lasted for five hours, until three p.m. Meanwhile there was a general pillage of the building. The archive room was forced and the estate papers carried away; a maid trying to escape by a ladder was hurt when the ladder was pulled down. The Countess herself and her two children were shut up in a room with a crowd of angry rebels, a noose was put round the Countess' neck by a peasant woman, sabres and a bayonet were flourished over her, cutting her on the arm and the forehead, while, weeping, she was forced to sign a succession of papers thrust at her by her captors. Not until that afternoon were the prisoners allowed to escape, packed into a cabriolet, driving off through the pouring rain, and thankful to get away alive.

The kind of Jacquerie I have been describing is, of course, a commonplace of the history of the French Revolution. However the Davenescourt riot quickly became a national *cause célèbre*. The Countess de la Myre was well connected, and her sufferings touched the heart of the leading Royalist editor Mallet du Pan, editor of the influential *Mercure de France*, who, a few days later, printed an indignant account of this "horrible outrage of the popular tyranny".[1] The Countess also knew Duport du Tertre, the Minister of Justice in the new Government in Paris, and it was not long before the ringleaders of the Davenescourt Jacquerie found themselves, in the spring and summer of 1791, on trial for their lives. Indeed they might well have perished but for a curious accident.

Thrown into prison in Montdidier, for a few days they chanced to share a cell with a notorious local agitator: François-Noel, or "Camille" Babeuf. Babeuf is chiefly known to history as the author of the so-called "Conspiracy of the Equals" of 1796, an attempt to overthrow the Directory and to create a communist régime in France. All that was, of course, a long way in the future in 1791. But already Babeuf had made a name for himself, in his home province, Picardy, as a leader of popular and peasant protest movements.

In 1790, in particular, he had led a revolt against indirect taxation which had ended in his being gaoled in Paris for some months.[2] This time he was in the Montdidier gaol for leading a crowd of "squatters" onto the commons belonging to his home town, Roye, and dividing the land out among his followers.

Once he had secured his own release, Babeuf took up the defence of the Davenescourt peasants, and he eventually succeeded in winning them an amnesty. In the meantime the Davenescourt Affair broadened out into a kind of national test case. On the one hand Babeuf published a propaganda pamphlet to demonstrate how the Davenescourt villagers had been goaded into violence by the unremitting and heartless feudal tyranny of the Countess de la Myre;[3] on the other the Countess' chaplain published a defence, in some ways, ironically, even more damning than Babeuf's indictment, to demonstrate that the Countess had acted at all times perfectly within the law and in defence of her legitimate rights.[4]

It is a curious reflection on the continuity of French history that this battle was still not yet fought out a century later, in 1888, when the local radical newspaper, the *Journal de Montdidier,* unearthed Babeuf's pamphlet, and reprinted it as electoral ammunition against a descendant of the Countess de la Myre, in the middle of a struggle for the control of the municipal council of Montdidier.

The wealth of documentation which was invoked by both sides in the controversy over the 1791 trial makes the Davenescourt Affair of particular interest to the historian of the French Revolution. In 1954 Professor Georges Lefebvre, the great French pioneer of studies of the Revolutionary peasantry, investigated another "peasant outrage" which took place about the same time, the murder of the Count of Dampierre.[5] Dampierre was a Royalist seigneur who joined a select group of the faithful who rallied to Louis XVI as the King passed by on his way to the frontier in June 1791. This was the occasion of the dramatic attempt of the French Royal family to escape which is known as the "flight to Varennes". While trying thus to do his chivalric duty the Count was pulled down by a group of peasants and shot.

While probing into the background of this apparently gratuitous piece of savagery, Lefebvre was able to show that for many years before the Revolution the Count and his tenants has been engaged in a bitter conflict over feudal rights on his estate in Champagne, and it was this conflict which finally erupted in the violence of 1791. The point that Lefebvre sought to illustrate was that this sudden outburst of violence was not therefore sudden at all, nor was it politically motivated in any superficial sense. Instead, the Count's murder had a generation of growing class hatred behind it, and it is to this general and intensifying bitter conflict in the villages in the years immediately before 1789 that we must look for an explanation of a great deal of the violence in the Revolution.

The extent of the "seigneurial reaction" remains an issue. Whether the last decades of the Old Régime were characterised by a significant intensification of feudal exploitation, by both noble and non-noble owners of feudal rights, is still a subject of controversy amongst historians.

In standard works like Philippe Sagnac's social history of modern France[6] and Gérard Walter's history of the French peasants[7] the seigneurial reaction is regarded as a general and important historical fact. Specialist studies such as Lefebvre's *Paysans du Nord*[8] and Saint-Jacob's *Paysans de la Bourgogne*[9] provide massive documentation of the actuality of such a reaction in widely separated regions of France, while Robert Forster's accounts of the transactions of the landlords of the Toulouse region and of the Burgundian family of Saulx-Tavanes offer clear illustrations of the methods involved.[10] Two of Forster's Toulouse seigneurs dug back respectively as far as 1235 and 1280 to prove their entitlement to lapsed feudal payments;[11] when the Count of Saulx-Tavanes was elevated to a Dukedom in 1786 he doubled his feudal dues for that year by reviving a right that had not been exercised for more than four hundred years. Between 1754 and 1788 the Saulx-Tavanes family raised income from their estates, a quarter derived from feudal dues and incidents, by more than forty percent, from 49,000 livres to 86,000 livres.[12] Alun Davies found evidence of a seigneurial reaction in Normandy, where the Duke of Harcourt sought, about 1752, to revive a whole series of ancient charges, which would have made his tenants pay, for example, "12 deniers from each house or cottage having a fire at Michaelmas, 2[d] for stabling a horse, 1[d] for a cow or pig, 1 *maille* for a sheep for one night and one day anywhere on the manor, 1[d] for any cow slaughtered and 4[d] as customs due if a coffer or chest were removed", and so on.[13]

In Picardy itself, the pre-revolutionary career of Babeuf himself as a *feudiste,* or specialist in feudal estate administration, provides a further illustration of the methods of the seigneurial reaction. In 1787, for example, Babeuf offered to double the Marquis de Soyecourt's income from *cens* or quitrent by reorganising his *terriers,* the records of feudal obligation, which had fallen into disarray over the past fifty years.[14]

The author of an influential recent revision,[15] William Doyle, nevertheless challenges the reality of the pre-revolutionary "feudal" or "seigneurial" reaction. Doyle does not doubt the evidence for attempts by nobles to assert and reassert their seigneurial rights at the expense of the peasants during the eighteenth century. Instead he argues, firstly, that other evidence indicates that these attempts were not universal throughout France, and, secondly, that such pressures were not a new phenomenon, but were "processes as old as the system". Thus "feudal reactions" in the sense of a rigorous insistence on legitimate rights, may be discovered occurring in various regions of France at various times over the centuries, and the case for a particularly significant intensification in the years immediately before 1789 has consequently not been established.

There is some force in these arguments; but whether the abundant pre-revolutionary examples of the vigorous pressing of seigneurial claims were widespread enough and significant enough to be qualified as a distinct and separate "seigneurial reaction" must continue to depend, granted the scattered and uneven nature of the evidence, largely on the intuition and judgment of the historian.

In this context the events in Davenescourt can only add support to those who believe that there was such a seigneurial reaction, and that that reaction contributed to the intensification of class-conflict and the building up of a revolutionary mentality in the French countryside during the years before 1789.

But first let us consider the parties in conflict. On the one hand, the village of Davenescourt, a typical Picard village, low-lying, with peaty soil, growing wheat and rye, with some cattle and sheep. About a hundred and sixty households, perhaps five hundred inhabitants, with a château on the river bank, a parish church, a mill, and fairly extensive common meadow on the marshy land by the river. On the other, the seigneurial family, the inhabitants of the château, Counts of La Myre, Barons-chatelain both of Davenescourt and the adjacent manor of Hangest.

Down to 1777 the holder of the title was Gabriel Melchior de la Myre, a naval officer, who died in that year, leaving his widow, Philippine, with three young children, two sons and a daughter. The eldest son, Joseph-Gabriel, was still only nineteen or twenty in 1791. Thus the administration of the family estates in Picardy, and also in Normandy, where there was other property, was the sole responsibility of the Countess.[16]

However, she was not without advisers. On his deathbed the Count had entrusted the protection of his children to their tutor, the Abbé Pierre Tournier, one-time professor of Philosophy at the Collège of Arras. The villagers' account presents Tournier as a character straight out of Beaumarchais, both comic and sinister, at the same time the Countess' evil genius and the scourge of the rustic ungodly. He was said to take a keen interest in the moral welfare of the maids at the château, even to the extent of shooting one of their suitors in the legs during a quarrel. And then there was the famous occasion of the midnight "owl hunt", which took place some time in 1780, but was never forgotten by the village.

Some of the village lads had fallen into the habit of taking an evening swim in the Countess' river, which they would round off in a suitable manner by raiding the Countess' orchard and vegetable patch for a snack. On the night in question the good abbé organised an armed posse from the château to check these depredations. According to Tournier's own version the guns all had powder but no shot — except his own, which he had charged just in case the party should start up an owl. The banging of the guns and the whistle of shot proved very effective in frightening off the invaders — and in building up the reputation of the "murderers at the château" also.

The Countess could rely also on a second adviser: Vincent Le Sueur, her steward, who had been at the château since about 1772. Le Sueur was particularly hated by the peasants since he was a former peasant himself and let nothing past him. Significantly, whenever they spoke of Le Sueur, the peasants tended to drop the Le, and called him simply Sueur ("Sweat"), as a measure of their affection.

Almost as soon as Count Gabriel had breathed his last, this triumvirate, the Countess, the Abbé and the steward, put their heads together to work out the plan of campaign of a private "seigneurial reaction". The Countess had a use for the money: the records show that she built a new Presbytery for the parish priest in the 1780s,[7] and, on the eve of the Revolution, in 1788, she began to build a new château which was to cost 25,000 livres.

The first opportunity presented itself when a lawsuit over the seigneurial mill was decided in favour of the Countess by the *Parlement de Paris* in 1781. The roots of this particular quarrel dated back centuries; in fact, they dated back to 1120. The crux of the matter was a dispute between the La Myre family and the Chapter of the Priory of Saint-Quentin in Beauvais over seigneurial rights and particularly over the ownership of the banality of the mill, that is, the sole right to licence grain milling within the barony of Davenescourt and Hangest. For centuries, down to 1780, the Priory had managed to maintain a mill in Hangest. In 1781, however, the Parlement de Paris ordered the Chapter to demolish their mill, and the Countess promptly announced her intention of enforcing a monopoly. Henceforth no grain was to be carried out of Davenescourt to "foreign" mills. All must be ground at the seigneurial mill. The Countess was gracious enough to concede that if the villagers did not like this arrangement, she had no objection to their going to one of the three mills in Hangest, all of which now belonged to her.

The Davenescourt villagers decided to resist, and fifty heads of households got together an appeal to the Intendant of Picardy, D'Agay de Mutigny, who backed the Countess, and refused leave to appeal to the royal court. Two leading citizens, Cusset, the King's Surveyor (Arpenteur du Roi) and Masson, the Syndic or secretary of the village community, took the case instead to Paris and appealed to the Parlement. Their argument was that, according to the local custom of the Bailliage of Péronne, the ban of the mill applied only to outsiders, and that vassals, or genuine tenants, were entitled to have their grain milled where they wished. It might or might not have been good law, but that did not greatly affect the issue. What did affect the issue was the close friendship between the Countess and Miromesnil, First President of the Parlement de Rouen, who was Keeper of the Royal Seals at Paris from 1774 to 1787. At the time of Maupeou's exile of the Parlements ten years earlier, it was at Davenescourt that Miromesnil had chosen to take refuge.

Now the influence of this legal and political heavyweight was thrown into the scales of justice on the Countess' side. In July, 1784 the Parlement de Paris declared that the seigneurs of Davenescourt had the right to compel all the inhabitants without exception to use the seigneurial mill, and to extract *mouture,* a special toll, from those who obtained permission to take their grain elsewhere. The cost to the Davenescourt commune of the three years' proceedings was four thousand livres. At that they got off lightly. When the inhabitants of another village in Picardy, Decalogne, sued the Comtesse de Ligny in a similar case, the proceedings took twenty-two years and in the end Parlement awarded twelve thousand livres in damages and fees against the suitors.[18]

As soon as she learned of the Parlement's verdict, the Countess de la Myre started to turn the screws as tightly as possible, posting lackeys along the roads in and out of Davenescourt, and demanding the payment of *mouture* on the bread which the stubborn villagers insisted on buying in the nearby town of Montdidier, rather than have any dealings with the grasping miller to whom the Countess had leased her mill. Even one of the workmen coming in to help build the new château had a single loaf of bread snatched away from him, although the Countess was afterwards shamed into giving it back.

The same decision of 1781 which had confirmed the Countess' sole ownership of the banality of the mill had also confirmed her in sole possession of another seigneurial right, the right of *Voirie*. By this right the seigneur was entitled to plant trees along the sides of the public roads passing through his fief. There was also a similar, but distinct, right of *Plantation* by which the seigneur could plant on the common lands within the fief.

As a result of the exercise of the right of *Voirie* the countryside of North-Eastern France was beautified with pleasing avenues of apple trees, but there was more to *Voirie* than beautification. Apples, chiefly for cider, were an important cash crop, and, as the eighteenth century drew to a close, the growing shortage of timber for building and for fuel led the seigneurs to seek to make the most of their rights, either directly, or by leasing them out. But as the avenues extended and grew thicker, and as smaller and smaller by-lanes began to turn into avenues overnight, the rural atmosphere was poisoned by a growing conflict of interest.

All over France the peasants whose land abutted on the roads protested that the shade of the avenue trees made their land infertile. The situation was further aggravated by two royal edicts of 1778 and 1780 which laid down firstly, that highways should be at least ten feet wide, and secondly, placed the trees along the verges under the safeguard of the village communities. What this meant in practice was that the seigneur was entitled to chop down the existing hedges which closed off and protected the peasants' field from marauding animals, so as to widen the highway and plant his own saplings, but if these were then torn up, the peasants had to stand the cost.

At Davenescourt the "War of the Trees" had some unusual features. The main highways were already seventy-two feet wide, with hedges at the sides. They were used for sheep pasture, and there were constant conflicts between the shepherds and the cultivators over encroachment on the pasture by peasants whose lands abutted on the roads. At the beginning of the 1780s the Countess intervened to plant two rows of apple trees along the roads, with thirty feet between the rows. The villagers promptly pulled them up and the Countess appealed to a royal court to declare that the plantation was, according to law, under the protection of the Commune of Davenescourt, and that the villagers must therefore pay compensation through the Commune. The villagers contested the case and lost, and it cost them six hundred livres; this was in 1783. The next conflict seems to have resulted from a counter-attack by the villagers following the episode of the roadside trees.

There was a river running through the village and past the château, which also drained a swampy area, the *Marais de Davenescourt,* a common pasture for the inhabitants. Between them the hundred and sixty households of the village were able to muster 150 cows, ninety-two horses, and forty-two mules or donkeys, and the marshy common was an important part of the village economy. As well as pasturing their beasts the inhabitants were entitled to cut fodder with a sickle, but not to reap with a scythe.

The river fishing-rights were reserved to the seigneur. However, soon after the Countess won her case over the trees, fishing suddenly became a lot more difficult, when the Davenescourt villagers planted a string of willow trees right on the bank and across the footpath, barring access to the river. Willows were, of course, very useful in the rural economy for fencing, basket-weaking and many other crafts. When the Countess asked that the willows should be planted at least three feet from the river's edge she met a blank refusal. So she invoked the right of *Triage* to teach the villagers a lesson.

The right of *Triage* had been regulated by an ordinance of 1664. In effect it was the right of any seigneur to divide up and enclose the common land within his fief, taking one-third for himself, and leaving two-thirds for the peasants. However there were certain conditions. The onus was on the seigneur to prove that the two-thirds of the commons left to the tenants was adequate for their needs, and that the original grant of the commons to the inhabitants had been a free concession by the seigneur and not made by a charter which specified payment by the inhabitants for the use of the common.

The Davenescourt villagers were now on their mettle, and they dug up a charter of 1258 which seemed to show, firstly, that there had already been, even by that date, a "Triage" -- a partition of the commons -- and that the section left to the inhabitants had been granted in return for considerations, and not as a free concession.

The Countess took the whole matter to the special court which dealt with such questions, the *Maîtrise des Eaux et Forêts,* at Clermont en Beauvaisis. The resulting lawsuit lasted eighteen months before the villagers ran out of money and nerve and gave up. During this time the Syndic, who represented the Commune, had to attend court for 160 days. The result was a declaration in favour of the Countess, in 1785. Not only was the Countess given the right to enclose a third of the commons, but she was allowed to choose her own third. According to the villagers she promptly seized the five best patches, which were worth the entire remainder of the commons put together. To demonstrate the impartiality of French justice under the Old Régime, when the bill for legal fees came in, the villagers found everything divided in its proper proportions, according to the principle of *Triage:* one-third as to be paid by the Countess, two-thirds to be paid by the Commune.

As soon as everything was settled the Countess decided to drain the whole marsh. The abbé Tournier described it as "one of her charities". The villagers were strangely lacking in gratitude. They pointed out, in a carping spirit, that the drainage works involved a network of eight- or nine-feet ditches which made access difficult and use dangerous for the village cattle. It looks as though what happened was that the Countess turned her piece into an enclosed and improved meadow, while the villagers continued to use theirs, as best they might, as rough pasture.

The triumvirate at the château had now won three victories in eighteen months; in the battle of the mill, the battle of the trees, and the battle of the commons. There was still more to come. A common feature of the seigneurial reaction in the 1780s was an attempt to revive and perpetuate ancient feudal dues and incidents. A seigneur, or the Prior of an Abbey, would get his own steward, or an outside expert, to go through the archives digging out old rights and payments and consolidating them into a new *Terrier* or statement of feudal obligations binding on all the tenants. Once the new *Terrier* had been completed, each tenant was compelled to agree to its terms, with perhaps a demand for twenty years or so of arrears. If he resisted he was fined in the seigneurial court; if he then appealed to a higher court he would be fought to a standstill, and ruined by the costs, in order to encourage the others.

Inevitably, the abbé Tournier and Le Sueur eventually turned their attention to the *Terrier* of Davenescourt. First, however, they waited until August 1786, when a royal edict raised the fees for the drafting of a *Terrier,* which were payable by the tenants, six times over. Then Tournier went round the village, allegedly with pistols at the ready, compelling all the tenants to accept the new conditions, while Le Sueur waited in reserve in case anybody decided to defy the abbé and his pistols and to take the matter to the seigneurial court, where he presided.

The new *Terrier* itself was not an exceptionally oppressive document, but it did include two new obligations. Firstly it made the inhabitants responsible for the repair of the highway and the bridge. Secondly, and this must have rankled most of all, it incorporated the recent decision which awarded the seigneur the absolute monopoly of the mill. In 1786 there seemed nothing the villagers could do about it, and they were compelled to submit — not entirely without protest, however. Even before the outbreak of the Revolution in 1789, if the abbé Tournier can be believed, there was a kind of permanent "cold war" at Davenescourt. On Sundays and feast days drunken crowds would gather around the château throwing stones and pebbles and flaunting "foreign millers" at the doors and windows.

After 1789, of course, the balance of forces in the village began to change. The famine of 1789 which contributed to the revolutionary discontents of that year was particularly severe in Picardy, thanks to a summer hailstorm in 1788 which destroyed food crops and flax across large stretches of the countryside, and the events of July 1789 in Paris were accompanied by a general uprising in the North-East of France, with attacks on excise barriers and grain convoys and warehouses.

The inhabitants of Davenescourt were preserved from complete destitution after the hail by another of the Countess' "charities", the rebuilding of the château. According to Tournier, when the château barns were empty, in 1789, he scoured the roads of Santerre to buy grain for the village, which he sold to the "workers" (*les ouvriers*) at a third of the going price. The Countess rose to the crisis by giving interest-free loans to ruined peasants and by allowing the tenant farmers a two-thirds rebate on their rent.

It was not enough. On 17 July 1789 an early outbreak of the curious phenomenon known as the *Grande peur* reached Davenescourt. The *Grande peur,* or "great fear", was a wave of mass hysteria which spread across the French countryside from village to village in 1789. It was sparked off by rumours of huge armies of desperate bandits and vagabonds wandering about pillaging and murdering. In response to such rumours the villagers would turn out in armed, excited bands. When the bandits failed to turn up, they usually went home tamely enough, but sometimes the peasant crowds themselves turned and attacked the local châteaux.

At Davenescourt it was a very near thing. Whilst the villagers were marching about the countryside searching for "bandits", Tournier and Le Sueur hurriedly got bread made at the mill for baking and free distribution to the crowd, but the château was only saved by a rally of peasants from other parishes, including Hangest, who gathered there to protect the Countess. Even so, it cost the Countess about five hundred livres in "refreshments" and cash contributions to her loyal vassals before things calmed down again.

One consequence of the revolutionary crisis of 1789 was an attempt by the Royal Government to control food prices, including millers' charges, and the Davenescourt villagers were quick to seize their advantage. Since 1787, in common with all other French village communities, they had had a formal municipal council and administration.

In December 1789 the Davenescourt municipality complained to the Intendant of Picardy that the Davenescourt miller was charging more than the price that he, the Intendant, had himself fixed the previous month. The Countess also wrote to explain to the Intendant that if she adhered to the official tariff, the mill would become "a charge rather than a revenue". What was the poor man to do? Precisely: he did nothing.[19] But clearly the villagers were beginning to assert themselves with a new confidence. In January, 1790 it was the Countess' turn to complain, to the National Assembly, that the secretary of the Municipality had been encouraging the inhabitants to cut branches from the roadside trees she had planted. The Assembly duly ordered the local Bailliage court to take action.[20] In June, 1790 the Countess was complaining to the Assembly again, but this time over a more serious matter.

In May, 1790 the National Assembly had abolished the right of *Triage,* leaving it open to peasant communities to challenge any enclosures made within the last thirty years. As soon as the news of this edict filtered through, the Davenescourt inhabitants decided to take direct action and occupy the land taken by the Countess in 1785, and they seized the "harvest" (presumably an early crop of hay) in the process.[21]

All in all it was not a happy time for the Countess. The August decrees of 1789 which abolished feudalism had swept away the monopoly of the mill without compensation; fresh decrees in the summer of 1790 abolished the right of *Voirie,* even though they compelled the peasants to pay compensation for existing trees. Meanwhile the Countess' eldest son, Joseph-Gabriel, had joined the aristocratic refugees from the Revolution and was far away in Hamburg.

Still, things were not all entirely bad, either. As a result of the nationalisation of the church lands in 1789 the extensive local estates of the old enemy, the Chapter of Saint-Quentin, were thrown on the market. The Countess de la Myre bought them, over the heads of the sitting tenants, to consolidate her own property.

Nothing, even so, could really compensate for the new, insubordinate attitude of the Davenescourt villagers. Things were changing, had changed, irreversibly. One of the leaders of the peasants in the quasi-uprising of July, 1789 had been a certain Alexis Bailli, whose nickname, incidentally, was "La Giberne", or "Cartridge-pouch", and while "Cartridge-pouch" was terrorising the Countess in her château at Davenescourt, away in Paris Pierre-François Bailli, his eldest son, was playing his part in the capture of the Bastille. Later Pierre-François came back to the village, resplendent in his uniform as a member of the Paris National Guard, to stiffen the rebellious spirit of the stay-at-homes. And so, under the influence of the Baillis, at the beginning of 1791, the villagers decided to have a settling of accounts with the Countess.

On the evening of 24 February the municipal council held a meeting and decided to press certain demands in a deputation to the château on the next day. They were determined that the commons should be given back to the village, that the Countess should refund the 600 livres costs of the 1784 decision on the trees, and that the additions made to the *Terrier* in 1786 must be dropped, where they were still applicable.

In the morning the Mayor and council duly presented themselves at the château and were admitted. I have already described the sequel: the humiliation of the Countess and her children, a manhunt for Le Sueur and especially for Tournier (who hid in a loft), the destruction of the manorial archives, finally the success of the villagers in driving the Countess and her household out of Picardy.

But the Jacquerie of 25 February was by no means the end of the story. Contrary to a common misconception, France was not in a state of unbridled anarchy after 1789. There were certainly attacks on châteaux in 1789 and 1790, but unrestrained lawlessness was not typical. There were laws to protect life and property, and there were new courts to administer them.

The Davenescourt rioters had committed assault and possibly murder, and they had engaged in pillage. Before long seventeen of them, including "Cartridge-pouch", his wife, and his two sons, found themselves on trial before the tribunal of the Montdidier District, facing the death sentence if convicted.

Babeuf's task in organising the defence of the Bailli family was not an easy one. The Countess was already pulling political strings to get the Minister of Justice to transfer the trial to Paris, away from the influence of local prejudices. Babeuf had to organise counter-pressures. At the beginning of May two hundred Davenescourt villagers marched on Montdidier armed with sticks and clubs to demand an early trial and to present a petition carrying sixty-nine signatures. This was the origin of the pamphlet in which Babeuf appealed over the heads of the Court, to the French public, seeking to show that the Jacquerie was not a blameworthy crime, but simply a just act of vengeance.

The trial stayed in Montdidier, but it dragged on and on, and despite the intimidation of witnesses by the crowd, and Babeuf's vigorous defence tactics, things began to look black for the prisoners. By the beginning of September 1791, Babeuf was convinced that his clients were doomed. "Tomorrow the scaffold will be their lot" he wrote in an appeal to the deputies of the National Assembly, "but the day after tomorrow, when the feudal horde conquers, they will send you too to execution".

Suddenly, on 14 September, the whole picture changed. As a parting gesture, before dissolving itself in preparation for new elections, the National Assembly decided to grant a general amnesty for cases which had arisen out of "revolution" and "rebellion". But the Baillis were not quite out of the woods yet. It was still necessary to demonstrate that the Jacquerie at Davenescourt was a political conflict, and not just a criminal enterprise, and Babeuf got to work, writing to Duport du Tertre, the Minister of Justice, and to well-disposed deputies to win their support. In the end the Minister was forced to concede the point, and the scene was now set for the final act.

The time and place: market day, Saturday 15 October, in the small town of Montdidier, the streets filled with peasants from the surrounding villages. As defence counsel, Babeuf attended the session of the District tribunal and delivered his submission. Then he led out the liberated prisoners onto the public square amid the cheering crowds. Next began a triumphal progress through the countryside.

"All the villagers, to the accompaniment of music, greeted us a league before Davenescourt", Babeuf wrote. "On our arrival in the village the tocsin was rung, and everyone set out for the church, and they played 'We praise thee, Lord', and then the dancing began; this continued all the following day, the Sunday. The festival was concluded by fireworks; citizens of all ages assembled, to complete the celebration of a victory over hated feudalism".[22]

In the end, of course, the La Myres came back again after all. In 1796 La Sueur was mayor of the commune, and in 1842 a member of the La Myre family held the same office.[23] But things were never quite the same again after February 1791.

In what ways does the narrative of these spirited events contribute to our understanding of the shape and development of popular protest in eighteenth-century France? Evidently no sweeping conclusions can be based on one episode in the history of one small village. On the other hand we know, from the researches of Lefebvre and others, that the story of Davenescourt illustrates in dramatic and idiosyncratic fashion aspects of French rural history that were quite general at the time.

A very common stereotype of the French revolution is that of the ragged and starving peasant mob storming the gates of the château with murder, lust and rapine in their hearts. "The mob plunder, burn and destroy in complete ignorance", Arthur Young noted at the end of July 1789. For the conservative historian Hippolyte Taine "Robbers, convicts, the worthless of every species, ... were to form the advanced guard of insurrections and lead the peasantry to the extreme of violence". George Rudé has castigated Taine and Gustave Le Bon for adding their scholarly authority to a general conception of the French Revolutionary crowd as composed of criminal elements, degenerates and persons with destructive instincts, who blindly responded to the siren voices of "leaders" or "demagogues".[24] Rudé would agree with Lefebvre that the student of popular disturbances must penetrate beyond facile generalities such as the deficiencies of human nature and the hidden hand of agitators. He must attempt to place the participants in their historical context, to explore carefully the origins of collective grievances, and to identify the mechanisms by which such grievances are, in certain circumstances, transformed into violent outburst.[25]

While Rudé did not include the phenomena of "Jacqueries" or anti-seigneurial peasant disturbances in his work on the French rural riot of the eighteenth century, he has shown that particularly in the food riots and episodes of *taxation populaire,* or popular price-fixing, that were common in the period, a quite different pattern to that posited by Taine and Le Bon prevailed. These were occurrences in which the ordinary inhabitants of the countryside, moved by a readily comprehensible response to economic pressures, joined in rational and often surprisingly orderly manner to make their collective protest, using traditional and time-honoured methods.[26]

It would be foolish to maintain that attacks on noble châteaux during the French Revolution were not often accompanied by extortion, pillage and arson. Amongst other studies, Lefebvre's account of the rural unrest of 1789 provides plentiful evidence that they were.[27] Yet Lefebvre also concludes that there were, characteristically, limits even to such violence. If the seigneur agreed to abandon his feudal rights then the violence came to an end; there were no attacks on women, and no deliberate murders.[28] Sydney Herbert writes of the same uprising that "the main object of the peasants was to destroy the hated manor-rolls which were the charters of their servitude, along with other documents which seemed capable of bearing witness against them".[29]

In this context the Davenescourt Affair may be seen, not as a blind outbreak of terror and looting by criminals, but as a typical application of limited violence in furtherance of rational objectives, precipitated by a final crisis in a long drawn-out and embittered conflict between the seigneur and the peasant community. Nor was the outbreak an unthinking reflex of unbearable immediate suffering, the generous alibi conceded by liberals for incomprehensible and impermissible violences: "Famine always lies at the bottom of insurrection", writes Louis Madelin of the rural uprising of 1789. At Davenescourt the rioters of 1791 were spurred on not so much by hunger as by the memory, shared by other peasant communities, of a generation of injustice at the hands of the courts of the Old Régime, and a consciousness, in the aftermath of 1789, that things were changing, and might change further, with a little courage.

Herbert points out, rightly, that the violent destruction of feudal archives, as a peasant tactic, dated at least from the original "Jacqueries" of the fourteenth century. The same tactic was central to a peasant uprising in Britanny in 1675.[30] The Davenescourt peasants, like their contemporaries in other villages, were thus remembering, or rather rediscovering, traditional and very long-established modes of peasant protest.

What was new about the Davenescourt episode was the unrepentant politicisation of the defence of the rioters, and, of course, the eventual victory of the peasants. Both were a consequence of the fact that the original confrontation had taken place in the second year of a revolution that had displaced and largely demoralised traditional authority.

The defender chosen by the peasants, Babeuf, had already become, by 1791, a skilled agitator, adept at seizing on particular local grievances to make general political capital. In 1790 he had launched his attack on the continued collection of indirect taxes against a background of widespread riots against the collectors. In a published petition on the issue, he urged the peasants and artisans of Picardy to intervene directly in politics by participating in petitions and public meetings to exert pressure on the authorities from below. During the autumn of 1790 he had launched a newspaper, the *Correspondent Picard,* which opened its pages to complaints by village correspondents. On the very eve of the Davenescourt outbreak, at the beginning of February 1790, Babeuf had drafted a petition in defence of the refusal by the inhabitants of Méry in the Oise Département to pay feudal dues. The Méry petition was also published, together with a general demand for the abolition of feudal dues without compensation, and the nationalisation of the domain land of the seigneurs.[31] Babeuf's pamphlet defence of the Davenescourt rioters originated as another petition which, while addressing itself to the particular case, amounted also to a general attack on feudal tyranny. The revival of Babeuf's indictment of the Countess de la Myre by the *Journal de Montdidier* almost a hundred years later is a tribute to its effectiveness in helping to create the greatly simplified but highly potent democratic image of the French Revolution as a struggle between virtuous peasants and oppressive aristocrats.

Thanks to the intervention of a popular leader of a new type, making inspired use of new opportunities, the Davenescourt Affair was thus transformed from a purely parochial conflict about particular grievances to an exemplary episode in a far wider and on-going political struggle. This transition, from sporadic and intermittent popular protest to generalised and organised political pressure, was a characteristic feature of the new departures in popular politics, inaugurated during the French Revolution, that would be seen as more appropriate to the industrialised Europe of the following century.

# *NOTES*

[ Acknowledgment is due to the Tasmanian Historical Research Association for permission to use materials in this article already published in the Association's *Papers and Proceedings.* ]

1. *Mercure de France,* 19 Mars 1791, no. 12, p. 225.

2. I have described this campaign elsewhere: R. B. Rose, *Gracchus Babeuf 1760-1797, The First Revolutionary Communist* (Stanford, 1978), pp. 55-71.

3. *Opprimés et oppresseurs: mémoire des habitants de Davenécourt aux représentants de la Nation* (Imprimerie du *Journal de Montdidier,* Montdidier 1888): a reprint of *Affaire de la commune de Davenécourt, district de Montdidier, département de la Somme, contre Philippine de Cardevac, veuve de Gabriel Lamire et ci-devant dame de Davenécourt... Dans l'exposé de laquelle on démontre combien sont encore formidables, les restes de la puissance féodale...* (Devin, Noyon, 1791). Only the reprint survives, in the Bibliothèque Nationale, at 4° Lk⁷ 26158.

4. *Dénonciation à M. l'accusateur public du tribunal de Montdidier et réfutation d'un libelle infâme intitulé Affaire de la commune de Davenescourt contre Philippine Cardevac, veuve de Gabriel La Myre et Ci-devant Dame de Davenescourt:* No publication details, but from internal evidence published in 1791. Copy in Bibliothèque Municipale d'Amiens, France.

5. Lefebvre, G., "The murder of the Comte de Dampierre" in Kaplow, J., ed., *New Perspectives on the French Revolution* (New York, 1965), pp. 277-286.

6. Sagnac, P., *La formation de la société française moderne,* 2 vols. (Paris, 1945-6).

7. Walter, G., *Histoire des paysans de France* (Paris, 1963).

8. Lefebvre, G., *Les paysans du Nord pendant la Révolution française* (Bari, 1959), pp. 157-171.

9. de Saint-Jacob, P., *Les paysans de la Bourgogne du Nord au dernier siècle de l'Ancien Régime* (Paris, 1960).

10. Forster, R., *The Nobility of Toulouse in the Eighteenth Century* (Baltimore, 1960); *The House of Saulx-Tavanes* (Baltimore, 1971).

11. Forster, *Nobility of Toulouse,* pp. 50-51.

12. Forster, *Saulx-Tavanes,* pp. 100-101, 107.

13. Davies, A., "The Origins of the French Peasant Revolution of 1789", *History,* XLIX (1964), 24-41.

14. Rose, *Babeuf,* pp. 21-6.

15. Doyle, W., "Was there an Aristocratic Reaction in Pre-Revolutionary France?", in: Johnson, D., *French Society and the Revolution* (Cambridge, 1976), pp. 3-28.

16. *Le Cabinet Historique de l'Artois et de la Picardie,* 111ᵉ Année, no. 2 (juin 1888), p. 85.

17. Archives départementales de la Somme, C. 874, Intendance de Picardie, Administration Communale.

18. Fournier, M.L., "Les paysans de l'Ancien Régime en Picardie", *La Révolution française* [periodical], VI (1884), p. 1087.

19. Arch. dep. de la Somme, C. 875, Intendance de Picardie, Admin. communale.

20. Archives Nationales, DXXIV bis 313 pièce 17: Comtesse de la Myre to M. l'Évêque, le Comte de Chalons, le 22 janvier 1790.

21. Sagnac, P., and Caron, P., *Les comités des droits féodaux et de législation et l'abolition du régime Seigneuriale, 1789-1793,* Collection de documents inédits sur l'histoire économique de la Révolution française (Imprimerie Nationale, Paris, 1907), pp. 545-6. The President of the Assembly at the time was Brioıs de Beaumez, deputy of the Noblesse of the neighbouring province of Arras, who was reminded by the Countess of "Le marques d'intérêt et d'amitié que j'ai toujours éprouvée de la part de votre famille".

22. Dalin, V. M., *Grakkh Babef; nakanune i vo vremia Velikoi Frantsuzkoi revolutsii, 1785-1794* (Izdatel'stvo Akademii nauk SSSR, Moscow, 1963), pp. 398-9.

23. *Opprimés et oppresseurs,* p. 89.

24. Rudé, G., *The Crowd in the French Revolution* (Oxford, 1959), pp. 2-3; *The Crowd in History* (New York, 1964), pp. 8-11.

25. Lefebvre, G., "Revolutionary Crowds", in Kaplow, *New Perspectives,* pp. 173-190.

26. Rudé, *Crowd in History,* pp. 19-32; see also my own similar conclusions in Rose, R.B., "18th Century Price-Riots, the French Revolution and the Jacobin Maximum", *International Review of Social History,* IV, no. 3 (1959), pp. 432-445.

27. Lefebvre, G., *La Grande Peur de 1789* (Paris, 1956).

28. *Ibid.,* p. 143.

29. Herbert, S., *The Fall of Feudalism in France* (London, 1921), p. 92.

30. Bernard, L., "French Society and Popular Uprisings under Louis XIV", in Kierstead, R.F., *State and Society in Seventeenth-Century France* (New York, 1975), p. 172.

31. Rose, *Babeuf,* pp. 79-85.

William J. Murray

# A PHILOSOPHE IN THE FRENCH REVOLUTION: DOMINIQUE-JOSEPH GARAT AND THE JOURNAL DE PARIS

Among the host of colourless characters who drifted across the stage of the French Revolution, few rose to high office and yet remained as colourless as the lawyer from the Basque country, Dominique-Joseph Garat. Yet he is surely not so deserving of the obscurity to which he has been consigned[1], or of the obloquy that was bestowed on him by contemporaries for his role in the Revolution.[2] From the time when he was elected, with his elder brother, to represent the bailliage of Labourd at the meeting of the Estates-General, and arrived at Versailles, his mind brimming with the ideas of the philosophes and his heart filled with hopes for a new future for mankind, he was seldom far from the political scene. Garat played a silent role in the National Assembly, but recorded its sessions in glowing terms in the *Journal de Paris* from 20 May 1789 until the close of that body on 30 September 1791; although he failed to get elected to the National Convention he replaced Danton as Minister of Justice on 9 October 1792, and then took over as Minister of the Interior in March, 1793. He held on to that position until 19 August, after which date his career was under a cloud which did not lift immediately on the fall of Robespierre the following summer. During the Directory Garat rose to a position of importance in the Council of Ancients, tied his star to Napoleon's and became a Knight of the Empire, but failed to have his merits recognized by the restored Bourbons in 1815, after which period he retired, returned to his native Ustaritz in 1826 and died there, aged eighty-four, in 1834.

Garat lived through and survived, then, the most tempestuous years in French history. Before the Revolution he was sought after in the salon society where plans to renew the world were eagerly proposed; his optimism survived the setbacks of the Constitutional Monarchy; his liberal humanitarianism was shaken but unbroken during the Terror, while every ideal he had ever upheld was set the test of Bonaparte's imperialism. He emerged sorely battered from the Empire and during the Restoration Garat is said to have turned into a bigot, and so finally to have turned his back on the philosophical idealism of his younger days. The year before he died, however, his services to France were recognized by the sixth régime he had lived under, when the bourgeois monarchy of Louis Philippe restored him to the Institute, to which he had been appointed by Napoleon and dismissed by the Bourbons.

The main interest in Garat lies in his very insipidity. He never made the impact on the public of his close friends Brissot and Condorcet, whose ideals he shared, nor of Danton, whom he admired as "un grand seigneur de la sans-culotterie";[3] neither, however, did he renounce the Revolution, as did another of his friends, Suard, whose biography he came to write in his later years. The interest in Garat lies precisely in that he lived through the Revolution and, like the vast majority of French people, he survived. Unlike the vast majority, however, he attained a position of great influence and recorded his reactions to the events of the time. Garat's success story began before the Revolution, when he emerged from provincial obscurity to acceptance in Parisian salon society in the 1780s. Although he several times complained of poverty, his was the poverty of the rich, more aware of the wealth above them than of the real poverty that surrounds them. A study of Garat, then, is not "history from below" in the sense of the Lefebvre school; it is closer to Robert Darnton's studies of the nobodies who roamed the French Grub Street on the eve of the Revolution, and whose reactions to the events of 1789 were in large measure conditioned by these years of frustration. Darnton has never claimed that the denizens of Grub Street automatically welcomed the Revolution (for some there was more money and fame to be found in opposition); nor does he claim that those in the hallowed halls of the establishment opposed it.[4] Garat belongs to the latter category, and a study of his reactions to the Revolution allows insights into one of its greatest strengths, and its greatest weakness: the secular humanist drive that tried to keep alive the spirit of 1789, and a belief in an economic system that contradicted these goals. A full-scale biography of Garat is still to be written; in the meantime the following is a study of his attitude to the Revolution in the crucial first three years, as recorded largely in the columns of the *Journal de Paris* where he was political editor.[5]

Garat, son of a respected but impecunious Basque doctor, was born at Bayonne on 8 September 1749. His education was erratic: as a young man he would wander over the countryside of his native Ustaritz, a Locke in one pocket, a Virgil or a Montesquieu in the other, and in this latter-day Elysium his sole conversations were with these "children of the gods." He had to make some contact with reality, however, and this he did when he became a lawyer and practised with his oldest brother at Bordeaux.[6] But it was history and literature that he loved best, and so he left his homeland, like thousands of other ambitious young men, to try his luck in the capital. There he arrived, in 1773 or 1774, a country bumpkin with a thick accent, and only thirty-six louis and an unfinished drama in his pocket.[7] He was also shy, short-sighted and far from robust, but it seems he did have talent, at least enough to impress his landlord, Suard. With such a connection many opportunities were opened to him: through Suard he met Panckoucke, and as well as being engaged on the *Encyclopédie méthodique* was employed to write articles for the *Mercure de France,* signed "Cosseph d'Ustaritz". From 1781 he was writing articles on philosophy and literature, as well as book reviews, for the *Journal de Paris,* by which time his name had been made. In 1778 he had published an "éloge" for Michel de l'Hôpital; subsequent "éloges" in 1779, 1781 and 1784, won first prize in these annual talent quests run by the French Academy.[8] By this time, too, his financial situation was secure, and not without a certain priggishness he rejected two offers of pensions: the first was twelve-hundred livres previously paid to the abbé Raynald, which he rejected because he did not want "to enrich himself at the expense of the living"; the second was for one-hundred écus, offered by the Baron de Breteuil for his work on the *Mercure,* which he dismissed because he was not "reduced to a state of humiliation and distress" that forced him to accept such a sum.[9] In 1786 he was employed to give lectures on Greek and Roman history at the newly-founded Lycée. The young Basque was now firmly established in Parisian society where he was introduced to most of the people a would-be philosophe should have met, including Rousseau, Diderot, d'Alembert, Condillac and Buffon.[10] However well he knew them he did become a close friend of Condorcet, who lived in the same stairway as the Suards, and so became a neighbour of Garat's when he arrived in Paris. Among Garat's other friends of this period were Brissot, for whom he had the most unqualified admiration, Dupont de Nemours and Rabaut de St. Etienne.[11]

Accepted in the salons, writing for the top newspapers, and attracting crowds to his lectures at the Lycée, Garat's hopes and ambitions were given a tremendous boost by the advent of the Estates-General. Now the time for talk gave way to the time for action, and the dreams of the philosophes became a practicable proposition. Garat returned to his native province, where he was successful in gaining representation for the bailliage of Labourd. Now he found himself on the national stage, where, however, he was threatened with anonymity amid the 1,200 other deputies; for Garat was a man of words rather than of action, and of the written rather than the spoken word. His feeble voice and his need for calm consideration before presenting a balanced argument were out of place in an arena whose violence and vituperation shocked him. He took consolation, however, in his position with the *Journal de Paris,* to which he was appointed as political editor on 20 May 1789, for whereas the most powerful voice at the tribune could be heard only in the Assembly, his could be heard throughout France. In addition to promoting his own ideas, he saw his task as editor as that of converting the heat generated at the debates into the light of reason in the columns of the *Journal.*[12]

Garat was just one of dozens of politicians who used the press as a springboard to action.[13] Unlike most Garat did not have to establish his own paper, but merely renewed his old association with France's first daily, a paper which in 1789 was a household name among the literate classes throughout France.[14] Like the other newspapers of the old régime, political censorship determined that it deal with controversies of a reasonably innocuous nature. The *Journal* was never entirely to lose its literary character, but with the advent of the Revolution, it too was caught up in the general fever, and before the end of 1789, matter other than the main political issues of the day was removed from the *Journal's* daily four pages, to be printed in special supplements. Garat's reporting of the National Assembly then dominated the paper, which maintained its pre-revolutionary success despite the intense competition it had to face after the fall of the Bastille.

In the pre-Bastille period, the *Journal* had maintained a reputation as an arbiter of good taste and a channel for expounding views of orderly social progress. Its subject matter varied from medicine to agriculture, from astronomy to street-cleaning, and from science to art[15]. The editors would answer questions on the gender of Latin nouns or confirm that vapours from the earth contributed to stomach upsets, and a lengthy argument might develop in the correspondence columns as to whether frozen sea-water, on melting, takes on the properties of fresh-water. Morals, too, came into the *Journal's* wide field and it added its approval to the advice given to a young "seigneur" about to go out into the world, that he must not contract debts and should always act as "l'homme d'honneur".[16] It sought also the protection of the fair sex, and an establishment for bringing up young girls was welcomed by the *Journal* as an asylum for innocence to avoid the traps of seduction.[17]

The *Journal* regarded slavery as "a deplorable institution",[18] but nevertheless it counselled that it had to be borne until it could be gradually modified before being abolished completely, and when it reviewed John Howard's famous book, *The State of Prisons, Hospitals and Asylums,* it was with fulsome praise for his having taken on a noble task, motivated solely by a pity for suffering prisoners and a love of humanity.[19] But it saw the spread of humanity, also, in the progress of the physical sciences, and there were few issues of the *Journal* that did not report progress in this field. Articles suggested methods of improving agriculture, and lengthy reports by the Academy were regularly printed, along with its announcements of coming competitions for methods of improving technology. The general tone of the *Journal* was one of optimism — the then-current optimism that in the advancement of science lay the key to knowledge and happiness.

In all this the *Journal* bore the imprint of the professional and the leisured propertied classes, but more particularly, it reflected the influence of the "philosophes".[20] A regular feature of the *Journal* was the column "Bienfaisance" where the aged, the unemployed, and pregnant mothers were all accorded sympathy, and methods were suggested whereby their plight could be eased. A request by the *curé* of Sainte-Marguerite for donations to buy soup-pots was more than fulfilled[21] and a similar enthusiastic and generous response greeted the story of an aged couple reduced to beggary.[22] These stories show a compassion for the unfortunate. But it was no doubt other than political censorship that dictated the non-reporting of the Réveillon riots. This sort of response by the poor to their problems was beyond the ken of the proprietors of the *Journal,* who at all times deplored civil disturbances.[23] But this was not an issue on which the proprietors and their new political editor were to agree, and it was to play its part in their parting of the ways at the close of the Constituent Assembly.

This was in the future, however. In the middle of 1789 the optimism of the *philosophes* was matched to the political optimism generated by the calling of the Estates-General. The *Journal* showed itself as siding with the aspirations of the bourgeoisie, although more by implication than by direct comment. Its reports of the elections of local deputies always stressed the way in which the interests of the three orders were being merged into one, with the privileged orders willingly making common cause with the Third. It was critical of particular interests which might harm the cause of the Nation as a whole; in a review of a book on the history of the Roman *comices,* the Estates-General in France and the British Parliament, the *Journal* remarked hopefully that this book should awaken and strengthen the generous resolution to sacrifice petty vanity, provincial interests, and separate bodies, in favour of the salvation and prosperity of the common fatherland.[24] It also denounced by implication the British Constitution where "... a thousandth part of the Nation ruled as mistress over the rest", and issued a warning to the apostles of Montesquieu that this constitution, "better praised than understood", should be examined and familiarised before attempting to imitate it.[25] The proprietors, like the vast proportion of the French people -- despite the cahiers --, clearly favoured the creation of a Constitution that would abolish the three orders. In a review of a book critical of how the interests of the "suffering people" at the meeting of the Estates-General at Blois, in 1588, were over-ridden by the "first two orders, always certain of the majority of the votes", it pointedly expressed the hope that the example of the past would serve as a warning to the present.[26]

It was a long way from supporting the creation of a National Assembly to applauding its institution by a popular revolution, however. The proprietors may have had many reservations about this, but Garat had none.[27] Still, his impact on the *Journal* was at first barely noticeable. The *Journal* had been permitted, along with the other "authorized" newspapers, on 19 May, to print verbatim reports of the meeting of the Estates-General, but imposed its own censorship on 28 May.[28] Nevertheless the *Journal* welcomed the king's acceptance of the Revolution on 17 July, and Garat allowed a certain note of triumph to sound in its columns when he reported the session of August 4.[29] He then allowed himself some cautious reflections on the introduction of an upper house[30] and his first words of criticism appeared in some comments on the king's veto, when he suggested that the king should be allowed to oppose only the power of reason to resist the will of the people.[31] At the same time he warned that too short-term a legislature would allow mediocre talents to push themselves forward at the expense of good laws, but that if the assembly's sessions were too long "an aristocratic spirit" would develop, and "a great power always corrupts to a greater or lesser extent those who exercise it."[32]

The October days marked a watershed in the Revolution, and even prompted the proprietors of the *Journal* to explain their policy of "prudent moderation" — that they did not wish to spread error or inflame passions. The radical press was not impressed by this statement, and continued to attack the *Journal* as a privileged paper still tainted with the corruption of the old regime. They accused it of being able to speak of liberty only in the language of slavery and of having abandoned its defence of the old aristocracy to serve in a more cowardly fashion the new aristocracy in process of being formed. It was under pressure of such attacks that Garat finally made a stand. On 5 November he proclaimed that the enemies of the French Empire who were trying to split its loyalties were being confounded by repeated expressions of respect and gratitude to the Assembly; that not only was the genius of the Assembly spreading throughout France, but it was going to "faire le tour de l'Europe". Less than a week later he refuted those aristocrats who were "malignantly" trying to split the Assembly and the Ministers: he asserted that relations between the Assembly, the King and his Ministers had never before been so harmonious and that they were guided, and always would be guided, by the same hope and the same heart.[34] And as Garat challenged the opponents of the Revolution, so he staunchly championed the work of the Assembly against its critics. He reminded his readers that the Assembly was dealing with first principles which had to be discussed carefully, and added that:

> Throughout the history of man and nations nowhere will there be found an example of such a great revolution brought about in such a short time at so little cost in money and blood, so many wise laws made in such short time... better could be done but the intelligence [*esprit*] of the Assembly is far from being exhausted.... But its work, such as it is, is still the best of its type that has been accomplished on earth.[35]

Moreover, as the Revolution appeared to near completion he declared that the last hopes of its enemies were vanishing[36] and that for every action of the former aristocracy against it, there were twenty demonstrations in its favour.[37]

The proprietors of the *Journal* may have been less enthusiastic than Garat about the progress of the Revolution, but he was maintaining their enterprise as one of the best-selling newspapers in the country, despite the revolution in newspaper reporting since the previous July. Moreover Garat was forwarding the pre-revolutionary ideals of the paper in regard to the *philosophes* and social progress through the spread of reason. Reason was to become, with humanity, the panacea which would solve the problems of slavery, war, prejudice and intolerance. The divine right of kings was to be replaced by the divine right of thought[38] and all royal commands should be reasoned requests.[39] It was reason and liberty that combined to reform criminal law and which dictated that reform of criminals was more important than punishing them;[40] the rivalry of nations would be extinguished by the spread of reason, and as liberty broke their chains all would be bound together in a new enlightened confederation.[41] Admittance of non-Catholics to rights of "active" citizenship was seen as a victory for reason and humanity[42] and the problem of religious tolerance, "delicate but not difficult",[43] was to be easily overcome by making a law to this effect.[44] Referring to Guillotin's proposals for reform in capital punishment, Garat claimed that prejudice in general would be doomed before the dual onslaught of reason and law.[45] He denounced slavery,[46] prejudice and fanaticism, and strongly defended both Jews and actors against the Abbé Maury's attempts to prevent them recovering their full civic rights.[47] He considered that monks were living a particularly unnatural and oppressive life which destroyed their reason, and when they were released from their vows remarked that even if they could not understand why they were being lightened of this burden, then at least they would feel the effects of this humane action.[48]

Garat was not to be entirely carried away on the flood of his own rhetoric, however. When the Assembly introduced its franchise qualifications in October 1789 he issued his first major censure of that body. Certainly it was the "silver mark" decree, rather than the creation of "active" and "passive" citizens, that injured his pride, but he opposed this decree, and others which restricted the right to vote by imposing financial qualifications, on the grounds of reason, humanity and man's "natural" rights; and because they dishonoured the Constitution of a people which regarded liberty as the right of all men.[49] When the Assembly refused Charles de Lameth permission to speak against this decree, Garat took up the cudgels on his behalf, claiming:

> A man can be silenced, but human reason, which the concerted efforts of the despotic tyrannies of Europe could not extinguish [*étouffer*], will doubtless not be destroyed, or reduced to silence, under the empire of a liberty which would not exist without the progress of reason. We will say then, in the name of that reason, the one true law of rational beings, that no authority on earth has the right to exclude man from the exercise of rights which he has received from nature; that his rights belong only to the quality of the man and not to silver marks; that if land-owners judge in favour of land-owners, humanity judges in favour of humanity; that it will never be understood what relationship exists between plots of ground and the genius and virtues of the legislators....[50]

Finally, Garat declared that it was impossible to "see a law of the nation in a decree that excluded from representation nine-tenths of its citizens". He apologized for this frankness, but added that unless worthy citizens were to judge as well as obey laws, Constitutions and laws would become themselves but despotisms. The extension of this dispute in that of the "tribut civique" evoked a similar response.[51] But Garat abandoned his criticism and claimed to be grief-stricken at the dilemma in which he found himself. Reason commanded that there should be no disabilities placed on an individual simply because he was not rich or a property owner, and yet the Assembly was doing just that. Torn between the rule of reason and the law of the land, Garat gave up in despair and could offer no solution.[52]

In the first months of 1790 it was the "aristocrats" and not the radicals who were denouncing the *Journal de Paris*. None other than Desmoulins welcomed Garat into the ranks of the democrats, alongside such other worthies as Carra and Marat.[53] This was too good an opportunity for the satirists to miss, and so were invented the new words in honour of "le beau triumlatronat": "caramaragaratiser" for a verb and "carramaragarage" for a noun, each in reference to some revolutionary atrocity or other.[54] Rivarol, with his usual acuity, commented on Garat's ability to "chanter une insurrection",[55] but what finally carried Garat into the camp of the radicals was taking the side of the peasants in a riot in the Limousin that ended in bloodshed. Who were the more criminal, Garat asked: the peasants milling around the castle or the owner of the castle who fired on them without warning? One thing was certain, he emphasized: there were many peasants lying dead, but no castle owner had been killed, and after an unjust trial many peasants had been sent to the dungeons to be tortured and others has been led to the gallows.[56] This was forthright reporting that went beyond class interest, and kept Garat to the fore in the right-wing satirical press which played up the notion of aristocrats burning themselves up inside their castles in order to play tricks on the democrats.[57]

The issue of popular violence was the most important factor in pushing bourgeois supporters of the Revolution into reaction. The other was the matter of the king's duplicity, suspected before his flight and made manifest thereafter. These major issues also troubled relations between Garat and the proprietors of the *Journal,* but it was not until after the king's flight and the subsequent massacre on the Champ de Mars that this issue blew open. In the Assembly's reform of the Church Garat was able to laud its intentions and effect without qualification, sharing the bourgeois anti-clericalism of the majority of the deputies.[58] His position in regard to the monarchy and popular violence was much more ambivalent.

Garat was later to show himself to be a decided republican, but even in this earlier period there were occasions when he barely concealed such ideas. In June, 1790 he claimed to see in the monarchy of Henri IV, a king who sought the interests of his people, the exception, and in that of Louis XIV, who sought only his own interests, the rule. Kings, claimed Garat, were guilty of many outrages to humanity: in addition to oppressing the people and keeping them in a state of ignorance, their most detestable crime was the instigation of war. War, he believed, was little more than a game for kings, provoked to break the boredom of life at court or for other trivial reasons.[59] In this game the people were no more than pawns pushed around to satisfy personal caprice. However, when the people ruled there would be no more wars; unlike negotiations between kings, negotiations between peoples would always result in peace,[60] and Garat looked to that day when there would be no more masters and slaves, and war would disappear, consummated in the "Pact of Federation of the Human Race".[61] Garat castigated kings for the artificial life which they created in a court far removed from "nature"[62] and praised instead the Americans Washington and Franklin as representing true greatness, and considered how ridiculous or puerile any titles would be beside their names.[63] He welcomed the abolition of hereditary nobility and titles in June 1790, as a victory to "be greeted with song", and acclaimed it as an occasion equalled only by the night of August 4 and the proclamation of the Declaration of the Rights of Man.[64] Six months later he was praising another step forward in the progress towards that simplicity of taste and habits that had to accompany liberty, when appanages to the Princes of the Blood were abolished. In cutting off this source of luxury to the throne he saw a "corrupting example to the people" removed. It meant, too, the end of that "magnificence of fantasies and frivolities" which served as substitutes for real merit.[65]

Kings might be subjected to temptation and misguided by a scheming court, but luckily for France, according to Garat, it had an exceptional king in Louis XVI. In him, France had a monarch who loved liberty and who willingly supported the Revolution. His reward for this was the true homage that only liberty could show: slaves might prostrate themselves, but they did not know how to "admire, esteem and love".[66] Garat seized on every opportunity to show just how exceptional a king Louis XVI was. His February 4, 1790 speech to the Assembly pledging patriotism and expressing distress at the evidence of counter-revolution, Garat greeted with feelings of "profound emotion", and, entering into the spirit of the Assembly, dramatically asked how, on the king's departure, normal work could be resumed.[67] Four months later (29 April, 1790), after the Assembly had stripped the executive of many of its former powers and Bailly, the mayor of Paris, persuaded the disgruntled king to make himself popular with the nation by again declaring his solidarity with the Assembly, Garat again acclaimed this further evidence of the king's goodwill.[68] He may have been trying to convince himself as much as his readers of the king's good intentions, but even the radical press was not yet ready to denounce the king.[69]

By April 1791, however, the situation had changed significantly. The furore over the departure of the king's aunts for Rome in February of that year, and the refusal of the Parisians to allow the king to leave Paris on 18 April to hear mass from a refractory priest at St. Cloud, reflected a general fear that the king might try to flee the country. Montmorency, the king's foreign minister, therefore urged the king to send a letter to all France's ambassadors and foreign agents re-affirming his allegiance to the principles of the Revolution. The radical press was not so impressed by this letter,[70] but Garat was "overcome" by it.[71]

Garat was desperately anxious that the king should be portrayed as a friend of the Revolution; in this he echoed not only the majority in the Assembly, but the vast majority of the French people who still saw in the king a father-figure. Garat denied that the king had any links with the counter-revolution. In any case he pretended this was not a serious problem: like the hopes of the priests, the hopes of the aristocrats were as stupid as they were criminal.[72] In November, 1790, Garat was no more than repeating an oft-quoted claim when he declared that the troubles upsetting France were not as bad as its enemies made out, and that "the pride of the aristocracy and the delirium of fanaticism... are capable of being cured."[73] Despite such oft-repeated declarations the *Journal de Paris* was accused in the National Assembly of saying that the queen, and, implicitly, the king, was not in favour of the Revolution. This allowed Garat ("profoundly upset") to embark on a eulogy showing how the king had smashed the hopes of these counter-revolutionaries (if there were any left) who thought that he favoured counter-revolution, and went on to add -- as he had done "a hundred times before" -- that he was loyal to the king "not out of habit, or mesmerized by the brilliance of the throne, but because the king had saved the

Constitution from being founded on bloodshed, and this reminder, which has inspired in us an unshakeable confidence in his virtues, has informed [*pénétré*] all we have had to write about his person."[74]

There is a decided ambivalence in such praise, however, for it was based on the assumption that the king favoured the Revolution. When he tried to flee the country in June, 1791 he destroyed this assumption and left to those who had been basing their opinion of the king on it to bury their heads in the sand or call for the nullification of the king's powers. In the National Assembly the ostrich solution was adopted with the fiction of the kidnapping, but Garat was not so quick to adjust to the new situation. The king's signed proclamation, which he expected to be read when he was safely across the frontier, revealed his true thoughts on the Revolution. It provoked Garat to express a disappointment that was probably at the same time a criticism more genuine than the praise lavished in the past. In this document the king complained about the Constitution and his part in it, about the loss of respect, dignity and freedom of movement he had suffered, and of the various outrages committed in the name of the Revolution. To Garat this was just one more proof of how far kings were divorced from reality. The king complains of his impoverished condition, Garat admonished, and yet he is living in lodgings in Paris that took the accumulated wealth of centuries to satisfy successive monarchs' "taste of grandeur, of comfort, of fantasy". He complains of his lack of funds and yet the twenty-five million livres granted from the civil list are more than some European nations have to spend on their State, let alone a single house. It is true, Garat went on, that he does not have such a large part to play in the government as formerly, but this has not resulted in a lack of respect, and it is an unjust calumny that portrays the "founders of liberty" as necessarily the destroyers of thrones and altars. The king might well have been horrified at some of the excesses committed in the name of the Revolution; so was every good citizen. But he should have realized that this was an inevitable concomitant of the transition from despotism to liberty.[75]

In his more theoretical discussions of sovereignty Garat had often praised Montesquieu and criticized Rousseau,[76] but in his fear of allowing the king, as head of the executive, any real power, Garat appeared to be paying only lip service to the separation of powers, and indeed drew closer to Rousseau's concept of a weak executive. On one occasion he even used Rousseau's metaphor when he claimed that "by the eternal nature of things, the executive power must be submitted to the legislative power as the force of a reasonable man is to his thought and will".[77] Following the king's flight Garat stated quite definitely that the king had no separate part to play in the Constitution. In a clash between the interests of the king and the interests of the people, it was the interests of the people that had to be upheld. In the past the king's happiness had never been imperilled by the elections rigged by his officials; now the people, who knew the kingdom as the king had never had, would suffer or profit by their own incapacity or merit to elect their officials. In short, it was the sovereign power, the people, who had to nominate those who executed the laws, just as it did those who made them. In more circumspect language Garat claimed that the granting of even a suspensive veto could be seen as a violation of "the principle of reason" and that it was indeed a marked concession to the king.[78]

As a result of the king's flight the more reactionary deputies sought means of stemming the rising radicalism. Garat was not one of them: while some proposed ways of strengthening the king's executive authority he calmly considered the respective merits of a monarchy and a republic, and after pointing out how Rousseau had shown that a monarchy was in fact a republic if it expressed the general will, went on to add that "this does not necessarily prove that a monarchical government is best suited to faithfully execute the laws and will of a free people".[79] In the following issue Garat again defended the supremacy of the general will against encroachments on its power by the king. Barnave had convinced the Assembly that the king was a representative of the nation in the same way as the legislature, and, in such matters as in his exercise of the veto and in foreign affairs, actually willed for it. Garat, on the contrary, pointed out that the king could only recognize or obstruct the general will in his exercise of the veto, and that in foreign affairs his decisions became the will of the nation only when they were ratified by its representatives. Garat feared the word "representative" as the thin end of the wedge of despotism; for if a king could represent a part of the general will, he asked, why not the whole?[80] This same reasoning roused his opposition to the suggestion that the king's family should form a distinguished class of citizens: he pointed out how, by heredity and by a virtual geometric increase in the number of families, this would give rise to a new nobility of princes.[81] Reason and discussion, not privilege and authority, was the true sovereignty. The "natural right" of the people, in replacing the "divine right" of kings, had restored a right which was "anterior to all others".[82]

But the Assembly was nearing the completion of its work. Time for a general amnesty was approaching and Garat's health was troubling him. When the king was called in to sanction the Constitution Garat once more donned his rose-coloured glasses and claimed to be (again!) "deeply moved" by the king's letter accepting the Constitution, and added that this letter was "an expression of truth that could not be simulated...and about which it would be criminal to have doubts."[83] In his final article for the *Journal de Paris,* in which he reported the king's last speech to the Constituent Assembly, Garat praised the king in what could also be seen as a challenge or a threat: "Kings of the earth, read these lines and see if in your absolute powers you can find anything that is worthy of these thoughts, these sentiments, these emotions".[84]

Garat's faith in the "people" was much more firmly based than his faith in the king, and survived much longer, despite his constant fear that those who had saved the Revolution might in turn destroy it. He recognized that the passage from despotism to liberty would be a stormy one, as "reason" had warned[85] and a quick look at the history of France during interregna indicated, but he claimed that the eventual outcome was never in doubt.

As reports of rioting came into the National Assembly, Garat tended to exonerate the people, whose only fault was their ignorance. But he was worried about the use the "aristocrats" made of these upheavals. His apologetic tone did develop a note of impatience from time to time, especially when the crowd took the law into its own hands. "'There is the people,' they say, 'and you unleash them'," admonished Garat, repeating the claims of the aristocrats, and although in the same article he went on to excuse the people on the usual grounds of ignorance resulting from despotism, and claimed that such outbursts were becoming fewer as the initial shocks of the Revolution died away, he emphasized that in the meantime the law must punish — and severely.[86] But unlike others who were more concerned with laws than justice, Garat believed that the people should make the laws. If the people allowed themselves to be provoked into violence by those very people who professed horror at it, these same critics would be further vindicated when they said that the people were fit only to be governed, to obey laws and not to make them.[87]

It was particularly frustrating to Garat that the principle he held the most essential to the happiness of the people -- the free circulation of grain -- was that which they seemed least able to comprehend.[88] This was the blind spot that he shared with most of the radical bourgeoisie — like Robespierre and his "paltry grocery goods" he could not understand what hunger or want were really like. Like other radical bourgeois, too, he was clearly anti-clerical and saw in the cry of "accapareur" a means of leading the people astray and inciting them to rebel second only to the impostures of the priests.[89]

The essence of the free enterprise ideal is that the private property of the individual be protected from the State or the jealousy of others; since the bourgeois had restricted government to property owners it was the latter who concerned them most. This concern gave rise to a fear that their property was continually at the mercy of those who had none; it was a fear more in the minds of the property owners than in any real desire on the part of the people to despoil them. It was a fear, moreover, that had a deadly effect on the progress of the Revolution, as behind all the crises -- from the attacks of the aristocrats on absolutists to the struggles between Girondins and Jacobins -- violence was provoked by conservatives who, having set out to achieve their own ends, chose resistance or repression, rather than concessions, when faced by the demands of others.[90] Garat's belief in free enterprise was more a belief in its supposed virtues than an expression of any selfishness on his own part; nor was he obsessed by the conservative bourgeois' fear of an attack on property. He denied that the people had designs on the property of others, and when a report came in from the country saying that the people had sought a new partition of property he dismissed this as a farfetched calumny against both liberty and the people, for they knew that, "if the revolution was necessary, if it was to be of great good, it is above all because it will make properties more respectable [*respectables*]."[91] Garat, however, did not consider property a "natural" right of man as set out in the Declaration, for he recognized that there were millions of men who did not possess a square inch of ground. Indeed, he argued, there were and could be systems of society and government without landed and individual property, and this proved that it was not a "natural" right; but he hastened to add that such societies were of other worlds, and disputed the abbé Mably's claim that they were better. What was undeniable was that everywhere that society had established the right of property, this was a "sacred and imprescriptible right".[92]

Despite his adherence to the absolute rights of private property, Garat shared the common eighteenth-century belief that a reduction in the extremes of wealth was essential for a healthy society. Where there were wide extremes of wealth, he noted, the wealthy tended to fear that their vested interests were under a constant threat from those who had nothing. The result of this had always been that the wealthy, who invariably controlled the government, devised barbarous laws designed solely to subdue.[93] But Garat could not have tolerated Helvetius' solution — that the wealthy be taxed out of existence. His solution to the evils inherent in excessive wealth lay in the inculcation of enlightenment. When it was proposed that the land tax should be spared at the expense of luxury goods, such as servants, horses and carriages, Garat considered this the idea of those "simple souls who love nature and morality". If luxury was to be proscribed it had to be done by changing the ideas and habits of the people, and not by taxation. With proper education they would no longer seek luxury and, then healthy ideas and a righteous mind would become the true sumptuary laws.[94]

Nevertheless Garat was not completely opposed to State intervention, and on occasions saw the need for the government to intervene on behalf of the weak. This action he regarded as most necessary in the relations between the individual and the law. Garat believed in the abolition of capital punishment,[95] favoured the introduction of juries,[96] and championed the principle that a man is innocent until proven guilty.[97] He also saw the need to protect petty offenders from the evil influence of hardened criminals,[98] and thought that prisons should be for reformation rather than punishment.[99] These, of course, are sound humanitarian principles and completely in consonance with the views held by the *Journal* even before the fall of the Bastille. In addition to supporting penal reforms, Garat attacked the tax on bread as "inepte", "inique" and "barbare";[100] praised the change in State policy that allowed a more prompt payment of allowances to the poor;[101] and lauded a decision of the State to take on itself the care of foundling children. He added that whereas previously the State had trampled the people underfoot as "savages did young plants", now it would care for them and bring them up to become an advantage to the State, and a credit to themselves and to the progress of reason.[102] In the case of unemployment relief Garat was torn between the "political evil" of encouraging laziness and its contingent vices, and a failure to help unwarranted indigence, which would be a crime against humanity.[103]

Overall, however, Garat did not see frequent government intervention as necessary in a free society. This was perhaps a natural reaction in a country that had only just rid itself of the strait-jacket of royal absolutism and its ruinous restrictions. Moreover, Garat believed that "liberty and equality" were complementary. With liberty, equality would follow naturally, because as man was inherently good or perfectible he would not take an unfair advantage of the weak. Thus he would be guided by motives of co-operation rather than competition, and this would ensure a reasonable equality. The harder fact, that liberty was more likely to become a liberty to oppress and, in the absence of State control, to result in gross inequalities, was not yet obvious in pre-industrial France.

If Garat saw little need for state intervention in economic affairs, he believed that all Frenchmen, regardless of wealth, should have the right to participate in government: his opposition to the franchise restrictions based on wealth had provoked his first serious criticism of the National Assembly. In October 1790, a motion was put to the Assembly that by paying a voluntary tax equivalent to three days' work a citizen should be admitted to the rights of an "active" citizen. It was defeated on the grounds that it might lead to corruption, with the rich buying the votes of the poor. In commenting on this motion, Garat objected to the idea that someone who needed all of his wages just to live, should have to sacrifice part of them "to exist politically", and stressed that it was essential that they should participate in the affairs of the country. He pointed out how in many countries where the poor were told to pay nothing, to meddle in nothing and to be nothing, the result of this pact had always been that they were more "robbed than relieved [*dépouillé que soulagé*]". But although "with trepidation" [*en gémissant*], he had to compromise his ideals with reality, and agreed that the eternel laws, the rights that came from nature - - in this case a universal franchise - - had to be reached by provisional laws.[104] Even after the Champ de Mars massacre, Garat was still critical of franchise restrictions and saw in them a real danger for the future. In August 1791, the "marc d'argent" qualification for deputies was suppressed at the expense of tighter restrictions on the qualifications to enter into rights of "active" citizenship. One of the arguments used to justify this was that voting was a political function, and not a natural right. Garat was not convinced by this: the chance to vote should be given to all, he declared, and should not be proscribed by law; the Constitution promised equality and this was what the Revolution was for. To the argument that the Revolution was for civil and not for political rights, Garat replied that this was the language of despots — that good rule is better than self-rule. More pointedly, Garat declared that the same complaints as had been made against absolute kings could now be legitimately made by those people excluded from political rights against those who were monopolizing these rights. He did conclude with the consoling thought, however, that as the exclusion was based on wealth and not on class, it was reasonable to expect that with the general increase in wealth, everyone would eventually be able to enjoy these rights.[105]

With such sentiments Garat was proposing a justification for the action that would eventually topple the monarchy — although in more muted form he was anticipating Guizot's "get rich" admonitions to those deprived of political power. Garat's philosophic humanitarianism was constantly plagued by doubts, but he seldom let these show through in the columns of the *Journal de Paris*. He had followed the mistake of the Assembly in seeing Bouillé's repression of the garrison at Nancy as necessary - - one of the few occasions when he was in direct conflict with the radical press - - but above all he let his irritation show when he reported the Champ de Mars massacre. This incident, prepared by Barnave in the Assembly and Regnault de Saint Jean d'Angély in the press,[106] brought Garat's latent fears to the surface, as he admitted that after two years of internal crises and convulsion, France

> has not yet repressed, destroyed these hordes of rogues who devastate and despoil her; has not yet punished their ferocious instigators; and that these monsters are still considered for important functions. The Assembly has never decided upon a more firm resolution to punish them, never has it been more clearly approved by the wishes of every citizen.[107]

This was a unique outburst, however (if indeed it came from him). More than Garat were misled in their approval of the juridical killings of mid-July 1791: the Jacobin Club was almost destroyed by the secession of members to found the Feuillant Club. Most of them returned, and in the *Journal de Paris* Garat's continued faith in the people was evident less than a month later, when he argued in favour of a more universal franchise.

Garat's criticism of the king and his continued support for popular sovereignty after the crisis of June and July 1791 was increasing tension between him and the *Journal's* proprietors. On 20 and 21 September 1791 two reports under the rubric "National Assembly" must have come as a shock to the regular readers of the *Journal*. These reports expressed the hope that France's "cruel agitations" would soon be at an end, since the barbarities committed previously in the name of the law, but after the Revolution in contempt of the law, were at last being suppressed. Popular violence was easier to excite than to contain, the articles went on, and the greatest achievement of the National Assembly had been the way it averted "eternal revolution". On 23 September Garat inserted a notice informing his readers that he had not been responsible for these articles. These articles -- as he pointed out in his notice -- were contrary to the spirit and principles that had guided Garat in his writing for the *Journal.* They were an anticipation of the changes that were taking place behind the scenes at the newspaper's office.

Nevertheless, Garat was allowed to nominate his successor, and chose Condorcet. For two weeks from 23 October Garat's friend regaled the *Journal's* readers with the same principles, but in a language harsher to the ear, especially if the reader did not in fact believe that all Catholics were "vile slaves of Roman superstition".[108] The proprietors of the *Journal* claimed that they had chosen Condorcet because of his patriotism, but the *Révolutions de Paris* might have been nearer the truth when it claimed that he had been appointed to attract more subscribers.[109] However that may be, Condorcet's more direct approach antagonized many subscribers and this, together with a growing belief by the management that the Revolution needed to be brought to a halt, resulted in his being sacked.

The proprietors then appointed the experienced journalist Regnault de Saint Jean d'Angély as political editor, while Suard wrote articles on the importance of the king's veto. But the slide towards reaction was most noticeable in the supplements, where a group of anti-Jacobin writers, most notably André Chénier, kept up a constant barrage of criticism of Brissot and his associates, a campaign which, despite the disclaimers of the proprietors, had their full support.[110] The *Journal de Paris* suffered with other Feuillant newspapers after August 10, perhaps even more so, as the patriots answered its insulting appearance on the eleventh and twelfth August by ransacking its offices and breaking its presses. Garat, on the other hand, returned to the politics he had claimed to detest. On leaving the *Journal de Paris* he had bought a house with the money he earned as a journalist, where he was surrounded by "more rocks than people"; but in 1792 he went to Great Britain in the suite of the French Embassy. Angered at the way the Revolution was being misrepresented he returned to France and wrote a defence which was translated into English. Back in Paris he participated in the "Brissotin" dinner parties and later claimed that he urged those discussing the republic to spend less time talking about it and to take more action to bring it about.[111]

Garat's support of the August 10 revolution was perfectly in keeping with the opinions he had made clear in the *Journal de Paris:* he had never supported the prerogatives of the monarchy, but instead held fast to the supremacy of the "general will", interpreted in a broad sense; nor had he condemned popular violence when directed towards the proper political end. This policy he continued in the disputes between the Jacobins and Girondins. His personal sympathies were almost entirely with the Girondins, where he had many friends, but he saw in the Jacobins, despite a very real personal revulsion against many of them, the spirit and force that was necessary to save the Revolution from its enemies. Although one of his solutions to the problem -- taken characteristically from his study of Roman history -- was a somewhat histrionic suggestion that the leaders of the two factions retire to voluntary exile, he also had a realistic appraisal of the problems facing France. He never condemned the September massacres, and as Minister of the Interior he presided over the expulsion of the Girondins on 2 June 1793. This event pained him greatly, but it was not necessarily out of pusillanimity that he took no official action to save his friends; in this crisis the safety of the Republic counted more than mere emotion.[112] It was pressure to introduce the Maximum that finally forced Garat to retire from politics: the concerted action of the people in the key events of the Revolution he approved of; the incidence of sporadic popular violence he deplored but did not condemn indiscriminately; but the continued refusal of ordinary French people to appreciate the virtues of free enterprise was too much for him to bear.

It is with justice then, that Garat has been called the "Jacobin malgré lui". Lacking Brissot's craving for popularity and Condorcet's strength of character, he survived both his friends and in doing so served the Revolution in the same way as countless thousands of Frenchmen who remain unknown. But this very naivety might also have saved him from the suspicion bordering on paranoia that eventually destroyed the political judgement of Robespierre. At the National Assembly Garat had voted with Robespierre on every issue, and even a few months after the latter's fall from power he still managed to mingle high praise with the obligatory criticism.[113] Garat's career thereafter might give some justification to accusations of him being a weathercock; but in the Directory he was known as an "ideologue", and when he served Napoleon there were the odd occasions when he alone dared to criticize him.[114] The restored Bourbons save him the dishonour of serving them by making it clear that his services were not required, and if he did become a practising Catholic later he was by then a very old man, surviving like so many other philosophes into his eighties.

Despite the accusation of weakness or even cowardice, which certainly were part of Garat's character, he was more than the eternal public servant, dedicated to whatever regime he happened to be serving. He could legitimately claim that his first interest was that of the Republic, and this in terms of the broad aspirations of the philosophes. After the fall of Robespierre, perhaps even just before it, the popular movement was finished and the triumph of the bourgeoisie more or less complete. Exile or retirement was one choice for those who despaired of the failure of the Revolution to live up to the hopes of 1789; for others a shaky belief in parliamentary democracy might give way to Napoleon's populism; the fate of those who chose revolutionary conspiracy was illustrated by Babeuf. The Revolution had no room for popular leaders after 1794, and the popular movement itself would lie dormant for more than a generation thereafter. The fate of a philosophe in the French Revolution could not have been so very different from that of Garat, unless it was that of his friend Condorcet or his associate Robespierre.

## *NOTES*

1. For instance he is barely mentioned in Soboul's standard text on the French Revolution or in Patrick's *Men of the First French Republic.*

2. A "political eunuch" known above else for his "faiblesse"; such are the usual judgements of Garat. Although Madame Roland supported him in 1792 her revised opinion of him in her *Mémoires* was of a "sickly little man and a detestable administrator"; Danton thought him constitutionally incapable of elevating himself "à toute la hauteur révolutionnaire"; Robespierre accused him of believing the aristocrats could come to like the Revolution; Marat dismissed him as a "disguised royalist"; while Momoro denounced him as a counter-revolutionary more perverse than all the Girondins put together.

   There is a long entry on Garat in the Michaud *Biographie universelle...*, by Villenave, and shorter entries in J. Sgard (ed.), *Dictionnaire des journalistes du dix-huitième siècle,* Grenoble, 1976; and the Prévost, d'Amat and Marembert (eds.), *Dictionnaire de biographie française,* Paris, still in progress, but the entry on Garat appeared in 1980. The most revealing work on Garat is his own *Mémoires sur la Révolution, ou Exposé de ma conduite dans les affaires et dans les fonctions publiques,* Paris, year III, reproduced in vol. xviii of Buchez et Roux, *Histoire parlementaire de la Révolution française.* All subsequent references to Garat's *Mémoires sur la Révolution* are taken from this edition. There is also some interesting information in "L'Arrestation du ministre Garat", *Archives historiques de la Révolution française,* vol. IX (1932), pp. 156-162, and in Garat's *Mémoires historiques sur la vie de M. Suard,* 2 vols. (Paris, 1820). Most of Garat's writing, however, is in the *Journal de Paris,* and it is this which forms the basis of the above article. On Garat and the *Journal de Paris,* Gallois's *Histoire des journaux et des journalistes,* 2 vols. (Paris, 1845-6), is on this as on most of his entries, useless, while Hatin's *Histoire politique et littéraire de la presse en France,* 8 vols. (Paris, 1859-61), still survives the test of time, particularly for its superb collection of extracts from the newspapers. The most recent general history of the French press makes the misleading statement in regard to the *Journal de Paris* that it was counter-revolutionary in the period of the Constituent Assembly; C. Bellanger, *et al., Histoire générale de la presse française,* I (Paris, 1969), p. 464.

3. Garat, *Mémoires sur la Révolution,* p. 447.

4. Darnton's "enlightenment from below" approach to eighteenth-century studies, the most refreshing and exciting contribution in this field for many years, has recently been crowned with his massive *The Business of the Enlightenment: a Publishing History of the Encyclopédie* (Cambridge, Mass., 1979), a work which fully lives up to the promise of the earlier articles.

5. This article issued from an "honours" dissertation originally presented as part requirement for the Honours degree of the University of Adelaide in 1966. It was my great pleasure, and privilege, to have had, as supervisor for this work, George Rudé.

6. On early "education" see his *Mémoires sur la Révolution,* pp. 465-6. Garat's older brother, Dominique (1735-1799), who accompanied him to Versailles in 1789, was more conservative in his politics, but had an eccentricity of character that once had him, a respectable *parlementaire,* leap on the stage at Bordeaux to show a troupe of dancers how properly to execute a Basque dance. Garat remained fiercely loyal to his family, including his sister the nun and his nephew the singer. Although he declared that he never used his influence to aid his relations, despite the urging of friends from the Gironde, he did take his nephew Francisque (1768-1850) to Naples with him when he went as ambassador there in 1798. (Much of this information comes from the biography of Pierre-Jean Garat, son of Dominique and a famous singer, by Paul Lafond, *Garat* [ Paris, s.d. — late 1890s ].) Garat himself had one son (b. 1791) by Marie Sainjal, a woman with whom he lived for many years and may have married.

7. In "L'arrestation..." he says he came to Paris in 1777, but in his *Mémoires sur la Révolution* he says that he was twenty-five when he came to Paris.

8. These three prize-winning *éloges* were included in a selection published in 1812: *Choix d'éloges couronnés par l'Académie française,* 2 vols. (Paris, 1812).

9. On the first see Hatin, II, pp. 416-8; on the Breteuil offer see Grimm's *Correspondance littéraire,* XIV, pp. 173-4 (June, 1785).

10. Michaud *Biographie universelle....*

11. His friendship with Rabaut probably dated from the period of the Constituent Assembly. In his *Mémoires sur la Révolution* (p. 345) he said of Brissot: "His manners were simple and pure, his ambition liberty and the happiness of all people...and although he loved glory he would have consented to an eternal obscurity to be the Penn of Europe, to create a society of Quakers and to make of Paris a new Philadelphia".

12. See his "open letter" prompted by Desmoulin's comment that the *Journal de Paris* had been astonished to find itself "patriotic" during the editorship of Condorcet. Part of this letter was published in the *Journal de Paris,* 29-12-1791.

13. Brissot, Marat, Fréron and Hébert are merely the best known. For the most recent consideration of work on the revolutionary press see Jeremy D. Popkin, "The revolutionary press: new findings and new perspectives", *Eighteenth Century Life,* vol. V, No. 4 (Summer 1979), pp. 90-104.

14. The introduction to the facsimile reproduction of selected numbers of the *Journal de Paris* (Éditions les yeux ouverts, 1968) gives the figure of 7,000 subscribers on the eve of the Revolution and 12,000 in 1790. This could well be the case, as Garat's salary was increased with his success in maintaining the *Journal* as a profitable enterprise -- see my *The Right-wing Press in the French Revolution, 1789-1792,* to be published by *The Royal Historical Society.*

15. Under this latter heading were the latest developments in the manufacture of false teeth, and advertisements for the cure of breast cancer (these were repeated in many issues).

16. *Journal de Paris,* 13-2-1789.

17. *Ibid.,* 1-2-1789.

18. *Ibid.,* 4-1-1789.

19. *Ibid.,* 11-4-1789.

20. Almost the whole issue of 9 February, 1789, was given over to an obituary for the Baron d'Holbach, atheist, humanist, and author of *Le Système de la Nature.*

21. *Ibid.,* 2-1-1789 for original letter: thereafter frequent references.

22. *Ibid.,* 31-3-1789 for original letter: thereafter frequent references.

23. In reporting the October Days the proprietors explained that they had preferred not to report popular disturbances because of the inflammatory effect this might have (9-10-1789). In September, however, the reviewer of Réveillon's *Exposé justificatif* sympathized with the "unwarranted persecution" to which the famous manufacturer had been subjected. The extract from this work, however, included with the review, also emphasized Réveillon's rise from obscure origins to that of a philanthropic employer anxious that others might be given the chance to rise in the world as he had done (4 September 1789). Prior to this, in the issue of 27 August 1789, under the rubric *Académie,* notification of a prize to one of Réveillon's servants was accompanied by a remark on her "unshakable courage... in the midst of the horrible pillage of her master's house in the faubourg Saint-Antoine."

24. *Ibid.,* 6-3-1789.

25. *Ibid.,* 13-2-1789.

26. *Ibid.,* 16-2-1789.

27. Garat preceded Robespierre in the National Assembly to speak on the disturbances of July as obviating the greatest of all crimes: an attempt on public liberty. The people armed itself against the plotters and blood flowed, but it was only that of the guilty *(Réimpression de l'Ancien Moniteur,* 30 July 1789, vol. 1, p. 255.) The proprietors showed much more sympathy for individual victims, and of course Garat's outburst in the Assembly was not reported in the columns of his paper. Early in 1790 when Garat was defending the

peasants in a riot in the Limousin, they were reminding their readers that the "seigneurs" had made their sacrifices and now had as much right to the protection of the law as anyone else (14-2-90).

28. *Journal de Paris,* 28-5-1789.

29. *Ibid.,* 6-8-1789: "We do not usually permit ourselves any reflections in these notices, but there is one that we cannot resist making: could such good be done so rapidly anywhere other than in a National Assembly!"

30. *Ibid.,* 6-9-1789.

31. *Ibid.,* 14-9-1789.

32. These words are more an echo of Montesquieu than an anticipation of Lord Acton.

33. *Journal de Paris,* 8-10-1789; see also 12-9-1789, 8-10-1789.

34. *Ibid.,* 11-11-1789.

35. *Ibid.,* 20-11-1789.

36. *Ibid.,* 25-11-1789.

37. *Ibid.,* 4-12-1789.

38. *Ibid.,* 4-12-1789.

39. *Ibid.,* 22-9-1789.

40. *Ibid.,* 11-10-1790.

41. *Ibid.,* 26-11-1789.

42. *Ibid.,* 25-12-1789.

43. *Ibid.,* 24-12-1789.

44. *Ibid.,* 22-12-1789.

45. *Ibid.,* 29-11-1789.

46. *Ibid.,* 1-11-1789.

47. *Ibid.,* 25-12-1789.

48. *Ibid.,* 7-11-1789.

49. *Ibid.,* 30-10-1789.

50. *Ibid.,* 4-11-1789.

51. *Ibid.,* 4-12-1789.

52. *Ibid.,* 8-12-1789.

53. *Révolutions de France et de Brabant,* IV, no. 48, p. 415, and V, no. 63, p. 512.

54. Particularly the *Actes des Apôtres.* I have expanded on this in my *Right-wing Press in the French Revolution.*

55. Hatin, II, p. 129. Citing from Rivarol's *Petit dictionnaire des grands hommes de la Révolution.*

56. *Journal de Paris,* 8-3-1790.

57. See especially Marchant's *Chronique du manège,* no.5, p.3 and no.15, p.12.

58. I have treated this issue in detail in my Adelaide honours dissertation, "The *Journal de Paris* and the French Revolution: 1789-91".

59. *Journal de Paris,* 18-6-1790.

60. *Ibid.,* 28-6-1791.

61. *Ibid.,* 27-8-1790.

62. *Ibid.,* 24-6-1790.

63. *Ibid.,* 4-10-1789.

64. *Ibid.*, 21-6-1790.

65. *Ibid.*, 22-12-1790.

66. *Ibid.*, 6-1-1790.

67. *Ibid.*, 6-2-1790.

68. *Ibid.*, 30-5-1790.

69. Hébert reflected public opinion, and was popular-royalist at this time; even after the king's flight Marat was more concerned about an oligarchy than a monarchy; Desmoulins and Robert were the only journalists forwarding republican notions before 1791.

70. Marat correctly told his readers of the secret covering letter advising sympathy for individual victims, and, again, Garat's outburst in the Assembly was not reported in the columns of his paper. A letter to Desmoulin's *Révolutions de France et de Brabant* in the first weeks of 1790 noted how Gouy d'Arsy appeared without title in the *Chronique de Paris* but became the comte de Gouy in the *Journal de Paris (Révolutions de France et de Brabant*, Vol. III, No. 30). In February 1790 Garat felt compelled to add a postcript to his *Assemblée nationale* column, pointing out that he had nothing whatsoever to do with any other part of the paper (*Journal de Paris*, 28-2-1790.) See also footnote 23 above.

71. *Ibid.*, 22-4-1791.

72. *Ibid.*, 23-12-1790.

73. *Ibid.*, 25-11-1790.

74. *Ibid.*, 24-12-1790. The king's interpretation was completely unjustified: the *Journal* was no more than reporting what someone else had said, and elsewhere in the same issue it showed warm praise for him.

75. *Ibid.*, 26-6-1791.

76. See, for example, *Journal de Paris*, 16-5-1791 but especially 15-6-1791; also 23-6-1790.

77. *Ibid.*, 27-2-1791.

78. *Ibid.*, 24-6-1791.

79. *Ibid.*, 11-8-1791.

80. *Ibid.*, 12-8-1791.

81. *Ibid.*, 25-8-1791.

82. *Ibid.*, 11-7-1790.

83. *Ibid.*, 14-9-1791.

84. *Ibid.*, 1-10-1791.

85. *Ibid.*, 15-12-1790.

86. *Ibid.*, 1-11-1790.

87. *Ibid.*, 3-6-1791.

88. Stated frequently, but see especially *ibid.*, 18-8-1790.

89. *Ibid.*, 15-2-1791.

90. I have developed this theme at length in my *Right-wing Press in the French Revolution.*

91. *Journal de Paris*, 4-12-1790.

92. *Ibid.*, 8-8-1791.

93. *Ibid.*, 2-6-1791.

94. *Ibid.*, 22-9-1790.

95. *Ibid.*, 4-2-1791

96. *Ibid.*, 9-4-1790, 30-4-1790.

97. *Ibid.*, 3-2-1791.

98. *Ibid.*, 3-12-1790.

99. *Ibid.*, 4-6-1791.

100. *Ibid.*, 22-7-1790.

101. *Ibid.*, 1-1-1791.

102. *Ibid.*, 30-11-1790.

103. *Ibid.*, 17-6-1791.

104. *Ibid.*, 24-10-1790.

105. *Ibid.*, 13-8-1791.

106. There is an excellent account of this in G. Michon, *Essai sur l'histoire du parti Feuillant: Duport* (Paris, 1924), pp. 225-258.

107. *Journal de Paris,* 18-7-1791.

108. See for example *ibid.,* 23-10-1791.

109. *Révolutions de Paris,* no. 123, 12/19 November 1791, pp. 308-310. This dispute is well-documented in Hatin, II, pp. 141-149.

110. Murray, *Right-wing Press in the French Revolution,* "A New Right"

111. Garat, *Mémoires sur la Révolution,* pp. 295, 346, 467.

112. Buchez and Roux do well to place Garat's *Mémoires sur la Révolution* as an introduction to their volume dealing with the Girondins and Jacobins, for Garat has many penetrating remarks to make on this issue.

Garat claims to have made a suicide pact with Condorcet, but when it came to the point Condorcet took the poison alone. After the expulsion of the Girondins Garat says that he offered Condorcet a refuge at the very offices of the Ministry of the Interior, and failing that at his private home ten leagues from Paris. Garat claims also to have rushed to the aid of Clavière and Lebrun *(Mémoires sur la Révolution,* pp. 324, 459-61.) Garat was here replying to the many accusations of weakness or even cowardice made against him.

113. In his *Mémoires sur la Révolution* Garat discerned amidst Robespierre's "constant drivel" [*rabâchage éternel*] on the rights of man and so on, the germs of a talent with a great capacity for good or for evil (p. 333); and in his *Mémoires sur Suard* (II, p. 339) he angered some people by what they saw as a comparison of Robespierre with Jesus Christ.

114. At least in the years of the Consulate: see comments by Villenave in the Michaud *Biographie universelle....*

Albert Soboul

# SUR LES « CURÉS ROUGES »
# DE QUATRE-VINGT-TREIZE

Le 5 juin 1790, C. Fricaud, député du Tiers État du bailliage de Charolles, présentait à l'Assemblée constituante, au nom du Comité des rapports, une affaire offrant « les plus étonnantes singularités »; « d'après le récit des faits vous verrez qu'elle tient absolument du délire »:[1]

> « Le 6 octobre dernier [1789], M. l'abbé Carion, curé d'Issy-l'Évêque [au bailliage d'Autun], sous prétexte d'établir un grenier de subsistance pour les pauvres, a convoqué une assemblée de paroisse. La séance a commencé par la lecture d'un cahier ayant pour titre: *Formation du Comité et Conseil d'administration de la ville et commune d'Issy-l'Évêque.* Ce cahier contient des lois sur la police de la ville, la réparation des prisons, l'administration de la justice, le régime des gardes nationales, les amendes et confiscations, les emprisonnements des citoyens sur simple ordre écrit du comité, les alignements des rues et des places publiques, les corvées, les prix des grains, en un mot tout ce que l'imagination exaltée de ce pasteur a pu réunir pour enfanter une législation. Le curé, le casque en tête et l'épée au côté, allait chez tous les laboureurs s'emparer de leurs grains; en vertu de son règlement, il en fixait le prix. Ce nouveau législateur n'a point reconnu la séparation des pouvoirs; car il ordonnait, jugeait, exécutait ses propres jugements. [...] Un jour, M. le curé partit, tambour battant; et arriva dans les Grandes Bruyères; il y rendit et y fit exécuter sur le champ ses lois agraires, s'adjugea à lui-même une portion du territoire, sous le prétexte que c'était une ancienne commune. Ses prônes étaient un mélange de faits de guerre, de menaces séditieuses, d'explications de ses règlements, avec le moyen de les faire exécuter. À l'aide de ses troupes (car il en avait), il a établi et perçu des octrois, fait abattre des murs de clôture, arracher des haies. [...] il nous reste à désarmer ce redoutable curé ».[2]

L'affaire fut renvoyée au Comité des rapports. Décrété de prise de corps, l'abbé Carion fut transféré à Paris. Le 10 février 1791, une députation d'Issy-l'Évêque et de cinq autres municipalités (« nous sommes venus à pied de quatre-vingts lieues ») réclama sa liberté à l'Assemblée constituante. « Nous devons faire connaître à cette auguste Assemblée, au sein de laquelle il a été faussement inculpé, les faits qui lui sont réellement personnels. Il a débité à 50 sous des blés qu'il avait achetés très cher; il a sacrifié une partie de son jardin pour l'utilité de la communauté; il a donné des secours aux ouvriers qui étaient sans travail; il a donné à la commune le prix des baux qu'elle ne pouvait pas payer ». Quant au comité permanent et à la garde nationale établis « pour les subsistances et pour la police, [...] notre curé ne fit qu'exécuter les délibérations prises par l'assemblée générale de la commune ».[3] Le 17 mars 1791, l'Assemblée nationale décréta l'élargissement de l'abbé Carion.[4]

Le curé d'Issy-l'Évêque était-il un « curé rouge »? À travers la dénonciation de Fricaud, avocat, ci-devant subdélégué de l'intendant de Bourgogne, et ses accusations, nous constatons que s'affirmèrent dès 1789 les traits essentiels des «curés rouges» de Quatre-vingt-treize. Revendication de la taxation des grains et du partage des biens communaux: il n'y a là rien que de très banal et sans doute pourrait-on citer bien d'autres cas analogues dès 1789. Et de même le recours à la pratique populaire de la démocratie directe. Il y a plus: le ton prophétique («Ses prônes étaient un mélange de faits de guerre, de menaces séditieuses»...), l'imagination exaltée, la vision utopique incitant à légiférer et à réglementer en tout, jusqu'au régime des prisons et aux «alignements des rues et des places publiques». Plus encore, l'abbé Carion est un homme d'action. Il est maire de sa commune, président du comité permanent, membre de l'état major de la garde nationale. Le voici «casque en tête, épée au côté», faisant abattre les murs de clôture, arracher les haies, en un mot «exécuter... ses lois agraires». Les temps étaient enfin révolus: le peuple rentrait dans la plénitude de ses droits.

Au delà de cette esquisse que suggère un texte de 1790, il est nécessaire de pousser l'analyse plus loin et de préciser ce que furent les «curés rouges» de Quatre-vingt-treize.

## I

«Curés rouges»: s'agissant de la Révolution française, l'expression est anachronique. Le rouge n'y fut jamais la couleur symbolique de la révolution. C'est à la loi martiale du 21 octobre 1789, que se rapporte le nom et le signe: «drapeau rouge». On doit le déployer quand on veut faire usage de la loi. «Cette déclaration se fera en exposant à la principale fenêtre de la maison de ville, et en portant dans toutes les rues et carrefours un *drapeau rouge*...».[5] On sait ce qu'il en fut au Champ de Mars le 17 juillet 1791. S'il fut question à la veille de l'insurrection du 10 août 1792, de faire marcher les insurgés sous un drapeau rouge portant l'inscription «Loi martiale du peuple souverain, contre la rebellion du pouvoir exécutif», la proposition n'eut pas de suite.[6] Quant au bonnet rouge, si son port se généralisa dans les masses populaires au cours de l'été 1793, il ne fut jamais entouré d'un respect unanime. Marat était coiffé d'une casquette, non pas du bonnet rouge; et le jour où Armonville arbora cette coiffure à la tribune, il souleva une telle tempête qu'il fut contraint de l'enlever. Pour Robespierre, le 19 mars 1792 aux Jacobins, imposer le port du bonnet rouge aux orateurs et au bureau de la société, ce serait «affaiblir l'énergie» du seul emblème national, la cocarde tricolore.[7] Nous n'insisterons pas plus longtemps: il fallut attendre la Seconde République pour que s'affirme la symbolique politique du rouge. *Rouge,* selon Littré (1876): «Républicain avancé acceptant le drapeau rouge pour symbole».

L'expression *curé rouge,* qui n'apparaît pas dans les travaux de Lichtenberger sur «le socialisme» au XVIIIe siècle et pendant la Révolution, ni dans l'œuvre d'Aulard, semble avoir été utilisée pour la première fois par G. Brégail en 1901.[8] Elle fut reprise par Ed. Campagnac en 1913 à propos de Métier, curé de Saint-Liesne de

Melun, alors qu'en 1903 ce même auteur (qui ignorait sans doute, à cette époque, l'étude de G. Brégail) avait qualifié Petit-Jean, curé d'Épineuil (Cher) de *prêtre communiste.*[9] Remarquons qu'aucun de ces deux auteurs ne s'est efforcé de préciser ce qu'il entendait exactement par *curé rouge.* On retrouve l'expression en 1937 sous la plume de F. Brunot dans son *Histoire de la langue française,* entre guillemets, mais sans aucun commentaire.[10] Il semble bien que, dans la sphère des études révolutionnaires, ce fut M. Dommanget qui popularisa l'expression, publiant en 1948 une brochure consacré à *Jacques Roux, le curé rouge,* en 1955 un article dans *L'École libératrice* intitulé « Curés rouges et prêtres ouvriers ».[11]

À la lumière de ces auteurs, nous nous garderons, dans une tentative de définition de toute extension abusive, précisant d'abord ce que n'est pas ou n'est pas seulement un curé rouge.

Première extension abusive, celle que présente souvent l'historiographie religieuse traditionnelle, pour qui les curés déprêtrisés et mariés sont nécessairement rouges. Ainsi de F. Bridoux dans son *Histoire religieuse du département de Seine-et-Marne pendant la Révolution*[12]: mais Parent, curé de Boissise-la-Bertrand près de Melun, prêtre déchristianisateur, est-il vraiment un curé rouge? Ainsi de l'abbé J. Gallerand qui dresse une liste de 77 prêtres mariés desquels émergent Gabriel Bayeux et Alexandre Dubreuil.[13] Mais pour être qualifiés de curés rouges suffit-il qu'Alexandre Dubreuil ait été le bras droit d'Hésine, l'un des défenseurs des Babouvistes lors du procès de Vendôme, que Gabriel Bayeux ait persisté à donner des prénoms révolutionnaires à ses enfants jusqu'en 1810? Et nous dirons de même s'agissant dans le Louhannais d'Antoine Thomas qui brûla ses lettres de prêtrise au pied de l'arbre de la Liberté à Chalon et du curé Maître qui laïcisa son nom en Égal...[14]

Élargissant la notion, Ed. Campagnac assimila curé rouge et curé patriote. « Métier subit ici le sort commun à tous les curés patriotes qui méritèrent l'appellation de curés rouges »[15]: ses accusateurs lui reprochaient d'être prêtre, bien qu'il ait remis ses lettres de prêtrise. Né en 1758, devenu prêtre, Métier avait exercé le sacerdoce en diverses communes de Seine-et-Marne, Melun en dernier lieu. « Le caractère ferme et énergique et la tête révolutionnaire », selon le représentant Du Bouchet en mission en Seine-et-Marne, Métier avait été secrétaire de la réunion des électeurs du bailliage de Melun en 1789, membre de la première municipalité de Melun en 1790, l'un des deux secrétaires de la Société des Amis de la Constitution en 1791. Prêtre constitutionnel, Métier occupait une place de premier rang dans la ville de Melun. Au moment de l'arrivée de Du Bouchet, Métier était à la fois juge au tribunal, président de l'Administration départementale, président de la société populaire. Le voici, le 11 septembre 1793, commissaire délégué du représentant du peuple, avec des pouvoirs illimités dont son énergie révolutionnaire allait user amplement. Carrière révolutionnaire exemplaire. Si Métier abjura finalement, ce ne fut que le 22 brumaire an II (12 novembre 1793), au lendemain de l'abjuration de Gobel. « Les déclarations antireligieuses de Métier sont plutôt rares, remarque Ed. Campagnac, et celles qu'il fait sont exprimées en termes modérés ». Métier: un curé jacobin qui, avant même que Robespierre ait protesté contre les violences des déchristianisateurs, comprit le danger de la propagande anti-religieuse, — curé rouge, certainement pas.

De même que ne peuvent être qualifiés de curés rouges les ci-devant prêtres déchristianisateurs acharnés: tels Parent, curé de Boissise-la-Bertrand, « un curé rouge de la première heure» selon Ed. Campagnac, «le plus apostolique et le plus obstiné» des curés rouges de Seine-et-Marne selon M. Dommanget. C'est lui qui, dès le 14 brumaire, écrit à la Convention: «Je suis prêtre, je suis curé, c'est-à-dire charlatan». Commissaire du district de Melun, Parent fut un prêtre patriote, mais il semble bien que son action militante fut essentiellement déchristianisatrice et n'alla pas au delà. Parent: un prêtre déchristianisateur, curé rouge, certainement pas.

Ce sont ces mêmes prêtres déchristianisateurs que S. Bianchi qualifie de «curés démocrates».[16] Encore que le terme *démocrate* soit ambigu (démocratie politique ou démocratie sociale?), peut-on ranger dans le même groupe le déchristianisateur Parent et ces véritables démocrates que furent Petit-Jean, curé d'Épineuil, ou Dolivier, curé de Mauchamps? Force est bien de tenter une définition plus précise: qu'est-ce donc qu'un curé rouge de Quatre-vingt-treize?

Nous emprunterons des éléments de définition à M. Dommanget. Dans son article de *L'École libératrice,* en 1955, il remarque combien "certains termes forgés par les historiens comme représentatifs d'un mouvement de masse ou d'un courant d'idées sont historiquement faux. Tel est le terme de *jacquerie* pour désigner ce qu'à l'époque on appelait les *effrois*; tel est le terme de *curé rouge* pour désigner les prêtres qui, au XVIIIe siècle et surtout pendant la Révolution, se sont placés à l'avant-garde du clergé en fait, en parole ou en écrit». Ayant souligné combien le terme est vague et prête à équivoque, M. Dommanget distingue les curés rouges «se tenant sur le seul terrain philosophique, c'est-à-dire des prêtres qui se sont débarrassés des préjugés religieux, mais conservent des préjugés sociaux», et les curés rouges «qui se sont débarrassés de tout ou partie des préjugés sociaux, mais conservent des préjugés religieux». Il y eut enfin ceux que M. Dommanget appelle les curés rouges *intégraux,* «débarrassés à la fois des préjugés religieux et des préjugés sociaux».

Que le curé rouge combatte sur le plan social, nous en sommes bien d'accord, encore convient-il de préciser le sens de ce combat. Mais compatissant à la misère populaire, épris de charité, pénétré des enseignements de l'Évangile, le curé rouge a conservé ses «préjugés religieux». Il ne fut point déchristianisateur. C'est comme chrétien et patriote à la fois qu'il mena son combat social.

## II

A tenter d'esquisser un portrait du prêtre rouge, il nous apparait dès l'abord dans la force de l'âge. En 1793, Croissy, curé d'Étalon au district de Montdidier (Somme), a 35 ans; Jacques Roux de la section parisienne des Gravilliers, 41 ans; Dolivier, curé de Mauchamps au district d'Étampes, 47 ans; Petit-Jean, curé d'Épineuil au district de Saint-Amand (Cher), 53 ans.[17]

Voici, d'après son signalement envoyé à tous les districts du département après l'insurrection d'Épineuil, le curé Petit-Jean. "Âgé de 52 ans [ nous sommes en 1792 ], mais paraissant plus jeune; très droit, portant naturellement la tête haute, les cheveux et sourcils châtains, barbe de même, le front bien fait [...]; en tout un bel homme et qui a l'air de le savoir par son regard et son maintien». Nous savons aussi de Jacques Roux qu'il était bel homme, d'un sang vif, en pleine possession de ses moyens.

À nous en tenir à ces quatre exemples, ces prêtres rouges ont été ou sont encore curés de paroisses rurales. Avant d'être « *prêtre vicaire* » de la paroisse de Saint-Nicolas des Champs, comme il le déclare au Département de police de la Commune de Paris, lors de son interrogatoire du 23 août 1793, Jacques Roux a été curé de Cozes, puis de Saint-Thomas de Conac au diocèse de Saintes. Avant de desservir la paroisse de Mauchamps, Dolivier a été vicaire de celle de Condat en Auvergne. Tous ont une expérience directe du peuple des campagnes, de ses besoins, de sa mentalité, de ses revendications. Nul doute que l'égalitarisme paysan ne soit l'une des sources vivantes de la vocation militante des prêtres rouges.

Tous ont prêté serment et ont gardé la foi. Curés constitutionnels, ils ne renièrent pas leur serment, ou ne le firent que sous la contrainte.

Quant à Jacques Roux, M. Dommanget remarque qu'« il ne semble pas avoir été aussi hardi sur le plan religieux que sur le plan politique et surtout sur le plan social ». S'il flétrit en effet les « charlatans ultra-montains », Jacques Roux s'en prend tout autant aux « athées sanguinaires ». « Le sacerdoce est un état, écrit-il dans le numéro 264 (septembre 1793) de son *Publiciste de la République française;* on ne peut faire un crime à l'homme de l'exercer, si un homme professe publiquement les principes de la véritable morale, s'il inspire l'horreur de la tyrannie. Un prêtre de cette nature n'est pas odieux à la société, avec d'autant plus de raison qu'on ne rend pas vingt-cinq millions d'hommes tout à coup philosophes ».

Petit-Jean qui, lui, vécut la déchristianisation, ne s'est pas déprêtrisé, ne s'étant jamais détaché de la religion, croyant parmi les paysans croyants, « surtout les femmes » au dire du procureur de la commune écrivant au district de Saint-Amand, le 26 septembre 1792. Arrêté le 19 décembre suivant, condamné à un an de prison, Petit-Jean fut libéré le 27 septembre 1793 par le représentant Laplanche en mission à Bourges qui, le 5 octobre, le nomma à la cure de Saint-Caprais « pour le soustraire à la malveillance de ses ennemis et prévenir toute discorde ». Petit-Jean refusa: il écrivit à l'évêque Torné qu'il voulait être curé d'Épineuil ou ne l'être nulle part. Il donna finalement sa démission, mais ne se déprêtrisa jamais.

On connait l'affaire du curé d'Étalon, Louis-Pierre Croissy, si bien démontée par Georges Lefebvre. À Montdidier, la municipalité décida le 8 frimaire an II (28 novembre 1793), de fermer les églises. « Que le curé d'Étalon, écrit Georges Lefebvre, se soit senti offensé dans sa foi, il n'y a pas de raison d'en douter ». Il continua a célébrer le culte, soutenu par une partie de ses paroissiens, portant aux mourants la communion et l'extrême-onction. Il déclara plus tard, quand on l'interrogea, qu'il n'avait pas porté le bon Dieu dans sa poche, ainsi qu'on le prétendait, mais à la manière accoutumée, c'est-à-dire évidemment avec tintement de clochette et un porte-croix. Finalement, le district fit enlever l'argenterie de l'église et celle-ci fut fermée; puis le 17 ventôse (7 mars 1794), Croissy remit ses lettres de prêtrise à la municipalité, sur invitation circulaire du représentant en mission, André Dumont. Mais il ne cacha pas qu'il aurait souhaité conserver sa cure et poursuivre son sacerdoce. Les notables qui avaient contre lui de tout autres griefs, profitèrent de la déchristianisation pour s'en débarrasser. Il est bien probable que les jurés du Tribunal révolutionnaire qui le condamnèrent à mort le 21 prairial (9 juin 1794), n'attachèrent pas grande importance à l'accusation de prédication de la loi agraire, mais condamnèrent en Croissy un prêtre qui avait accueilli avec colère la déchristianisation.

L'abbé Dolivier, curé de Mauchamps, fut l'un des premiers prêtres à se marier. On est frappé par le ton philosophique du discours qu'il prononça le 21 octobre 1792, à l'issue des vêpres, pour annoncer son mariage à ses paroissiens.[18] C'était là le résultat d'une longue évolution, et non pas un quelconque coup de tête ou simplement le désir d'imiter ses confrères qui, tel l'abbé Cournand, l'avaient précédé dans cette voie. Tout comme la pétition du printemps précédent en faveur des émeutiers d'Étampes, le discours du 21 octobre 1792 n'est pas autre chose qu'un manifeste du droit naturel appliqué au problème du célibat des prêtres, cette «superstition», cette «imposture» contraire aux lois de la nature. Demeuré profondément religieux, Dolivier ne se déprêtrisa que sous la contrainte et avec la plus grande discrétion. Il réprouvait la déchristianisation menée à grand fracas par Couturier en mission dans le district d'Étampes d'octobre à décembre 1793, qui ordonna le 29 novembre la fermeture de toutes les églises. Pour l'abbé Dolivier, le «sentiment» religieux était nécessaire à l'harmonie de l'édifice social. Il est impossible de fixer avec précision la date de déprêtrisation du curé de Mauchamps, elle était effective au 1er décembre 1793. L'abbé Dolivier abandonna Mauchamps pour se réfugier à Paris auprès de son frère.

Hommes de foi, les curés rouges furent aussi hommes d'action. Qu'il suffise d'évoquer le rôle de Dolivier dans l'affaire d'Étampes en mars-avril 1792, celui de Petit-Jean dans l'émeute d'Épineuil du 23 septembre 1792, la vie militante de Jacques Roux. Le dimanche 23 septembre, à l'issue de la grand'messe, Petit-Jean rassemble les paysans qu'il a convoqués par affiches. Il place devant l'autel une table qui lui sert de tribune. Une centaine de ses partisans l'entourent, il leur présente une pétition à signer... Dans la rixe qui suit, Petit-Jean excite les paysans: « Tuez tous ces gueux-là»! L'agitation reprend à l'issue des vêpres. Petit-Jean rassemble à nouveau ses partisans et les mène sur les terres de Clermont, officier municipal, l'un des plus riches propriétaires d'Épineuil, pour en abattre les haies. Vers la fin de la journée, le bruit se répandant qu'un détachement de la garde nationale de Saint-Armand s'avançait, Petit-Jean ordonna de donner le tocsin...

Plus que des révoltés, les curés rouges furent, par tempérament, des révolutionnaires. On ne peut de ce point de vue les comparer au curé Meslier comme nous y invite M. Dommanget. Le curé d'Étrépigny: révolté plus que révolutionnaire. Il a manqué à Meslier l'influence enrichissante de l'événement et de l'action: pensons à Jacques Roux. Similitude et contraste à la fois de ces deux tempéraments: chez l'un et l'autre, la révolte. Mais chez Jacques Roux, l'audace de l'action, le sens de l'agitation révolutionnaire, la persévérance et le courage jusqu'à la mort. La conduite prudente de Meslier étonne, mis à part l'esclandre de 1716, affrontée à la hardiesse de sa pensée.[19]

Prophète, a-t-on dit du curé Meslier. À poursuivre la comparaison avec les curés rouges de Quatre-vingt-treize, on constate combien ces derniers dépassent le prophétisme du curé d'Étrépigny. Chez les uns et les autres, la même force de dénonciation contre toutes les injustices, tous les abus, toutes les oppressions, la même vigueur de la révolte contre les grands et les rois, les aristocrates et les accapareurs. Chez les uns et les autres, la même ardeur de compassion pour les pauvres et les déshérités, la même exigence de justice totale, la même soif d'absolu, la même intolérance au temps. Le même souffle prophétique les anime. Écoutons Petit-Jean. Il annonce, le 1er septembre 1792, que «le massacre général de tous les aristocrates va s'opérer pour établir l'égalité», «qu'avant un mois les maisons des riches seront détruites». Dans un écrit adressé au district, au département et à la France entière: «C'est un prêtre qui a perdu la France [l'abbé Maury?]; c'est un prêtre qui la sauvera»: Petit-Jean lui-même. «Que la contre-révolution commencerait à Épineuil, et que de là elle se répandrait par toute la France et qu'il se mettrait à sa tête; que le nom de Petit-Jean serait mémorable; que l'égalité et le partage des biens se ferait sous peu de temps; que l'on avait vu déborder les rivières, mais que l'on verrait couler beaucoup de sang».

Mais le prophète, s'il dénonce l'ignominie du présent et annonce l'avenir, ne se soucie pas de la construire. Le prêtre rouge au contraire se lance dans l'action avec toutes les audaces, il aide l'histoire à accoucher de l'avenir.

L'action révolutionnaire des curés rouges se caractérise, dans sa pratique, par le recours constant à la démocratie directe. À ses ennemis qui le menacent des juges, Petit-Jean répond «qu'il ne reconnait la compétence d'aucun juge; le juge naturel est le peuple souverain». Méprisant les institutions officielles, il convoque de sa propre autorité une assemblée des villageois; au maire qui lui demande pourquoi il a convoqué cette assemblée, alors que c'est un délit prévu par la loi, il répond que c'est pour obéir «à la loi et à l'humanité». Quant à Croissy, il avait dit souvent, chez son ami Dumont, que «le peuple étant souverain pouvait prendre ce qui lui convenait sans qu'il fût besoin de recourir à des arbitres ou aux tribunaux, et que les communes étaient absolument maîtresses». Pareils propos conformes à la mentalité et au comportement populaires et qui légitimaient pour le moins la reprise sans formalités des biens communaux usurpés, ne pouvaient que déplaire foncièrement aux notables.

La pensée politique de l'abbé Dolivier s'était affirmée dès 1790 avec *Le Voeu national*[20]: critique sévère de l'organisation politique élaborée par l'Assemblée constituante et esquisse d'un système original de démocratie populaire. Les Constituants ne parlent d'égalité des droits que pour mieux maintenir l'inégalité *naturelle* des moyens. « Je voudrais au contraire, affirmait Dolivier, que l'état social établisse une juste égalité des moyens... en sorte que chaque associé puisse parvenir à l'entière jouissance du droit qui lui est propre». Droits, moyens: «Je n'entends point cette distinction lorsque ce que l'on appelle moyen est précisément ce qui constitue le droit». À peine a-t-on proclamé les principes d'égalité qu'on s'est hâtés de les enfreindre. «Il faut avouer que si on a eu l'intention d'établir l'aristocratie des riches, on ne pouvait faire un meilleur choix pour y réussir».

La pratique politique de Jacques Roux dans le cadre de la section des Gravilliers est trop connue pour que nous y revenions ici. Rappelons seulement le souci constant de Jacques Roux de prendre appui sur les organisations populaires de base. Ainsi à l'occasion de sa fameuse pétition du 25 juin 1793. Le 20 juin, aux Cordeliers, il propose que soit ajouté à la Constitution, déjà presque entièrement votée, un article portant peine de mort contre l'agiotage et l'usure. Le lendemain, au Conseil général de la Commune, il propose de se transporter en masse à la Convention pour qu'elle décrète comme article constitutionnel que «la liberté ne consiste pas à affamer ses semblables». Obstiné, Jacques Roux revient à la charge générale de la section des Gravilliers à l'unanimité; l'impression en est ordonnée. Le 25 enfin, Jacques Roux se présente à la barre de la Convention à la tête d'une députation des sections des Gravilliers et de Bonne-Nouvelle et du club des Cordeliers. Plus encore peut-être que par le contenu, c'est par le ton qu'il heurte l'Assemblée. Au nom du peuple souverain, il tance les *mandataires*: «Depuis longtemps vous promettez de faire cesser les calamités du peuple; mais qu'avez-vous fait pour cela? [...] Députés de la Montagne, fondez les bases de la prospérité de la République; ne terminez pas votre carrière avec ignominie». Il ordonne: «Prononcez donc, encore une fois... Les sans-culottes avec leurs piques feront exécuter vos décrets».[21]

Prenant appui sur la pratique de la démocratie directe, la revendication sociale des curés rouges, en harmonie profonde avec les tendances populaires, porte essentiellement sur le droit à l'existence et donc sur la critique du droit de propriété, sans toutefois que nous trouvions chez eux (Dolivier mis à part) une théorie élaborée. Il s'agit plus simplement d'un égalitarisme viscéral, s'entendant essentiellement des conditions d'existence. On a pu parler d'égalitarisme de la consommation. «Chacun doit avoir de quoi vivre paisiblement», écrivait le curé Meslier. À l'autre bout du siècle lui répond Jacques Roux: «L'égalité n'est qu'un vain fantôme quand le riche, par le monopole, exerce le droit de vie et de mort sur son semblable». Le droit à l'existence l'emporte sur le droit de propriété. «Eh quoi! Les propriétés des fripons seraient-elles quelque chose de plus sacré que la vie des hommes?» Le droit de propriété ne saurait exister pour «les sangsues du peuple».

Exerçant leur sacerdoce au sein de communautés rurales, les curés rouges ne pouvaient qu'être sensibles aux problèmes de la terre, essentiellement de la propriété et de l'exploitation. «La terre prise en général, écrit l'abbé Dolivier dans son *Essai sur la justice primitive,* doit être regardée comme le grand communal de la nature, où tous les êtres animés ont primitivement un droit indéfini sur les productions qu'il renferme. [.... dans l'ordre social ] chaque individu doit trouver son droit de partage au grand communal». De là des revendications très concrètes: la reprise des biens communaux usurpés, la division des grandes fermes.

Pour une juste appréciation de l'action militante des prêtres rouges au sein de la communauté villageoise, il serait nécessaire d'avoir une analyse précise des structures sociales d'Épineuil, de Mauchamps, d'Étalon. Rappelons que la paroisse de Mauchamps comprenait 135 à 140 habitants groupés en 34 foyers: une petite paysannerie de vignerons et de manouvriers dominés par deux laboureurs qui à eux seuls payaient, à la fin de l'Ancien Régime, 800 livres de taille, 18 journaliers n'en payant que 600. Alors que les villageois détenaient en propre ou à loyer à peine plus de 86 arpents, les fermiers «en corps de ferme» en cultivant 92. De là, la revendication essentielle de la petite paysannerie que Dolivier transcrivit dans son *Essai sur la justice primitive*: «la division de la terre entre tous les citoyens qui n'en ont point ou qui n'en ont pas suffisamment», de telle sorte qu'une exploitation «ne surpasse point le labourage d'une charrue».

À Épineuil, la communauté villageoise était dominée par trois paysans plus qu'aisés qui s'adjugèrent de surcroît une partie des biens nationaux mis en vente, si bien que le curé Petit-Jean put les traiter à plusieurs reprises d'accapareurs et exciter contre eux la jalousie des petits paysans. Le pouvoir politique allant de pair avec le monopole foncier, ces paysans aisés dominaient la municipalité. Quand commença l'action militante et la propagande égalitaire de Petit-Jean? On ne peut le préciser. Les premières traces en apparaissent, d'après les dénonciations postérieures, en août 1792. « Il leur dit tous les jours que les biens vont être communs; cherche à les persuader par les propos les plus insinuants, en leur disant qu'il n'y aura qu'une cave, qu'un grenier, où chacun prendra tout ce qui lui sera nécessaire ». On reconnaît là l'un des thèmes essentiels de l'utopie égalitaire. Petit-Jean conseillait à ses paroissiens « de former des dépôts dans les caves et dans les greniers, où ils iront puiser en communauté », ajoutant que « l'on n'aurait plus besoin d'argent ». Le 1er septembre 1792, il adresse au district, au département, à l'Assemblée législative, un libelle « où il annonce que le massacre général de tous les aristocrates va s'opérer pour rétablir l'égalité; et il invite les citoyens à suivre ses conseils, à consentir librement l'abandon de toutes leurs propriétés et le partage général de tous leurs biens ».

Cette prédication égalitaire, quel qu'ait été son caractère utopique, ne pouvait qu'effrayer les possédants. « Il prêchait la violation des propriétés ». Selon le rapport du commandant de la garde nationale de Saint-Amand, « le sieur Petit-Jean tenait les propos les plus incendiaires et les plus inconstitutionnels en prêchant comme à sa coutume la loi agraire ». Le curé Petit-Jean ne se contentait pas de prêcher, il agissait. Il conseillait à ses paroissiens de ne pas payer « l'indemnité de la dîme », entendons la redevance (dite *colonique* en Auvergne) en sus du métayage (le Berry était pays de fermage général). Lors de l'émeute du 23 septembre, dans l'après-midi, Petit-Jean prend la tête des paysans armés « de fourches, de palissades », et les mène sur les terres de Clermont pour en abattre les haies: les textes ne permettent pas de préciser s'il s'agissait de biens nationaux ou d'une reprise de biens communaux usurpés. Le sens de l'action n'en est pas moins clair: pour le prêtre rouge, c'était le geste annonciateur de la société égalitaire à venir; pour les paysans, la main-mise sur la terre tant convoitée.

Nous ne reprendrons pas ici, après Georges Lefebvre, l'analyse de l'affaire de Croissy, curé d'Étalon. Accusé d'avoir prêché la loi agraire, Croissy s'en défendit, et il se peut qu'il ait été sincère. « Jamais je n'ai parlé de cette loi que pour la combattre [...]; observant qu'il fallait distinguer, que ce n'était point des biens propres, mais des terres de fermage qu'on diviserait en plusieurs lots, afin que le peuple pût y prétendre. [...] On a confondu les terres de fermage avec les terres en propre ». Croissy distingue avec soin la division des grandes fermes de la loi agraire, tout comme Dolivier qui, à Mauchamps, avait borné sa propagande au premier objet. Mais il est clair qu'aux yeux des paysans aisés et des gros fermiers, coqs de village ou matadors comme on les appelait dans le Nord, la confusion allait de soi entre division des fermes et partage général des terres. Croissy n'avait-il pas, au surplus, justifié l'abattis des arbres des chemins, propriété seigneuriale sous l'Ancien Régime, restitués aux communes par la Révolution, et légitimé ainsi, au nom de la souveraineté populaire, la reprise des biens communaux usurpés? Il y avait là de quoi inquiéter les notables. Les membres de la municipalité d'Étalon, paysans aisés tel Hadingue, le maire, étaient peut-être jacobins, mais jacobins conservateurs. Ils avaient la loi agraire en horreur, et de même tout ce qui pouvait porter atteinte à leur prépondérance foncière et donc à leur profit. La déchristianisation leur fournit un prétexte pour se débarrasser du curé Croissy, qui, s'il n'était pas communiste, s'avouait sûrement partisan de la démocratie sociale.

### III

Au terme de cette esquisse sur ce que furent, nous semble-t-il, les curés rouges, une double direction de recherche s'impose quant à l'origine historique et à l'impulsion sociale des idées et de l'action de ces prêtres: quelles furent les sources de leur égalitarisme agraire? Sources livresques sans doute, mais aussi expériences vécues.

Sources livresques: l'Évangile certainement pour ces prêtres qui gardèrent la foi, et le souvenir mythique de « la communion des premiers chrétiens », des communautés évangéliques du christianisme primitif. Et tout autant vraisemblablement, chez ces hommes pénétrés de culture classique, le mythe de l'âge d'or tel qu'il apparaît chez Virgile ou chez Ovide ou dans telle œuvre moderne; que l'on se reporte à la description de la Bétique dans le *Télémaque* de Fénelon.

Expériences vécues: on ne peut douter que les curés rouges, comme Meslier en Champagne, comme Babeuf en Picardie, n'aient tenu des communautés villageoises au sein desquelles ils vivaient, leur vif sentiment du droit social, leur exigence égalitaire. Picardie de Croissy (Étalon est à quelques kilomètres au nord de Roye qui fut le quartier général de Babeuf), Berry de Petit-Jean: provinces où les communautés rurales s'affirmaient toujours vivaces pour la défense de leurs droits collectifs, de leurs traditions communautaires, et avaient soutenu contre leurs seigneurs une âpre lutte pour la propriété de leurs biens communaux. La communauté villageoise conservait le sentiment très vif d'un droit social, sans doute depuis les plus lointaines origines: les justes besoins de la communauté dont tous les membres ont droit à l'existence, sont supérieurs à la propriété, qui doit être aménagée en conséquence. Encore faudrait-il être mieux renseigné sur les communautés d'Épineuil ou d'Étalon, sur celles où Jacques Roux exerça le sacerdoce avant de se fixer à Paris. Quelles étaient exactement leurs structures sociales? De quel poids, face aux paysans aisés, pesaient les paysans parcellaires ou sans terre dont les prêtres rouges épousèrent la cause? Comment fonctionnait, jusqu'à la réforme municipale de 1787, la démocratie villageoise? Expériences qui ne pouvaient que vivifier les souvenirs livresques et nourrir la réflexion critique.

On ne peut cependant que souligner l'écart entre la violence de la dénonciation sociale, la hardiesse des affirmations abstraites, et les remèdes proposés. Au terme de son *Essai sur la justice primitive,* Dolivier rassure les propriétaires: « Quant à présent, il ne doit être question que de remèdes provisoires tels que peut les comporter la situation actuelle des choses ». Et de demander la division des corps de ferme, division des exploitations, non des propriétés. Les sans-culottes des campagnes ne demandaient pas autre chose. Tant le champ idéologique général s'imposait même aux plus hardis. On ne peut de ce point de vue que souligner le réalisme de la pétition de Jacques Roux du 25 juin 1793. Il reprenait en un programme cohérent les revendications essentielles des militants sectionnaires les plus conscients, sans cependant que l'on puisse parler d'un corps de doctrine. « Le prêtre socialiste », écrit A. Mathiez de Jacques Roux: anachronisme. Disons un prêtre égalitaire, un militant lié au peuple et qui sut en traduire les aspirations avec une pénétration d'esprit, une sincérité, une chaleur peu communes.

Petit-Jean disparut de la scène politique dès fin 1793, Dolivier en janvier 1794, Jacques Roux se suicida, Croissy fut guillotiné. Mais quel qu'ait été l'échec, ces prêtres rouges, face à un monde d'imposteurs et d'exploiteurs, ont voulu construire la communauté fraternelle de l'avenir. Par leur dénonciation du présent, par leur audace, ils ont devancé l'histoire. Jacques Roux se suicide de désespoir, mais la Convention a voté la loi du maximum général le 29 septembre 1793. Un exemplaire de l'*Essai sur la justice primitive* de Dolivier fut saisi dans les papiers de Babeuf.

# NOTES

1. *Moniteur,* IV, 560.

2. *Ibid.*

3. *Ibid.* VII, 356. Issy-l'Évêque, district d'Autun, département de Saône-et-Loire.

4. *Ibid.* VII, 651. Sur cette affaire, voir P. MONTARLOT, *Un essai de commune autonome et un procès de lèse-nation. Issy-l'Évêque. 1789-1794,* Autun, 1898. Simple mention dans A. LICHTENBERGER, *Le socialisme et la Révolution française. Étude sur les idées socialistes en France de 1789 à 1796,* Paris, 1899, p. 158. Voir aussi *Cahiers des paroisses et communautés du bailliage d'Autun pour les États généraux de 1789,* publiés par A. de CHARMOYSE, Autun, 1895. Le cahier de doléances de la paroisse et communauté d'Issy-l'Évêque (p. 109 et p. 111) demande en particulier la suppression de la gabelle et des corvées, le rachat des droits de mainmorte et de banalité; « qu'il soit prélevé sur la dixme tout ce qui est nécessaire pour la subsistance d'un vicaire, d'un maître d'école, pour l'entretien de la sacristie, de l'église et pour le soulagement des pauvres de la paroisse ». Article 4 (p. 110): « les pauvres désolent les campagnes et mettent souvent les laboureurs à contributions par leurs menaces; qu'il soit ordonné que chaque paroisse sera tenu de nourrir ses pauvres ».

5. DUVERGIER, I, 52.

6. Voir M. DUMMANGET, *Histoire du drapeau rouge,* Paris, s.d., p. 30.

7. *Jacobins,* III, 443; Moniteur, XI, 693. Voir A. SOBOUL, *Les sans-culottes parisiens en l'an II,* Paris, 1958, p. 650.

8. G. BRÉGAIL, *Les curés rouges et la Société montagnarde d'Auch,* Auch, 1901, in-8°, 16 p. (B.N., Lk 7 33035).

9. ED. CAMPAGNAC, « Un prêtre communiste: le curé Petit-Jean », *La Révolution française,* novembre 1903, p. 425; "Un curé rouge: Métier, délégué du représentant du peuple Du Bouchet », *Annales révolutionnaires,* 1913, p. 477. Ed. Campagnac utilise à nouveau l'expression en 1922: "Une chanson patoise contre un curé rouge", *Annales révolutionnaires,* 1922, p. 430.

10. T. IX, *La Révolution et l'Empire,* Deuxième partie, p. 628.

11. M. DOMMANGET, *Jacques Roux, le curé rouge. Les Enragés contre la vie chère sous la Révolution,* Paris, Spartacus, Cahiers mensuels, décembre 1948; « Curés rouges et prêtres ouvriers », *L'École Libératrice,* juin 1955, n° 37.

12. F. BRIDOUX, *Histoire religieuse du département de Seine-et-Marne pendant la Révolution,* Melun, s.d., 2 vol.

13. Abbé J. GALLERAND, *Les cultes sous la Terreur en Loir-et-Cher,* (1792-1795), Blois, 1928.

14. L. GUILLEMAUT, *Histoire de la Révolution dans le Louhannais,* Louhans, 1899-1903, 2 vol.

15. ED. CAMPAGNAC, «Un curé rouge: Métier»..., *article cité.*

16. S. BIANCHI, «La déchristianisation de l'an II. Essai d'interprétation», *Annales historiques de la Révolution française,* 1978, n° 3, p. 354.

17. Nous suivons ici pour Petit-Jean, ED. CAMPAGNAC, article cité ci-dessus, note 9; pour Dolivier, J. MARTIN, Diplôme d'études supérieures, Institut d'histoire de la Révolution française, Paris, 1968 (dactylographié); pour Jacques Roux, M. DOMMANGET, brochure citée ci-dessus, note II, et l'ensemble de l'œuvre de W. MARKOW, *Jacques Roux oder vom Elend der Biographie,* Berlin, 1966, *Die Freiheiten des Priesters Roux,* Berlin 1967, *Jacques Roux. Scripta et Acta,* 1969, *Excurse zu Jacques Roux,* Berlin, 1970; pour Croissy, G. LEFEBVRE, «Où il est question de Babeuf», *Annales d'Histoire sociale,* t. VII, p. 52, repris dans *Études sur la Révolution française,* 2° éd., Paris, 1963, p. 406.

18. *Discours à ses paroissiens pour leur annoncer son mariage,* B.N., 8° Ln 27 6141, imp. in-8°, 22 p.

19. Voir Jean MESLIER, *Œuvres complètes,* t. I, Paris, 1970, p. CI; A. SOBOUL, «Le critique social devant son temps».

20. *Le vœu national ou système politique propre à organiser la nation dans toutes ses parties et à assurer à l'homme l'exercice de ses droits sociaux,* B.N., 8°Lb 39 8241, imp. in-8°, 78 p., suivi d'une *Première suite...* (B.N., 8°Lb 39 4448) et d'une *Seconde suite...* (B.N., 8° Lb 39 4448bis).

21. Sur ce contexte politique de démocratie directe, voir A. SOBOUL, *Les sans-culottes...,* op. cit., pp. 56-58.

Walter Markov

# "CURÉS PATRIOTES" AND SANS-CULOTTES IN THE YEAR II

The epoch in which revolutionaries -- from the Taborites to Cromwell's godly Ironsides -- waved the banner of religion had given way, in the sphere of Western civilization, to a philosophy which in the eighteenth century was ill-disposed towards any transcendence. From then on, rebels -- at least in our latitudes -- clothed themselves neither as religious warriors nor as confessional combatants nor as fighters *against* the Church. Nevertheless, the French Revolution drew the *Ecclesia Gallicana* into its vortex. The hierarchy at the highest level was connected by a long process of symbiosis with the titled beneficiaries of the Ancien Régime. The lower clergy had a more direct relationship with its parishioners and, consequently was not only acquainted with their spiritual requirements and needs but, to a large extent, with their earthly burdens as well, not infrequently sharing them in one way or another. The Revolution offered refuge to neither, whether they wanted it or not: the one and the other, hierarchy and lower clergy -- as "the church in this world"-- had to take sides, for or against. Both the old and the new order found among them impassioned defenders.

This was in no sense unusual. It happened to everybody, including secular groups of some significance, and in our case with the result that, at the Convention, about three dozen clergy, to the rank of bishop, had taken their seats, some still in, some out, of office. As a consequence of the Revolutionary Church legislation of 1790, the First Estate of the Kingdom, in about equal parts, not only split into *assermentés* (juring) and *insermentés* (non-juring), but the clerics, like other citizens, were divided according to their political convictions. From then on one could find them -- though in different strengths -- in every camp: together with the old Royalists and Feuillants, and with the Girondists and the Montagnards. Finally some joined those "extremists" -- or *exagérés* -- to whom even the Jacobins, either in regard to principles or to their implementation, appeared delinquent in furnishing full proof of their close ties with the people.

Certainly, such intransigents formed a minority, even an insignificant one, unequal in power to those they challenged. Yet, on closer examination, it seems they were by no means only "flotsam" washed ashore by the *mouvement populaire,* people who, in despair, helplessness and perplexity, had left the right way. Quite the contrary: one encounters *curés patriotes* of the sort of a Carion[1] or Dolivier[2] among the first who, already in 1789, advocated a "People's Revolution". In other words, they are not satisfied only with the rise of the propertied and the educated middle class to power and prosperity; neither do they accept the meagre outcome of events for the most needy. It is true that, with varying intensity, the Church had engaged herself in *social* change. Nevertheless, a red thread, already perceived by Chassin, runs through the "rising of the priests" against their aristocratic episcopate during the election of 1789,[3] to Métier, Petitjean, Croissy and Roux of the year II.[4]

The ecclesiastical advocate of the poor, too, had certainly been influenced by the Enlightenment: Voltaire as the prophet of humanity and tolerance was highly regarded and Rousseau, his beloved "Jean-Jacques", as a *démocrate populaire,* stood in even higher esteem. Yet this explains little, since in matters of philosophy the better-read followers of moderate political shadings exceeded such a cleric by a large measure. Georg Buechner in *Dantons Tod* expressed this most vividly in the prison scene between Thomas Paine and Chaumette. I would, therefore, hesitate to count the village or suburban priest among the "intelligentsia", something J.M. Sacher[5] is inclined to do. Access to the armoury of the Enlightenment and its corresponding thought-exercises does not alone engender sufficient motivation. This is to be found elsewhere.

To the *Lumières* and their revolution-bent disciples, the achievement of a bourgeois constitution was synonymous with the realization of practical reason, of common sense. Interest, ideal and ideology were in an exemplary fashion all one for them. In 1789 their expectations had been fulfilled: the historical parameters were right, and they had no reason to question -- in anticipation of the young Marx, so to speak -- the postulated equation between *citoyen* and *bourgeois*. There were those however, like the *curés patriotes,* who, turning towards sans-culottism, felt called upon, for religio-ethical as well as socio-political reasons, to take care of the humble and the suffering. They sought to find for them in the Revolution -- and *only* in the Revolution -- a chance to obtain justice, human dignity *and* their daily bread. This issued from a sense of "evangelical humility" (this latter, however, not taken entirely literally) and the spirit of the Sermon on the Mount, combined with personal courage (without, that is, "turning the other cheek"). To such priests it hardly mattered whether clever businessmen, as yet without a coat-of-arms, replaced blue-blooded seigneurs well-versed in chicanery.

Marx declared as "failed", in his well-known dispute with Bruno Bauer, "the revolution only for the masses which, in its *political* 'idea', did not possess the idea of their real interest, whose true life-principle thus did not coincide with the life-principle of the revolution and whose real conditions of emancipation are essentially different from the circumstances under which the bourgeoisie was able to emancipate itself and society."[6] It was not for this objective that the servants of the Church, in the footsteps of the *Vicaire savoyard,* edged near the precipice of heresy, nor did the poor wish to die as the unsung footsoldiers of a revolution benefitting only others.

I do not believe, however, like Daniel-Rops,[7] that the *"curé rouge"*[8] had for that reason been the "precursor of Christian collectivism" or, like Richard Cobb, that he was, simply, "too good a priest".[9] He had already thrown himself into the totality of his historic moment and did not withdraw into a new exegesis of the Holy Scripture. Usually, in reponse to the impact of a radically changing situation and in full awareness, he quite intentionally and forcefully expanded the limits of his *clerical* mandate. Where this was not the case, where the foundation and the devotion *sola fide* are manifest, as with the mystic Claude de Saint Martin,[10] he maintains his distance from the actions of the *mouvement populaire,* although he shows sympathetic compassion for George Rudé's "crowd". When, however, he joins the *sans-culottes,* he joins at the base and without inner reservations, and he might also advance into the ranks of their *meneurs* and even turn into an *Enragé,* the egalitarian revolutionary *sans phrase.*

Nevertheless, the *curé patriote's* different point of departure has its consequences: he cannot deny his original leitmotif, to bring the good news *(evangelion!)* of a "new heaven and a new earth". Malicious opponents--or competitors--will constantly remind him of the "Nessus shirt of his class". He would commit treason against his God (even against a deistically or pantheistically watered-down God) and against the "widows and orphans" in his trust -- so ran the *topos* of that time --, were he satisfied to take form for content: Liberty for the hungry? Equality, where one class of man oppresses the other? Fraternity, where brother lives off the exploitation of brother?[11]

This is why Jaures had drawn attention to the Nazarene background of a Dolivier or a Jacques Roux: to them the equality and opportunity provided by Creation appeared irreconcilable with an unbridled striving for profit. Whoever was content to accept such an outcome of the Great Revolution was either a profiteer working only for his own advantage, the *"rich égoïste"* of the pamphleteers, or an acquiescent, unfaithful shepherd. Considered in such a way, other impulses and motives had given a different meaning to original evil, if not to original sin. Yet the *bonheur terrestre,* Saint-Just's *idée nouvelle,* appeared to the oppressed as distant as ever, even under the Jacobin heaven: at best a future prospect, if not simply a cheap promise. The clerical advocate of the people had, therefore, to remain "radical" ("at the root"): looking forward he dreamed himself an *Enragé,* obsessed, for whom the social (and with it his own moral) revolution took precedence over the political-institutional revolution. Dreaming backwards, into the past, he saw himself as the Romantic cruelly taught by Thermidor (Coleridge: *France, an Ode...*), who, disappointed and pouring the baby out with the bathwater, laments the lost totality of the Middle Ages and, not infrequently, finally submits to the ultramontane legitimism of a de Maistre.

Incontestably, there have been very few *sans-culotte* preachers of the old stamp who, having taken the leap over the abyss, remained true to themselves, even in the face of death. Conventional Catholic historiography until the pontificate of John XXIII has, at least under the *nihil obstat,* contested the fact--without, however, giving proof--that a genuine, religiously-inspired commitment can compel one to the farthest Left. It was left to secular history to ask: did those *curés* who in the Year II still counted themselves among the *patriotes avancés* (even if they all too often were not taken seriously) belong to the "good people" of the *sans-culottes?* Did they still form part of this group -- earlier pitied, now being wooed by all, but soon again to be cast away -- or were these *curés,* despite their innermost striving, nevertheless an unassimilable foreign body?

The *option civique* of the priest for a revolutionary cathechism was not suf-ficient to supply the answer. He likewise had to face the theological demands of the day. It is simpler said than done, however, to relate adequately one with the other. The "Cold War" trenches dug by the *Kulturkampf* of the Third Republic at the turn of the century associated the Church history of the Revolution with more or less biased apologists.[12] Bernard Plongeron, by borrowing from the Frankfurt School, had to create the term "political theology" in order simply to escape the traditional *circulus vitiosus.*[13] He defines it as a "theological reflexion on a political set of facts", with the objective, in the light of Christian revelation, to attribute content and meaning to the evolution of society in time. To Plongeron, this would presuppose a dialectic between continuity (the dialogue Church-world) and discontinuity (possible contradictions between the Christian imperative and the options of lay society); a dialectic between faith and hope (read: "liberty"), and charity (read: "justice"). In this way *"théologie politique"* would, in relation to society, act as critical stimulus rather than dogmatic assurance.

There are here certainly links to Karl Barth and Teilhard de Chardin, which do not meet all the desiderata of a strict historiographical methodology. In this Plongeron falls behind even such a standard classic as Latreille. Nevertheless, his method amounts to a surrender of the tacitly-alleged identification of the Church opposition with the Right's store of arguments concerning each stage of the Revolution. In addition it means the acknowledgement of the revolutionary drama as an historical expression which theology cannot evade but must face. This point, however, is precisely the one which all investigations have up to now always circumvented.

Naturally, this view is considerably easier for a retrospective analyst to adopt than for a contemporary; and Bishop Dillon of Narbonne reduced this problem to a disarmingly sincere formula: he could, possibly, have given in as a spiritual leader — as a nobleman, never. Consequently, the Catholic hierarchy, after some famous as well as futile attempts on the part of Boisgelin and Emery, in fact produced no official theory of revolution — not to mention a theology of sans-culottism. Instead, referring to the guidelines of Pius VI, it single-mindedly formulated a theology of counterrevolution. This provoked a decidedly antipapist current among the loyal, that is pro-revolutionary, clerics, which in turn evoked an inevitable counterreaction: such clerics left the church, noisily or quietly, with or without regret — but they left it.[14] Opposing apostolic leadership, to fight for "the rock of Peter" appeared to them as either hopeless or no longer satisfying. They followed in the course of time the "well-meant" advice which mockers of the *Révolutions de Paris* had long ago given them: the very best the *curé patriote* could do, as an interim solution acceptable to the nation, would be to let his Estate totally disappear. Patriot -- yes; *curé* -- no?

It was hard for him. The handwringers of both sexes, the *dévotes,* indignantly rejected him because he had injured or deeply insulted long-rooted custom. The enlightened ones, again, ridiculed him: for what purpose still so much foolery, so much expensive spectacle which sustains superstition? Jacques Roux himself estimates that "three-quarters of the people" detest such a "caste of charlatans". Yet even from the perspective of Paris this is too high a percentage, and it certainly is totally wrong for the countryside. It is true that anticlericalism established itself there, too: otherwise the dechristianization campaign, whatever its starting point, would never, even if only temporarily, have experienced such a mass following. However, the average *sans-culotte* (not to mention his wife) desired a *different* priest, rather than none at all. His feelings were certainly expressed by Radet and Desfontaines (on November 4, 1793):

> J'ons un Curé Patriote,
> Un Curé bon Citoyen,
> Un Curé vrai Sans-Culottes,

Un Curé qui n'fait qu'du bien.
Chaqu'paroissien trouve en lui
Son modéle, son appui;
Et nos coeurs sont tous a lui,
Sont tous à lui.

Désormais le presbytére,
Séjour de la liberté,
Par un froid célibataire
Ne sera plus habité;
Not' curé vivra chez lui.
Et sans dîmer sur autrui,
Il aura sa femme à lui,
Sa femme à lui.

Sans l'secours de la soutane
Et, com'nous, coiffé vetu,
Y r'mettra celui qui s'damne
Dans l'chemin de la vertu:
Y prech'ra l's enfants d'autrui.
Puis le soir, en bon mari,
Il en f'ra qui s'ront à lui,
Qui s'ront à lui.

Si le vieux évêque d'Rome
Dit quelqu'mauvaises raisons,
Contre un prêtre qui s'fait homme,
S'il braque ses saints canons,
Notre curé, dieu merci,
N'en prendra point de souci,
Il aura d'au'canons qui s'ront pour lui,
Qui s'ront pour lui.

Nevertheless, the Revolution in the Year II thrust itself forward more and more as the desired synonym for total secularization (which it called "dechristianization"), and in its linguistic usage the *Sans-Culotte Jesus* maintained a certain popularity, in the columns of the *Pere Duchesne* and elsewhere. The *défroqué* married and took bourgeois employment in which, under certain circumstances, he could go far -- as Fouché, the Minister of Napoleon's Police, shows -- or at least, like Dolivier, found refuge from the adversity of the times. Some -- Louis Roux comes to mind -- took up arms against the Vendée. Others, like Eulogius Schneider, former Professor of Theology in Bonn, got caught in the machinery of the Terror.

\*     \*     \*

It should not be forgotten that the Church of France, already during the Ancien Régime, had been anything but monolithic, something which the periodical assemblies of the prelates intentionally demonstrated. Disputes about what direction to take between Jansenists, Richerists, Febronians and Martinists at times touched on heresy, and continued into the Revolution as they tried to determine a new position.

Natural religion, Gallicanism and Pascal's posthumous revenge for the Bull *Unigenitus* were godfather to the *Constitution civile du clergé* in 1790. The Thomistically-grounded resistance-theory of Suarez turned into the first attempt to rationalize a theology of revolution, by the former Court preacher Claude Fauchet. His Te-deum in Notre Dame for those who had stormed the Bastille heralded the *aggiornamento* of a bourgeois Reform Church, based on fundamental teachings assumed to be unchangeable.[15] From the *Être suprême* he theologized Christian succession on earth in the spirit of a conciliatory postcartesian Masonic philosophy, and obstinately evaded the clean separation of Spinoza's *"deus sive natura"*. This revealed Fauchet's readiness to compromise with the agnostic free-thought of his friends from the Voltairian Gironde-intelligentsia circle — an intermediate position undermined politically as well as theologically as the Revolution progressed from liberal to democratic Republic in 1793.

It may be surprising that a man of the determined Left like Henri Grégoire, a fellow-traveller of the Montagnards, showed himself far less compliant as a theologian. A revolutionary of high repute, by far less in need than others of a philosophical alibi, his thought nevertheless reflected the unmistakable separation of the spiritual and the worldly, of Church and State. This was offensive, it is true, to the sectarian dechristianizers, but not, however, to those responsible for the Revolutionary Government or for the Club at the rue Saint-Honoré. Such a binding distinction between dogma and church policy (consequently not a theology of the Revolution but a theology in the Revolution) remained unacknowledged by the Vatican (and not only by it). Finally, one hundred years later Leo XIII endeavoured to come to terms with the bourgeois French Republic on the basis of this distinction. This is not without an inner logic, because the Gallican Bishop of Blois kept his humanistic credo within the permissible range of theological thought. His advance beyond the political Middle (but not too far towards "the people") assured him, within necessary limitations, of greater flexibility — and of survival.

Quite differently with Saint-Martin, *"le philosophe inconnu"*. Long before the Revolution his thoughtful book, *Des erreurs et de la vérité* (1775), caused controversy. At the same time he gathered around himself a small yet deeply-moved circle of followers. He interpreted the ongoing upheaval as the confirmation of his apocalyptic warnings and prophesy. To this seeker, inspired by Jacob Boehme, Swedenborg and Martinez Pasqualis, the Revolution was ground repeatedly broken by a *"deus lo vult"*; in this ground alone could the seed of His Word, to change one's ways, grow and nurture a people that, unknowingly, acted as God's instrument.[16]

The absolute claim of a radical theology at the revolutionary cross-roads of the Year II thus might move towards the political praxis of the Left and even beyond the "Jacobin bloc" to an extreme Left. What remained to be decided, however, was the precise direction.

As the main combatants had changed, the Left had drifted with the *circonstances:* from Mirabeau beyond Brissot and Chabot to Robespierre.The most daring views of 1789 were by 1793 legislatively insufficient; those of the Year II had, at the beginning of the Revolution, attracted only a few estranged enthusiasts, but not the acknowledged spokesmen — and not those now at the head of the *Enragés* and the *Hébertistes.* "Relative" extremists, therefore, are encountered in all phases of the Revolution — someone must, finally, stand at both ends of the revolutionary scale. "Absolute" extremism, however, appears only at the vortex of the conflagration, where a whole basket of real or hypothetical or imaginary possibilities is being offered, to the "chosen" and the "un-chosen" alike. Do these so-called

Ultras embody the ideal sum of social change or, rather, its aberration, the way to hell, which as we know is paved with good intentions?

In our view[17] the formation of the "extreme Left" expresses the fact that the so-called historical Left as a whole had a very broad class base. The congruence of their objectives, however, was expressed in action against the common enemy: at the moment of danger the image of the enemy acts as a binding force. However, when those progressing towards the exercise of power intend to realize their declared (or, even more, their undeclared) intentions, and as soon as their opponents, defeated, no longer prevent this, it soon proves impossible to do simultaneously what is contradictory. It is quite possible for compromises to be found on a middle ground, and also in mixes of policy, because the Revolution does not simply turn things inside out, but is able also to modify considerably the social structures themselves. Thus, it is not surprising that a rural *crème des coqs de village,* strong in economic power and prestige, can come to terms with the new governing exponents of the bourgeoisie, just as, on the other side, judicious *ci-devants* -- not necessarily at a loss -- exchange their feudal rents for agrarian-capitalist accumulation. As a parallel development, the Revolution makes it easy for a not-inconsiderable part of the more mobile urban middle class (and in addition, for a smaller segment of the lower class) to rise by one, and sometimes even two, rungs.

There is nothing irreconcilable in this. For such groups the "Jacobin" question is reduced to tactical usefulness: when the new order requires a strongly coordinating hand in the face of tense internal and external situations, one "requires" Jacobinism. The battle won, one "does away" with the embarrassing midwives: they have done their work (really quite properly, it is whispered) with an iron broom. As long as they are still "useful", one conforms -- this one willingly, the other gnashing his teeth -- to their dictatorship, since the figures add up and, taking all in all, they are doing the work of the (bourgeois) nation as as whole.

The situation is quite different among the lower element within the *menu peuple,* which, far from gaining anything from the more rationalized forms of production and exploitation, has to pay for them. Certainly, there are two factors which retard its migration into the camp of the "extreme Left". For one, it cannot see into the future. It does not know that a consequence of the concentration of capital and labour is the demise of many crafts, that the industrial revolution in its initial stage does not lessen pauperism, that it dissolves the *"Sans-Culotterie";* this becomes common knowledge only around 1831, 1848 and, finally, 1871. Secondly, the Republic in 1793 is still encircled by deadly enemies: by the Vendée and the European Coalition of princes. All these factors force the underprivileged, even where they suffer from drastic treatment at the hands of the Jacobins, to persevere in supporting them so as not to go down with them. In this way the Nation, not only in exalted imagination but also in a very real concrete sense, takes precedence over social divisions and interests.

"Extreme Leftists", therefore, must remain restricted to weak vanguards (or even single sentries), which assume the risk of breaking out of this dilemma: on the one hand, to defend the Revolution, good or bad, with all those who are willing, against the Counterrevolution; on the other, to take up the more radical demands of the underprivileged and, in their name, to call for a social, as well as a political, democracy, to go beyond liberty and equality as merely formal legal concepts. This is, it should be understood, neither socialism nor anarchism, but egalitarianism in *sans-culotte* fashion.

They had unachievable expectations of the Revolution. It was not within their historical grasp to understand that the little man, to whom no alternative method of production was then available, would, in the future, rule. The prophet with his peers, therefore, had, after an ephemeral beginning, to fail; despite this, we regard him as a necessary building block for the new order. First, because only the call for the political emancipation of the *sans-culottes* could induce the radical-bourgeois leadership, which otherwise would lose its fighting columns, to extend the Revolution to its last "possible" (as opposed to the extreme Left's "impossible") stage. Further, because in approaching the boundaries which restricted the Revolution, in the knowledge that the ideal and the real did not correspond, the thoughtful were forced to find ways to reflect upon the problems which the Revolution did not and could not solve, and to take bearings on "what comes after us" (to borrow an expression from Werner Krauss). To put it differently, the defeat of the *Enragés* meant the discovery of the dead-end at which the plebeian notions of equality had arrived, and were bound to arrive at, as they changed sides: no longer against the *"aristocrates"*, yesteryear's enemies, but against the "rich", tomorrow's enemies; not for establishing a new class rule, but against any class rule. This defeat prepared the ground for the rise later of a viable antithesis through viable supporters. In this respect, such an "extreme Left", sacrificing itself for a greater, if unachievable, goal, was indirectly effective and appears to have found its social "place", and historical justification, at a crucial turning point.

Now, to be sure, there are Lefts and "Lefts". Besides the Left, it is true, one notices another "revolución en la revolución", historically premature, yet originating in a straight line from the protest of social segments shut out of the Revolution. In the first case, we are dealing with the carrying too far of still-immature, but already socially-embedded, potentials; in the second, we note an escalation of ideas which become independent of social facts, the dogmatization of an abstract maximalism.

As thought-process this seems useful evidence of the agility of the human mind, rather than a flaw. As soon as social fetters are broken, the mind tries playfully to explore the consequences which follow — it does not wait for their appearance. Already directed towards such an objective (the ideological "incubation-phase" of the Revolution), its fantasy is set free. Its tinkering with utopias, no more than a stimulating literary motif in static-evolutionary periods, can make the unconscious conscious and reinforce moral, social and political awareness. This is the ultimate purpose of every enlightenment, to anticipate the necessity of social change and the means which will bring it about, to replenish the necessary reservoir of power. In short, revolutionary theory precedes the revolution, either as a chimera or as an instruction for action, and, like a "mole", digs into it, breaking the soil: if the theory does not simply flow from a social point of reference, but remains functionally connected with it, then the ideal framework is created for the "currents" it identifies with. It can, however, be deflected and, losing its social contact, become isolated.

Sometimes this happened peacefully, and even to a certain degree "unpolitically" in a positive sense. Some authors, looking -- once the Revolution had arrived -- for the social *perpetuum mobile* in the form of a *liberté* or *égalité parfaite* in the traces of Freemasonry, did so as an exercise in diligence. They conceived poetically, for themselves and for others, the "highest bliss on earth", not infrequently painted in communist colours, and carefully filled out prescriptions (which Ioannissian has collected in a remarkable book),[18] which were also submitted in the form of petitions to the Convention. Yet they had no intention of getting involved in everyday politics. The distance between their dream-castles and even the best of the very best of revolutionary parties was too great; and so, while the daily political struggles were going on, people like Rabaut, Cournand, Taboureau, Boissel, Grenus, Laussel and Momoro remained good Girondists, Jacobins or Cordeliers, with a little personal "tic", so to speak.

In addition, however, one finds adventurers linking dream and action together impurely; the "never satisfied" and "never-to-be-satisfied" who, always finding fault, meandered through the new order as they had previously through the old one, ceaselessly seeking to outdo the good by the still better, recluses lacking creative power who yet wished to impose their will upon the situation. They were bustling "benefactors" of mankind who cared no more about classes as yet unborn than about those already in existence. "Condottieri", often intelligent and sincere (if we exclude the play-acting "casual thieves" present in all camps), yet without real perspective. The situation threw up missionaries in boots, exalted without quite knowing why, without measurable goals, giving in to, and provoking, emotions: purpose-less terror, continuous rebellion, dechristianizing by decree — men like Rutledge and Fournier, Vincent and Duret. They constituted a political Bohemia; they were sometimes absolutely charming yet, more often and against their intentions, badly harmed the causes they supported. This was the world of shifting sand which every Revolution, sooner or later, must filter out or risk its own destruction.

With this distinction in mind, should one add the *curés rouges* as a fourth component to the category "Left radicalism", which already includes class-congruent practice, literary-utopian ideas, and abstruse, excessive action?

This could be inappropriate, because they are of course already represented, if only sparsely, in all three categories, and are related more strongly to these than to each other.[19] Their standards and values differ widely. Millenarian concepts had either to be total, or not be at all, and Saint-Martin's design for salvation did not shrink from invoking the worldly sword of the *sans-culottes.* It bestowed upon them a positive worth in a scale of values *sub specie aeternitatis.* If it accepted terror, it did so within the framework of the *dies irae,* as a purgatory for the Whore of Babylon and, ultimately, as a gateway to a transcendent point of reference.[20] The *curé patriote,* on the other hand, trying to gather the poor around an adequate social programme, felt he lived in an age which fulfilled itself *in this world.* The sermon of Jacques Roux *(Le triomphe des braves Parisiens sur l'ennemi public)* explicitly called attention to this, although he hardly knew the Greek expression *"Kairos": Le temps déterminé par les décrets de la Sagesse éternelle...est enfin arrivé.*[21]

\*       \*       \*

We may now perhaps be permitted to draw a first conclusion. The *Ecclesia Gallicana,* much as her superiors tried to isolate her from it, could not close her eyes to the revolutionary summons: but she answered with many voices. On either side of the barricades it proved impossible clearly to separate *temporalia* and *spiritualia*. This led to a manifold intertwining of developing political ideologies and faith: it led to confrontation and to coordination, to a theology of counterrevolution and, likewise, to different drafts of a theology of revolution. There is no reason to question her honest efforts, despite the fact that her system was not geared to the new tasks and the obviously immense difficulties involved. She sought in one of her branches, and into the Year II, to understand the specific historic mission of an egalitarian *sans-culotte* radicalism and to justify it by spiritual means.[22]

The question, however, whether she herself became a constitutive part of the Revolution, would have to be answered in the negative. It deserves attention as a subordinate, *sui generis* question which throws light onto a hitherto dark corner of revolutionary history. Although not at all *"marginaux",* the *curés rouges* do not enlarge the social catalogue offered by the extreme Left by anything new or different. The reason is not that both sides -- it was entirely inevitable -- committed errors; nor that the *curés* were overshadowed or crowded out by substitute religions like the prerevolutionary hagiolatry, the "Goddess Reason", the Supreme Being or theophilanthropy. Rather, by the end of the eighteenth century the emancipation of bourgeois society in France had progressed so far that its system appeared sufficiently rational and explainable in itself, and that it could, likewise, stamp its mode (and method) of thinking on the social periphery. The process of secularization introduced by the militant Enlightenment proved during the Revolution an already-irreversible threshold. This dispensed with the objective, as well as subjective, need for that sacral legitimation which, at the time of Fra Dolcino, John Ball, Prokop, Thomas Muentzer or Gerrard Winstanley, had been indispensable for the rebellious people; and which is still indispensable well after the French Revolution, in as yet historically "late" societies, the Third World, for instance.

# NOTES

1. P. Montarlot, *Un essai de commune autonome et un procès de lese-nation* (Issy l'Évêque, 1789-1794; Autun, 1898).

2. Dolivier has not yet found his authoritative biographer. J.M. Sacher (Zakher) in *Pierre Dolivier* (Leningrad, 1925) and M. Dommanget in "Pierre Dolivier, curé rouge, 1746-1817", *Cahiers Spartacus,* Série CN 70 (Juillet / Août 1976) offer only outlines. The thesis submitted for a diploma (D.E.S.) by J. Martin (Paris, 1968) is unpublished, and A.R. Ioannissian (see below) deals only with his ideas. Early writings: *Discours sur l'abus des dévotions populaires* (1788); *La voix d'un citoyen sur la manière de former les États-Généraux* (1788); *Lettre d'un curé du bailliage d'Étampes à ses confrères* (1788); specifically, however: *La Vœu national ou Système politique propre à organiser la nation dans toutes ses parties et à assurer à l'homme l'exercice de ses droits sociaux* (1790, with two additions.)

3. Ch. L. Chassin, *Les cahiers des curés. Études historiques d'après les brochures, les cahiers imprimés et les procès-verbaux manuscripts* (Paris, 1882 — an annihilating rejoinder to H. Wallon); *Le clergé en Quatre-vingt-neuf* (Paris, 1876).

4. The -- fairly common -- names stand for "left", but not in every case simultaneously for "red", priests. E. Campagnac, "Un prêtre communiste, le curé Petit-Jean", in *La Révolution française,* 1903, no. 2.; *idem,* "Un curé rouge: Métier, délégué du représentant du peuple Du Bouchet", in *Annales révolutionnaires* (1913), p. 477 ff.; G. Lefebvre, "Ou il est question de Babeuf", in *Études sur la Révolution française* (Paris, 1954; 2nd ed., 1963); M. Dommanget, *Jacques Roux, le curé rouge. Les Enragés contre la vie chére* (Paris, 1948; 2nd ed., 1976); W. Markov, *Die Freiheiten des Priesters Roux* (Berlin, 1967); *idem, Exkurse zu Jacques Roux* (Berlin, 1970).

5. J.M. Sacher (Zakher), "Beshenye" (Enragés) (Leningrad, 1930; *idem.,* Dvizhenye "beshenych" ("Movement of the Enragés") (Moscow, 1961).

6. K. Marx and F. Engels, *Werke,* vol. II (Berlin, 1957), pp. 85-86.

7. Daniel-Rops, H., (i.e., H. Petiot), *L'Église des révolutions,* vol. I: *En face de nouveaux destins* (Paris, 1960), p. 645.

8. Undoubtedly this expression is meant metaphorically and, as a result, is admissible only "entre guillemets". During the Revolution and long afterwards it was not in use. Only the rising socialist movement introduced the political symbolism of the colour red and applied it retrospectively to "pre"-socialists. If "socialism" is imputed thereby, this would have to be refuted, as much as the reverse tendency to extend it to all *curés patriotes.* See G. Brégail, *Les curés rouges et la société montagnarde d'Auch* (Auch, 1901). The later popularization of the expression goes back to M. Dommanget.

9. *The Times Literary Supplement,* March 30, 1967.

10. "J'ai dit dans ma lettre sur la Révolution française que cette révolution était faite de la part de Dieu, quoiqu'elle ne fût pas encore faite de la nôtre." — L.C. de Saint-Martin, *Mon portrait historique et philosophique (1789-1803),* ed. R. Amadou (Paris, 1961), p. 366.

11. Jacques Roux, *Scripta et acta* (Berlin, 1969), "Le Manifeste des Enragés", p. 141.

12. A. Sicard, *L'ancien clergé de France,* Vols. I-III (Paris, 1893-1903); *idem, Le clergé de France pendant la Révolution,* Vols. I-II (Paris, 1912-1927); O. Delarc, *L'Église de Paris pendant la Révolution française, 1789-1801,* Vols. I-III (Paris, 1895-1898); *L'Église de Paris et la Révolution,* Vols. I-IV (Paris, 1908-1911); P. de La Gorce, *Histoire religieuse de la Révolution française,* Vols. I-V, (Paris, 1909-1925).

13. B. Plongeron, *Conscience religieuse en révolution. Regards sur l'historiographie religieuse de la Révolution française* (Paris, 1969).

14. Newer insights into this in M. Vovelle: *Religion et révolution. La déchristianisation de l'an II* (Paris, 1976); S. Bianchi, "La Déchristianisation de l'an II. Essai d'interprétation", in *A.H.R.F.* (178), no. 3.

15. Claude Fauchet, *Discours sur la liberté française,* Vols. I-III (Paris, 1789).

16. "Vrai commissaire de Dieu" and "l'exécution d'un décret formel de la Providence", for people and Revolution, respectively, in *Lettre à un ami* (Paris, s.d.), *loc. cit.,* pp. 60, 73.

17. W. Markov, "Von einigen Dimensionen der Jacobinerfrage", in: *Evolution und Revolution in der Weltgeschichte,* Vol. I (Berlin, 1976), pp. 157-167; *idem., "Die Gleichheit des Jacques Roux"* in *Lendemains* (Cologne) (1978), no. 12.

18. A.R. Ioannissian, *Kommunisticheskiye ideyi v godi Velikov frantsusskoy revoliutsii* (Moscou, 1966).

19. A. Soboul. "Sur les 'curés rouges' dans la Révolution française", in *A.H.R.F.* (1981) no. 2. In reference to this Soboul and Bianchi started a highly welcome new round of discussion. Quite correctly, both object to the blurred outline of the group in the literature. One should, however, not overlook the fact that "completeness" and "chemical purity" are seldom encountered in a historical phenomenon, and certainly not when politico-ideological attitudes are related to social structure. One should, perhaps must, concede a certain tolerance. Soboul, however, with good reason insists that the "curé rouge" has to meet at least two minimal criteria: he has to emphasise the social aspect of the people's action and, at the same time, he has to remain a *curé.* Vehemently to participate in a *société*

*populaire,* or in dechristianization taken by itself, will not suffice *ex definitione,* anymore than will unreserved endorsement of all aspects of the Terror. Naturally, the circle of true *curés rouges* becomes such smaller: one can count on the fingers of one hand those known (and, at best, add heuristically a few dozen [still?] unknown) to us. Bianchi operates with the considerably extended concept of the *prêtre démocrate,* which allows us to multiply the figure to two to three thousand (?). Out of their number, the social-radical militants (i.e., "our" *curés rouges)* would stand out like the tip of an iceberg.

20. "Le bien-être terrestre m'a paru si bien un obstacle au progrès de l'homme, et la démolition de son royaume en ce monde un si grand avantage pour lui, qu'au milieu des gémissements qu'occasionnait le renversement des fortunes pendant la Révolution, par une suite de la maladresse et de l'ignorance de nos législateurs, je me suis souvent trouvé tout prêt à prier que ce genre de désordres s'augmentait encore afin de faire sentir à l'homme la nécessité de s'appuyer sur son véritable soutien dans tous les genres." *(Mon portrait historique et philosophique,* p. 271).

21. *Scripta et acta,* p. 8.

22. W. Markov, "La collera del prete rosso", in *Studi Storici* (1965), no. 4.

Pierre H. Boulle

# IN DEFENSE OF SLAVERY: EIGHTEENTH-CENTURY OPPOSITION TO ABOLITION AND THE ORIGINS OF A RACIST IDEOLOGY IN FRANCE*

Among social scientists, it is customary to differentiate between modern racism and the various forms which prejudice took in earlier times. As a recent work puts it:

> Racism emerged at a relatively recent date. Before the nineteenth century, relations between men were marred, of course, by all sorts of inequalities, of flagrant injustices or willful cruelties, and no-one would dare pretend that racial differences were unrelated to it.... Nonetheless, it is only truly since the nineteenth century...that expressly racist phenomena have manifested themselves and multiplied.[1]

Such a view is not altogether surprising, given the evidence from the nineteenth century. Such statements as those of Victor Courtet de L'Isle, positing in 1847 the existence of "naturally predominant races" and "naturally weak [*débiles*]" ones,[2] are too frequent not to suggest that a fundamental shift had occurred, away from the standard Enlightenment view of the perfectibility of mankind.

Yet a growing corpus of documentation suggests some difficulty with this view. Were the break from eighteenth-century thought as sharp as it has been argued, one should find it reflected in differing linguistic formulations. A recent study of French abolitionist texts suggests the opposite. Comparing the use of the pejorative "nègre" with its more objective counterparts, "esclave" and "Noir," it finds no statistically significant difference between eighteenth- and nineteenth-century usage.[3] Similarly, the apparently "racist" remarks of such major Enlightenment figures as Hume, Jefferson or Voltaire[4] need to be explained, rather than merely labelled as unrepresentative statements or the results of their authors' personal aberrations.

What characterizes modern racism for most observers is the link made between race and the natural sciences:

> Racism is any set of beliefs that organic, genetically transmitted differences (whether real or imagined) between human groups are intrinsically associated with the presence or absence of certain socially relevant abilities or characteristics, hence that such differences are a legitimate basis of invidious distinctions between groups socially defined as races.[5]

It is this scientific base which provides not only "objective", but also apparently immutable, grounds for prejudice: it is the immutability of traits ascribed to distinct human groups which permits the identification of so-called "inferior races" and their exploitation by races deemed "superior." Here again, as any perusal of encyclopedias will show,[6] the nineteenth century is particularly rich in texts making such connections — yet the origins of modern science predate the nineteenth century.

221

On this basis alone, one must look before the 1800s for the roots of modern, "scientific" racism.

Given recent history, it is perhaps not surprising that the first serious attention paid to eighteenth-century racism has focussed on antisemitism. Two major works on the subject were simultaneously published on either side of the Atlantic.[7] Each forthrightly tackled the antisemitic statements found in mainstream French Enlightenment writings; each argued not only the representativeness of the position, but also its essential connection with the secularization of thought and the emergence of a scientific approach. For each, it is in the eighteenth century that modern antisemitism first developed and spread, to pass without significant transformation into the nineteenth.[8]

A number of studies have since been published on the racial views of the Enlightenment, one of which, at least, focusses on attitudes toward Blacks.[9] Basing himself on these studies, William B. Cohen concludes:

> In the first half of the nineteenth century, attitudes toward non-European peoples were influenced by two trends of thought that remained unresolved at the end of the eighteenth century. The first was evolutionist.... The second was racist and saw the destiny of peoples as shaped by their racial makeup.[10]

The racist strain thus is now recognized as part and parcel of eighteenth-century rationalist thought, and indeed as one logical outgrowth of this thought.

On the other hand, Cohen's identification of racist elements in eighteenth-century thought rests in part on a mistake in translation. Misreading the French term *race* (originally meaning lineage or generational links) for its modern English counterpart (inferring different biological species), Cohen inappropriately argues a direct connection between sixteenth-century nobiliar usage and the nineteenth-century meaning of the term. It is along this continuum that he sees eighteenth-century statements take their place.[11]

Such an anachronism cannot serve as an adequate basis for understanding the origins of modern racism. Therefore, it still remains to identify precisely when the historically specific type of racism termed "modern" replaced older forms of ethnocentricity. Even more significant, one must establish whether eighteenth-century racism was merely one trend of thought, as Cohen asserts, or whether it had already become by then an operating ideology, meant to legitimate contemporary forms of colonial exploitation.

*    *

The standard approach to eighteenth-century thought has been to study legal formulations and the major texts of the Enlightenment. As a first step, therefore, we will take a brief look at this type of evidence.[12]

Laws are especially useful indicators of shifts in social attitudes, permitting the rough dating of such shifts. Thus, the Letters-Patent of October 1685 -- Colbert's famous *Code noir* -- are usually regarded as a crucial document for the understanding of the French plantation system: they fix the relationships between colonial white masters and black workers, which had slowly evolved in the preceding decades as a result of the introduction of slavery. A similar set of documents, modifying the terms of the Black Code, can provide a useful guide to the dating of transitions in eighteenth-century perceptions of race relations. Of particular interest are those which deal with the growing problem of slaves brought to France and sometimes abandoned there.

A first decree was promulgated in 1716,[13] in response to planters' fears that the slaves they brought to France would be deemed to have been freed. The fear was not unfounded, for the practice of bringing slaves into the country ran counter to the Black Code, which stipulated that slaves remain in the colonies, and also to metropolitan jurisprudence, which did not recognize the institution of slavery. The edict granted satisfaction to the planters, but, in a formulation which would be repeated in all subsequent acts, limited the purposes of such visits to reasons of religious instruction and training in some craft. The act was declared a specific derogation to French jurisprudence: any contravention of its clauses by the slave owner would result in the freeing of his slave. Most significant, in light of subsequent concerns about miscegenation, a slave could marry in France with his owner's permission, which was considered to have the same effect as manumission. Clearly the act, while granting the demands of the planters, was meant essentially for the benefit of the colonies. No particular concern was expressed as to the existence of a free black population in France, nor for that matter as to the dangers of mixed marriages.

The same can be said of the 1738 Declaration,[14] which tightened the clauses established in 1716, arguing that

> most of the Negroes contract [in France] habits and a spirit of independence which could have unfortunate results…and that [among those who remain in France]…there are some who are for the most part useless and even dangerous….

What concerned the government was a matter of public order, and Blacks were obviously lumped together with an equally "useless and dangerous" white population of masterless poor and semi-employed workers. Similarly, the government obviously worried that the "habits and spirit of independence" which the slaves contracted in France would occasion disorders in the colonies when they returned there. No clear "racial" sentiment can be inferred from the act. Even the prohibition of marriages, which the Declaration contained, is most properly read as a means of hastening the return of slaves to the colonies, rather than as a result of emerging fears of miscegenation, as Cohen claims.[15]

The letter published in 1763 by the Duke of Choiseul, the Minister of the Marine (under whom colonial matters fell), is another matter altogether.[16] Also meant to stop excessive advantage being taken of the 1716 permission, the letter ordered the immediate return of all slaves to the West Indies. One reason given was the need of colonial agriculture for labour, an understandable concern following the catastrophic interruption of the slave trade during the Seven Years' War. But the letter also spoke of

> putting an end to the disorders that they [the slaves] have introduced in the Kingdom by their communications with the Whites, from which has resulted a mixed blood, which increases daily.

A first rough dating may thus be proposed. Sometime between 1738 and 1763, the racist approach began to assume a dominant position, at least in French law. Indeed, Choiseul's letter marked the start of a new policy towards Blacks in France. The Letters-Patent of 1685 had placed black freedmen on the same footing as the white colonial population. Two acts posterior to Choiseul's letter imposed on them the registration requirements until then reserved to slaves, and thereby created in France itself the clear racial line between Whites and Blacks already in place in the colonies.[17]

The new treatment of Blacks in French law, reflecting a new attitude among the upper classes,[18] was due in part to the growing role the planters played in elite and government circles.[19] It had to do as well with a new attitude expressed among intellectuals.

The middle of the eighteenth century marks in the Enlightenment an important shift from Newtonism, the application to human society of the fixed principles of physical science, to an interest in the natural sciences, from which the *philosophes* took their idea of race. The identification of distinct races predates our period, but it was only in the mid-eighteenth century that the concept was systematized and given the aura of unimpeachable scientific authority, principally by its publication in Buffon's *Histoire naturelle, générale et particulière* (1749-1788), and especially in the sections first published, "On Man's Nature" and "The Varieties in the Human Species."[20]

Buffon's categorization of human "races" was based on climate, which he claimed had created hereditary differentiations which only the vastness of time could erase. He viewed the Europeans, living between the fortieth and fiftieth parallels, as the original type of mankind, from which others had "degenerated." As the two extremes from the European model, the African and the Laplander suffered most from the comparison. They were "the furthest away from the true and the beautiful"; they were "equally gross, superstitious, stupid."[21] Culturally sterile,[22] they possessed a mind akin to a *tabula rasa*,[23] which could be developed only in contact with superior races. It was precisely because the Africans were in contact with Europeans, through West Indian slavery, that Buffon preferred them to the Laps.[24]

Buffon's views were adopted by other scientists, becoming the standard opinion among late eighteenth-century naturalists.[25] More to the point, the *Histoire naturelle* became the vade mecum of the Enlightenment.

Statements of racial prejudice are common among the *philosophes,* especially among those who wrote in the second half of the century. Even such opponents of slavery as Montesquieu, Abbé Raynal, or even Abbé Grégoire can at times be shown to have held disparaging views concerning Blacks, though they often ascribed the "defects" they perceived to social or environmental, rather than to racial, factors.[26] But it was not merely a matter of prejudice. Voltaire, for example, could speak of the Jews as "born with raging fanaticism in their heart, just as the Bretons and the Germans are born with blond hair."[27]

His view of the Blacks was no more charitable. He likened them to animals, whose physical features and mental processes, he believed, they approximated, and suggested that "abominable matings" with monkeys had created the "monstrous species" described by the Ancients. He chastised Christians for believing that black Africans were made in God's image, and he declared slavery, which he condemned elsewhere for its effects on the white masters, to be the condition which "nature" had reserved for Blacks.[28]

Voltaire's polygenetic beliefs, borrowed from Paracelsus and Malpighi as a means of combatting Christian tradition, no doubt influenced him in adopting these views. Yet, polygenesis was not for him a matter of mere tactics. It led him, on the basis of a pseudo-scientific apparatus, to stipulate the existence of fixed species, possessed of innate qualities (or defects), and to develop a distinctly modern concept of racial superiority. Whites, he said, are "superior to these Blacks, just as Blacks are [superior] to monkeys, and monkeys to oysters and other animals of that kind."[29] More to the point, it led him to moral judgments as to the appropriateness of a given race's existence.[30]

Most *philosophes* saw mankind, more traditionally, as the result of evolution. But, as nineteenth-century Social Darwinism shows, such a position did not preclude a concept of European, even racial, superiority. Quite the contrary, for the "Great Chain of Being" thesis suggested precisely the ranking of species. Thus, Helvétius posited a spectrum of human types, from the "lazy" Africans and Caribs, representing inertia and childhood, to the Europeans, representing civilization and maturity, to the Asians, representing decadence ("*mollesse*") and old age.[31] Evolution was specially noticeable in colour, which graphically described for eighteenth-century thinkers the degenerate status of the Blacks.[32] As the most visible symbol of distance from European civilization, blackness was a sign of brutishness.[33]

The fear of miscegenation and its implied degenerative consequences would become common among the elite in France at approximately the same time as law became concerned with racial purity. Thus, such forceful opponents of slavery as Abbé Raynal and the *bailli* of Mirabeau would speak in the last half of the eighteenth century of black blood as "one of the yeasts which alter, corrupt and destroy our population," and of mulattoes as "vile...children of the most detestable debauchery, a sort of monster always composed of the knavery of the two colours."[34] It is perhaps for similar reasons that Rousseau, who argued that the Jews were not a race but a cultural entity and that humanity was so mixed as to render the concept of race meaningless, specifically excluded the Africans from this last remark.[35]

Physical characteristics, and principally colour, assumed by the middle of the eighteenth century the quality of fixed attributes which, whether one perceived them as expressions of moral traits or not, whether one understood them to be absolutely immutable or merely evolving over centuries, indelibly marked one set of individuals as different from another, and focussed racial prejudice on them. As the *bailli* of Mirabeau, governor of Guadeloupe, noted, "Slavery...in this country is the most powerful it has ever been, not because of the laws but...[because] colour adds to it an indelible physical stain."[36]

\*   \*

The racist outlook was first developed in the plantation colonies. There, the christianization of a substantial number of slaves made a mockery of the convenient religious justification for slavery, and demanded a new secular rationalization for the institution.[37] There, as well, proximity fostered a sense of racial distinction.[38] There, finally, the growing problem of mulattoes and freedmen, threatening the Manichaean vision of society created by slavery, led to the first regulations concerning interracial marriage and the first enactments against non-slaves of African descent.[39] To these facts may be added in the mid-century a growing sense that slavery was on its way out, or rather that, if it were to survive, a new set of defenses against such detractors as Montesquieu, Diderot and Raynal was required.[40]

Summarizing the position of the planters, a series of systematic defenses of slavery were written in the 1770s.[41] They contained all the traditional arguments (no justification was too petty to be ignored) but included a number of new ones as well. If, for instance, the old religious rationalization continued to be put forward,[42] it was reinforced with more secular arguments. Old beliefs concerning the bestial practices of Africans were reaffirmed, but they were now couched in more modern garb. Thus, a colonial, speaking of the Black as part of a distinct "species," argued that "his colour has made him into a slave and...nothing can make him the equal of his master."[43]

Reference to the naturalists became common. As early as the 1760s, one planter turned to his own purposes Buffon's argument for monogenesis, based on all human species' ability to speak, and therefore to think. "Were it not that they have the power of speech," he noted of Africans, "they would possess of Man only the shape.... One would be tempted to believe...that Blacks form a race of creatures by which nature seems to mount from orangutans to pongos to man."[44] Even more specific were the references made to those among the *philosophes* who had argued against slavery. Such propositions could not be taken lightly; they had to be countered directly. For example, Montesquieu's famous passage on the subject (*L'Esprit des lois,* XV, 5) was dismissed by one author as "a joke...not serious...so frivolous" that one might question whether it did not consist of "some fragments from another work, inserted by error in this famous treatise which promises the development of the *Spirit of the Laws.*"[45]

Slavery continued to be described as indigenous to Africa (hence exonerating Europeans from all blame) and coupled there with the most bloodthirsty practices.[46] On the other hand, in an obvious response to the humanitarian sentiments expressed by the *philosophes,* the West Indian institution was depicted in well-nigh idyllic tones. Masters were the kindest of men, and slaves the best cared for of servants: "...in his old age, he [the slave] sees his infirmities cared for, and his children following the same career [*sic*] as he, without a care or need."[47]

Should such justifications not convince, a more serious argument was advanced in law, the more effective because it placed the institution of slavery in the context of proprietary rights, then advanced by the *philosophes.*[48] Such an argument, stressing the legal similarity between slaves and other forms of chattel, also served as a stepping-stone for the presentation of the now standard stereotype, the more insidious for being couched in legal terms:

> This word [slave] withdraws all the rights of humanity from the being to which it is applied. He is no longer a man: he is, according to circumstances, an instrument with feelings or an acting beast of burden.... Save for the fact that he still walks on two feet, save [also] that he knows not how to moo or neigh, and

that no use of his flesh or skin is made upon his death, there is no longer any difference between him and an ox, or a horse.[49]

The final nail was driven in by drawing attention to the threat which the liberalization of slavery posed for European society itself:

Surely no-one will make us desire the incorporation and the mixing of Races? Yet, slavery is essential if we wish to avoid this. Only the ignominy attached to an alliance with a Black Slave secures the Nation's own filiation. If this prejudice is destroyed, if the Black man is assimilated to the Whites among us, it is more than probable that in short order we shall see Mulattoes as Nobles, Financiers [ and ] Traders, ... [ and that their ] wealth will soon procure wives and mothers [ with coloured skin ] to all Estates within the State. It is thus that individuals, families [ and ] Nations become altered, debased, and that they dissolve.[50]

The campaign of the 1770s did not have the expected effect, and in the 1780s the abolitionist movement in France assumed disturbing proportions. Most threatening perhaps was the establishment of the well-connected *Société des amis des noirs* on the eve of the 1789 meeting of the Estates-General, the more so because a number of its most influential members were elected to this assembly and showed every sign of wishing to raise there the matter of abolition.[51] Faced with such a threat, some planters demanded and finally obtained the representation of the colonies in the National Assembly, as a means of opposing there the measures advocated by the abolitionists.[52] More subtly, others founded a counter-society, the so-called *Club Massiac,* whose purpose was to protect planter interests and, more specifically, to orchestrate a campaign against the *Amis des noirs.*[53]

It is not the purpose of this article to describe the various measures of the French Revolution concerning the slave trade and slavery.[54] It is enough to say that the planters viewed with increasing alarm the steps taken by the National Assembly: most notably the abolition of privilege on the night of 4 August, during which a first attempt seems to have been made to deal with slavery,[55] and the Declaration of the Rights of Man, from which the abolition of slavery could logically be deduced. This last document was particularly worrisome, and the planters, while they based their defense of the institution on the section dealing with property, sought and finally managed to exclude the colonies from the new constitution by claiming an associate status for the West Indies, precisely on the basis of the existence of slavery there.[56] By waging a protracted rear-guard action against the liberalization of their own society, the planters involved the Assembly in extensive and at times acrimonious debates on the colonies. Though they succeeded in delaying the inevitable,[57] and even for a while in limiting the rights of black freedmen and mulattoes,[58] they did so at enormous cost to themselves and to their metropolitan advocates, most of whom, accused increasingly of "aristocratic" leanings, ended up, with the planters, either in exile or on the scaffold.[59]

What strikes the reader when perusing the post-1788 colonial discourse is not its originality, but rather the frenzy of the arguments, owing no doubt to the growing concern the authors felt for the preservation of their way of life. Attacks on the *Amis des noirs* verge on hysteria. The latter are labelled "negrophiles," a not altogether innocent insult, given the planters' ambivalent view of sexual relations with Blacks;[60] they are accused of causing "sedition" in the colonies and of being enemy agents.[61] Similar linguistic excesses are replete in the presentation of the old arguments, revealing, if nothing else could, the frankly racist vision, spurred on by fear, which buttressed the planters' prejudices. Stressing the animalistic practices of some Africans, one such writer warned that, as rebellious slaves, they would atavistically "change themselves into tiger[s] in order to tear and devour all."[62]

On the whole, the contribution of planters' deputies to the National Assembly debates show more moderation, no doubt because such speeches were meant to convince. Much was thus made in the Assembly of the political, though unfortunate, "necessity" of racial prejudice.[63] While the colonial deputies stressed the guarantees which the Constitution provided to the planters as proprietors, they could at times nevertheless claim to at least envision with equanimity the end of the slave trade.[64]

And yet, when protracted debate raised their hackles, colonial deputies too could express sentiments not unlike those of the propagandists. The revealing comment of the scholarly deputy from Saint-Domingue, Moreau de Saint-Méry, can be ascribed to such a case of frayed nerves. Though retaining some of his usual caution, he nonetheless clearly inferred that West Indians would secede, rather than accept as equals the sons of slaves.[65] His more hot-tempered colleague, Gouy d'Arsy, revealed his true feelings when pushed by the seven-day debate leading to the Decree of 15 May 1791, which granted civil rights to a few freedmen. Racial discrimination, he said, was "an ancient prejudice" (hence, presumably, a respectable one). Freedom and equality could never be given to Blacks, for it required that they reach the appropriate "intellectual development," and that was "a mathematical impossibility."[66]

As characteristically, another deputy caused to be published, as a means of deflating the arguments of the *Amis des noirs,* a document purporting to issue from black freedmen and opposing the pretentions of the mulattoes. It began as follows:

The Negro is born of a pure blood. On the contrary, the mulatto is of mixed blood; he is a composite of black and white, a sort of bastardized species.

From this truth, it is evident that the Negro is superior to the mulatto, as it is evident that pure gold is superior to mixed.[67]

Though presumably meant as an absurd statement, this stress on racial purity, replicating the planters' own views on the subject, could hardly be treated as a joke. Colonial society, as Malouet informed the National Assembly, was based on strict colour lines, which defined the status of groups:

The prejudice of colour against Blacks is for them [the mulattoes] what it is for us against mulattoes, that is to say, a mulatto believes himself superior to a free Black, just as a White [believes himself superior] to a mulatto.[68]

Even more telling was Malouet's view that a mere drop of black blood, or even marriage to a mulatto, excluded a given individual from white status.[69]

It was not to a planter, however, that the dubious honour of most fully expressing the colonial point of view fell, but to Mirabeau's aristocratic younger brother. Climate, the Viscount of Mirabeau argued, did not permit Frenchmen to work in the colonies. The labours of agriculture thus fell to the Blacks, "this degraded species." Blacks possessed an "infinitely limited intelligence," and thus stood far below the "superior race" of their masters. Their "carefree character" [*insouciance*] and their "laziness" and "aversion to work" were "natural" attributes of Africans. Freedom thus would be "a fatal gift" to West Indian slaves, for they "would immediately cease to work"...and cause "several million [white] French-men" to be reduced to poverty. "If humanity orders me to improve the conditions of the Blacks," the Viscount concluded, "reason commands me to confirm them into slavery."[70] The planters could not but approve.

*      *

The merchants of France, and especially those *armateurs* whose livelihood rested on colonial trade, form an especially interesting group to study. They possessed a culture at least equal to that of the planters, and yet had the advantage of relative distance from the colonial world. Among them stood individuals of distinct intellectual ambitions, who served as conduits between the "Republic of letters" and merchant thought. Their privileged institutional connections to the State allowed them readily to pass their views to society at large.

It should not surprise anyone that such ports as Bordeaux and Nantes, for all their disagreements with the planters, at times shared common interests with the latter. Their merchants were involved in the West Indian trade, and more impor-tantly with the slave traffic, and were often absentee planters themselves. It is precisely this conjoining of merchant and planter interests which makes suspect the many addresses supporting the slave system sent to the National Assembly by the merchant towns, for it has been argued, on the basis of a fair amount of evidence, that the campaign was orchestrated by the representatives of planters in Paris.[71] If so, these merchant petitions must be used with caution, for they cannot serve as altogether reliable guides to commercial opinion. Fortunately, another type of documentation is available, which suggests that the attitudes of merchants involved in the colonial trade, and notably those of the Nantes commercial community, paralleled the views expressed in the sectors of society already studied.

A 1716 document drafted by Gérard Mellier, the city's mayor, provides a first look at Nantes attitudes.[72] Mellier's advice was being sought on the planters' peti-tion concerning slaves residing in France. The document is particularly interesting because it clearly forms the basis for the Edict of October 1717, already cited, which, with one notable exception, follows the sense and even the language of the mayor's recommendations.[73] The date is equally significant, for Mellier's draft predates the great period of Nantes' slave-trading activities, though the city already possessed some experience in the traffic.

Trying to explain the reasons for the slave system, the mayor argued:

> This [slave] trade which, by the greed of men turns [some of] them into cattle, would not be permitted without the indispensible need we have of their services in the colonies, and if the Negroes we transport there did not escape error and idolatry to receive baptism and to be instructed with care in the Roman religion by priests and missionaries sent there for this purpose.
>
> In any event, the *Nigritie* is a vast region of Africa, divided into several kingdoms. Its people are so numerous that they would find it difficult to survive, were it not that the slave trade relieved them each year of a number of inhabitants. They would be led to kill the captives they take in war, were it not that they have to keep them alive in order to sell or exchange them against goods

and merchandise brought either by our ships or those of the English, the Dutch and the Portuguese.

The statement is striking because, while it exculpates Europeans from blame -- and even turns them into humanitarians--it stresses only the most traditional explanations. Moreover, it lays no emphasis on a supposed African barbarity, but rather provides in demographic pressures a rational explanation for the alleged slaughters so heavily stressed by other European sources.

Yet, when contemplating the permanent residence of slaves in Europe, Mellier charges their character with more ominous traits:

> When all is said, Negroes are naturally inclined to theft, larceny, lechery, laziness and treason. And if we can put faith in the philandering annals and anecdotes of Spain, they are used for means which are best kept away [ from our shores ]. In general, they are only fit to live in servitude, and to be used in the labours and in the cultivation of land on the continent of our American colonies.

The statement is significant because it appears so totally gratuitous, the more so since Mellier advanced a better reason for keeping slaves in the colonies: "All those who would remain in France would diminish what must be part of our colonies." This was the reason picked up in the Edict. Foreshadowing the words of the Edict, Mellier saw no difficulty in the existence of a small free black population in France. He proposed that visiting slaves be permitted to marry, although he did not advocate their automatic freedom, as the Edict would provide. Instead, he recommended freedom only for the slaves' children born in France. Despite his relatively liberal views concerning marriages, the mayor's recommendations clearly demonstrate that there already existed in 1716 Nantes, if not the start of a truly racist outlook, at least an already firmly established prejudice against Blacks. At the same time, the inclusion of a rationalization of the slave trade, in a document which hardly required it, suggests that the author still felt some twinges of conscience.

The years following the War of the Spanish Succession mark the beginning of Nantes' true vocation as a slave-trading port.[74] If Nantes *armateurs* were to be slave traders, they could not afford to retain such reservations. It is therefore not surprising that a process of objectifying the trade occurred in these years. The traffic in slaves became known as the trade in "ebony wood," a term clearly meant to transform the unfortunate victims into dehumanized articles of trade. It also permitted those who suffered permanent physical harm from the middle passage -- not to mention the dead -- to be treated as so many "rejects," to be deplored only as net losses on the account books.[75] So inured did the slave traders become to the human sufferings they caused that one of them, Jean-Gabriel Montaudouin de La Touche, is reported to have called one of his ships the *Social Contract,* after Rousseau's famous work.[76] No less significant was the practice adopted by the merchant community of Nantes in the 1760s, of decorating the facades of their newly-built urban mansions with sculpted masks of Africans, thereby proudly announcing the source of their fortune.[77]

A look at the many memoirs on the slave trade produced by the Nantes commercial representation during the middle years of the century confirms this trend. For the most part, they pay no attention to the human dimension of the trade and concentrate instead on the economic gains and losses associated with it.[78] Nor, for that matter, did other cities' chambers of commerce dwell on the issue, showing that Nantes' lead was quickly picked up by its rivals.

A survey of the many commercial guides published in the eighteenth century shows the same process taking place. While the very popular seventeenth-century *Parfait négociant* contained as late as its 1713 edition the traditional religious excuses for the slave trade, its eighteenth-century sequel significantly toned down these considerations to focus on the economic factors.[79] Conscience, however, returned toward the end of the century, no doubt as a result of the humanist campaign conducted by certain *philosophes,* whose culture the commercial establishment laid claim to share. Thus, the author of a commercial guide of the late 1760s, while declaring all Africans in general to be "thieves," footnoted a chart showing the economic gains that could be derived from the slave trade with a comment roundly condemning the immorality of the practice.[80]

It was, however, the French abolitionist campaign of the late 1780s, specifically directed at the livelihood of the slave-trading towns, which triggered there a renewed attention to the human effects of the traffic. Towns less directly involved in the colonial traffic began to take their distance; they could at times afford to express some moral reservations.[81] Those which were more closely involved could not.

With the calling of the Estates-General, Nantes merchants took good care that their views would be represented in the *sénéchaussée's* list of grievances, arguing there, among other things, that the protection of the slave trade ought to be continued.[82] They were less successful in having members of their community named as deputies to the Estates. Out of eight members representing the County of Nantes, five came from the port city, but only one of them, Jacques-Nicolas Guinebaud de Saint-Mesme, was a merchant.[83] Other commercial centres were no better served, so that there was a real danger that "...the voice of your six merchant deputies from the seaports, to whom the total representation of commerce in the Estates-General is limited," would not be heard.[84] For this reason, Nantes and other French commercial ports sought, as the planters did, to gain their own representation to the National Assembly. When the request was refused, they organized a parallel deputation of commercial and manufacturing towns, the so-called *députés extraordinaires,* whose purpose was at once to keep the Assembly informed of merchant concerns and to watch with care the actions of the towns' official deputies, judged to be lukewarm to merchant interest.[85]

Nantes' special deputies were two brothers, Jean-Baptiste Mosneron *(l'aîné)* and Alexis Mosneron de Launay. Coming from a family of *armateurs* -- a third brother kept up the affairs of the firm in Nantes -- and allied by marriage to the merchant elite, they each had had experience in trade, but were no longer actively involved in it. The elder brother abandoned trade for literature as a young man; more traditionally, the younger brother had spent sixteen years in Saint-Domingue and had only returned to France in 1783. Mosneron de Launay had served on the Consulate, and both had experience in representing Nantes commerce on special missions to Versailles and to the Estates of Brittany in Rennes.[86] It is principally through the work of the Mosneron brothers and through the official deputy François-Pierre Blin that Nantes sought to protect its slaving interests during the seating of the National Assembly. To them fell the task of forwarding Nantes' petitions. While Blin kept up a decorous dialogue on the Assembly's floor, the Mosneron brothers were left the crasser lobbying tasks.

Blin and certain of his colleagues from merchant towns participated in the campaign against emancipation and against the extension of rights to free Blacks and mulattoes. They joined the more cautious planter representatives, Moreau de Saint-Méry and, principally, the *Abbé* Maury, in derailing the debate whenever an embarrassing question came up.[87] Blin saw his principal role, however, as that of defusing the campaign of the *Amis des noirs.* Always avoiding abusive characterizations, he at times even managed to turn the abolitionist arguments to his own purposes.[88] Occasionally, however, he and his colleagues used certain excessive phrases, as when the Normand deputy Jacques-François Begoüen, a West Indian-born leading merchant of Le Havre, referred to the "moral bases" on which slavery rested.[89] With one notable exception, however, the tone of merchant representatives remained on the whole moderate when addressing their colleagues, even if the opinions they offered on colonial matters clearly identified them with the Right of the Assembly. As one of them stated: "Gentlemen, it is not enough to be just; we must be just with prudence."[90]

Merchant representatives sought to avoid an open confrontation on the matter of slavery.[91] In the process, they came to suggest a non-racial criterion for the institution. The matter at issue was not one of colour, they hinted, but one of differing interests between foreigners (that is, Africans) and "the French population of the colonies, the citizens, the one[s] truly attached to France by ties of patriotism and consanguinity."[92]

The one notable exception to the moderate tone of merchant intervention was a speech which the Nantes lawyer Joseph-Michel Pellerin had published when a closure of debate prohibited its delivery.[93] Attacking the *Société des amis des noirs* by name, Pellerin sought to counter their argument by showing the advantages which could derive from the slave trade, not only to France but also to the Blacks themselves. In the process, he repeated the usual description of African conditions, by now so familiar as no longer to be worth reporting. A number of revealing comments, however, deserve mention.

Tellingly, the Nantes deputy distinguished White-owned from Black-owned plantations. Slaves on the latter were treated with infinitely more harshness, for West Indian freedmen, like all sons of Africa, lacked natural humanity and considered only their own self-interest. His use of the Caribs to show what a system of free labour would mean for West Indian agriculture is equally revealing:

> Negroes, when freed, will no longer work, because free Negroes do not work. Caribs, who own the best land on Saint-Vincent Island, only cultivate a bit of corn. Hunting and fishing are their [main] occupations, and even so they hunt and fish only when pressed by hunger; at other times, they sleep. Here is the life of these Negroes in their indolent free state. And we would want to entrust the cultivation of our Colonies, the resources of France, the soul of its commerce to them? What a policy!

Leaving aside the heavy-handed irony of the tone, the confused identification of the Caribs and Blacks, by lumping together two colonial peoples into one inferior non-white group, was a significant step in the emerging racist, Manichaean, vision of the world.[94]

The special deputies of commerce too showed some moderation, at least when speaking publicly.[95] The Mosneron brothers in particular sought to present themselves as dignified, justifiedly sorrowful merchants, reproaching their opponents for their unwarranted accusations and urging upon them the adoption of sweet reason. However, their role as lobbyists permitted them more freedom, and Alexis Mosneron de Launay, for one, adopted positions strikingly similar to those of Pellerin.

Even when assuming a reasonable tone, as in an Open Letter to Condorcet, the younger Mosneron described Blacks as "perverted men" with raised knives at the throat of their masters. More significantly, they were "instruments of cultivation." He adjured the President of the *Amis des noirs* to lead his Society into becoming "the friends of the Whites, the friends of the French."[96] The Letter to Condorcet drew an anonymous response, to Mosneron's obvious delight, for it allowed him to push his own arguments further, while taking on the air of an aggrieved correspondent. In his reply, the special deputy noted the pre-existence of slavery in Africa, citing English Parliamentary evidence, and drew, on the basis of alleged personal interviews with West Indian slaves, a horrifying picture of African cannibalism. As to freedmen, they were at once lazy and cruel. They "do not cultivate the land; they have slaves [to do it], which they treat with a hundred-fold more severity" than the white plantation owners do.[97]

In a subsequent speech to the Jacobin Club, Mosneron heaped up new details. Painting a rosy picture of the treatment reserved to Blacks on slave-trading ships and on West Indian plantations, he dismissed those who had died in the process of creating the French sugar empire as "the unavoidable wastage [*frottements*] of a vast and complex machine whose returns are immense"; in effect, they were necessary losses in a quasi-industrial process. Of course, Mosneron was referring only to Whites, for the Blacks remained for him mere "instruments of agriculture."[98]

The most interesting document is an incomplete, undated and unsigned draft for an address to the National Assembly. Internal evidence suggests that it was written by Mosneron de Launay, though it is possible that it was merely influenced by him. The proposed speech focusses on the "moral" and "political" aspects of the slave trade, and as such on the principal grounds upon which the abolitionists laid their case. Addressing the first question, the author started by admitting, following Rousscau:

> I do not pretend to support the slave trade by arguing morality in its [most] rigorous sense. I know that no man has the right to take freedom away from his kind, that no man can alienate his own freedom. If he were for a moment to forget the rights which nature has given him, to degrade himself and give himself up [into slavery], he would always be free to demand and to take back this inalienable property.

However, he hastened to add, these principles do not apply to the slavers, who do not enslave free men. Far from causing slavery to flourish in Africa, they protect its inhabitants from its consequences and, by shipping them to the West Indies, provide them with the gradual benefits of freedom. Neither do strict principles of morality apply to the Blacks, for they have always been slaves and, in Africa, have treated each other in abominable ways, presumably thereby excluding themselves from the very name of men. "Thus, on moral grounds, the slave trade must not be abolished."[99]

                                    *         *

Was there a racist ideology in eighteenth-century France? To conclude with
this question may seem by now redundant. But if racism there was -- and it seems
certain--there still remain questions to be answered. How deep-rooted was the
racism? Did it form a dominant ideology or, as Cohen asserts, was it merely one
trend among others in eighteenth-century thought, a trend which would become
dominant only in the nineteenth century? How closely tied is eighteenth-century
racism, dominant or not, to the more familiar strain of the nineteenth century?

Starting with the last question, it is helpful to draw a parallel between
eighteenth-century statements and the description which Albert Memmi gives of the
modern colonist's racism.[100] Racism, he notes, is not "a more or less accidental
detail, but...a consubstantial element of colonialism." Modern racism, he argues,
develops as a three-step process, only the last two of which are truly racist:

> 1) The discovery and the putting in evidence of the *differences* between colonizer
> and colonized; 2) the placing of *value* on these differences, at the profit of the
> colonizer and at the expense of the colonized; 3) the transformation of these
> differences into *absolutes,* by claiming that they are permanent, and by acting in
> such a way as to make them so.

"Self-absolved" as the civilizing agents of his inferiors, the colonizer further
legitimates his own position by ascribing to "natural laws" the differences which he
perceives. When all is said and done, he is not altogether sorry to find negative
qualities -- sloth, a propensity to petty theft -- in those whom he exploits, for these
qualities "define" the colonized and further legitimate the domination exercized over
him. Ultimately, they lead to the denial of the very humanity of the exploited, who
thus become mere objects, existing only to serve the colonizer.

Clearly the process described by Memmi was in full operation in the eighteenth
century. *Differences* between Europeans and others were identified by the scientists
and a *value* placed on them by the philosophers. These differences were transformed
into *absolute* and permanent racial characteristics, especially by those most closely
identified with the exploitation of Blacks, and by no means only in the colonies.
Negative qualities were everywhere ascribed to Blacks, and we have shown significant examples of the latter's dehumanization. It can no longer be in doubt that
Memmi's description applies as equally well to late eighteenth-century attitudes as to
more recent ones. Far from being a new kind of racism, the nineteenth-century brand
merely refined and generalized the approach which had come to light in the second
half of the eighteenth century.

How wide-spread in the eighteenth century, then, were the attitudes we have
described? Not all *philosophes* by any means subscribed to them, but even those most
closely associated with the humanitarian campaign, including the abolitionists,
ascribed negative qualities to the slaves. No doubt, racial prejudice was prevalent as
well among planters and slave traders. There remains, however, a question as to how
far down the social ladder -- even within the merchant class -- such attitudes spread.

In this respect, one may note certain distinctions, in terms of period, geography
and class. As to the first factor, evidence from every group studied shows that a shift

in attitude took place in the middle of the century, which can be given as the date of birth of the modern racist approach. As to geography and class, it should be noted that the documentation marshalled for this article comes from those groups which, at one and the same time, were most closely associated with elite culture and with slavery or the institutions which controlled it: the colonists themselves, port merchants, government officials. Does racism assume less clear forms as one moves further away from Paris and the port cities, and from the elite? The evidence available to us on this score is very scanty, and more work will have to be done before we can settle the issue. Nonetheless, what we know suggests a gradual blurring of racist themes.

Race riots did occur in the eighteenth century, but they appear to have taken place only in the port cities and in Paris,[101] probably because it was there that the bulk of the Blacks had settled. Inland merchants, as we have shown, quickly took their distance from the anti-abolitionist campaign waged by their port colleagues. Similarly, those *cahiers* which advocated in 1789 the abolition of the slave trade came almost exclusively from the inland regions or from the clergy.[102] Most significant, perhaps, is the fact that mixed marriages appear to have been more readily accepted in the provinces and among the lower classes than in Paris and among the elite.[103]

Dominant ideology may be defined as particular to the upper class, spread by its intellectual agents as a non-violent means of legitimizing its control over society by providing "objective," that is, non-class, explanations for, and hence perpetuation of, its domination. Not until the advent of an "immigrant" work-force in the twentieth century could racism serve directly to objectify labour relations in France itself, though it was used for that purpose in the colonies and may have reinforced at home the time-honoured upper-class prejudice against lower-class swarthiness. Similarly, as the evidence of race riots shows, racism may have served, much as it did in the nineteenth century, to provide the white labouring class, in cities where it was confronted with Black competitors, with a sense of "belonging" linking it to its "betters." For all these reasons, one should not be surprised to find racism, as part of the dominant ideology, partially adopted but not fully shared by the lower echelons of society.

The Enlightenment, especially after 1750, has at times been crudely defined as "bourgeois ideology," the essential precursor of the bourgeois revolution. The emergence of racism at precisely that time might support this view, especially when one sees its full flowering among nineteenth-century capitalist societies. Our study suggests an alternative to this interpretation. Those who adopted racist views in the eighteenth century can hardly be linked to modern capitalism, whether they were government officials, West Indian planters or port merchants. They all took positions on the Right during the French Revolution, and saw their status overthrown in the upheaval. Racism, like the Enlightenment itself, of which it was part, was a bridge between late Ancien Régime and modern capitalist societies. And like most significant intellectual movements, it fully defined the outgoing social regime, at the same time as it elaborated the values which the new society would adopt. If so, it is little wonder that racism, as well as slavery, survived the French Revolution.

The identification of colour with less than human characteristics became by the late eighteenth century an essential part of the process by which the French defined

their role as colonizers. As Barnave noted in the Revolutionary debates, the West Indies were divided into three classes: the African slaves (whose existence he merely inferred), the French planters, and the "native born" Blacks and mulattoes (*"la race"* or later *"les races des ingénus"*). It was precisely because of the colour of the latter that the prejudice against them, which he claimed to deplore, had to be enshrined in law.[104] Similarly, the abolitionist Grégoire reproached the planters for having instituted a difference not found among white Europeans:

> In France, the status of active citizen is an inequality owed to wealth, which each individual can hope to surmount, whereas in the colonies this inequality results from the difference in colour, which is insurmountable. In France, the declared [in]equality is not visible; it is not inscribed on [one's] forehead; it has not created insolence on one side and humiliation on the other. In the colonies, on the other hand, this inequality is written on the forehead of man himself, and man cannot escape the humiliation [associated with it].[105]

Blacks had, by then, been relegated to the permanent status of racial inferiors.

## NOTES

\*   Research for this article was started in France in the Summer of 1981, thanks to a McGill University Social Science Summer Travel Grant and to funds from the Interuniversity Centre for European Studies (Montreal). I also benefitted from the assistance of M. Alain Tremblay during the academic year 1981-1982, made possible by Quebec Government funds under the Programme à la Formation des Chercheurs en Action Concertée. My thanks go also to Roberta Rothstein and Frederick Krantz for their comments on earlier drafts.

1. Gilbert Varet, *Racisme et philosophie* (Paris, 1973), p. 47.

2. Quoted in Michèle Duchet. "Le Mouvement anti-esclavagiste: théorie et pratique," in *Racisme et société,* ed. Patrice Comarnond and Claude Duchet (Paris, 1969), p. 130.

3. Serge Daget, "Le mot esclave, nègre, Noir et les Jugements de valeur sur la traite négrière dans la littérature abolitionniste française de 1770 à 1845," *Revue française d'histoire d'Outre-mer,* LX:4 (1973), 511-48.

4. On Hume, see Richard H. Popkin, "The Philosophical Basis of Eighteenth-Century Racism," *Studies in Eighteenth Century Culture,* III (1973), 245-46; on Jefferson, Winthrop D. Jordan, *White Over Black: American Attitudes toward the Negro, 1550-1812* (Durham, N.C., 1968), pp. 429-81; on Voltaire, see below p. 224-25 and no. 27.

5. Pierre Van den Berghe, *Race and Racism. A Comparative Perspective* (New York, 1967), p. 11.

6. Among others, see the art. "Nègre" in Pierre Larousse, *Grand dictionnaire universel du XIXe siècle,* 15 vols. (Paris, 1866-1876), V, 903-04.

7. Léon Poliakov, *Histoire de l'antisémitisme,* 3 vols. (Paris, 1968); Arthur Hertzberg, *The French Enlightenment and the Jews* (New York, 1968).

8. The key passages are found in Poliakov, *Histoire de l'antisémitisme,* III, 87-173; in Hertzberg, *The French Enlightenment,* pp. 6-7, 268-313.

9. Michèle Duchet, *Anthropologie et histoire au siècle des Lumières* (Paris, 1971); Carminella Biondi, *Mon frère tu es mon esclave: teorie schiaviste e dibattiti antropologico-razziali nel settecento francese* (Pisa, 1973).

10. William B. Cohen, *The French Encounter with Africans. White Response to Blacks, 1530-1880* (Bloomington, Ind., 1980), p. 210.

11. *Ibid.,* pp. 96-99, and for his evidence on the eighteenth century, pp. 110-13.

12. Owing to space requirements, this section has been reduced to its simplest expression. Full elaboration will be made in a forthcoming work, provisionally entitled *Essays on Early Modern Racism.*

13. Royal Edict of Oct. 1716, Bibliothèque Nationale (Paris) [henceforth: Bibl. Nat.], Impr. F.23621 (525).

14. Royal Declaration of 15 Dec. 1738, *ibid.,* Impr. F.23624 (772).

15. *French Encounter,* p. 110. Cohen, however, cites the Declaration of 1738 from Lucien Peytraud, *L'Esclavage aux Antilles françaises* (Paris, 1897), and places particular emphasis on the phrase, "for they give the occasion...of the mixing of black blood in the kingdom." No such statements has been found in the act.

16. Choiseul to Lebret *(Intendant* of Brittany), 30 June 1763, Archives Départementales de la Loire-Atlantique [henceforth: A.D. L.-Atl.], C742, no. 2.

17. Royal Declaration of 9 Aug. 1777, Bibl. Nat., Impr. F.20987(36); *Arrêt* of 23 Mar. 1783, A.D. L.-Atl., C742, no. 6. For colonial legislation, see Gabriel Debien, *Les Colons de Saint-Domingue et la Révolution: Essai sur le Club Massiac* (Paris, 1953), pp. 35-36, and Léo Elisabeth, "The French Antilles," in *Neither Slave nor Free: The Freedmen and African Descent in the Slave Societies of the New World,* ed. David W. Cohen and Jack P. Greene (Baltimore, Md., 1972), pp. 153-54.

18. See, for instance, the protest of two music professors to the appointment of a mulatto as director of the Academy of Music in 1770. Michèle Duchet, "Esclavage et préjugé de couleur," in *Racisme et société,* ed. Comarnond and Duchet, p. 127.

19. On the general growth of planter influence, see Jean Tarrade, *Le Commerce colonial de la France à la fin de l'ancien régime: l'évolution du régime de "l'Exclusif" de 1763 à 1789,* 2 vols. (Paris, 1972).

20. On Buffon, see espec. Duchet, *Anthropologie et histoire,* pp. 229-80; on his influence, Daniel Mornet, "Les Enseignements des bibliothèques privées (1750-1780)," *Revue d'histoire littéraire de la France,* XVII (1910), 460.

21. Quoted in Duchet, *Anthropologie et histoire,* pp. 259 and 269.

22. George Louis Leclerc, comte de Buffon, *Les Époques de la nature,* ed. Jacques Roger (Paris, 1962), pp. 211-12.

23. Buffon, *De l'homme,* ed. Michèle Duchet (Paris, 1971), p. 283.

24. Duchet, *Anthropologie et histoire,* p. 260.

25. For the followers of Buffon, see Poliakov, *Histoire de l'antisémitisme,* III, 152-58, and *Le Mythe aryen* (Paris, 1971), p. 165. See in particular the work of the Dutch naturalist Cornelius De Pauw, *Recherches philosophiques sur les Américains ...,* 2 vols. (Berlin, 1768-1769); also that of the French medical doctor Claude Nicolas Le Cat, *Traité de la couleur de la peau en général, de celle des nègres en particulier* (Amsterdam, 1765), espec. p. 5, which reproduces Buffon's theses.

26. Cohen, *French Encounter,* p. 75.

27. *Lettres de Memmius à Cicéron* (1771), in François-Marie Arouet de Voltaire, *Œuvres complètes,* ed. Louis Moland [henceforth: O.C. Moland], 52 vols. (Paris, 1877-1885), XVIII, 440. The fullest treatment of the Jews by Voltaire is in his art. "Juifs" (1765 and 1771), *Dictionnaire philosophique,* in *O.C.* Moland, XIX, 511-41.

28. *Traité de métaphysique* (1734), *Lettres d'Amabed* (1769), and *Essai sur les mœurs et l'esprit des nations* (1753-1763), in *O.C.* Moland, XII, 191-92 and 210; XXI, 462; XI, 7 and XII, 380-81. On Voltaire's condemnation of slavery, see Biondi, *Mon frère tu es mon esclave,* pp. 150-51, and Duchet, *Anthropologie et histoire,* pp. 163n. and 320-21.

29. *Traité de métaphysique,* in *O.C.* Moland, XII, 192-93.

30. Most clearly in the case of the Jews. *Lettres de Memmius à Cicéron* and *Il faut prendre un parti, ou le principe d'action* (1772), in *O.C.* Moland, XXVIII, 440 and 549.

31. *De l'esprit* and *De l'homme,* in Claude-Adrien Helvétius, *Œuvres complètes,* 4 vols. (Liège, 1774), I, 380 and 593-98; IV, 312-13. On the "Great Chain of Being" thesis, see Cohen, *French Encounter,* pp. 86-89, and Jordan, *White Over Black,* pp. 219-20.

32. Pierre-Louis Moreau de Maupertuis, *Dissertation physique à l'occasion du Nègre blanc* (1744), quoted from Poliakov, *Le Mythe aryen,* p. 161.

33. See in particular Louis-Antoine de Bougainville, *Voyage autour du monde* (1771), cited by Duchet, "Esclavage et préjugé de couleur," p. 122, as well as by many others.

34. Guillaume-Thomas-François Raynal, *Histoire philosophique et politique de l'établissement et du commerce des Européens dans les Deux Indes* (1770 ed.), quoted from Poliakov, *Le Mythe aryen,* p. 166; Jean-Antoine de Riquetti, bailli de Mirabeau, quoted in Duchet, "Esclavage et préjugé de couleur," p. 126.

35. Unpublished manuscript of Rousseau, quoted from Poliakov, *Histoire de l'antisémitisme,* III, 122.

36. Quoted in Duchet, *Anthropologie et histoire,* p. 161.

37. The point is made for English America by Jordan, *White Over Black,* pp. 180-87, but it can be applied as readily to the French West Indies.

38. See the curious example of the early eighteenth-century New England traveller, Sarah Kemble Knight, who objected to eating at the same table as black slaves: "... into the dish goes the black hoof as freely as the white hand" (quoted in *ibid.,* p. 231).

39. Examples cited by Cohen, *French Encounter,* pp. 50-51. See also Duchet, "Esclavage et préjugé de couleur," pp. 121 and 124-25; David Lowenthal, "Free Colored West Indians: A Racial Dilemma," *Studies in Eighteenth Century Culture,* III (1973), 335-54.

40. Duchet, *Anthropologie et histoire,* pp. 137ff., espec. pp. 158-59.

41. Most notably Pierre-Victor Malouet, *Mémoire sur l'esclavage des nègres* (Neufchatel, 1788), written in 1775. A number of these apologies, published in the 1770s, are analyzed by Biondi, *Mon frère tu es mon esclave,* pp. 16-95.

42. As late as 1793, by Louis-Narcisse Baudry-Deslozières, *Les Égarements du nigrophilisme* (Paris, Year X [1802]), written for the most part in the previous decade (pp. x-xi).

43. Memoir dated 1777, quoted in Cohen, *French Encounter,* p. 107.

44. Jacques-Philibert Rousselot de Surgy, *Mélanges intéressants et curieux ...,* 10 vols. (Paris, 1763-1765), X, 161.

45. Simon-Nicolas-Henri Linguet, *Théorie des loix civiles* (1767), vols. III-V of his *Œuvres,* 6 vols. (London, 1774), V, 46.

46. Joseph-Gaspard Dubois-Fontanelle, *Anecdotes africaines ...* (Paris, 1775), Part VIII, pp. 29, 43-44, 52-58.

47. Malouet, *Mémoires sur l'esclavage des nègres,* p. 27.

48. The argument is everywhere subjacent in Linguet's treatment of slavery, *Œuvres,* V, 38-314. See also the 1777 memoir quoted by Cohen, *French Encounter,* p. 107.

49. Linguet, *Œuvres,* V, 40.

50. Malouet, *Mémoire sur l'esclavage des nègres,* p. 40.

51. Shelby T. McCloy, *The Negro in France* (Lexington, Ky., 1961), pp. 66-67. On the Society, see C. Perroud, "Le Société des amis des noirs," *Révolution française,* LXIX (1916), 122-47, and Daniel P. Resnick, "The Société des amis des noirs and the Abolition of Slavery," *French Historical Studies,* VII:4 (1972), 558-69.

52. Debien, *Club Massiac,* pp. 71-75.

53. *Ibid.,* pp. 63-64.

54. The vast documentation on the subject has been gathered in a collection, *La Révolution et l'abolition de l'esclavage,* 8 vols. (Paris, 1968). On the Revolutionary debates, see, among others, David B. Davis, *The Problem of Slavery in the Age of Revolution, 1770-1823* (Ithaca, N.Y., 1975), pp. 137-48.

55. Jean-Pierre Hirsh, *La Nuit du 4 août* (Paris, 1978), pp. 155-58 and 167; "Confession d'un député ... Louis-Marthe de Gouy d'Arsy," 15 Sept. 1791, in Jérome Mavidal and E. Laurent, eds., *Archives parlementaires de 1787 à 1860, première partie (1787-1799)* [henceforth; *Arch. parl.* ], 92 vols. to date (Paris, 1862-1981), XXXI, 301.

56. Decree of 8 Mar. 1790, confirmed by those of 12 Oct. 1790, 13 May and 24 Sept. 1791, *Arch. parl.,* XII, 72; XIX, 570; XXVI, 62; and XXXI, 288.

57. When slavery was finally abolished, in 1794, it was done mainly in a last-ditch attempt to safeguard the West Indian islands from rebellion. George Lefebvre, *La Révolution française* (Paris, 1951), p. 635, who notes as well that the decree had little effect in the colonies, where slavery was replaced at best with forced labour. Slavery, of course, was re-established under Napoleon.

58. Decree of 15 May 1791, *Arch. parl.,* XXVI, 97.

59. For instance Barnave, executed in 1793, whose vast reputation was first tarnished in his defense of the planters' cause as *rapporteur* for most of the measures proposed to the National Assembly by its colonial committee. See Rewbell's comment, 15 May 1791, *ibid.,* p. 92; also the violent exchange between Robespierre and Barnave on 5 Sept. 1791, *ibid.,* XXX, 235-39. On the link that was increasingly made between planters and aristocrats, see various remarks made during the long debate leading to the Decree of 15 May 1791, especially Pétion (*ibid.,* p. 641) and Robespierre (XXXI, 9), and during that leading to the abolition of slavery (15-16 Pluviôse Year II [3-4 Feb. 1794]): Danton (LXXXIV, 257), Maribon-Montaut (*ibid.*), Dufay (p. 281) and Levasseur (p. 283).

60. The term seems first to have been used by a member of the *Club Massiac,* David Duval de Sanadon, in his *Réclamations et observations des colons sur l'idée de l'abolition de la traite* [9 June 1789] (Debien, *Club Massiac,* p. 69). It soon became a favourite label in private communications among planters (e.g. Gouy d'Arsy, "Confessions d'un député...", *Arch. parl.,* XXXI, 302-03 and 308.

61. See the document in annex to the Meeting of 12 May 1791, *ibid.,* 25-26, in which opponents of the planters are described as having "voté pour l'Angleterre contre la France." The most extreme statement is found in Dominique Harcourt Lamiral, *L'Affrique et le peuple afriquain* (Paris, 1789), p. 372.

62. Beaudry-Deslozières, *Egaremens du nigrophilisme,* pp. 18-20 and 42.

63. "Opinion de M. Chabert de La Charrière, député de la Guadeloupe ..." 12 May 1791, *Arch. parl.,* XXV, 28; "Opinion de M. Malouet ..." 24 Sept. 1791, *ibid.,* XXXI, 294.

64. Speech by Cocherel (Dep. Guadeloupe), 26 Nov. 1789, *ibid.,* X, 267.

65. 7 May 1791, *ibid.,* XXV, 639.

66. Speech of 11 May 1791, *ibid.,* pp. 748-49.

67. "Réclamation des nègres libres, colons américains, adressées à l'Assemblée nationale", in annex to Meeting of 28 Nov. 1789, *ibid.,* X, 329. Debien, *Club Massiac,* p. 170, suggests Cocherel as the author.

68. "Opinion de M. Malouet..." 24 Sept. 1791, *ibid.,* XXXI, 297.

69. *Ibid.,* p. 294. The same opinion is found in the unsigned planter memoir of 1777, quoted in Cohen, *French Encounter,* p. 107.

70. "Opinion...[de] M. le vicomte de Mirabeau," in annex to Meeting of 8 Mar. 1790, *Arch. parl.,* XII, 76.

71. Debien, *Club Massiac,* pp. 103-11.

72. [Gérard Mellier], "Réponse en Mémoire...concernant les Nègres Esclaves..." A.D.L.-Atl., C742, no. 12.

73. On the purpose of the memoir, see the two letters of Ferrand (*Intendant* of Brittany) to Mellier, 11 July 1716 and undated 1716, copied at the end of *ibid.*; on Mellier's career, Gaston Martin, *Nantes au XVIIIe siècle: l'administration de Gérard Mellier* (Toulouse and Nantes, 1928).

74. Statistical calculations from Jean Mettas, *Répertoire des expéditions négrières françaises au XVIIIe siècle,* vol. I: *Nantes,* ed. Serge Daget (Paris, 1978), show the slave trade to have been on an ascending curve from the 1710s to the Seven Years' War, to pick up again in the very last years of the Ancien Régime. The record years of 1789 and 1790 have much to do with Nantes' sentiments concerning the abolitionist movement.

75. "Calcul sommaire...tendant à établir quel est le bénéfice de l'exemption du Demi-droit par chaque tête de Nègre", July 1767, A.D. L.-Atl., C741, no. 103.

76. André Ducasse, *Les Négriers ou le trafic des esclaves* (Paris, 1948), p. 61.

77. A substantial number of these "mascarons" can still be seen on *hôtels* in the slave traders' *quartiers* of La Fosse and Ile Feydeau.

78. One such memoir does call the slave trade a "Commerce si scabreux", but the context shows that the term is used in its eighteenth-century sense, implying risk rather that impropriety. "Mémoire des Négociants de Nantes...Envoyé à M. le Duc de Choiseul le 9 février 1764," A.D. L.-Atl., C742, no. 2.

79. Jacques Savary, *Le parfait négociant; ou Instructions générales pour ce qui regarde le commerce des marchandises de France et des pays étrangers...,* 7th ed. (Paris, 1713), p. 540; [Jacques] Savary des Bruslons, *Dictionnaire universel de commerce...,* ed. Philémon-Louis Savary, 3 vols. (Paris, 1723-1730), art. "Nègre", and *ibid.,* new ed., 5 vols. (Copenhagen, 1759-1762), art. "Commerce des côtes d'Afrique," V, 1108-22.

80. C.-F. Gaignat de L'Aulnay, *Guide du commerce* (Paris, n.d. [post-1764]), p. 309, table betw. pp. 232-33, verso, and p. 338.

81. E.g. "Addresse à Nosseigneurs de l'Assemblée Nationale..." 3 Dec. 1789, Archives de la Chambre de Commerce de Lille, Recueil de la Correspondance (5 Apr. 1786-16 Aug. 1790), pp. 93-100.

82. "Cahiers de Doléances...de la ville et comté de Nantes..." 16 Apr. 1789, A.D. L.-Atl., C580, no. 19.

83 Guinebaud de Saint-Mesme had sat as Judge on the commercial consulate of Nantes. He was relatively silent in the Assembly's colonial debates and did not say a word on slavery. Thus, the onus of defending Nantes commerce fell to a lawyer (Joseph-Michel Pellerin), who resigned early, and to a medical doctor (François-Pierre Blin). *Arch. parl.,* XXXIII, 19; Adolphe Robert *et al., Dictionnaire des parlementaires français,* 5 vols. (Paris, 1891), *passim.*

84. Unnamed deputy to Michel (Nantes *armateur*), 1 July 1789, A.D. L.-Atl., 6-JJ-22, no. 6; see also Mosneron brothers to Nantes Consulate, 2 and 15 Sept. 1789, *ibid.,* C626 (2), nos. 176 and 177. Among the deputies who contributed to the slavery debates, I have been able to identify as *négociants* only three: Begouën from Le Havre, Nairac from Bordeaux, and Roussilou from Toulouse. To these may be added Delattre (Abbeville), who had been involved in maritime trade, and the three Monneron brothers, bankers in Paris, but representing respectively the Ardèche district of Annonay, the Indian Ocean island of Ile de France, and the five French factories in India.

85. On the merchants' efforts to have themselves seated as a corps, and on the origins of the commercial commitee, see J. Letaconnaux, "Le Comité des députés extraordinaires des manufactures et du commerce et l'œuvre économique de l'Assemblée nationale, 1789-1791," *Annales de la Révolution,* VI (Mar.-Apr. 1913), 149-208; Frederick L. Nussbaum, "The Deputies Extraordinary of Commerce and the French Monarchy," *Political Science Quarterly,* XLVIII (Dec. 1933), 534-55; Jean Tarrade, "Le Groupe de pression du commerce à la fin de l'ancien régime et sous l'Assemblée constituante," *Bulletin de la Société d'histoire moderne,* 14th ser., no. 13 (1970), 23-27; Jean-Pierre Hirsch, "Les Milieux du commerce, l'esprit de système et le pouvoir à la veille de la Révolution," *Annales: Économies, Sociétés, Civilisation,* XXX:6 (Nov.-Dec. 1975), 1337-70.

86. The Mosnerons are sometimes given as Monneron, but I have chosen the former spelling, which they used, to distinguish them from the Parisian bankers, cited above, to whom they were not related. On their careers, see Steve Chaigneau, "Un exemple de mobilité sociale dans le monde de l'armement nantais: les Mosneron," D.E.S. thesis (Univ. Nantes, Fac. Lettres), 1967, espec. pp. 12-14 and 115-18; on their pre-1789 missions, Tarrade, *Le Commerce colonial*, II, 504, 519-22, 527 and 576, and A.D. L.-Atl., C626(1), nos. 95 and 96.

87. See Begouën's and Maury's interjections, Meeting of 2 Mar. 1790, *Arch. parl.*, XII, 4 and 6. For other cases, see Meetings of 28 Mar. 1790 (Charles de Lameth) and 12 and 16 May 1791 (Maury), *ibid.*, p. 383; XXVI, 12 and 123.

88. "Opinion de M. Blin..." in annex to Meeting of 2 Mar. 1790, *ibid.*, XII, 12; also Roussilou's speech, 24 Sept. 1791, *ibid.*, XXXI, 273.

89. "Opinion de M. Begouën..." in annex to Meeting of 24 Sept. 1791, *ibid.*, p. 289. On Begouën's early life and career, see Maurice Begouën-Demaux, *Mémorial d'une famille du Havre*, 4 vols. (Le Havre, 1948-1958), vols. III and IV: *La grande époque: Jacques-François Begouën, 1743-1831.*

90. Speech by Roussilou, 24 Sept. 1791, *Arch. parl.*, XXXI, 274.

91. In this, they rejoined the Left, which kept the Assembly from "dishonouring" itself by specifically using the term in its decrees (e.g. Meeting of 13 May 1791, *ibid.*, XXVI, 60-61).

92. "Opinion de M. Begouën..." *ibid.*, XXXI, 289.

93. *Réflexions sur la traite des noirs par M. Pellerin, député du Comté-Nantais* (Paris, 1790), 15 pp., in A.D. L.-Atl., 6-JJ-29, no. 80 (also reproduced in annex to Meeting of 1 Mar. 1790, *Arch. parl.*, XI, 768-71).

94. It is revealing that, precisely at the same time, light-skinned Tahitians were being extolled for having exactly the same attitude toward work that Pellerin condemned in dark-skinned peoples.

95. E.g. their Address, read to Meeting of 25 Feb. 1790. which nonetheless repeats the old saw about the West Indian climate and speaks of "ces hommes bornés [the Blacks]" *(ibid.*, XI, 699).

96. Open Letter of 16 Dec. 1789, in *Journal de Paris*, suppl. to no. 362 (28 Dec. 1789), pp. 1701-04.

97. Letter to the Editors, 17 Jan. 1790, in *ibid.*, suppl. to no. 6 (24 Jan. 1790), pp. 1-2.

98. *Discours sur les colonies et la traite des noirs, Prononcé le 26 Février 1790... à la Société des amis de la Constitution* (n.p.n.d.), in A.D. L.-Atl., 6-JJ-29, no. 70, espec. pp. 8, 10, 12-13.

99. "Mémoire sur la traite des noirs [1790?]," *ibid.*, C740, nos 123-34.

100. *Portrait du colonisé* (Montréal, 1972), pp. 75-79 and 84-89.

101. Cohen, *French Encounter*, p. 113.

102. Beatrice F. Hyslop, *French Nationalism in 1789 According to the General Cahiers* (New York, 1934), pp. 142 and 276-77.

103. McCloy, *The Negro in France*, p. 53; also p. 62.

104. Report of 23 Sept. and Speech of 24 Sept. 1791, *Arch. parl.*, XXXI, 256 and 281-82.

105. Speech of 14 May 1791, *ibid.*, XXVI, 70.

Carolyn Fick

# BLACK PEASANTS AND SOLDIERS IN THE SAINT-DOMINGUE REVOLUTION: INITIAL REACTIONS TO FREEDOM IN THE SOUTH PROVINCE (1793-4)

The Saint-Domingue revolution of 1791-1804 constituted the only successful slave revolt in history, and from it emerged the second independent nation in the New World. But more than that, the former French colony of Saint-Domingue became the first independent black nation in the long history of indigenous struggles against colonial imperialism. The struggle of the slaves was a two-fold one. While they achieved the total abolition of slavery in 1793, they did not achieve a permanent guarantee of that freedom until they had defeated and driven out the colonialist powers of Spain, Britain and, finally, France herself.

Toussaint Louverture, in many ways the most astounding black leader to emerge from that revolution, had inauspiciously joined its ranks in the fall of 1791 under the command of the two slave leaders, Jean-François and Biassou, allied with Spanish forces from Santo-Domingo.[1] When France ratified the abolition of slavery in 1794, Toussaint abandoned his black comrades and their Spanish protectors, joined the republican cause and entered the French army as brigade general. He succeeded in expelling first the Spanish, then the British forces (both at war with France since 1793) and rapidly thereafter became the chief, if not the sole, military and political authority in the colony. In 1801 he was made Governor for life, while in France Napoleon Bonaparte, now First Consul, began preparing the restoration of slavery in the French colonies.

An expeditionary army of some twelve thousand troops arrived on the shores of Saint-Domingue early in January 1802. The continuing black struggle for freedom now merged with and necessitated the struggle for national independence. During the course of this war, Toussaint was captured, deported and left to die a tragic death in an isolated prison cell in the French Alps. The task of leading the struggle for independence thus fell to Dessalines, Toussaint's staunchest general and comrade-in-arms from the early days of the revolution. After two thoroughly devastating years of war, the blacks defeated the Napoleonic army and achieved the final stage of the revolution. Independence was proclaimed on 1 January 1804. In this two-fold struggle for freedom, the mass of black laborers and their popular leaders played both an instrumental and often a decisive role.

This essay will limit itself to one aspect of that revolution in a single province, the South.[2] It will examine this popular movement, and its ideology, from the

243

vantage point of these black laborers and their chosen leaders at that stage of the revolution marked by the abolition of slavery and the transition to a semi-wage labor system.[3] First, however, a brief background account is needed to place in their historical context this particular stage of the Saint-Domingue revolution and the popular resistance movement in the South.

\*     \*

The revolution started with the revolt of a group of aristocratic white planters in the North province seeking colonial representation in the newly-convened Estates General in France. Through their representatives they aimed to achieve greater autonomy from the metropolis and to modify in their favor the restraining aspects of the Crown's mercantile policy. Opposed to them were the royalists who supported the colonial regime and its bureaucracy and were therefore against any substantial shift in power. Only after colonial representation was granted, however, did the white planters fully comprehend the inherent dangers for them, as slave owners, of being represented in a national revolutionary body. For during this time, the free mulattoes and free blacks, or *affranchis,* constituting the intermediate sectors of the population as a buffer between the white ruling class and the mass of black slaves, had organized a parallel movement for their own representatives in France and for full political and civil rights in the colony.[4] By 1791 divisions amongst the white colonists reached a peak. Another faction, calling itself the "patriot" party, had coalesced around the issue of near-total independence as a solution to the quagmire of colonial representation and the inevitable treatment of the mulatto question in the National Assembly.

On 15 May the mulattoes won a partial victory with the passage by the Assembly of a decree granting political equality to those *affranchis* born of free parents and who possessed the requisite age and property requirements. The white colonists reacted with fear and violence. In the name of white supremacy, they forgot their differences and hastily formed a united front to subvert the application of the 15 May law. To allow even a few mulattoes to vote would immediately open the whole question of those mulattoes still in slavery or born of only one free parent, and from there, they believed, the abolition of slavery would be but a step away. The entire social and economic structure of the colony -- slavery itself and the fortunes derived from it--were at stake. Thus the mulattoes, in their defense against the inevitable violent onslaughts directed against them by the white colonists, now turned to armed rebellion. A few months earlier, the slaves in the North had already revolted massively and were by this time in control of most of that province.

\*     \*

That the slaves were fighting for their freedom when they revolted in 1791 can hardly be denied. And while freedom may be the political watchword of most revolutions, for the black slave masses of Saint-Domingue it had a particular meaning, grounded in the human realities of slavery. For the slave freedom meant, first of all, freedom from his material conditions; that is to say, from the absolute rule of the master and from a system of lifelong forced labor, regimented by the whip and controlled by fear. Secondly, it entailed the liberty to do with that freedom as he wished. In short, it meant (his) private ownership of both the land upon which he labored and the fruits of his own labor. Thus, for the inarticulate slave, freedom was not a philosophical concept or ideal, nor was it a complex existential problem. It was a concrete reality that he strove to create for himself, a reality emerging from and at the same time opposed to the very conditions of his existence as a slave. The initial reactions and resistence of the black laborers to the official abolition of slavery in the South province offer us a glimpse of how they themselves perceived their freedom and their future, and also illuminate the substance of that freedom for which they had so bitterly and so tenaciously fought.[5]

When the mulattoes revolted for political equality in the West and the South, they had solicited the support of the black slaves, armed them and extended varying promises: of freedom, three free days per week, and even, in one instance, the sharing of plantation profits once the whites were defeated — anything to get them to join their ranks and increase their forces. Actually, a rumor had been circulating throughout the colony since early 1791 that the King had granted the slaves three free days per week, but that it was the white masters who refused to consent. Though the precise origins of the rumor are somewhat unclear, what is certain is that it was capably used both by the slave leaders in the North as a political organizational tool for their revolt of August 1791 and by the mulattoes inciting the blacks in the West and South to join them.[6] The rumor was, of course, false, but it represented the nearest thing to freedom they knew; they accepted it as a fact and expected its application as a right.[7]

The slaves in the West and the South had not yet entered the revolution as an independently organized, collective force, as did their rebel counterparts in the North. By the beginning of 1792, however, those in the South had been swept from one end of the province to the other into the armed struggles of the mulattoes, whose diverse promises of freedom corresponded to their own independent aspirations to be free.[8] On the other side were the white planters who, without adequate military support in the face of the widespread and growing revolts of the *affranchis* and their slave allies in the South, had in turn freed a portion of their own slaves and armed them to defend the white masters.[9] So the slaves in the South were now fighting each other in enemy camps and at the same time were rapidly acquiring valuable military skills and political experience. It was from this situation, then, that they emerged as the active agents of their own struggle for freedom, organized on their own terms and directed by their own popular leaders.

By the end of the summer of 1792 a new stage was reached. News had reached the colony of the 4 April decree passed by the National Assembly in France according full and unconditional rights of French citizenship to all free persons of color. In addition, France would send a civil commission accompanied by six thousand troops to restore order and ensure the application of French law in the colony. A tremendous victory for the mulattoes, it was but the beginning of the armed struggle of the slaves in the South who, as in the West, were now to be disarmed, disbanded and sent back to work on the plantations as before.

Encamped in the mountainous region known as les Platons were a considerable number of slaves who, still armed and taking advantage of their position, refused to surrender their arms and organized themselves in open opposition to the proclamation ordering them to return to their respective plantations.[10] Whether armed by the mulattoes or by the whites, their experience in arms had transformed them. They had fought as equals and considered themselves free; to return now to their plantations to work as they had before, as slaves, was impossible. By the end of July they were over four thousand strong and their numbers continued to increase as slaves from the surrounding plantations deserted throughout the summer to join their forces.[11]

The two most prominent slave leaders, Armand, a *commandeur* (the head man or foreman of the field slaves) from the Berault estate, and Martial, known as Maréchal, from the Pemerle plantation, put forth their demands to the provincial and military authorities: freedom for three hundred of their leaders; three free days per week for every slave; and the abolition of the whip as a means of punishment.[12] Seven hundred of these who had been armed by the mulattoes were offered freedom, but only after they had totally defeated a military expedition launched against them in August.[13] The majority of the slaves, however, remained entrenched at Platons along with Armand and Martial, in addition to several other major popular leaders, Jacques Formon, Félix, Gilles Bénech and Bernard. By January, 1793, when a second expedition was led against them, they constituted a fully organized maroon community of ten to twelve thousand men, women and children.[14] In their defense, they had built entrenchments of earth or rock above mountain precipices descending three thousand feet or more.[15] They built homes for themselves; in fact, as one astonished soldier reported, there were as many cabins here as there were houses in les Cayes. They constructed two infirmaries for the sick; the soil permitting, they began to grow crops and stockpile food supplies.[16] They had, in effect, begun a rudimentary form of civil government, calling their newly acquired territory the Kingdom of Platons and choosing for themselves a ruler whom they designated as King.[17] During the January 1793 attack that finally dislodged them, they made their attitudes clear, treating the attacking soldiers as the "brigands", and telling them

> ...'nous après tandé zaute,' which is to say, we had expected you, and we will cut off your heads to the last man; and that this land is not for you, it is for us.[18]

Although the bulk of the civilian population was dispersed, the armed nucleus of the movement, including all of the principal leaders as well as the ablest and most experienced of the insurgent slaves -- several thousand in all -- retreated higher into the mountains at Macaya where they remained in armed camps for yet another seven to eight months.[19]

By that summer the entire colony had been driven to a state of administrative chaos. Both Britain and Spain had declared war against France and were now her official enemies. What this meant was that the counter-revolutionary royalists in the colony now had powerful foreign allies. The rebel slaves in the North, led by Jean-François and Biassou and allied with Spain, were already in possession of most of that province. British forces, already in control of the western extremities of the colony, were beginning to make dangerous inroads into the interior. The salvation of the colony for France depended directly upon winning over the black rebel armies to the republican side. This could only be done by guaranteeing them, in the name of the French government, that freedom they had already in fact acquired through armed struggle. In a desperate move, the civil commissioners, Léger Sonthonax and Etienne Polverel, sent by France the previous year to restore order to the colony, issued a proclamation on 21 June 1793 guaranteeing freedom and full rights of citizenship to all slaves in the North who would join in the defense of France against her enemies.[20]

On 25 July the same offer was extended to all slaves in the South who had fought in arms, whether for the whites or for the mulattoes, as well as to the Macaya insurgents who were still armed to conquer their freedom and who would deliver their arms, "...including Armand, Martial, Jacques Formon, Gilles Bénech and the other leaders."[21] Their freedom depended, however, upon two conditions. First, they would be enrolled in companies or "legions of equality" to fight for France as an integral part of the French army; secondly, as an "indispensable duty", they would have to make the rest of the slaves return to their respective plantation and assure that order and a regular work rhythm be maintained.

The initial reactions of the slaves and their leaders to the 25 July decree were mixed. While all of the principal slave leaders accepted the government's offer of conditional freedom and were made company captains, they remained nonetheless skeptical, distrustful and, as for Jacques Formon, openly defiant.[22] In fact, he alone of the principal leaders remained consistently faithful to the original goals of their revolutionary struggle, though it later cost him his life.[23] André Rigaud, the leading mulatto spokesman in the colony and military head of the Legion of Equality in the South, singled Jacques out as the most uncompromising of the leaders:

> Under the pretext of carrying out the orders I gave him to make all of the slaves from Macaya come down and return to work, he would visit various plantations and play the Tartuffe, delivering speeches to the slaves, telling them to work and not to go up into the mountains anymore. I have been assured that those under his command have incited them to do just the opposite.[24]

Armand, Martial, Bernard and Gilles Bénech seemed the most inclined to conform to the conditions of their new role. But the majority of the rebel slaves from Macaya, those who were destined to return to the plantations as slaves, were furious over their leaders' acquiescence in the government's offer of freedom, an act by which they rightly felt betrayed. At one point, they even took Armand and Gilles prisoner.[25] When they finally did descend, they promised to be obedient and submissive, but continued to pillage and ransack the plantations, and here and there were even audacious enough to disarm a white planter.[26]

Within the ranks of the Legion, Rigaud complained only two weeks after the 25 July decree that the new citizens "were still given over to committing acts unworthy of their new condition; they spread themselves out over the plantations, attempting to destroy citizens' property."[27] The *légionnaires* were chronically being arrested and imprisoned in the les Cayes jails for crimes ranging from insubordination, refusal to obey orders, and agitation, to horse thievery and even desertion.[28] These initial forms of resistance characterized the mood and temperament of the newly emancipated black soldiers who, having taken up arms and risked their lives in open revolt to obtain their freedom, now constituted the rank and file of the French army. The total abolition of slavery was but a step away. Sonthonax had already proclaimed general emancipation in the North on 29 August, an act which Polverel did not fully endorse until 21 September in the West and 10 October in the South.

For the black laborers, however, the new system of emancipation brought with it very few changes in material conditions, and fell far short of their own expectations and aspirations. Among these, the desire for land remained foremost. What the ex-slaves were aiming at may perhaps best be summed up as subsistence farming based upon the individual, or personal, ownership of small property; or, put in another way, the freedom to possess and to till their own soil, to labor for themselves according to their own needs and to dispose, in their own interest, of the products of their labor.

The transitional system instituted by Polverel flew directly in the face of these aspirations. First of all, the ex-slaves were forced to remain on their respective plantations and to continue working for their former masters, as before; the plantations would remain undivided; the whip as a form of punishment was abolished and would be replaced by a forthcoming penal code. The new system would be regulated by a work code that systematically delineated the specific hours and conditions of work, as well as the proportional salaries of the laborers.[29] They still had to work six days per week from sunrise to sundown, their only free day besides holidays being Sunday, as under slavery. They could no longer be whipped, mutilated or tortured as they were in the past, for if the work code carried restrictions upon the activities of the worker, it also limited the extent of the authority the former owner could exercise. The latter now had to use the force of persuasion to make recalcitrant workers produce.

To make this freedom meaningful, Polverel included in his system of emancipation certain "property rights" for the ex-slaves. They were, according to the commissioner, to be "co-owners" of the land to which they were assigned and would receive collectively one-third of the net plantation revenues. Whereas as slaves they had received nothing for their work, now they would receive a small recompense as an incentive to increase production and thereby, theoretically at least, to increase their own revenues as well. So instead of being the property of the master and of having only the illusory incentive of an eventual grant of freedom by a humane master, the blacks were now legally free persons and were given a minimal pay incentive; yet they were still legally bound to specific plantations. Though the mode of production, and consequently the set of social and economic relationships prevalent under slavery, had been altered, the change had little effect upon the mentality, the aspirations and the predispositions of the workers. One thing however, had fundamentally changed: they were now free persons. And they defined what that meant to them through their demands and their acts of resistance to Polverel's system, especially during the initial period of administrative chaos when the work codes were not yet published.

In the preamble to his 7 February 1794 proclamation on wage allocation and distribution of agricultural produce between the owners and the laborers, Polverel spoke of the "errors" the workers had committed during the first months following emancipation.[30] On some plantations, they took advantage of the absence of the owner and the relative state of abandon in which he left his plantation to expand the size of the small lots provided them under slavery for subsistence. In this way they began cultivating portions of the plantation property for their own use. They also helped themselves to the uncultivated fruit of the land such as wood, fodder and other products that grew spontaneously and that existed abundantly in a natural state. They also helped themselves to the plantation rations and sold what they could at the market, using the horses and mules belonging to the plantation for personal pleasure and to carry their stolen goods to market. On some plantations, the workers had effectively taken over the land for themselves. As they were organized in brigades, each group would cultivate that portion of the land assigned to it, and the workers would then sell the products that were superfluous to their needs.

The problems for the administration were even more acute on plantations that had been sequestered from émigré planters who had fled the revolution. In the parish of les Cotteaux, a group of blacks had established itself on the abandoned Condé plantation. They cut down, burned and literally devastated the coffee grove to build houses for themselves in its place.[31] Now that they were free, it seemed only logical that the land they had labored on for so long should rightfully belong to them.

On those plantations where the owner or a manager was present and where a somewhat regular work schedule was imposed, the most persistent of the workers' demands was the five-day working week. Under slavery, their only day off was Sunday; they now expected that to change and demanded Saturday as a free day, too. But they often refused to work altogether; they arrived in the fields late in the morning and quit early in the evening. When they did work, their work was slack and unproductive. They often resisted the new system as they had resisted slavery, by running away, or becoming fugitives.

The women, too, were now demanding equal pay for equal work. As slaves, they had worked in the fields alongside the men and under the same conditions. Now, as laborers receiving a recompense, their role in the work force was no different and, excepting pregnancy and childbirth, they were subject to the same regulations as their male co-workers, but received only two-thirds the pay: Why should we receive less pay than the men? Do we come to work later than they? Do we leave earlier? They might have added: Do we not receive the same punishments as the men for refusing to work? Simply stated, the women saw themselves as laborers. Moreover, they were not fighting against the men but against the new system and its inequalities. The men apparently raised no objections to the women's demands. In fact, Polverel had to try to convince the men they should put these women back in their "proper place".[32]

According to the stipulations of the work code, the workers' collective allocation of one-third the plantation revenue would be based solely upon an arduous six-day work week. When the question was later put to them in accordance with Article 23 of the work code, a good number of them persisted in demanding the five-day work week. The owners or managers of each plantation were instructed to read and explain intelligibly to the assembled workers and *conducteurs,* or foremen, both the preamble and the articles concerning the work expected of them, as well as the allocated earnings due to them. If they agreed to work a full six-day week, they would receive collectively one-third of the net profits. If, in addition to Sunday, they chose to take one day per week for themselves, their collective revenues would be cut by one-half; if they desired more than two free days per week, they would get nothing at all and would be removed, by force if necessary, from the plantation. In the parish of Cavaillon, just outside the Plaine-Des-Cayes, the workers on one plantation out of three adamantly insisted upon a five-day work week, reserving Saturday for themselves, even after they were reminded that their earnings would be reduced to one-sixth.[33]

Of course one cannot hope to make any sort of statistically precise generalization as to worker attitudes toward the six-day week throughout the province based on the reports of just one parish. The type of plantation and the specific nature of the work required are significant factors that might influence the decisions of the workers on the number of days they would want to work. However, based on the evidence available, it seems the five-day work week was not an uncommon or untypical desire, at least among the black workers in this middle region of the South, an area where insurrectionary activity was always particularly prominent.[34] More than that, the demand for the five-day week was something entirely new. For the blacks, as laborers, it was an attempt at defining for themselves and at controlling, even though in a limited way, their own working conditions within the new system.

At this point one may be tempted to interpret these acts of resistance as merely the ephemeral expression of exuberance on the part of the newly-freed blacks at being free, or as a "test", as it were, of the extent and validity of their freedom. Yet, following the publication of the 7 February work code and the accompanying penal code of 28 February, the black workers continued to resist in great numbers and in a variety of ways.[35] Most often, workers were punished with imprisonment and forced labor on public works without pay, the length of time depending upon the gravity of the offense. For example, according to the 28 February police code for plantation workers, disobedience or refusal to carry out the orders of one's superior warranted a sentence of one month for a field worker and twice that for a secondary *conducteur*. If a subordinate threatened his or her superior, either with words or by gesture, he or she would receive a two-month sentence, while that of a secondary *conducteur* was double. In the case of an armed threat, the corresponding punishments were tripled. If a worker or subordinate actually carried out his threat by striking the head *conducteur*, he would then be removed from the plantation for the remainder of the year, arrested and tried by a civil court. If the majority of the workers on a plantation were guilty of any one of the above offenses, the entire work force would be sent away and replaced by the owner with day laborers.[36]

Another common form of resistance was theft. Here, the thief was required to pay into the plantation treasury the value of the stolen goods; in addition, he or she would pay the same value again, this time as a fine. Half was given to the informer, half to the government. If the stolen products were from the rations storehouse or were among the uncultivated fruits of the land growing freely but belonging to the plantation, the fines would be evaluated at the potential market value of the products. For stealing or "borrowing" a plantation animal, the thief would be fined a given sum per day until the animal was returned, the fine depending upon the animal's utility. Here, as for ordinary thievery, a second fine was imposed and divided between the informer and the government. Damage to any form of plantation property was treated in the same way as theft.

Naturally, plantation workers who resisted the regulations of the work code almost never had sufficient funds to cover their fines. Thus they purged their sentences in prison and labored on public works until such time as their potential earnings, based on the inferior wage-rate for public workers, equalled the amount they owed. If they repeated an offense after this, they would be removed from the plantation, declared unworthy of participation in the plantation community, imprisoned and sentenced to public works without pay for one year.[37]

Despite these coercive regulations, punishments and incentives, many black workers openly refused to submit themselves to a system of regimented labor. The most immediate and the most widespread form of resistance was, as one may expect, the refusal to work, usually practiced by individual workers or groups of workers in varying numbers, and occasionally even by entire plantation labor forces.[38] Often workers were caught breaking or damaging the sugar cane in order to get out of work or to lighten the work load. For the same reasons, they continually deserted their assigned plantation to attach themselves to another where, depending upon the nature of the plantation, the type of work required would be less intensive. Or simply, they might desert to another plantation, there to hide out and not work at all.[39] While some remained errant in various regions throughout the plain, others sought refuge in the military camps in the mountainous areas where they could be sheltered by their black comrades in the Legion. In a letter to Salomon, the military commander of les Cayes, Sonthonax gave orders to have three runaway workers from the Collet plantation arrested and sentenced to public works: "I have been told that you might be able to find them in the cabin of a *légionnaire* named Zamore, formerly belonging to the Collet plantation...."[40] Some workers were even audacious enough to pass themselves off as *légionnaires.* Petit, commander at Camp Périn, wrote to ask Polverel to designate a plantation for over fifty workers who had tried to infiltrate the ranks of two companies, specifying that the plantation should be a safe distance from the camp. In less than two weeks he wrote Polverel again, stating that he had arrested and was sending back twenty-nine black soldiers from the same two companies, to be reintegrated into the plantations: "It is absolutely necessary that they be uprooted from the military milieu."[41]

On most plantations, insubordination was more often the rule than the exception. The hierarchy of labor established under slavery and perpetuated by the work code placed the *conducteur,* a black and an ex-slave like the workers, in a position of direct authority over the latter. And, as in the days of slavery, the *conducteur* often played a pivotal role vis-à-vis the mass of workers in his charge. Thus production or resistance generally hinged upon his inclinations and pre-dispositions, as well as the strength of his influence over the workers. In some cases, the relationship between the *conducteur* and the workers might be one of solidarity. For example, on the sequestered Champtois plantation in the Plaine-du-Fond, indolence, refusal to work and insubordination among the workers were seriously hindering production. Polverel sent Petit to visit the plantation and arrest the agitators. Having assembled the workers, he discovered the *conducteur* was absent and sent one of his soldiers to bring him back from the nearby plantation where he had spent the night. Petit demanded that the *conducteur* denounce on the spot the six worst troublemakers. The *conducteur* refused to name a single one and was arrested along with four others finally singled out by the second *conducteur.*[42]

On the other hand, as an authority figure, as the one responsible for executing the orders of the manager or owner, the *conducteur* was often taken to task by dissenting or resisting workers. Sometimes worker insubordination resulted directly from the *conducteur* either surpassing his authority or being forced by the manager-steward to mistreat his charges.[43] In many instances, though, workers simply refused to obey the legitimate orders of the *conducteur* and usually accompanied their refusal with verbal threats and slanderous insults; a few even backed up their threats with arms. Nearly every plantation throughout the plain had agitators and proselytizers of this sort, and one or two sufficed to disrupt the already irregular rhythm of work.[44]

The newly enfranchised slaves expressed through their acts -- including refusal of night work on the sugar plantations, thefts of plantation products, prison escapes and subsequent flights into hiding -- what they thought of Polverel's type of freedom, of his work code and of the new regime. They were now workers and free citizens; and yet this freedom had brought about no fundamental change in the system of production, and only insufficient change in their relationship to the products of their labor. The land did not belong to them. Polverel had made that explicitly clear in his 7 February proclamation. When they took surplus crops to market, when they started using portions of the plantation to expand their own minimal plots of land, they were merely taking and appropriating for themselves what they felt rightly belonged to them by virtue of their constant labor under slavery. This attitude was, as we have seen, most vigourously expressed by the slaves while defending the Platons region they had conquered with arms in 1792-3.[45] They would work, and would work cheerfully, but only if it meant that they were the independent owners of the land they cultivated, of their own labor and the fruits of that labor. For better or worse, this was how they felt, and neither Polverel nor Sonthonax, nor even Toussaint Louverture, could ever substantially change that mentality. Polverel now told them point-blank: "This land does not belong to you. It belongs to those who purchased it [or] to those who inherited it from the original owners..."; in other words, to their former masters.[46]

This contradiction between the aspirations of the newly freed black laborers and the harsh realities imposed by the system had generated certain patterns of resistance and had stimulated a sense of solidarity. So, when the workers pillaged the plantation rations, they used their own methods of dividing them up; if they sold stolen surplus, it was often for the benefit of other workers. They covered up for one another, organized themselves to help get a co-worker out of prison; they sheltered their comrades who had run away or who were being pursued. And if disobedience and flagrant insubordination toward one's superior were common, the incidence of *conducteurs* being arrested along with groups of workers was equally common, despite the increased severity of their sentences.[47]

Among the former slave leaders of the earlier Platons insurrection many had become company captains, either in the Legion of Equality or in the local militia units that had been created to police the countryside and maintain the subordination of the black workers to the new work regime. But workers and soldiers often carried out acts of resistance in mutual complicity. As we have already seen, it was not uncommon for a *légionnaire* to provide shelter for fugitive workers. At the same time, *légionnaires* could be found agitating amongst the workers on the plantations: Beauregard, military commander of Cavaillon, wrote to Polverel concerning the effect of his 28 February proclamation on the plantations he visited. He discovered several workers who, having disrupted the working order on their own plantations, had taken cover on various others. Along with these agitators, he found two deserters from the Legion

...who serve as models of indolence for the rest.... It would be impossible for me to depict the new order of things without making mention of the runaways, and I would not be surprised at all, citizen commissioner, if before long the runaways follow one another with the same rapidity as in the days of despotism. That, effectively, is the success of the regenerating principles of liberty, equality and humanity.[48]

Nicolas, a dragoon in the Legion of Equality, was arrested in early April and sentenced to public works without pay "until all the plantation workers in the parish of Baynet return to an orderly, disciplined work routine". On the same day, thirty-one workers, including the two *conducteurs* from the La Cour plantation in Baynet, were arrested along with Nicolas.[49] Yet imprisoned workers would sometimes escape under the dissimulating eye of the black militia guards responsible for their surveillance.[50]

The subversive activities of the *légionnaires* were not always covert, and in one instance would have resulted in armed rebellion had the plot not been discovered. Under the leadership of Apollon, a lieutenant in the local militia at Petit-Goâve, the blacks on several plantations around the area had organized mass meetings to oppose an ordinance published by Faubert, a mulatto division commander of the Legion in the South. The ordinance concerned an aspect of the·work code and had originally come from Polverel, but Faubert had rewritten it so as to make it harsher than Polverel had ever intended. Apollon knew this and made it known to the workers that it was a false proclamation. However, his underlying purpose in organizing these gatherings was to agitate the workers, using this issue as grounds to assassinate Faubert.[51] As a popular leader, Apollon had been actively agitating for quite some time amongst those he was supposed to police. Polverel said of him that

...his spirit of domination and insubordination, his influence over the Africans and the misuse he has been making of that influence, the stockpiles of powder and cartridges that he had accumulated behind the backs of his superiors, prove that he had been contemplating armed rebellion for a long time.[52]

Given the high rate of insubordination, indolence and persistent resistance to his work code among the black workers of the Plaine-du-Fond, especially on the sequestered plantations. Polverel had found it necessary to introduce additional measures of control. At the end of March, he established a team of regional inspectors, each inspector being responsible for the surveillance of a given number of plantations. The commissioner believed that to increase their productivity, the workers needed only to be directed by men who knew the nature of the land, the temperature, the climate, the variations of the seasons, the influence of these variations upon production, and the type of agriculture best suited to the Plaine-du-Fond. These supervisors would stimulate the "lazy", denounce insubordination to the authorities, stir the zeal of the managers and reinforce the discipline demanded by the *conducteurs.* Above all, they would be chosen from actual or former agricultural laborers.[53]

Of the principal insurrectionary leaders of the Platons revolt of 1792-3, Armand and Bernard were perhaps the most diligent in carrying out their new duties as captains in the Legion and members of the French army. And so, for "their zeal, talents and intelligence," they were both chosen, along with six others, as regional inspectors.[54] For the time being, Martial and Gilles Bénech retained the positions they occupied in the Legion. Jacques Formon, the most uncompromising of the popular leaders, had already been court-martialled and shot for perpetuating insurrectionary activity and refusing to follow Rigaud's leadership.[55]

This, then, was the republic's new army of black peasants and soldiers, and it was upon them that the government depended to sustain the war against the counter-revolutionary colonists and their foreign allies, Britain and Spain, now in military possession of the greater part of the colony. The defense of Saint-Domingue depended upon the black army, but without the arduous and constant labor of the agricultural workers, the government, as the commissioners realized, "would have neither the rations with which to feed the soldier nor the revenue with which to pay his salary."[56] If the attitudes, aspirations and activities of a considerable portion of the blacks in the South ran counter to the pressing economic and military necessities of the situation, they nevertheless were the direct product of slavery itself. The new system of freedom, in spite of its incentives, had done little to change the conditions out of which these aspirations emerged.

\*     \*

For the black laborer, the desire for land was a necessary and an essential part of his vision of freedom. For without land and the possibility to work for himself and his own family, freedom for the ex-slave was more a legal abstraction than a concrete reality. To continue to labor for others, to be tied in perpetuity to property that was not his own, meant he was not entirely free. One is reminded here of the aspirations of the Platons rebels who, having developed a vast maroon community in the mountains, had dared to demand full territorial rights to the region. During the transitional period from the abolition of slavery to the institution of the new labor system, some ex-slaves had literally appropriated the land and its products in what may seem on the surface to be a somewhat chaotic, almost anarchistic, manner. Underlying these activities, however, one can discern a distinct aspiration toward economic self-determination.

Within the system itself, popular protest may be seen as an attempt by the ex-slaves, insofar as it was materially possible, to define for themselves and to control in some measure their own working conditions. The demand on the part of some laborers for the five-day work week; the women's demand for equal pay; the refusal of night work on the sugar plantation — all were attempts to impose their independent will upon the restrictions of a system that did not seem too far removed from slavery. Popular resistance was even carried to the brink of organized armed rebellion (as in the case of the *légionnaire* Apollon) in order to safeguard their rights under the new system.

Following this transitional period, the civil commissioners had been recalled to France, thus leaving the South to the political and economic domination of a mulatto elite that, in fact, maintained its hegemony well into the post-revolutionary era. In part because of the South's isolation from the ongoing political and military upheavals of the revolution in the rest of the colony, the autonomous protest movements of the blacks had markedly subsided. However, during the French expedition to restore slavery, and the ensuing war for independence, these movements resurfaced, at first clandestinely and then gradually proliferating until a province-wide network of resistance was formed. And it was this popular resistance, once again in the name of freedom, that had prepared the groundwork for the military liberation of the South and the final defeat of the French troops.

Permanent freedom from colonial slavery had been won through independence, but the deeply entrenched aspirations of the masses for land ownership were left to be fulfilled. In the North the preservation of the large estates that had formed the base of the colonial economy was generally fostered, while the task of land distribution was never seriously undertaken until the presidency of Alexander Pétion (1807-1818) in the South.[57] Here the persistent demands of the black Haitian masses for small property ownership had forced Pétion to effect a stabilizing compromise between the politically hegemonic mulatto elite and the economically dispossessed masses. From 1809 on, a series of measures were passed involving the parcellization and distribution of state land, previously owned by white colonists, to officers and soldiers of the army, as well as to civil servants, invalids, and even squatters.[58] On the other hand, the large coffee estates -- and therefore a monopoly of the colony's single most important export crop since the demise of sugar -- remained in the hands of the dominant mulatto elite that had now replaced the white planter class of colonial days.

Though many a slave had by now made the transition to landed peasant in an economy that tended, on one level, toward peasant proprietorship and strict subsistence farming, many more were left to struggle for their survival, as they had in the past and would continue to do into the future. The nature of that struggle in Haiti today is not much changed, but the solutions to it will, of necessity, be fundamentally different.

# *NOTES*

1. At this time, the French colony of Saint-Domingue, the present-day Haiti, occupied the western half of the island of Hispaniola; the Spanish Colony of Santo-Domingo, today the Dominican Republic, comprised the eastern half.

2. In the eighteenth century Saint-Domingue was divided into three regional and administrative units, referred to as the North, the West and the South provinces.

3. The transitional labor system that replaced slavery in the colony was neither wholly a free labor system nor was it, strictly speaking, a system of share-cropping. The emancipated black laborers were paid a wage for their labor, but were bound to their respective plantations by yearly contracts. For a fuller discussion of this transitional system, see pp. 247-52 below.

4. Though legally free, the *affranchis* existed in a state of public bondage, or "public property," by virtue of a wide range of discriminatory legislation rendering impossible their assimilation into white society. See Auguste Lebeau, *De la condition des gens de couleur libres sous l'ancien régime* (Poitiers: Masson, 1903) and Beauvais Lespinasse, *Histoire des affranchis de Saint-Domingue,* 2 vols. (Paris: Kugelman, 1882), vol. I.

   The population figures for Saint-Domingue on the eve of the revolution run roughly as follows: 30,826 whites, 27,548 *affranchis* and 465,429 slaves. See M. Placide-Justin,

*Histoire politique et statistique de l'île d'Hayti* (Paris: Brière, 1826), p. 144. In the West, the *affranchis* were nearly as numerous as the whites and in the South were in the majority.

5. While similar studies dealing with the same problems may be undertaken for the other two provinces, the abundance of prison records, official registers, reports and correspondence for this transitional period, located in the Archives Nationales (Paris) and the Public Record Office (London), lends itself most readily to a particular study of the South, a province too often neglected in the general histories of the Saint-Domingue revolution. See also, Adolphe Cabon, *Histoire d'Haiti,* 4 vols. (Port-au-Prince: Éditions de la Petite Revue, 192?-1940), 3:145-186 and 4:80-87. Paul Moral, *Le paysan haitien, étude sur la vie rurale en Haiti* (Paris: Maisonneuve et Larose, 1961), pp. 12-17. Gérard Laurent, *Quand les chaines volent en éclats: un moment de réflexion* (Port-au-Prince: Imp. Deschamps), pp. 131-191 and Annexes 3 and 6 pp. 215-231 and 242-278 respectively.

6. See J. Ph. Garran-Coulon, *Rapport sur les troubles de Saint-Domingue,* Commission des Colonies, 4 vols. (Paris: Imp. Nationale, 1795) 2:211-12.

7. In fact, the slaves of the Port-Salut/les Cayes districts in the middle region of the South had, as early as January 1791 -- six months prior to the massive slave insurrection in the North -- organized a rebellion precisely around the demand for three free days per week. AN DXXV 63, 638. Extrait des registres de l'Assemblée Provinciale du Sud, les Cayes, 21 janv. 1791. The slaves' demand for three free days per week persisted throughout the colony during the early stages of the revolution up to general emancipation. It was used as strategy in negotiations with the colonial authorities and was put forward, once again, by organized rebel slaves in the South in 1792. See pp. 249-50, below. See also Garran-Coulon, *Rapport, 2:570.*

8. AN DXXV 61, 613. Extrait des pièces déposées aux archives de l'Assemblée Coloniale. La Municipalité de Torbeck à MM. de l'Assemblée Coloniale, signé, St. Martin, maire *et al.,* Torbeck, 15 janv. 1792. DXXV 61, 613. Conseil Général de la commune de Tiburon et de Dame-Marie réunies à l'Assemblée Coloniale, signé, Gachet *et al.,* Tiburon, 29 janv. 1792. DXXV 62, 626. L'Assemblée Provinciale du Sud à l'Assemblée Coloniale, les Cayes, 5 janv. 1792. DXXV 61, 613. Assemblée Provinciale du Sud à l'Assemblée Coloniale, les Cayes, 26 janv. 1792. DXXV 63, 638. Adresse de l'Assemblée provisoirement adminis-trative de la partie du Sud à l'Assemblée Nationale de France, signé, Billard, prés., Les Cayes, n.d. DXXV 63, 637. Adresse de l'Assemblée Provinciale et provisoirement administrative du Sud à l'Assemblée Nationale de France, les Cayes, 23 fév. 1792.

9. On 25 December 1792, the Provincial Assembly of the South approved a decree from the municipalities of Torbeck and les Cayes to arm one-tenth of their slaves in defense of the white masters against the mulattoes and free blacks. AN DXXV, 61, 637. Adresse de l'Assemblée Provinciale et provisoirement administrative du Sud, les Cayes, 23 fév. 1792. DXXV 62, 626. L'assemblée Provinciale du Sud à l'Assemblée Coloniale, les Cayes, 5 janv. 1792. Pauléus Sannon, *Histoire de Toussaint L'Ouverture,* 3 vols. (Port-au-Prince: A. Héraux, 1920), 1:102.

10. The word *platons* was generally used in reference to mountain gorges, and because of its multiplicity of gorges and precipices, this particular area of the South came to be designated as a distinct region, les Platons. See Garran-Coulon, *Rapport,* 2: 582-83.

11. AN DXXV 66, 671. La municipalité des Cayes à M. Delaval, député de la paroisse des Cayes à l'Assemblée Coloniale et secrétaire de sa députation, les Cayes, 27 juillet 1792.

12. Garran-Goulon, *Rapport,* 2:570. These demands were similar to those put forward in November 1791 by Jean-François and Biassou in the North. The slaves never demanded the outright abolition of slavery by means of negotiation. Rather, the slaves proceeded tactically with limited demands and thus contributed to the creation of a situation for which general emancipation later became the only solution.

13. *Ibid.,* 3:151. Their freedom was, however, conditional upon their enrolment into contingents to police the countryside and maintain order among the slaves on the plantations. It should be mentioned, though, that only 350-400 of the slaves accepted the offer of freedom. PRO HCA 30, 393. Demoncour to Meunier, les Cayes, 22 Dec. 1792.

HCA 30 393, 238. M. Bergeaud to M. Faucher, Cayes St. Louis, 16 Jan. 1793. HCA 30 393, 248. Ferrand to Salenave, aîné, les Cayes, 30 Nov. 1792. The slaves knew that under colonial law only a master could officially grant freedom, and so unshakeable was their desire for permanent freedom that nearly half of them refused to accept an affidavit signed by Rigaud and the Provincial Assembly, an act that, in times of political upheaval such as these, might later be nullified.

14. In plantation slave societies, the maroons were fugitive or runaway slaves. Within the broader context of the revolutionary upheavals in Saint-Domingue after 1791 the desertion of the slaves from the plantations became an integral part of their collective struggle, culminating in general emancipation.

15. PRO HCA 30 394, 8. Dubreil to LeJeune, Cayes St. Louis, 19 Jan. 1793.

16. PRO HCA 30 394, 15. Billard, fils to Mmes. Billard, Moreau et Amand Billard, les Cayes, 16 Jan. 1793. Also, HCA 30 395, 143. Dubreil to citoyenne Piquot, les Cayes, 17 Jan. 1793. HCA 30 394, 8. Dubreil to LeJeune, Cayes St. Louis, 19 Jan. 1793. HCA 30 392, 146. R. Bouard to Dervillé, les Cayes, 14 Jan. 1793.

17. PRO HCA 30 394, 8. Dubreil to LeJeune, Cayes St. Louis, 19 Jan. 1793. Actually, full territorial possession of les Platons had, at one point, been put forward by Armand during the negotiations with the colonial authorities following their crushing defeat of the first expedition in August 1792. Garran-Coulon, *Rapport,* 2:610.

18. PRO HCA 30 393, 189. Gensterbloom to his mother, les Cayes, 16 Jan. 1793. (Author's translation. Unless otherwise indicated, all other translations of French passages will be those of the present writer.)

19. One colonist placed their numbers at over three thousand. PRO HCA 30 392, 34. H. Duvau to M. Duvau, les Cayes, 17 Jan. 1793. Also, HCA 30 392, 129. Sainet to Mme. veuve Sainet, les Cayes, 19 Jan. 1793. HCA 30 395, 254. St. Martin to Duplessy, les Cayes, 16 Jan. 1793. Among those who chose not to retreat to Macaya, a considerable proportion had divided themselves into bands and remained as maroons around the plantations of the area; others returned to their masters seeking pardon. However, it is nearly impossible to accurately determine how many actually did return. While one colonist reported that they were very few in number, another estimated their numbers had reached roughly three thousand. PRO HCA 30 393, 5. F. Peche to Mme. Peche, Fond de l'Isle-à-Vache, 17 Jan. 1793 and HCA 30 392, 55. Martin to M. Party, n.p. (?Jan. 1793).

20. AN DXXV 40, 400. Registre servant à la transcription des proclamations, ordonnances et autres actes de la commission civile, imprimés depuis le 13 juin jusqu'au 13 mai 1794, Haut du Cap, 21 juin 1793. The civil commission, composed of three members, Sonthonax, commissioner for the North, Polverel for the West, and Ailhaud for the South, arrived in the colony in September 1792. The latter member abandoned his post after one month in the colony, leaving the administration of both the West and the South to Polverel. The commissioners were accompanied with six thousand troops to ensure the application of the 4 April 1792 decree [see p. 245, above.] and to defeat the slave insurrections throughout the colony. Within two months, over half of these troops were killed off by the climate.

21. AN DXXV 97, 849, Ds. 18. Proclamation de Polverel et Sonthonax du 25 juillet 1793, le Cap, 25 juillet 1793.

22. AN DXXV 27, 281. Prison records for les Cayes, Sept. 1793 to Jan. 1794.

23. AN DXXV 12, 116. E. Polverel à Sonthonax, les Cayes, 30 Nov. 1793. See p. 253, below.

24. AN DXXV 21, 212. Le colonel Rigaud, commandant provisoire de la province du Sud au citoyen Polverel, commissaire civil de la république, les Cayes, 22 août 1793.

25. *Ibid.*

26. *Ibid.*

27. AN DXXV 21, 212. André Rigaud, colonel, commandant provisoire de la province du Sud, les Cayes, 14 août 1793.

28. From October 1793 to the end of the year the prison records for les Cayes, the capital city of the South just outside the Plaine-du-Fond where the insurrectionary movement had germinated, indicate over three hundred entries for arrests of black *légionnaires,* many of these for second and third-time offenders. AN DXXV 27, 281 and 282.

29. AN DXXV 41, 404. Procès-verbal de la célébration de la fête de la république française au Port-au-Prince, E. Polverel, Port-au-Prince, 21 sept. 1793. Also, Proclamation of 27 August 1793, printed in Garran-Coulon, *Rapport,* 2:215.

30. AN DXXV 28, 286. Règlement sur les proportions du travail et de la récompense, sur le partage des produits de la culture entre le propriétaire et les cultivateurs, petite habitation O'Sheill, Plaine-du-Fond de l'Isle-à-Vache, 7 fév. 1794, signé, E. Polverel. Unless otherwise indicated, the following section will be based on the statements made by Polverel in his 7 February proclamation. Prison records and other related documents for this transitional period, indicating a constant flow of arrested black workers, as well as soldiers in the Legion, are found in AN DXXV 27, 281 and 282. DXXV 37, 373 and 374. DXXV 41, 404. DXXV 44, 421.

31. AN, DXXV 41, 404. Registre d'ordres et décisions, petite habitation O'Sheill, Plaine-du-Fond de l'Isle-à-Vache, 25 mars 1794.

32. See n. 30, above.

33. AN DXXV 28, 286. Procès-verbaux de la commune de Cavaillon sur la lecture faite aux cultivateurs du règlement du 7 février 1794, Cavaillon, 21-28 fév.; 13-5 mars 1794. Of the twenty-three written reports available for the plantations in the parish of Cavaillon regarding the workers' intentions, twenty final decisions are recorded. Thirteen plantations opted for a full six-day work week, and seven chose to work only five days per week.

34. The prominence of organized insurrectionary activity here may be explained partly by the high concentration of sugar plantations and the corresponding organization of slave labor in massive numbers. In the les Cayes plain alone, by far the wealthiest section of the province, there were nearly a hundred sugar plantations, roughly half of the total for the province, and over twenty thousand slaves. See Bernard Foubert, "Colons et esclaves du Sud de Saint-Domingue au début de la Révolution", *Revue française d'histoire d'Outre-Mer,* 61 (1974):200. Regarding the five-day work week, the workers on the la Haye plantation in the les Cayes plain stated that "since many other plantations were operating on five days per week," they too wanted an extra day and chose Thursday. AN DXXV 44, 421. Sonthonax à Blanchet, petite habitation O'Sheill, 22 mars. DXXV 37, 374. Blanchet, commandant militaire à Aquin à Polverel, commissaire civil, Aquin, 28 Mars 1794.

35. Polverel sincerely believed that, once properly understood, the work code would enlighten the workers as to their true interests and thereby create harmony between them and the owners, both parties being engaged in a collective enterprise, each having specific duties and responsibilities, the whole being based on a hierarchy of labor and the unequal distribution of wealth.

36. A majority comprised one-half of the plantation workers, plus one.

37. AN DXXV 28, 287. Règlement de police sur la culture et les cultivateurs, E. Polverel, commissaire civil de la république, petite habitation O'Sheill, 28 fév. 1794. Of the hundreds of workers arrested on the plantations in the Plaine-du-Fond, roughly from the end of February when the police code was published to the beginning of April 1794, the cause of arrest is not always indicated. However, in most cases, the black workers were condemned to "public works without pay until further orders," a sentence which could apply to nearly all of the offenses specified in Polverel's 28 February police proclamation. AN DXXV 27, 281 and 282. DXXV 37, 373 and 374. DXXV 41, 404. DXXV 44, 421.

38. AN DXXV 41, 404. Registre d'ordres et décisions, petite habitation O'Sheill, 19 fév.; 10 mars; 4, 8 avril 1794. DXXV 37, 373. Dalesme, gérant sequestre de l'habitation Formon au citoyen commissaire, au Vieux Bourg, 17 mars 1794. DXXV 37, 374. Petit, commandant au Camp Périn à Polverel, commissaire civil, Camp Périn, 25 mars 1794. DXXV 37,

373. Salomon, commandant militaire à Polverel, commissaire civil, les Cayes, 19 mars 1794. DXXV 44, 421. Sonthonax à Lachapelle, petite habitation O'Sheill, 24 fév. 1794.

39. AN DXXV 41, 404. Registre d'ordres et décisions, petite habitation O'Sheill, 16, 24 fév.; 12, 17, 20, 21, 27 mars 1794. DXXV 44, 421. Sonthonax à Lachapelle, petite habitation O'Sheill, 24 fév. 1794. Sonthonax à Boury, petite habitation O'Sheill, 9 mars 1794. Sonthonax à Baulos, petite habitation O'Sheill, 11 mars 1794. DXXV 22, 226. Beauregard, commandant militaire à Étienne Polverel, commissaire civil, Cavaillon, 2 avril 1794. DXXV 37, 373. Thiveruy, gérant de l'habitation Labiche et Dunezac au commissaire civil, au Fond, 20 mars 1794. DXXV 37, 374. Attestations of concierge, les Cayes prison, les Cayes, 28 March 1794. Petit, commandant militaire à Polverel, commissaire civil, Camp Périn, 25 mars 1794. Salomon, commandant militaire à Polverel, commissaire civil, les Cayes, 30 mars 1794. Poulain, économe-gérant de la deuxième habitation Laborde à E. Polverel, deuxième habitation Laborde, 23 mars 1794.

40. AN DXXV 44, 421. Sonthonax à Salomon, petite habitation O'Sheill, 2 avril 1794.

41. AN DXXV 37, 374. Petit, commandant au Camp Périn à Polverel, commissaire civil, Camp Périn, 27 mars 1794.

42. AN DXXV 37, 374. Petit, commandant au Camp Périn à Polverel, commissaire civil, Camp Périn, 25 mars 1794.

43. AN DXXV 41, 404. Registre d'ordres et décisions, petite habitation O'Sheill, 2, 9 mars 1794. DXXV 44, 421. Sonthonax à Marin, procureur de la commune de Torbeck, petite habitation O'Sheill, 16 mars 1794.

44. AN DXXV 41, 404. Registre d'ordres et décisions, petite habitation O'Sheill, 20, 31 mars; 3 avril 1794. DXXV 44, 421. Sonthonax à Salomon, petite habitation O'Sheill, 20 mars 1794. DXXV 37, 373. François Médor au citoyen commissaire civil, au Fond, 20 mars 1794. Elie Boury, commandant militaire de Torbeck à Daniel Gellée, secrétaire à la commission civile, Torbeck, 13 mars 1794.

45. See p. 246, above.

46. AN DXXV 28, 286. Règlement sur les proportions.

47. AN DXXV 37, 373. Dalesme, gérant sequestre de l'habitation Formon, au Vieux Bourg, 17 mars 1794. DXXV 37, 374. Salomon, commandant militaire au commissaire civil, les Cayes, 26 mars 1794. Attestations of concierge, les Cayes prison, les Cayes, 29 March 1794. Petit, commandant au Camp Périn à Polverel, commissaire civil, Camp Périn, 25 mars 1794. DXXV 41, 404. Registre d'ordres et décisions, petite habitation O'Sheill, 25, 29 mars; 6, 8 avril 1794.

48. AN DXXV 22, 226. Beauregard, commandant militaire à Étienne Polverel, commissaire civil, Cavaillon, 2 avril 1794. Also, DXXV 41, 404. Registre d'ordres et décisions, petite habitation O'Sheill, 3 avril 1794.

49. AN DXXV 41, 404. Registre d'ordres et décisions, petite habitation O'Sheill, 6, 8 avril 1794.

50. AN DXXV 37, 373. Lachapelle, capitaine à l'adjudant général au citoyen Polverel, commissaire civil, les Cayes, 20 mars 1794. Salomon, commandant militaire provisoire aux Cayes à Duboisquéheneul, secrétaire *ad hoc* de la commission civile, 21 mars 1794.

51. The sparse evidence available concerning this incident does not allow for a more precise determination of why Apollon wanted to assassinate Faubert. However Faubert may have pushed too far this time, thus becoming the target of armed rebellion organized by the blacks to safeguard their newly-established freedom.

52. In addition to Apollon, two black workers, Atity and Tausia, were also arrested as active instigators who, knowing that the plot was to kill Faubert, approved of it and agitated amongst the other blacks to solicit their adherence. AN DXXV 43, 418. Les commissaires civils à Figuière, faisant fonction de commissaire instructeur à St. Louis, Port-Républicain, 20 mai 1794.

53. AN DXXV 28, 288. Proclamation of 31 March 1794, signed, Polverel, petite habitation O'Sheill, Plaine-du-Fond de l'Isle-à-Vache.

54. AN DXXV 41, 404. Registre d'ordres et décisions, petite habitation O'Sheill, 31 mars 1794. The other six were: Bartholo, Baptiste, Jacquet, Jean Créole, Thomas and Amant. DXXV 28, 288. Tableau des habitations séquestrées dans la Plaine-du-Fond... distribuées en sections par ordre du commissaire civil, petite habitation O'Sheill, 31 mars 1794.

55. See p. 247, above.

56. AN DXXV 44, 421. Les commissaires civils à Simonet, préposé de l'administration à Jacmel, Port-Républicain, 6 mai 1794.

57. The plantation system was favored both by Dessalines, who ruled from 1804 until his assassination in 1806, and by his successor, Christophe, who, like Dessalines, had been one of Toussaint's staunchest generals. Christophe's succession was contested by Alexander Pétion, the foremost mulatto leader of the South, thus causing the bifurcation of the country and the creation in the North of the State of Haiti under Christophe and, in the South, of the Republic of Haiti under Pétion.

58. Rodman, S., *Haiti: The Politics of Squalor* (New York, Houghton Mifflin, 1971), pp. 60-61.

John F. Laffey

# CONCORD AND DISCORD IN FRENCH SOCIAL THOUGHT IN THE FIRST HALF OF THE NINETEENTH CENTURY

The great square telescopes a history in its names: *place Louis XV, place de la Révolution, place de la Concorde.* George Rudé has mastered the history expressed in these names, and enriched our understanding of it. His achievement rests upon a steadfast refusal to sanction a social world of masters and subjects. More at ease in the Faubourg Saint-Antoine than in the large, cold square, my friend and colleague at Concordia University has also moved about in a greater and much less geometric *place de la Révolution.* Broad and generous concerns and sympathies have fused with specific, painstaking scholarly endeavours. Certainly, few are better prepared to comment upon the change in name, after Thermidor, from *Révolution* to *Concorde.*

If the consolidation of the French bourgeoisie's gains from the Revolution demanded harsher measures, the fixing in stone of the ideal of *Concorde* was not without its significance. However shabby the motives behind it, the Thermidorians displayed a certain crude sense in changing the name. They tried to appeal, after all, to genuine, profound, and long-lived aspirations. The vision of concord stretches back, beyond Roman temples to the Bible, and forward, to a society from which exploitation will actually have been banished. The very attraction of this perennial vision of social peace has rendered its use in buttressing the hegemonies of ruling classes all too easy. Yet the same vision of concord has on occasion provided the ruled with a stimulus for moving beyond situations which too obviously give the lie to its ritualistic invocations from above. Aimed at the obfuscation or transcendence of social struggle, differing versions of the vision and, equally important, of the means of realizing it do come into conflict. At any given time the hegemonic version of concord can sanctify, but cannot permanently ensure, a social *status quo*: the raw Thermidorian usage, in the interests of ideological mystification, marked a symbolic terminus *within,* but not *of,* the Revolution.

The effects of the upheaval begun in 1789 would be felt until 1848 and, indeed, beyond that great and tragic year. Sanctioning much that had been claimed in 1789, the Restoration restored little. And the feeble efforts in the direction of a more genuine revival of the *ancien régime* ended in the collapse of the Bourbon monarchy. Installed amidst hopes for improvement, the Orleanist regime presided over a deepening social crisis. If a minority responded successfully to Guizot's *"Enrichissez-vous,"* the condition of many worsened. While the amount of industrial development in France before 1848 should not be exaggerated, steam power did come to play a role in production and transportation, the number of spindles multiplied significantly, and the factory began to encroach upon the small workshop. Not only were the horrors first wrought in Britain by the Industrial Revolution seen on a smaller scale

261

in France, where wages declined drastically in some industries, but Britain also provided the spectre of what the future might hold for France. Justified by the economic teachings of Jean-Baptiste Say and Charles Dunoyer, the Liberal bourgeoisie opposed any efforts to remedy the situation. Inevitably social unrest increased: Lyon and Paris witnessed short-lived insurrections, embryonic trade unions took shape, the strike began to eclipse the food riot in social importance, and secret societies proliferated. Daumier summed up the other side of the coin, savage repression, in *La Rue Transnonain.*

Social conflict and, equally important, fear of it ravaged France during the first half of the nineteenth century. In such circumstances the appeal of concord increased. A new concern with social reconciliation emerged, encompassing solutions to conflict as widely diverse as those of the political economist and historian Sismondi (1773-1842), the defrocked abbé Lamennais (1782-1854), the utopians Saint-Simon (1760-1825) and Fourier (1772-1837), and the anarchist Proudhon (1809-1865). It would not be difficult to add others, including those of a much more explicitly reactionary stamp, to such a listing.[1] Whatever the divisions among such men, their differing pursuits of social reconciliation transcended in seriousness, in sophistication, and often enough in intent the crude maneuver of the Thermidorians. Horrified by the disintegration of society into a chaos of struggling individuals and classes, all preached the need for the establishment of a new social harmony. Opposing the reigning Liberalism, all condemned discord and exalted concord.

The theorists of reconciliation looked forward to a time when the more ferocious struggles among men would cease. But if they sought the end of class conflict, they did not necessarily envision the end of classes. Often enough their arguments came down to the perception that the position of the different classes in the social hierarchy could and should be altered. Even those bold enough to envision a class-less society usually believed that, ideally, the change to it could and should be brought about with a minimum of violence. Such emphases sprang from several sources. These theorists were for the most part convinced that the violence of the French Revolution had solved little or nothing. Many believed that love, essentially a more or less secularized Christian *caritas,* should be the strongest bond among men, no matter what their social class. The glorification of human ties also reflected the continuing appeal of the message of companionship in a world still deeply marked by the existence of the small workshop and farm and, perhaps more important, coloured by distorted images of how good life had been before the advent of larger concerns and the consequent hardening of class divisions. For some, yet another reason behind the provision for the continued existence of classes lay in the appeal of the revolutionary idea of "the career open to talent," the idea that the higher positions in society should be rewards for ability and effort. A more mundane reason resided in the reformers' need for capital in order to implement their schemes. While denouncing present abuses and threatening employers and politicians with the disastrous consequences of their policies, these theorists often enough found themselves soliciting help from those same employers and politicians. Given the limited number of such potential supporters, as well as the mutually exclusive nature of their projects, the proponents of universal concord often quarrelled bitterly among themselves.

If such internal discord weakened the movement on behalf of class reconciliation, other factors damaged it more severely. The politics of reconciliation remained largely apolitical or, more accurately, remained at best a politics of influence. Given the circumstances in which these theorists found themselves, that was probably inevitable. No matter to which class or group they primarily addressed themselves, the advocates of reconciliation had little to rely upon but their persuasive powers. They grasped, moreover, the need to understand the deeper forces behind the shadow-play of contemporary politics.[2] Yet their spurning of politics rendered the theorists of reconciliation especially inept when confronted with the great events of 1848. Greater political sagacity alone, however, could not have prevented their failures in that year. Their fundamental commitment, the dedication to social concord, rendered them unfit to cope with the situation when the bloodbath of June followed February's feasts of fraternity and the realities of class conflict revealed the possibility of social reconciliation to be, at best, a generous illusion.

Jean-Charles-Leonard Sismonde de Sismondi did not live to witness the events of 1848, but he interested himself in political matters more than most of those considered here. In his early *De la richesse commerciale* (1803), a none-too-original statement of the principles of Economic Liberalism, he maintained that "the science of government is. . . the science of rendering men happy," and, in the far more critical *Nouveaux principes d'économie politique* (1819; second edition, 1826), he argued that "the science of government proposes, or should propose, for its goal the happiness of men united in society."[3] How such an aim was to be achieved posed a problem, for Sismondi feared the advent of democracy, had little good to say about constitutional monarchy, and loathed centralized regimes, whether Absolutist, or Jacobin, or Bonapartist. Ideally, with power rooted in municipal and provincial centres, a federal republic would be served by "eminent men" and "the aristocracy of talent" who would perceive the need for government to intervene in economic life in order to exercise "on the pursuit of wealth a regulating and moderating influence."[4]

The introduction of the graduated income tax would constitute one form of such intervention, for Sismondi believed that the wealthier a person, the more he should be willing to pay for the protection which the State rendered him. That implied, of course, the continued existence of classes, and, indeed, he thought it "necessary" for society to "contain some wealthy, some men of average condition, and some poor."[5] But he insisted on the need for cooperation between the two great classes, the wealthy and those who possessed only their labour power. If the State had to favour one of these classes, it should be the latter. Thus, contrary to existing society, the classes would be bound together in a new social solidarity. That end, however, could only be achieved through "the slow and indirect methods of legislation."[6]

If Sismondi admired "the republics of the Middle Ages which, with less brilliant theories, practiced liberty more than we do," he denied any hankering for a vanished world: "I have been represented as being, in political economy, the enemy of the progress of society, the partisan of barbarous and oppressive institutions. No, I do not wish for that which was, but I do wish for something better than that which is. I can only judge that which is by comparing it with the past, and I am far from wanting to revive ancient ruins, when I demonstrate by them the eternal needs of society."[7] Although he disagreed with them vehemently in regard to the means of ending social conflict, this concern with "the eternal needs of society" led him to acknowledge a certain intellectual kinship with Robert Owen and Charles Fourier.

Sismondi praised, in past and present, peasant proprietorship. Behind his excessively idyllic picture of peasant life lay a keen awareness of the role of the peasantry in maintaining social stability. That perception dictated his evaluation in 1819 of the French Revolution: "this revolution, in the midst of a deluge of evils, has left several benefits behind it, and perhaps one of the greatest of these is the guarantee that such a scourge will be unable to return. The revolution has multiplied tremendously the class of peasant proprietors."[8] By then he had abandoned his earlier faith in the power of *laissez-faire* economics, industrial concentration, and the Liberal State to produce human happiness. A sober question had replaced the youthful idealization of Britain: "Has not England, by forgetting men in the pursuit of things, sacrificed the ends to the means?"[9]

If his emphasis on the role of under-consumption in causing business crises constituted Sismondi's most probing contribution to the criticism of capitalism, it hardly exhausted his strictures. The theory and the practice of the existing economic system revealed basic faults. Adam Smith's "fundamental dogma of free and universal competition" had led, indeed, to "a prodigious development in the powers of industry," but such progress had been accompanied by an enormous growth in human suffering.[10] David Ricardo had only worsened matters by making "an abstraction of man" and setting up the unlimited growth of wealth rather than the happiness of mankind as the supreme social good.[11] Sismondi judged the whole perspective of the Economic Liberals to be fundamentally wrong: "political economy is not a science of calculation, but a moral science. It is misguided when one believes it guided by numbers; it only leads to the goal when one appreciates the feelings, needs and passions of men."[12] He worried especially about "the trans- formation of the nation into a great factory" and the sacrifice of "men to things, individuals who can suffer to abstractions."[13]

More textiles, of course, were being produced than ever before, but at the cost of the labour of children who had never known any of the joys of life. More generally, not only was the worker forced to live in degrading conditions and deprived of all hope of advancement, but he now lacked any way of judging what the demand for his labour would be and, hence, had been hurled into an entirely new world of chance, uncertainty, and insecurity. Oppressed by hunger and suffering, and with all their faculties stupified by "constant, stubborn, and uniform work," the moral sentiments of the workers disintegrated.[14] In brief, although the Industrial Revolution might have brought happiness to one man in a thousand, it had reduced others to less than animals and certainly had not brought happiness to mankind.

For Sismondi, liberal capitalism, and the industry associated with it, had produced a fundamental conflict between "all those who possess and all those who work," a bitter struggle between "the owners of accumulated labour" and "the men who can sell only their strength."[15] Implicit in this situation lay the threat of social revolution, a threat which could not be contained through coercion alone. Confronted with the crushing of the insurrection in Lyon in 1834, Sismondi concluded that "if the war declared by the proletarians on the established order must inspire a just fright, it must be said that the manner in which the defenders of this order have triumphed over them can scarcely inspire less terror."[16] Never a friend to revolution, he still proclaimed in outrage that "the massacre of inoffensive people by the moderates and the friends of order is the greatest atrocity in forty-five years of revolution."[17] In other words, having plumbed the horrors of the Industrial Revolution, Sismondi now accepted the thesis that the continuing crisis in French society could be traced back to 1789.

Hugues-Felicité-Robert de Lamennais also defended the insurgents of 1834. In succession theocrat, liberal Catholic, and radical democrat, he appears to have lived a life riven by sharp discontinuities. Yet, as Saint-Beuve remarked in 1834, the year Lamennais' powerful *Paroles d'un croyant* appeared, the former priest had always been concerned with society and the need to reform it. Unable to accept that the deity could have created the misery of the poor, Lamennais concluded that men themselves had made it and, hence, could themselves remedy it. Its origin, like the source of the divisions within society, lay in "the insatiable passion for acquiring and possessing."[18] He argued, in traditional Christian terms, that those who benefited from the workings of the society of the day would eventually have to answer to divine justice. But impelled by hatred of existing conditions, he overstepped the bounds of Christian orthodoxy by introducing a distinctly Manichean note in his depiction of the conflict between the majority and the minority, the people and the privileged, the poor and the rich, the children of God and the children of Satan. He continued to look forward, however, to a final reconciliation in a society where "the social organization will emanate from the holy and immutably established maxims of equality, liberty and fraternity. Private interests will gradually come to rest in a single interest, that of all, because, freed from the influence of cold and sterile egotism, *all* will understand…there is life only in love."[19]

Lamennais endeavoured to set this goal in an historical context. While he argued that revolutions made for progress because post-revolutionary situations never quite degenerated to the level of pre-revolutionary conditions, he remained harshly critical of what the revolutions of 1789 and 1830 had achieved for the mass of the population: "You were promised freedom; and you were given slavery."[20] More specifically, he argued that, if

> equality and liberty are written into the laws, it is still only a vain formulation in opposition to the facts; the people still vegetate under dependence upon men and things; upon men, because of the concentration of power in the hands of a few privileged; upon things, because of the concentration of wealth in those same hands Thus, in reality, the people are denied any participation in power, the only guarantee of property, and property itself, the only guarantee of liberty.[21]

The acknowledgement of the right to property, however, did not imply an acceptance of a capitalist world which had reduced even marriage to "only a calculation, a speedy way of enriching oneself, a business affair."[22]

With the overthrow of the Orleanist regime in 1848, Lamennais entered the Chamber of Deputies where he devoted himself to abortive plans for a constitution which would provide for decentralization of the administration, the separation of Church and State, the right to an education and freedom of teaching, a graduated tax system, and the organization of credit. Preoccupied with such projects, he refused to expend any love upon those "systems which, since Saint-Simon and Fourier, have multiplied in all parts and whose general character is the negation, explicit or implicit, of the family, of property."[23] But his commitment to the preservation of property did not prevent the forging of the closest links between the unfolding of the revolution and the life-span of his newspaper, *Le Peuple constituant.* Its last issue appeared on June 11, 1848 and carried a biting farewell message: *"Le Peuple constituant* began with the republic; it ends with the republic. For what we are witnessing today is certainly not the republic, it is only its name."[24] With "the people decimated and driven back into its misery, more profound now than ever before ... the saturnalia of reaction" reigned.[25]

Although he changed his positions even more frequently, Claude-Henri Saint-Simon never embraced Lamennais' democratic convictions. Believing politics to be "the science of production," a science which should benefit the poorest and most numerous class, he stressed the need for an elite which would justify itself by working for the good of the entire society.[26] Unfortunately, most elites, including those courted by Saint-Simon, refused to act in such a fashion. This was all the more dangerous in that "revolutions are inevitable evils, because the progress of enlightenment moves faster than social progress" and "the idea of equality acquires a deadly prestige when the necessary inequalities are not justified."[27] When a socially incompetent class continued to rule, "the situation is revolutionary."[28] If Saint-Simon remained an heir of the revolution of 1789 in his concern with the provision of "careers open to talent" and in his vaunting of the merits of the industrious, both capitalists and workers, his juggling of various elites and classes in his numerous ideal schemes of society reflected a continuing dedication to the construction of a social order from which the spectre of revolution would be banished.

The problem came down, in the end, to how to bind together the new hierarchical society. Spurned by his previous patrons in the banking community and dissatisfied with earlier efforts constructed on the bases of physics and physiology, Saint-Simon turned towards the end of his life to religion as the cement with which to replace the disruptive tendencies of Liberal society. He contended in *Nouveau Christianisme* (1825) that "the immense majority of the population could enjoy a moral and physical existence much more satisfying than that which it has enjoyed until now" and that "the rich, by increasing the happiness of the poor, could improve their own existence."[29] Such goals could be realized through the introduction of a new Christianity which he differentiated from its earlier form. Whereas the old Christianity had made love of neighbour a matter of individual morality, Saint-Simon's version transformed it into "the rule of social morality, the dogma of all politics."[30] And whereas the aim of early Christianity had been the destruction of slavery, the new Christianity sought "to establish a social organization which assures uninterrupted work to all proletarians, a scientific education to all members of society."[31] It proposed that all "must work for the amelioration of the moral and physical existence of the poorest class."[32] But his concern for the poor did not lead Saint-Simon to abandon the rich and powerful. He still believed that it was "obviously impossible to improve the moral and physical conditions of the poor by means other than those which tend to increase the pleasures of the wealthy class."[33] Fusing the claims of idealism and self-interest, he ended the *Nouveau Christianisme* with an appeal to princes.

The Saint-Simonians devoted themselves to developing the implications of their master's teachings, a process which provoked schism and led to such bizarre undertakings as the search conducted in the Near East for the Female Messiah. Yet crucial threads remained unbroken. Rejecting "the unbridled competition" which was nothing "but murderous war," Saint-Simon's disciples denounced a society divided into two classes, "one of which considered the other as an instrument."[34] Fortunately, they had arrived "to bring peace...by proclaiming a doctrine which preaches not only its horror of blood, but the horror of strife under whatever name it may disguise itself."[35] They proclaimed "to the rich and to the poor, to employers and wage-earners...humane fraternity, UNIVERSAL ASSOCIATION, THE BASING OF CLASSES UPON ABILITY, REWARD ACCORDING TO WORKS."[36] Fired by such a message, proletarian and privileged youth were supposed to have discovered, at the Saint-Simonian "altar of reconciliation," that they were alike children of God.[37]

If Saint-Simon had opposed the class of *industriels,* composed of capitalists and workers, to the unindustrious and parasitic within society, the most magnetic of the Saint-Simonians, Père Enfantin, looked to the reconciliation of capitalists and proletarians as fellow *travailleurs.* But by 1835 Enfantin had decided that "our popular apostolate, our appeal to the people, is finished...the royal apostolate, the appeal to the great, to the princes of the world, begins."[38] He went on to invite Louis Philippe to become king of the workers. While this appeal could be amply justified by reference to Saint-Simon's own proclivities, it posed special problems when the July Monarchy came crashing down. Yet Enfantin was not caught completely by surprise, for in January, 1848 he predicted the rapidly approaching "liquidation of the regime," a "liquidation" which would benefit "the most numerous and poorest class" just as that of 1814 had benefited the nobility and clergy and that of 1830 had benefited the bourgeoisie.[39] Presumably still working towards such an end, he busied himself towards the end of 1848 with the founding of a new journal, *Crédit,* which espoused "not the republic of the heartless, not the republic of the *sans-culottes,* but a humane, intelligent, liberal, magnanimous republic which the workers defend, the bankers credit, the women and priests bless, the poets praise."[40] Such notions, however, had been outdated by the bloody events of June, and in the end Enfantin, like so many old Saint-Simonians, would make his peace with Louis Bonaparte.

The Saint-Simonians never disguised their hostility towards the Fourierists, whose emphasis upon personal liberty threatened to seduce some of their own members. Fourier replied in kind with works like *Pièges et charlatanisme des deux sectes Saint-Simon et Owen qui promettent l'association et le progrès* (1837). The differences between the two groups, however, had more to do with their variant projections of the ideal society, as well as with the means of constructing it, than with the general thrust of their criticisms of existing conditions. Entertaining more respect for liberty and fraternity than for equality, Fourier subjected the revolutionary trinity to ruthless scrutiny. But equality was not the only danger, for, with the end of the Terror, the French had embraced the equally delusive visions provided by commerce. Having lost his "best years in the workshops of deceit," Fourier eventually came to isolate thirty-two ugly characteristics of civilized commerce.[41] If he devoted far more attention to the workings of commerce than to the impact of industry, he still hurled what was becoming an almost standard reproach against England: "You have become a rich nation whose soil is covered with the poor."[42]

According to Fourier, not even the wealthy benefited from the conditions spawned within existing society: "Does the torture of the people make the rich happier? Not really. They increase the waste of wealth by appearing to increase their enjoyments, most of which are illusionary."[43] The unhappiness of the wealthy led him to expect the emergence from their ranks of "another Isabella who... will take in hand the cause of humanity and elevate it, through the easy proof of passionate harmony, to the throne of universal unity."[44] This *nouvelle Isabelle* would support, of course, his system, which promised happiness to "the entire society, to the three classes of rich, middle and poor, to the three sexes, men, women and children, to the four ages and to all other divisions."[45] Whatever the tribulations he encountered, Fourier had no doubt that social reconciliation could and should reign globally: while the establishment of world-wide economic unity would pose no problem, the securing of administrative unity would require another six to eight years and the emergence of religious unity another thirty-five to forty years.

While fully sharing Fourier's ideal of social concord, his followers proved themselves more latitudinarian in their dealings with fellow critics of the established order. Acknowledging Saint-Simon as "a man of genius" who had grasped the outlines of the evolution of society, they praised his insistence that the nineteenth century had "to pass from a governmental, feudal, and military regime to an administrative, industrial and pacific regime."[46] But they also argued that his analyses did not do full justice to the complexity of the historical process and that his flirtations with "financial feudalism" and theocracy posed genuine dangers.[47] Even the Saint-Simonians possessed some merits: "they have launched erroneous views on women, on property, on the principle of authority, on the mode of hierarchical classification... but their general views... contain may insights, many true ideas."[48] More generally, the Fourierists decided that "the organization of the reign of justice on earth is the common goal of all socialists, who differ only as to the means."[49] Falling back upon Fourier's notion of the passions, they concluded that the form of socialism focused upon egalitarianism corresponded to "the sensual passions" which marked "the material man," that the communist form corresponded to "the affective passions" characteristic of "the spiritual man," and that their own variety corresponded to "the distributive passions" and satisfied "the complete man."[50] During the heady days of 1848 the Fourierists rejoiced not only in their own influence, but in that of the Saint-Simonians and Icarians in France, the spread of communism in Switzerland, Germany and even Russia, and the strength of Chartism in England.

While this degree of toleration for fellow socialists was unusual, Fourierist criticism of existing conditions moved along more conventional lines. Like others, they argued that France had been in revolutionary crisis for decades. Tracing the unrealized ideals of the revolution of 1789 back to Christ, they argued that, in reality, this upheaval had but added yet another distinction to those forged under the *ancien régime;* a "distinction more profound than all the others: there is a class which possesses and another which has nothing."[51] Moreover, the "new feudalism" which had arisen in England illustrated how "simple liberty engenders monopoly and pauperism."[52] The reign of "anarchical competition" had turned that unhappy country into "the most opulent and the most starved of nations."[53] But conditions were hardly better at home: "France is only an immense grave into which fall pell-mell, weakened by deprivation and all kinds of illnesses, almost all the citizens."[54] Capitalism's unhindered workings threatened even the capitalists: "they go bankrupt and become the agents, the foremen, or simply the workers of their more fortunate adversaries."[55] Those strong or fortunate enough to survive the competitive struggle faced yet another danger, for industrialists and workers had become completely estranged. And the situation had become explosive. The upheavals in Paris, Lyon and elsewhere were "only symptoms which will sooner or later lead to an eruption; and all these tumultuous revolts are the prelude to the horrible war which threatens us, the war between the man who possesses and the man who has nothing."[56]

The Fourierists promised to provide the means of escape from that bloody prospect. They claimed that the implementation of their system would achieve the reconciliation of order and liberty through organization; of progress and conservatism through association; of facts and ideas through science; of individual interest and general interest through hierarchy; and of the State and the provinces through graduated centralization. Their refusal to accept egalitarianism dictated the delicate balancing of such factors: "universal observation proves that there are not in all men equal measures of intelligence and morality, and even that a great number of the members of humanity are almost entirely deprived of these precious attributes of human nature."[57]

This position allowed the Fourierists to call for the provision of a basic minimum for all and to proclaim the right to capital accumulation. While taking vital differences into account, they promised to bring together capital, labour and talent, the two sexes, and all ages in a form of association which would allow for the reconciliation of the "absolute order of the whole" with the "absolute independence of the parts."[58] It turned out that their central goal, "universal association," was in fact the same as Christ's.[59] Depicting the bourgeoisie as the real materialists and the socialists as the true Christians of the nineteenth century, they announced that the implementation of their system would realize in this world "the splendours of the celestial Jerusalem."[60]

The events of 1848 and 1849, however, revealed the barriers (and barricades) on the road to the new Jerusalem. Victor Considérant, leader of the Fourierists, participated in the writing of the Second Republic's constitution, and, while admitting its imperfections, he deplored its betrayal in the attack upon the Roman republic, the failure to aid the cause of revolution elsewhere in Europe, and the suppression of the Fourierist *Démocratie pacifique.* If the very name of the journal reveals an essential weakness in his position, a new grimness did pervade his analysis of what went wrong:

> The suddenness of the February victory, the ravages of corruption, the concert of the terrified, the egotists, and the cowardly; the intrigues of the factions of the past, of the partisans of the monarchies; the exploitation of the inevitable defects; the ignorance of social questions on the part of men of good will who were the first depositories of the revolution; all joined with the extreme forbearance of the triumphant democracy to give power to the same oligarchic influences whose egotism and incapacity had provoked it.
>
> Today we again have 1847 and 1815.[61]

But all he could recommend was "a pacific insurrection, constitutional and legal, against the violators of the constitution."[62] Considérant found solace, however, in the notion that the people would come to "understand that the Idea is the irresistible artillery of the modern world" and that then "the walls of Jericho will fall before its all-powerful word, and it will conquer the Jerusalem of the promised land."[63] Once again the persuasive orientation of the politics of reconciliation had triumphed.

Formulated in such a fashion, this kind of message only aroused the scorn of Pierre-Joseph Proudhon. He charged that "the metaphysics of Fourier is only rhapsody and plagiarism, his classification of the passions erroneous, his 'laws of analogy' chimerical, and most of his pretended formulas just as infantile."[64] The Saint-Simonians hardly fared better: "If I had the honour of living in the Church of Saint-Simon, my first move would be to box the ears of the pontiff."[65] And Proudhon simply dismissed Lamennais for the "excessive mediocrity" of his thought.[66] Behind such fulminations lay a suspicion of those "beautiful but barren words" so often invoked by the proponents of social concord, "love one another, love your neighbour as yourself."[67] Prizing justice more than love, Proudhon admitted frankly: "You speak to me in vain of fraternity and love: I remain convinced that you do not love me, and I know that I do not love you."[68] Such a perspective led him to identify "utopia" as the "greatest enemy" of socialism and to pose a pivotal question: "Has one ever seen a capitalist, tired of gain, conspiring for the general good and making the emancipation of the proletariat his latest speculation?"[69]

Yet this self-proclaimed anarchist confronted the same issues faced by those he castigated, and pursued, in his own fashion, the common goal of social concord. He too returned to the Revolution of 1789 which, he argued, had remained incomplete, because Rousseau's misunderstanding of the social contract had led inevitably to the excesses of 1793. Those who embraced Rousseau's ideas, the "makers of bloody homilies," the "friends of the people," the "friends of the working class," the "friends of mankind", the "philanthropists," only filled Proudhon with "pity and contempt."[70] Industrialization roused a more active hatred, for it entailed "the stoppage of work, the reduction of wages, over-production, congestion, the alteration and falsification of products, bankruptcies, the declassing of the worker, the degeneration of the species, and finally sickness and death."[71] The nature of the July Monarchy, rightly seen by Proudhon as a *"bancocratie,"* only worsened the situation.[72]

Proudhon terrified the Orleanist ruling class by insisting that property was theft. But like too many subsequent historians, they seized upon that celebrated phrase without noting his qualifications. He used it in his *De la Célébration du Dimanche* as an illustration of the critical tendencies of the nineteenth century.[73] He returned to it again, in a sense closer to that in which it is usually interpreted, in *Qu'est-ce que la Propriété* (1840), but he immediately went on: "Reader, reassure yourself, I am not an agent of discord, an incendiary of sedition."[74] However, that denial did not prevent his landing in court where he defended himself by pointing to others who had defined property in much the same manner: Beccaria, Pascal and Considérant.[75] If he did not abandon the phrase, he hedged it round with more qualifications in *Système des contradictions économiques, ou philosophie de la misère* (1846):

> Property is the right of occupation; and at the same time the right of exclusion.
> Property is the price of work; and the negation of work.
> Property is the spontaneous product of society; and the dissolution of society.
> Property is an institution of justice; and property IS THEFT.[76]

In the end, if property was theft, it was also "possession."[77] Such a balancing depended, in turn, upon Proudhon's belief in the contradictory nature of human existence: "The life of man is a tissue of contradictions. Each of these contradictions is itself a monument of the social constitution...which is only produced by the mysterious contradiction of the extremes."[78]

Convinced that such contradictions produced equilibrium, Proudhon claimed that his system represented "a synthesis of community and property" which gave rise, in turn, to true liberty.[79] More specifically, his version of the good society encompassed an equality of conditions which was not an equality of well-being; personal independence derived from differences in talents and abilities; and the recognition of a proportionality in regard to intelligence and sentiment, but not in regard to the mere possession of things. The ideal society would be egalitarian, but it would also still reward talent and hard work. Proudhon, the champion of the small workshop, the peasant holding, and the family, staunchly defended the right of inheritance. If he did not expect the bourgeoisie to fund his schemes, he hardly excluded the possibility of coming to terms with them. After all, he claimed to respect diverse traditions, and his appreciation of the revolutionary tradition of the bourgeoisie carried him as far as the striking dedication of his *Idée générale de la révolution au XIXe siècle* (1851): "To you, the bourgeois, the hommage of these new essays. You were in all times the most intrepid, the ablest of revolutionaries."[80] In words which might have come from any of the figures considered here, Proudon proudly proclaimed: "All my philosophy is nothing other than the perpetuation of reconciliation."[81]

Once again, that orientation posed special problems in 1848. Having acted in that year less intelligently and less courageously than some of the other proponents of reconciliation whom he had so fiercely attacked, Proudhon later devoted a volume to explaining his behaviour. The explanation, in essence, came down to the following:

> For me, the memory of the June Days means eternal remorse....After having placed my foot on the parliamentary Sinai, I ceased to have any relation to the masses: forced to absorb myself in legislative affairs, I entirely lost sight of current affairs. I knew nothing of the situation of the national workshops, nor of the policies of the government, nor of the intrigues in the Assembly.[82]

But he might have devoted more attention to the "Programme révolutionnaire" which he published in his *Représentant du peuple* in late May and early June, 1848. There he proclaimed:

> My principle is yours, that is, property itself.
> I have no other symbol, no other principles than those of the Declaration of the Rights of Man and the Citizen: liberty, equality, security, property.[83]

There he invoked a liberty which was not that of Babeuf, Saint-Simon and Fourier, but rather that of Franklin, Washington, Lafayette, Mirabeau, Casimir-Périer, Odilon Barrot and, finally, Thiers. In brief, Proudhon's search for social concord had brought him into the camp of the bourgeoisie on the eve of the outbreak of the bitter struggle which pitted the people of Paris against that very bourgeoisie.

If there seems to be little need to revise the Marxist indictment of Proudhon, the more general Marxist treatment of theorists of reconciliation calls for some reexamination. Rightly convinced of the superiority of their grasp of social dynamics, with its focus upon the centrality of class struggle, Marx and Engels had scant patience with "duodecimo editions of the New Jerusalem."[84] Such attitudes, however, could become excessively rigid, and their codification in Engels' *Socialism: Utopian and Scientific* (1880) has been sharply questioned. Yet, whatever their polemical excesses, Marx and Engels provided more balanced assessments of various manifestations of the drive towards social concord. The "petty-bourgeois Socialism", best represented by Sismondi, won their praise in important respects:

> This school of Socialism dissected with great acuteness the contradictions in the conditions of modern production. It laid bare the hypocritical apologies of economists. It proved, incontrovertibly, the disastrous effects of machinery and the division of labour; the concentration of capital and land in a few hands; overproduction and crises; it pointed out the inevitable ruin of the petty bourgeois and peasant, the misery of the proletariat, the anarchy in production, the crying inequalities in the distribution of wealth; the industrial war of extermination between nations, the dissolution of old moral bonds, of the old family relations, of the old nationalities.[85]

That kind of appreciation can be extended. The theorists discussed here were at their best in describing and denouncing the social conditions spawned by the triumph of capitalism in the French Revolution and then exacerbated by the initial impact of the Industrial Revolution. They were at their worst in seeking to escape class conflict through the provision of detailed and conflicting blueprints of the good society in which concord would reign and happiness prevail.

To use terms favoured by the Saint-Simonians, the great achievements of the proponents of social reconciliation were "critical," their "positive" accomplishments few. Yet these same Saint-Simonians perceived themselves as moving beyond the critical to a new positive or organic stage in human affairs. The confusion reflected the circumstances in which the theorists of concord found themselves: a new kind of society, with capitalism triumphant, was establishing itself in the France of their day, but class relations had not yet been clarified sufficiently to allow for anything approaching scientific analysis and prescription. As Engels commented, "To the crude conditions of capitalistic production and the crude class conditions corresponded crude theories."[86]

George Rudé, most notably in *The Crowd in History, 1730-1848* (1964), has lent living flesh to that remark. More recently, this master of "history from below" has also raised a problem extending beyond the confines of this essay in intellectual history. In *Ideology and Popular Protest* (1980), he emphasized the convoluted relations in popular ideology between "inherent" and "derived" elements and the "sea change" which the latter undergo "in the course of transmission and adoption."[87] Viewed in these terms, it might well be that, whatever their shortcomings in 1848, the theorists of concord contributed to the social and ideological discord they so desperately wished to resolve. This problem, involving the *counter*-hegemonic appropriation of the idea of concord, cannot be resolved from the ideological perspective of the *place de la Concorde:* it must be approached "from below", from the perspective, that is, which George Rudé has done so much to illuminate.

# *NOTES*

1. Given Professor Rudé's interests, I regret my inability to include Louis Blanc, Jules Michelet, and Étienne Cabet in the following discussion. For a manifestation of the more conservative tendency, see John F. Laffey, "Auguste Comte: Prophet of Reconciliation and Reaction," *Science and Society,* XXIX, 1 (Winter, 1965), pp. 44-65.

2. The Saint-Simonians summed up a more general attitude in a query: "What matters a white flag or a tricolor if it is not really the symbol of a new order of things?" *Globe,* February 18, 1831, quoted in Sebastien Charléty, *Histoire du Saint-Simonisme (1825-1864)* (Paris: Paul Hartmann, 1931), p. 105.

3. J.-C.-L. Sismondi, *De la richesse commerciale, ou Principes d'économie politique, appliqués à la législation du commerce* (Genève: J.J. Paschoud, An XI (1803), pp. viii-ix; J.-C.-L. Sismonde de Sismondi, *Nouveaux principes d'économie politique ou de la richesse dans ses rapports avec la population,* I (Genève: Éditions Jeheber, 1951), p. 33.

4. J.-C.-L. Sismonde de Sismondi, *Études sur les constitutions des peuples libres* (Paris: Treuttel et Würtz, 1836), pp. 67, 312: Sismondi, *Nouveaux principes,* I, p. 308.

5. J.-C.-L. Sismondi, "Études sur l'économie politique, sixième essai," *Études sur les sciences sociales,* III, in Élie Halévy (ed.), *Sismondi* (Paris: Librairie Félix Alcan, 1933), pp. 106-07.

6. J.-C.-L. Sismonde de Sismondi, *Nouveaux principes d'économie politique ou de la richesse dans ses rapports avec la population,* II (Genève: Éditions Jeheber, 1953), p. 22.

7. Sismondi, *Études sur les constitutions,* p. 109; Sismondi, *Nouveaux principes,* II, p. 289.

8. Sismondi, *Nouveaux principes,* I, p. 148.

9. *Ibid.,* p. 22.

10. *Ibid.,* p. 68.

11. Sismondi, *Nouveaux principes,* II, p. 248.

12. Sismondi, *Nouveaux principes,* I, p. 242.

13. *Ibid.,* pp. 83-84, 279-80.

14. Sismondi, *Nouveaux principes,* II, p. 209; Sismondi, *Études sur les constitutions,* p. 94.

15. Sismondi, *Nouveaux principes,* II, pp. 292, 232.

16. J.-C.-L. Sismonde de Sismondi, "Du sort des ouvriers dans les manufactures," *Revue mensuelle d'Économie politique,* 1834, in Halévy, *Sismondi,* pp. 97-98.

17. Quoted in *Ibid.,* p. 21.

18. F. de La Mennais, *Paroles d'un croyant, Oeuvres complètes,* XI (Paris: Paul Daubroc et Caillaux, 1836-1837), p. 109.

19. F. de Lamennais, *Le livre du peuple,* quoted in Charles Boutard, *Lamennais, sa vie et ses doctrines,* III (Paris: Perrin et Cie, 1913), pp. 223-24. Throughout this essay all emphases appear in the texts quoted.

20. La Mennais, *Paroles,* p. 125.

21. H.-F.-R. Lamennais, *Du passé et de l'avenir du peuple,* quoted in Jacques Poisson, *Le Romanticisme sociale de Lamennais* (Paris: Librairie Philosophique J. Vrin, 1931), pp. 287-88.

22. H.-F.-R. Lamennais, *Amchaspands et Darvands* (Paris: Pagnerre, 1845), p. 133.

23. H.-F.-R. Lamennais, *Le Peuple constituant,* n.d., quoted in Poisson, *Le Romanticisme sociale,* p. 303.

24. H.-F.-R. Lamennais, *Le Peuple constituant,* July 11, 1848, quoted in Boutard, *Lamennais,* III, pp. 422-23.

25. *Ibid.*

26. C.-H. de Saint-Simon, *Lettres à un Américain,* quoted in Henri Gouhier, *La Jeunesse d'Auguste Comte et la formation du positivisme,* III (Paris: Librairie Philosophique J. Vrin, 1941), p. 142.

27. C.-H. de Saint-Simon, *Introduction aux travaux scientifiques du XIXe siècle,* quoted in Henri Gouhier, *La Jeunesse de Auguste Comte et la formation du positivisme,* II (Paris: Librairie Philosophique J. Vrin, 1936), p. 155.

28. *Ibid.*

29. C.-H. de Saint-Simon, *Nouveau Christianisme: Lettres d'Eugène Rodriques sur la Religion et la Politique; L'Éducation du genre humain de Lessing* (Paris: Au Bureau du Globe, 1832), pp. 9-104, 26-27.

30. Charléty, *Saint-Simonisme,* p. 20.

31. C.-H. de Saint-Simon, *Opinions littéraires, philosophiques et industrielles,* in Jean Dautry (ed.), *Saint-Simon, Textes choisis* (Paris: Éditions Sociales, 1951), p. 178.

32. Saint-Simon, *Nouveau Christianisme,* p. 83.

33. *Ibid.,* p. 90.

34. *The Doctrine of Saint-Simon; An Exposition,* translated with an Introduction by Georg G. Iggers (New York: Schocken Books, 1972), pp. 102-03; Barthélemy-Prosper Enfantin, *Producteur,* in Sebastien Charléty (ed.), *Enfantin* (Paris: Librairie Félix Alcan, 1930), p. 20.

35. *The Doctrine of Saint-Simon,* p. 1.

36. B.-P. Enfantin, "Économie politique et sociale," *Globe,* July, 1831, in Charléty, *Enfantin,* p. 29.

37. *The Doctrine of Saint-Simon,* p. 40.

38. Quoted in Charléty, *Saint-Simonisme,* p. 245. Enfantin announced the new apostolate in a letter to Heine, who had dedicated the first edition of his *De l'Allemagne* to him. Explaining that "the martyrs no longer carry the cross, they wear the Legion of Honour; they no longer cross the desert barefooted, they are married like good bourgeois, and found railroads," Heine deleted the dedication from subsequent editions of his work. Quoted in *Ibid.,* p. 248.

39. Enfantin, January 30, 1848, quoted in *Ibid.,* p. 292.

40. Quoted in *Ibid.,* p. 297.

41. Charles Fourier, "Analyse du mécanisme d'agiotage," *La Phalange,* VIII (1848), pp. 5-32, 97-136, 193-244, 9-10. For the characteristics of commerce, see Charles Fourier, "Section des trois unités externes," *Ibid.,* I (1845), pp. 3-46, p. 8.

42. Charles Fourier, "Crimes du commerce," *Ibid.,* II (1845), pp. 5-32, 193-224, p. 24.

43. Charles Fourier, "Des diverses issues de civilisation," *Ibid.,* X (1849), pp. 184-256, p. 211.

44. Charles Fourier, "L'Inventeur et son siècle," *Ibid.,* IX (1849), pp. 193-240, p. 240.

45. Fourier, "Des diverses issues de civilisation," p. 236.

46. E.B., "Le triomphe de saint-simonisme," *Ibid.,* III (1846), pp. 117-21, p. 117; Paul de Baurelle, "Saint-Simon et sa doctrine," *Ibid.,* IV (1846), pp. 537-57, p. 545.

47. F. Cantagrel, "Du Droit au travail et son organisation pratique," *Ibid.,* V (1847), pp. 152-82, p. 158; Baurelle, "Saint-Simon," p. 556.

48. E. B., "Le triomphe," p. 117; Cantagrel, "Du Droit au travail," p. 158.

49. Clovis Guyornaud, "Caractère socialiste de l'héresie en France," *Ibid.,* VII (1847), pp. 317-36, p. 335.

50. *Ibid.*

51. Fr. Cantagrel, "Du Droit au travail et son organisation pratique," *Ibid.,* II (1845), pp. 261-91, p. 270.

52. *Ibid.*, p. 276.

53. *Ibid.*, pp. 267-68.

54. M. Perreymond, "Bilan de la France, ou la crise, la misère et le travail," *Ibid.*, VIII (1848), pp. 175-288, p. 216.

55. Cantagrel, "Du Droit au travail," p. 269.

56. *Ibid.*, p. 286.

57. Victor Meunier, "L'Esprit de l'histoire," *Ibid.*, IX (1849), pp. 501-25, p. 503.

58. (Victor Considérant?), "Introduction -- Système des développements de l'école sociétaire," *Ibid.*, I (1845), pp. i-xliv, p. ii.

59. *Ibid.*, p. iv; Victor Considérant, "Simples explications à mes amis et à mes commettants," *Ibid.*, X (1849), pp. 113-30, p. 113.

60. *Ibid.*, p. 129; Meunier, "L'Esprit," p. 525.

61. Considérant, "Simples explications,"p. 114.

62. *Ibid.*, p. 126.

63. *Ibid.*, p. 130.

64. Pierre-Joseph Proudhon, *Avertissement aux propriétaires, ou Lettre à M. Victor Considérant* (Paris: Marcel Rivière, 1938), p. 213.

65. Pierre-Joseph Proudhon, *Justice,* I, quoted in an an editorial note in Pierre-Joseph Proudhon, *Système des Contradictions économiques ou Philosophie de la Misère,* I (Paris: Marcel Rivière, 1923), p. 137.

66. Pierre-Joseph Proudhon, *Deuxième mémoire sur la propriété* (Paris: Marcel Rivière, 1938), p. 139.

67. Pierre-Joseph Proudhon, *De la Création de l'ordre dans l'humanité, ou Principes de l'organisation politique,* quoted in Henri de Lubac, *The UnMarxian Socialist, A Study of Proudhon* (New York: Sheed and Ward, 1948), p. 187.

68. Proudhon, *Système,* I, pp. 257-58.

69. Pierre-Joseph Proudhon, *Système des Contradictions économiques ou Philosophie de la Misère,* II (Paris: Marcel Rivière, 1923), p. 85; Proudhon, *Système,* I, p. 366.

70. *Ibid.*, p. 350; Pierre-Joseph Proudhon, *De la Célébration du Dimanche* (Paris: Marcel Rivière, 1926), p. 55.

71. Proudhon, *Système,* I, pp. 188-89.

72. Pierre-Joseph Proudhon, *Les Confessions d'un révolutionnaire pour servir à l'histoire de la révolution de février* (Paris: Marcel Rivière, 1929), p. 97.

73. Proudhon, *De la Célébration,* p. 31. Due to space restrictions, I have hitherto tried to avoid citing the sources of paraphrased material. But Proudhon's treatment of property calls for specific citations.

74. Pierre-Joseph Proudhon, *Qu'est-ce que la Propriété? ou recherches sur le principe du droit et gouvernement, première mémoire* (Paris: Marcel Rivière, 1926), p. 131.

75. Pierre-Joseph Proudhon, *Explications présentées au ministère public sur le droit de propriété* (Paris: Marcel Rivière, 1938), p. 273.

76. Proudhon, *Système,* II, p. 182.

77. Proudhon, *Qu'est-ce que la Propriété,* p. 157.

78. *Ibid.*, p. 87.

79. *Ibid.*, p. 342.

80. Pierre-Joseph Proudhon, *Idée générale de la Révolution au XIXe siècle* (Paris: Marcel Rivière, 1923), p. 93.

81. Proudhon, *Système,* I, p. 398.

82. Proudhon, *Confessions,* p. 169.

83. Pierre-Joseph Proudhon, *Programme révolutionnaire* (Paris: Marcel Rivière, 1938), p. 304.

84. Karl Marx and Frederick Engels, "Manifesto of the Communist Party," in Karl Marx and Frederick Engels, *Selected Works,* I (Moscow: Foreign Languages Publishing House, 1958), pp. 33-65, p. 63.

85. *Ibid.,* p. 57.

86. Frederick Engels, "Socialism: Utopian and Scientific," in Karl Marx and Frederick Engels, *Selected Works,* II (Moscow: Foreign Languages Publishing House, 1958), pp. 92-154, p. 121.

87. George Rudé, *Ideology and Popular Protest* (New York: Pantheon Books, 1980), pp. 35-36.

# PART FOUR

Neal Wood

# AFRICAN PEASANT TERRORISM AND AUGUSTINE'S POLITICAL THOUGHT

No contemporary historian has done more than George Rudé to call our attention to the importance of "history from below,"[1] and probably no scholars could benefit more from his approach to the past than historians of political thought. They have tended to neglect the fact that most classic political theorists, from Plato to Max Weber, in their speculations about the nature of the state have usually been engaged in writing "history from above." Indeed, with some notable exceptions, the major political theorists have in the Gramscian sense been among the most active intellectual agents of class hegemony.[2] The history of political thought is a history of ideas, and as such is generally history from above, but it is always a history of ideas situated within a specific social context. Once this is acknowledged, it is apparent that the historian of political thought, if he is to do justice to his subject, must establish the connection between the political ideas to be examined and history from below. Historians cannot afford to ignore that classic political theories are rooted in the everyday life of their times as well as in the realm of ideas. In the precapitalist era this has meant that the political theorist had to deal with the central problem of lord versus peasant, a concern to be taken seriously by the analyst of his ideas.

So for instance, little systematic effort in the history of political thought has been made to study St. Augustine's ideas within the predominantly agrarian setting of fourth- and fifth-century North Africa. From the time of Augustine's return from Milan in 388 until his death in 430, Africa was plagued by acute economic troubles, widespread rural unrest, serious religious schism, and popular revolt against Roman colonial rule. In order to suggest how this turbulent history from below can be related to Augustine's "history from above", the example of the Circumcellions may be instructive. They were bands of fanatical Donatist peasants who terrorized parts of Roman North Africa during Augustine's residence prior to the composition of *The City of God*. Perhaps the nature of the Circumcellions can be better grasped by reference to Augustine's outlook, and conversely, certain elements of his political thought may be illuminated by a fuller appreciation of these armed peasants.

## I

A discussion of the Circumcellions must begin with a brief summary of the economic and religious difficulties in Africa.[3] By Augustine's day Roman North

Africa (Proconsularis, Byzacena, Numidia, Mauretania Sitifensis, Mauretania Caesariensis) including much of modern Algeria and Tunisia and excluding Egypt and Cyrenaica, may possibly have had a population of seven million or more with fewer than six-hundred towns and urban centres.[4] Roman colonial rule had been inflicted upon a numerous indigenous and predominantly peasant people, speaking Punic, and more commonly Libyan in the immense rural interior. Latinization was confined to a small proportion of the natives, largely the better-off townsmen. The seat of colonial administration, Carthage, the second city of the Empire, perhaps exceeding three-hundred thousand free inhabitants,[5] together with the coastal area, constituted a significant cultural sector in the third great period of Latin literature that had flourished since the reign of Constantine.[6] Africa had long been of critical economic importance to the Empire. The principal granary of Rome and the province with a reputation in the past for being the wealthiest,[7] Africa was "the classical land of great estates,"[8] owned by a "substantial class" of patrician millionaires,[9] by Crown and Church. Huge wheat producing latifundia and extensive olive orchards were evidently worked not by agrarian slaves,[10] but by dependent, often tied peasants, the *coloni.* In addition, there were peasant freeholders, and many small farmers with perpetual leaseholds on marginal land known as Mancian tenures. The *coloni* were sharecroppers, and Mancian tenants paid rent in kind, normally one-third of their produce.

Since the third century the Empire had been suffering from an agricultural decline, accompanied by inflation, depopulation, a chronic shortage of manpower in the countryside, and an increasing polarization of rich and poor. Despite the tightening vise of burgeoning taxes and rents and multiplying social discontents, rural Africa appears to have been relatively better off than elsewhere in the Empire. Society, economy, and government were in the grip of a tiny affluent elite separated from the vast peasant masses by an annual income differential of as much as or more than ten-thousand to one.[11] Special circumstances in Africa seem to have contributed to economic stagnation and impoverishment during Augustine's lifetime, creating a social atmosphere of hostility and insecurity.[12] Taxation, differing from that of other provinces, was at a flat-rate, regardless of the quality or use of the holdings. Since an appreciable part of the whole consisted of marginal lands, including the Mancian tenures, much of it was abandoned by impoverished peasants, particularly in Numidia and Byzacena. By the second decade of the fifth century the loss of land due to this primary cause was enormous, up to fifty per cent, as compared to a maximum of twenty per cent in other regions. Moreover, the frequent forays of unfriendly nomads along the southern borders, and the expenses incurred by the need for maintaining large defensive garrisons, may also have been a source of economic hardship in Numidia and Byzacena. Rural unrest, nevertheless, was far more serious in Numidia than Byzacena, in spite of the higher proportion of *agri deserti* in the latter area. This was perhaps because Numidia unlike Byzacena was characteristically a locale of huge estates that, in view of the scarcity of labour, came to depend increasingly upon the services of itinerant agrarian workers forced to give up their holdings on the marginal lands. Under such conditions exploitation proliferated and antagonisms were inflamed. Also in Numidia peasants may have been more subject to the harassment of stewards and landlords since villages were often situated within the boundaries of the latifundia.[13] Bad as economic affairs were in Numidia, however, the plight of the peasant was not completely unrelieved. Olive production was on the upswing, and a revival of native art and culture signaled a developing peasant vigour and awareness. Popular protest on a broad scale rarely occurs in an environment of utter impoverishment, degradation and hopelessness.[14] Deprivation in rural Numidia was not so severe as to prevent the peasantry from being conscious of their oppression and victimization and from violently reacting to it.

A classic revolutionary situation, therefore, seems to have been in the making among the Numidian peasants, one to which Christianity made a notable contribution. During the era of religious toleration in the latter part of the third century, Christianity developed in the Empire primarily as an urban phenomenon, appealing greatly to the lower classes. Little head-way was made in the countryside, with the three important exceptions of Africa, Anatolia, and Egypt. In rural Africa the first surviving dated Christian inscriptions begin in 266 and by the end of the century the total number of sees in town and country doubled to about 250. The rapid conversion of the African peasantry may have been connected to their increasing cultural consciousness and self-awareness, to economic conditions of relative deprivation, and in view of the perceived failure of the pagan gods, to the prospect of social justice offered by the new faith. Christian belief in rural Africa appears from the beginning to have had puritanical and apocalyptic leanings, with an affinity for martyrdom and the idea of the elect, and a vague identification of poverty with righteousness. The Great Persecution of the first years of the fourth century, Diocletian's ill-fated attempt to suppress Christianity, may well have failed because of its popularity among the peasantry of Africa, Anatolia, and Egypt. Although urban Christians presented comparatively little opposition to the inquisition, the rural populace, most prominently in Africa, actively resisted with stubborn fervour.

Donatism was born in Africa out of this particular social and religious configuration and in reaction to the oppression of Diocletian. Certain prelates were accused of collaboration with the state and branded "*traditores*" (those who "hand over") for surrendering the Holy Scriptures for burning by the magistrates. Whatever the truth of such accusations, in 311 eighty Numidian bishops protested that the ordination of Caecilian, Bishop of Carthage and "primate" of Africa, was performed by a *traditor.* They elected Majorianus to the post, soon to be succeeded by Donatus after whom the new schismatic faith was named. Until 412, when Donatism was outlawed by civil authority in concert with the Catholic episcopacy, Africa was witness to the bitter struggle of the two Christian Churches. While the Donatist leaders and some of their followers were cultured, Romanized men of distinction from the urban upper classes, their broad base of support was among the peasantry and the lower orders of the towns. Catholicism, in contrast, rested primarily upon the propertied classes -- their dependents and clients -- and upon a host of public officials. Donatists were convinced that they were the true believers who had remained pure in faith, refusing to submit to the dictates of the state in the time of the Great Persecution. They thought of themselves as martyrs, willing to sacrifice their lives for the preservation of an undefiled Church. Sacraments administered by the *traditores* and their successors were simply illicit. Hence, all that was impure must be cleansed, and Catholics, voluntarily or forcibly converted, must be rebaptised. Members of the Donatist Church, an untainted haven in a tainted world, were free from sin, and could be sure that their prayers alone were heard by God. Donatism seems to have had no distinct social ideals, although it tended to equate poverty and moral virtue. After several failures to heal the rupture between the two Churches, Constantine resorted to persecution of Donatism, but eventually relented. Peasant uprisings in Numidia were initially backed by the Donatist Church, until they went too far, and some support was also given to the revolts of two local counts, those of Firmus (372-4) and Gildo (397-8). Under the powerful Bishop Optatus of Thaumugadi (Timgad) in southern Numidia, Donatism attained the zenith of its influence in the nineties, when Catholicism had been reduced to the minority Church, as Augustine was to find it in Hippo in 391.

Little is known about the Circumcellions, and their identity is a matter of scholarly controversy.[15] Not to be confused with the Donatist Church, they were extremists of the schism, religious zealots described by Brown as "a combination of gipsy and itinerant Hot Gospeller,"[16] by Jones as the "storm-troopers of the movement,"[17] and by MacMullen as the "shock troops of Donatism."[18] Bishop Optatus of Milevis emphasized their madness, as did Augustine.[19] To the Donatists they were "holy combatants" *(agonistici)*, "holy men" or "saints" *(sancti)*, and "soldiers of Christ" *(milites Christi)*. To their Catholic opponents they were *circumcelliones*, a pejorative term compounded from *circum* and *cella*, probably meaning "around the shrine," denoting their typical mode of living in the vicinity of the rural shrines of martyrs from whose usual facilities for grain storage food could be obtained.

Apparently the Circumcellions consisted mainly of landless peasants of various kinds with some renegade slaves: illiterate, Libyan-speaking countrymen concentrated in the regions of the large estates in southern Numidia, around Hippo Regius, and possibly in parts of Mauretania. Many seem to have been farmers who, having been forced to abandon their small holdings, formed a pool of itinerant agricultural workers. One suggestion is that they were migratory labourers making a circuit of the olive orchards.[20] Their leaders may have been Donatist priests, and possibly they were recipients of material support from local bishops in times of adversity and for the launching of especially ambitious projects. Dressed in monastic garb and accompanied by women sworn to chastity, Circumcellions led ascetic lives and carried and sold religious relics. These bands of peasants may have been wandering monks, precursors of the marabouts or dervishes and African counterparts of a common religious phenomenon in the East.[21] Their weapons were clubs called "Israels," although upon occasion more formidable instruments of violence, such as swords, axes, and slings, might be used. Engaging in ritual drinking and dancing, they would attempt to martyr themselves by attacking the villas of Catholic landholders and their churches, amidst war-cries of *Deo laudes*. A traveller might be waylaid by a group of the saints and be given the choice of killing them or being killed. Martyrdom was even carried to the extreme of ritualistic mass suicide.

Augustine, himself narrowly escaping an ambush by the saints, depicts in detail their methods of terrorizing the countryside: murder, beating, mutilation, blinding by "acid," "tar and feathering", and kidnapping.[22] Not the least of their atrocities was violence against property: "They live as bandits, they die as Circumcelliones, they are honoured as martyrs!"[23] Villas were pillaged and burned; Catholic churches destroyed; and altars and shrines, demolished. Promissory notes were stolen and creditors frightened from collecting debts. Slaves were incited against their masters, aided in seeking freedom, and given refuge. In fact, the Circumcellions seem to have been so numerous, their migratory labour so much a part of the rural scene, and their armed terror so infamous that they were accorded the status of an *ordo* in an imperial edict of 412 stipulating the fines for Donatist belief.[24]

A history of the Circumcellions can only be outlined in an imprecise way. Their first recorded appearance was in 340 under the leadership of two unknowns, Fasir and Axido, in a peasant uprising in southern Numidia. Saintly agitation, especially at the great markets or public fairs so common in the area, reached such proportions that the Donatist episcopacy appealed to the Roman authorities for the reestablishment of law and order. In a grave incident at the market of Octava partisans were killed resisting imperial troops and given martyrs' burial by the lower Donatist clergy in contravention of their Bishop's stipulation. Although in this early period Circumcellions were banned by their Church, their terrorism seems to have increased. The Donatist hierarchy apparently used them when it was advantageous to do so, disowning them, however, if matters went too far. In 347 Donatus, Bishop of Bagai, relied upon the saints to oppose by force the recently instituted governmental investigation of the relations between the two churches. After he lost his life in the hostilities, a time of relative quiet ensued, only to be disrupted in the sixties by an outbreak of Circumcellion atrocities protesting an imperial decree uniting the churches. Later in 372-4 Circumcellions were at the forefront of a full-scale revolt in protest against excessive taxation organized by the native Count Firmus.

The height of Circumcellion activity was reached in the last decade of the century, when Optatus, Bishop of Thaumagadi since 388, armed them for the purpose of crushing the Catholics and imposing Donatism on the whole of Africa. His ambitions were abruptly terminated, however, with the suppression of the Donatist-supported revolt in 397-8 of Count Gildo, younger brother of Firmus. In the next years Donatism was exposed to constantly increasing pressure from the authorities, culminating in the proscription of 412 and the subsequent suppression. The Circumcellions, possibly hindered from spearheading a massive Donatist counter-offensive by the withdrawal of leadership and aid from the beleaguered mother church, ended its reign of terror with a bloody rash of mass suicides.[25] So serious was the Circumcellion threat to the unity and peace of African society, one historian has concluded that the "destruction of Roman landed civilization must be laid at their door, and in this they were a far more terrible enemy than the Bagaudae in Gaul and Spain."[26]

## II

Were the Circumcellions a social protest movement? Professor Frend is the leading British scholar who answers the question in the affirmative. In *The Donatist Church* (1952) he argues that the Circumcellions, although "above all, religious fanatics," protested "against clearly defined economic grievances," thereby reflecting "the union of social and religious discontent in the Donatist movement."[28] He contends, furthermore, that the Numidian uprising of Fasir and Axido in 340 in which the Circumcellions had a prominent role is "the prototype of every agrarian revolt inspired by the teaching of the Bible down to John Ball and the German Peasant Revolt of 1524-25."[29]

Frend's estimate of the Circumcellions (and the Donatists), however, has been vigorously disputed by several eminent authorities. Among the first, Professor A.H.M. Jones in 1959 rejected the thesis that the Donatists were "at bottom a social movement."[30] The "real moving force" of Donatism and other ancient heresies was religion, not "national or class feeling." This theme was to be taken up again in *The Later Roman Empire* (1964): "In general, it would seem, the religious struggles of the later empire were in reality what they appeared to be. Their bitterness demonstrates the overwhelming importance of religion in the minds of all sorts and conditions of men."[31] Yet, as will shortly be seen, Jones' evaluation of the Circumcellions, as distinguished from the Donatists, is more equivocal than that of the other critics. One of them, Augustine's distinguished biographer, Peter Brown, held in 1967 that the notion of Donatism as an expression of popular protest obscures the role of Augustine and his associates in fomenting trouble by their "doctrinaire persecution from above, which, in turn, can only be resisted by mounting violence from below."[32] Earlier, in 1964, Brown had written: "... even the word 'movement' applied by historians to the Circumcellions contains the insidious *praeiudicium* that their activity must have been directed 'against' something."[33] Nor should we "assume without question that the origin of such activity must lie in a reaction to Roman society." In examining the Circumcellions, according to Brown, we are confronting a "'crisis', such as frequently affects the religion of primitive communities; and...the social repercussions and intentions of this religious 'crisis' were largely wished upon it by the more easily shocked, or the less scrupulous, members of the African episcopate." Finally in 1967, Professor MacMullen of Yale University flatly denied that either "the Circumcellions or the Donatists had enlisted in a class struggle or that they were social revolutionairies."[34] Instead, the Circumcellions possessed a "religious orientation," and their "schismatic violence was just what everybody thought who could observe it at first hand, that is, basically religious...."[35]

A fundamental shortcoming of the scholarly opponents of Frend's position is an apparent oversimplification of human motivation and action. Their assessment of the Circumcellions is of an "either/or" kind. The saints are said to have acted solely for religious reasons and for no other. Unlike Frend's more balanced approach, his critics claim the Circumcellions to be either religious zealots or social protestors, and deny the latter. Oswyn Murray has emphasized the difficulties of the approach in a review of MacMullen's book: "The question is not whether the *circumcelliones* or *bagaudae* were proletarian Marxists or tribal nationalists, but whether there was not also some element of economic or national motivation in these movements."[36] He continues by pointing to a common error in studying agrarian unrest, "that of believing that when the major cause is identified, no other factors are relevant...." In our critics' model of human behaviour, no allowance is made for a possible mixture of motives and reasons, or for an ambiguity of incentive and outlook. A clear-cut and conscious means-end rationality seems to be ascribed to the peasant actors, as if they were always fully aware of what they were doing and precise in regard to the ends being pursued. These are particularly dangerous assumptions to make about anyone, much less the Circumcellions. Moreover, in the world of classical antiquity, where from our standpoint distinctively economic, social, political, and religious phenomena were complexly intertwined and often conflated, it would be highly misleading to reduce the psychology of popular protest to a single factor, religious or otherwise. The fact that the Circumcellions offered no definite programme of social reform or distinct set of social ideals by no means rules them out as a social protest movement, contrary to the contention of two of the critics.[38] Considering the nature of the saints, it would be surprising indeed had they articulated any social objectives.

More specifically, the scholarly sceptics have asked this question about the Circumcellions, in the words of MacMullen: "Was their ferocity aimed at the rich as such or at the rich as Catholics?"[39] The critics agree that the available evidence suggests: 1) Catholic not Donatist landlords were terrorized, 2) renegades from Donatism were especially persecuted, and 3) Catholic landlords who did not interfere with the religion of their tenants and servants were seldom victimized.[40] Nevertheless, Professor Jones has admitted that "some features of a class war" can be found in the religious struggles in Africa, and that "some solid evidence" exists for the conclusion that peasant terrorism was in part, at least, a revolt of the poor against the rich.[41] Circumcellions, not to be confused with Donatists in general, "were no doubt not averse from paying off old scores against oppressive landlords and extortionate moneylenders when they had a good excuse for doing so in the name of religion."[42] The "solid evidence" Jones has in mind are the first-hand accounts by such Catholic dignitaries as Bishop Optatus of Milevis, Augustine, and his friend and biographer, Bishop Possidius of Calama. Their reports suggest that, in addition to pagans and schismatics within Donatism like the Maximianists, true-blue Donatists were themselves sometimes the victims of Circumcellion atrocities. Possidius, in his life of Augustine, states that the rural terrorists "spare neither their own kind nor others,"[43] and Augustine in 398 affirmed that Donatists as well as Catholics were among the injured.[44]

Other portions of their testimony tend to confirm that Catholics were not the only victims, and that Circumcellions were something more than itinerant holy zealots determined to harm and eradicate their religious foes. Some descriptions of the objects of Circumcellion terror are worded in a very general way with no effort to identify them specifically as either Catholic or Donatist. Moreover, the conflict depicted clearly indicates elements of class struggle. For example, Optatus said that "...no man could be secure in his possessions. Bonds of indebtedness were without value: no creditor at that time was free to exact payment. All were terrified by the demands of those who boasted that they were leaders of the holy men...."[45] Augustine, writing to the Donatist Bishop Macrobius of Hippo in 409, referred to the Circumcellion incitement to war: "Unity is shattered as peasant boldness is directed against their landlords, and fugitive slaves, contrary to apostolic discipline, are turned not only against their masters, but even threaten them, not simply threatening, but subjecting them to violent attack."[46] A few sentences later he mentions a heavily indebted subdeacon who became a Donatist, in part, at least to escape his creditors.[47] About 417 and after the threat of the Circumcellions had passed, Augustine recalls their terrorism:

> What master was there who was not compelled to live in dread of his own servant, if he had put himself under the guardianship of the Donatists? Who dared even threaten one who sought his ruin with punishment? Who dared to exact payment of a debt from one who consumed his stores, or from any debtor whatsoever, that sought their assistance or protection? Under the threat of beating, and burning, and immediate death, all documents compromising the worst of slaves were

destroyed, that they might depart in freedom. Notes of hand that had been extracted from debtors were returned to them. Any one who had shown a contempt for their hard words were compelled by harder blows to do what they desired. The houses of innocent persons who had offended them were either razed to the ground or burned. Certain heads of families of honourable parentage, and brought up with a good education, were carried away half dead after their deeds of violence, or bound to the mill, and compelled by blows to turn it round, after the fashion of the meanest beasts of burden. For what assistance from the laws rendered by the civil powers was ever of any avail against them? What official ever ventured so much as to breathe in their presence? What agents ever exacted payment of debt which they had been unwilling to discharge? Who ever endeavoured to avenge those who were put to death in their massacres?[48]

But the thesis that Catholics were the sole victims of Circumcellions by no means weakens the case for their being a social protest movement. For it can be argued that the behaviour of Circumcellions, broadly speaking, was a manifestation of "popular culture."[49] We know practically nothing about the feelings, thoughts, and aspirations of the African peasantry. Nevertheless, it would seem safe to assume that from their perspective an unbridgeable gulf existed between themselves and the Catholic Church. Catholicism stood for an alien and hostile world. It was the religion of magistrate, tax collector, and landlord. The Church itself possessed large properties worked by peasants and slaves. Catholicism and all it represented were a foreign urban culture imposed upon a subject rural people. Most of the clergy could not even speak the language of the peasant. To the ordinary Donatist countryman the Catholic Church must have come to mean all that was impure in the world, secular as well as religious, all the oppression and exploitation that he bore.

In the relatively primitive society of rural Africa steeped in the custom and superstition of an age-old tradition of peasant culture, the potency of such symbolism cannot be discounted. Catholicism proved to be a lightning rod for the discharge of peasant frustration and discontent. Social protest in Africa, therefore, was inextricably bound up with religious protest. The two could hardly be separated in the peasant mentality. An attack upon the Church was in effect an assault upon the established social order. Re-baptism, so central a sacrament to Donatism, was not only a purifying release from the impurity of Catholicism, but also may have been something of a symbolic act of defiance against ruling class hegemony and of a ritualistic gesture of freedom from the Roman yoke. In brief, the Circumcellions in their conflict with Catholics, were not simply religious protestors, but a counter-hegemonic force.

The argument that the Circumcellions were engaged in social protest is generally bolstered by the work of some contemporary social historians on more recent problems. In the first place, to refer to the most obvious matter, Circumcellion terrorism cannot be categorized "criminal" in the customary sense, a point reinforced by the distinction made by George Rudé between "ordinary crime" and "social protest crime."[50] Protest crimes, he maintains, are not simply private acts for self-aggrandizement and revenge, although these may be motives. Most character-istically, however, protest crimes are collective rather than individual acts, usually extending over a considerable time-period, and committed by some kind of organized, popular movement. The typical social protest crime appears to aim at some kind of social goal, albeit not always clearly and distinctly expressed. According to these criteria, the illegal acts of Circumcellions against Catholics seem to have been protests against the worst features of oppression and exploitation, as they directly affected day-to-day agrarian life in a disintegrating patriarchal society.

On the face of it, the Circumcellions are akin to what E.J. Hobsbawm, in quite another historical context, has called "social banditry," a rural protest movement of illiterate peasant primitives.[51] As he explains, social banditry is a pre-political movement, without organization or ideology, that may arise before the generation of genuine class consciousness and a political focus. The protest of social bandits is directed not against oppression and poverty *per se,* but their excess. To quote Hobsbawm, social banditry

> ... is little more than endemic peasant protest against oppression and poverty: a cry of vengeance on the rich and the oppressors, a vague dream of some curb upon them, a righting of individual wrongs. Its ambitions are modest: a traditional world in which men are justly dealt with, not a new and perfect world. It becomes epidemic rather than endemic when a peasant society which knows of no better means of self-defence is in a condition of abnormal tension and disruption.[52]

The existence in a time of economic decline and social decay of pre-political protest movements among peasants before the emergence of class consciousness, such as Hobsbawm postulates, is a view not dissimilar to E.P. Thompson's contention that in pre-industrial society class struggle often precedes mature class formations.[53] Circumcellion protests can perhaps be described in precisely this way. Since fully conscious classes did not exist, at least in the classic nineteenth-century English sense, and because no written record of the ideas and ideals of the peasant protestors has survived, we must, following Thompson's suggestion, look to the hegemonic class for any articulation of the fundamental clash of interests in Africa.

It has already been noted that the portrayal of the Circumcellions by Optatus and Augustine is sometimes formulated in what we readily recognize as the language of class struggle: peasant versus landlord, slave versus master, and debtor versus creditor. Often, however, the accounts are not in such obvious terms, and to reveal more fully the nature of the basic social antagonisms in rural Africa, we must, to use Thompson's expression, "decode" the vocabulary employed by the hegemonic class.[54] For Optatus and especially Augustine the peasant terrorists were not what their own partisans would call them, "holy combatants," "saints," and "soldiers of Christ," but *circumcelliones,* "around the shrines," a label that would immediately set them apart as peculiar and unnatural creatures. They are bandits *(latrones),*[55] but certainly not ordinary ones. Their abnormality is denoted particularly by the use of *furor,*[56] and to lesser extent of *dementia* and *insania.* They are mad, frenzied, fanatical bandits. Apart from this demented character, and perhaps more important, is their boldness, brazenness, impudence, and insolence. The key-word, appearing with great frequency, is *audacia,* employed in the derogatory sense rather than with the meaning of courage or daring.[57] Boldness or brazenness is often a term of abuse in both ancient Greece and Rome and even in the modern world, applied by the gentlemanly classes to social inferiors, hoi polloi who do not know their place and defy the authority of their betters. Augustine refers to their onslaughts against landholders as *"audacia rusticana,"* rustic or peasant boldness.[58] *Rusticus* also meant simple, clownish, boorish, all that a refined and cultured urbanite was not. Circumcellions, then, were criminal dregs, simple-minded and uncouth zealots of brazen demeanour who scorned all discipline *(disciplina)* imposed from above,[59] and consequently challenged the unity *(unitas)* of both religion and society.[60]

Possibly the trait of the Circumcellions stressed most by the agents of hegemony was their rootlessness and wandering nature. Their vagrant and nomadic character is depicted by the use in particular of "herd" or "troop" *(grex)*,[61] which is coupled with "abandoned" or "wretched" *(perditus)*.[62] So they are herds of abandoned men, or as it were herds of sheep without their shepherds insanely roaming the countryside and insolently committing crimes against their betters. In one passage Augustine portrays them as "those herds of abandoned and most demented men."[63] The words *vagus* and *vagor* are sometimes employed.[64] They are vagabonds, living a shiftless, worthless, and irresponsible existence. Augustine and his peers were apparently deeply concerned that Circumcellions had no permanent residence or fixed abode upon the land as peasants should, subject to the secular authority of a specific landlord and magistrate. Unlike the *peregrini* or pilgrims, Augustine's designation of the condition of the elect in the inhospitable temporal world,[65] the Circumcellions were vagabonds who knew no authority, neither that of God nor man. For Augustine, they must have been a terrifying instance of his precept that a "people" without the external unity and harmony created by a hierarchical system of institutional order would degenerate into a "disordered multitude" or unruly mob.[66]

The Circumcellions, consequently, from the vantage of Augustine and his associates, are one of the first extensively documented historical examples on a mass scale of the social phenomenon of "masterless men,"[67] dreaded ever since by magistrate, landlord, and priest for their disturbance of rural and urban tranquillity. In the language of Marx and Engels, masterless men are "social scum," "proletarian rabble," "lumpen proletarians," "vagabonds," *"lazzaroni," "gens san feu et aveu."*[68] They are propertyless paupers with no occupation, those "who have no master, and who have too many," and must prostitute themselves for the sake of survival. Engels uses the phrase of Oliver Goldsmith, "the bold peasantry of England," who, since the Middle Ages, having been gradually dispossessed of their land and forced to turn to poaching, smuggling, and pilfering, become the basis of the future industrial proletariat.[69]

Augustine is fearful of the masterless Circumcellions and what they spell for African society as well as for his Church and religion. His horror is the time-honoured dread of the "many-headed beast"--the "mob" on rampage--so characteristic of the entrenched propertied classes and their spokesmen from Plato's day to our own. He dwells upon the irrationality of the saints, their boldness, their vagrancy, and criminal defiance of law and order. Singularly absent from his remarks is any real sign of fellow-feeling, much less understanding, for their pitiable lives. He is deeply perturbed by their non-conformity and violations of all social discipline, by their threat to established authority and disruption of religious and secular unity. Hence, the nature of the social forces of Africa in opposition, the lines of battle, and the interests at stake are now clearly discernible.

## *III*

Any remaining doubt, however, that the Circumcellions were a social protest movement, a counter-hegemonic force in Africa, may be dispelled by closer scrutiny of Augustine. An examination of his life and political thought attests that he was a leading intellectual agent of class hegemony. Once we recall his status in the Roman world, his conception of society, his attitude toward rich and poor and the peasant, and his notion of the state, we should be in a better position to understand his profound concern over the saints. Apart from their actual violence against the person and property of Catholics, their very being and abnormal mode of life threatened the crucial principles of order, unity, and authority upon which, for Augustine, a viable temporal realm depended. Our comprehension of the Circumcellions and of Augustine's political thought, hence, are mutually interdependent. A knowledge of each may help to elucidate the other. Through Augustine's political thought we can perhaps more readily perceive the nature of the Circumcellions and their social significance within the context of Roman Africa. And conversely, by thus enhancing and enriching our knowledge of them, certain salient aspects of Augustine's social and political ideas will be brought into sharper relief and thereby rendered more intelligible. Indeed, the spectral saints may possibly have been a factor in shaping his later outlook.

Although the son of a poor property-holder of the curial class of Thagaste in Numidia (Souk Ahras, Eastern Algeria), Augustine's early career was typical of the increasing upward social mobility since the reign of Constantine. His rapid ascent of the social ladder was at each step forwarded in Africa and Italy by wealthy and powerful patrons, friends, and associates.[70] Had he not returned from Milan and entered the Church, his upward climb, so he tells us in the *Confessions,* would have been furthered by the probable award of high governmental rank and marriage to a rich heiress.[71] As a Bishop of Hippo Regius he had become an eminent figure of the cultured and affluent Romanized colonial establishment. With little or no knowledge of the indigenous languages, and restricting his life mainly to the urbanized coastal sector, he was effectively cut off from contact with the labouring poor of the countryside. If not before, certainly after the publication in 413 of the first books of the *City of God,* his name became well known to sophisticates throughout the Empire. His influence among the ruling circles was promoted by a peripatetic "literary agent" and a distinguished "lobbyist" at court. If he had ever felt free to retire from the pressing duties of episcopal office, his personal ideal would have been a gentlemanly and monastic leisure devoted to contemplation, writing, and discussion with like-minded souls, free from the "turbulent molestations of human life."[72] His heroes were the highly educated members of the aristocracy who had turned to Christianity, renouncing their riches for an ascetic, reflective regimen. They were refined, austere, persevering, God-fearing patricians like Ambrose and Paulinus of Nola. The audience for which Augustine intended the *City of God* was of much the same breed, with the important difference of being pagan: wealthy, cultured refugees in Carthage from the barbarian invasion of Italy.

Augustine's view of society is in keeping with these features of his life.[73] It is a vision which largely accepts the status-quo and justifies the prevailing polarities of noble and servile, rich and poor, propertied and propertyless, leisured and labouring, master and servant. In this inegalitarian society of wide disparities in wealth and rank, each person has been assigned a station by divine providence and is expected to accept his status and its duties humbly and without complaint.[74] Rich and poor are divinely ordained, but morally equal.[75] Riches do not prevent one from entering heaven, although perhaps rendering such entry more difficult, nor is poverty a guarantee of celestial beatitude.[76] Covetousness, of which rich and poor alike can be guilty, is a sin and not wealth as such. The rich should not strive for more than they have, live in moderation, use their wealth with benevolent intent, and treat their inferiors humanely.[77] The poor should be content with their lot, and conscientiously obey their superiors, neither stealing from the rich, nor glorying in their own poverty, or struggling to improve their wordly condition:[78] "...ye poor, refrain from plundering....ye poor bridle your desires."[79]

Harmony, order, and peace, not strife and conflict, should characterize human relations. Following the teachings of St. Paul *(Romans,* xiii, 1-2) and St. Peter (1 *Peter,* ii, 13), Augustine urges respect for an unswerving obedience to all secular authority.[80] As he conceives of it, authority is patriarchal and paternalistic and should be unquestioned. Properly constituted society is a natural hierarchy of the higher and lower, each level and rank taking its orientation and values from the one above it: Church from God, state from Church, household from state, wife from husband, child from father, and slave from master.[81] Any active resistance to established authority is sinful. No matter how badly he may be treated by his superior, the social inferior should always be obedient and submissive, never defiant and insolent. Augustine endorses the apostolic teaching (*Ephesians,* vi, 5; *Titus,* ii, 9) that slavery is a divine penalty for human sin.[82] However, if anyone is required to violate a divine command, he is morally obligated to disobey passively, and to accept dutifully the punishment for such disobedience. Augustine's conception of society is informed by the principle that the things of the temporal world are essentially unimportant. As long as external order is maintained so that men live in peace and security, and can safely worship their true God, material conditions are negligible. The primary concern of the Christian should be the state of his soul, not the world about him. What Augustine says about slavery in the *City of God* can be taken as an apt summary of his social outlook:

> And beyond question it is a happier thing to be the slave of a man than of a lust; for even this very lust of ruling, to mention no others, lays waste men's hearts with the most ruthless dominion. Moreover, when men are subjected to one another in a peaceful order, the lowly position does as much good to the servant as the proud position does harm to the master. But by nature, as God first created us, no one is the slave either of man or of sin. This servitude is, however, penal, and is appointed by that law which enjoins the preservation of the natural order and forbids its disturbance; for if nothing had been done in violation of that law, there would have been nothing to restrain by penal servitude. And therefore the apostle admonishes slaves to be subject to their masters, and to serve them heartily and with good-will, so that, if they cannot be freed by their masters, they may themselves make their slavery in some sort free, by serving not in crafty fear, but in faithful love, until all unrighteousness pass away, and all principality and every human power be brought to nothing, and God be all in all.[83]

Augustine seems to have lacked any genuine understanding of Africa's labouring millions, nor did he ever demonstrate great sympathy or compassion for their plight, except to emphasize that this was the changeless way of things. He was out of touch with them,[84] unfamiliar with their wretched living conditions. Only with difficulty did he overcome his initial aversion to the masses.[85] No doubt he shared in the ancient gentlemen's disdain for banausic labour. Despite his perseverance in becoming well-disposed toward the working poor, an occasional note of contempt creeps into his thoughts. Labourers are simple folk with no understanding of causes, possessing as they do only an outer and not an inner eye.[86] There was hardly an artisan, "who does not practise his own art for the purposes of pecuniary gain...."[87] The world of the peasantry was beyond the ken of a confirmed townsman like Augustine who had originally foresaken the backwaters of rural Numidia for the culture and refinement of Carthage, Rome, and Milan. He judged shepherds and plowmen to be foolish creatures because they are not ruled by their minds.[88] The juxtaposition and opposition of terms in one of his writings suggest something of the nature of his feelings: "the few," "the learned," "the city-dwellers" in contrast to "the many," "the ignorant," "the peasants."[89] His few concessions to rural life were to speak nostalgically of gardening as a "bracing exercise," to remark that Adam and Eve had the good fortune to be gardeners, and to recall his own youthful hunting of birds.[90] The countryside where most Africans lived and worked at a bare subsistence level was *terra incognita,* the heart of darkness, the centre of ignorance, superstition, and unreason. It was as if he had projected the dualism of his early Manichaeism upon his native soil, dividing it between the enlightenment of the Romanized coastal areas and the impenetrable blackness of the Numidian hinterland. If Catholicism was the focus of all the grievances of protesting Donatist peasants, the Circumcellions must have symbolized to Augustine all that was uncouth, uncultured, and irrational about the countryside and its denizens. The rural saints were disciples of the Devil endangering the whole complex edifice of social relationships inspired by God and established by his flock over the centuries.

To be a bastion of "enlightenment" withstanding the forces of evil, however, the requisite social system does not develop on its own, but rests upon a stern disciplinary order imposed from above by government and law. Before the Fall, according to Augustine, man was by nature gregarious, an authentic social being, but the sin of Adam transformed him into a political creature. After Adam succumbed to temptation, thus poisoning the human race with pride, the law of nature inscribed upon the human heart was no longer sufficient to guide our lives in an Eden of psychic and social bliss. Because of man's lustful, fallen nature, the state became essential as a divinely ordained penalty and remedy for the prevention of mutual destruction and anarchy. The state, instead of being natural, is a God-inspired convention devised by men for the preservation of their lives and possessions. It is basically a repressive agency with violence at its disposal to control sinful man through fear of law resting upon coercive sanctions.[91] The state's purpose is solely the secular one of maintaining external harmony and unity under the moral guidance of the Church. While a relatively uncorrupt people like the ancient Roman republicans were able to govern themselves, when a society has declined to the abysmal circumstances of his own, Augustine believes the only feasible mode of government to be the severe, but beneficent rule of patriarchs like the Christian Emperors Constantine and Theodosius.[92] Just as true peace is that of the soul in harmony with God, so true justice is not of this world, which is merely a way station in the passage to eternal salvation or damnation.

A Christian state like the one fashioned by Constantine and Theodosius, of course, enables the faithful to worship and perform good works in tranquillity without fear of interference. The Christian polity, moreover, is the most conducive to unity and stability because of the mutual bond joining man to man through a common love of God.[93] In sum, Augustine was thoroughly committed in theory and practice to a hierarchical, authoritarian society and an autocratic, patriarchal state guided by a unified Christian Church. He "was able to identify in general terms the cause of the Catholic Church with that of *Romanitas* in Africa," and insisted upon "the virtue of the framework of Roman laws and institutions in which that Church was living."[94] Such a stand entitles him to be called the "theorist of the Constantinian Revolution,"[95] or perhaps somewhat less euphemistically, one of the foremost intellectual agents of class hegemony during the later Roman Empire.

What effect the masterless and brazen saints had upon this grim and brooding statuary of ideas must remain a matter of conjecture. Perhaps the "profound and ominous changes" occurring between 395 and 405 in Augustine's attitude toward state and religion were in part reflective of a gnawing anxiety over the escalating terrorism of the Circumcellions, who for him represented Donatism carried to its most frightening and destructive extreme.[96] First-hand experience from his episcopacy of the growing ferocity of rural turmoil must have alerted him to the hopelessness of the social situation and been vital to his eventual decision in 405 to approve the use of state power for the extirpation of heresy, a reversal of his previous positions. Prior to about 398 he believed that Donatists might be persuaded of their errors. Then, even after Donatism had been declared a heresy, he argued that the state should only act against those responsible for criminal acts, for example, against lives and property. Now, he thought that rational discussion and legal protection against criminality were no longer sufficient for dealing with the anarchic potential of these lustful men. They must be more firmly disciplined, more completely subjected to the punishing prophylaxis of social authority and governmental pressure. Admittedly, to be guided by Brown's subtle and penetrating analysis: "...the violence of the Donatists, alone, cannot explain Augustine's change of attitude."[97] It was rooted in his past thinking on the subject of religious coercion -- he did not hesitate to advocate suppression of paganism in 399-401 -- and on the question of freedom of choice as related to the problem of enforced conversion.[98] The significant point, however, is that Donatist violence, i.e., Circumcellion activity, was a major factor, if not the only one, accounting for Augustine's dramatic change of mind. Commenting to Januarius, the Donatist primate, in 406, Augustine leaves no doubt about the matter: "...the clemency of the Catholic Church would have led us to desist from even enforcing these decrees of the emperors, had not your clergy and Circumcelliones, disturbing our peace, and destroying us by their most monstrous crimes and furious deeds of violence, compelled us to have these decrees revived and put in force again."[99]

But violence, in and by itself, probably did not so much worry or move Augustine, as did the portent of violence, its significance in the greater scheme of things. The degree to which the established religion and the political and social status quo were threatened by the anomalous way of life and eccentric frame of mind and motives of those who used violence, was a greater consideration than the violence itself. Even had the Circumcellions not resorted to violence, he might have still decided to urge their forcible repression, as he did in the case of the Rogatists, a peaceful Donatist sect.[100] This may be why Augustine, if Brown is correct, "deliberately emphasized their [Circumcellion] rôle as potential troublemakers in order to induce the authorities to suppress them as a religious group."[101]

All of this tends to be obscured by those who insist that the Circumcellions were motivated solely by religious considerations. For if their protests were social in addition to being religious, and considering Augustine's apparent awareness that such was the case, then surely he had an additional and most pressing incentive for his volte-face in urging civil coercion of the Donatists. The bold and masterless peasants, to Augustine, must have become a dire threat in principle as well as actuality to the divinely ordained social hierarchy of ranks and stations. Their behaviour called into question the very axioms of order and hierarchy upon which a stable and enduring society was constructed. The brazen saints were flagrantly disavowing the supreme canon of Scriptural authority: that one should always bow before the higher powers. Likewise, Holy Writ had decreed that servants and slaves, no matter what the provocation, should be the docile subjects of their masters. Not only were all their crimes sins against God,[102] but also by usurping the coercive functions of the law, the Circumcellions were guilty of the basest conduct, which if unchecked would destroy society.[103]

No alternative was left to Augustine, if a fragmenting social order were to be salvaged, than to oppose their subversive outlook and ruinous violence with the legitimate and creative coercion of the state. Masterless men must be mastered and subordinated to duly constituted secular and religious authority, if catastrophe were to be avoided. They must be crushed, punished, and disciplined by the armed might of civil authority. Without state intervention to uphold law and order, "...the reins placed on human licence would be loosened and thrown off: all sins would go unpunished. Take away the barriers created by the laws! Men's brazen capacity to do harm, their urge to self-indulgence would rage to the full."[104] Although rational discussion and admonition may be sufficient to correct the minority, the better sort of men, fear of punishment is the only method of handling the meaner and inferior types, those making up the vast majority.[105] They are like wayward sons or straying sheep who need to be "recalled" by "the stripes of temporal scourging" just as if they were "evil slaves" and "good for nothing fugitives". Furthermore, to coerce some is to save the many from doom: "For there are actually not so many persons who thus perish of their own free will, as there are estates, villages, streets, fortresses, municipal towns, cities, that are delivered by the laws under consideration from that fatal and eternal destruction."[106]

A final question remains about Augustine's perception of the Circumcellions. Why, in all his writing, is there no sustained and explicit discussion of their threat to society? He describes in detail their violent activities, of course, and by reading between the lines, as it were, we realize that he was aware of their social implications. But why does he never expressly evaluate them as social as well as religious dissenters? The explanation, for what from our standpoint is a curious omission, is that Augustine was at root a religionist and theologian, and not strictly speaking a social and political theorist or commentator. Religious non-conformity was not differentiated by him from social subversion. Any attack upon the doctrine and institutions of his Church undermined the very structure of Roman society. For Catholicism legitimized and gave authority to the already weakened system of social relationships against which the religious protests of the Circumcellions were aimed. He, no more than they, made the kind of distinction that is so obvious to us.

Since 395, on becoming Bishop of Hippo, until death in 430, Augustine, overburdened by the onerous responsibilities of office and ever more aware of the collapse of his civilization, grew socially more conservative and pessimistic about the possibilities of human action. His intellectual position was hardening and in some ways becoming more extreme.[107] He was increasingly convinced of the necessity of drastic measures for the containment of fallen man, sceptical of the capacity of free will, and committed to the doctrines of grace and predestination. Strengthened also was the conviction that true freedom was solely a matter of the inner life. He even went so far as to reject Cicero's conception of the state, redefining it so as to omit the criterion of justice.[108] No state can possibly be just, but not all states are tyrannical. Although, ever since his conversion he had believed that earthly justice was an image of divine justice, now not only had the image become so faint as to be non-existent, but also the archetype itself was beyond the grasp of the human intellect. To argue that this changing consciousness was due to the impact of the Circumcellion menace upon African society would obviously be reckless. It might, however, be equally foolhardy to discount the terrorism of these bold and masterless peasants in shaping Augustine's political thought. In studying the great precapitalist political thinkers of the past their history from above cannot with impunity be treated in isolation from history from below as it was being made by voiceless and faceless peasant masses.

# NOTES

1. Esp. *The Crowd in the French Revolution* (Oxford, 1959); *Wilkes and Liberty: A Social Study of 1763 to 1774* (Oxford, 1962); *The Crowd in History: A Study of Popular Disturbances in France and England, 1730-1848* (New York, London, Sydney, 1964).

2. Cf. Rudé, *Ideology and Popular Protest* (London, 1980), 22-4.

3. On the African economy see: R.P. Duncan-Jones, "City Population in Roman Africa," *Journal of Roman Studies,* LIII (1963), 85-90; "Some Configurations of Landholding in the Roman Empire," *Studies in Roman Property,* ed. M.I. Finley (Cambridge, 1976), 7-33; "Costs, Outlays and Summae Honorariae from Roman Africa," *Papers of the British School at Rome,* XXX (1962), 47-115; *The Economy of the Roman Empire: Quantitative Studies* (Cambridge, 1974); "Wealth and Munificence in Roman Africa," *Papers of the British School at Rome,* XXXI (1963), 159-77; W.H.C. Frend, *The Donatist Church: A Movement of Protest in Roman North Africa* (London, 1952); A.H.M. Jones, *The Later Roman Empire, 284-602: A Social Economic and Administrative Survey* (Oxford, 1973), esp. II, chs. xx, xxv; *The Roman Economy: Studies in Ancient Economic and Administrative History,* ed. P.A. Brunt (Oxford, 1974); B.H. Warmington, *The North African Provinces from Diocletian to the Vandal Conquest* (Westport, Conn., 1954); C.R. Whittaker, "Agri Deserti," *Studies in Roman Property,* 137-65.
   For religion: Peter Brown, *Augustine of Hippo, A Biography* (London, 1967); *Religion and Society in the Age of Augustine* (London, 1972); Gerald Bonner, *St. Augustine of Hippo: Life and Controversies* (London, 1963); Herbert A. Deane, *The Political and Social Ideas of St. Augustine* (New York and London, 1963), esp. ch. VI; W.H.C. Frend, *The Donatist Church;* "The Failure of the Persecutions in the Roman Empire," *Studies in Ancient Society,* ed. M.I. Finley (London and Boston, 1974), 263-87; *Martyrdom and Persecution in the Early Church* (Oxford, 1964); "The Roman Empire in the Eyes of Western Schismatics during the Fourth Century A.D.," *Miscellanea Historiae Ecclesiasticae* (Stockholm, 1961), 9-22; Jones, *The Later Roman Empire,* esp. II, chs. xxii-xxiii; "Were Ancient Heresies

National or Social Movements in Disguise?," *The Roman Economy,* 308-29; B.H. Warmington, *The North African Provinces;* G.G. Willis, *St. Augustine and the Donatist Controversy* (London, 1950).

4. These figures are an extrapolation of the "tentative estimates" of the mean total between 98 and 244 of a population of 8 million and 600 towns of urban centres made by Duncan-Jones, "Wealth and Munificence," 167, 170.

5. Duncan-Jones, *The Economy of the Roman Empire,* 260 n. 4, 276.

6. Brown, *The World of Late Antiquity: From Marcus Aurelius to Muhammed* (London, 1971), 116.

7. Whittaker, "Agri Deserti," 150.

8. Jones, *The Later Roman Empire,* II, 779.

9. Duncan-Jones, "Costs, Outlays and Summae Honorariae," 69.

10. Jones, *The Later Roman Empire,* II, 793: "In Egypt the papyri prove that agricultural slavery was virtually unknown, and there is no allusion to it in the abundant literary sources for Africa. These two regions, both famous for their teeming peasant population, may have been exceptional."

11. Based on the calculations of Duncan-Jones, "Wealth and Munificence," 163-71.

12. The following relies on Jones, *The Later Roman Empire,* II, 812-23; and Whittaker, "Agri Deserti."

13. Warmington, *North African Provinces,* 100.

14. A point stressed by Frend, *Martyrdom and Persecution,* 463.

15. For the Circumcellions, in addition to the works on religion cited above in n.3, the following are useful: Jean-Paul Brisson, *Autonomisme et christianisme dans l'Afrique romaine* (Paris, 1958), 325-56; Theodora Büttner and Ernst Werner, *Circumcellionen und Adamiten* (Berlin, 1959), 21-72; Salvatore Calderone, "Circumcelliones," *La Parola del Passato,* CXII (1967), 94-109; Hans-Joachim Diesner, *Kirche und Staat im Spätrömischen Reich: Aufsätze zur Spätantike und zur Geschichte der Alten Kirche* (Berlin, 1963), 53-90; Ramsay MacMullen, *Enemies of the Roman Order* (Cambridge, Mass., 1966), 198-207; Emin Tengström, *Donatisten und Katholiken: soziale, wirtschaftliche und politische Aspekte einer nordafrikanischen Kirchenspaltung* (Göteborg, 1964), 24-78.

16. *Augustine of Hippo,* 229.

17. "Ancient Heresies," 324.

18. Macmullen, *Enemies of the Roman Order,* 201.

19. For references, see below, n. 56.

20. The argument of Tengström, *Donatisten und Katholiken,* 44-56. He also suggests that their clubs may have been the characteristic implements used in olive culture, and that the *"cella"* of "Circumcellion" instead of referring to shrine might mean *"cella olearia,"* a store house for olive oil. See the negative comments on this theory in Calderone, "Circumcelliones", 99-103; and in Brown, *Religion and Society,* 336.

21. Calderone, "Circumcelliones", 102-07; Brown, *Religion and Society,* 114 n.7, 247. The Circumcellions may possibly have been widespread in Africa and not confined to Numidia alone.

22. For examples of their activity, see Augustine *Letter* LXXXVIII, 6-8; CXI, 1; CXXXIII, 1; CLXXXV, 15, 27. Latin titles will be given in English.

23. Augustine, *Letter* LXXXVIII, 8: *"uiuunt ut latrones, moriuntur ut Circumcelliones, honorantur ut martyres...."* Translations other than my own will be so indicated. Latin texts are those of the *Corpus Scriptorum Ecclesiasticorum Latinorum.*

24. For an enumeration of the penalties of the various classes, see Warmington, *op. cit.,* 87.

25. Brown, *Augustine of Hippo,* 335.

26. Frend, *The Donatist Church*, 248. Warmington, *North Africa Provinces*, 86, 100, does not believe they were as serious a threat as the Bagaudae. On the Bagaudae, see E.A. Thompson, "Peasant Revolts in Late Roman Gaul and Spain," *Studies in Ancient Society*, ed. M.I. Finley, 304-20.

27. It is not my purpose in what follows to enter the larger controversy as to whether Donatism as a whole was a social protest movement with nationalistic features.

28. *The Donatist Church*, 172, 173, 176. Also see his "Failure of Persecutions," 284. Frend's position is seconded by Brisson, *Autonomisme et christianisme*, 341. He describes the Circumcellions, on the basis of the testimony of Optatus of Milevis and Augustine, as possessing "...les traits de l'organisation d'une classe économiquement opprimée dans sa lutte pour la vie." He concludes "...avec une assez grande sûreté sur ce point de notre enquête: nous sommes en présence d'un phénomène économique, la réaction d'un prolétariat agricole réduit à la misère." The Circumcellions are "...un exemple de révolution économique assez exceptionnel dans l'antiquité." Also, Büttner and Werner, *Circumcellionen und Adamiten*, 41-52; and Diesner, *Kirche und Staat*, 53-90.

29. *Martyrdom and Persecution*, 556.

30. "Ancient Heresies," 324-5. The views of Frend's British and North-American critics are supported by Tengström, *Donatisten und Katholiken*, 66-78, and Calderone, "Circomcelliones," 108-09.

31. *The Later Roman Empire*, II, 970.

32. *Augustine of Hippo*, 228.

33. *Religion and Society*, 333. A review of Diesner, *Kirche und Staat*, in *Journal of Theological Studies*, n.s. XV (1964), 409-11.

34. MacMullen, *Enemies of the Roman Order*, 203.

35. *Ibid.*, 201, 206.

36. Oswyn Murray, *Journal of Roman Studies*, LIX (1969), 264.

38. Jones, "Ancient Heresies," 324-5; MacMullen, *Enemies of the Roman Order*, 201. Jones here is referring to the Donatist Church as a whole.

39. MacMullen, *Enemies of the Roman Order*, 201.

40. *Ibid.*; also Jones, "Ancient Heresies," 325; *The Later Roman Empire*, II, 811, 969-70.

41. *The Later Roman Empire*, II, 970; "Ancient Heresies," 324.

42. "Ancient Heresies," 324.

43. *The Life of St. Augustine (Sancti Augustini Vita a Possidio episcopo)*, 10, as quoted in MacMullen, *Enemies of the Roman Order*, 354 n. 10.

44. *Letter*, XLIV, 9.

45. *On the Schism of the Donatists*, III, iv.

46. *Letter*, CVIII, 18.

47. *Letter*, CVIII, 19.

48. *Letter*, CLXXXV, 15. Marcus Dods translation.

49. See Rudé, *Ideology and Popular Protest*, 27-38.

50. *Protest and Punishment: The Story of the Social and Political Protesters transported to Australia, 1788-1868* (Oxford, 1978), 1-7.

51. *Primitive Rebels: Studies in Archaic Forms of Social Movement in the 19th and 20th Centuries* (New York, 1965), 3-6, 13-29.

52. *Ibid.*, 5.

53. "Eighteenth-century English society: class struggle without class?," *Social History*, 3 (May 1978), 133-65.

54. *Ibid.,* 150. I perhaps am taking a liberty with Thompson's use of "decoding." He writes: "In the eighteenth century resistance is less articulate, although often very specific, direct and turbulent. One must therefore supply the articulation, in part by de-coding the evidence of behaviour, and in part by turning over the bland concepts of the ruling authorities and looking at their undersides. If we do not do this we are in danger of becoming prisoners of the assumptions and self-image of the rulers: free labourers are seen as the 'loose and disorderly sort,' riot is seen as spontaneous and 'blind'; and important kinds of social protest become lost in the category of 'crime'."

55. For example, Augustine, *Letter* LXXXVIII, 8; *Against the Letters of Petilian,* II, 184. For a valuable discussion of the Roman use of *latros* and *latrocinium,* see Brent D. Shaw, "Bandits in the Roman Empire," *Past and Present,* 105 (November, 1984), 3-52.

56. Augustine, *Letter* LXXXVIII, 6; CVIII, 18; CLXXXV, 7, 18, 29, 41; *Against the Letters of Petilian,* I, 26; II, 184; *Against Cresconius,* III, 47; *Against Gaudentius,* I, 33. Optatus, *On the Schism of the Donatists,* III, iv. On the use of *furor, audacia, perditus, grex, latro,* see my essay, "*Populares* and *Circumcelliones:* the Vocabulary of 'Fallen Man' in Cicero and St. Augustine," to be published in *History of Political Thought;* also Guy Achard, *Pratique Rhétorique et Idéologie Politique dans les Discours "Optimates" de Cicéron* (Leiden, 1981). On *audaces,* Ch. Wirszubski, "*Audaces:* A Study in Political Phraseology," *Journal of Roman Studies,* 51 (1961), 12-22.

57. *Letter* XCIII, 2; CVIII, 18, 19, 20; *Against Cresconius,* III, 47.

58. *Letter* CVIII, 18.

59. *Letter* XXV, 2; XCIII, 3; CVIII, 19, 20; CLXXXV, 7, 11; *Against Gaudentius,* I, 33. On *disciplina* see Brown, *Augustine of Hippo,* ch. 21.

60. *Letter* CVIII, 17, 18, 19, 20; CLXXXV, 4, 12; *Against the Letters of Petilian,* I, 26; II, 52.

61. *Letter* XXXV, 2; XCIII, 5, 11; CLXXXV, 15; *Against the Letter of Parmenian,* II, 19; III, 18; *Against the Letters of Petilian,* II, 184. "Herd" as a translation of *grex* probably conveys Augustine's meaning better than "troop," and certainly fits his bucolic imagery.

62. *Letter* XCIII, 3; "*violentas perditorum hominum;*" CVIII, 19, 20; CLXXXV, 15, 16, 23.

63. *Letter* CLXXXV, 15: "*illos perditorum hominum dementissimi greges*".

64. *Letter* XXXV, 2; "*vagabundos;*" *Against the Letter of Parmenian,* II, 19. Optatus, *On the Schism of the Donatists,* III, iv.

65. Brown, *Augustine of Hippo,* 323 ff.

66. *Sermon* LIII. The term "*multitudo*" is applied to the Circumcellions by Optatus, *On the Schism of the Donatists,* III, 61.

67. See Christopher Hill's superb treatment of "masterless men" in seventeenth-century England, *The World Turned Upside Down: Radical Ideas during the English Revolution* (London, 1972), ch. 3. Also, the 1965 essay, "The Many-Headed Monster," reprinted in his *Change and Continuity in Seventeenth-Century England* (London, 1964), p. 188.

68. See, for instance, Marx and Engels, *Collected Works* (New York, 1975-   ), IV, 251, 551-2; V, 84, 202; VI, 246-7, 494; VII, 25, 142-3, 505; IX, 43-4; and *Selected Works* (Moscow, 1962), I, 155, 294-5, 341. John Locke, as a Commissioner of the Board of Trade, in his famous proposal for poor law reform of 1697 applies the label "idle vagabonds" to vagrant and unemployed paupers who require control and discipline by the authorities. The memorandum is reproduced in H.R. Fox Bourne, *The Life of John Locke* (London, 1876), II, 377-91.

69. *The Condition of the Working Class in England* (1845) in *Collected Works,* IV, 551-2. The reference is to "a bold peasantry, their country's pride," in Goldsmith's *The Deserted Village.* Engels proceeds to explain (553-4) that incendiarism (true also of the Circumcellions), was their "favourite method of social warfare" and to discuss "Swing". For a detailed analysis of this social phenomenon in England, see Hobsbawm and Rudé, *Captain Swing* (New York, 1968).

70. Brown, *The World of Late Antiquity,* 30. The following details of Augustine's life are largely derived from Brown, *Augustine of Hippo.*

71. *Confessions,* VI, xi.

72. Such is the ideal expressed in *Confessions,* VI, xiv, Loeb Classical Library translation.

73. By far the best general treatment of Augustine's social and political thought is the previously cited volume by Herbert A. Deane. I have relied in what follows upon his work, although my interpretation is not necessarily his own. The citations to Augustine serve simply as illustrations and are by no means exhaustive. Also of value is R.A. Markus, *Saeculum: History and Society in the Theology of St. Augustine* (Cambridge, 1970).

74. For example, *Of True Religion,* 76-8.

75. *Sermon* VI, IX, X, XXXV, CXIII.

76. *Sermon* XXXV.

77. *Sermon* CXXXVII.

78. *Sermon* XI, XXX.

79. *Sermon* XXXV. Marcus Dods translation.

80. *Sermon* XII; *Of True Religion,* 77.

81. *City of God,* XIX, 16.

82. *Sermon* XLIV; LII.

83. *City of God,* XIX, 15. Marcus Dods translation.

84. A point emphasized by Brown, *Augustine of Hippo,* 21.

85. *Ibid.,* 208-09.

86. *Of True Religion,* 59.

87. *City of God,* VII, 3. Marcus Dods translation.

88. *On Free Choice of the Will,* I, ix.

89. *On Cathechizing the Uninstructed (De catechizandis rudibus),* Migne, *PL* 40, 310-47, quoted in Jacques Le Goff, *Time, Work, and Culture in the Middle Ages,* trans. Arthur Goldhammer (Chicago and London, 1980), 94.

90. Brown, *Augustine of Hippo,* 21, 143.

91. *On Free Choice of the Will,* I, xv.

92. *On Free Choice of the Will,* I, vi; *City of God,* V, 24-26.

93. *Letter* CXXXVII.

94. Frend, "The Roman Empire in the Eyes of Western Schismatics," 13.

95. Brisson, *Autonomisme et christianisme,* 288. The expression is that of Brown, *Religion and and Society,* 257.

96. Brown, *Augustine of Hippo,* 235; also the whole of ch. 21.

97. *Religion and Society,* 263 n. 2.

98. *Ibid.,* 260-78.

99. *Letter* LXXXVIII, 6. Marcus Dods translation.

100. Brown, *Religion and Society,* 263 n. 2; "The Rogatist sect had no record of violence, yet Augustine would not exempt them from the laws against heretics...."

101. *Ibid.,* 318. Cf. Frend, *The Donatist Church,* 298: "The vehemence with which Augustine describes the outrages of the Circumcellions and the Donatist *sanctimoniales* who accompanied them suggests comparative helplessness."

102. *Enchiridion,* LXIV.

103. *Sermon* CCCII, 14.

104. *Against Gaudentius,* XIX, 20, cited and translated by Brown, *Augustine of Hippo,* 238.

105. *Letter* CLXXXV, 21. Marcus Dods translation.

106. *Letter* CLXXXV, 33. Marcus Dods translation.

107. Brown, *Augustine of Hippo,* 235 ff. Of importance for tracing the changes in Augustine's views between 386 and 400 is F. Edward Cranz, "The Development of Augustine's Ideas on Society Before the Donatist Controversy," *Harvard Theological Review,* 47 (1954), 255-316.

108. *City of God,* II, 21; XIX, 21, 24, 27.

J.S. Bromley

# OUTLAWS AT SEA, 1660-1720: LIBERTY, EQUALITY AND FRATERNITY AMONG THE CARIBBEAN FREEBOOTERS

Two societies, two conceptions of justice, collaborated and collided when French forces stormed Cartagena of the Indies in May 1697. For their commander, the baron de Pointis, a naval captain in the mould of Drake, this bloody if strategically pointless success fulfilled a long-postponed design "that might be both honourable and advantageous", with ships lent and soldiers (but not seamen) paid by the King, who in return would take the Crown's usual one-fifth interest in such "prêts de vaisseaux", the remaining costs falling on private subscribers, in this case no less than 666 of them, headed by courtiers, financiers, naval contractors and officers of both pen and sword.[1] According to Pointis, peace rumours restricted the flow of advances and the expedition, nearly 4,000 strong when it sailed out of Brest, was weaker than he had planned, especially if it should prove difficult to use the ships' crews ashore. At St Domingue, however, the experienced governor Jean Ducasse, who had risen by his own business abilities from relatively humble origins in Béarn, had orders to place another thousand men at the baron's disposal, in locally armed frigates and sloops. Some of these seasoned warriors were garrison soldiers, others militiamen and small settlers; there were also 180 negroes, some free and others lent by their owners with a promise of manumission if the enterprise went well. But the majority, at least 650 and probably more, were *flibustiers,* freebooters whom Ducasse had called from the sea and detained for months pending the late arrival of the squadron. With their long, light muskets known as *boucaniers*--from their original use by those earlier huntsmen who smoke-dried their meat *(boucane)* Indian-fashion--these were crack marksmen, well able to board ships or Spanish trenches, if not ramparts, with little use for artillery.

According to the careful historian, Fr Charlevoix, who had access to government records as well as to the manuscripts of a fellow Jesuit, Le Pers, who was serving on the Coast of St. Domingue at the time, Ducasse's contingent, amounting in the end to more than a fifth of the whole force, acquitted themselves with their usual audacity and resourcefulness.[2] Even Pointis, in his *Relation,* praised the negroes. The *flibustiers,* however, were "a troop of *Banditti* ... idle Spectators of a great Action ... this Rabble ... that base Kind of Life", gifted only with "a particular Talent at discovering hidden Treasures". He had resented having "to court them in the most flattering Terms". They, in their turn, were quick to object to "le bâton haut" of naval officers, as happened again when Le Moyne d'Iberville brought his last privateering armament to Martinique in 1706.[3] It was because they would serve immediately only under a man they knew, preferably one whom they had elected, that Governor Ducasse himself joined the expedition. Even so, they would have sulked in the woods had he not obtained from Pointis some prior agreement about sharing the plunder. A notice was accordingly posted at Petit Goave--by this date as much the principal privateering base of the Coast as the island of Tortuga had been in the earlier decades of "la flibuste"--announcing simply that the St Domingue contingent would participate "homme par homme" with the crews of His Majesty's ships.

Ducasse took this vague undertaking to mean that his men would share in the booty in the same proportion as their numbers bore to those from France. Pointis, mindful of the claims of his shareholders but entirely overlooking the modest investors of the Coast, allowed this assumption to rest until he was ready to embark the booty, provisionally estimated at not more than nine million in *livres tournois*. Ducasse and his followers, who had not been allowed into the counting-house where the gold and silver and precious stones had been collected, suspected that it would add up to twice as much; in any case, they expected over two million for themselves. Word came back, for the two leaders were no longer on speaking terms, that they were entitled to 160,000 *livres tournois* in silver crowns or pieces of eight, as their proper proportion of what was due to the French crews — a tenth of the first million and a mere thirtieth of the rest. This worked out at twenty-five crowns a man instead of an anticipated 1500 or 1600, including three months' wages. The freebooters' answer was to return to the city, against the appeals of Ducasse, and sack it all over again. They came away with enough precious metal to distribute a thousand crowns to each man by weight, as their custom was, before sailing, but also with fabrics and other merchandise which they would later have parted with for much less than they were worth. Four of their larger ships were soon intercepted by the British navy, the cargo of the *Cerf Volant* allegedly being sold in Jamaica for £100,000.[4]

The quarrel between Pointis and Ducasse reverberated for years. A royal *arrêt* awarded the flibustiers something near seventeen per cent of the ultimate net sum available for distribution, but it was remitted to St Domingue in goods, piecemeal, and much of this "masse de Cartagennes" never reached its intended destination, partly because it passed through dishonest hands but also because many of the tropical claimants had dispersed or died.[5] It was precisely the flight of its warriors that every good governor of St Domingue, thinly populated and exposed to attack from many quarters, most feared; and Ducasse too had a substantial personal stake in the *masse* or stock out of which the tropical investors should recover their outlay. Nevertheless, the "perfidy" of Pointis rankled most in that he had caused the governor to break faith with his prickly following.[6] He had already experienced their stubborn refusal to go to sea whenever they had money to spend, and their strong preference for the occasional Spanish prize over regular cruising against the English or Dutch, as distinct from tip-and-run descents on Jamaica for slaves. Moreover, they were still grumbling that they had not received justice after Ducasse's own attack on Jamaica in 1694. Beeston, governor of Jamaica, referred to this when reporting the state of mutiny which preceded the departure for Cartagena — "they to fight and the great only to take away the money from them."[7]

This feeling about "the great" marks the whole history of seventeenth-century privateering in the West Indies, and indeed finds echoes among the pirates, properly so called, documented by Defoe. "They were poor rogues", said some, of those strung up at Cape Coast in 1722, "and so hanged, while others, no less guilty in another way, escaped."[8] The resentments of pirates, generally recruited from merchantmen, were most specifically directed at the despotism of shipmasters: after seizing a ship, "Captain Johnson" tells us, "the Pirates began to take upon themselves the distribution of justice, examining the men concerning their master's usage of them, according to the custom of other Pirates".[9] On privateers, impeccably commissioned by a sovereign prince, a kind of class consciousness revolted against the larger shares of prize and plunder allotted to the officers, often numerous because crews were not under naval discipline; and there was sometimes distrust of the owners as well, usually entitled in France and Britain to two-thirds of the net takings, though there was no rule about this and it looks as if such "gentlemen adventurers" came to be contented with half at a later date. The well-known cruises of Woodes Rogers and George Shelvocke into the Pacific, respectively in 1708-11 and 1719-22, provide rich evidence of both attitudes, and are especially relevant here because they carried old campaigners from "the Jamaica [buccaneering] discipline". They evidently drew on what William Dampier, himself a buccaneer from 1679 to 1688 and chief pilot to Rogers, calls "the Law of Privateers", meaning in effect what in St Domingue was known as "the Custom of the Coast" — a corpus of practices which also left a strong mark on those of the common pirates, many of whom originated in the Caribbean after the proclamations of peace in 1697 and 1713, and sometimes while formal hostilities continued between their princes.

Shelvocke's account largely consists of his encounters with mutineers. Their first petition, moderately worded by comparison with what was to come, he described as "needless tautologies, insignificant expressions, and dull confusion". It referred to the treatment of Rogers's two crews, who carried their "Case" against the Bristol owners to the House of Lords, though in vain.[10] The agreements Shelvocke had to make at sea defining and dividing plunder--those articles in a prize to which the captors had sole claim, such as the personal possessions of prisoners--follow almost word for word those made by Woodes Rogers and his fellow captain, Stephen Courtney, whose grand stroke was to surrender "the whole Cabin-Plunder", that is, the contents of "the Great Cabbins" of captured shipmasters and often therefore the best of the pillage. Their object was to prevent both indiscriminate plunder and its concealment by securing every man's interest. To do so they had to extend their definition well outside the limits (all above deck, roughly) recognised in European courts and eventually to shut their eyes to the embezzlement of "Arms, Chests, Knives, Roman Relicks, Scizzars, Tobacco, loose Books, Pictures, and worthless Tools and Toys, and Bedding in use...". Shelvocke's chief enemy, William Betagh, his captain of marines, wanted to go much further — "to oppose the owners having a part of any thing but what was upon freight, or mentioned in bills of lading".[11]

Cheating the owners by excessive pillage was inherent in privateering. Thanks to "riflinge", Elizabethan "owners and victuallers" may have received less than half the value of their prizes, instead of the nominal two-thirds; and the *armateurs* of Louis XIV's numerous corsairs never ceased to complain of pillage, and of the laxity of the courts in repressing it. Temptation mounted when wages were substituted for shares, for then a ship's company was entitled in France only to a tenth of the prize money in place of a third, the same as in the navy. The naval bureaucracy preferred wages ("à la solde") to shares ("à la part") in privateers, because of the tricks and delays for which the directors of armaments were notorious; but "à la part" remained the prevailing system at Dunkirk and St Malo, if not in Provence.

Rogers's "undertakers" neatly combined wages and shares, wages halving a man's share whatever his rank. There was no universal method and no uniform tariff of shares, though Trinity House had long ago tried to establish one.[12] At St Malo the company's portion was distributed by a panel of ship's officers in the light of performance, but at Calais and probably Dunkirk shares were allotted before sailing, as was the English practice, where all depended on the negotiating strength of owners, officers and seamen in each case. Thus Woodes Rogers was to enjoy twenty-four shares in his company's third, the master and surgeon ten each, and so on down the scale to the sailor at two and a half, the landman at one and a half. Exactly the same sub-division was observed in their agreements about plunder; Rogers exchanged his "Cabin Plunder" for an extra five per cent on his shares. These were high in proportion to the sailor's; at Calais, for example, a captain got only four or six times the "lot" of a *matelot*.[13] But Rogers was about to cruise for as many years as a small Calais corsair would be away for months; the investment, risks and objectives were in no way comparable. Nevertheless, his company alleged that the officers "could not possibly in a Privateer deserve what they were allow'd in proportion to the rest". Shelvocke's boatswain called them all *"Blood-suckers"*. The *syndic* of St Malo implied as much of some of his own captains.[14] That Shelvocke was on the British navy's half-pay list would not have worked in his favour either. Naval officers were notoriously avaricious about prize-money, which engendered constant friction between them. One who knew them well told King William in 1699 that some commanders kept their men out of their money for years, "until not a man concerned was to be found", while James Vernon, a secretary of state and prize commissioner, considered that this particular fraud contributed to desertion and piracy.[15]

Although their codes of punishment were wide apart, harsh treatment in navy and merchant navy alike fed these animosities. In the latter, however, arbitrary and even savage conduct by a master was less likely to be corrected by other officers or the employer. There was a great gulf fixed between shipmasters, with their powers and responsibilities and prospects, and even their first mates. The powers and responsibilities were as old as the Laws of Wisby and Oléron, themselves only compilations of earlier decisions or customs; masters were responsible to their owners for the offences of their crews, a member of whom had little right to defend himself against the boss's physical blows, while any refusal of duty might forfeit all title to wages. Once he had signed articles, a seaman's life was no longer his own. Meanwhile, the privileges and social position of masters had gone forward by leaps and bounds, at least in England. In the late seventeenth century a body of attorneys is said to have lived on encouraging seamen's claims against them.[16]

It is essential to keep this background in mind if we are to understand the originality of the Caribbean freebooters in dealing with plunder, and indeed freebooting itself. However, it would be wholly erroneous to suppose that "flibustier", *alias* "buccaneer", necessarily implies a seaman. This "fanciful kind of inversion" itself implies that the English were confused by the interchangeability of *flibustier* and *boucanier*, who in the opinion of James Burney, still the best of their English historians, "are to be considered as the same character, exercising sometimes one, sometimes the other employment".[17] Charlevoix, steeped in the "société des ordres", was distinguishing functions rather than men in describing them as separate "corps", as he did also the settlers *(habitants)* and their indentured white servants *(engagés)* in that "République des Aventuriers" which preceded royal government in St Domingue and long lived side by side with it. It was all a matter of less or more, the *gens du métier* (without fixed property unless or until they settled down, as some did) and the part-timers, who might also be settlers or traders rather than huntsmen — a dying profession long before 1700.[18]

What *flibustier* and *boucanier* most obviously had in common was their accuracy with small arms, the principal weapon of the privateering *barques* or sloops, which called for the minimum of seamanship. Fr Labat, who sometimes sailed with them and counted some of their captains among his friends, attributes their preference for a simple sail-rig to a dislike of work in the first place; Pointis' sailors were "nègres blancs" to them.[19] In any case, "roving on the account" included land operations, all the way from Trinidad to Campeche and ultimately the Spanish Pacific coasts as well. Sir Henry Morgan's ransom of Panama in 1671, to recall only the most famous of these episodes, was the reward of sound military tactics as well as tough marching by a miscellaneous Anglo-French force which knew how to draw itself up "in the form of a tertia"; in Cuba earlier, says Esquemeling, "the Pirates marched in very good rank and file, at the sound of their drums and with flying colours".[20] Their standard method of levying contributions from coastal villages, under threat of burning, is reminiscent of the Thirty Years War. In Dampier's and other contemporary narratives there is mention of "the forlorn", the European soldiers' term for the advance guard, also known among the freebooters as the "enfants perdus". [21] Their habit of assuming *noms de guerre* was also common with those impoverished noblemen and others who made a profession of war in mercenary armies; and we know that privateering captains from Europe could often be described, like Nathaniel Butler of the Old Providence Company, as "an ancient soldier at sea and land".[22]

Even more evocative of the European military background, ignored by our buccaneering historians, was the role assigned to the quartermaster, the second man to the freebooter captain and elected like him, but more especially entrusted with the interests of "les garçons", above all in the distribution of booty, "une espèce de procureur pernicieux qui règle leurs comptes", as an unkind planter official put it. This "trustee for the whole", as Defoe described him, enjoyed the chief authority also on pirate vessels, except in chase or action: among the Caribbean privateersmen, "his opinion is like the Mufti's among the Turks".[23] Such a magistracy can have had little to do with the humble role of quartermasters at sea, who were petty officers ranking only a shade above the ordinary seaman. This fact may well have rendered his title agreeable, and it is true that seagoing quartermasters took charge of boats during disembarkations; but, as an infallible sign of "the Jamaica discipline", he resembles those officers who saw to the billetting, feeding, clothing and accounts of a body of troops, once known as harbingers, highly respectable and well enough remunerated for their duties to be worth the attention of commissioned officers.[24]

Freebooters -- a "softer" word than "pirates" and not yet common robbers -- got their name from an old tradition of soldiers serving for booty only, like those privateersmen who signed "on the old pleasing account of no purchase no pay [*à la part]".*[25] Even after 1700, while pay mutinies remained "so endemic that they were almost condoned" in Europe, "plentiful campaigns" meant good plunder.[26] The prospect of loot was a friend to the recruiting sergeant, conjuring up that dream of sudden wealth which was also a powerful if illusory inducement to many a West Indian immigrant, thanks to travellers' tales and the eloquence of those who traded in indentured servants. To illustrate the lure of pillage to officers as well as men, we need look no further than the restlessness of the land forces engaged in Cromwell's Western Design when it was at first proposed to "dispose of all Preys and Booties... towards the carrying on of the present Service", many officers, on the contrary, "coming in hopes of Pillage into a country where they conceiv'd Gold as plentiful as Stones". Venables and Penn wished to meet this pressure, in effect, in much the same way as the *flibustiers* managed their booty, by throwing all into a common stock, with fierce penalties on concealment and a view to distribution "according to every Mans quality and Merit". There was no reference to special recompenses for the loss of limbs or eyes, characteristic of privateering and piratical charter parties, but the generals referred to David's military law (1st *Sam.* xxx. 24) "to give equal share to every person of the Army though not present in the Action".[27] Whether or not Levelling teachings came to the West Indies in 1655, we can be certain that the Civil War experience abundantly did — and Irish experience long before that, especially through its victims. So, too, through Dutch and French, the pitiless, *sauve-qui-peut* mentality of the long Continental strife, as we see it through the eyes of *Simplicissimus.* Whether any significant number of our Caribbean freebooters had endured the tyranny and rapacity of military commanders there is no means of telling, but in nothing were these "pay-grabbers" and "military enterprisers" more distrusted than in the sharing of loot. What is of even more interest for present purposes, military workforces showed talent in organizing their mutinies, under elected leaders — the *Ambosat* or *electo* of the sixteenth century.[28]

We shall never know the individual buccaneer, not even most of the captains, with anything like the intimacy which the devotion of George Rudé has recovered for participants in urban riots, or even as well as we know the leading figures in Warwick's and Pym's Old Providence Company. This is because buccaneering proper, unlike the long history of earlier privateering and armed trade in the Caribbean, was by definition locally based and early West Indian records are scarce. It is conventionally dated from about 1640, from the use of Tortuga, with its comfortable anchorage and strong natural defences, by bands of rovers from the recently settled British and French islands in the outer chain of the Antilles, as distinct from earlier occupation by the *boucaniers* who hunted hogs and cattle for barter with vessels from Normandy, which frequented those parts well before 1600.[29] Under the suggestive name of Association Island, Tortuga had also been briefly taken over by the Old Providence Company in the 1630s. There is no need to recapitulate the early vicissitudes of this privateering nursery, except to stress the brutality of Spanish attempts to expel the intruders. Like the harsh treatment of prisoners later--though these were more usually treated as convicts than pirates--it was enough to feed the flames of hispanophobia, so harsh a characteristic of some of the earlier *flibustiers* as to afford their marauding an ideology of sorts.

Tortuga, alternately dominated by French and English leaders, always elected but sometimes tyrannical, until formally adopted by the French Crown in 1657, received several increments of Huguenots, beginning with the fall of La Rochelle: St Domingue itself, with its English and especially Dutch elements, offered them a more attractive asylum than the more strictly governed Martinique.[30] Whether Montbars of Languedoc, soaked in Las Casas, or the merciless L'Ollonais (of Sables) were of Protestant origin is unproven, but two other leaders particularly feared by the Spaniards, Roche Brasiliano and Laurens de Graaf, were Dutchmen. Calvinism, it is true, did not flourish in the West Indies, as the example of Providence Island (Santa Catalina) showed, and such traces of religion as we find among the *flibustiers* were Roman: Ravenau de Lussan, referring to one of the many discords which marred their collaboration with the British in the South Sea (after 1680), expresses shock at the iconoclasm of the buccaneers, who were yet capable of sabbath observance "by command and common consent" under Captains Sawkins and Watling. Ravenau, a Parisian and an example of the gentleman adventurer in debt, was shrewd enough to see that Creole hatred of impiety rubbed off on French Catholics.[31] Walking off with the altar candlesticks, on the contrary, was necessary to "la bonne guerre" and we are not obliged to believe Labat's assertion that the Martinique privateers always donated captured church ornaments to sacred uses.[32] Spanish churches were also regularly used as the *corps de garde* for prisoners and pillage, apart from the intrinsic value of their contents. The aggressors had their own share of superstition, however, and there were good and able men among them, like the incomparable Dampier and his "ingenious Friend Mr Ringrose".[33]

If the ideological bitterness of the sixteenth century was receding, it is hardly credible that the Freebooters could have acted so fiercely towards Spanish Creole civilians without the moral self-righteousness conferred, in their turn, by Spanish atrocities and intolerance, real or mythical. It was still what the Elizabethans called a war of reprisals: "our Men", wrote Dampier, "were very squeamish of plundering without Licence", even if it meant getting one from an Asian prince in the faraway Philippines. This was in 1686, several years after the supply of French or Portuguese commissions had dried up.[34]

In the violent, mobile West Indian scene the freebooters necessarily suffered heavy casualties. Losses were particularly heavy following the grand exodus to the Pacific in the 1680s, so much so as to create anxiety for the security of Jamaica and St Domingue when the islands were divided by the Nine Years War. Yet, so long as Spain was the enemy, their forces soon built up again. Ducasse once remarked that the *flibuste* renewed itself every ten years.[35] A reliable analysis of 1706, admittedly from Martinique, which succeeded where St Domingue failed in organizing a prosperous cruising war against English and Dutch, breaks in down into three human elements: a sprinkling of young men from the best families; impoverished settlers "et des engagés qui ne veulent point s'assujetir au travail de la terre"; and ("la plus forte de la flibuste") deserters from merchantmen, hiding behind their *noms de guerre.* Sailors from Europe, however, needed time to become acclimatized and there is evidence that they did not take to the staple diet of the freebooters, manioc. Morgan in 1680, when he had turned King's evidence, told London that buccaneering tempted "white servants and all men of unfortunate and desperate condition".[37] Pointis saw them as seamen deserters or else vagabonds sent out to work in the plantations: "at the End of the Term of Servitude, some Body lends them a Gun, and to Sea they go a Buccaniering".[38] As an excellent intendant of Martinique pointed out, the *engagé,* though he served shorter articles than his British counterpart, usually wanted to go home after eighteen months: the habit of hard work had to be acquired, and there were also bad masters who underfed and worked them beyond their strength.[39] The blacks were said to be better treated, unless the bond-servant exercised some skill as artisan, in which case he was more like a European apprentice, though earning higher wages. But artisans too joined the freebooters, "We had Sawyers, Carpenters, Joyners, Brickmakers, Bricklayers, Shoemakers, Taylors, &c.", says Dampier.[40] Because they frequently adapted prizes for their own use, and were as often wrecked, the buccaneers set a high value on carpenters, as on surgeons or apprentice surgeons.

Paid off with a few hundred pounds of tobacco at the end of his articles, the *engagé* had not the means to set up planter, as the English often had before Barbados and the Leewards filled up; but even there, as is well known, the "sugar revolution" (1640-60) spelt doom to the small planter. Captain William Jackson, who "kept the Indies in an uproar", could have manned his ships threefold at Barbados in 1642, on the basis of no purchase no pay, "every one that was denied entertainement reputing himselfe most unfortunate".[41]

Jackson and his "vice-admiral", both old Providence hands, armed ships in England, but increased their fleet to seven in Barbados and St Christopher, with an additional 750 men. Can we doubt that the obscure beginnings of a Caribbean-based privateering industry are connected with the mid-century decades of growing displacement and indebtedness, when the struggle for existence, among those who survived the appalling mortality rate of immigrants, quickened movement from island to island? In these conditions a bond-servant might change masters many times, as bankrupt planters swelled the ranks of runaways and derelicts, naturally disposed to soak the wealthy Spaniard.

The plight of the British has been movingly described by Carl and Roberta Bridenbaugh, who consider that from 1640 the "parent islands" contained "the greatest concentration of poverty-stricken freemen in any of England's dominions before 1776", boom or slump.[42] The parent islands of the French reached demographic saturation somewhat later, but their social experience was not dissimilar. In both cases, of course, the run of first-generation immigrants were men and women without resources, buying their passage by selling themselves to a known or more often unknown settler. Some would have borne the scars of pressures and oppressions, if not persecutions, at home. More than half the population of the British West Indies in 1650 were Irishmen, the latest arrivals soldiers from Drogheda; Barbados alone received thousands of war prisoners before the transportation of felons began in 1655. Numerous anabaptists came out with Penn and Venables in that year.[43]

Gabriel Debien's patient combing of the "actes d'engagement" in the notarial minutes of La Rochelle, Nantes and Dieppe points to a preponderance of day-labourers, textile workers and other *ruraux* making for the islands, and not least St Domingue, where one might become a "valet de boucanier"; many sailed in the winter months, when jobs were relatively scarce.[44] Although we are now more vividly aware of seasonal and other kinds of vagabondage along French roads and rivers, it seems significant that so many came from areas affected by peasant risings against the royal *fisc* and the proliferation of crown agents, not to mention plunder by unpaid soldiers, in the 1630s; the *Croquants* of Saintonge, Angoumois and Poitou, the *Nu-Pieds* of Normandy. These violent events would not have been soon forgotten. Emotive, visceral, spontaneous gestures they may have been, devoid of revolutionary content: nevertheless, large assemblies of aggrieved taxpayers had shown a capacity for self-organization, the constitution of "communes", election of deputies and promulgation of *Ordonnances:* "L'assemblée du Commun peuple, le Conseil tenant, a esté ordonné ce qui s'ensuit...". Revealing, indeed startling, is the image they had of themselves as forgotten men, "comme si on ne songeait à nous que comme des pièces perdues".[45]

Well might Mazarin fear the contagion of English example in 1647.[46] Two years later republican placards appeared in Paris, also a major source of West Indian immigrants, often from the building trades. The presence of a substantial, literate working-class élite among the emigrants is fully established. A rector of Kingston was to say that in the Jamaica of 1720 there were not six families of "gentle descent": tavern-keepers, tailors, carpenters and joiners called themselves Colonel, Major, Captain, Honourable or Esquire.[47] So respectable a picture may be corrected, however, by the critical comments of the priest who sailed with an ill-fated party for Cayenne in 1652: "toutes sortes de personnes...enfants incorrigibles...gens qui avoient fait faillite...Plusieurs jeunes débauchez...des Moines Apostats...Et le pire de tout, quantité de femmes...". They had not got far before their "General" accused them of aiming at "un corps de Republique, voulant y establir des Présidents, Conseillers...un Parlement".[48]

A president, councillors and other officers were certainly elected for the baptismal ceremonies, followed by protracted drinking, when newcomers to the tropics crossed the Line. Charlevoix has it that these mysteries were held in St Domingue to release a man from all antecedent contracts.[49] Even there life was never so simple, but for some decades it preserved in exaggerated forms that libertarianism which in some degree splintered all the English colonies, as was demonstrated from the start in the radical politics of Bermuda and Barbados. A governor of Jamaica, within ten years of conquest, could describe his people as "generally easy to be governed, yet rather by persuasion than severity"; as late as 1692, Ducasse wrote of "cette colonie n'ayant esté formée que selon le caprice de chaque particulier, elle a subsisté dans le désordre"; not a man, said another, "qui ne se croie plus que nous officiers du Roy".[50]

The early history of "the Coast" was stamped by a series of revolts, especially against French monopoly companies, from the time when Governor d'Ogeron (1665-75), "whom nature had formed to be great in himself", began "to establish the regularity of society upon the ruins of a ferocious anarchy".[51] The supreme embodiment of this impatience of authority, this drive to absolute freedom, was *la flibuste,* in Jamaica "roving on the account". Dampier, who called it "the other loose roving way of Life", notes that "Privateers are not obliged to any Ship, but free to go ashore where they please, or to go into any other Ship that will entertain them".[52] The authorities agree on their self-will, caprice, dislike of work; on their disordered and unwashed clothing, their habit of singing while companions tried to sleep and shooting to make a noise; on their blasphemies and debaucheries. So long as they had cash to spend, it was difficult to persuade them to the sea. In this they resemble the typical *pícaro,* willing to lose everything on the throw of a dice, then begin all over again; and the picaresque novel, though seldom set in the New World, contains some profound truths about it. Living from day to day, at the mercy of events, the picaresque rogue is seldom his own master for long, yet living on his wits he can assert his independence and turn the table on masters no more virtuous than himself.[53] There was more than this, however, to the libertinism of the buccaneers. They were not merely escaping from bondage. In their enterprises at least, they practised notions of liberty and equality, even of fraternity, which for most inhabitants of the old world and the new remained frustrated dreams, so far as they were dreamt at all — more than we usually suppose, perhaps.

The first such notion was familiar enough to Croquants and Levellers: the right to be consulted. Elizabethan seamen, according to Monson, had claimed a say in the conduct of their voyages and freedom to adopt at sea a casual privateering consort — unpremeditated agreements which owners might disown.[54] Both were standard features of buccaneering practice. Before ever a ship's company left on the account, however, articles had to be agreed regarding future dividends, captains and quartermasters elected. Later might follow "consults" about consortship with other companies encountered, or about tactics, especially in tight situations. Thus L'Ollonais "called a council of the whole fleet, wherein he told them he intended to go to Guatemala. Upon this point they divided into several sentiments.... But the major part of the company, judging the propounded voyage little fit for their purpose, separated from L'Ollonais and the rest."[55]

Far from base, especially on the far side of the Isthmus of Darien, such secessions were commonplace. After the death of Richard Sawkins, "the best beloved of all our company or the most part thereof", records the scholarly Basil Ringrose, Captain Sharp "asked our men in full council who of them were willing to go or stay, and prosecute the design Captain Sawkins had undertaken, which was to remain in the South Sea...".[56] Those who stayed later deposed Sharp and subsequently reinstated him. So even when captains only consulted each other, they must have kept a finger on the pulses of their followings. Morgan seems only to have taken counsel with "the chiefest of his companions", but he had a record of success which removed all obstacles.[57] No doubt this and a reputation for personal valour go far to explain the election of other leaders. Yet powers of verbal persuasion must always have been requisite, another quality Morgan had in abundance. Governor Nathaniel Butler of Old Providence noted in his diary how Captain Parker "and his two Counsellors being obstinate to their owne Endes, went about to satisfie", with words, a starving crew which "in temperate waye desired to know what he meant to doe with them" — and buccaneers could be far more intractable than that.[58] It is unlikely that they could have been ruled by the methods of terror and delation attributed to Tuscan captains in the Levant by one who sailed with them in the 1690s.[59] As late as 1708, the Board of Trade in London thought that the "ill practices too frequently committed" by Bermudian privateers (clearly influenced by the Jamaica discipline) could be prevented if captains enjoyed "the sole command... whereas, as we have been informed, every seaman on board a privateer having a vote, it is not in the captain's power...".[60]

The balance between privateering democracy and dominant personalities is hard to strike, and commanders certainly enjoyed absolute power in action; but in this as in other respects there is a strong indication of the consolidation of a body of regulatory customs among the freebooters in the survival of references to them into the Spanish Succession War. In 1706 the "gouverneur par intérim" on the Coast, Charitte, in writing home, used such phrases as "les charteparties qui se font aux Isles Françoises" or simply "charteparties de l'Amérique". He was referring to the distribution of booty and provision for the maimed. The principles are the same as those briefly described by Esquemeling and Charlevoix for an earlier period.[61] No text of a "chasse-partie", as it was known (neatly translated by Burney as a "chasing agreement"), has come to light before 1688. It does not restate the basic egalitarian principle, "à compagnon bon lot", presumably because this could be taken for granted; it is an agreement between Captain Charpin and Mathurin Desmaretz "quartier maistre de l'équipage" and deals expressly with a very few departures from that rule, in defining the captain's dividend--ten *lots* and first choice of any captured vessels--and those of two surgeons, who in addition to the usual allowance for their chests were to keep captured instruments "qui ne seront point garnys d'argent".[62] Pillage included "or, argent, perle, diamant, musq, ambre, sivette, et toutes sortes de pierreries" as well as "tous balots entammez entre deux ponts ou au fond". That this was clarified is a sure sign that their ship, *St Roze,* was not owned by captain and crew.

The typical privateer seems usually to have been the crew's common property or that of their leader, in which case he was awarded extra shares. Morgan's captains in 1670 drew the shares of eight men for the expenses of their ships, besides their usual allotment, which Esquemeling elsewhere states as "five or six portions to what the ordinary seamen have".[63] It is to be noted that the largest part of the outlay in a European privateer consisted in victuals, arms and cash advances to the crew. None of these items counted for much or at all with the freebooters, who contributed each man the essential weaponry and often also his provisions, so far as they did not rely on what they shot or fished, gathered or seized; with a week's supply of food to start off with, the only big capital item was the ship and this itself might well be a cheap prize. Only a frigate would call for such resources as those of the royal officers on the Coast (usually also planters) could supply, and they might invest with the object of stimulating the "course aux ennemis", especially governors who shared the admiralty tenth in prizes.[64]

At the same time there was nothing to stop settlers from taking out an interest, and we have to allow for the debts piled up by freebooters with inn-keepers and others; the *cabaretiers* gave credit to the *flibustiers* in 1690, for example, to buy victuals, allegedly at inflated prices.[65] In St Domingue privateering retained the approval of the community long after it had begun to be opposed by a powerful interest in Jamaica, the Spanish traders. In 1709 Choiseul Beaupré, a governor who set himself to revive the waning *course,* claimed credit for restoring the classical "à compagnon bon lot", which meant that the chief fitter-out agreed with the ship's company for a certain number of *lots* amounting to never more than an eighth of the produce of a cruise, in place of his usual third — in metropolitan France, two-thirds.[66] As an interesting Guernsey charter party of 1703 suggests, this difference of a third may be accounted for by the fact that the crew provided their own food and drink; in earlier times, when *armateurs* were divided into owners and victuallers, armaments, including trading voyages to the Caribbean, had been split into thirds, so that "tiercement" in France came to be a synonym for whatever was owing to a crew. On the other hand, the buccaneering sloop was so cheap that it could have been mainly the cost of victualling that fell on the fitters-out, whether ship's company or not, allowing "victualling" to include such items as powder, lanterns and "menus ustensiles".[67]

The freebooters allowed "extraordinary shares" to other ship's officers besides the captain, but on a narrow scale: "the Master's Mate only two", says Esquemeling, "and other Officers proportionable to their employment". On a small sloop or brigantine they were not numerous. Defoe's pirates, who drew directly on the model of the freebooters, offered a bonus only to half a dozen officers, even captain and quartermaster receiving only twice (or less) the common dividend.[68] This was what they called "a free ship, that is, they agreed every man should have an equal share in all prizes".[69] Labat's friends among the freebooting captains received only a present in addition to the equal dividend when their ship was common property, though it might be substantial enough to multiply his dividend three or four times; otherwise the only special beneficiaries, rateably, were the quartermaster, surgeon and pilot.[70] But the freebooters liked to make merit awards. Morgan offered fifty pieces of eight for "entering the first any castle, or taking down the Spanish colours"; Rogers, twenty "to him that first sees a Prize of Good Value, or exceeding 50 Tuns in Burden", and "a good Suit of Clothes to be made for each Man that went up the River above Guiaquil[sic]". His owners had already agreed to a scale of compensation for widows and those "so disabled as not to get a Livelihood", as well as further rewards for "Whoever shall in Fight, or otherwise, signalize himself", notably in boarding.[71] Time had passed since it was possible to assert that English privateers could not afford to take care of their wounded or the relatives of their dead, and since the mercenary soldier's wage was expected to cover the cost of his injuries.[72]

The shipowners' duty to provide for a sick seaman is at least as old as the Laws of Oléron, but awards to the disabled originated much later. The mutual benevolent fund created by Drake and Hawkins in 1590, the Chatham Chest, marked a giant step forward for seamen, although its resources fell far below the claims made on it in wartime: by 1675 it was granting disability pensions for war wounds, "in its historic condition of insolvency".[73] At about that date the French government blazed a similar trail for its *troupes de terre,* and it was the first, though not until 1703, to set up a state fund for granting half-pay to men disabled in private armaments at sea, with small lump-sums for widows. The idea was born of a small tax on prizes levied in Brittany for the redemption of Barbary slaves, and its extension opposed by the Dunkirk owners, who pointed to the traditional responsibility of its *magistrat* for finding public employments, short of the "maison des pauvres"; even at St Malo there were many claims for unpaid nursing expenses in the admiralty court.[74]

Against this background it is not surprising that Esquemeling, who qualified as a surgeon at Amsterdam a year after his book was first published there, makes much of the smart money awarded in the *chasse-parties* for the loss of limbs and eyes. As with all such articles, there was room for variety, and doubtless evolution: an eye worth only a hundred piastres even in Morgan's grand scale-- 1800 crowns for the two hands as against 600 for one and 1500 for both legs-- equated with a thumb or index finger at 300 in Labat's account, in which the wearing of a cannula had gone up to as much as an arm (600 *écus,* without distinction between right and left). Defoe's pirates offered 600 dollars (about £150) to a cripple, according to the three sets of articles he came by — about the same as the governor of St Domingue offered for its defence in 1709, with the alternative of a life annuity.[75]

There is clear evidence of custom at work in these tariffs, except that the freebooters had no thought for pensions. That would have contradicted their mentality, which was to distribute dividends on the first possible occasion. Nor was there anything like a hospital on the Coast until 1710, when Choiseul created one for soldiers and *flibustiers,* partly to be funded by the *lots* of those killed without heirs.[76] But there were captured slaves. Negroes, though sometimes freed when they could be replaced, served as slaves until they could be sold. After money, plate and precious stones, they were the most easily convertible booty. Indeed, the crippled freebooter might elect to take a slave in lieu of 100 pieces-of-eight. Indeed, that might prove a sounder pension than any annuity — with up to six slaves in return for a wooden leg, a retired freebooter might set up planter, though he would need to be a good husband of his shares, as some were.[77]

Charlevoix tells us that the practice was for cruises to go on until enough had been earned to pay for the lamed and wounded — first charge on the common stock. There were other prior charges, including the claims of owners or victuallers ashore (if any) and the admiralty tenth, payable in Jamaica from the start and on the Coast by the 1690s, to judge by the disputes of Ducasse with the governor-general in Martinique.[78] Given a flexible attitude to plunder, which by definition belonged to the captors exclusively, and the sale of prize goods in neutral islands, especially Danish St Thomas, it is unlikely that these tithes were ever surrendered in full. But no doubt whatsoever hangs over the basic rule of the common stock. All our authorities refer to this, or to the punishment of theft, at the least by forfeiture of shares, at worst by marooning. The articles drawn up in 1697 for d'Iberville's projected Mississippi expedition--describing his Canadians as *flibustiers,* interestingly enough--impose both penalties, unless "selon le vol" the offender deserved shooting: the same with the pirates' articles. Woodes Rogers preferred to get agreement to a fine of twenty times the value for concealing plunder worth more than half a crown, besides loss of shares, the original penalty: that the terms were stiffened suggests trouble in the intervening year, but also that it was reprobated by the majority. It means something that Dampier never accused his fellows of the "many hundreds of little deceitful Acts" which he noticed among Dutch seamen in the Far East; in his "new voyage" of 1683-91, moreover, he reports only one case of theft, the offender being condemned "to have three Blows from each Man in the Ship...".[79]

Cheating would self-evidently be least tolerable under the system of "à compagnon bon lot", virtually a Rousseauistic contract rooted in self-interest. By this device the freebooters' democracy may be thought to have achieved an objective which eluded most commanders on land or sea, "everybody thinking they have a right to get what they can".[80] "Captain Johnson", who enjoyed exposing the hypocrisy of his readers, noted the paradox: "For these men whom we term, and not without reason, the scandal of human nature...when they judged it for their interest...were strictly just."[81] It is reasonable to assume that an outraged sense of justice, besides a cut in expectations, played its part in the Cartagena affair, and for that matter in the "obloquies and detractions" which drove Morgan to leave most of his followers behind when he sailed home from the Isthmus in 1671.[82]

Defoe relates with gusto a mock trial conducted by a crew of Caribbean pirates under the greenwood tree about 1720 — a parody of English institutions typical, apparently, of these outlaws.[83] But freebooter justice was deeply flawed in its own turn. We need not make too much of the fact, so much deplored by the earliest historian of the Coast, the Dominican Père du Tertre, that they were apt to be self-appointed judges in their own cause;[84] nor perhaps of acknowledged cruelties to Spanish civilians, which seem to have been largely confined to the extraction of information and of ransoms — manners in which they had little to teach European privateersmen, and nothing to European war lords. As Ducasse wrote after his descent on Jamaica in 1694, "Nous avons fait la guerre en gens désintéressés, ayant tout brûlé"; at Cartagena, thought Charlevoix, the *flibustiers* showed more ruse than violence, much of it feigned.[85] A calculated terrorism, as distinct from gratuitous cruelty, was inherent in this type of banditry, approximating most nearly to the "haiduk" variety in Eric Hobsbawm's classification.[86] Among the pirates proper, examples of sheer brutality are not hard to find; they made a point of recruiting prisoners, the freebooters in the end released them; but even the pirates, it was said, were most to be feared in the first flush of success.

The test of fraternity is how they treated each other. The freebooters' care for their sick and their solemn funeral rites are indications of that.[87] Farther, Esquemeling remarks that, among themselves, the buccaneers "are very civil and charitable... if any wants what another has, with great liberality they give it to one another".[87] Liberality, indeed a generosity "mieux qu'en aucun lieu du monde" (as Labat says of their hospitable customs), was as characteristic of the *flibustiers* as intemperate drinking, and neither trait was perhaps without a touch of that ostentation which to them would stamp a gentleman — "ce sont des dîners éternels".[88] But if high spending was a rule of "la bonne flibuste", as it was a habit of the European *pícaro,* so was gambling. What Bartholomew Sharp called "Confusion and strong Contests among the Men" were a necessary consequence of their "Consults", but drink and gaming engendered faction. A buccaneer would wager the clothes off his back. "The main Division", says Dampier of Swan's men at Mindanao in 1687, "was between those that had Money and those that had none." A little earlier, Sharp himself, wishing to go home with "almost a thousand pound", had been supported by the thrifty and turned out by those "scarce worth a groat", who were for staying in the South Sea.[89] Ravenau de Lussan had an even sorrier tale to tell of his return across the Isthmus in 1688: "Eighteen of those whom the luck of the play had most despoiled had determined to massacre those who were rich...". To save their heads, but also to solve a problem of portage, "the rich" shared again with "the poor", on condition of receiving back a half or two-thirds after reaching St Domingue.[90] No wonder d'Iberville, Rogers, and the pirate John Phillips, to mention but a few, treated gambling as an abuse only less heinous than theft, or that Sawkins cast the dice overboard.[91]

Fraternity "on the account", therefore, under stress of monotony and rum, might be less apparent than in times of danger or dividend distribution. Was it anything more than the camaraderie of the camp or the sociability of the village? "Pebble-Smasher" and "Never-Fail" were only variants of "Chasse-Marée" or "Passe-Partout", and of a thousand other such familiar vulgarities as helped cement the fellowship of military "chambers" and the inescapable collectivity of country communities.[92] Gildsmen were supposed to be brothers too — and George Rudé has taught us not to underrate the solidarity of the shop-floor, of the mentality common to masters and men among the *sans-culottes.* One could also invoke Professor Mousnier's "société des fidélités" for the seventeenth century, although his examples of total devotion are all of high-born men.[93] Further down the scale, however, out on the Coast, there was the well-established institution of *matelotage,* first among the *boucaniers,* who shared any property they had with their "mess-mate" and might bequeath it to him: when the early *habitants* combined to cultivate a plot, "ils s'amatelotaient".[94] What is less well known, something like *matelotage* prevailed among the log-cutters of Campeche and Honduras, the "Baymen" whose "Trade had its Rise from the decay of Privateering".[95] An anonymous but intelligent visitor to those parts in 1714-15 noted that they were hard drinkers and very quarrelsome, but that neighbours lived in common, under two elected governors and a short compendium of laws "very severe against theft and Encroachments".[96] Forty years earlier, Dampier noticed there how "every Man is left to his choice to carry what he pleaseth, and commonly they agree very well about it". And on Saturdays at least they hunted.[97] It looks as though "the Custom of the Coast", originally that of the *boucaniers,* being rooted in the wilderness and doubtless subject to Carib, Cuna and other Indian influences, possessed an extraordinary power of survival in suitable circumstances. But between Coast and Bay we need look for no stranger agency than the freebooters themselves. The code survived even while its adherents might fail it, as is true of any social group.

Among "fellow adventurers" as impulsive as the Brethren of the Coast it would be surprising to find consistency of conduct, especially with English and Dutch admixtures of differing backgrounds. And yet the outlines of a fairly homogeneous portrait can be put together. That Captain Andreas who called one morning on the Scots in Darien, and who claimed Swan and Davis as "his particular Friends", stands forth as a recognizable type: "He (as generally those People are) is of a small Stature. In his Garb affects the Spaniard as alsoe in the Gravity of his carriage. He had a red loose Stuff coat on with an old hatt and a pair of Drawers, but noe Shoes or Stockins."[98] The skills of a Rudé could uncover a crowd of such forgotten men.[99] There are sources still to be mined, especially Spanish, and short of them ample room for new perspectives. The freebooters astonished the world in their day and have attracted some sensational literature since. Sadly, very little has come from professional historians. As Una said to Puck in one of Kipling's stories, "pirates aren't lessons". But did she wish they were? And why not?

# NOTES

1. *An Authentick and Particular Account of the taking of Carthagena by the French... By the Sieur Pointis* (London, 1740: a late edition of the 1698 translation of the *Relation de l'expédition de Carthagene,* Amsterdam, 1698), p. 1; [Paris,] A[rchives] N[ationales], Marine B4/17, fos. 404-5; B[ibliothèque] N[ationale], Thoisy 91, p. 515. There is a modern narrative of this expedition in N.M. Crouse, *The French Struggle for the West Indies 1665-1713* (New York, 1943), ch. viii.

2. P. F.-X. de Charlevoix, *Histoire de l'Isle Espagnole de S. Domingue,* 4 vols. (Amsterdam, 1733), iv, 123 ff.

3. *Account,* pp. 42-3, 62, 69; AN, Col[onies] C8A/16, Vaucresson, 10 May 1706.

4. *Ibid.,* C9A/3, fos. 303 ff., 370 ff.; Anon, *An Answer to Mr. Paschal's Letter...* (London, 1702), p. 5; Charlevoix, iv, 106, 150 ff.

5. *Ibid.,* pp. 167-8; AN, Col. C8A/12, fos. 190 ff.; C9A/8, f.337ᵛ; BN, Thoisy 91, pp. 515-32.

6. AN, Col. C9A/4, fos. 272-4.

7. Charlevoix, iv, 44-5, 105, 110; C[alendar of] S[tate] P[apers,] Col[onial Series], 1696-7, p. 403.

8. Captain Charles Johnson, *A General History of the... Pirates,* ed. A.L. Hayward (London, 1926), p. 252. For Defoe's authorship, see J.R. Moore, *Defoe in the Pillory* (Bloomington, 1939), pp. 126-88.

9. *Ibid.,* 304.

10. G. Shelvocke, *A Privateer's Voyage Round the World* (London, "Travellers Library" edn., 1930), pp. 43-6; *The Manuscripts of the House of Lords,* new ser. vol. xii (London, 1970), pp. 235-6.

11. Woodes Rogers, *A Cruising Voyage Round the World,* ed. G.E. Manwaring (London, 1928), pp. 22-3, 114-6, 170-1, 206-7; Shelvocke, p. 114.

12. K.R. Andrews, *Elizabethan Privateering* (Cambridge, 1964), pp. 39-44, 167; Oxford, Bodleian Library, Rawl. A 171, fos. 63-4; AN, Marine G 144 and B 3/115, fo. 532.

13. Rennes, Arch. Dép. Ille-et-Vilaine, *fonds de notaires,* Pitot and Vercoutère-Le Roy *(actes d'engagement);* Arras, Arch. Dép. Pas de Calais, 13 B 156, 13 Feb. and 2 March 1694; Capt. Edward Cooke, *A Voyage to the South Sea,* 2 vols. (London, 1712), sig. b4ʳ⁻ᵛ·

14. Rogers, p. 173; Shelvocke, p. 40; AN, Marine B3/115, fos. 544-8.

15. *The Sergison Papers,* ed. R.B. Merriman (London, Navy Rec. Soc., 1950), pp. 8-9; G.P.R. James, *Letters Illustrative of the Reign of William III,* 3 vols. (London 1841), ii, 187.

16. C. Molloy, *De Jure Maritimo,* 5th ed. (London, 1701), pp. 220-4; R. Davis, *The Rise of the English Shipping Industry* (London, 1962), pp. 149-54.

17. *History of the Buccaneers of America* (London, Unit Library ed., 1902), p. 40. In 1657 the first of Jamaica's governors refers to "buccaneers" as "French and English that kill cattle" in Hispaniola: "Edward D'Oyley's Journal, Part 2", *Jamaica Hist. Rev.,* xi (1978), 69.

18. Charlevoix, iii, 11, 54-67; P. Constantin, "Jacques Yvon sieur des Landes (1645-1698), Lieutenant du roi à Saint-Domingue", *La Province du Maine,* xxxvi-vii (Laval, 1957), 7-48.

19. *Nouveau Voyage aux Isles de l'Amérique,* 2 vols. (The Hague, 1724), I, ii, 77; Charlevoix, iv, 137.

20. *CSP Col. 1669-1674,* p. 202; John Esquemeling, *The Buccaneers of America,* ed. W.S. Stallybrass ("Broadway Translations", London, n.d.), p. 131.

21. Cf. Defoe's description of seamen as "Les Enfants Perdus, the Forlorn hope of the World", *An Essay upon Projects* (London, 1697), p. 124.

22. F. Redlich, *The German Military Enterpriser and his Work Force,* 2 vols. (Wiesbaden, 1964), i, 117; A.P. Newton, *The Colonising Activities of the English Puritans* (New Haven, 1914), p. 252.

23. AN, Col. C9A/9, fo. 217; Johnson, pp. 184-5, 400.

24. C.G. Cruickshank, *Elizabeth's Army* (Oxford, 1966), p. 49; R.E. Scouller, *The Armies of Queen Anne* (Oxford, 1966), p. 66.

25. Shelvocke, p. 30; Redlich, i, 134; M. Pawson and D. Buisseret, *Port Royal Jamaica* (Oxford, 1975), p. 29.

26. Scouller, pp. 130, 267.

27. *The Narrative of General Venables,* ed. C.H. Firth (Camden new ser. no. 60, 1900), pp. 14-16.

28. Redlich, i, 135; G. Parker, *The Army of Flanders and the Spanish Road 1567-1659* (Cambridge, 1972), pp. 188-90.

29. See K.R. Andrews, *The Spanish Caribbean: Trade and Plunder 1530-1630* (New Haven, 1978), esp. pp. 181-7.

30. G. Debien, *Les Engagés pour les Antilles 1634-1715* (Paris, 1952), pp. 188-9; Newton, pp. 103-10, 192-3, 211-16, 279-82; cf. Charlevoix, iii, 46.

31. I have used the translation of his "Journey to the Southern Sea from 1685 to 1686" in M. Besson, *The Scourge of the Indies* (London, 1929): see pp. 115-16. Cf. Basil Ringrose's journal in Esquemeling, pt iv, p. 398.

32. *Nouveau Voyage,* I, i, 75-6. Louis XIV did his best to return the church treasures taken by Pointis: AN, Marine B 4/18, fos. 348-65. It should be recalled that Spanish American churches were "the place of all publick Meetings, and all Plays and Pastimes are acted there also": William Dampier, *A New Voyage Round the World,* ed. Sir A. Gray (London, 1927), p. 93.

33. *Ibid.,* p. 189. Dampier's veracity can be checked by reference to Ringrose's journal (and vice versa) till the latter's death in 1686.

34. *Ibid.,* p. 211. Jamaican commissions were no longer obtainable after 1670, when many buccaneers resorted to St Domingue. Conversely, some of the *flibustiers* served in Jamaican privateers during the Spanish Succession War. See generally A.P. Newton, *The European Nations in the West Indies 1493-1688* (London, 1933), pp. 286 ff., and C.H. Haring, *The Buccaneers in the West Indies in the XVII Century* (New York, 1910). Cf. the design of Capt. Nathaniel North's men, "not intending to Pirate among the Europeans, but honestly and quietly to rob what Moors fell in their way, and return home with clear consciences...".

35. AN, Col. C9A/4, fo. 446 (15 Oct. 1698).

36. *Ibid.,* C8A/16, "Mémoire sur l'état présent des Isles. Remis par Mr Mithon et Mr de Vaucresson...à son arrivée", 10 May 1706; *ibid.,* 8, fo. 75, Blénac to Pontchartrain, Martinique, 23 March 1694.

37. *CSP Col. 1677-1680,* p. 565.

38. *Account,* p. 10.

39. AN, Col. C8A/10, fos. 350-3, Robert to Pontchartrain, 11 July 1698.

40. *New Voyage,* p. 240. Cf. C. and R. Bridenbaugh, *No Peace Beyond the Line: The English in the Caribbean 1624-1660* (New York, 1972), pp. 106, 118-20. Half a dozen types of *engagement* are described by G. Debien in "L'émigration poitevine vers l'Amérique au XVIIe siècle", *Bulletin de la Société des Antiquaires de l'Ouest,* sér. 4, t. ii (1952), pp. 273-30.

41. *The Voyages of Captain William Jackson, 1642-1645,* ed. V.T. Harlow (Camden 3rd ser. no. 34), p. 2; cf. Newton, *Colonising Enterprises,* pp. 267-8, 315-17.

42. *Op. cit.,* p. 113.

43. *Ibid.,* pp. 17, 102-3, 196; A.P. Watts, *Une Histoire des colonies anglaises aux Antilles* (Paris, s.d. [1925]), p. 134.

44. Debien, *Engagés,* ch. v.

45. R. Mousnier, *Fureurs paysannes* (Paris, 1967), pp. 72, 90, and review by R. Mandrou in *Rev. Hist.,* ccxlii (1969), 29-40.

46. C. Hill, *Puritanism and Revolution* (London, 1958), p. 136.

47. Debien, *Engagés,* pp. 109, 131; L. Lewis, "English Commemorative Sculpture in Jamaica", *Jam. Hist. Rev.,* ix (1972), p. 12.

48. A. Biet, *Voyage de la France Equinoxiale en l'Isle de Cayenne* (Paris, 1664), pp. 8, 56f.

49. Charlevoix, iii, 55.

50. Sir Charles Lyttleton, quoted by F. Cundall, *The Governors of Jamaica in the Seventeenth Century* (London, 1936), p. 19; P. de Vaissière, *Saint-Domingue* (Paris, 1909), p. 55.

51. Raynal, *A Philosophical and Political History of the Settlements and Trade of the Europeans in the East and West Indies,* 8 vols. (London, 1783), vi, 125-6.

52. *New Voyage,* pp. 30, 238.

53. F.W. Chandler, *Romances of Roguery: An Episode in the History of the Novel* (New York, 1961), esp. pp. 47 ff., and A. Valbuena y Prat, *La Novela picaresca espanola* (Madrid, 1956), pp. 14 ff.

54. *The Naval Tracts of Sir William Monson,* ed. M. Oppenheim, 5 vols. (Navy Rec. Soc., 1902-14), ii, 247; *English Privateering Voyages to the West Indies 1588-1595,* ed. K.R. Andrews (Hakluyt Soc., Cambridge, 1959), p. 162.

55. Esquemeling, p. 112.

56. *Ibid.,* pp. 333-4.

57. *Ibid.,* p. 130.

58. [London,] B[rit.] L[ibrary], Sloane MS. 758, entry for 25 Aug. 1639.

59. W. Hacke, *A Collection of Original Voyages* (1699), pt iv (Roberts); cf. AN, Col. C8A/6, fos. 446$^v$-7.

60. Quoted by H.C. Wilkinson, *Bermuda in the Old Empire* (Oxford, 1950), p. 24.

61. AN, Col. C9A/7, fos. 322-3.

62. AN, Col. C9A/2, fo. 357, Isle à Vache, 18 Feb. 1688.

63. Esquemeling, pp. 60, 177. Charlevoix (iii, 68) grants the captains only a double lot.

64. Ducasse's running quarrel with Blénac, the governor-general at Martinique, who claimed the *dixième,* suggests not only that it was a useful source of income, but that the disposal of prizes was now coming under official control, although Danish St Thomas remained a favourite mart for them: see (e.g.) AN, Col. C9A/2, fos. 322, 328-9, 362, 418-20, 471. Ducasse lost this battle in 1696 *(ibid.,* 3, fo. 231), but in 1702 the Amiral de France awarded half his tenths to the governors of both islands *(ibid.,* 6, fo 130$^v$). Governor d'Ogeron's more direct involvement in the *flibuste* should be clarified by the edition of his correspondence now being prepared by M. Michel Camus.

65. *Ibid.,* 2, fo. 130.

66. *Ibid.,* 8, fo. 394.

67. I am most grateful to Dr Alan Jamieson of University College, London, for communicating a copy of the charter party of the *Defiance* of Guernsey, possessed by the Priaulx Library; it is impossible to be sure that it was typical of the numerous Channel Island privateers of the time. For illuminating examples of *tiercements* see C. Bréard, *Documents relatifs à la marine normande et à ses armements aux XVIe et XVIIe siècles pour les Antilles, le Brésil et les Indes* (Rouen, 1889), pp. 11-25.

68. Esquemeling, p. 60; Johnson, pp. 184, 274, 307.

69. *Ibid.,* pp. 535-6.

70. *Nouveau Voyage,* I, i, 74-5.

71. Esquemeling, p. 178; Rogers, pp. 23, 171; Cooke, i, sig, b4.

72. G. St Lo, *England's Safety* (1693), in *Somers Tracts,* ii (1814), 72; Redlich, i, 122.

73. J.J. Keevil, *Medicine and the Navy,* 2 vols. (Edinburgh, 1957-8), ii, 135-6.

74. *Arrêt du Conseil,* 31 March 1693, text in Citoyen Lebeau, *Nouveau Code des Prises,* 3 vols. (Paris, an VII), i, 137, 273-5; AN, Marine B4/25, fos. 410-11; H. Buffet, *Répertoire numérique de la sous-série 9 B: Amirauté de Saint-Malo* (Rennes, 1962), pp. 188-206.

75. Esquemeling, pp. 60, 177-8; Labat, I, i, 75; Johnson, pp. 184, 274, 307; AN, Col. C9A/8, fos. 402-3. I have found only one French agreement, probably of 1702, offering compensation for disablement, but the sums are well below West Indian rates — e.g., 150 *livres tournois,* or roughly thirty-eight piastres, for an eye (AN, Marine B4/23, fo. 134).

76. AN, Col. C9A/9, fo. 51; cf. *ibid.,* 2, fo. 204.

77. The phrase is Dampier's, *New Voyage,* p. 246. Cf. Pawson and Buisseret, p. 31; G. Debien, *Une Plantation de Saint-Domingue: La Sucrerie Galbaud du Fort, 1690-1802* (Cairo: Institut Français d'Archéologie Orientale, 1941), p. 34; Labat, II, 237.

78. Charlevoix, iii, 68; AN, Col. C8A/6, fo. 407 (on provisions, 1691). On admiralty tenths see H.J. Crump, *Colonial Admiralty Jurisdiction in the Seventeenth Century* (London, 1931), p. 105, and *supra,* n. 64.

79. P. Margry (ed.), *Découvertes et établissements des Français dans l'Ouest et dans le Sud de l'Amérique Septentrionale, 1614-1754,* pt iv (Paris 1880), p. 17; Johnson, pp. 182-3, 274, 307; Rogers, pp. 22, 206; Dampier, pp. 195, 219.

80. Sir C. Wager to Admiralty, 1727, cit. R.G. Marsden (ed.), *Documents Relating to Law and Custom of the Sea,* 2 vols. (Navy Rec. Soc., 1915-16), ii, 266. Cf. T. Hesketh, *A Discourse concerning Plunder* (London, 1703), arguing, with reference to the plunder of St Mary's and of the Vigo galleons in 1702, that booty belongs to him who takes it; and more generally, F. Redlich, *De Praeda Militari: Looting and Booty 1500-1815* (Wiesbaden, 1956).

81. *Op. cit.,* p. 545.

82. Esquemeling, pp. 222-3: *pace* D. Pope, *Harry Morgan's Way* (London, 1977), p. 246, the charge was supported by Morgan's surgeon-general, Richard Browne, in *CSP Col. 1669-1674,* p. 252.

83. Johnson, pp. 259-60. Cf. the parody of Lords and Commons, *ibid.,* pp. 166-8.

84. *Histoire générale des Antilles habitées par les François,* 4 vols. (Paris, 1667), iii, 151.

85. AN, Col. C9A/3, fo. 47; Charlevoix, iv, 163-4.

86. *Bandits* (London, 1969), esp. pp. 50, 62-4.

87. Charlevoix, iii, 246-7. Ravenau de Lussan suggests a care for sick comrades reminiscent of the Yugoslav partisans: Besson, pp. 98, 137, 147. Dampier, p. 155, notes the willingness of his companions to stay behind on one of their marches to protect "a stout old Grey-headed Man, aged about 84, who had served under *Oliver...*". Cf. Lionel Wafer, *A New Voyage and Description of the Isthmus of America,* ed. L.E. Elliott Joyce (Hak. Soc., Oxford, 1938), p. 5: "There had been an Order made among us at our first Landing, to kill any who should flag in the Journey. But this was made only to terrify any from loitering, and being taken by the Spaniards; who by Tortures might extort from them a Discovery of our March." The wounded Wafer owed his life to the kindliness of the "wild", unconquered Cuna Indians of the Isthmus, indispensable allies of the buccaneers.

88. Esquemeling, p. 61; Labat, II, 244, 249.

89. Hacke, pt ii (Sharp), p. 14; Dampier, p. 252; Esquemeling, pp. 273, 341, 398.

90. Besson, p. 153; cf. Charlevoix, iii, 243.

91. Margry, iv, 17; Rogers, p. 207; Johnson, p. 307; Ringrose, *apud* Esquemeling, p. 398.

92. On the sharing of possessions and profits by the half-dozen men who composed a *camera* in the Army of Flanders, see Parker, p. 177; and Cruickshank, p. 114, for Elizabethan *cameradas.* Debien, *Engagés,* pp. 136-7, offers a rich selection of nicknames in France.

93. *Les Institutions de la France sous la monarchie absolue,* i (Paris, 1974), pp. 85-9.

94. Charlevoix, iii, 55; Labat, I, i, 75; Debien, *Galbaud du Fort,* p. 33; Burney, p. 41. Cf. London, Public Record Office, Admiralty 1/3930, Paris, 28 Oct. 1701, reporting a new Line of Battle: "the *Prompt* is in the midst of them as being Matelot, or assistant to the Vice-Admirall."

95. Dampier, p. 163.

96. BL, Add. MSS 39, 946, fo. 10ᵛ·

97. Dampier, *Voyages and Discoveries,* ed. C. Wilkinson (London, 1931), p. 181.

98. *Papers Relating to the Ships and Voyages of the Company of Scotland Trading to Africa and the Indies 1697-1707,* ed. G.P. Insh (Scottish Hist. Soc., 3rd ser., 6, Edinburgh, 1924), p. 81.

99. Some freebooter captains, mostly English, are to be found in P. Gosse's *The Pirates' Who's Who* (London, 1924), which draws on a narrow range of well-known sources. Gosse at least considered that more of them deserved a place in the *Dictionary of National Biography.*

Pierre Vilar

# RÉBELLIONS PAYSANNES, RÉBELLIONS OUVRIÈRES, RÉBELLION « NATIONALE ». LE CAS DE LA CATALOGNE DU 19ième SIÈCLE

George Rudé et Eric Hobsbawm nous ont appris à regarder en historiens les formes diverses des rébellions « primitives ». Et, dans cette revision éclairante de vieux phénomènes, les regards se sont plus d'une fois reportés sur le pays classique des contrebandiers et des bandits, sur cette Espagne méridionale telle que Gautier, Dumas et Mérimée avaient cru la voir, et telle que l'ont décrite plus récemment de sérieux historiens et sociologues. Je n'ajouterai, à cette bibliographie bien connue, qu'une note personnelle: un de mes amis, grand ingénieur des Ponts et Chaussées, à peine plus âgé que moi, m'a conté que lorsqu'il construisait des routes en Andalousie, dans ses années de jeunesse, il entendait souvent, au cours d'un repas pris en commun avec trente ou quarante « peones », s'élever une plaisanterie qui semblait classique (et peut-être nostalgique?): « Don X…, et si nous formions une « partida »?…nous avons tout pour cela…» Ainsi, le souvenir des formations rebelles spontanées ne s'était pas entièrement effacé dans la mentalité populaire des premières décennies du 20e siècle. Et quant aux groupes armés politiques, aux « guerrillas », on sait qu'il en a existé en Espagne, dans le prolongement de la guerre civile, jusqu'au delà de l'année 1950.

Il peut pourtant sembler paradoxal d'évoquer ces vieilles images - - « bandolerisme » ou « guerrillas » - - à propos de la région actuellement la plus modernisée de la Péninsule, de cette Catalogne où la paysannerie ne représente plus aujourd'hui que quelque 7% de la population active, où tout s'organise en fonction d'une agglomération surindustrialisée, où enfin une autonomie semble s'installer sans agitation ni problèmes graves.

Or si nous revenons de cent-dix ou cent-trente ans en arrière, un peu après 1870 ou un peu avant 1850, nous découvrons une montagne catalane sans cesse parcourue, parfois dominée, par les bandes armées traditionnalistes, « carlistes », et une Barcelone déjà en pointe dans la pensée et dans l'action ouvrières révolutionnaires. Un texte de 1849 accuse la Catalogne d'être tout entière « *un levain de rébellion contre toute autorité constituée* », de nourrir un peuple « *sans frein et sans police* «, habitué à « *arracher par la bouche du tromblon ce qu'il ne devrait gagner que par le travail et le respect du droit d'autrui…* »[1]. Bien entendu, des jugements aussi passionnels sont le fait d'un responsable de la répression, d'un agent de l'autorité centrale espagnole. Encore faut-il qu'ils prétendent s'appuyer à la fois sur une situation d'actualité, et sur une tradition plus que séculaire. Et il s'agit en effet d'un article inspiré à un général, dans la *Revista militar* madrilène, par la double rébellion catalane de la montagne carliste et de la Barcelone ouvrière et progressiste, en pleine conjoncture européenne révolutionnaire: 1846-1849.

L'intérêt de ce cas régional, dans une atmosphère de tension sociale généralisée, réside donc à la fois dans les formes, encore souvent «primitives», de la rébellion, et dans la conjonction paradoxale de deux inspirations idéologiques de signe contraire, ainsi que dans l'interprétation de ce paradoxe par les forces répressives: «ces gens-là»-- montagnards carlistes et ouvriers barcelonais révoltés-- n'ont en commun que *d'être catalans:* c'est donc *en tant que tels* que nous devons les combattre. On passe ainsi de la vision idéologique d'un conflit, politico-social à ses origines, à la vision d'un conflit *de groupes.* Ceux qui se croient désignés comme garants naturels de l'unité espagnole se mettent à caractériser si fortement l'originalité catalane qu'ils suggèrent de mettre en doute cette unité espagnole même, donnant des arguments aux futures dissidences, et aux historiens «catalanistes» d'aujourd'hui toujours à la recherche du «fait différentiel». Pour une analyse de ce problème historique fondamental--celui des rapports entre unité d'un État, structures nationales internes, et luttes classiques sociales--cet épisode catalan des années 1846-1849, et les textes qu'il inspire, se révèle donc riche de leçons.

Il est d'abord curieux de suivre à travers les siècles une association d'idées —souvent répétée par des textes savants ou pseudo-savants, mais qui peut fort bien traduire une image *populaire:*[2] le relief heurté, la structure labyrinthique du territoire catalan, seraient au moins le symbole, peut-être la cause, du caractère âpre, belliqueux, séditieux, habituellement prêté à la population catalane. Le texte de 1849 donne à cette vieille croyance une forme particulièrement caricaturale:[3]

> «...les Catalans obéissent à des conditions fatales, impérieuses... le soleil fertilise chez eux les pitons rocheux, la vigne naît dans le nid des aigles, le vin n'y fermente que pour être bu par des titans, l'eau a des effets pléthoriques qui forment des protubérances dans les gosiers, la langue est brève et dure, la terre sécrète en surface une croute de salpêtre qui pénètre et sature tout ce qu'elle nourrit,... Les pâtures et les eaux, ou le climat, comme on dit vulgairement (sic), font des Catalans une race insubordonnée...»

Cet étrange déterminisme géographique mêle le souvenir de vieux proverbes dont les Catalans eux-mêmes sont assez fiers («le Catalan tire du pain de la roche»), et les images, encore récentes en 1849, où l'on voit de beaux messieurs et de belles dames en costumes romantiques, arrachés d'une diligence, au sortir des terribles défilés subpyrénéens, par des bandits bien armés, tandis qu'un couple assez dérisoire de policiers ruraux en espadrilles s'efforce de courir à leur aide.[4]

Le simple rapprochement entre une représentation contemporaine d'une scène de ce genre, et la photographie d'une gorge de montagne, que certaines routes catalanes doivent emprunter,[5] justifie cette relation spontanément établie entre les conditions naturelles du pays et les facilités offertes au banditisme, aux «guerrillas», sans oublier la contrebande à travers une frontière d'État, qui ne sépare ni les types humains, ni les formes de vie montagnarde, ni les langues populaires.

Aussi bien s'agit-il de phénomènes multiséculaires. Le général Fernández San Román, en 1849, n'a aucun mal à découvrir, à l'appui de ses affirmations sur les Catalans, des textes du 17ème siècle:[6]

«Même les laboureurs, les hommes des champs, auxquels leur métier a donné partout un caractère égal, et pacifique, subissent ici les effets de cette coutume (à savoir le banditisme routier), de telle sorte que tout le monde y est exposé aux vengeances et à la discorde, à la fois par les caractères de la nature, par les formes de l'habitat, et par la force de l'exemple.»

Est-il besoin d'ajouter que cette explication par la nature et par le tempérament (même «acquis») ne satisfait pas l'historien, qui constate de très fortes variations dans l'intensité et les formes de ces désordres latents, suivant les conjonctures démographiques, économiques, sociales, politiques, non seulement locales, mais très générales.

Ainsi, aux 14ème et 15ème siècles, c'est une «guerre de cent ans» entre seigneurs et serfs «de remensa», combinée aux rivalités entre féodaux et pouvoir royal, qui agite la Catalogne entière, mais qui, si l'on considère le petit nombre des hommes engagés dans les rencontres les plus connues, ne doit guère dépasser la dimension des guerres de «bandes». Il n'empêche que le fond social--une lutte de classe bien caractérisée--en est le moteur.[7]

Au contraire, au 16ème et au 17ème siècles, une meilleure stabilité sociale dans les campagnes, et même une solide prospérité dans les «masies» isolées (et fortifiées!), donnent une autre forme et un autre sens au banditisme latent. Les châteaux haut perchés, «qui serviraient bien d'hermitages aux gentilshommes qui ne désirent compagnie», n'inspirent guère confiance aux voyageurs étrangers appelés à passer de France en Castille, et qui pourtant préfèrent l'itinéraire de terre à celui de mer, car «par celuy de terre au pis aller on ne perdait ordinairement que la bourse, de la mer il n'en eschappait rien».[8] Et l'on tombait pourtant, aux abords du royaume de Valence, de la menace des «bandouliers» dans celle des dissidents morisques!

Cela signifie qu'après la prospérité médiévale et la grande crise (à fond démographique) des 14ème et 15ème siècles, les structures de l'Espagne ont été bouleversées, et la Catalogne n'est plus, dans le système impérial espagnol, qu'une région de passage (incommode) entre les lieux où se recueille l'argent des Indes, et les lieux où, dépensé d'avance, il doit finalement aboutir. Or, dans ce même 16ème siècle, la population catalane s'est mise à croître rapidement, et ne trouve pas à s'occuper tout entière. Cadets de petite noblesse ou de souche paysanne, valets sans place, artisans ruinés, soldats sans maître, étrangers réfugiés, se mettent au service de chefs de bande, qui guettent les convois d'or et d'argent destinés à l'Italie, les cortèges de riches marchands génois ou de fonctionnaires d'empire, dont les déplacements sont signalés aux bandits par leurs agents dans les administrations et les banques. Et, pour jouer sur l'inflation interne qui monte, on fabrique de la mauvaise monnaie divisionnaire de cuivre, «boscatera», c'est-à-dire «faite dans les bois».

Il est exact, naturellement, que de tels phénomènes ont coloré la vie quotidienne de toute la Catalogne. Une enquête du 16ème siècle y a recensé un «pedrenyal» (tromblon) par foyer rural. Aux mêmes dates, un simple artisan peut se proclamer, moyennant une déclaration à son seigneur naturel (l'Église parfois!) en état de «guerre privée» avec un de ses semblables, c'est-a-dire avec droit de rencontre armée.[9] Et, dans l'ensemble, la population protège les hors-la-loi, ou en tout cas ne s'unit pas à la répression, soit par peur, soit par sympathie pour l'une des deux grandes «bandositats» («nyerros» et «cadells») que ces hors-la-loi soutiennent.[10]

La répression existe pourtant. Pouvoirs locaux et pouvoir central s'en renvoient réciproquement la responsabilité. Et elle est à la fois terrible et inefficace. C'est sous des grappes de bandits morts, pendus de vingt en vingt ou de trente en trente, que don Quichotte se heurte à «quarante bandits vivants», «ce qui me donne à penser», dit-il, «que je suis proche de Barcelone». J'ai montré ailleurs comment on peut, par recoupements, vérifier que la version romanesque de Cervantes, autour de la figure du bandit «Roque Guinart», est bien une allusion «d'actualité», malgré la distanciation nécessaire à l'œuvre d'art.[11] Et on est loin d'avoir encore tout dit sur les rapports entre mythe populaire et vérité sociale à propos des figures de hors-la-loi présentes dans les chansons, comme celle du célèbre Joan Serrallonga.

Or c'est du temps de Serrallonga -- autour de 1620-1630 -- que cette agitation désordonnée des campagnes en arrive à apparaître non plus divisée, mais comme une manifestation commune *d'opposition*. Elle se dresse contre un gouvernement lointain, que chacun croit corrompu, et qui au bout du compte est étranger «à la terre». Les «bandes» prennent à leur compte les cris de «vive la terre», «mort aux traîtres», «mort au mauvais gouvernement». Et quand, pour des raisons stratégiques en face de la France, des troupes espagnoles (souvent mercenaires) sont installées en Catalogne et s'y conduisent en armées d'occupation, c'est la révolte catalane de 1640, où la riche municipalité barcelonaise n'hésite pas à annoncer la participation efficace des *«hommes des bois et des grottes».*[12] Le général Fernádez San Román aurait donc raison? L'affirmation catalane s'exprime-t-elle toujours, finalement, «par la bouche du tromblon» (on dit aujourd'hui «au bout du fusil»)?

Deux objections à cela. D'abord l'objection géographique: les arguments et les souvenirs mis en avant par le général semblent s'appliquer surtout à l'intérieur du pays catalan, assimilé à sa partie montagneuse; or les agitations (et même le banditisme, si l'on en croit don Quichotte) si situent aussi bien «aux portes de Barcelone»; le phénomène profond, les rapports (oppositions et rapprochements) entre ville et campagne, mer et montagne, doivent donc être examinés dans leur complexité, ne pas être réduits aux contrebandes de frontière et aux guet-apens de routes.

L'autre objection est historique: le phénomène des actions «hors-la-loi» *n'est pas continu*. Dans certaines conjonctures, quand la prospérité du pays dans son ensemble est réelle, quand certaines formes de développement (industrielles par exemple) se révèlent capables d'absorber la croissance de la population, on voit les formes désordonnées des luttes sociales et politiques s'atténuer, disparaître. Ainsi, dans la Catalogne du 18ème siècle, que j'ai particulièrement étudiée, je n'ai rien observé qui rappelle massivement les types d'agitation que nous venons de décrire. Même les classiques crises de subsistances qui agitent le reste de l'Espagne (1766), ou Barcelone pendant quelques jours (1789) ne donnent lieu qu'à des incidents mineurs, vite résorbés. C'est qu'une marine rénovée, une participation directe au trafic colonial, une industrialisation naissante, acheminent la Catalogne vers une modernisation rapide de ses structures, très en avance sur l'Espagne intérieure, et qui suggère à certains esprits une comparaison avec l'Angleterre.

Mais nous savons aujourd'hui que -- fût-ce pour l'Angleterre -- les survivances et les phénomènes marginaux ne s'effacent pas d'un coup. Des reculs, même, peuvent survenir. Et ils surviennent en effet, pour la Catalogne, avec la «Guerre d'Indépendance». Coupée de ses marchés--espagnol, coloniaux--et malgré une participation d'un instant aux avantages du «système continental», la Catalogne, spontanément dressée contre l'occupant français, a retrouvé ses traditions «guerrilleras». Antonio de Capmany, député catalan aux Cortes, animateur et théoricien de la résistance antifrançaise, n'hésite pas à compter les «*facinerosos*» (les criminels) au nombre des composantes du mouvement patriotique de 1808.[13] Il y compte aussi, malgré les méfiances exprimées par les libéraux, la plus grande partie de la noblesse et des moines. Autant d'éléments qui n'entraînent pas l'Espagne sur les chemins de la modernité et de la révolution! Si l'on ajoute qu'en 1812-1813 la guerre tourne à la catastrophe démographique et économique (des villages catalans perdent plus de la moitié de leurs habitants), et que Ferdinand VII, en 1814, annule d'un trait l'œuvre révolutionnaire des Cortes de Cadix, on peut affirmer sans exagérer que l'Espagne de 1814-1820 ressemble davantage à celle de 1714, des lendemains de la «Guerre de Succession», qu'à ce qu'elle était devenue vers 1792-1793, à la fin de sa période «éclairée». À la brusque faillite de la révolution de 1810-1812 succède, plus étalée dans le temps, la «*faillite de la monarchie absolue*»,[14] dans le domaine intérieur et le domaine colonial. Et aussitôt renaissent, dans le Sud andalou comme dans les défilés pyrénéens, les vieilles formes de vie irrégulière, de banditisme routier et de contrebande organisée. Au point que l'image romantique de l'Espagne va s'identifier à ces formes. Barcelone même, en 1820, en proie à l'épidémie, devient en Europe une sorte de symbole de la détresse des pays «du Sud», au secours de laquelle il convient de mobiliser la charité des pays plus fortunés.[15]

Pourtant (mais ce n'est sans doute pas par hasard), 1820 est aussi la date initiale de l'épisode «libéral», «constitutionnel», qui s'ouvre avec le «pronunciamento» du général Riego, et se clot, en 1823, par l'intervention militaire française en faveur de l'absolutisme du roi Ferdinand.

Les débats de 1820-1821, aux «Cortes» constitutionnelles, permettent justement de saisir et de mesurer la profondeur de la double crise catalane: à Barcelone, misère *de chômeurs,* à la campagne *chute généralisée du revenu agricole.* L'effort législatif des «Cortes» pour remettre en application la suppression des droits seigneuriaux solennellement décrétée en 1811, et pour annoncer la sécularisation des biens d'Église, semble inquiéter, plus que rassurer, la majorité des paysans, dont les plus aisés sont surtout préoccupés du poids croissant de l'impôt royal (payé en argent), et dont les plus pauvres comptent encore beaucoup sur l'usage des communaux et les secours ecclésiastiques (couvents et paroisses). Le clergé mobilise alors facilement les bandes paysannes des sans-travail et des sans-ressources, habituées depuis 1808 à se former en «guerrillas». Et dans le même esprit que contre Napoléon: au nom de la religion, contre les idées venues de France (même si la France a changé!), pour les droits locaux et ce qui reste des anciens usages communautaires, contre l'individualisme libéral. C'est pourquoi l'action de bandes armées, en haute et moyenne Catalogne, commence dès les lendemains de 1815,[16] la réaction au sommet opérée par Ferdinand, trop lointaine et trop politique, ne suffisant évidemment pas aux exigences religieuses, sociales, et décentralisatrices, des chefs de bande «ultras», qui souvent sont les religieux eux-mêmes.

Cette agitation «ultra» redouble, bien entendu, au cours du «trienio» libéral, alors qu'à Barcelone triomphent les «exaltés», organisateurs des «milices» urbaines révolutionnaires, et qui répandent à profusion la littérature de la liberté. Dès lors, au cœur des Pyrénées, se constitue une «régence» (dite «d'Urgell»), le roi étant considéré comme prisonnier des libéraux. La frontière catalane devient aussitôt un lieu d'intrigues compliquées, préparant l'intervention militaire française (ainsi que d'une activité accrue de la contrebande, qui ajoute à la ruine de l'industrie).

On pourrait croire que «l'ignominieuse décennie» absolutiste qui suit le rétablissement de l'autorité de Ferdinand par l'expédition du duc d'Angoulême (1824-1833), est bien faite pour satisfaire les tenants de l'extrême réaction. Mais la mentalité «apostolique», et les noyaux d'agitation qu'elle inspire, tiennent à leur implantation locale et se méfient de Madrid: les trois dernières années du règne de Ferdinand (1830-1833) les inquiètent de plus en plus: libéralisation relative, peur inspirée par les révolutions de 1830, intrigues autour du mariage du roi et de la naissance d'une future reine. À la mort de Ferdinand, tout est prêt pour une division de l'Espagne entre partisans de la Régente, Marie-Christine, libérale et constitution-naliste par position, et partisans du prétendant don Carlos, frère du roi défunt, dont l'absolutisme doctrinaire à fond religieux a fait depuis longtemps le candidat au trône idéal pour toute l'Espagne traditionaliste: Pays basque, Navarre, haut Aragon, Catalogne intérieure, confins montagneux du royaume de Valence. Cette fois, il s'agit d'une véritable dissidence (presque d'une «guerre de Sécession»), où des généraux «carlistes», comme un Zumalacarreguí, feront preuve d'un vrai génie militaire, et où des généraux «cristinos», comme Espartero, gagneront des batailles, des titres de noblesse ronflants, et finalement des rôles politiques de premier plan, destinés à marquer la physionomie des pouvoirs dans l'avenir de l'Espagne.

Mais, régionalement, et particulièrement en Catalogne, la «guerre carliste» n'est souvent qu'un état latent de désordre, de successives main-mises de bandes armées sur tels villages ou telles vallées, suivies, à chaque changement de pouvoirs, d'assez horribles vengeances. Ces va-et-vient tournent plus d'une fois au simple règlement de comptes entre bandits et contrebandiers. Et c'est ainsi que la Catalogne retrouve sa réputation farouche des siècles passés -- en même temps, d'ailleurs, que l'Andalousie de «Carmen», qui cependant n'est pas traversée des mêmes courants idéologiques ni des mêmes types d'opérations militaires -- ce qui engage à bien limiter la portée explicative du «carlisme» comme phénomène social de fond.

Pour la Catalogne, Josep Fontana a bien cerné, récemment, les rapports entre «crise paysanne» et «guerre carliste».[17] Il écarte plaisamment les interprétations du «carlisme» qui n'invoquent que d'obscures querelles entre une infante et ses belles-sœurs, ou que de fumeuses considérations juridiques sur les normes de succession (la «loi salique»!). Il montre comment l'idéologie non pas «immobiliste» mais franche-ment «passéiste» (rêve d'un *retour en arrière* vers des traditions plus ou moins mythifiées) a inspiré très tôt des actions armées. Elles seront menées, de plus en plus, par les formations dites de «volontaires royalistes», dont les ambassadeurs français ont vite décelé, non sans inquiétude, le caractère *populaire,* en tout cas *antibourgeois.* Après tout, la plupart des «riches» passent pour «libéraux», et les «milices» urbaines, qu'on croit «révolutionnaires», se recrutent parmi les «classes moyennes». Les «volontaires royalistes», eux, sont des paysans ruinés par la crise agricole et par les impôts, des artisans sans travail, des jeunes qui n'absorbe pas une économie devenue stagnante. L'Église offre à ces marginalisés (qui tendent à devenir de purs «marginaux») une idéologie non exempt de démagogie (la «démocracia frailuna» a toujours plus ou moins dénoncé «les riches») et non exempt de superstitions (on dit couramment que le «trienio» libéral, par malédiction de Dieu, a correspondu à trois ans de sécheresse).[18]

Sans doute convient-il de ne pas simplifier: les paysans (mais peut-être, il est vrai, les plus aisés parmi eux) luttent encore contre les vestiges féodaux, et paient la dîme de mauvais gré. Mais, dans le «Camp de Tarragona», région côtière relativement riche pourtant, on note que les paysans «ne pouvant payer les contributions et n'ayant rien à manger, se lèveront plus facilement pour la défense de S.M., si on les paie comme on l'a promis...»[19]

Ce qui signifie que les «ultras» (les couvents en tête) sont prêts à encadrer, et à financer, tout mouvement antilibéral, le recrutement réussissant particulièrement bien quand s'achèvent les récoltes, parmi ceux qui y ont participé, et seraient sans travail s'ils n'entraient dans les «guerrillas». Paysans aisés contre les impôts, ouvriers agricoles contre le chômage, telles sont donc les bases des formes carlistes d'opposition.

Il faut dire qu'en quinze ans, au delà du quinquennat 1814-1818, le prix du blé et celui de l'huile ont baissé de 50%, celui de l'eau-de-vie - - produit d'exportation classique de la viticulture - - de 60%. La «trilogie» agricole méditerranéenne est en mauvaise posture. On peut objecter que, pour les grains, l'autoconsommation, la semence et les droits payés en nature, ne dépendent que du niveau des récoltes (très variable, il est vrai). Il reste que le poids relatif de l'impôt-argent, et celui de tout achat opéré dans le commerce, a pratiquement doublé entre le retour de Ferdinand en 1814 et sa mort en 1833.[20]

Un remarquable document - - comptes et «livre de raison» quotidiens d'un paysan aisé de la «Conca d'Odena», bassin et passage accidentés, mais proches de Barcelone, - - a permis à une excellente étude récente[21] de reconstituer la physionomie de la «première guerre carliste» (dite «guerre des sept ans», 1833-1840), telle que l'a vue, et vécue, un personnage de culture moyenne, sérieux gestionnaire et bon observateur, représentatif d'une catégorie sociale peu engagée dans la lutte active (et qui voudrait probablement en être mieux dégagée), mais qui, par cela même, révèle les solidarités, les indifférences, les sympathies et les méfiances spontanées, dont le sens peut changer suivant les attitudes successives des deux factions en lutte.

Le «journal» de Martí Vidal, du «mas Gallardes», constate un jour que la guerre, «partie de peu est devenue beaucoup».[22] «De peu», cela veut dire qu'on a d'abord vu descendre de la montagne, faisant passer de mauvaises nuits aux habitants des «masies» isolées, des «lladres», c'est-à-dire des voleurs en troupes, commandées par des chefs dont les noms deviendront célèbres (mais on ne le sait pas encore, car on les déforme singulièrement). Comme l'observe Fontana, le paysan moyen n'entre donc pas dans la guerre carliste au nom de Cristina, ou de don Carlos, ou même de Cabrera, dont il ne sait rien, ou pas grand-chose; il constate simplement une recrudescence de l'activité des «lladres». Pourtant cette guerre, de «peu», deviendra «beaucoup». Dans quelle mesure y participera-t-on, idéologiquement et pratiquement?

Ce qui est clair, c'est qu'on n'est pas «libéral», moins par hostilité raisonnée, que par *incompréhension,* ignorance, manque d'outillage conceptuel. On constate, dans les comptes du «mas», un effacement progressif, une usure par les circonstances, entre 1808 et 1834, des droits féodaux encore payés tout le long du 18ème siècle.[23]

Or on ne semble nullement rattacher cela aux législations de 1811, 1820, 1837, contre le principe du «señorío». Tandis que, dans les mêmes comptes, on voit s'accroître nettement les exigences de l'impôt royal, perçu par Madrid. L'hostilité sous-jacente est celle de la campagne contre la ville.[24] La ville des hommes de loi, des agents commerciaux, des collecteurs d'impôts (et, longtemps, des droits féodaux eux-mêmes, car ils étaient toujours affermés à des compagnies urbaines).[25]

Autre point clair: on sait que *l'Église,* dans ses diverses institutions, penche pour le carlisme. Or on a *besoin* de l'Église. Les sacrements rythment la vie. On croit combattre la sécheresse, les épizooties, par les prières des prêtres.[26] On supporte mal que pendant six mois le village soit privé de ses desservants, et de ses cloches. Inversement, les troupes libérales soupçonnent volontiers les curés de sonner contre elles le tocsin (le «somatén»), l'appel aux armes;[27] et, dans ce cas, elles punissent sévèrement. On est assez près de Barcelone pour savoir que les émeutes urbaines (les «bullangues») s'en prennent volontiers aux couvents. Cela scandalise, et probablement fait peur (le massacre par surprise d'une troupe libérale est attribuée à la vengeance d'une image religieuse profanée).[28]

Dans cette atmosphère, le carlisme, à ses débuts, monte allègrement. On s'engage dans ses bandes, quand on est jeune, «comme on va à la fête du village».[29] Mais on dit clairement pourquoi: les carlistes *ont de l'argent,* celui des couvents, la «bourse des moines». Ils réquisitionnent les armes (comme au 16ème siècle, il y en a partout); mais ils les paient! Ils paient même les rations de nourriture qu'ils consomment ou prélèvent! *Employeurs* et *clients,* ils sont la solution providentielle contre la crise. Et on les qualifie alors de «bona gent».[30]

Mais cela ne dure pas bien longtemps. Quand s'épuisent les ressources des «guerrilleros» carlistes, on recommence, dans les «masies», à ressentir la terreur nocturne des «patuleias». Car elles imposent des «compositions», avec séquestra-tions, au besoin tortures.[31] Un phénomène non moins important se renverse aussi. Un des grands griefs de la paysannerie contre les pouvoirs a toujours été la haine des «quintas», c'est-à-dire du recrutement militaire forcé, avec tirage au sort des partants; les Catalans n'ont jamais admis de bon gré qu'on le leur applique; or le système (assorti du possible «rachat» en argent pour les conscrits malheureux... et riches) fut généralisé, pour les besoins de la guerre civile, par le gouvernement de Madrid: autre raison d'être contre lui.[32] Hélas, au bout d'un certain temps, les carlistes, dans les régions qu'ils dominaient, procédèrent à leur tour à l'appel des «quintas». C'est la preuve que le recrutement «volontaire» était épuisé.

Dès lors, c'est avec soulagement -- mais sans enthousiasme, sans le moindre revirement idéologique -- que le mas Gallardes observera la retraite vers la France du chef carliste Cabrera, avec 8 000 hommes, et le passage vers Barcelone de la Régente et de la jeune reine, «entourées de beaucoup de troupes», mais victorieuses (7-06-1840).[33] Il n'empêche qu'un an plus tard encore, le «journal» consacre une sorte d'épitaphe aux chefs de bande Casurellas et Marimón, survivants de l'aventure carliste, tués le jour de l'Ascension 1841, après avoir «causé bien des maux, assassiné bien des gens, détruit bien des foyers».[34] Décidément, l'installation de la société bourgeoise libérale, dans la campagne catalane, n'a pas été sans problèmes. L'intelligent découvreur du journal de Martí Vidal ne manque pas de rapprocher ces problèmes de ceux qu'ont éclairés Thompson, Hobsbawm et Rudé, sur d'autres fronts du monde «préindustriel» finissant.[35]

Cependant, au cours des mêmes années, le monde industriel, avec ses propres conflits «primitifs», s'installait à Barcelone. L'alliance, scellée dès les «Cortes» de 1820, entre propriétaires céréaliers du centre espagnol, et fabricants catalans de cotonnades, autour d'un double protectionnisme,[36] est peut-être ce qui a permis à Marie-Christine de se défendre du carlisme en Castille, et à la Catalogne de conserver, en face du populisme «ultra» de ses montagnes, un bastion urbain (avec quelques annexes côtières) ouvert au progrès matériel, à l'idéologie bourgeoise avancée, à une première prise de conscience ouvrière.

En effet, c'est dans l'«ominiosa decada» (1824-1833), et en pleine guerre carliste (1834-1840), que l'industrie cotonnière catalane a acquis du souffle: consommation annuelle de coton brut est passée de 1 424 tonnes en 1816-1820 à 3 906 en 1834-38 et à 5 636 en 1839-43; avec mécanisation (27 000 broches mécaniques en 1835, 346 000 en 1841).[37] Or, en 1835, une émeute urbaine, qui avait commencé par l'incendie de couvents, s'est terminé par celui de la fabrique la plus mécanisée. Typique geste «luddiste». Mais qui a inspiré une des analyses prémarxistes les plus remarquables sur les rapports entre mécanisation et partage capital-travail dans le produit, ainsi que sur les effets à termes divers du progrès technique: à long terme, économiquement favorable à tous, mais, dans l'immédiat, désastreux pour la classe ouvrière comme telle.[38] Or, cet article fouriériste, signé «Proletario», parut dans le journal «El Vapor», dont le titre est un programme, et qu'animait Aribau, romantique du progrès scientifique et technique, esprit «européen», collaborateur, à Madrid, du banquier catalan Remisa, et futur haut fonctionnaire des douanes.[39] Tout cela alors que le «mas Gallardes» (à peine à 50 kilomètres) passe ses nuits sous la menace de «lladres» organisés, avec ou sans prétextes politico-religieux! Il est vrai que cet étrange contraste entre Barcelone et ses environs immédiats avait déjà frappé don Quichotte!

Et l'on est en droit de se demander, comme fera un peu plus tard le général San Román, ce que peuvent bien avoir en commun ces ouvriers révoltés, ces paysans en colère? D'abord, bien entendu, une peur instinctive de la société qui s'annonce, prête à les réduire à l'état prolétarien, sans le soutien matériel de l'Église, cette «sécurité sociale» d'autrefois, et sans le soutien moral d'une foi élémentaire, dont les uns subissent encore la pression, tandis que d'autres y ont déjà renoncé. Mais les uns comme les autres réagissent d'une façon «primitive»: dans les campagnes choix de la vie rebelle, à la ville gestes destructeurs.

Faut-il ajouter qu'ils ont en commun d'«être catalans»? Il est certain que dans la mentalité «carliste», le *particularisme* est une importante composante. Il est communément admis aujourd'hui qu'elle est le signe d'une continuité des consciences de groupe, l'annonce des futurs «nationalismes» basque et catalan. Dans cette perspective, il est significatif de constater qu'au populisme passéiste des montagnards répond un particularisme progressiste, à ouvertures révolutionnaires, qui préfigure le futur «fédéralisme» républicain et le «catalanisme» démocratique, puisque plus d'un émeutier populaire barcelonais crie «Vive la République catalane» et même «Vive l'état catalan!»[40] En fait, c'est là un autre aspect du refus de la société qui s'annonce: le refus de l'état-nation bourgeois, qui, indifférent aux misères sociales, qu'il croit inhérentes, voire nécessaires, au progrès matériel, se montre politiquement autoritaire et administrativement centralisateur.

Sur ce point, jusqu'à la fin du 19ème siècle, le patronat catalan a une position ambiguë. Le territoire espagnol est son marché, l'État espagnol sa garantie d'ordre dans la rue; il dénonce donc toute manifestation particulariste comme une aide offerte à «la fraction» (c'est-à-dire au carlisme réactionnaire).[41] Mais dès que le libéralisme madrilène menace de se teinter de libre-échangisme (et cela arrive), l'industriel catalan n'hésite pas à faire appel à la solidarité de ses ouvriers pour la défense des intérêts «catalans». On voit combien d'obstacles se sont dressés, parfois contradictoires, parfois convergents, sur le chemin d'une «révolution bourgeoise» espagnole à l'européenne: libéralisme économique interne mais continuité d'une défense solidaire envers l'extérieur, cohérence, sur tout le territoire national, de la politique des classes dirigeantes, envers le double danger de réaction et de révolution.

Aussi bien, les secousses socio-politiques vont-elles se répétant, moins décisives, mais plus fréquentes, qu'en France même. Entre les troubles de 1835 et la crise de 1846-1848, Barcelone se soulève au moins trois fois: pendant l'été 1840, elle aide Espartero, «progressiste», à s'emparer de la Régence, à la place de Marie-Christine, trop «modérée»; mais elle tend aussitôt à se gouverner elle-même, par ses «milices» et ses «juntes»; on en arrive, en novembre 1842, à chasser de la ville l'armée régulière! Espartero soumettra Barcelone en la bombardant. Moins d'un an plus tard, ayant collaboré au renversement d'Espartero, la capitale catalane était de nouveau en dissidence et subissait un siège en règle.

Les aspects purement politiques de ces révolutions (souvent étendues à toute l'Espagne) ne peuvent nous retenir ici. Mais les *aspects sociaux* et *style populaire* qu'elles présentent en Catalogne touchent au problème que nous avons posé: s'agit-il, dans ces mouvements, de formes spontanées d'inquiétudes sociales? s'agit-il (davantage ou en partie) d'un mécontentement *de groupe,* d'un désir d'échapper à un pouvoir central mal accepté?

Pour novembre 1842, voici comment les événements sont jugés par le consul de France (il mérite confiance, c'est Ferdinand de Lesseps!):

> «Le mouvement de Barcelone n'a eu d'autre cause que l'irritation des Catalans contre les rigueurs militaires du général Zurbano, et contre les projets de négociations commerciales attribués au gouvernement de Madrid. L'établissement de la «Quinta», ou loi de recrutement, a achevé de soulever les esprits.»[42]

Intéressante combinaison de griefs! 1) L'un d'eux touche la classe des entrepreneurs: c'est la menace d'un traité libre-échangiste (Espartero est lié à l'Angleterre); cela explique la participation des hautes classes barcelonaises à l'opposition, aux «juntes» antiesparteristes, avec, dans une première phase, appel à la solidarité des ouvriers; 2) L'autre grief est la loi de recrutement, la «quinta», tirage au sort avec possibilité de rachat, qui fait peser la servitude militaire sur les seuls pauvres, et devient par là, à travers tout le siècle, le symbole de l'inégalité sociale et de la duperie des appels patriotiques; déjà, sous l'ancien régime (1770), tout essai d'appliquer en Catalogne un recrutement forcé avait causé des émeutes; mais on invoquait alors le vieux droit des Catalans à assurer leur défense eux-mêmes; un siècle plus tard, la résistance aux «quintas» sera devenue plus sociale que particulariste, mais, dans les deux cas, les arguments sont mêlés, par le vieux réflexe populaire: nous voulons bien des armes, mais pour notre cause; c'est la Commune; «*soldados no, milicianos sí;*[43]
3) reste le troisième grief: «les rigueurs militaires» du général commandant la place:

les heurts entre Barcelonais armés (corporations, ou émeute improvisée) et «soldats du roi» (ou marins) sont aussi vieux que les histoires de «bandolers»;[44] aux deux sens des deux mots, le «*language*» de «*l'armée*» choque Barcelone: l'idiome des soldats (qui n'est pas celui du peuple), le discours des généraux; en 1842, si on entend dans la rue «mort aux soldats», «mort aux Castillans», c'est que selon Lesseps, Zurbano aurait dit «L'Espagne peut bien exister sans la Catalogne».[45] Authentique ou non, le propos a le tort de passer pour vraisemblable. Il suffit de regarder le Pays Basque aujourd'hui pour saisir le même type de relations.

Pourtant, cette rancoeur commune aux Barcelonais ne peut effacer leur division en classes hostiles. Au début des événements, c'est la «milice nationale», organe de bourgeoisie moyenne, qui oblige l'armée régulière à se retirer hors des murailles. Aussitôt pèse sur la ville la menace du bombardement. Et les possédants, les bien pensants, quittent Barcelone. Les «juntes» passent aux mains des exaltés, des activistes, des «républicains». Au dessous de la «Milice» surgit un *troisième niveau de formations militaires*: les «fusiliers de la Patrie»... mais la rue leur applique, comme aux irréguliers, le terme moins respectable de «*patuleies*».[46] Ce sont des jeunes (chômeurs?) recrutés pour quatre réaux par jour et la soupe: on en trouve 1 500. On menace en vain de confisquer les biens des bourgeois en fuite. Et c'est le dur bombardement, la capitulation à merci, les exécutions. Cabet, qui a des amis en Catalogne, publie à Paris: «Le bombardement de Barcelone ou voilà les Bastilles» (1843).[47]

Or, quand parut le livre, la situation était déjà renversée. L'autoritarisme d'Espartero avait provoqué des «pronunciamientos» en chaîne. Et la première «Junte centrale» qui le destitua siégeait à Barcelone. Cependant, le gouvernement modéré qui s'installa à Madrid s'affirma le seul légal. Et Barcelone déclencha le mouvement bizarrement connu sous le nom de «centraliste» (à cause de la Junte «centrale») alors qu'il est, de nouveau, une dissidence régionale, avec «dérapage» révolutionnaire rapide.[48] Toujours sur les mêmes divergences: impôts, contrebande, «quintas», choix des pouvoirs locaux, acceptation ou désarmement des «bataillons francs» urbains. Cette fois la situation est complexe, parce qu'en haut les militaires sont divisés, et qu'en bas on espère voir d'autres villes d'Espagne rejoindre la «Junte». Or ce sont surtout de petites villes catalanes qui «se prononcent» («se prononcer» est une habitude militaire, mais aussi municipale). La dernière réduite sera Figueres, place-frontière,[49] qui avait pour maire Abdon Terrades, poète populaire républicain. Rappelons qu'une de ses chansons demandait au peuple de renverser «la Cour et la noblesse — l'orgueil de la richesse», en somme les deux révolutions.[50]

Une autre chanson barcelonaise de 1843 voulait faire «frire dans la poêle» le général Prim, devenu trop modéré, et continuait ainsi:

«Mort aux aristocrates / ils ont fait trop de mal / le peuple est le seul maître / bon Dieu, il le sera — Si nous risquons nos vies / pour notre liberté / que notre vote vaille / pour faire un député / — Que jamais plus les pauvres / ne paient contribution / que les riches les paient / ces voleurs de millions / — et que pas davantage / il n'y ait tant d'employés / trop, pour les faire vivre / on nous a dépouillés.»[51]

Ce sont là griefs d'artisans, de boutiquiers, des espoirs de «sans-culottes». Mais les ouvriers ne sont pas absents. Un bataillon de la milice est dit «*de la blouse*».[52] La bonne société appelle ces combattants «*la jamància*», mot méprisant d'argot gitan. Et certains «*jamàncios*» arborent le drapeau noir. Bien entendu, leur coiffure est la «barretina», traditionnel bonnet catalan de paysan ou de marin, mais qui a quelque chose du bonnet phrygien.[53]

S'agit-il de bandes irrégulières, indisciplinées? Il est intéressant de voir un militaire castillan, de tradition libérale, qui les a commandés, leur faire ainsi ses adieux:

> «Fidèles et braves camarades...une croyance est assez enracinée en Espagne, selon laquelle les Catalans sont insurbodonnés...j'ai appris grâce à vous que les Catalans peuvent être, et sont en effet insubordonnés, mais seulement lorsqu'ils bataillent en faveur du despotisme, car ils sont très dociles et soumis lorsqu'ils suivent imperturbablement un chef qui, au nom de la liberté, les conduit à la mort ou à la victoire...»[54]

Un peu gêné, ce militaire ajoute qu'il espère que personne ne commentera injurieusement son départ pour l'étranger! Et l'on constate en effet que, à cause sans doute de la division des militaires, l'épisode se termina plus modérément qu'en 1842. On signa de véritables traités. Mais Barcelone avait reçu 8 615 obus selon les uns, 11 893 selon d'autres.[55] Curieuse comptabilité!

En 1845, les modérés de Madrid, avec une Constitution censitaire et une bonne réforme fiscale, semblent devoir stabiliser la situation. Mais la grande crise économique gagne le pays. De 1846 à 1848, à Barcelone, l'indice des prix du blé passe de 79 à 199; le chômage atteint 49% dans certaine branches. Politiquement, le problème du mariage de la reine ranime la querelle dynastique, où interviennent Français et Anglais. La frontière pyrénéenne fourmille de nouveau d'intrigues...et de contrebande: Lesseps écrit «il n'y a plus de Pyrénées».[56] Et quand le prétendant carliste («Charles VI», comte de Montemolín) quitte clandestinement Bourges pour l'Angleterre et y lance un manifeste conciliant, les «guerrillas» reparaissent en Catalogne: «jeunes qui ne veulent pas être soldats réguliers, chômeurs urbains, paysans ruinés, anciens carlistes de la précédente guerre, simples 'bandouliers'...»[57] Les chefs? Les mêmes que dix ans plus tôt: le chanoine Tristany, Ros d'Eroles, Borges, Vilella, et de moindres, aux surnoms plus pittoresques,[58] qui occupent un instant les villages, pillent les magasins publics, affectent d'épargner les paysans, et sont appelés «*matiners*» (lève-tôt).[59] Leur nombre se situe entre 3 500 et 4 000, mais ils semblent être partout. On leur oppose une armée doublée, 22 000 hommes, puis 40 000, avec, successivement, trois généraux énergiques: Pavía, de la Concha, Fernández de Córdova. Comme il arrive souvent, Pavía a cru en finir en capturant, et en fusillant spectaculairement, Benat Tristany et Ros d'Eroles.[60] En fait, comme dans la guerre précédente, les bandes carlistes ne perdirent la partie que quand elles furent obligées, faute de ressources, d'être plus exigeantes, en hommes, en argent, et en vivres que l'armée et le pouvoir réguliers. En janvier 1848, on annonçait la «pacification», l'amnistie. Mais le consul de France n'attribuait le calme qu'aux «rigueurs de l'hiver».[61] Et en effet, au moment où Narváez croit pouvoir procéder aux «quintas» de 1846 et 47, les «matiners» reprennent séquestres, pillages de trésors, et exécutions d'officiers «isabelinos».

Surtout, la révolution française de février est sur le point de modifier les conditions militaires et idéologiques de la révolte catalane: les progressistes, les anciens «centralistes» de 1843, les républicains (par exemple Abdon Terrades depuis

Paris) tentent de relancer, partout où ils le peuvent, l'agitation contre le dur conservatisme de Narváez: ils négocient avec les «montemolinistes», parfois combattent à leurs côtés: «qui nous eût dit, écrit le *Diario de Barcelona,* que la cause de Montemolin était liée à celle des communistes français?»[62]

À vrai dire, le comité révolutionnaire formé à Barcelone se contentait de demander la suppression des «quintas», des impôts de consommation, le suffrage universel, la milice nationale, la liberté de la presse, l'enseignement primaire gratuit et obligatoire.[63] Il fut arrêté. On était encore en 48. Mais déjà en août! En janvier 1849, un curieux document,[64] rédigé par de soi-disant «paysans» de La Garriga, gros bourg à mi-chemin entre Barcelone et la «montagne», fait la leçon, justement, aux «montagnards» ralliés aux *«matiners».* Le carlisme, leur dit-on, était bon quand toute l'Europe opposait «absolutisme» à «libéralisme». C'est fini. La cause de don Carlos est morte. Si elle admet la constitution, autant choisir le pouvoir en place, car, désormais,

> «ce n'est ni le roi constitutionnel ni d. Carlos qu'on veut instaurer, non, montagnards, c'est le fatal *communisme,* dans son extension et son horreur; c'est ce système désorganisateur du monde, *le terrible combat de celui qui ne possède pas contre celui qui possède,* la destruction de la propriété, des familles, de la religion, où 'les biens seront communs, à tous en général et non à chacun en particulier, où les pères n'auront plus autorité sur les fils ni les fils de devoir envers les pères, où les temples seront abolis, et leurs ministres...' Tel est le communisme».

Eh oui! «Un spectre hante l'Europe»! Les *«matiners»,* devenus alliés des républicains, tiennent des discours *«ouvertement démocratiques et désorganisateurs, en un mot communistes».* (Après tout, le dernier prétendant carliste, en 1975, se dira bien trotzkiste!). Les hommes de La Garriga se rassurent en constatant que les Français ont déjà élu un Bonaparte, qui met en prison les Espagnols antigouvernementaux, qu'ils désirent passer la frontière, ou la repasser quand ils ont été battus. Le dernier cas est celui du général Ametller, ex-chef «centraliste», l'autre cas celui de Montemolín lui-même, et aussi d'Abdon Terrades, surveillé à Perpignan.[65] Conservateurs de tous les pays unissez-vous! «Libéralisme»? «absolutisme»? Non pas. Mais sécurité bourgeoise. Passéistes et utopistes n'ont pas dit leur dernier mot en Espagne.[66] Mais ils ne trouvent plus guère de chefs. Concluons, avec Jaume Vicens Vives:[67]

> «Les hommes qui, en 1846, prirent leur tromblon et partirent en campagne venaient de camps politiques divers: carlistes, républicains, démocrates, d'autres — la majorité peut-être, inadaptés. Mais nous ne les appellerons pas «latrofactieux», mot méprisant par lequel la presse bien-pensante et domestiquée de Narváez croyait les humilier. S'ils devaient vivre et lutter à la façon des «bandolers» du 16e et 17e siècles, c'est qu'ils se heurtaient à un État qui non seulement ne satisfaisait pas leurs aspirations, mais qui contrariait leurs impulsions politiques élémentaires. Seule la puissante reprise de l'agriculture et de l'industrie catalanes après 1856 évita de garder le «trabucaire» comme symbole de protestation populaire. Il ne fut pas apprivoisé par le pouvoir. Il fut digéré par l'expansion économique».

Encore deux réflexions, qui nous ramènent vers l'actualité.

1) Dans la convergence d'un instant entre «matiners» traditionalistes et velléités révolutionnaires, aperçoit-on l'amorce de ce *«catalanisme»* qui marquera si profondément un siècle (1880-1980)? Un personnage oublié vient d'être redécouvert:

Tomás Bertrán i Soler,[68] qui tenta, en 1848, non seulement la négociation entre toutes les forces d'opposition catalanes, mais encore la création d'une «Députation générale de Catalogne», résurrection historique qui annonce la «Généralité». Ses écrits condensent déjà l'idéologie «nationaliste». Son échec, son isolement, montrent qu'à cette date il est encore un «inadapté». Mais enfin, dans les composantes du futur «catalanisme», convergeront bien (même s'ils s'y contredisent) un traditionalisme catholique, un rêve bourgeois de contrôle et d'expansion des marchés, et la résistance instinctive, commune aux intellectuels, aux couches populaires et aux ouvriers, contre un autoritarisme centraliste ressenti comme étranger, incarné surtout par les militaires.

2) Et ceci nous ramène aux dires — et au *style* — de la *Revista militar* de février 1849, exactement contemporaine du document de La Garriga:

a) La Catalogne y est traitée en *corps historique,* des prétentions des Comtes à celles des «Consellers» barcelonais, «vrais souverains», dit-on, non sans rancœur contre le *bourgeois* catalan, contre son chantage protectionniste:

«chaque Espagnol jette son obole dans une sébille pour soutenir une fraction des Catalans appelée 'les ouvriers', car, si on ne le fait pas, ou bien ils meurent de faim, ou bien ils se soulèvent et tuent leur prochain.»[69]

b) Mais les adjectifs globaux (insubordonnés, ingrats, tyrans) s'appliquent aux «peuples».[70] Le carlisme est mort. La révolte continue. Elle est donc contre «l'Espagne». Peut-être vaudrait-il mieux opposer aux Catalans la «nationalité castillane». Ils devraient alors financer leur guerre. Ils hésiteraient![71]

c) En guerre, on ne discute pas de la bonne foi de l'adversaire, et, donc,

«il faut trancher le nœud gordien»,[72] «le seul procédé de conquête est la terreur salutaire»,[73] «nos pères se sont arrangés comme ils ont pu dans les questions catalanes, nos fils devront en faire autant...»,[74] «qu'est-ce qu'une 'transaction'? tailler les branches ou couper l'arbre? on sait que la taille fait reparaître les branches avec plus de sève...il est sûr, si on coupe l'arbre, que les branches disparaîtront».[75]

d) Et c'est tout le vocabulaire «antisubversif»: «*nettoyer*», «*balayer*»,[76] «*occuper*» (il y a des pages entières sur ce concept).[77] Les *guerrillas* sont insaisissables, fantomatiques, ont leur langue, sont informées par la population, muette devant l'armée. On a même pensé à «reconcentrer» les populations éparses.[78]

e) Des articles plus généraux font de l'Armée «*le bras de l'autorité*» partout en Europe: «la société allait à l'abîme, l'armée la préserve; la civilisation allait disparaître sous les pas d'un prolétarisme barbare; l'armée la remet en place.»[79]

On s'en prend à «l'ultralibéralisme», à l'abominable révolution de février, heureusement endiguée; et on note que le «Times», «journal le plus libéral de tous ceux qui se publient dans la nation la plus libérale», s'en félicite. Si l'Allemagne avait disposé de «généraux accrédités» (sic),[80] «la jacobinique et ridicule assemblée de Francfort aurait-elle converti la raisonnable et droite nation germanique en un abîme de désordres et de crimes?»[81] Même chose, bien entendu, pour l'autre malheureuse nation, «où un avocat nommé Robespierre commença sa carrière de même façon qu'aujourd'hui un autre avocat appelé Ledru-Rollin.»[82]

Quand le militaire dénonce «l'avocat» comme danger principal, la «révolution bourgeoise» est-elle accomplie? Quand le «nationalisme catalan» en est encore aux escarmouches des «matiners», et au rêve solitaire de Bertrán i Soler, les généraux le dénoncent. On pourrait dire qu'*ils le créent,* en décelant, à travers le temps et l'espace social, une *nation* sous-jacente, en transformant en lutte contre «le peuple catalan» une répression contre «le peuple» tout court, celui qui croyait au ciel, celui qui n'y croyait plus. Depuis lors, les généraux ont plus d'une fois essayé de «couper l'arbre». En 1985, ils se montrent prudents envers la Catalogne. Est-ce parce qu'elle s'est mise à rassembler à l'Angleterre du «Times»? Mais il y a Euskadi! Les généraux n'ont pas encore fini de réemployer leur vocabulaire.

# *NOTES*

1. FERNANDEZ SAN ROMÁN, General Eduardo, «Consideraciones sobre la guerra de Cataluña», *Revista militar* (Madrid), T. IV. février 1849, pp. 130-131.

2. SALES, Núria, *Els botiflers, 1705-1714,* Barcelone, 1981, p. 14, cite ce texte populaire des débuts du 18ème siècle: Fortelesa inexpugnable — que entre valls y entre montanyes — La naturalesa sola — forma fossos y murallas.

3. *Revista militar,* art. cit. pp. 132-133.

4. VILAR, Pierre, *La Catalogne dans l'Espagne moderne,* Paris, 1962, T.I. pp. 328-329, planches 42 et 43.

5. *Ibid.*

6. *Revista militar,* art. cit., pp. 133, et pp. 143-144, longue citation de MELO, Francisco Manuel, *Historia de los movimentos, separación y guerra de Cataluña en tiempos de Felipe IV* (1645) (Cf. BAE.XXI.)

7. Je renvoie ici au t. I. de *La Catalogne dans l'Espagne moderne,* pp. 466-471 et 497-503.

8. *Ibid.,* pp. 579-586. Les textes sont de CAVEREL, Philippe de, *Ambassade en Espagne et Portugal en 1582 du R.P. en Dieu J. Sarrazin, abbé de Saint Vaast* (P. en 1860 par l'Académie d'Arras).

9. *Ibid.,* p. 585.

10. *Ibid.,* pp. 62 -624

11. VILAR, Pierre, «Les fondements d'un irréalisme, l'Espagne de 1600», *Beiträge sur Romanischen Philologie,* 1971, pp. 207-216.

12. *La Catalogne...,* pp. 623-625.

13. VILAR, Pierre, «Patrie et Nation dans le vocabulaire de la Guerre d'Indépendance espagnole», *Annales historiques de la Révolution Française,* oct.-déc. 1971, pp. 503-534.

14. FONTANA, José, *La quiebra de la monarquía absoluta,* Barcelone, 1971.

15. Cf. HOFFMANN, Léon-François, *La peste à Barcelone,* Princeton et Paris, 1964, et, du même, *Romantique Espagne, l'image de l'Espagne en France entre 1800 et 1850,* Princeton et Paris, 1961.

16. TORRAS ELIAS, J., *Liberalismo y rebeldía campesina,* Barcelone, 1976.

17. FONTANA, Josep, «Crisi camperola i revolta carlina», in *Recerques,* No. 10 (Barcelone, 1980), pp. 7-16.

18. Art. cit. p. 13.

19. *Ibid.,* p. 14.

20. *Ibid.,* pp. 13-14.

21. PASCUAL I DOMENECH, Pere, «Carlisme i societat rural, la Guerra dels Set Anys a la Conca d'Odena», in *Recerques,* No. 10 (Barcelone, 1980), pp. 51-92.

22. Art. cit. p. 53 «esta guerra se comensa per poch, però ara arivat a mol...».

23. *Ibid.,* Paragraphe intitulé «La incomprensió de la societat rural davant la 'revolució liberal'».

24. *Ibid.,* pp. 57 et suiv.

25. *Ibid.,* p. 61, et *La Catalogne...,* t. II. pp. 419-481.

26. Art. cit. p. 55.

27. *Ibid.,* p. 56 «estigué al poble de Tous casi un any sense tocà campanes», et l'incident du 26-02-37 où une troupe libérale emprisonne le recteur de Tous «per abé tocat las campanas a morz, dién que tocava a somatén» (Le «somatén» est le traditionnel appel aux armes en cas de danger). Observons qu'en 1936 encore des incidents semblables auront lieu. Même page, même incident, plus grave, un prêtre tué.

28. Toujours p. 56.

29. P. 65: «que los parexia que se anaven a une festa majó.»

30. *Ibid.,* «primerament, els pirons éran mol bona gent...» Le mot «pirons», pour désigner les carlistes, est d'origine incertaine *(ibid.* n. 36); en revanche, le mot «patuleia», pour désigner une troupe irrégulière, est employé pour toutes les formations politiques. En 1846 au Portugal, la révolution «de la patuleia» gardera ce nom (faut-il entendre «pata-ao-léo» —nus-pieds»? (HALPERN, Myriam, *Livre Câmbio e desenvolvimento económico* Lisbonne, 1971, p. 328). Les précédents espagnols me font douter de cette étymologie).

31. Art. cit. pp. 69 et suiv. et surtout 83 et suiv.

32. *Ibid.,* p. 76.

33. *Ibid.,* p. 91.

34. *Ibid.,* p. 69, fin de la note 44.

35. *Ibid.,* note 49.

36. Cf. VILAR, Pierre, communication au colloque de Lisbonne de février 1984, «Libéralisme politique et libéralisme économique dans l'Espagne du 19ème siècle» (À paraître dans les *Actes* du Colloque).

37. NADAL, Jordi, *El fracaso de ka Revolución industrial en España, 1814-1913,* Barcelone, 1975, pp. 207 et 196.

38. J'ai utilisé cet article dans «Le socialisme espagnol» (chap. de DROZ. *Histoire générale du socialisme,* T. II, Paris, 1975).

39. Cf. *La Catalogne...,* t. I, p. 157, pour la place d'Aribau dans l'idéologie progressiste européenne, alors que son «Oda a la Patria» inaugure le mouvement littéraire de la «renaissance» catalane.

40. Ce caractère populaire --et non bourgeois--d'une appartenance catalane, aux origines du «catalanisme», a surtout été mis en valeur par TERMES, Josep, «El nacionalisme català. Problemes d'interpretació, *«Colloqui d'historiadors,* Barcelone, 1974. Toutefois, la *théorie* et la *politique* d'un nationalisme catalan de modèle 19ème siècle seront bien édifiées par une bourgeoisie déçue.

41. Cf. *La Catalogne...,* t. I, p. 49 (texte de 1836).

42. CAMPS I GIRÓ, Joan. *La guerra dels matiners i el catalanisme polític 1846-1849,* Barcelone, 1978 utilise, grâce à la documentation française réunie par J. FONTANA, les archives consulaires françaises (Af. Etr.). En annexe, le remarquable rapport économique de Lesseps, pp. 149-174.

43. Formule des anarchistes combattants en 1936.

44. Dans l'article cité ci-dessus note 11, j'ai comparé le récit fictif d'une nouvelle de Cervantes avec un rapport municipal *postérieur,* qui prouve la réalité de ces chocs entre 1600 et 1620.

45. RISQUES, Manel J. «La insurrecció de Barcelona pel novembre de 1842. La seva dinàmica social», *Recerques,* No X, 1980, pp. 93-112, p. 95 et p. 96.

46. *Ibid.,* p. 102. Pour «patuleia», cf. ci-dessus, note 30.

47. Utilisé par RISQUES, art. cit. pp. 101, 107, etc..

48. Sur ce mouvement, cf. un récit anonyme («por un testigo de vista»), au jour le jour du 2 septembre au 3 décembre, avec documents annexes, *Revolución de Barcelona proclamando la Junta Central,* Barcelone, 1844. Aucun commentaire mais une profusion de textes utiles.

49. VICENS VIVES, Jaume, *Industrials i politics del segle XIX,* Barcelone, 1961, pp. 227-256 («La revolució burgesa») fait un remarquable résumé des événements confus du milieu du siècle. Pour la fin du mouvement «centraliste» cf. pp. 256-257.

50. Nombreux textes de Terrades in TERMES, José, *Anarquismo y sindicalismo en España,* Barcelone, 1971.

51. Texte intégral in *Revolución de Barcelona...,* appendice IV.

52. *Ibid.,* p. 16: «à midi, ceux de la blouse et une partie des francs de Riera étaient déjà en possession de la Loge...» (francs = corps francs). Et *passim.*

53. Cf. CARR. Raymond, *España, 1808-1939,* Barcelone, 1968. Hors-texte, p. 232, planche 49: un «jamàncio» brandissant le drapeau noir, et arborant une tête de mort sur sa barretine (mais l'imitation des gravures révolutionnaires françaises est patente; il est vrai qu'elles pouvaient inspirer aussi les combattants de rue; ceux de 1936 aimaient s'habiller en sans-culottes!).

54. *Revolución de Barcelona,* p. 203, note I.

55. *Ibid.* Appendice III.

56. CAMPS I GIRÓ, ouv. cit. p. 37.

57. *Ibid.,* p. 48.

58. «Griset de la Cabra», «Anton de la Puda», «L'hereu lladre», «L'estudiant de Grau», «Bou (ou Pep) Milisera», «Gravat de l'Ase» etc..

59. Le général Fernández San Román (art. cit. p. 132) trouve ce nom significatif, «il ne manque que l'heure, on n'attend que le signal...»

60. CAMPS I GIRÓ, ouv. cit. p. 58-59, publie l'ordre du général Pavía (17-05-47). Le cadavre de Ros d'Eroles, préalablement assassiné, sera exposé sur les lieux de l'exécution de Tristany, le glas sonnera trois heures; tout le clergé est convoqué (Benet Tristany est chanoine de Solsona).

61. Ouv. cit. p. 70.

62. *Ibid.,* p. 77.

63. *Ibid.,* p. 78.

64. *Ibid.,* texte intégralement cité pp. 222-230 (Annexe 30). Issu, officiellement, d'«une réunion de paysans». En fait, il exprime l'opinion depuis longtemps en germe chez les traditionalistes modérés (Balmes), et on y devine la plume de quelque ecclésiastique.

65. Abondance de textes d'archives françaises sur les ordres de surveillance et de sanctions (ouv. cit., annexes 31, 34 etc.).

66. L'épisode des années 1868-1873 abondera encore en formes primitives ou utopiques chez les carlistes comme chez les «cantonalistes» républicains ou anarchisants.

67. *Industrials i polítics* (ouv. cit. note 49) p. 264, lucide conclusion sur une époque confuse.

68. CAMPS I GIRÓ. ouv. cit. a reconstitué la biographie et analysé l'idéologie de ce personnage, qui semble bien en effet, mais isolément, avoir exprimé l'essentiel d'un projet «nationaliste».

69. FERNÁNDEZ SAN ROMÁN, art. cit. p. 141. Le chantage est décrit p. 140.

70. *Ibid.,* p. 132.

71. *Ibid.,* p. 142.

72. *Ibid.,* p. 134.

73. *Ibid.,* p. 131.

74. *Ibid.,* p. 133.

75. *Ibid.,* p. 136.

76. «limpiar», «barrer», etc.

77. En particulier dans l'article «Observaciones acercas de las consideraciones...», qui commente et critique l'article précédent; plus techniquement, l'auteur cherche à analyser comment réaliser «occupation», «persécution», «domination». Les auteurs ne semblent pas sensibles à ce qu'un tel vocabulaire a de surprenant dans une guerre civile.

78. CAMPS I GIRÓ, ouv. cit. pp. 66-67, ordre du général Pavía, qui annonce les méthodes de Weyler à Cuba en 1896-97.

79. *La Revista militar,* juillet 1848 (t. III) avait publié «El ultra-liberalismo. Los ejercitos y la sociedad» (pp. 65 et suiv.). Cf. aussi «Sobre la indiferencia lamentable de nuestros generales hacia la cosa pública», titre stupéfiant d'inconscience quand on parcourt l'histoire de l'Espagne aux 19ème et 20ème siècles!

80. «El ultraliberalismo...» p. 66.

81. «Sobre la indiferencia...» p. 745.

82. *Ibid.,* p. 741.

Kåre Tønnesson

# POPULAR PROTEST AND ORGANIZATION: THE THRANE MOVEMENT IN PRE-INDUSTRIAL NORWAY, 1849-55

In 1848, at Christmas, Marcus Thrane, the radical editor of the *Drammens Adresse,* founded the Drammen Workers' Association. From Drammen, a town some thirty-five kilometers south-west of Kristiania (Oslo), the movement expanded between 1849 and 1851 over large parts of the country. Workers' Associations *(Arbeiderforeninger)* sprang up, first in towns, then in the countryside. Quantitatively the Thrane movement was impressive, even by international standards: the organization gave its membership as 20,854 by the end of June 1851. Two series of nominative sources, from 1850 and 1851 respectively, show that the number of men who were members at one time or another must have been between 20,000 and 30,000, probably closer to the latter than to the former figure. The male population of Norway, above twenty·years, was at the time approximately 400,000, and the Workers' Associations did not cover the whole territory. The Associations also constituted an organized movement at the national level. A Central Board in Kristiania edited a weekly paper and arranged two national meetings of delegates, in 1850 and in 1851.

One precondition for the movement was the liberal Norwegian political regime after 1814: no permissions had to be asked for in order to agitate, to organize and to publish. For two years the authorities respected these rights, but tensions developed as the movement was radicalized and socialist ideas were opposed to property rights, and the government turned towards repression. In 1851 it found it possible, on the basis of cases of actual and threatened breach of the law, to start criminal proceedings. In July Thrane and other leaders and militants were arrested. After years in custody they were brought to trial, several of them being sentenced to long terms of imprisonment.

This spelled the end of the movement. In custody, it is true, Thrane was able to edit the weekly, and this is the period where socialist ideas were most extensively discussed. But, beset by internal dissensions, the central organization disintegrated, and only a few local organizations lingered on. By 1858, when Thrane was released, the movement had ceased to exist.

The Thrane movement was the first mass, organized political movement in Norway. Marcus Thrane himself is counted as the first Norwegian socialist. The man and the movement have attracted considerable attention in Norwegian historiography, but as all the literature is in the vernacular, they are practically unknown outside Scandinavia. In the words of Bjørklund, his latest biographer, Marcus

Thrane, by "raising a mighty labour organization of socialist tendency in a pre-industrial society... ought to loom large among the pioneers of the labour movement of the world."[1]

To vindicate such a position for Thrane is not the object of this article. It will, however, endeavour to show that the movement he triggered and led is of international interest. Central to our discussion will be the opposition, in Bjørklund's statement, between *pre-industrial society* and *pioneering a labour movement.* In *The Crowd in History* George Rudé, distinguishing "the typical popular disturbance of the new industrial society from that of the 'pre-industrial age'", justifies a dividing line in England and France around the 1840's by pointing to such innovations as "factory towns, railways, stable trade unions, a labour movement" as evidence "that a new age was not only in the making but in being".[2] On all these counts Norway in 1850 was still at the pre-industrial stage. Studying the Thranites one would be well advised to keep in mind not only contemporary, but also earlier, social movements in other countries.

There is, in fact, a close historiographical parallel between the evolution of Thranite studies and that of research and interpretation in the field of pre-industrial social movements in England and France. Discarding older tendencies to ante-date the modern labour movement, the latter studies have shown, in Rudé's words, that the participants were "sometimes peasants (as in the past), but more often a mixed population of what in England were termed 'lower orders' and in France *menu peuple* (or, for a short period in the 1790's, sans-culottes)...".[3] The classical picture of the Thrane movement, as drawn by Halvdan Koht, was one of class conflict between the rural proletariat and the owners of the means of production.[4] Modern research, questioning this interpretation, has demonstrated the socially heterogeneous character of the movement.

Yet, there are traits that, at least partly, satisfy some of Rudé's criteria for the historically significant disturbance in industrial society, such as demonstrations being led by political organizations and objects tending to be "well defined, forward looking, and rational...".[5] This would point to the Thrane movement as a transitional phenomenon. It also reminds us that Norway should not be considered in isolation: the position of a pre-industrial country in a pre-industrial world is different from that of a less-developed country closely connected with more-developed ones. The Thranites must be envisaged both in an international context and in their indigenous social setting.

## Norwegian Society around 1850

Norway in 1850 was only on the threshold of modern industrialization, through the introduction, in the forties, of the textile and mechanical industries, based on machines and technology imported from Britain.[6] Norway was predominantly preindustrial; of the 1845 population of 1.3 million some twelve percent lived in the towns; eighty percent is classified as "agricultural" population. That term, however, must not be taken to mean that such a proportion of the population lived essentially from agriculture. Indeed, most of the non-agricultural production of pre-industrial Norway was provided by the peasantry.

There were four traditional major non-agrarian industries: fisheries, forestry and lumbering, metallurgy and shipping. The typical Norwegian fisher was a peasant-fisherman. In forestry and saw-milling the number of workers completely divorced from agriculture was insignificant compared to the mass of peasants working in felling and rafting. This holds good also for the workers in iron and copper works in relation to the peasants attached to the industry through deliveries of charcoal and timber and transport services. Shipping also, in the time of wood and sails, was closely connected with agriculture. The sea provided seasonal and youth occupation for members of peasant households, and the construction of ships was as much a countryside as an urban industry.

The social effects of the various extra-agricultural pursuits created considerable regional differences of great importance for the local character of Thranite associations. The fisheries contributed to relative equality inside the peasant community. Forestry, on the other hand, based on real estate property, drew a line between the farmers who could draw revenues from the farm's own woodland and the smallholders who had to eke out a living by working for others.

In law, however, the farmers as a whole, i.e. freehold and copyhold users of matriculated farms, were singled out as one large group, often referred to as the *independent* peasantry. Irrespective of wealth and the size of holdings, they acquired the right of vote and eligibility through the constitution of 1814 and the Local Government Act of 1837. Correspondingly, the *dependent* rural population, i.e. those who did not hold land on the two conditions mentioned above, were excluded from political rights, again without regard to the poverty or prosperity of the individual.

The distinction between the dependent and the independent and the divisions within the dependent class are vitally important for the social analysis of the rural Thrane movement. Analysis is often an arduous task as contemporary sources such as censuses -- and the lists of Thranites -- hesitate between occupational categories and denomination indicating the relation to land and housing. Thus, as dependent groups, we are faced by the categories of servants and day-labourers, but also by those of *"innerst"* and *"husmann"*. An *"innerst"* was a lodger with separate household, usually in a farmer's house. A "houseman" (in opposition to "farm-man"), was one who rented a house with a holding or just a small lot which was not matriculated separately, but was a dependency of the main farm and taxed along with it. The rent was usually acquitted by doing work for the owner. In this article "houseman" and "cottar" will be used as synonyms.

While "innerst", or lodger, does not say anything about the source of livelihood, "houseman" may or may not denote occupation. The so-called "work-housemen" *(arbeidshusmenn)* were in fact agricultural labourers, who, when the rent was paid, still had to work for the owner whenever called for. This work was remunerated, but at a rate lower than that of the day-labourers. For the farmers the houseman system was a means of providing stable, low-cost labour. "Places", on the other hand, were sought after by young people as almost a necessary condition for marrying.

Work-housemen, naturally, were found in greatest numbers in the large-farm districts of the East and of Trøndelag; they are therefore referred to as the "Eastern type". "Western-type" housemen, also to be found in the East, did not have any duties to perform for the owner once the rent was paid. They therefore cover a wide occupational spectrum: rural artisans, fishermen, "free" agricultural and forestry labourers.

A strategic group in the Thrane movement, the housemen were an expanding social category. Norway, in fact, in the first half of the nineteenth century, went through a period of rapid demographic growth. From 883,000 in 1801, the population rose to 1.3 million in 1845 and to 1.5 million ten years later. Both the independent and the dependent groups swelled in numbers, the latter somewhat more than the former. In 1855 they comprised fifty-seven and forty-three percent, respectively, of the rural population. Housemen holdings numbered 77,000 in 1845 and 87,000 in 1855, as against 113,000 farmer households in the latter year, but there were districts in Eastern Norway where housemen outnumbered farmers.

With the advent of the big cohorts of young people of the forties, the tensions within this structure were brought to a head. Houseman holdings were scarce. The bargaining power of the farmer who could offer one was strengthened. Labour obligations were extended to the houseman's wife and children. The eviction of old people also created tensions with the small farmers without housemen, who yet, through the poor-tax, had to pay for the up-keep of the big farmers' discarded labourers. Locally the number of the completely landless day-labourers increased as young people were unable to secure positions as housemen.

The social structure of the towns lends itself more easily than that of the countryside to a summary account. Towns were small. With suburbs Kristiania (Oslo), the capital, had 38,000 inhabitants in 1850; the fourth on the list, the plank-and-beam-town of Drammen, had 9,000. In contemporary consciousness the town population fell into three ranks: the "better rank" of state servants, great merchants, and some industrialists; the "middle rank" of smaller merchants, artisans, shippers and employees; and the "humble rank" of day-labourers, sailors, servants and paupers. Within the artisan group, at least in larger towns, the dividing line between masters and journeymen sharpened, as the journeyman's prospect of becoming a master diminished.

As in rural electoral districts, active political rights were based on the concept of independence. The suffrage was enjoyed by state servants and all registered burghers: merchants, master artisans, and shippers. A non-burgher could have the right to vote if he owned a house of a fixed minimum value.

National politics were dominated by the officers of state, generally supported by the bourgeoisie, the more so as the natural bourgeois leaders, the great eighteenth-century plank-and-beam houses, had been largely ruined by the economic crisis after the Napoleonic wars. Civil servants, military officers and clergy monopolized governmental positions. In Parliament, the opposition was constituted by the farmer deputies, with only a sprinkling of bourgeois.

This society, already in a structural crisis due to population growth, was hard-hit by the European economic crisis of the late forties. Lumber exports suffered badly. In the face of foreign competition Norwegian charcoal-based iron production was drawing to a close. Newly-introduced measures of economic liberalism disrupted traditional structures. In the towns day-labourers and artisans were the first to suffer, but it will be apparent from what has been said about the mixed rural economy that the crisis affected great regions of the country-side as well. A series of bad harvests made matters worse. The number of suits for debt and forced sales rose steeply, provoking anger and bitterness the more as free interest on short-term loans had recently been introduced as part of a policy of economic liberalization, throwing borrowers on the mercy of usurers. Owners of real property were in a more favorable position, since mortgage loans were unaffected by this law. It was thus in an atmosphere of crisis, coinciding with exhilarating news from the Continent, that Marcus Thrane issued his call to the workers to organize in order to better their condition.

## *The Leader and the Organization*

Marcus Thrane was déclassé.[7] He was born in 1817 into one of the richest of Kristiania's merchant families, although its fortunes were only created by Marcus' grand-father Paul. A few months after Marcus' birth disaster overtook the Thrane family, as his father David, one of the directors of the Bank of Norway, was arrested for improprieties committed after heavy losses in his private businesses. Relatives and friends covered the loss to the bank; David escaped prison but left the country.

His wife Lena stayed on with the children in Kristiania; her economic position grew worse as one after another in the Thrane family was crushed by the post-war crisis which ruined a great part of the Norwegian "plank aristocracy". After her death in 1831 the youngest children were taken care of by Lena's womanservant. During one period Marcus and a brother went round the town to a number of rich families, which had agreed to take the Thrane boys in for dinner in a fixed rotation.

From this tale of woe the conclusion seems clear: Marcus Thrane became a social rebel out of a personal grudge against society. But this explanation clashes with the testimony both of his own writing and of descriptions by others of his character. A sanguine person, cheerful and friendly, Marcus had a strong sense of the vitality of life. Two other traits in the Thrane family are important for an understanding of Marcus' career. Wide cultural interests and artistic gifts were characteristic of Paul Thrane, his wife and their descendents. Marcus' grand-parents were also notorious in the 1790s for pro-revolutionary opinions and were described as "democrats". Above all Marcus sucked radicalism in with his mother's milk.[8] Lena Bull, a strong and wilful character, was something of an *enfant terrible* at the time of the French Revolution.

Family background, then, on the one hand gave Marcus Thrane the self-assurance of the born gentleman; unlike the lowly-born he was uninhibited by deference to the great. On the other hand, unlike many other young men of the upper classes who toyed with radical ideas, Thrane was not held back by social loyalty to his class of origin. These bonds had been severed by the family disaster.

Thrane, in fact, did not, as many a son of the ruined merchant aristocracy did, reintegrate himself into the upper class through the University and government service. He broke off formal schooling just before the University entrance examination, and, in 1838, went on foot to Paris where, if his autobiography is to be trusted, he studied socialist writers.[9] On his return he did the matriculate and studied theology, supporting himself by teaching. But in 1841 he married one of his French-students, a woman of brains and character, who was to prove an asset to the Workers' Associations. The couple started a private school in the small inland town of Lillehammer, where they became a centre of cultural life. When the year 1848 opened Thrane was a teacher in the small agglomeration of Modum, west of Kristiania, and his stay there marked the turning-point of his career.

The cobalt works at Modum were, at the time, the biggest industrial enterprise in the country, with some seven hundred workers and many more attached through deliveries and transport services. The company was hard hit by the crisis of 1847, and bankruptcy was only avoided by the British owners selling out to German interests. Here Thrane witnessed stark poverty; and then, in March, the exhilarating news from Paris came in. Thrane now, in his own account, saw the direction his life should take. According to his autobiography he felt "a personal responsibility for mending things"; a less solemn and typically self-ironic expression from 1849 is that the February revolution gave him "an irresistible desire to get into the political opera house".[10]

Fortune smiled on him, and by the summer of 1848 Thrane was a newspaper editor in the plank-and-beam town of Drammen, close to Kristiania. For five months the *Drammens Adresse* was a radical paper, calling for the formation of a democratic party or a "People's party", and introducing, if not agitating for, socialist ideas. The subscribers were annoyed, and the printer-owner, alarmed by the diminishing circulation, gave his editor notice at Christmas. At that time Thrane was switching over to new ground. He had got in touch with a handful of workers, and on 27 December, 1848, after ten days of preparation, the *Drammens Arbeider-forening* was founded with 160 members. In March, 1849, after a spell of serious illness, he moved to Kristiania, where he founded a Workers' Association and, on 5 May, published the first issue of the Associations' weekly, the *Arbeiderforeningernes Blad*.

Kristiania, in 1848 and the following years, witnessed an upswing in radical opinion and activity. Artists and intellectuals in 1848-49 returned from abroad, bringing with them fresh impressions from radical circles and revolutionary events. In the spring of 1849 a "Democratic Association", working for extension of the suffrage, was formed. A new radical journal was launched in January 1851 by three students, later to become great literary figures. One of them, Henrik Ibsen, who was the room-mate of Thrane's lieutenant and rival T. Abildgaard, also contributed small pieces to Thrane's paper.

There were also movements at a more popular level. The capital saw some small rioting in March 1848. An opposition newspaper printed an editorial acclaiming the revolution in Paris and expressing the hope that this would permit a change of regime also in Norway. Pro-government students staged street demonstrations against the editor. This, in turn, provoked violent popular counter-demonstrations, in which artisan journeymen were conspicuous; there is also discernible in this movement a protest against police regulations which interfered with the right to buy food on Sunday morning[11].

Nor were direct contacts with events abroad limited to members of the educated classes. Recent investigations of artisans' journeys have brought new knowledge about contacts with revolutionary movements.[12] The custom of journeying abroad developed in Norway particularly from the middle of the eighteenth century. In 1848, journeymen finding it difficult to get jobs in France returned home. A local newpaper, reporting the arrival of seven journeymen from Paris on 2 June, noted that they "had taken part in the latest February revolution".[13] One of them became a member of the Kristiania Workers' Association and of the Thranite Central Board.

But more foreign artisans went to Norway than Norwegians abroad, and a good number stayed in the country. Slightly over half the master bakers of Kristiania in 1865 were German-born. Police records and newspaper notices make it possible to follow the itineraries of foreign artisans and to identify the radical and socialist agents. Conspicuous among those who appeared in 1848 and 1849 were Georg Fein, a German of Mazzini-Garibaldi connexions, as well as the Swedish tailor Carl D. Forsell and the German printer Heinrich Anders, both of them agents of the London *Bund der Kommunisten* and attached to the Stockholm Götrek circle, which advocated a Cabet-inspired Christian and peaceful communism.[14] Although nothing precise is known about their audience in Norway, there can be little doubt that new knowledge and ideas were introduced into the Norwegian artisans' milieu. Wilhelm Weitling, it should be noted, could be studied first-hand, as his "Garantien der Harmonie und Freiheit" was published in translation in Kristiania in 1847. Two years later, in a series of articles, a prominent Kristiania newspaper presented Engels' analysis of the state of the working class in England.[15]

The foreigner who by far attracted most notice was the republican Harro Harring (1798-1870), who had been active in Greece and Poland and was linked with Mazzini and Garibaldi.[16] A Frisian, born a subject of the King of Denmark, he spoke and wrote Danish, and thus, when arriving in Norway towards the end of 1849, easily got in touch with radicals in Kristiania, who helped him launch the weekly *Folkets Røst* ("The Voice of the People"). At the end of May, 1850 Harring was expelled by the government.

Between Harring and Thrane there were contacts, but no close cooperation. Their outlook and methods were too different. Thrane in fact distinguished himself from all other radical tendencies. The journeymen agitators probably did not reach beyond the world of artisans. Radicals of the educated classes, like Harro Harring, addressed themselves to educated people, trying to convince them to adopt a policy of political and, in some cases, of social reform. Here, Marcus Thrane was in several respects an innovator.

In the first place Thrane addressed himself to what he called the workers or the working class. He divided society into two parts, "the producing and the consuming classes" ("nærende og tærende klasser"). The dichotomy has been thought to be inspired by Saint-Simon, which is quite possible, but not certain, as the same division had been made earlier by farmer and bourgeois oppositions. What was new with Thrane was that he drew the dividing line lower than had ever been done in Norway, relegating farmers and the bourgeoisie generally to the "consuming class" together with great merchants and government servants. From 1851 Thrane increasingly used the expression "capitalist versus labourer", which reflects his reading in economics and socialism.

The message Thrane rammed home was that the workers themselves had to fight for their interests. In the first issue of his paper, in a proclamation headed "Workers! *God* be with you! *God* be with us all; a strife will begin; a strife *must* begin", he writes: "Wake up then, workers! Unite, and agree to act *yourselves* for your own best future, for you have long enough experienced that you wait in vain for others to do something for you when you yourselves keep quiet."[17]

Addressing a public, of whom many could not read and would therefore have the paper read aloud, Thrane developed a new style, direct, concrete and simple, explaining all difficult words. Although a moralist, he put little moral or social pathos into his writing, but he did use humour and irony to great effect. The paper was enlivened by engravings, the social sting of which was also expressed through humour, rather than sentimentality.

Thrane, finally, was an organizational innovator. Formal political organizations did not exist in the country, and organizational work on a large scale had only just started in the temperance and Christian missions' movements. The Thranite organization was built up at three levels. The local association, under a chairman, was either grouped with neighbouring associations under a super-chairman or subdivided in sections. Demarcations were always on a geographical, never on a trade, basis. At the top the central organization at first consisted of Thrane and his wife, but in April, 1850 Thrane had a Central Committee elected by the Kristiania and neighbouring associations. The central organization was financed by the weekly paper and by membership fees coming in through the local associations (with considerable difficulties and arrears). This hierarchical set-up grouped associations spread over large regions and of widely different social composition.[18]

The economic and social situation in the forties, as well as Thrane's addressing his agitation to the "workers", lend *a priori* plausibility to the interpretation of the movement as a class-conflict between the have-nots and those who disposed of property and authority. This is again reinforced by the territorial extension of the Thranite associations, which coincides with the agriculture-cum-forestry regions, and with the towns in the same counties. From Drammen and Kristiania through 1849 to 1851 associations spread over the South-East plains and valleys and across the mountains to Trøndelag, the districts around the town of Trondheim; another current went down the south coast. There were no associations in Northern Norway, and very few in the Western fjord region. Yet the lists of members in 1851, as established by the police, do not warrant such clear-cut conclusions.[19]

Addressing himself to the towns, Thrane, feeling that the journeymen artisans considered themselves above the common labourer, made a point of convincing them that they ought to identify themselves with the workers. In fact the artisans, and not only journeymen and apprentices, were to form the mainstay of the associations in many towns.[20]

In the larger towns the weight of the artisans varied considerably. In Trondheim, where the day-labourer contingent was important, they only made up twenty-five percent of association membership. But in the big Kristiania association, which reached 1,030 members in the spring of 1850, up to eighty percent were journeymen and apprentices. Very few masters can have joined, as only thirteen have been identified with certainty.[21] In the small association of Lillehammer, also, artisans dominated; eighteen of thirty-five identified members were artisans. But in this little town the composition of the artisan contingent was utterly different, as fifteen were masters, which is to say that one out of four of the artisan burghers was a Thranite. Pryser finds that the Thranite artisans were small masters working alone; both the employers and their men stayed out of the movement. All the bourgeois members -- there were also two merchants -- classify as petty bourgeoisie by tax assessments. Of the town's about thirty day-labourers, ten were Thranites; these were not among the most indigent, since none received poor law allowances.[22]

In the towns generally the Thranites do not seem to have been recruited among the very poorest, and as a group the day-labourers did not dominate, even quantitatively. The leading element were artisans and other specialized labour, like the ship-carpenters of the southern towns. Through the master artisans the movement passed the dividing line of legal privilege to make some incursion into the petty bourgeoisie. This pattern concurs with what has been experienced time and again in pre-industrial *menu peuple* movements, and also in the first stages of modern labour organizations.

The social composition of the rural associations, more than that of the urban Thranites, has been felt by historians to be decisive in judging the over-all character of the movement. Thrane himself drew attention to the rural orientation as a specific feature, when he noted as a "not insignificant difference between our labour movement and the foreign ones, that ours particularly focuses the condition of the rural population, while abroad they chiefly concentrate on the organization of factory production."[23]

In the classic picture, as noted above, the Thranites appeared as a movement of the rural proletariat. That small farmers also joined has, it is true, always been known. But Koht annexed these to the working class, and they do not hold an important position in his class pattern. A regional case supporting the Koht model is the Hedemarken district on the eastern shores of Lake Mjøsa, analysed in a pioneering local study by Ingrid Semmingsen in 1934.[24] Hedemarken was one of the richest agricultural districts of Norway. It was characterized by big farms, a surplus production of cereals, a large cottar population, and much poverty. The call to form workers associations was brought to Hedemarken in March, 1850 by the chairman of the Kristiania association, the journeyman mason Bernhard Hansen. In one month thirteen associations were founded, with nearly seven hundred members; rather more than one year later, according to police lists, membership had risen to 1,883.

Of these members thirty-seven per cent were "housemen" without indication of profession, but the majority must have been agricultural labourers, or "work-housemen". Twenty-seven percent were farm servants or day-labourers. To Semmingsen, that as many as eighteen percent were farmers and sons of farmers appeared to be a problem needing explanation. Even in the parish most strongly dominated by large farms, and having the highest ratio of "housemen" to farmers, there were a considerable number of farmer Thranites. The explanation was found through the farm names: the Thranite farmers were backwoodsmen occupying newly-cleared ground on the outskirts of the parishes. Several of these farms were former cottar holdings, transformed into (pitifully small) matriculated farms as the cottar bought his independence.

A farmer element of this type is not immune to intense enmity towards big farmer-bosses or "sofa-farmers", to use a word which appeared in the Norwegian language at this period. As Thranite processions toured Hedemarken with flags and music, saluting with cannons, cheering their friends and booing their enemies, farmers were reported to have gone into hiding. Hedemarken, as we shall see, was also the scene of Thranite crowd violence.

Later local studies have taken Hedemarken as a frame of reference. While Semmingsen found the eighteen percent farmer figure surprisingly high, the point driven home in some studies is that the figure is too *low* to be nationally representative. Thus it has been found that among the rural Thranites of South Trøndelag county (745 members on whom we have sufficient data), 30.7 percent were farmers and farmers' sons. As opposed to Hedemarken the farmers here constituted the politically leading element of the associations. A different farm structure and a lower cottar-to-farmer ratio must essentially account for the difference.[25]

Along the south coast and in its hinterland, where the big farm in the East-Norwegian sense does not exist, and where there was a great wealth of extra-agrarian occupations, the social distinction between farmers and dependent groups was perhaps less than in most other Thranite districts. Farmers' relative participation varied widely according to whether or not there were saw-mill plants or an iron-works in the community, which invariably brought up the number of working-class members. The peak farmer membership (58.3 percent) was held by a small association whose chairman was the mayor of the commune.[26]

Recent investigations of some East Norwegian associations have enlarged the statistical basis by drawing also on the 1850 petition.[27] This increases farmer membership both because farmers were the first to quit as tension developed between the Thranite organization and the government and, one suspects, because local police covered the socially prominent. Yet the wide local variations are corroborated. At Bærum, later to become part of the Oslo agglomeration, four associations grouped one-third of the adult males. One important contingent was composed of iron-works labourers, the others were members of rural dependent groups. Farmer membership was insignificant.[28]

At the other extreme, there is the result of the most important revisionist study: Pryser's investigation of the Thranites of Ullensaker.[29] In this parish, on the Romerike plain between Hedemarken and Oslo, the biggest groups were farmers and sons, forty-seven percent, cottars and sons, thirty-eight percent, and lodgers and day-labourers, nine percent. But beyond these contemporary social categories Pryser, through an analysis of all relevant material, aims at a prosopography of the Ullensaker Thranites, 173 men, rather more than ten percent of the adult male population. The result is to show that the Thranites constituted a cross-section of the population, on counts such as relation to land, size of holdings, occupations, age, family size and past political experience (seven had been members of the municipal council). The exceptions were that servants were under-represented, and that the really large farmers were represented by only one man, and he was on the way down, having lost his several farms after unfortunate speculations.

Investigating the sources of livelihood, of the relation-to-land-and-housing categories of farmers, cottars and lodgers, Pryser uncovers the importance of incomes from sources other than land and the farmers' own woodland. Thus, while only one percent of the Ullensaker Thranites were listed as artisans, twenty-one percent were found to live partly or mainly from handicrafts. Ullensaker was indeed economically complex, with a considerable element of money-economy involvement characterizing the social groups. Above all, Ullensaker was the plank-driving parish *par excellence.*

The large Kristiania lumber export had for centuries been based on intercepting the timber rafted down the Glomma river about the point closest to the city. There the Kristiania companies had their saw-mills, and the planks and boards were sledged in winter along the "plank road" to the export harbour. Drivers and horses came essentially from the Romerike plain. Cutting transport costs through the construction of a canal had been studied several times, but given up. In 1850, however, the first Norwegian railway, from Kristiania to Lake Mjøsa, was about to materialize, largely financed by the lumber companies.

The Ullensaker Thranite associations were, *inter alia,* an anti-railway movement. At a public sale of railway shares they staged a successful demonstration to dissuade prospective buyers. Opposition to the railway scheme created a bond of interest between farmers and the dependent categories. Farmers and their sons drove planks themselves; cottars were plank drivers both on their own account and on that of their landlord. More than those directly engaged were involved. Inn-keepers were prominent in the movement; they must have realized that they would be among the first sufferers if the cash-flow from the plank road were to dry up.

## *Vertical and Horizontal Bonds.*

One important object of the Ullensaker investigation is to consider the Thrane movement as a collective phenomenon in the stage of transition from pre-industrial to industrial society. As an organization, the movement was of the modern *Gesellschaft* type. But Pryser's thesis is that the association developed as a super-structure built on the traditional *Gemeinschaft* social units of neighbourhood and family. Pryser in fact finds such relations highly characteristic of the Ullensaker Thranites. Here, some objections must be made. It is convincingly demonstrated that the limits to geographical expansion in Ullensaker can be explained by lines of communication: The bulk of the Thranites lived along the main roads and round the principal community centres. Now, this implies neigbourhood. As for family ties, it is again convincingly demonstrated, particularly at the leadership level, that kin provided a channel for recruitment. But marriage inside the parish was so frequent that Pryser's finding that 123 of the 173 Thranites had family ties to other members asks for comparison with a control group.

Inspired partly by British research in the social transformation effected by the industrial revolution, Norwegian social historians have lately been much occupied by the transition from the paternalism and the vertical bonds of the old society to the horizontal identification and class-consciousness of the modern. Paternalism, it is true, has always been seen as relevant to the Thrane movement, but it has been observed invariably as a negative factor, as an obstacle to be overcome. The

*Arbeiderforeningernes Blad,* by way of warning and "punishment", published lists of farmers who ordered their day-labourers and cottars to stay out of the movement. Cases were reported of saw-mill owners and other employers who compelled their workers to quit the associations.[30]

For Kristiania, where the Thranite organization was above all a movement of artisan journeymen, an analysis has been made of the correlation between proportion of Thranites and modernity of trade, when modernity is measured by high marriage frequency among journeymen, little living-in with the masters among the unmarried, and high pay.[31] The correlation is striking between the masons on the top, the joiners in the middle, and the bakers at the bottom of the Thranite scale. It is less convincing among the shoemakers, tailors and printers; the latter ranked high in modernity but low in Thranite participation, although some decades later they were to pioneer the labour movement. Generally speaking, the evidence points to the breaking-up of the old household organization of artisanal work and life as a precondition for horizontal identification and Thranite activity. But among the tailors there is some indication of the *positive* value of paternalist ties and influence for Thranite recruitment, as masters joined the movement taking their journeymen with them.

Pryser finds such positive effects - - not at Lillehammer where we have seen that the Thranite artisans were small masters with no men to wield authority over - - but in the rural setting of Ullensaker. This is somewhat surprising. As cottars and labourers everywhere joined the movement in considerable numbers, it would not seem necessary to explain it through the influence of Thranite farmers. High *farmer* membership was the Ullensaker problem to be solved, and we have seen that Pryser argues that the plank-driving interest brought both cottars and farmers into the movement. It would seem, therefore, that a very high farm coincidence between farmer and dependent membership would be necessary to prove the effect of paternalistic influence.

According to Pryser's findings seventeen out of thirty-five farm units had Thranites of both categories, eighteen of only one. Of the Thranites from the dependent groups ninety-nine lived on units with farmer Thranites, seventy-four on other farms.[32] This can not be taken as evidence of a positive effect of vertical ties. It is, however, sufficient to confirm the negative conclusion that antagonism between cottar/labourer and landlord/employer is not an important element in the Ullensaker Thranite movement. As such it is interesting to compare Pryser's findings with what results from applying his method to a community with big farms and an over-crowded and depressed proletariat. In Fåberg close to Lillehammer, five percent of the Thranites were farmers, fifty-nine percent were cottars; six percent of the parish's farmers as against almost half the cottars and day-labourers joined the movement. Here, as in Ullensaker, there were "clusters" of Thranites on farm units, but with very few exceptions they were to be found on farms where the farmer was not in the movement. Of the 468 Thranites in the parish twenty percent lived on nine farms which grouped eight percent of the adult, male population. From one such farm in the district there is an eyewitness report that the "housemen" sat at their masters' table discussing how they would distribute the farm between them, when, hopefully, it would be divided up.[33]

## The Local Leaders

No systematic study on a large scale of the leadership of the associations has been undertaken. By local leadership is understood the section leaders, chairmen, super chairmen and delegates to the central meetings. The latter, who naturally overlap with the former, are the only group on which comprehensive figures can be given.

At the central meeting of August 1850 there were 102 delegates from ninety-nine associations, all of them in the East and the South. Farmers, cottars, and artisans (masters and journeymen) constituted just over one-quarter; the remainder was made up of twelve labourers and six schoolteachers and others with some education. The central meeting of June, 1851 was attended by seventy-eight delegates from 120 associations; this time a couple of associations in Trøndelag and in the West were also represented. The social level had risen. The relative membership of farmers and of people of some education had gone up, cottars were stable, artisans had declined, and labourers had dropped sharply.[34]

There can be no doubt that the chairmen also came predominantly from the farmer, cottar, and artisan groups. A study of twelve neighbouring associations in the East in 1851 relates chairmen to composition of members. Seven associations had a cottar chairman, four a farmer, and one a lodger. Three of the four farmers were elected by the associations having the highest proportion of farmer members (upwards of nineteen percent). The fourth, unfortunately for the correlation, was the only farmer in his association.[35]

But the categories of farmer and cottar, if they do tell something about status, are only vaguely indicative of an individual's occupational and economic situation. Recent investigations at the parish level have penetrated deeper.[36] One of the Ullensaker findings is that a prominent feature of a large proportion of Thranite leaders, as indeed among the rank-and-file, is social mobility, up or down or both in succession. This has been confirmed by later local studies. Conspicuous examples -- which should not be generalized -- are the degraded *coqs de village,* such as, in Fåberg, the ruined owner of the farm Storhaave (*stor* =big), a man more interested in reading and in politics than in agriculture. Ullensaker also had one specimen, or rather three. The delegate to the 1850 meeting, known as Stor-Randbye, had lost his several farms after unsuccessful speculations; his two sons, farmer and mason respectively and both of them in financial straits, headed two of Ullensaker's associations.

There are cases of moving up from cottar to free-hold status, but also instances of inability to meet, in time of crisis, the mortgage-debt obligations incurred. Such was the fate of the son of a cottar, who after two years as a Thranite leader emigrated to America in 1852. Or again the leading Thranite of Bærum, whose *curriculum vitae* reads: born a cottar's son, a tailor's apprentice at ten, six years in the army, a tailor and small freeholder, numerous entries in the Debts Conciliation Board register, a copyholder in 1855, and a lodger in a cottar-tailor's house at the census of 1865.[37]

It appears, as could be expected, that the Thranite leaders classified as "housemen" were rarely "work-housemen". These indeed were the most dependent of all, as they were subject to their master both through their holding and as wage-earners. Rather, the leaders based their living on a houseman's holding plus odd trades and handicrafts. A fine, but no doubt too beautiful, example, is a parish top-leader by the name of Grødeknap *(Poorcrop),* a type of name often given to cottars' holdings. Grødeknap was tailor, shopkeeper and "vaccinator". He became in 1852 the cashier of the local savings-bank established by the Thranites, and, not least, he was married to the midwife. One wonders whether four of the other eight cottager chairmen and section-leaders in the same parish in mountainous Telemark did not also enjoy some local standing, when one learns that two of them practiced the prestigious art of bear-hunting, and that the other two were renowned for physical strength and prowess.[38]

*    *    *

Marcus Thrane, then, called into being a broad popular movement in town and countryside, composed of social elements whose relative strength varied greatly from place to place. In reality the Thranite organization included, in the words of J.A. Seip, "several more or less independent 'movements'". There was "a farmer movement, an artisan movement, a cottar movement, and a labourers' movement."[39] The ability to appeal to many different dissatisfactions gave the organization immediate strength, but not solidity. We must now turn to the programme of the central organization, but we shall also see how popular ideas and beliefs, aims and methods emerged at the local level. It will appear that there was in the movement a coming together of traditional -- or in George Rudé's terms, *inherent* -- beliefs and modern -- or *derived* -- ideology.[40]

## Aims, Beliefs, Methods

The programme of the Thrane organization as a whole was expressed in the petition to the King, written by Thrane and a few collaborators in 1849, and the resolutions of the two Central meetings of 1850 and 1851. The petition was very respectful in form and moderate in content. The demands were set forth in ten points, of which only universal male suffrage can be considered radical. The deepening of the economic crisis in the country, the influence of local leaders, as well as the rejection of the petition by the King in October 1850, brought about a radicalization of the movement in its two last stages. It is not possible here to account for all aspects of the programme; only a few main areas will be considered.

Equality, understood as a natural human right, appears as the supreme value, as it does in Thrane's own writings. The conscious and gradual movement towards equality was what Thrane understood by socialism, as when he opposes Proudhon and socialism to Cabet and communism. If he did not disapprove of Icarian communism he considered it utopian, and although we have seen that some of the foreign socialist agents in Norway belonged to this school of thought, Icarianism does not seem to have had any real influence in the Thrane movement. Proudhon, "no doubt the greatest genius of our time", Louis Blanc, and Cabet seem to have been the socialists with whom Thrane was chiefly familiar. Only during his term of imprisonment from the autumn of 1851 did Thrane study socialist thought systematically. He does not seem to have known Marx until after he was released in 1858.[41]

Two of the ten points of the petition asked for the immediate application of the right to equality. One was that the principle of universal military service embodied in the constitution be put into practice; the other was the demand for the enactment of universal male suffrage. But although the latter claim was justified as a human right, it was conceived above all as a means of enabling the workers to better their condition through parliament and local government. Abolishing what the Thranites considered the "aristocratic" regime was a pre-condition of equality and welfare. For Thrane it was by no means obvious, however, that democracy was the best alternative to aristocracy. He had misgivings about the practical value of giving the right to vote to poor and ignorant masses, and was continually discussing the relative merits of democracy and absolutism. In this he reflected feelings that were widespread among the common people. An interesting document shows by its wording that ideas and concepts popularized at the time of the French Revolution lived on in the people. In one rural community the instruction to the delegate to the 1851 Central meeting was dictated by a seventy-year-old blind man of the dependent class.[42] Before 1814, the instruction reads, "when legislation was in the hands of the King", who cared for his subjects like a father and set limits to each man's ability to harm another, there was general prosperity among the common people. In 1814, when Norway was in danger of becoming a province under Sweden, "Democracy won us the suffrage and the legislation." But then "Aristocracy chose in its own midst certain men to come together and give laws with no other object than to serve their own interests and repress Democracy." Parliament was all to blame, as there were "good reasons to excuse the King and the Government…who do not know how Aristocracy has tyrannized and impoverished us." Yet the old man did not think it commendable to try to restore the King's absolute power; the solution now must be to give the workers influence in legislation through the franchise.

Less elaborate expressions of popular royalism and antiparliamentarism were often met with, as Thrane himself reported. This may be one reason why it was decided to address the petition, which was avowedly inspired by the Chartist example, not to Parliament, nor to the government, but to the King in person. The petition was important immediately as part of agitation and organizational work: signing the petition and joining an association went together; addressing the king no doubt increased the petition's popular appeal.

The demand for universal male suffrage initially met with some positive response in the ministerial press, while it was sourly received by the farmers' opposition newspapers. Together with the town bourgeoisies, the farmer minorities in large-farm and great dependent-class districts were indeed the people most likely to see their political power diminished by an extension of the suffrage. The Thranite economic claims also menaced the large farmers, particularly those with a grain surplus, who in Thranite eyes were guilty on the one hand of sweating their cottars and labourers and on the other of using their political influence to keep up the price of bread.

Typically for pre-industrial popular movements, a low price for necessities was the central issue, rather than the question of wages. The petition asked for the abolition of protective tariffs and particularly for the abolition of, or a considerable reduction in, the import duties on grain. It would also have restored the traditional right of the individual consumer to buy directly from foreign ships for a limited number of days.

Protection of the workers against the big farmers was the object of the Thranite demand for a new cottar law. This is a field where the radicalization of the movement expressed itself very clearly. The petition asked for investigation into and improvement of the condition of the cottars. It also suggested that the government sell untilled reclaimable soil at cheap prices to the landless, both from the crown domains and private land which the government would be able to buy. The Central meeting of 1850 presented a project, against Thrane's moderating counsel, for a new cottars' law which would give the cottar families hereditary rights. It went on to demand a radical splitting-up of great estates, thus conjuring up the spectre of disregard for property and of socialist policies. Indeed, the 1851 Central meeting, echoing Proudhon, proclaimed that "property is theft".

Socialist measures also appeared with regard to manufacturing. The *Arbeiderforeningernes Blad,* in 1849, printed letters from journeymen artisans proposing that cooperative workshops be established in Norway, as in France. The 1850 Central meeting asked for government support for such cooperatives, as several practical projects by workers had been given up because they were unable to raise the necessary capital. But at Kristiansand in 1854 workers started a co-operative ship-yard, and in Kristiania some journeymen smiths formed a co-operative workshop, which had to be given up when buyers did not present themselves (which, the journeymen thought, was due to active opposition by smith masters).

The Thranite Workers' Associations, indeed, were not only a political party or a pressure group trying to impress and to influence the political institutions of the country; the principle of association also meant that the workers would themselves implement practical innovations to improve their condition. More local instances of this will be seen below. There were complementary, but also competing, parliamentary and extra-parliamentary tendencies in the movement. These were to clash on the question of reform or revolution.

Marcus Thrane expressly and openly justified the workers' moral right to make a violent revolution, but invariably concluded that the use of force should be avoided, as it would be sure to fail. The rejection by the king of the petition in November, 1850 brought this conflict to a head. On the one hand the parliamentarian tendency was strengthened. The Thranites would now have to address themselves to Parliament, and at the 1850 elections the chiefly farmer-based opposition had been strengthened and radicalized, although only Thranites had been elected. This, for some, held out hopes for close cooperation with the parliamentarian opposition. On the other hand, a sense of deception by the king's refusal exasperated the revolutionary tendency, the chief protagonist of which was the hatter Halstein Knudsen, the violently radical leader of the Thranites from the large-farm and forest district of Ringerike, north-east of Kristiania.

The Central meeting of 1851 became the scene of strong conflicts of opinion and of personal rivalries. A vote was taken on whether one should or should not make a revolution. The majority was for revolution, but the next day Thrane intervened and had the vote retracted. There was considerable confusion among the delegates; many quite clearly did not understand "revolution" to involve a violent taking of power, but rather saw it as a massive demonstration of the people, which would peacefully compel the authorities to carry out its will.

Where Halstein Knudsen came from, strange mythical memories had surfaced during discussion of the delegates' instructions. Concerning revolution, no vote was taken. Instead, it was said that they would all have to join if "the 'Northern power' came to 'sweep everybody with it'". There would then be only one choice: to go along with it, or to be crushed. The "Northern power", also called the "Hun army", is known in Norway and Sweden from the sixteenth century. In 1541, in a Norwegian valley, eighteen peasants tried to call up a "Hun army" which would kill all bailiffs and lords and "then raise the common people and march all the world over".[43]

The debate and vote in the Central meeting provoked the government to repressive measures. These were caused equally, however, by local events.

## The Local Level

The activity and the duration of the Thranite local organizations varied widely. When active they did not content themselves with working through the national organization; they also took initiatives to improve conditions at the local level. This naturally led to political divergences and contradictions.

The local activity of Thranite associations can be summarized under a few headings. As pressure groups they addressed themselves to local authorities. They acted as social rallying points; meetings were often accompanied by festivities and processions. Measures to improve the members' self-respect, their moral and educational standing, were important. Associations fought against bad drinking habits, regarded as important factors in social degradation and political passivity. They established Sunday schools to teach adults to read and write. Material self-help was an important field of initiative, as can be seen in the starting up of mutual insurance associations and of local savings banks.

The question of credit, the passionate anger at the abolition of interest regulation and the exploitation of this by usurers, provoked the first crowd actions by Thranites. One of the Hedemarken associations decided in November, 1850 to protect two of their members (one of them, Mons the Clockmaker, a very active militant) against forced sales. The decision was endorsed by the district super-chairman, who wrote a justification which was read aloud at the church beforehand. The plan was successfully put into operation by a crowd which turned up at the auction, and the super-chairman published a report in which he called on others to take similar measures. This led to arrests, and a move to liberate Mons by force failed.

In Trøndelag, in February 1851, the "Levanger war" was a successful crowd action to set free an arrested Thranite agitator. There was some rioting, and street fighting with a small military force which was called up.[44] These outbreaks of popular anger caused grave concern in the government, the more so as there were troubles in different regions of the country, more or less connected with Thranites: illegal, overt and defiant felling in forests, which was only stopped by military force, and disquieting movements of protest among saw-mill workers. But the biggest crowd action, the "Hatters' war" in Ringerike, was provoked by the arrest of Halstein Knudsen, during the repression after the Central meeting of 1851.[45]

## The End of the Thrane Movement

On 7 July 1851 Marcus Thrane and other leaders were arrested, documents were confiscated, local police were ordered to set up lists of all members of the associations, and judicial procedures were started to have Central committee members and delegates to the Central meeting brought before the courts. Thrane and a number of other members spent several years in custody, as judgment in first instance and by the High Court followed only in 1854. Altogether, 127 were condemned and another seventy were convicted of illegal acts in connection with the Hedemarken and Levanger affairs. Halstein Knudsen got nine years and died in prison; Thrane was condemned to four years of prison and as no reduction was accorded for the time in custody, he was only released in 1858.

By then the Thrane movement had faded away. As the organization itself was not criminalized, historians have asked why it did not survive the arrest and condemnation of its leaders. One explanation has been found in the economic upswing of the 1850's; Norway enjoyed good conditions during the Crimean War. But the movement was on the wane earlier than that. The repression itself must have been a very important element, the more so as all Thranites had reason to feel in danger when local police, in the late summer of 1850, were ordered to set up lists of all association members.

Even earlier many of the "respectable" associations, that is, those dominated by petty bourgeois or by farmers, had ceased their activities as tension with the constitutional authorities worsened. Important dates were the rejection of the petition in November, 1850 and the "crisis" of February, 1851 — repression of the Levanger affair and the prohibition of the Kristiania demonstration. In Ullensaker the last known association meeting was on 16 February 1851.[46] During the years that the leaders were in custody, the big journeymen and labourer associations of Kristiania and Drammen were the most active ones. Thus, while the "proletarian thesis" cannot be upheld with regard to the total membership of the Thrane movement, workers and journeymen did constitute the most resistant core.

Some local studies indicate that former Thranites were over-represented in the emigration to America in the 1850's.[47] Some chose to leave the country because they had been Thranites, feeling the bitterness of defeat and fearing prosecution. But no doubt Thranite opposition and emigration must also be seen as two different acts, proper to men who refused to bow to God-given destiny.

Among the late emigrants was Marcus Thrane himself. In 1863, after the death of his wife, he went to the United States with his five children. There he lived as a journalist, newspaper editor and lecturer. He was now more of a religious free-thinker in opposition to the Scandinavian Lutheran churches than a social reformer, though he became a member of one of the Chicago Scandinavian sections of the First International. When he died in 1890, he was living with his son, a physician, in easy circumstances.

What were the lasting effects of the Thrane movement? It hastened the split in the farmers' opposition between the majority, which became a mainstay of the Liberal party, and parts of the Eastern large farmers who joined the Conservatives. Local innovations, like some of the savings banks, survived the movement. The government was prompted to undertake tariff reform and to propose a new cottars' law.

The most important question, however, involves the possible continuity between the Thrane movement and the modern Norwegian labour movement. As the latter started in the 1870's with trade unions in the artisan trades of Kristiania, political and organizational experience from the Workers Association of that city may have been of some importance. But comparison with the Thrane movement as a whole brings out differences rather than similarities. The new movement proceeded carefully and methodically, setting itself modest immediate goals. It lacked the great visions and the daring of the Thrane movement, but had much more solidity. The distance between them was considerable, as Thrane himself was made to feel, when he visited Norway in 1883. He was shunned as a compromising figure, or met with a sheer lack of interest. Marcus Thrane was re-discovered as a pioneer of the labour movement only well after the turn of the century. In 1949 his remains were brought home, to be buried in the Oslo cemetery of honour beside Henrik Ibsen and other national glories.

# *NOTES*

1. Bjørklund, O., *Marcus Thrane* (Oslo, 1951); rev. ed., *Marcus Thrane, sosialistleder i et uland* [*"Socialist Leader in an Underdeveloped Country"*] (Oslo, 1970), p. 340.

2. Rudé, George, *The Crowd in History: A Study of Popular Disturbances in France and England, 1730-1848* (New York, 1964), p. 5.

3. *Ibid.*

4. Koht, H., *Marcus Thrane* (Kristiania, 1917), pp. 1-5.

5. Rudé, *op. cit.,* p. 5.

6. For an account of Norwegian economic history, see Dyrvik, S., *et al, Norsk økonomisk historie 1500-1980,* Vol. I, *1500-1850* (Bergen, 1979).

7. Thrane's biography and the general account of the Thrane movement here is based on Bjørklund, to whom reference is made in specific instances.

8. Seip, J.A., *Utsikt over Norges historie* [*"Perspective on the History of Norway"*], Vol. I, *1814-ca. 1860* (Olso, 1974), p. 187.

9. The Norwegian original of Thrane's autobiography has been lost. An English translation, by his daughter, is in the University Library, Oslo (Department of Manuscripts).

10. Bjørklund, *op. cit.,* pp. 66-67.

11. Pryser, T., "Mars-urolightene i Kristiania 1848" ["The Riots of March 1848 in Kristiania"], *Tidsskrift for arbeiderbevegelsens historie* (Oslo), I (1981), 19-45.

12. Pryser, T., "Internasjonale 'revolusjonære' strømninger i Norge 1847-1849. Noen forbindelser på individplanet" ["International Revolutionary Currents in Norway, 1847-1849: Some Connections at the Individual Level"], *Historisk Tidsskrift* (Oslo), 1981, 105-132.

13. *Ibid.*, pp. 120-121. Five other journeymen were sent home from Paris at the cost of the Consulate.

14. *Ibid.*, pp. 105-118, 121-125.

15. *Den Norske Rigstidende*, 21, 27-29, 31 December 1849.

16. Koht, H., *Menn i historia* (Oslo, 1963); Pryser, "Internasjonale 'revolusjonære' strømninger i Norge, 1847-1849", pp. 125-129.

17. Lorenz, E., ed., *Marcus Thrane, Arbeidere, Forén Eder! Politiske skrifter av Norges første sosialist* ["*Workers, Unite! Political Writings of Norway's First Socialist*"] (Oslo, 1969), p. 43.

18. Svåsand, L., "The Early Organization of Society in Norway. Some Characteristics", *Scandinavian Journal of History*, Vol. V (1980), pp. 185-195, puts the Thrane movement into the context of early Norwegian mass organizations.

19. The police lists of July-August 1851, comprising 17,654 names, provide professional titles and/or land-relation designations.

20. Grankvist, R., *Thranitterbevegelsen i Trøndelag* (Trondheim, 1966), p. 228; Bull, E., "Håndverkssvenner og arbeiderklasse i Kristiania. Sosialhistoriske problemer" ["Journeymen and Labouring Class in Kristiania. Problems of Social History"], *Historisk Tidsskrift* (Oslo, 1966), 89-114.

21. Pryser, T., "Thranitterbevegelsen på Lillehammer", *Heimen* (Oslo, 1977), 415-429.

22. Try, H., in Pryser, T., ed., *Thranerørsla i norske bygder* ["*The Thrane Movement in Norwegian Rural Communities*"] (Oslo, 1977).

23. *Arbeiderforeningernes Blad*, 14 October 1954, quoted by Bjørklund, *Marcus Thrane*, p. 117.

24. Gaustad (Semmingsen), I., *Arbeiderklassen på Hedemarken 1850-1900* (1934, unpublished); I. Semmingsen and T. Moshaug in Pryser, T., ed., *Thranerørsla i norske bygder* ["*The Thrane Movement in Norwegian Rural Communities*"] (Oslo, 1977), pp. 93-109.

25. Grankvist, R., in Pryser, *idem.*, pp. 166-67.

26. Tveiten, H., in Pryser, *idem.*, p. 59; H. Try, *idem.*, pp. 36-55.

27. Pryser, T., "Thranitterbevegelsen i Norge 1850-51. Seks mikroundersøkelser fra Østlandsbygdene" ["Six Micro-Investigations in Eastern Norway Rural Communities"], *Tidsskrift for arbeiderbevegelsens historie*, No. 2 (1980), 27-79. The petition carries 12,833 signatures, some signed more than once. Since these lists do not provide occupational and land-relation information as regularly as the police lists, they have to be analyzed with the aid of sources like parish registers and tax rolls.

28. Myhre, J., *Bærums historie 1850-1980* (to be published).

29. Pryser, T., *Klassebevegelse eller folkebevegelse? En sosialhistorisk undersøkelse av thranittene i Ullensaker* ["*Class Movement or Popular Movement? A Socio-Historical Investigation of the Thranites of Ullensaker*"] (Oslo, 1977).

30. Bjørklund, p. 166.

31. Bull, E., "Håndverkssvenner og arbeiderklasse", pp. 91-97.

32. Pryser, *Klassebevegelse eller folkebevegelse?*, pp. 237-243. By "farm unit" is understood one farm or a group of farms with the same name resulting from the splitting-up of an original farm.

33. Handgaard, B., in Pryser, T., *Thranerørsla i norske bygder*, pp. 126, 128-130; Pryser, *Thranitterbevegelsen i Norge 1850-51*, p. 71.

34. Seip, J.A., *Utsikt over Norges historie*, p. 191.

35. Hvamstad, P., in Pryser, *Thranerørsla*, p. 80.

36. Pryser, *Klassebevegelse eller folkebevegelse?* and *Thranitterbevegelsen i Norge, passim.*

37. Myhre, J., *Bærums historie 1850-1980.*

38. Pryser, *Thranitterbevegelsen,* p. 47.

39. Seip, J.A., *Utsikt over Norges historie,* Vol. I, p. 192.

40. Rudé, G., *Ideology and Popular Protest* (London, 1980), pp. 31-37..

41. Bjørklund, p. 126; *cf.* Skard, S., *Til Marcus Thranes idéhistorie* (Olso, 1949).

42. Ropeid, A., in Pryser, *Thranerørsla i norske bygder,* p. 29-30.

43. Ropeid, in Pryser, *Thranerørsla,* p. 34.

44. Grankvist, R., *Thranitterbevegelsen i Trøndelag,* pp. 196-208; Grankvist also analyzes other disturbances in Trøndelag.

45. Ropeid, in Pryser, *Thranerørsla,* p. 33.

46. Pryser, *Klassebevegelse eller folkebevegelse?,* pp. 107-108.

47. In Bærum, where one-third of the males were Thranites, Myhre *(Bærums historie)* finds that 12.7 percent emigrated from 1851 to 1860, while the emigration frequency among non-Thranites was about 3.3 percent. Family members included, sixty-four per cent of Bærum's emigrants were Thranites.

Caroline Ralston

# EARLY HAWAIIAN CONTACT HISTORY, 1778-1854: WHAT HAPPENED TO THE ORDINARY HAWAIIANS?

## Hawaii 1778-1845: A Preliminary Chronology

*In 1778 the Hawaiian archipelago was given a permanent location on Western maps by its European discoverer Captain James Cook, who was killed there. Numerous foreign traders, attracted to the fur resources of the North-west coast of America, called in at Hawaii between the 1780s and the 1810s and large quantities of Western goods, particularly armaments, were exchanged for food supplies. Through warfare and diplomacy the high chief Kamehameha brought all the islands except Kauai under his control in 1795. No major battle was waged after 1795, but Kamehameha did gather a large naval and military force on Oahu in 1804 in an unsuccessful attempt to conquer Kauai, which finally accepted his sovereignty in 1810.*

*Sandalwood, which grew in the upland areas on several islands, became the major export from Hawaii between 1815 and the late 1820s. Kamehameha I died in May 1819 and later the same year the ruling elite overthrew the traditional religious system, which provoked only limited resistance. The first company of American Protestant missionaries arrived in 1820 and were joined over the next twenty-eight years by another eleven companies, bringing a total of more than 130 mission workers to Hawaii. Kamehameha II, who died in London in 1824, was succeeded by his twelve year-old brother, Kamehameha III, but real power was exercised by the regent, Kaahumanu, the late Kamehameha I's favorite wife. Under her aegis Christianity was imposed on all Hawaiians in 1825. Servicing the whaling industry became the major foreign economic activity during the 1820s and remained so until the 1860s. The port towns of Honolulu and Lahaina grew rapidly attracting large foreign and Hawaiian-born populations.*

*In an attempt to improve political and economic relations between the Hawaiians and the foreigners, which had become increasingly intractable in the late 1830s, a series of political, legal and land-holding reforms was introduced in the 1840s. Without exception these reforms concentrated power in the hands of foreigners and a tiny Hawaiian elite. When Kamehameha III died in 1854, Hawaii, a nominally Christian country, governed by quasi-democratic institutions, was on the brink of massive expansion into a plantation economy that was to be organised and controlled by foreigners.*

*

While in European historiography the validity and importance of people's histories is well established, in the newly developed area of Pacific history research into the lives of the ordinary islanders has only just begun.[1] Since Pacific history broke its essentially imperial and eurocentric mould in the 1950s and '60s historians have concentrated their attention either on island populations as a whole or upon island leaders, big men and chiefs, those people who had most contact with the incoming foreigners.[2] To differentiate between social groups and to consider how contact with Western personnel, goods and ideologies specifically affected the lives of ordinary islanders has, to date, attracted less attention. However, the early contact history of Hawaii (1778-1854) offers an ideal context in which to make such an attempt.[3] A number of general histories of Hawaii have been written, in contrast to many other Pacific island groups, but none of these has revealed much detailed evidence concerning the lives of the *maka'ainana* (the majority of the Hawaiian population).[4]

In the established versions of early contact Hawaiian history one moves from the death of Cook at Kealakekua Bay, Hawaii Island, in 1779, to Kamehameha's successful unification of all the islands (except Kauai) in 1795, with the aid of men and material from foreign fur traders. Between 1796 and 1810 Kamehameha I consolidated his rule and finally came to an understanding with Kaumualii, ruling chief of Kauai, which left the latter sovereign ruler over his own island but with certain obligations to Kamehameha. Sandalwood, which grew throughout the archipelago but most prolifically on Hawaii Island, Oahu and Kauai, opened Western and Chinese warehouses to Kamehameha and Kaumualii and certain selected chiefly companions. In return for sandalwood these chiefs received European ships, alcohol and manufactured goods and Chinese fabrics, furniture and porcelain. Inevitably, given the ruthless extraction of the wood, the boom was short-lived, and the Hawaiian chiefs were left with no significant access to the market economy, which became increasingly dominated by Americans engaged in the whaling industry. New England missionaries arrived in 1820 and ten years later Christianity was the established religion; Honolulu expanded rapidly as the major whaling port in the north Pacific, and Kamehameha I was succeeded by Kamehameha II and III, both of whom were flanked by very much more powerful chiefly women. Reforms in the 1840s and '50s limited the powers of the ruling elite, introduced the rudiments of a democratic political system, and set in motion a transformation in land-holding.[5]

Most Western minds have interpreted this as a pageant of economic development, religious conversion and political progress; behind it, the experience of the Hawaiian people is only briefly and sporadically glimpsed. Life for them did become more secure and settled with the cessation of fighting in 1795, after two decades of frequent, bitter warfare. Later, chiefly demands for sandalwood drove bands of men and sometimes women into the mountains to cut and carry the desired timber. The hewers suffered unaccustomed cold and rigorous working conditions, gardens were temporarily neglected and the ordinary people had no right to trade sandalwood on their account. The overthrow of the traditional *kapu* structure (see below p. 368) and the later acceptance of Christianity, both initiated and enforced by the ruling elite, compelled the people to conform, at least outwardly, to new religious practices and beliefs, and to change daily living patterns to accommodate attendance at compulsory church, school and prayer meetings. Finally the land reforms left many people not as the independent yeomen farmers that some at least had desired, but as landless peasants with only their unskilled labour to call on.

Such are the insights that the general histories offer into the lives of the ordinary Hawaiians. There is no sustained study of the processes which changed their lives from affluent subsistence farmers, albeit in a politically rather unstable world, to a group of unskilled and increasingly landless peasants who were becoming alienated from their chiefs--those beings who in pre-contact times had been revered as almost godlike--the source of life, fertility and all good fortune.

Reasons for this neglect are not difficult to discover. Problems of evidence must predominate. Any study of non-literate peoples presents the historian with difficulties which are now well-known and fully discussed by social historians of the lower classes in pre-twentieth century Europe.[6] To attempt to write the history of the lower classes in a culture that is as a whole non-literate compounds the problems. In the European context most historians can refer to evidence of the people recorded by the literate ruling class, but for pre-contact Hawaii there is no contemporary literary evidence at all, and post-contact the record is predominantly European in origin. These evidentiary problems can be partially overcome for pre-contact times by using the myths, legends and other materials collected by foreigners and Hawaiians in the decades after contact.[7] Comparison of anthropological data collected this century from other Polynesian islands less frequented than Hawaii can give some insights into patterns of Polynesian beliefs, life-styles and material culture, and present-day archaeology is providing more information about housing and population densities before contact. Used with critical caution all these avenues can help to illuminate the pre-contact past of Hawaii's people. The post-contact record, while predominantly Eurocentric, poses fewer problems and there are the works of the Hawaiian-born historians, including Malo, Ii, Kamakau and Kepelino, to redress the bias a little.[8] But their description of life and history must be read with a sensitive awareness of the Christian education and conversion these authors had experienced, and their tendency to describe chiefly living conditions and customs as if they pertained to the community as a whole.

A further reason for the neglect of the ordinary Hawaiians has been, I believe, the extreme scarcity of evidence that the ordinary people ever questioned the changes wrought in their lives or the roles the chiefs played in the transformation. It has been too easy to see them submitting willingly, or passively, depending on interpretation, to chiefly dictates. Certainly there was no outspoken protest or resistance against the sandalwood trade or the land reforms: series of events which to some Western eyes were highly detrimental to the well-being of the Hawaiian people. But to the historian searching for a people's history there are fragmentary bits scattered throughout the historical records of Hawaii to suggest that acquiescence and acceptance on the Hawaiians' part were not automatic or unthinking. In this article I want to give some examples of the limited protests that have been recorded and also to suggest why dissatisfaction never developed into sustained resistance.

In contrast to most other pre-contact Polynesian societies Hawaii was already highly stratified and politically centralised, with chiefs clearly distinguished from the people by known rank, control over resources and religious regulations. To succeed to the highest political position, the *alii nui* (the ruler over an entire island or over a number of districts within an island) required political acumen and military skills as well as claims to high genealogical rank. Below the *alii nui* were serried ranks of chiefs who served the government, many of them in full-time specialised roles as priests, warriors and administrators. The bulk of the population, the farmers, fishermen and certain craftsmen and women, laboured in their various capacities and on communal projects to support themselves and this chiefly bureaucratic system. Tax or tribute for the chiefly elite was collected annually during a major religious festival, which had developed from an earlier first-fruits offering into a more formally regulated taxation system. But demands on the ordinary people did not end there. Warfare always required extra manpower and supplies, and even during peace the itinerant court of a high chief lived off the land through which it moved. Special areas had to be regularly cultivated by corvée labour for chiefly use, and any object -- a fine hog or calabash -- belonging to an ordinary person could be requested by a chief and refusal was not possible. In return for this substantial investment of labour and goods the ruling élite provided the supervisory and technical skills for large communal activities, offered justice and security and, of paramount importance, had the religious connections and knowledge to ensure the well-being of society.[9]

Territorially and administratively the islands were divided into segments *(ahupua'a)*, which ideally stretched from the uplands through the alluvial plains to the inshore reefs and the sea, offering a complete range of resources necessary for subsistence to the inhabitants within their bounds. The *ahupua'a* formed both the basis of community and the unit for tax assessment and collection. Although the people were deeply attached to the lands they lived on, cultivated, and in which they buried their dead, they had no absolute rights to them. A local chief could deny usage rights if the land were not properly cultivated or the correct taxes not forthcoming. The people, however, were not bound to a particular chief or area and could move away if conditions became oppressive. Ultimately the land belonged to the ruling chief, on whose accession a wholesale redistribution of land occurred amongst his immediate chiefly supporters, who further apportioned rights to their subordinates, who in turn became the new district chiefs. This redistribution of rights in land occurred after the death or military defeat of each *alii nui*. For chiefly followers of an *alii nui,* office and its rewards were never likely to be permanent. At the lowest level, however, while new chiefs were imposed above the people to supervise communal labour and collect taxes, the people's usage rights were rarely disrupted. Thus, although it was possible for the people to move or be removed from their land, in practice they usually were the more permanent fixtures in the Hawaiian polity. The chiefs, who depended on patronage, lived with the *alii nui* or became supervisors of agricultural production in communities where frequently they had no kin.

Even before Western contact, processes were at work in Hawaiian society weakening the links between chiefs and people and undermining the people's ability to organise effectively to protect their standard of living. At the local level people worked for and obeyed chiefs imposed from above. Moreover, they were denied the right to genealogical knowledge amongst themselves. The chiefs had full-time experts to learn, safeguard and pass on their genealogies, which were an essential ingredient in any struggle for power, but the people had no such knowledge or experts, nor the advantages they afforded.[10] Within the *ahupua'a* community endogamy was the predominant marriage pattern and it was encouraged by the local chief to protect the labour supply available to him for communal and taxation purposes.[11] This led to numerous marital and blood ties between the people but little sense of lineage or acknowledged leadership based on kin. Because notions of kinship were not exclusive, well-defined and tightly-knit, economic and political groups with recognised leaders did not develop.

The elite methods of political control and resource management, seen in conjunction with the weakness of local-level leadership, reveal the political and economic gap that had developed between the non-labouring chiefs and the people. But before contact this stratification cannot be called a class division, in part because the complex gradation of status and rank throughout society amongst chiefs and people did not give rise to such clear-cut divisions, and also because many aspects of life still linked chiefs and people closely together.[12] The chiefs tempered their demands on the people's labour and produce because they still needed their support in all political/military struggles. Further, despite the fact that local chiefs were imposed from above, a spirit of mutual goodwill grew between them and the people, who accepted chiefly rule as god-given and inevitable. On the other hand most local chiefs must have recognised that their term of power was likely to be limited and that their futures lay with the community and their ability to live with its members. From the legends there is a little evidence of *maka'ainana* rebellion against local or higher chiefs, but most of it pertains to only one district on Hawaii Island, and none of it suggests that the people questioned the rule of chiefs *per se,* only the rule of certain chiefs.[13] No fundamental breach had appeared in the all-encompassing inherent ideology of rule by the chiefs, who were believed to be descended from the gods and through whom all life and welfare flowed.

The subsistence, non-industrialised nature of pre-contact Hawaiian life acted as a further brake on chiefly demands. While *tapa* cloth, feather work and wooden artefacts were accumulated, no basic Hawaiian crop could be stored for long periods. Large quantities of foodstuffs could be collected at any one time but rapid redistribution was also necessary. This limited the chiefs' ability to hoard consumable wealth. Contact with the West broke this subsistence nexus and offered certain chiefs opportunities for political and economic aggrandizement, often at the people's expense.

Given this background of extensive stratification and subordination in pre-contact Hawaiian society, a brief review of the major changes in Hawaii, 1778-1854, with particular focus on the lives and reactions of the people, provides new insights into the period. From the moment of contact and throughout most of the period under consideration, it is clear that many newly-introduced Western goods were siphoned upwards to the highest chiefs. Not only goods with special prestige value like red cloth or luxury items, but also ironware, from simple adzes to firearms and ammunition, were accumulated and at times monopolized by the chiefs, who had previously enjoyed the right to requisition any goods they coveted from their followers.[14] On Oahu in December 1786 the high chief found means of acquiring many of the newly-introduced goods, even before the ship which was the source of supply had sailed:

> [W]hen this [the storehouse] was compleated, he [the high chief] caused the
> bay to be tabooed, and convened a general assembly of the inhabitants at the top

of this mountain, directing them at the same time, to bring whatever trade they had got, that it might be deposited in his new-erected edifice. This being effected, he found means, on some pretext or other, to appropriate one-half of these stores to his own use. We now no longer wondered at the old priest venting his reproaches so very liberally, as it was pretty evident Teereteere [the high chief] had exerted his authority contrary to the rules of justice and equity.[15]

Throughout the following decade, 1786-1795, while civil warfare was intense, guns and ammunition were the major, sometimes the only, demand made on the foreign fur traders who sought provisions from Hawaii.[16] When a vessel first came to anchor, the people flocked out to trade but, once the high chief was told of its arrival, trade usually diminished until the chief had been received on board, and the bulk of the trade, especially in hogs, was then collected from the people and channelled through chiefly agents, who ensured that guns and ironware demanded in exchange went to the chief.[17] On many of these occasions there is no evidence that the people gained anything in recompense. Thus from contact onwards a growing quantity of food supplies was drained out of the system without any commensurate return to the producers, while the chiefs gained the wherewithal to enhance their rapidly expanding political and economic interests.

With the cessation of warfare and planned invasion in 1804, chiefly demand for foreign goods altered, but the basic pattern of exchange between chiefs and foreigners, based on unrecompensed *maka'ainana* labour or produce, remained. The development of the sandalwood trade, 1810-1830, provided Kamehameha I and later II, and certain high-ranking chiefs, with an opportunity for unprecedented goods accumulation. In exchange for sandalwood, which was cut and carried from the mountains by the people, these chiefs received European vessels, crystal, silver and frame-houses, Chinese porcelain and brocades, none of which was available to their followers who had no right to trade in sandalwood and who were not always fed when cutting and handling it on the chiefs' behalf. In pre-contact times labourers working for the chiefs were never expected to provide their own food, and on many projects, such as building fish ponds or irrigation channels, the resultant benefit to the community as a whole was clear. In the sandalwood trade recompense and long-term community benefits were slight.[18] While the hewers suffered harsh working conditions, and food shortages due to the periodic neglect of gardens did occur, there is no evidence that the trade was directly responsible for causing famine or that it fundamentally changed the people's living conditions. The most influential long-term effect of the sandalwood trade occurred amongst the chiefly participants, who had become accustomed to a standard of living which was increasingly difficult to maintain once the sandalwood resources dried up in the late 1820s.

In desperate attempts to create new avenues of wealth the chiefs attempted to monopolize any product that had a marketable potential. From first contact the chiefs had revealed engrossing tendencies over the sale of food supplies, especially hogs, and with the decline in sandalwood resources these monopolistic instincts intensified. A resident missionary on Kauai in the early 1830s exposed the chiefs' predicament and their solutions:

> The chiefs are continually in debt to the merchants, hence when an article is found capable of being turned to their account, the sale of it is usually prohibited; or such a tax is laid, to be paid in said article, as amounts to a prohibition or nearly so.[19]

In 1820 the Hawaiian governor of Oahu discovered there was a short-term demand for oakum from old rope and he "immediately prohibited the sale of it [rope] that he might engross this small trade himself."[20] Similarly in the early 1830s on Kauai when goats' skins sold for 6¼ to 12 cents each, all goats were claimed the property of the chiefs.[21] In this way taxes and other demands on the people's labour and property increased. Traditional customs of offering a gift on the completion of a chiefly building or on the birth of a chief became occasions for very specific demands, often in coin. Kamehameha II expected to raise $5,000 from chiefs and people from his new house completed in 1823.[22] Silver dollars were collected on the birth of a daughter to the district chief of Waialua in the early 1830s.[23] Fifty per cent or more of any money gained from provisions sales to whalers was collected from the people by government inspectors at the Honolulu and Lahaina markets from the 1820s onwards.[24] A special tax in money was suddenly demanded from the Lahaina people in the early 1830s when the chiefs there realised that a few dollars had been accumulated from the whalers.[25]

Throughout the period, because of the upward movement of certain goods and the people's limited access to the market, their opportunities to acquire even the basic items of European trade were restricted. Evidence of the scarcity of such goods is apparent as late as the 1820s and 1830s when people demanded simple iron implements and cloth whenever an opportunity to trade materialised.[26] The recognized advantages of iron over stone, cloth over *tapa*, did not benefit the Hawaiian people individually during the early decades of contact as much as might have been expected. As late as the 1820s most Hawaiians outside the port areas still dressed predominantly in *tapa*, which was also used in bed coverings and demanded for taxes.[27] Throughout the period most agricultural production relied exclusively on traditional Hawaiian implements. Access to tools and skills such as carpentering, coopering, shoe-making and blacksmithing was denied to many people as late as the 1840s.[28] Before the late 1820s when missionary-inspired laws altered consumption patterns, several traders and naval captains remarked on the people's willingness to accept alcohol and tobacco in exchange for foodstuffs or labour performed; a request at least partly conditioned by the fact that these were readily consumable items that could be kept out of the clutches of the chiefs.[29] Given the volume of trade transacted at Hawaii between the 1780s and 1850s, the *maka'ainana's* acquisitions or benefits from it were not substantial.

This lack of participation in and benefit from trade in foreign goods cannot be explained in terms of the people's lack of interest or desire for manufactured goods. Iron was recognized and demanded from Cook's first landing,[30] and throughout the period, whenever chiefly monopolies were lifted or surveillance lessened, the people traded eagerly. In 1827 when the chiefs made a concerted effort to pay off their debts, which had accumulated during the sandalwood boom, all adult males were ordered to deliver to the government half a picul (one picul = 133⅓ lbs) of sandalwood and as a concession they were allowed to trade a further half picul of wood on their own account, a privilege never granted before.[31] The resultant activity was unusual: "indeed this indulgence has produced a complete change in the feelings and habits of this people, each one is anxious to get all the wood he can and thinks of nothing but accumulating property."[32] During the 1840s the missionaries lamented that the little money that came into the people's hands was spent on lavish clothing, horses and their equipment, rather than on what they considered more useful household goods.[33] The seemingly unlimited market for provisions opened up by the Californian gold rushes in the late 1840s stimulated great exertions amongst the Hawaiians, who cultivated large fields to supply the trade.[34] So many vessels seeking provisions arrived at different anchorages throughout the islands that chiefly monopolisation of the trade was impossible. Even in remote Kohala, Hawaii Island, where access to incoming vessels was difficult, the resident missionary wrote, "Never since our knowledge of Hawaiian affairs had so great an amount of labor been expended on the soil." But the result of all this activity pleased the missionary not at all: "the people were getting wild with prosperity."[35] The total collapse of the trade with the decline of the gold-fields was seen, by missionaries at least, as a just punishment for this cupidity. Whatever label was put on the people's desires there can be little doubt that aspirations had risen, but opportunities to satisfy them were rarely adequate.

While the political changes in 1795 had little impact on the people's economic position or trading opportunities, the end of active warfare did have profound repercussions on *maka'ainana-alii* relations. Once Kamehameha I had won political supremacy and warfare was no longer a vital issue for the rival factions, a major constraint on chiefly expropriation from the people was removed. After 1804 the people were not conscripted for chiefly armies, neither was their produce liable for requisition for military purposes.[36] Life and livelihood were more secure from the vicissitudes of war, but to offset these gains the chiefs were no longer so concerned to foster the loyalty of the people. After this period new trading opportunities prompted them to use their followers' labour and produce to finance buying sprees with little concern for the people's well-being. Further, after 1795, Kamehameha I, through right of conquest of the islands of Oahu to Hawaii, reorganized the patterns of land-holding amongst the high chiefs. In the past chiefs had been given rights to large areas of contiguous lands, but under Kamehameha I smaller areas of land in different districts and even islands were parcelled out, diminishing any one chief's chances of raising a rebellion. Kamehameha I introduced another safeguard against rebellion by insisting that the more influential chiefs live at his court rather than on their own lands. An important effect of these changes was to increase the alienation between chiefs and people, the former having less contact with and responsibility for the latter than in pre-contact times.[37] By 1800 two crucial events for the welfare of the *maka'ainana* had occurred in Hawaiian society: the restraints on accumulation, typical of a Pacific subsistence economy, had been broken and the political bond between chiefs and people, already tenuous in pre-contact times, was further weakened by the cessation of warfare and Kamehameha's reorganisation of chiefly land-holding patterns and rights of residence.

The overthrow of the *kapu* system in 1819, symbolized by the introduction of free eating, formalised and extended the process of state formation which had been occurring throughout Hawaii since 1795.[38] The magnificent public religious ceremonies which required large quantities of food and artefacts from the people, but denied them any participation, were abolished, along with the priestly class who serviced them. The high chiefs' political and economic power was consolidated at the priests' expense, and the previous flow of goods and labour into major religious concerns was now available for use in other chiefly activities, especially the sandalwood and provisions trade.[39] The abolition of *kapu* allowed all men and women to eat together and the women to eat foods earlier forbidden to them, two dispensations which seemed to be widely appreciated. Also the diverse demands on the ordinary people's labour and goods were rationalised and centralised, if not reduced. On the religious level, however, the people's belief and commitment to their ancestral deities and local gods, the mainsprings of the religious life, were less seriously affected.[40]

All available evidence suggests that this dramatic reorganisation was initiated and executed by a clique of high chiefs on Hawaii Island, and that it provoked only two instances of resistance, both on that island. One, the larger and potentially more serious, was led by the high chief and priest, Kekuaokalani; the other, which occurred in the Hamakua district, northeast Hawaii Island, was apparently an uprising of commoners without chiefly leadership.[41] Both groups were defeated in battle, and apart from the statements that the Hamakua uprising was led and composed of commoners, there is little evidence about the people's reactions to the abolition of the *kapu* or their motivations for joining Kekuaokalani or the Hamakua group. No overt resistance to the overthrow surfaced on any other island and for the people it can be argued that this religious upheaval was less intrusive and traumatic than the later enforced conversion to Christianity, which occurred after 1824.

The final major political changes of the period occurred in the 1840s. New codes of law were promulgated, a quasi-democratic form of government with some elected representatives was introduced, a number of foreigners became paid advisors to the new government, and a massive redistribution of land and changes in land-holding rights were brought into effect between 1845 and 1854.[42] The processes and rationale cannot be detailed here, but the more influential effects on the people should be outlined. With the introduction of new legislation in the 1840s the people gained *de jure* a number of new rights and avenues of protection, especially from arbitrary taxation. But these changes took time to filter down and be understood, and even if this occurred, the people had little power to insist on their new rights.[43] Similarly the people's attempts to claim the lands they cultivated and on which they lived were frustrated, and sometimes denied, by avaricious chiefs or foreigners.[44] A number of missionaries and philanthropists had welcomed the land division and offer of freehold tenure to the ordinary Hawaiians, in the belief that it would free the people from the continual and excessive demands of the local chiefly agents, and would encourage them to become hard-working independent farmers enjoying the fruits of their own labour. In practice many people received no land at all. Some who gained freehold tenure to cultivated plots lost former communal rights to grazing land or collecting areas, which rendered independent subsistence farming impossible, and some, for this or other reasons, were unable to prevent the subsequent sale of their newly-acquired land.[45]

Overall the land division eliminated the group of local chiefly agents, who had overseen the collection of taxation and agricultural production for the chiefs, and released many of the *maka'ainana* both from those chiefly demands and from the land itself. They were free to become wage labour in the expanding plantation industry. Other processes were also at work removing commoners from the land, one of the very few sources of independent existence open to them. By the mid-1840s government taxes had to be paid in cash, not kind, which forced people in areas remote from foreign commercial activities into the port towns to earn the necessary tax money.[46] By the mid-1850s, with a growing proportion of men and women cut off from the land, the process of class formation was developing rapidly — the transition from affluent subsistence to landless, unskilled labour had for many already occurred. The divergence of chiefly and commoner interests had grown over the decade 1840-1850, and for some ordinary Hawaiians at least there was a sense of alienation between themselves and the small governing elite who were strongly influenced and often co-opted by foreign commercial interests.

At no stage between 1779 and 1854 did the people join together in any numbers to break the trading monopolies of the chiefs, to uphold the old religious practices or to refuse to provide the labour and taxes demanded from them; but individually or in small groups some did flout chiefly authority and thwart chiefly aspirations. People anxious to acquire foreign goods were always prepared to sell provisions from canoes, despite chiefly attempts to impose monopolies.[47] If caught, the total purchase price might be confiscated, but this does not seem to have prevented an illicit trade continuing. In Honolulu in 1830 the chiefs prohibited the people's access to the resident foreign traders, but as one merchant pointed out, the order "is evaded whenever we are not too closely watch'd."[48]

"Prostitution" would appear to be another means through which ordinary women and their menfolk were able to gain access to desired foreign goods. From Cook onwards women willingly offered themselves, or were offered, to foreign visitors.[49] At the beginning the economic motive does not appear:

> ... we found all the Women of these Islands but little influenced by interested motives in their intercourse with us, as they would almost use violence to force you into their Embrace regardless whether we gave them any thing or not....[50]

But as familiarity with the intruders and their goods grew and the chiefs' monopolistic tendencies were firmly established, prostitution provided an avenue to goods that was difficult to prohibit or police. As early as 1804 a foreigner claimed that there was a causal connection between increased chiefly exploitation and prostitution.[51] In 1835 a resident missionary at Waimea, Hawaii Island, explained the frequent lapses into prostitution amongst the females of his flock in similar terms: "their poverty is one reason why they often yielded."[52] Only one chief tried to cash in on the women's earnings, by supplying vessels in Honolulu harbour with women and claiming a cut.[53] Usually the business was conducted privately by the women or their male kinsmen.

Once the missionaries gained an ascendancy with certain chiefs, strong governmental pressure was imposed to stop women going out to vessels or frequenting the dance halls and grog shops in Honolulu and Lahaina.[54] But even after the nominal conversion of the entire archipelago in the late 1820s it is noteworthy that any disturbance or political upheaval was accompanied by a missionary outcry against increased prostitution and adultery[55]. During the provisional government of 1843, when laws prohibiting prostitution were temporarily lifted, women from the outer districts and islands flocked into Honolulu and Lahaina.[56] In 1847 two foreign physicians in Honolulu claimed that four-fifths of the money received in Honolulu and Lahaina by the people came from the wages of prostitution.[57] While the claim may be exaggerated, the people's arbitrarily limited access to the market economy made a certain dependence on prostitution inevitable.

During the sandalwood trade and later, individual instances of labour sabotage occurred. On Oahu and Molokai, and presumably the other islands, the sandalwood cutters deliberately destroyed young sandalwood trees in attempts to protect their children from the trade.[58] In 1837 some people were called out to cut timber for the chief in the mountains. Once there it was discovered that the people had brought only three ropes with them to haul the logs and those broke the moment they were attached.[59] By then the day of labour for the chiefs was over.

Demands on the people did not end with the sandalwood trade, and some became increasingly adept at evasion. In Waimea, Hawaii Island, the resident missionary claimed in 1835:

> There is no one branch better understood by the people of that region [Waimea]
> than running away from, and otherwise evading the orders of their chiefs.[60]

Where evasion was impossible, other means of quiet protest were sometimes employed. The district of Waialua on Oahu belonged ultimately to the Premier Kinau, who frequently sent a government vessel to the area to be filled with provisions for her retinue in Honolulu. After a period of particularly heavy demands, which had to be given over and above their ordinary taxation, the people protested, not verbally or by withdrawing labour, but by putting leaves, a whole taro and even dung in some of the bundles of *poi* (cooked taro paste) demanded by the voracious chiefess. Punishment was swift and heavy. When no-one admitted guilt, all but invalids and the young were sent to work for the government at a distant place for six weeks.[61]

Many missionaries lamented the apathy and laziness of the people, but at least some of them recognised that on many projects the people were conscripted and that even when working for themselves they had no guarantee that they would enjoy the fruits of their labour.[62] A particularly fine hog or field of taro could be commandeered by a chief or his agent, just as it was ready for consumption. While laziness and apathy are culturally loaded judgements, it seems highly likely that at least sometimes non-activity was a form of passive protection for the people. When the return for labour seemed fairly secure, for example during the 1827 tax concession or the gold rushes, the people were prepared to expend enormous amounts of energy.[63]

Resistance to imposed Christianity appeared in many muted forms. Not only adultery and prostitution increased at times of political upheaval, but also *hula* dancing, tatooing, *'awa* drinking and what the missionaries called heathenish practices. In 1827, on the death of one of the most powerful high chiefs who had been an ardent mission supporter, the Sabbath was desecrated in Honolulu and the *hula*, cards and rum reappeared.[64] On more remote mission stations reports came in throughout the 1840s of incidents of *'awa* drinking, tattooing and traditional religious practices, which frequently occurred when the local chief was absent.[65] In 1833 Kamehameha III himself publicly defied the missionary-inspired laws prohibiting drinking, gambling and prostitution, and throughout the islands, with the exception of Kauai, the people deserted the mission schools and eagerly resorted to former pastimes.[66] These outbreaks inevitably had political implications, especially amongst the different factions of the ruling elite, but the widespread support they evoked from the people and the spontaneous reversion to traditional activities by the people themselves in the absence of chiefly surveillance reveals the tenuousness of Christianity's hold on many people for whom ancient practices still offered greater efficacy and enjoyment.

The most concerted and well-organised popular opposition was a series of petitions which originated in Lahaina. The Lahaina one was signed by 1,600 of the "common people of your kingdom" and was sent to Kamehameha III and his council in June 1845. 1,344 signed a similar petition sent from Molokai in July 1845. Other petitions followed from Maui, and one from Kailua, Hawaii Island.[67] By 1845 a legislature had been introduced to Hawaii and a number of foreigners, after becoming naturalised Hawaiian citizens, had been appointed to the government in the most influential ministerial positions.[68] The petitioners questioned the independence of a nation that relied so heavily on foreigners, whom they wished replaced by Hawaiian chiefs, and they objected to the naturalised foreigners' right to buy land freehold in Hawaii. A letter signed by eighteen Hawaiian-born Lahaina residents published at the same time in a Hawaiian-language newspaper contained a perceptive analysis of the matters most concerning the petitioners.[69] Hawaii was becoming a nation of foreigners, any one of whom could take an oath of allegiance on stepping ashore, marry a Hawaiian woman and buy land. In contrast most Hawaiians had no cash income at all and even the educated Hawaiians, employed by the government, were paid in kind, not money. Thus no ordinary Hawaiian could compete with foreigners when land was sold.

> Foreigners come on shore with cash, ready to purchase land; but we have not the means to purchase lands; the native is disabled like one who has long been afflicted with a disease upon his back. We have lived under the chiefs, thinking to do whatever they desired, but not according as we thought; hence we are not prepared to compete with foreigners ... If we had not been loitering around after the chiefs, thinking to accustom ourselves to that mode of life, then perhaps we should be prepared to compete with foreigners. But now, where are our oxen and carts, ploughs and shovels, and other tools for cultivating the soil? In years which have past, we desired to pasture cattle, that we might have some property, but the most of us were forbidden to pasture cattle; therefore we have no cattle, nor anything with which to purchase cattle. And now the chiefs are admitting foreigners into the country to possess the good lands of Hawaii, and to deprive us of the same, with the exception perhaps of our small cultivated patches. Foreigners will say to us perhaps, purchase according to your ability to purchase and husband well.
>
> Very well; but why are we poor at this time? Because we have been subject to the ancient laws, till within these few years. Is it proper at this crisis that we should be turned in with wealthy foreigners to purchase ourselves lands? That is equivalent to the land with the life of the kingdom passing into the possession of foreigners.[70]

Some Hawaiians clearly understood the implications of the political transformations and the likely outcome for themselves. Kamehameha III's foreign advisors were anxious to establish that this agitation was the result of disaffected foreigners, but apart from the leading role of the mission-educated Hawaiian, David Malo, no evidence of foreign interference or inspiration could be produced.[71] Later explanation of the movement by a missionary resident at Lahaina revealed a widespread fear amongst the people that the foreign officers would only build up their own positions and that of the king, while their concern for the ordinary Hawaiians would be minimal. Some had prayed for months that the Lord would give them black rulers.[72] A reply to the petitioners, pointing out the need for well-educated foreign experts whose allegiance to the king should be predominant, was published in July 1845; and later that year Kamehameha III and a part-Hawaiian government official toured Maui, the centre of the opposition, to explain the government's policies.[73] The protest died out without having effected any visible change in those policies.

Such were the nature and extent of the Hawaiians' opposition to their enforced lack of involvement in the political and economic changes that were transforming Hawaii. Resistance ranged from individual acts of assertion or passive obstruction, to widely supported, perceptively argued petitions. None of them was violent or threatened violence, with the exception of the two groups who resisted the abolition of the *kapu* in 1819. Careful scrutiny of the evidence suggests, however, that changes in the lives of the people had been substantial and that even in places least affected by Western contact standards of living had deteriorated markedly. Basic changes in relations between the people and the chiefs, and between the people and their access to and use of subsistence resources, were crucial factors in this decline: the people's labour and cultivated foodstuffs were not only expended within a closed economic and political system to maintain a chiefly bureaucracy, but were also used to maintain the chiefs' expanding trading interests with the foreigners. Thus the chiefs enjoyed unprecedented opportunities to accumulate goods, while the people's aspirations were frequently frustrated and curtailed. Further, by the 1850s increasing amounts of prime, cultivatable land were being engrossed by foreigners and some Hawaiians were left without access to land. Progressively, under the impact of Western penetration and the changes associated with it, the interests of chiefs and people had diverged until, by the 1850s, it would appear to a modern-day Western analyst that in many senses two classes with opposed interests had emerged.

Despite this, active resistance was minimal. To analyse why raises a number of cultural and semantic problems: specifically, how does one define or identify exploitation in a Hawaiian context, or establish whether it increased after contact with the West? Evidence has been provided above to reveal the critical changes in relations that had occurred, but it has not been possible to quantify the amount of labour, or percentage of cultivated crops, animals or artefacts that were demanded by the chiefs. Neither can the reactions of most Hawaiians to these changes be precisely established. Did they experience and perceive the changes as exploitation, let alone *increased* exploitation? In pre-contact times a division in society in terms of those who enjoyed powers to requisition resources and deploy labour and those who provided the services had already occurred, but as was pointed out earlier, strong bonds still linked chiefs and people. To attempt to establish quantitatively that pre-contact relations were exploitative poses real problems, given a system in which tangible goods (labour, foodstuffs and artefacts) were exchanged for intangible goods (administrative, religious and horticultural skills and knowledge).[74] Post-contact, the difficulties of analysis and interpretation still remain. The traditional subsistence nexus was broken, and the chiefs used their followers' labour and provisions to pursue new commercial activities and to accumulate new goods; but did the people question the chiefs' long-established rights to act thus or to fill storehouses and caves with newly-acquired goods that were not used for community needs? In pre-contact times the well-filled storehouses of the chiefs had kept their people loyal and secure;[75] post-contact, the goods of the chief still proclaimed their status and prestige and reflected glory on their followers.[76] Despite the new demands made on the people perhaps they still saw the chiefs as reciprocating and fulfilling their expected roles satisfactorily. Any attempt to hypothesize about the ordinary people's reactions to the dramatic changes which had occurred between the 1780s and the 1850s in Hawaii, must be sensitive to the cultural patterns and predispositions which lay at the heart of chiefly/commoner relations.

Theories of exploitation that are quantitatively arrived at tend to be culturally biased, and to assume that people's perceptions of and reactions to events which the analyst sees as exploitative will be similar. But in any pre-industrial society the question of exploitation and resistance is "not just a problem of calories and income but is a question of peasant conceptions of social justice, of rights and obligations, of reciprocity."[77] And even if people perceive themselves as exploited, active resistance is not inevitable; in fact "exploitation without rebellion seems...a far more ordinary state of affairs than revolutionary war."[78]

In the Hawaiian context it is not possible to talk about a strong inherent ideology of protest.[79] Certainly the Hawaiians had clear notions about their right to the means of subsistence and of reciprocity between themselves and the chiefs, crudely calculated as their labour, food supplies and artefacts in return for the organisation of major agricultural projects, celebrations and feasts, and physical and spiritual protection.[80] But in normal times the Hawaiians did not press hard upon the bountiful resources available to them, and if particular chiefs proved oppressive, demanding goods to which they had no recognised customary right, the people could move to another district, or threaten to do so. In these circumstances no strong traditions of organised protest grew up amongst the people. On the few recorded occasions of popular uprisings, an unacceptable chief was automatically replaced by another chief — often the man who had fomented and led the rebellion.[81]

Over the people's modest conceptions of their rights towered the massive body of official ideology venerating the chiefs, investing them with god-like qualities and demanding for them absolute obedience and loyalty.[82] The people's reverence and awe were not to be effaced by four to five decades of chiefly indifference or refusal to respect customary ideas of reciprocity. These deep-seated ties to a chiefly ideology were one of the major reasons why militant resistance did not eventuate. Hawaiians found it extraordinarily difficult to confront their chiefs and demand justice. Their petitions were couched in the most deferential and self-effacing way, while personal, verbal confrontation was apparently unthinkable for most.[83] These habits of thought and action persisted despite the upheaval and insecurity many experienced.

On-going population loss was another factor militating against active resistance. Actual numbers, either of the absolute decline over the period or of the rate of decline during particular decades, cannot be established, but at a conservative estimate the total decrease was at least forty percent.[84] Thus the spectre of over-population and attendant famine, potent sources of popular unrest in other countries, played no part in Hawaii. One can also argue that repeated epidemics and periods of high death-rates from diseases whose nature and virulence were unknown before contact, undermined the people's self-confidence and weakened local coherence; and this in communities which were already lacking strong kin bonds between the people even before contact. The movement of young people, both men and women, into the port towns of Honolulu and Lahaina further compounded this problem of local organisation.

Finally, while contact with the West offered the possibility of access to new ideologies, the only one consistently and widely peddled to the ordinary Hawaiians was a form of evangelical, Protestant Christianity which, while it preached equality of all people in Christ, was totally dependent on the chiefly elite for its very existence in the islands and its acceptance as the official religion. Amongst the missionaries themselves there were uneasy divisions on this subject. Several railed publicly against the greed and tyranny of the chiefs, most of whom were church members. "[I]t is to a number of your missionaries a matter of deep regret that rulers, so manifestly covetous, & oppressive, as are most of the high chiefs, should be connected with the church."[85] Very rarely a particularly exploitative chief was disciplined by the missionaries, as happened to the high chief, Kuakini, governor of Hawaii Island, who was suspended from the church in 1840 for his prominent love of money and his "oppression of the people seeking his own interests in opposition to theirs or rather out of theirs."[86] But the majority of missionaries between 1820 and 1854 muted their criticisms, enjoying the security and influence which a close association between the Christian church and the ruling chiefly elite made possible. As a general mission letter to headquarters written in 1838 pointed out:

> To wink at the evasion or resistance of Government orders because they seem to impose heavy burdens, provided they do not require a manifest violation of God's commands, we are aware would tend to sedition and confusion, and a total defeat of our object and the proper object of government.[87]

Typical of Christian authorities in many other parts of the world, the mission in Hawaii offered the people an ideology that gave them little or no assistance in resisting the political power of the chiefs or the burgeoning interests of the foreigners.

Yet, despite present historiography, not all ordinary Hawaiians were just passive bystanders quietly accepting the massive political, economic, social and religious changes that swept Hawaii in the decades after contact with the West. While for most of them conscious recognition -- let alone any act of public defiance of the fact -- that the chiefs were pursuing interests in direct opposition to their own well-being was difficult, there were still groups of Hawaiians who ignored chiefly trading embargoes, temporarily sabotaged sandalwood-cutting expeditions, reverted to traditional pastimes when opportunity arose, and wrote and organised petitions. Yet they influenced the course of events not at all. The relentless pressure of foreign invasion by merchant companies, consuls and naval authorities, missions and large-scale planters, all of whom, except the consuls and naval personnel, enjoyed some form of chiefly co-operation, could not be resisted. By 1854 the ordinary Hawaiians owned only one per cent of the land[88] and their numbers were greatly reduced, while the sugar industry stood ready for enormous expansion, buying up more and more land and engulfing the remnant of Hawaiian population with migrant labour.[89] Even before this expansion, however, the possibility of effective opposition by the Hawaiians was minimal. Neither inherent nor derived ideologies prompted or promoted resistance, while the lack of effective community organisation and leadership, combined with on-going population decline, compounded the difficulties. While concentrating one's attention on the *maka'ainana* for the period 1778-1854 of Hawaiian history does not alter the broad outlines of change that have been already established, it does deepen knowledge of the period and suggest some of the costs the changes imposed. It also reveals the pervasive forces, both indigenous and introduced, at work in Hawaii to reduce and mute popular opposition. Clearly the Hawaiian people's experience of change was in many cases very different from that of the high chiefs.

# NOTES

1. Two such studies being undertaken at the moment are those by Rod Lacey, who is working on a general history of the people of Papua New Guinea, and John Waiko, who is preparing a Ph.D. thesis on the Binandere, a tribal unit within Papua New Guinea.

2. For example, Greg Dening, *Islands and Beaches. Discourse on a Silent Land: Marquesas 1774-1880* (Melbourne, 1980); K.R. Howe, *The Loyalty Islands. A History of Culture Contacts 1840-1900* (Canberra, 1977); Sione Latukefu, *Church and State in Tonga* (Canberra, 1974); and many of the chapters in J.W. Davidson and Deryck Scarr (eds), *Pacific Islands Portraits* (Canberra, 1970) and Deryck Scarr (ed.), *More Pacific Islands Portraits* (Canberra, 1979).

3. The stratification in traditional Hawaiian society facilitates an analysis of the differing experiences of the ruling elite and the majority of ordinary people once contact occurred. Interest in the lives and conditions of the ordinary Hawaiians has grown amongst Hawaiian specialists, pre-eminently from Marshall Sahlins, but it is also seen in the work of Timothy Earle, Marion Kelly and others. To date, however, a study concentrating on the ordinary Hawaiians has not been published.

4. These include Ralph S. Kuykendall, *The Hawaiian Kingdom*, 3 vols. (Honolulu, 1938-1967); Gavan Daws, *Shoal of Time. A History of the Hawaiian Islands* (New York, 1968); Harold W. Bradley, *The American Frontier in Hawaii: The Pioneers 1789-1843* (Stanford, 1942); Theodore Morgan, *Hawaii. A Century of Economic Change 1778-1876* (Cambridge, Mass., 1948); Jean Hobbs, *Hawaii. A Pageant of the Soil* (Stanford, 1935).

5. Kuykendall, *op. cit.,* Vol. 1, *passim*; Bradley, *op. cit., passim*; Daws, *op. cit.,* chs 1-4; Morgan, *op. cit.,*; Hobbs, *op. cit.*; Richard A. Pierce, *Russia's Hawaiian Adventure, 1815-1817* (Berkeley, 1965); Jon J. Chinen, *The Great Mahele. Hawaii's Land Division of 1848* (Honolulu, 1958).

6. Witness the works of George Rudé himself and those of many of the contributors to this volume. Several Pacific historians have also been concerned with the problems of evidence in pre-literate societies, including J.W. Davidson, "Problems of Pacific History," *The Journal of Pacific History,* I (1966), 5-21; Gregory Dening, "Ethnohistory in Polynesia," *The Journal of Pacific History,* I (1966), 23-42; Sione Latukefu, "Oral Traditions: An Appraisal of their Value in Historical Research in Tonga," *The Journal of Pacific History,* III (1968), 135-43; H.E. Maude, "Pacific History - Past, Present and Future," *The Journal of Pacific History,* 6 (1971), 3-24.

7. David Malo, *Hawaiian Antiquities,* trans. Nathaniel B. Emerson (Honolulu, 1951), John Papa Ii, *Fragments of Hawaiian History,* trans. Mary Kawena Pukui (Honolulu, 1959); Samuel M. Kamakau, *Ruling Chiefs of Hawaii* (Honolulu, 1961), *Ka Po'e Kahiko. The People of Old,* trans. Mary Kawena Pukui (Honolulu, 1964), *The Works of the People of Old Na Hana a ka Po'e Kahiko,* trans. Mary Kawena Pukui (Honolulu, 1976); Martha W. Beckwith (ed.), *Kepelino's Traditions of Hawaii* (Honolulu, 1932); *Ka Mooolelo Hawaii,* trans. Reuben Tinker in *Hawaiian Spectator,* II (1839), 58-77, 211-31, 334-40, 438-47 and continued but not completed in *The Polynesian,* 28 July, 1, 8, 15, 22 Aug. 1840; John F. Pogue, *Moolelo of Ancient Hawaii,* trans. Charles W. Kenn (Honolulu, 1978); Abraham

Fornander, *An Account of the Polynesian Race....,* 3 vols in 1 (Rutland, Vermont, 1969); Abraham Fornander, *Fornander Collection of Hawaiian Antiquities and Folk-lore,* 3 vols. (Honolulu, 1916-20); Martha Beckwith, *Hawaiian Mythology* (Honolulu, 1970).

8. Malo, *op. cit.;* Ii, *op. cit.;* Kamakau, *Ruling Chiefs....; Ka Po'e Kahiko...;* and *The Works...;* Martha Beckwith, *Kepelino's Traditions...; Ka Mooolelo Hawaii....*

9. In an essay of this length a detailed analysis of pre-contact Hawaiian society cannot be attempted. While the outlines of Hawaiian political and social hierarchy are rarely questioned, there is debate over local community organization, its degree of autonomy and the strength of the kin group. See Timothy Earle, *Economic and Social Organization of a Complex Chiefdom* (Ann Arbor, 1978), 143-45, for a brief resumé of the debate. A further problem is the degree of cultural differentiation amongst the ordinary Hawaiians. Kamakau, *Ruling Chiefs...,* 230-31, 238-39, suggests that there were marked differences in living conditions for the ordinary people throughout the islands, which can only be substantiated by further research. In this paper I have used the general term "Hawaiians", which is an oversimplification but not, I believe, for the purposes of my argument, misleading.

10. Kamakau, *Ruling Chiefs...,* 242; Fornander, *The Polynesian Race...,* II, 28-29, 63-64.

11. Earle, *op. cit.,* 145.

12. Malo, *op. cit.,* 60; Kamakau, *Ka Po'e Kahiko...,* 3-9. I Have used the terms "chiefs" and "people" throughout this paper, but I do not wish to imply that these were absolute or clear-cut divisions.

13. Malo, *op. cit.,* 195; Robert John Hommon, "The Formation of Primitive States in Precontact Hawaii," Ph.D. thesis, University of Arizona, 1967, 160-63.

14. Nathaniel Portlock, *A Voyage round the World...1785...1788* (London 1789), 310-11; Ii , *op. cit.,* 88; Lucia Ruggles Holman, *Journal of...* (Honolulu 1931), 18-28; Charles H. Hammett, *Journal of...,* 18 Aug. 1823, MS in Bryant and Sturgis Papers, Baker Library, Harvard University; Laura Fish Judd, *Honolulu, Sketches of the Life Social, Political and Religious in the Hawaiian Islands from 1828 to 1861* (Honolulu, 1928), 108.

15. George Dixon, *A Voyage round the World... 1785-1788* (London, 1789), 105-06.

16. John Meares, *Voyages made in the Years 1788 and 1789 from China to the North West Coast of America* (London, 1790), 354-56; George Mortimer, *Observations and Remarks made during a Voyage....* (London, 1791), 53; George Vancouver, *A Voyage of Discovery to the North Pacific Ocean....* (London, 1801), I, 403, III, 185-86.

17. Portlock, *op. cit.,* 154-99, 303; Dixon, *op. cit.,* 96-139, 252-61.

18. Kuykendall, *op. cit.,* I, 85-92; Bradley, *op. cit.,* 53-120; Pierce, *op. cit.;* Kamakau, *Ruling Chiefs...,* 204, 276; William Ellis, *Journal of...* (Rutland, Vermont, 1979), 214-15, 261, 265, 283; Daniel Tyerman and George Bennet, *Journal of Voyages and Travel....* (Boston, 1832), II, 43.

19. Peter Gulick to Anderson, Waimea, Hawaii, 22 Aug, 1833, ABC: 19,1, Vol. 5 #173, MS in American Board of Commissioners for Foreign Missions, archive in the Houghton Library, Harvard University (hereinafter ABC).

20. James Hunnewell Journal, 6 June 1820, MS in Baker Library, Harvard University.

21. Gulick to Anderson, Waimea, Hawaii, 22 Aug, 1833, as above.

22. Sandwich Island Mission Journal, 26 Apr. 1823, ABC: 19.1, Vol. 1 #1-111.

23. Elizabeth P.P. Pratt, *History of Keoua* (Honolulu 1920), 50-51.

24. Sandwich Island Mission Journal, 25 March 1822 as above; Gilbert F. Mathison, *Narrative of a Visit to...the Sandwich Islands during the Years 1821 and 1822...* (London, 1825), 452; C.S. Stewart, *Journal of a Residence in the Sandwich Islands, during the Years 1823, 1824 and 1825* (Honolulu, 1970), 151; Ellis, *op. cit.,* 299.

25. Gulick to Anderson, Waimea, Hawaii, 22 Aug. 1833, as above.

26. J.C. Jones to Marshall and Wildes, Oahu, 23 Dec. 1821, MS in Marshall MSS in Houghton Library, Harvard University; Sandwich Island Mission Journal, 16 Jan. 1822, as above; Sereno E. Bishop, *Reminiscences of Old Hawaii* (Honolulu, 1916), 27-29; Abner Wilcox to Anderson, Hilo, 4 Oct. 1839, ABC:19.1, Vol. 11 #177; C. Forbes to Anderson, Kealakekua Bay, Hawaii, 22 July 1841, ABC:19.1, Vol. 10 #119.

27. Use of *tapa* may at times have been preferred, but reports of the Hawaiians' love of extravagant clothing, when obtainable, suggest that many Hawaiians wanted Western cloth. James Macrae, *With Lord Byron at the Sandwich Islands in 1825* (Honolulu, 1922), 6; Bishop, *op. cit.,* 14, 44: Levi Chamberlain to Evarts, Honolulu, 19 Nov. 1830, ABC:19.1, Vol. 16 #161; *1831 ... 1834* (New York 1835), 400, 403, 414; Armstrong Letter Journal, 26 July 1837, Wailuku, Maui, ABC:19.1, Vol. 10 #100.

28. The Hawaiian digging stick was very effective for Hawaiian horticultural techniques and iron substitutes were probably not often sought, but other tools and skills were denied. Bishop, *op. cit.,* 27-29; Forbes to Anderson, Kealakekua Bay, Hawaii, 22 July 1841, ABC:19.1, Vol. 10 #119; Elias Bond to Secretary, Kohala, Hawaii, 8 Apr. 1844, ABC:19.1, Vol. 14 #259.

29. Isaac Iselin, *Journal of a Trading Voyage around the World, 1805-1808* (New York, n.d.), 77; Samuel Hill, Journal and Log of Two Voyages..., MSS in the New York Public Library and on microfilm in Pacific Manuscripts Bureau, PMB 512, 91; Otto von Kotzebue, *A Voyage of Discovery... Under taken in the Years 1815-1818* (London 1821), I, 331, 336; V.M. Golovnin, *Around the World on the Kamchatka 1817-1819,* trans. Ella Wiswell (Honolulu, 1979), 210; James Hunnewell Journal, 7 Sept. 1820.

30. J.C. Beaglehole (ed.), *The Journald of Captain James Cook on his Voyages of Discovery* (Cambridge, 1967), III, part 1, 264.

31. Kuykendall, *op. cit.,* 1, 92.

32. J.C. Jones to Captain D. Wildes, Oahu, 30 Sept. 1827, MS in J.C. Jones Letters 1826-1838 in Hawaiian Historical Society Library, Honolulu.

31. Kuykendall, *op. cit.,* I, 92.

33. Armstrong to Anderson, Honolulu, 12 Oct. 1842, ABC:19.1, Vol. 10 #90; Armstrong to Green, Honolulu, 11 Nov. 1845, ABC:19.1, Vol. 12 #23; Conde, Report of the Hana Station, July 1848, ABC:19.1, Vol. 15 #258; Bishop to Anderson, Ewa, Oahu, 26 Oct. 1849, ABC:19.1, Vol. 14 #249.

34. J.F. Pogue to Anderson, Kealakekua Bay, Hawaii, 14 July 1849, ABC:19.1, Vol. 16 #239; A. Thurston to Anderson, Kailua, Hawaii, 27 May 1850, ABC:19.1, Vol. 16 #315; G.B. Rowell, Waimea, Kauai Station Report, 1851, MS in Hawaiian Mission Children's Society Library, Honolulu (hereinafter HMCS Library).

35. Bond, Kohala, Hawaii, Station Report 1851, ABC:19.1, Vol. 13 #140.

36. Kuykendall, *op. cit.,* I, 49-51.

37. Stephenie S. Levin, "The Overthrow of the *Kapu* System in Hawaii," *Journal of the Polynesian Society,* 77 (1968), 420.

38. M.C. Webb, "The Abolition of the Taboo System in Hawaii, "*Journal of the Polynesian Society,* 74 (1965), 21-39, particularly 27; William Davenport, "The 'Hawaiian Cultural Revolution': some political and economic considerations," *American Anthropologist,* 71 (1969), 1-20); Richard H. Harfst, "Cause or Condition: Explanations of the Hawaiian Cultural Revolution," *Journal of the Polynesian Society,* 81 (1972), 437-71; Levin, *op. cit.*

39. Davenport, *op. cit.,* 17-18; Webb, *op. cit.,* 30-31; Ellis, *op. cit.,* 80-81.

40. Davenport, *op. cit.,* 18; Ellis, *op. cit.,* 34, 44, 198, 250.

41. Kuykendall, *op. cit.,* I, 65-69; Davenport, *op. cit.,* 16; Kamakau, *Ruling Chiefs...,* 225-28; Fornander, *Fornander Collection...,* Vol. 5, 478-82; Webb, *op. cit.,* 34; W.D. Alexander, "Overthrow of the Ancient Tabu System in the Hawaiian Islands," *Hawaiian Historical Society Annual Report for 1916,* 42.

42. Kuykendall, *op. cit.,* I, chs 10-15; Chinen, *op. cit.*; Lorrin A. Thurston (ed.), *The Fundamental Law of Hawaii* (Honolulu, 1904), I-168.

43. Kamakau, *Ruling Chiefs...,* 370; Bradley, *op. cit.,* 321; *Answers to Questions* (Honolulu, 1848), 13, 37-41; L. Lyons to Anderson, Waimea, Hawaii, 26 Mar. 1847, ABC:19.1, Vol. 16 #182.

44. J.S. Emerson to Anderson, Waialua, Oahu, 26 Oct. 1847, ABC:19.1, Vol. 15 #333; Gulick to Anderson, Waialua, Oahu, 11 Oct. 1850, ABC:19.1, Vol. 16 #18; Bond to G.M. Robertson, Kohala, Hawaii, 17 Feb. 1851, Land Commission Records in Archives of Hawaii; J. Fuller to J.H. Smith, Kailua, Hawaii, 11 Oct. 1852, Land Commission Records.

45. Chinen, *op. cit.,* 30-31; Marion Kelly, "Changes in Land Tenure in Hawaii 1778-1850," MA thesis, University of Hawaii, 1956, 138-42; Emerson, Waialua Station Report, 1848, MS in HMCS Library; Bishop to Amstrong, Ewa, Oahu, 30 April 1850, Public Instruction Land File, in Archives of Hawaii.

46. Robert C. Schmitt, *The Missionary Censuses of Hawaii* (Honolulu, 1973), 44; Thurston to Green, Kailua, Hawaii, 1 May 1844, ABC:19.1, Vol. 16 #306; J. Paris to Secretary, Waiohinu, Hawaii, 20 Apr. 1847, ABC:19.1, Vol. 16 #200.

47. Vancouver, *op. cit.,* III, 185-86; Alexander Ross, *Adventures of the First Settlers on the Oregon or Columbia River 1810-1813,* ed. R.G. Thwaites (Cleveland, 1904), 59; Pierce, *op. cit.,* 172; J. Ely to Evarts, Kaawaloa, Hawaii, 11 Oct. 1842, ABC:19.1, Vol. 2 #112, Stewart, *op. cit.,* 151.

48. James Hunnewell to J.P. Sturgis, Oahu, 10 Feb. 1830, James Hunnewell Papers in Baker Library, Harvard University.

49. The moral condemnation inherent in the word "prostitution" is not appropriate in traditional Hawaiian culture, which vaunted sexuality and placed no value on virginity or chastity except for certain persons and then for political/dynastic reasons, rather than moral ones.

50. David Samwell, Journal, in J.C. Beaglehole (ed.), *op. cit.,* III, part 2, 1085.

51. Urey Lisiansky, *Voyage round the World in the Years 1803...1806* (Amsterdam, 1968 facsimile), 128; Daniela D. Tumarkin, "A Russian View of Hawaii in 1804," *Pacific Studies,* 2, No. 2 (Spring 1979), 129.

52. Unsigned Waimea, Hawaii, Station Report 1835, MS in HMCS Library.

53. Gavan Daws, "The High Chief Boki," *Journal of the Polynesian Society,* 75 (1966), 66.

54. Kuykendall, *op. cit.,* I, 122-23; Hiram Bingham, *A Residence of Twenty-one Years in the Sandwich Islands* (New York, 1847), 284-89, 313-19.

55. For example, during the Kauai rebellion in 1824, after the death of Kalanimoku in 1827 and during the troubled year of 1833 when Kamehameha III rescinded many of the missionary "blue" laws.

56. Bond to Secretary, Kohala, Hawaii, 8 April 1844, ABC:19.1, Vol. 14 #259; Thurston to Green, Kailua, Hawaii, 1 May 1844, ABC:19.1, Vol. 16 #306.

57. *Answers to Questions,* 32; Armstrong to Anderson, Honolulu, 24 May 1847, ABC:19.1, Vol. 14 #84.

58. Bob Krauss, *Historic Waianae: A Place of Kings* (Honolulu, 1973), 18; George P. Cooke, *Moolelo o Molokai. A Ranch Story of Molokai* (Honolulu, 1949), 61.

59. Marshall Sahlins, Lecture III delivered in Honolulu, University of Hawaii, Feb./Mar. 1973.

60. Unsigned, Waimea, Hawaii, Station Report, 1835, MS in HMCS Library.

61. Emerson to Chamberlain, Waialua, Oahu, 19 Oct. 1835; Emerson to Chamberlain, Waialua, Oahu, 10 Nov. 1835, MS in J.S. Emerson Letters in HMCS Library.

62. Ely to Evarts, Kaawaloa, Hawaii, 11 Oct. 1824, ABC:19.1, Vol. 2 #112; Mary A. Richards (comp.), *The Hawaiian Chiefs' Children's School. A Record compiled from the Diary and*

*Letters of Amos Star Cooke and Juliette Montague Cooke* (Rutland, Vermont, 1970), 17; Paris to Anderson, Orange Hill, Hawaii, 16 July 1853, ABC:19.1, Vol. 16 #219.

63. See notes 32, 34.

64. F. W. Beechey, *Narrative of a Voyage to the Pacific...in the Years 1825...1828* (London, 1831), II, 103; Bradley, *op. cit.,* 164-65.

65. Conde to Green, Hana, Maui, 12 Feb. 1845, ABC:19.1, Vol. 12 #73; G.B. Rowell, Waimea, Kauai, Station Report, 1848, HMCS Library; Lyons to Anderson, Waimea, Hawaii, 6 Mar. 1848, ABC:19.1, Vol. 16 #183; *Answers to Questions,* 59-60.

66. Kuykendall, *op. cit.,* I, 134-36; Levi Chamberlain Journal, 1833, MS in HMCS Library; Chamberlain to Anderson, Honolulu, 26 Mar. 1833, ABC:19.1, Vol. 6 #163-64; Gulick to Secretary, Koloa, Kauai, 25 Apr. 1836, ABC:19.1, Vol. 5 #181.

67. *The Friend,* 8 Aug. 1845, 118-19; Petition from Molokai, July 1845, Petitions in Archives of Hawaii; Kuykendall, *op. cit.,* I, 257-60.

68. Kuykendall, *op. cit.,* I, ch. 4.

69. *The Friend,* 8 Aug. 1845; 119.

70. *Ibid.*

71. Kuykendall, *op. cit.,* I, 259; Judd, *op. cit.,* 114.

72. Baldwin to Green, Lahaina, Maui, 8 Nov. 1845, ABC:19.1, Vol. 12 #33.

73. *The Friend,* 8 Aug. 1845, 118-19.

74. Harfst, *op. cit.,* 455.

75. Malo, *op. cit.,* 195.

76. In February 1824 the missionaries were gratified at the number of people who attended church. Later they were told that the people had only come to see the new clothes of their chiefs. *Missionary Herald,* 1825, 280.

77. James C. Scott, *The Moral Economy of the Peasant....* (New Haven, 1976), vii.

78. *Ibid.,* 4.

79. George Rudé, *Ideology and Popular Protest* (London, 1980), 28.

80. Malo, *op. cit.,* 135-39, 190-96; Kamakau, *Ruling Chiefs...,* 226; E.S.C. Handy and Mary Pukui, *The Polynesian Family System in Ka'u, Hawaii* (Wellington, 1958), 198-204.

81. Hommon, *op. cit.,* 160-63.

82. Malo, *op. cit.,* 54, 190-92; Beckwith, *op. cit.,* 293-313; Kamakau, *Ka Po'e Kahiko,* 4-10, Handy and Pukui, *op. cit.,* 199-200.

83. See petitions in Land Commission — Incoming Correspondence, Claims and in Petitions in Archives of Hawaii.

84. Schmitt, *op. cit., passim;* Robert C. Schmitt, *Demographic Statistics of Hawaii: 1778-1965* (Honolulu, 1968), 10-45; Robert C. Schmitt, "New Estimates of the Pre-censal Population of Hawaii," *Journal of the Polynesian Society,* 80 (1971), 237-43; Norma McArthur, Review of Schmitt, *The Missionary Censuses* in Oceania, 45 (1974-75), 169; and personal communication with Norma McArthur, 12 June 1980.

85. Gulick to Anderson, Waimea, Hawaii, 22 Aug. 1833, ABC:19.1, Vol. 5 #173.

86. Thurston to Anderson, Kailua, Hawaii, 24 Apr. 1840, ABC:19.1, Vol. 9 #45.

87. Report of the Delegate Meeting to Anderson, Lahaina, Maui, 20 June 1838, ABC:19.1, Vol. 8 #10; see also Chamberlain to Anderson, Honolulu, 7 Feb. 1839, ABC:19.1, Vol. 9 #119.

88. Chinen, *op. cit.,* 31; Neil M. Levy, "Native Hawaiian Land Rights," *California Law Review,* 63, No. 4 (July 1975), 856.

89. Kuykendall, *op. cit.,* II, especially chs. 5-6; Schmitt, *Demographic Statistics,* 46-78.

William J. Fishman

# A PEOPLE'S JOURNÉE:
# THE BATTLE OF CABLE STREET (OCTOBER 4th 1936)

On October 4th 1936, an extraordinary political happening took place in the East End of London. The homegrown Fascist Leader, Sir Oswald Mosley, had attempted to carry out his threat to lead a great march of his blackshirt contingents through the Jewish quarter. It was an act of provocation, ostensibly aimed at the dual targets of Fascist attack: Jews and Communists. 3,000 mobilised at their start line in Royal Mint street, flanked by over double their number of police, who were to act as a protective shield. But they never set out. By late afternoon, the Fascist "army" was forced to turn about and march off in the opposite direction: through the deserted City, along the Embankment, where, in the absence of an audience, they quickly dispersed. That night there was dancing in the pubs and in the side streets of the East End. And thus was a legend born.

What were the political realities of this event? Why the East End as the major battle-ground between Fascist and anti-Fascist? Were there discernible short- and long-term consequences accruing from this local "defeat"?

The common factor in all this was the existence of a large Jewish concentration in a traditional, and vividly publicised, area of social and economic deprivation. By the 1930s, although sustaining a sort of quasi-ghetto (mainly through their persistence in adhering to "alien" customs based on ancient religious precepts), these Eastern European Jewish immigrants were slowly becoming integrated; their children, via school and club, more rapidly so.[1] The densest settlement was in the borough of Stepney. The *New Survey*[2] reported 43% of total London Jewish families located there (compared with 15% in Bethnal Green, which attracted the highest level of Fascist support), and the 1931 Census records Stepney as housing the largest number of foreign-born residents of any borough in England: 30,052, most of whom were of Eastern European (Russo-Polish Jewish) origin, and of whom 25,328 were registered aliens.[3] East End Jews were, generally, though not always, "different and readily identifiable".[4] This "difference" combined with a legacy of over-population pressing on unsanitary, and seemingly uninhabitable, slum dwellings, was easily associated with the immigrants. Politically the Jews were vulnerable as ready-made scapegoats for local discontent. In 1932, at the height of the recession, 18% of the population of Shoreditch, 17.8% of Bethnal Green and 15.5% of Stepney were estimated to be living on or below the poverty line.[5] Even whilst the high point of depression was already passing, unemployment was rife, in an area historically prone to it.

By 1934 the national budget was already showing a surplus and lower income tax was implemented. Bond sellers scooped in £224 million, and the unemployed faced a £7 million reduction in dole cuts. Even the Communist *Daily Worker* reported improvements on the economic front.[6] According to Party activist Phil Piratin "The deep crisis had passed, and Britain's industry was gradually recovering. The ground of middle class discontent was, therefore, beginning to recede."[7] Old Labour loyalties were returning. Locally, at the 1935 General Election, in those constituencies with known Fascist support, Labour party candidates won their seats comfortably. For example Labour gained Bethnal Green North East, with Dan Chater obtaining a majority of almost 5000 over the Liberals, whilst Sir Percy Harris, the popular established Liberal M.P. for South West Bethnal Green (he had held the seat since 1922), only just defeated his Jewish Labour opponent, George Jeger. Major Clement Attlee (Labour) was returned with a majority of 7000 for Limehouse, whilst at Mile End, Jewish Labour candidate Dan Frankel retrieved one of the three seats lost by the Party in 1931. J.H. Hall recaptured the second for Whitechapel against Liberal (and Jewish) Barnett Janner and Ernest Thurtle the third at Shoreditch from a National Liberal.

Mosley, understandably, refused to contest the election that year. His reasons were self-evident. The acts of brutality perpetrated against hecklers by Fascist stewards at the Olympia meeting (June 6th 1934) and widely publicised in the press, followed three weeks later by Hitler's "Night of the Long Knives", alienated his party, the British Union of Fascists (B.U.F.), from its more respectable Conservative sympathisers (it was at this point that the Press mogul, Lord Rothermere, withdrew the support of his powerful Associated Press from Mosley). The B.U.F.'s image had become disreputable, its violence and rhetoric already associated with those of Mussolini and Hitler. Party funds were short and there was a noticeable increase in drop-outs. Dr. Benewick listed the issues which kept the Fascists directly out of the hustings:

> Economic conditions and the political mood of the people were against a radical party, while the unemployed already had a champion in the Labour Party, and, in the distressed areas, the Communist Party was better organised and had enlisted the support of many malcontents. Finally Mosley could not afford an electoral disaster after the bitter experience of the New Party.[8]

Yet it was implicit in the Fascist appeal that the Leader must continue to dazzle and amaze. For Mosley there was an easy way to retain the limelight for himself and bring a renewed impetus to his movement. In 1935 diminishing fortunes and the hardening of anti-Fascist activity brought about an acceleration of the anti-Jewish campaign. The British Leader had gotten the message: here was a well-defined target against which he could muster wider support.

1936 was the year of opportunity. The King's death (January 20th) had evoked an outburst of patriotism. (*Britons First* was a populist Fascist slogan.) Above all, Fascist/National Socialist aggressive intent was seen to pay off. On March 7th German troops re-occupied the Rhineland and on May 9th Mussolini proclaimed the annexation of Ethiopia. The Western democracies appeared flabby and impotent against the powerful dynamic of the totalitarian powers. Mosley sought to present himself as the domestic symbol of the advance of Fascism in Europe. Now, he had to justify this.

Tension began to build up as the B.U.F. stepped up its operations in the East End. From all contemporary evidence, their purpose seemed obvious: to focus attack on the Jews (in all their vulnerability as a minority group) as a means of enhancing Fascist support, a policy in line with the Hitlerian creed. Yet forty years after the events, there has arisen a self-styled "revisionist" school of historians, which proclaims "the need for an interactionist analysis to understand the origins and development of... political anti-semitism in Britain." It would appear from the conclusions of one of its pioneers, R. Skidelsky, that

> A Jewish malaise of this time was to be obsessed by Fascism. If some Jews found it intolerably provoking they certainly went out of their way to be provoked. Fascist meetings drew them as a magnet.

After this extraordinary statement, Skidelsky gives us a clue, perhaps unwittingly, to this "obsession" by referring to a police arrest as far back as 30th April 1933, when seven blackshirts were remanded, whilst selling their paper in Piccadilly, ostensibly for provoking Jews. The Police Superintendent reported, "Since the Jewish persecution in Germany, the Jews have taken objection to the selling of the *Blackshirt* publication *which gives great publicity to the German point of view.*"[9] Given the treatment meted out to the Jews by Hitler and the attendant horrors already well known to the community, is it any wonder that East End Jews would be roused to oppose, at the least in self-defence, a uniformed and overtly pro-Nazi group? Who was provoking whom?

Another attempt to justify Mosley's incursion into the ghetto area contradicts the accepted view that he deliberately invaded East London to stir up a *Judenhetz*. "Rather what happened is that Gentile East Londoners sought out the B.U.F. in order to make it a vehicle for their local grievance. Mosley went to where his national support lay...".[10] The argument infers that *most* East End gentiles were anti-Semitic, and can be refuted. By 1936 Mosley was certainly making headway in Bethnal Green, and Poplar (Duckett Street area), but both were on or well beyond the periphery of Jewish settlement. For where Jew and non-Jew were neighbours in the same street they lived in reasonable amity, more often in friendliness, and there are innumerable examples of mutual aid — of the poor helping the poor, transcending ethnic bounds, during the Depression. As will be shown, it was the gentile dockers and their families who provided the vanguard during the battle of Cable Street.

1936 registered a peak build-up of Fascist activity and propaganda aimed against the Jews. They were accused of clannishness and filthy habits; of swindling the innocent gentiles and depriving them of jobs; of being, simultaneously, capitalist plutocrats and communist agitators. Ultimately these unwelcome strangers within the gates should be "excluded" from the host community.[11] The campaign was a deliberate ploy, playing on the irrational fears and hatreds of the slum dwellers. Piratin[12] rightly suggests that it was a populist "appeal to the basest sentiments" and founded on ill-informed accusations. With full-time organisers ensconced in strongholds in Green Street (Bethnal Green), Hoxton, and Salmon Lane (Poplar), Fascist incursions were mounted against the Jews. Attacks on individuals and shops were stepped up as gangs of Blackshirts made daily, more often nocturnal, forays into the ghetto. Local concern could not be divorced from the wider realities of Fascist and Nazi advances taking place in Europe. Evidence of Mosley's earliest sympathy and support for Mussolini and Hitler[13] brought the ghetto dweller out in defensive action to join "the struggle in the streets". East End Jews, in the front line of attack, had no alternative but to resist.

By February there was enhanced activity as Fascist and anti-Fascist forces clashed. For some time Jews had been faced with a dilemma, accruing from opposing advice, on how to conduct themselves in the face of aggression. The Jewish Board of Deputies, organ of the Anglo-Jewish establishment, warned that the community should not draw attention to itself by engaging in militant action in the streets, on the premise that it would only play into Mosley's hands, for he could then "prove" his accusation that the Jews were Communist troublemakers. The Board's plea was for dignified behaviour and trust in the authorities, especially the police, to contain the menace. Curious advice to offer to those exposed to daily abuse (the walls of Stepney were extensively daubed with slogans like "Get rid of the Yids" and "P.J" — *Perish Judah)* and threats of physical violence. The Labour Party tended to ignore the B.U.F., advising its followers to stay away from their meetings. Labour M.P.'s made loud noises of protest in Parliament, but this from a distance, far removed from the actual conflict played out in the streets of East London. "This left the Communist Party, and to a lesser extent the Independent Labour Party, to fill the vacuum."[14] Aided by strong minority groups such as "The Jewish People's Council against Fascism and Anti-Semitism", "The Jewish Ex-Servicemen's Association", and the "Labour Party League of Youth", a united body of activist opposition was rapidly taking shape, with the Communist Party (C.P.) assuming the role of vanguard.[15]

The Blackshirt concentration of resources in East London, with their campaign at its peak, approached a reign of terror. They offered, moreover, an excuse for the C.P., already well organised, to intensify and focus its own ideology.[16] The wider streets and open spaces of Stepney provided the battleground; Shoreditch, with its overcongested thoroughfares and narrow markets, was less well-endowed for street fighting than its neighbours. The East End was traditionally conducive to street-corner politics as one recreative diversion for people condemned to slum and sweatshop. Violence, too, always lay beneath the surface, ready to erupt. "When previously it might have been argued that the anti-Fascists made violence inevitable, political anti-Semitism deliberately invited its use."[17]

Rival meetings and clashes developed, as much a response to the European as to the home political barometer. On 17th February, a "Week of Peace and Democracy", initiated by the C.P., was marked locally by a grand exhibition at the St. George's Town Hall. It brought together a practical united front of diverse anti-Fascist leaders with visiting speakers including Labour M.P.s. Clem Attlee and George Lansbury, the radical priest Father St. John Grosser, some minor Trade Union officials and Mary Hughes acting as usher.[18] Contemporaneous with the Spanish General Election, where armed pro-Franco terrorists were already on the rampage, and with a physical assault on Léon Blum by French Fascists, Ernest Thurtle, M.P. for Shoreditch, was raising the question of B.U.F. violence against Jewish shopkeepers and a protest signed by over 1000 local tradesmen was presented to Parliament. March saw the formation of the *Left Book Club*[19] as an educative force to alert readers to the dangers of Fascism at home and abroad, whilst the Communist *Daily Worker* ceaselessly stressed the link between events in Nazi Germany and the extension of B.U.F. attacks in the East End.

On the 22nd March, Mosley, not to be outdone, organised a national B.U.F. meeting at the Albert Hall, London. There was a massive anti-Fascist response as vast crowds flocked to the vicinity, blocking the roads leading to the Hall. Huge traffic jams ensued, such that the "Leader" arrived fifteen minutes late to make his address. It was here that police protection manifestly ensured minimum disruption. (Under hard questioning the Home Secretary revealed that 2500 regulars and 400 police reservists were employed in maintaining order.) Outside, a peaceful meeting of opponents at Thurloe Square was brutally dispersed by an unwarranted baton charge by the police.[20] In France a Popular Front demonstration brought 80,000 supporters out into the streets and lent an additional impetus to British anti-Fascists eager to unite against the home enemy. The Stepney Communist Party stepped up its "agit-prop" for a united front, and was praised by the *Daily Worker* for topping sales in the *Daily Worker League* (21st March 1936). On May 1st, traditional Labour Day, when the Madrid workers declared a general strike, Mosley focused attention on his own cause by holding a rally at Victoria Park Square, Bethnal Green. The "Leader" appeared, resplendent in full panoply, on top of a loud-speaker van, surrounded by four or five hundred of his uniformed supporters. Although barracking by a large group of opponents led to fights and minor scuffles, police protection sufficed to enable the meeting to end without disorder. It was Mosley's cue to attempt a break-through into hostile territory: a deliberate plan to penetrate the outer ring of the ghetto, which harboured the enemy.

On the 5th June, a loudspeaker van, resembling a large troop carrier, filled with blackshirts appeared at the junction of Dellow and Cable streets, in the St. Georges precinct, where Anglo-Irish dockers and Jewish immigrants had been living amicably together for over a generation. A local docker, ex-boxer and gentile, Ernie Leek, led the assault against the intruders, who were forced to abandon the meeting, the van retreating under police escort. It was one of innumerable examples of Stepney gentiles coming to the defence of Jews. A minor triumph, it helped bring to a head the dilemma that was causing division within the ranks of the C.P. — particularly between the local, on the spot, activists and the distant party headquarters. To meet the earliest B.U.F. attacks, a young Stepney dissident group led by Joe Jacobs responded by direct action, that is, constant physical attack, wherever and whenever Mosley appeared on the streets. This was resisted by Party leadership, who argued that instead of immediate confrontation, it could be more fruitful, in the long term, to engage in the tactics of a circuitous entryism into the Trade Unions and reformist parties, thereby gaining control of a stronger force engaged in a broader struggle.[21] By this time, the long-term would be too late. A crisis was developing as the Fascists stepped up their attack, and rallies and counter-rallies reached a crescendo. It helped solve the dilemma in favour of the dissidents, but led, ultimately, to Jacobs' expulsion from the C.P. for his "lack of Party discipline".

A gloomy portent for East End Jews was expressed in the replies sent by the Under-Secretary at the Home Office to the complaints delivered by the M.P.s for Poplar (George Lansbury) and South West Bethnal Green (Sir Percy Harris) of attacks perpetrated against their constituents. It was cold comfort to be told that "steps *would be taken* to deal with Fascist violence and attempts to molest Jews", without promise of legal enforcements. "All I saw was massive police support for Mosley", notes Jacobs. On 7th June, a second large East End rally was called by the

B.U.F. in Victoria Park, heavily protected by the police.[22] On an open platform Mosley was seen free to pour out his venomous anti-Jewish tirades, apparently with the tacit approval of the law. On 14th July an outrage occurred in Petticoat Lane (following another, when, during a peaceful procession to Victoria Park, organised by the East London Trades Council, the main speaker 'Herbert Morrison' was bombarded with bags of flour and soot by Fascist hooligans). A van full of uniformed blackshirts suddenly drove in to the middle of the market. Thugs shouting anti-Jewish obscenities leaped out and proceeded to smash the stalls and beat up the stall-holders. Fortunately members of a nearby ex-Servicemen's anti-Fascist meeting were alerted and ran up to confront the attackers, who immediately took off and escaped in the crowd.

Fascist incursions were deliberately stepped up as daily reports of street fights and Jew-baiting poured in. The London Ex-Servicemen's Movement Against Fascism, formed in May, called for a massive demonstration of protest by all anti-Fascists on 30th August. A united front was already operating as a political collective, supported by the Jewish Labour Council, groups representing Trade Unions, the rank and file of the Labour Party, and allied social organisations in East London. The march to Victoria Park, led by Whitechapel M.P. J.H. Hall and veteran suffragette Sylvia Pankhurst, was attacked en route by Fascists who hurled stones at the leaders. Within the local C.P. the gap between the protagonists of street action and those opting for extended "agit-prop" within the Trade Unions was narrowing. The urgency of the struggle nationally (the B.U.F. seemed to be particu-larly spurred on to prove its own mettle by the news of Franco's rebellion in Spain) would bring an end to Party divisions. September heralded numerous meetings in support of the legally elected Spanish government.[23] In Leeds a march by Fascists into the Jewish quarter, blocked by a determined opposition, was only saved by a protective shield afforded by the police. It was a dress rehearsal for the great battle to come.

Tension was building up in the East End as September drew to a close.[24] The B.U.F., no doubt spurred on by the triumphs of their more successful European counterparts, was poised for a big showdown with the Left, which, at the least, would project them on the national stage. On 26th September, the *Blackshirt* proclaimed that a march would take place terminating in mass meetings in Stepney. The following issue gave further details. Blackshirt columns would march straight through the Jewish area and disperse to four support meetings — at Aske Street (Shoreditch), Salmon Lane (Limehouse), Stafford Park (Bow); and finally, at 6 p.m., the high point of the exercise, a triumphant gathering of the faithful at Victoria Park Square, where the Leader would address the people. (The square was conveniently sited opposite the B.U.F.-patronised pub *The Salmon and Ball,* where the prospect of a liquid celebration by the "victors" was well in the cards.) The date was October 4th. It was the very day that the Young Communist League had called for a mass rally in support of the Spanish Republic, at Trafalgar Square: leaflets publicising this had already been widely distributed.

The effect of Mosley's announcement brought to a head the dilemma which had bedevilled the C.P. At first it forced the leadership into a ludicrous stance. The District Committee's pronouncement that "It was going ahead with the Trafalgar Square demonstration... and *after* the demonstration to march through East

London to show their hatred of Mosley's support for Fascist attacks on Democracy..."[25] horrified the local party dissidents. They knew that the primary need to stop Mosley *on the streets* was agreed by all Stepney anti-Fascist organisations. It was activist spokesman Joe Jacobs who demanded an urgent meeting with the C.P. leaders on home ground to explain the realities of the situation.

In close touch with the grass roots, Jacobs would demonstrate to them that other groups were already committed, as first priority, to oppose Mosley's march by forceful action. "The slogan - - 'They Shall not pass' - - was already on everyone's lips and being white-washed on walls and pavements". The Party leaders agreed to discuss tactics with the Stepney delegates, but were adamant about not changing their policy of first supporting the Trafalgar Square meeting. Joe Jacobs, present at what developed into a dialogue of the deaf, described how far Party headquarters had lost touch with local sentiment.

> We were treated to a long talk on the world situation in which it was stated that the demonstration in support of Spanish Democracy was more important than Mosley's march in East London. Our leaders always talked about the world situation in a particular jargon which often impressed the rank and file... We argued that the best way to help the Spanish people was to stop Mosley marching through East London. It was, in fact, the same fight. If we said the Fascists should not pass, it was what the Spanish people were trying to ensure and giving their lives in the process. A victory for Mosley would be a victory for Franco. In any case the people of East London had their own ideas about all this and would oppose Mosley with their bodies, no matter what the CP said.[26]

Jacobs was, perhaps, stretching comparisons too far, but his assessment of local feeling was correct. There was a dramatic intervention as Pat Devine, a high Party official, burst in. Orders had been reversed. The call would go out to all branches to rally to Aldgate instead of Trafalgar Square. The slogan would be — *They shall not pass*! Reality had finally imposed itself on the leadership's thinking, and only just in time, for pressure by responsible public bodies on the Home Office to stop the march had proved futile. (A deputation of five East London Mayors had just called on the Home Secretary, Sir John Simon, to request a ban and been rebuffed. A similar plea by petition, organised by the Jewish People's Council against Fascism and containing 100,000 signatures, was also refused.) The signal was given. There could be no more passive acceptance on the part of the ghetto dwellers. They were already mobilising for the fray.

Piratin's claim, that once the C.P.'s decision to stop Mosley was announced "the most powerful campaign of propaganda and preparation took place, unequalled in any other action of recent working class history, with the exception of the 1926 General Strike", was no exaggeration. The national leaders, saved by the perspicacity and intransigeance of local members, now threw themselves into frenzied activity. There was no time to produce new leaflets. The old one, advertising the Trafalgar Square demo, was actually printed with a call to anti-Fascists to rally to Aldgate at 2 p.m. instead. They were faced with a threefold task: to rouse all anti-Fascists to participate in the action; to decide on tactics to halt the march; to set up a headquarters for logistics and intelligence and to direct the, hopefully, large number of protagonists involved. Before the great day, "Battle HQ" had been established at Manningtree Street (sixty yards from the "front line" at Gardiners Corner), with runners detailed to receive and despatch messages from there, as well as to act as a flying column to distribute posters and banners. First aid and command posts were set up at the Whitechapel Library, Toynbee Hall and Cable Street. Since Mosley had openly revealed his line of march, good strategy dictated that maximum opposition should be concentrated at Leman Street and Gardiners Corners, which if strong enough to halt the police and Blackshirts, would leave only one likely opening for the march — along Cable Street. Such intelligent preparation paid off. Meanwhile the unknown quantity, vital for success, was *how many* of the defenders would turn up on the day?[27] On the eve of confrontation the Mayors of the East End boroughs, rabbis, the *Jewish Chronicle,* the Labour *Daily Herald* and the Liberal *News Chronicle,* were all urging the people to keep away, so that the Fascist march could be converted into a farce — an advance into nothing. But it was the ILP demonstration in Hackney led by Fenner Brockway, the day before, that captured the mood of the locality, by calling for an overwhelming demonstration against the Blackshirts on the following day.

October 4th opened with a bright autumnal morning, the weather conducive for both sides to "do battle". Then an extraordinary scene took place. From out of the narrow courts, alleyways and main thoroughfares came the steady tramp of marching feet, growing in intensity as the columns were swelled by reinforcements. A forest of banners arose, borne aloft, with the watchwords *THEY SHALL NOT PASS* emblazoned in a multi-variety of colours, with red predominating. (Red flags adorned hundreds of windows from Aldgate to Stepney Green.) Youngsters clustered at the rear of the marchers chanting "Mosley shall not pass!" and "Bar the road to Fascism!" Loud-speaker vans manned by the C.P., I.L.P. and Jewish Ex-Serviceman's Association patrolled the streets booming out the message for *all* to rally to the defence lines at Cable Street and Gardiners Corner. Mass battalions, mobilising spontaneously from the ranks of mainly local folk of mixed ethnicity, swiftly filled up the streets adjoining the "front", that is, where the proposed Fascist incursions were to take place. By noon a huge, impassable, crowd had collected at Gardiners Corner, the confluence of the Whitechapel and Commercial Roads, with off-shoots extending south along Leman Street to Cable Street—the whole presenting a solid block to any would-be invader. The determination of an "expectant Madrid" had transformed East Enders into a fighting unity.[28]

On the other side of the line the police had also moved in early. It was a formidable display of the forces of law and order. "Six thousand foot police and the whole of the mounted division were on duty, posted between Tower Hill and Whitechapel. Sir Philip Game, the Commissioner of Police, had his headquarters in a side street off Tower Hill. Police wireless vans moved around reporting frequently. A police 'observation' aeroplane flew low overhead. Every police officer in the Metropolis was on duty. Special constables had been drafted in to take the place of the 'regulars' withdrawn from other parts of London."[29] The first contingents of Blackshirts, arriving by coach from all parts of the country, disembarked at their starting point, Royal Mint Street. Anti-Fascists had already filtered through the police cordon to make contact, and scuffles broke out; coach windows were smashed and the first group of casualties removed before the Leader arrived at 3:30 p.m., one and a half hours late for the time set to march off.

The prime task confronting the police was to clear Leman Street from the south (Dock Street end) to the north at Aldgate, which held a solid mass of anti-

Fascists. At Gardiners Corner an added obstacle was a tram left standing by its driver so that it traversed the conjunction of Leman Street and Commercial Road. Faced by this impregnable object, the harassed police charged again and again into the crowd. Piratin recalls:

> The Police were working in very difficult circumstances and, without doubt, the rank and file were carrying out their instructions, but they were as vicious in action as anything I have ever seen including some of the hunger marches.... And in one particular case, when I happened to be near Gardiners Corner where some of the plate glass windows were broken in, among the crowd that had to be picked up was my own young sister-in-law...and her back was lacerated as a result of this....She was then a kid about 17.[30]

Police violence begat violence. Fighting broke out and injuries and arrests mounted up. But the crowd remained firm. The police could make no impression on this immense human barricade. Orders from their headquarters revealed a plan to divert the march through the last possible route of entry — Cable street, which had already been anticipated by the foresight and tactics of the C.P. leaders.

It was a phone call from party "spy" Dr. Hugh Faulkner, who had infiltrated the Blackshirt ranks, that alerted C.P. headquarters of the proposed re-routing. Tubby Rosen, one of those in charge of operations in Cable Street, concurs with Piratin's account of the instant reaction, as the opening was quickly plugged by a surge of bodies from the rear:

> We were ready. The moment this became apparent the signal was given to put up the barricades. We had prepared three spots. The first was near a yard where there were all kinds of timber and other oddments, and also an old lorry. An arrangement had been made with the owner that this old lorry could be used as a barricade. Instructions had been given about this, but when someone shouted "Get the lorry!" evidently not explaining that it was in the nearby yard, some of the lads, looking up the street, saw a stationary lorry about 200 yards away. They went along, brought it back, and pushed it over on its side before anyone even discovered that it was not the lorry meant to be used. Still it was a lorry and supplemented by bits of old furniture, mattresses and every kind of thing you expect to find in box rooms, it was a barricade which the police did not find easy to penetrate.[31]

A dramatic exercise in mutual aid emerged as Orthodox Jew and Anglo-Irish docker laboured and fought side by side:

> On this occasion I saw the way in which they were stacking up the barricades with mattresses and the way in which these dockers and labourers were working alongside the bearded Jews. Now I had already lived in Stepney all my life...and I have never seen this before... the important point to me, and it struck me fiercely as I was driving around in a motor cycle, that Mosley was trying to divide the nation and this counter action against him helped in uniting the very people he was trying to split.[32]

An additional fillip, quite unexpected by the leaders, was the response of people housed on both sides of the street. As the police broke through the first barricade "from the roofs and upper floors, ordinary housewives and elderly women too, were throwing down milk bottles...other weapons and all kinds of refuse — on to the police". Other reinforcements, mainly dockers, moved in to form a tight defensive vanguard, which met the police baton charges with stones and bricks. One or two attackers, who managed to break through, were overpowered by the crowd in the rear and forced to surrender. (There are said to be helmets and batons still in possession of families, retained as souvenirs of their involvement in the "battle".)

At this juncture, for the police, enough was enough. Police Commissioner Sir Phillip Game finally accepted that the total force ranged against him was impassable. The Blackshirt columns were still immobilised on their start line in Royal Mint street. Having phoned the Home Secretary, who instructed him to make a decision on his own responsibility, he called Mosley and informed him that it was impossible to get through without mass bloodshed. "'As you can see for yourself, if you fellows go ahead from here, there will be a shambles. I am not going to have that. You must call it off.' Mosley asked, 'Is that an order?' 'Yes', replied Game. Mosley complied."[33] The Fascists lined up in column of route, turned about and, led by a drum and fife band, marched off in the opposite direction, through the silent streets of the City, on to the Embankment, where, with no audience to posture to, the Leader dismissed the parade.

Whatever the arguments, especially those posed by his apologists, it was a humiliating defeat for Mosley. All the boastful rhetoric of his acolytes in the days preceding the event had come to naught. His army had not passed; and, in the process of attempting it, a miserable outcome had ensued, with eighty-three anti-Fascists arrested and 100 (including police) injured. The victors, chanting jubilant slogans, assembled quickly and, led by the Young Communist League band, with a number of their injured still bandaged and bloody, moved off to celebrate at a monster meeting in Victoria Park Square — at the very spot designated by Mosley for his anticipated victory parade. There were still minor disturbances at some street corners on the outer borders of Stepney, where a few determined B.U.F. speakers attempted, unsuccessfully, to hold meetings, but, by nightfall, peace was restored. Whilst 3000 police remained on duty, the noise of festivities celebrating the "victory" in homes, pubs and clubs, went on into the early hours. Wild tales, true and false, exchanged by comrades throughout that night and passed on from generation to generation, would make for the creation of another East End legend — the Battle of Cable Street.

Two questions still require valid answers. First, where and amongst whom, did the B.U.F. gain their local recruits? In the absence of detailed research and categorisation, subsequent attempts to explain away home-based Fascism in terms of individual psychological aberrations, or as the activity of a mindless *lumpenproletariat,* no longer ring true. Perhaps the *Jewish Chronicle,* though no friend of the Fascists, managed to convey a more balanced appraisal of the basis of their support:

> There has been a combination of several types of working class element influenced by Fascism. They included some unemployed and many wives of unemployed workers, many *lumpenproletarian,* a number of municipal workers who held a Trade Union card and were dissatisfied with conditions under a Labour Borough Council, some Catholics, many unorganised workers in small workshops and factories ... costermongers and small holders who felt that the Jews were depriving them of their livelihood and a large number of shopkeepers ...voted Fascist.[34]

Yet only a minority of these were real activists who swallowed the Fascist theology and accompanied Mosley on his *grandes journées.* Secondly, how far were the police sympathetic to the Mosleyites? They were certainly *seen* to be forceful in protecting the Fascists and in arresting their opponents. But the answer is more complex. One important factor, omitted by both sides, that is, those accusing the police of pro-Fascist bias, as against the proponents of police "neutrality", is the locally-stationed (H Division) constable on the beat, who lived and worked among the immigrants, and was, therefore, disposed to be friendly towards the law-abiding Jews. (There is a wealth of evidence, written and oral, to sustain this, if some of the "historians" of the area and period had been perceptive enough to delve deeper into such sources.) The need to bring in a host of police from outside, including provincials of solid *petit-bourgeois* or farming stock, might account for the greater appeal afforded them by the B.U.F.'s uniform, military discipline and patriotic rhetoric. To them, the B.U.F. may have appeared to have been composed of kindred spirits. In the final count, some argue, police attitudes "were less pro-Fascist than pro-police... Metropolitan Police files... give a striking picture of the police conducting a war on two fronts, increasingly irritated by the problems posed by the B.U.F., yet hostile to the organised Left. If we were seeking an instrumental bias in the Metropolitan Police in those years it could be better to characterise it as anti-Left rather than pro-Fascist."[35] Certainly, after Cable Street, the police switched to backing a policy of restricting marches. B.U.F. demonstrations, with their concomitant violence and traffic obstruction, had become unsupportable; but above all, they resented the harassment and discomfort suffered by all ranks, on constant call, when the Blackshirts were on the march or rampage. Certainly, in their own view, it has always been the major function of the police to remain final arbiter of what is, or what is not, permissible on the streets of London, and they would surely brook no uniformed rival, such as the B.U.F., to usurp that rôle.

The affair of Cable Street was the turning point. It was this that finally prompted both government and police chiefs to opt for the Public Order Act which became law in December. This prohibited the wearing of political uniforms and proscribed what it called "quasi-military organisations". It gave to chiefs of police the power to ban processions for up to three months, subject to the Home Secretary's consent, and reiterated the law against insulting or abusive language likely to lead to breaches of the peace. Finally it legitimised charges that could now be brought by organisers of public meetings against disrupters, to strengthen "the right to free speech." Although aimed at both camps, Fascist and Communist (and it was the Communists who were quick to voice their suspicions of the dangers to free assembly accruing from the banning clause), the Act proved to be most effective against the Mosleyites. With the glamour of the uniform removed the B.U.F. rank and file were cut down to size, and the Leader deprived of his charismatic trappings. It marked the beginning of the decline of British Fascism. Never again would Mosley risk another march through the ghetto. For he faced not only the censure of the Public Order Act (it was actually invoked by the next Home Secretary, Sir Samuel Hoare, to abort a second attempt announced for July 14th 1937), but also the united front of East Enders, who had learned, through their own *journée* of October 4th, how to deal with the enemy.

**Post-script:**
One of the radical activists present in the crowd on that October day, a consistent fighter against fascism, was the young George Rudé.

# NOTES

1. As early as 1903 supporting evidence is given by the Headmaster of an East End school in the Royal Commission on Alien Immigration. Mr. J.M.P. Rawden of Deal Street Board School confirmed that in his school "practically the whole of these children are of foreign parentage. Notwithstanding this fact the lads have become thoroughly English. They have acquired our language. They take a keen and intelligent interest in all that concerns the welfare of our country. They are proud to be considered English boys." *(Royal Commission on Alien Immigration, 1903 cd. 1742 Min. 18,873.)*

2. *The New Survey of London Life and Labor,* ed. Sir H. Llewelyn Smith (London, 1934), Vol. VI, p. 293.

3. *Census of England and Wales* (London, 1931) *General Report* (1950), p. 178, table LXXVII; County of London tables 26 and 30.

4. According to R.D. Benewick, *The Fascist Movement in Britain* (London, 1969; rev. ed. 1972), p. 217.

5. *The New Survey of London Life and Labour* (London, 1934), Vol. III, pp. 345-6, and table III, p. 151.

   The poverty line was measured on an income of forty shillings a week for a moderate family (p. 101).

   The conventional definition of overcrowding was "more than two persons per room standard", with Bethnal Green and Stepney reckoned both at third place in the London Borough tables. (See *Census of England and Wales* — County of London [1932]; tables 3,11-13, XIX.)

6. *Daily Worker,* 18th April 1934.

7. Piratin, Ph., *Our Flag Stays Red* (London, 1948), p. 15.

8. Benewick, p. 202. Mosley's early New Party suffered a disastrous defeat in the first election attempt in 1931. It polled only 2% of the total vote with twenty-two out of the twenty-four candidates finishing at the bottom of the poll. Mosley was unwilling to risk a second disaster in 1935.

9. Skidelsky, R., *Oswald Mosley* (London, 1975), p. 381 for both quotations; my italics in the second. It would appear that Skidelsky may have also been attracted to Mosley's personality, for he admits that when he first saw him perform in a debate in the Oxford Union in 1961 "my interest was born in him. I greatly admire courage and intelligence...", which he immediately attributed to Mosley. His judicious attempt to act as a biographer "coming between a counsel for the defence and judge" falls short of the mark. Most of his evidence on B.U.F. activities in the East End is derived either from Mosley and B.U.F. (British Union of Fascists) sources or the police — neither of whom would be sympathetic in assessing the anti-Fascist activity. It is a pity that his research activities did not bring him to the East End in person to interview surviving anti-Fascists, and there are many, to ensure that "balance" he was purportedly seeking to obtain.

10. Skidelsky, p. 393. Again, this author and his fellow "revisionists" might well have interviewed surviving gentiles living with or near Jews in the East End during that period, to note their relationships with them.

11. After Cable Street, Dudley Barker in the *Evening Standard* (5th November 1936) argued that anti-Semitism had existed before advent of the B.U.F. due to the Jewish employers' propensity to exploit the recession, and the "alien habits" of the immigrants. *The Morning Post* (21st October 1936) declared that there was an established "identity between Jewry, sedition and Socialist malpractice".

12. Piratin, p. 16.

13. As early as 1931 Mosley was extolling the achievements of Mussolini (see *Action,* dated 27th November, December 24th and 31st, 1931) and the virtues of Hitler *(Action,* 10th

December 1931). In October 1936 Mosley secretly married Diana Mitford in Germany, with Hitler present as guest of honour at a luncheon given by Frau Goebbels. See O. Mosley, *My Life* (London, 1968), p. 363 and R. Skidelsky, *Oswald Mosley*, p. 341. On 18th April 1935 the Nazi Jew-baiter, Julius Streicher, had sent Mosley a telegram of congratulations.

14. Benewick, p. 223.

15. Joe Jacobs, *Out of the Ghetto* (London, 1978), p. 193. Jacobs, ex-C.P. member, locally engaged in the fight against Mosley, records that acceleration of Mosley's activities in the East End meant that a number of groups were taking to the streets in opposition, and the C.P., as a vanguard party, had no alternative but to join and head the struggle in the streets.

16. Evidence of the "terror" was reported widely in the press. After Cable Street, the *News Chronicle* (26th October 1936) observed a siege mentality amongst the Jews living near the borders of Bethnal Green: lighted fireworks thrown through letter boxes, threats, and actual physical attacks, such that people bolted doors and were afraid to venture out.

17. Benewick, *Ibid.,* p. 217.

18. *Daily Worker,* 14th, 19th and 21st February, 1936. Mary Hughes, daughter of Tom Hughes (author of *Tom Brown's Schooldays),* had founded a settlement in Stepney dedicated to help the poor and homeless. She was a staunch anti-Fascist.

19. Founded by Victor Gollancz, it achieved a membership of 16,000 by July 1936. It produced a book a month, at 2s.6d. per volume, by leading Radical authors.

20. For the Home Secretary's statement see *310 H.C. Dep 5s (25th March 1936) columns 1229-1230.* For conflicting reports of the meetings at the Albert Hall and Thurloe Square see *Action,* 19, 26th March 1936 and the *Daily Herald* and *News Chronicle,* both dated 23rd March. Also see the National Council for Civil Liberties, "Sir Oswald Mosley's Meeting March 22nd 1936 — extracts from statements of eye-witnesses, 1936, Statement 57."

The overwhelming evidence is that the police, in general, were more sympathetic to the Fascists than to their opponents. See below, pp. 389 and 390-91.

21. Opposing views are presented by Jacobs (pp. 186 and 205), who was urging instant and direct action, and Piratin (p. 18). The latter viewed the slogan "Bash the Fascists whenever you see them" as unproductive since it could not answer the question (i) How and why Mosley was able to recruit East End workers in spite of our anti-Fascist propaganda? (ii) Can we offer *effective* social and political counter-propaganda?

In the final count it was Piratin who changed tactics, and assumed top leadership in directing the Battle of Cable Street.

22. *Action,* 18th June 1936, inflated the audience numbers to 100,000. Local papers estimated 3000 and the police 5000 at the most.

23. These included a united front meeting in Trafalgar Square on 6th September, which attracted a huge crowd, and a public collection afforded £600. On the 9th a meeting of the Jewish Labour Council in the Ladies Tailors Union offices in Whitechapel was attended by immigrant TU leader and local magistrate J.L. Fine and Communist delegate Joe Jacobs. A collection was also made for Spanish aid.

24. For this paragraph, see Jacobs, *Out of the Ghetto,* pp. 235-37; on Mosley's "intensive campaign" after 1936, see Skidelsky, pp. 404-05.

25. *Daily Worker,* 30th September 1936.

26. According to Joe Jacobs, *Out of the Ghetto,* p. 241. Phil Piratin reports succinctly, in his own moderated version, of the internal clash: "At a joint meeting with officials of the London District Committee it was decided to ask the youth to call off their meeting in Trafalgar Square and devote the full resources of the Communist organisations to the anti-Fascist action against Mosley" (*Our Flag Stays Red,* p. 19).

27. Piratin, *Ibid.,* p. 20 and J. Jacobs, pp. 254-257 for details of the preparation and aims of the C.P. organisers.

28. The number estimated was around 100,000 (See Benewick, p. 227). Piratin suggests 50,000 were concentrated in the Gardiners Corner/Leman Street area alone, with an overall turn-out of a quarter of a million facing the police and fascists along the line. (See *Our Flag Stays Red*, p. 23 and BBC TV Documentary, *Yesterday's Witness: The Battle of Cable Street, script* p. 10. (Transmitted 4th January 1970).

29. Piratin, pp. 22-23; Benewick, pp. 226-228, and Jacobs, pp. 254-257; Skidelsky gives a very sketchy description, barely devoting a page to the action (p. 405).

30. Piratin, recorded in BBC TV, *Yesterday's Witness: The Battle of Cable Street,* p. 10.

31. Piratin, pp. 21-22; also Benewick, pp. 227, 228; BBC TV, *The Battle of Cable Street,* p. 11. Tubby Rosen, later prominent leader of the 1938/1939 rent strikes in Stepney, helped to turn over the lorry.

32. Piratin, *ibid.;* see too BBC TV, *Battle of Cable Street,* p. 7.

33. *East End News,* 10th October 1936, agreed that if the Fascists would have been allowed to march, 7,000 police would have been inadequate to protect them. *The Times,* 5th October, confirmed that the Commissioners' decision had the backing of the Home Office. For the dialogue between Mosley and Game see Skidelsky, p. 405.

34. *Jewish Chronicle,* 16th April 1937. See also J.H. Robb, *Working Class Anti-Semite* (London, 1954) and Colin Holmes' article "Anti-Semitism and the BUF", in *British Fascism,* ed. by Kenneth Lunn and Richard C. Thurlow (London 1980).

35. Skidelsky, p. 420, and article "The BUF, the Metropolitan Police and Public Order", in *British Fascism,* ed. by Kenneth Lunn and Richard C. Thurlow, pp. 147-148.

# INDEX

This "INDEX" was composed by Christine M. Jacobs.